My Giant Book of Animals

This book belongs to:

....

....

Mountain and Forest Animals

ant	
badger	4
beaver	5
bat	6
chamois	7
coyote	8
deer	9
eagle	10
falcon	11
fox	12
hare	13
hedgehog	14
marmot	15
lynx	16
mountain goat	17
owl	18
rattlesnake	19
marten	20
squirrel	21
spider	22
toad	23
woodpecker	24
wild boar	25
	26

Wild Animals

elephant	28
bison	29
water buffalo	30
camel	31
cheetah	32
chimpanzee	33
crocodile	34
gazelle	35
gorilla	36
gibbon	37
jaguar	38
hyena	39
lion	40
koala	41
panda	42
llama	43
flamingo	44
tiger	45
raccoon	46
zebra	47
toucan	48

Giant Animals

African elephant	50
giraffe	51
hippopotamus	52
rhinoceros	53
dolphin	54
orca	55
shark	56
whale	57
polar bear	58
bear	59
moose	60
kangaroo	61
Andean condor	62
ostrich	63
orang-utan	64
giant panda	65
Great Dane	66
lion	67
giant snake	68
giant squid	69
giant turtle	70
crocodile	71
walrus	72

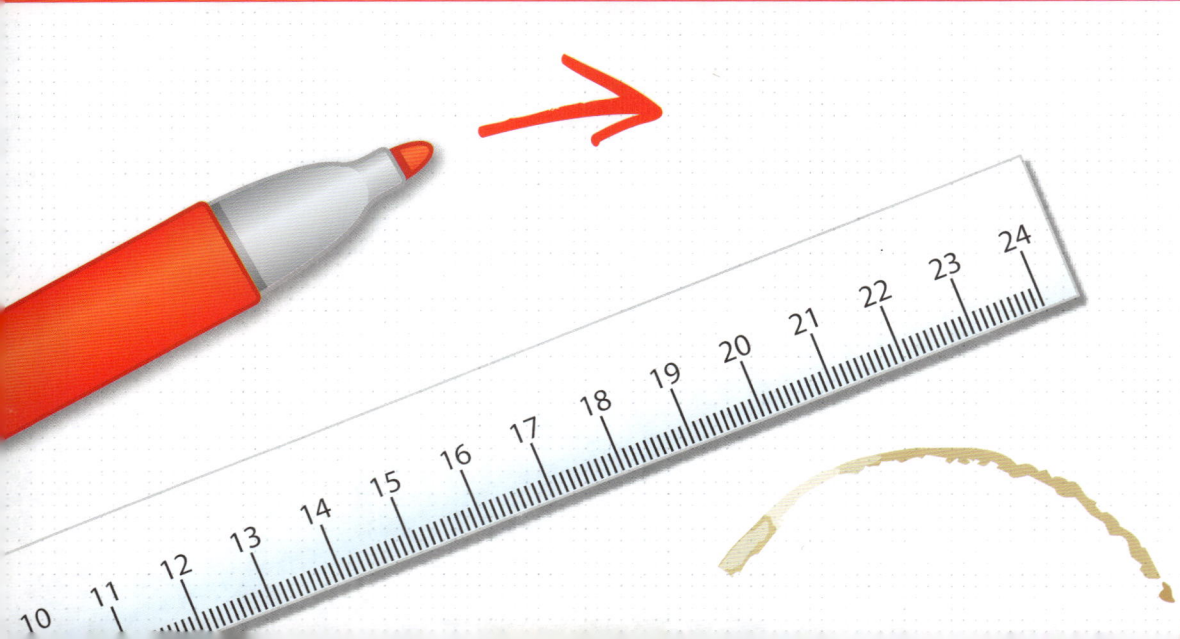

Mountain and Forest Animals

A lot of animals live in the woods and mountains. Some come out during the day and walk, crawl, climb, run, jump or fly through the woods or across the rocks. Others do not like daylight at all and are only active at night. In this chapter chock-full of fun animal facts, you can read about forest and mountain animals and test yourself. How much do you know about forest and mountain animals?

Ant

Weight: practically nothing!
Colour: black, brown, yellow, red
Mode of living: in a large colony
Life span: up to 25 years (queen)
Number of eggs: up to 30,000 per day

WHO?

Ants are insects and are related to wasps. There are many different kinds of ants. They always live in large colonies. The queen is the boss.

WHAT?

Forest ants are omnivores. They like leaves, but they especially love lice droppings and they feast on insects. Because they eat harmful insects, they are very useful animals!

WHERE?

Ants can be found all over the world. Some live above ground or underground, others only live in tree tops. You mostly find red forest ants in the woods.

DID YOU KNOW THAT...

... an ant can carry something that is 50 times its weight?
... ants communicate through scent?
... ants smell with their antennae?

Take the test!

1. What do you call a group of ants?
   A. Parade
   B. Colony

2. Where do red forest ants make their nest?
   A. Underground in the sand
   B. Above ground with pine needles

3. Ants usually walk...
   A. in a long line
   B. criss-cross

4

Badger

Weight: about 12 kg
Colour: grey, black, white
Mode of living: in a clan
Life span: 14 years
Gestation period: 7 weeks
Offspring: 5-6 babies

WHO?
A badger is a predator. It is about 1 m long and has black and white stripes on its head. It prefers to live with its family in a large den underground.

WHAT?
Badgers are omnivores. They like plants and fruit, but they also love to eat insects and small animals, such as mice and rabbits. Worms are their favourite!

WHERE?
Badgers live in a sett, or den, which they have dug themselves underground at the edge of the woods. The den has several halls and rooms and lots of exits. They make their beds from leaves and grass!

DID YOU KNOW THAT...
... a badger regularly changes its bed?
... a badger makes a special nursery where badger babies are born?
... people used to hunt badgers for their beautiful fur?

1. What is a badger's den called?
A.   Hallway
B.   Sett

2. Are badgers most active at night or during the day?
A.   At night
B.   During the day

3. Where does a badger stay during the day?
A.   Underground
B.   Above ground

1B/2A/3A

Beaver

WHO?

The beaver is a very large rodent. It is an excellent swimmer and uses its flat tail as a rudder. It can chew through trees with its large front teeth!

WHAT?

Beavers eat plants. They like twigs and leaves, but they also eat herbs, grass and berries. Bark is their favourite snack!

WHERE?

Beavers live in environments full of water, such as rivers and swamps. Their houses are called dens and are made from branches. They are half submerged in water, but on the inside they are dry!

DID YOU KNOW THAT...

... a beaver uses mud to glue together the branches for its den?
... a beaver's front teeth are orange?
... a beaver cannot walk fast on land?

1. Why does a beaver create the entrance to its den under water?
A.   So that wolves cannot get in
B.   Because it does not like climbing

2. When are baby beavers born?
A.   In spring
B.   In autumn

3. When a beaver slaps its tail on the water...
A.   it calls its babies
B.   it warns other beavers of approaching danger

1A 2A 3B

Bat

Weight: about 3.5–8 kg
Colour: grey, black
Mode of living: in a colony
Life span: 4–5 years
Gestation period: about 4 months
Offspring: 1

WHO?
Bats are the only mammals that can fly. There are 1,100 different kinds. Bats have excellent hearing. They sleep during the day and hunt for food at night.

WHAT?
A bat eats insects, such as flies, moths and mosquitoes. In one night, it can eat as many as 500 insects! In winter, it cannot find enough food, so it goes into hibernation.

WHERE?
Bats are found everywhere, except at the North and South Poles. During the day, bats sleep in a dark place like a hollow tree trunk or a cave.

DID YOU KNOW THAT...
... bats have poor eyesight but can hear where they are flying?
... bats have milk teeth at first, just like humans?
... bats make high-pitched squeaking sounds which people cannot hear?

Take the test!

1. How does a bat sleep?
A.   Upside down
B.   On its side

2. Can bats walk?
A.   Yes
B.   No

3. How does a bat find its prey in the dark?
A.   By using its ears
B.   By using its eyes

1A/2B/3A

Weight: 30-60 kg
Colour: red-brown, dark brown
Mode of living: in a group and alone
Life span: 15-17 years
Gestation period: 24-26 weeks
Offspring: 1-2

Chamois

WHO?

A chamois looks like a goat. It has coarse fur and 2 dark stripes on both sides of its head. Both males and females have horns.

WHAT?

In summer, a chamois lives off grass, herbs, twigs and bark. In winter, it mostly eats moss. Chamois are mostly active during the day.

WHERE?

A chamois lives high up in the mountains. Steep slopes are no problem for it: it is a good climber and can easily jump from rock to rock.

DID YOU KNOW THAT...

... male chamois usually live alone?
... female chamois and their babies live in a group?
... a male chamois raises his back hair to look impressive?

Take the test!

1. Does a chamois have a tail?
A. Yes
B. No

2. Does a chamois lay eggs?
A. Yes
B. No, a chamois is a mammal

3. What is a male chamois called?
A. Buck
B. Boar

1A/2B/3A

Coyote

WHO?

Coyotes are related to wolves, but they weigh much less. They can grow to about 90 m tall. Coyotes are predators.

WHAT?

Coyotes mainly eat rodents and rabbits and find snakes, insects and frogs delicious. But they do not only eat meat: they also love berries and grass.

WHERE?

Coyotes are mostly found on grassy plains, or prairies, and in not too dense forests. They do not like large groups, so they are solitary animals or they live in a small pack.

DID YOU KNOW THAT...

... a coyote is also called a prairie wolf?
... a 6-month old coyote already lives by itself?
... coyotes often go hunting in pairs?

Weight: about 15-20 kg
Colour: grey-brown
Mode of living: alone or in a small pack
Life span: 15-22 years
Gestation period: 60 days
Offspring: 6

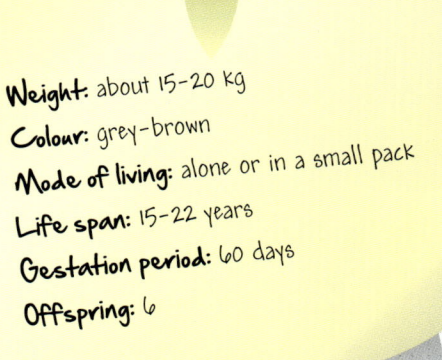

1. Is a coyote a nocturnal animal?
   A.   Yes
   B.   No

2. What is the sound called that coyotes make?
   A.   Whistling
   B.   Howling

3. Which animal is the coyote's biggest enemy?
   A.   Elephant
   B.   Wolf

1A/2B/3B

Deer

WHO?

A deer is a mammal. The male deer, or buck, has antlers, which it sheds each year. The female is called a doe.

WHAT?

Deer are herbivores. They are very picky and always smell their food first before they start to eat. A doe teaches her babies which plants to eat.

WHERE?

Deer mainly live in forests and woods but are also found on grassy plains. In autumn, males search for a female and try to impress them by bellowing.

DID YOU KNOW THAT...

... new antlers are usually larger than old antlers?
... moose are the largest deer?
... many young deer have a spotted coat?

1. Do deer have a long or short tail?

A. Long
B. Short

2. What do we call the sound a male deer makes when looking for a female?

A. Bellowing
B. Gurgling

3. Do deer digest their food by rumination?

A. Yes
B. No

1B/2A/3A

Weight: about 4-6 kg
Colour: brown, bald eagle: white head
Mode of living: alone or in pairs
Life span: 22 years
Gestation period: 35-45 days
Offspring: 1-3 eggs

Eagle

WHO?

Eagles are large birds of prey with very long and wide wings. They can fly very well and stay up in the air for hours. Eagles have a strong, hooked beak and sharp claws.

WHAT?

Eagles are carnivores. Thanks to their excellent eyesight, they can spot their prey from high up. They love eating other animals, such as rabbits, ducks, fish and snakes.

WHERE?

Eagles are found everywhere: in mountainous areas, but also in forests, grassland, swamps and along the shore. From a high tree or rock, they are on the lookout for food.

DID YOU KNOW THAT...

... female eagles are larger than male eagles?
... an eagle also eats fish and snakes?
... an eagle is the strongest bird of prey?

Take the test!

1. Are eagles diurnal or nocturnal birds?

A. Diurnal birds

B. Nocturnal birds

2. What does an eagle use to kill its prey?

A. Its claws

B. Its beak

1A 2A

Weight: 400 g–1.3 kg
Colour: blue, black, grey
Mode of living: alone
Life span: 20 years
Gestation period: 1 month
Offspring: 3–6 eggs

Falcon

WHO?

There are more than 65 different kinds of falcons in the world. Falcons have long, pointed wings and a straight tail. Male and female falcons often look the same.

WHAT?

Falcons eat animals such as grasshoppers, frogs and sparrows. Their favourite food is mice! They swallow the animal whole or in two pieces and later they cough up pellets, which contain the bones.

WHERE?

Most falcons do not make their own nests but instead steal the nests of other birds to brood in! They also brood in hollow trees or holes in cliffs.

DID YOU KNOW THAT...

... peregrines are faster than a car?
... a kestrel can spot a mouse from a distance of 100 m?
... a kestrel can hang motionless in the air?

Take the test!

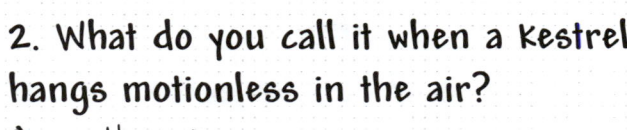

1. Is a falcon a bird of prey?
A. Yes
B. No

2. What do you call it when a kestrel hangs motionless in the air?
A. Hovering
B. Being lazy

Fox

WHO?

There are more than 10 different types of fox. The red fox is the most famous. It does not like to live in large groups, so it usually lives alone or with a few other foxes.

WHAT?

Foxes are real carnivores. In the woods, they can feast on small animals, such as birds, mice, rabbits and insects. They also like fruit.

WHERE?

Foxes like living in the woods. If there is not enough food there, they move to another spot. Once in a while, a fox ends up in a city!

DID YOU KNOW THAT...

... a fox has excellent hearing?
... a fox buries its food so it can be eaten later?
... the coat of an arctic fox is grey-brown in summer and white in winter?

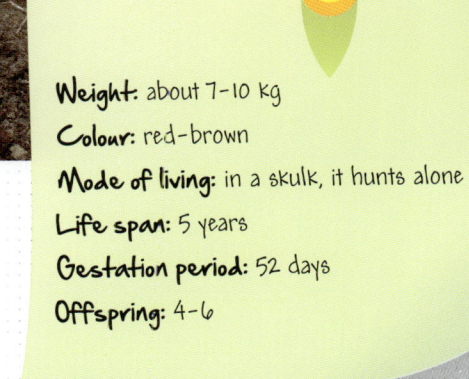

Weight: about 7-10 kg

Colour: red-brown

Mode of living: in a skulk, it hunts alone

Life span: 5 years

Gestation period: 52 days

Offspring: 4-6

1. **When does a fox bark?**

A.   When it is happy

B.   When there is danger

2. **Are foxes easily scared?**

A.   Yes

B.   No

3. **Does a fox always dig its own den?**

A.   Yes

B.   No

Weight: 3-7 kg
Colour: grey-brown, white, black with a white tummy
Mode of living: alone
Life span: 7 years
Gestation period: 6 weeks
Offspring: 1-9

Hare

WHO?
There are 30 different types of hares. Hares have large hind legs and long ears. The tips of their ears are black. Hares can run very fast for long distances!

WHAT?
Hares like plants. They love to eat grass, herbs and seeds. They also like to nibble on a piece of bark or a thin twig.

WHERE?
Some hares prefer living on open grass plains and in deserts. Others like the woods better. During the day, they lie on their tummy in a hole, a form, which they have dug themselves.

DID YOU KNOW THAT...
... hares can reach speeds of up to 75 km per hour?
... hares do not dig burrows?
... hares prefer to live alone?

1. A newborn hare...
A. can already walk
B. cannot walk yet

2. Where does a hare sleep?
A. Underground
B. Above ground

3. When 2 hares fight over a female...
A. they hit each other with their forelegs
B. they bite each other

1B/2A/3A

Weight: 500 g–1.5 kg
Colour: grey, brown
Mode of living: alone
Life span: 8 years
Gestation period: 31–39 days
Offspring: 3–6

Hedgehog

WHO?

The hedgehog is famous for its prickly hair and long snout. Because hedgehogs are mammals, they do not lay eggs. Small hedgehogs are born completely bald.

WHAT?

Hedgehogs love insects, worms, snails and caterpillars. They hunt for food in the dark. They go into hibernation because they cannot find any food in the winter!

WHERE?

Hedgehogs are frequent visitors to people's back gardens. They also like the woods and parks. They prefer to hibernate underneath a thick blanket of dead leaves!

DID YOU KNOW THAT...

... a hedgehog rolls up into a ball in case of danger?
... the spikes of a newborn hedgehog start growing after a couple of hours?
... hedgehogs have poor eyesight?

Take the test!

1. Can hedgehogs make sounds?
   A.   Yes
   B.   No

2. Can hedgehogs swim?
   A.   Yes
   B.   No

3. Does a hedgehog prefer to drink milk or water?
   A.   Milk
   B.   Water

Marmot

Weight: about 4-9 kg
Colour: brown, black, grey
Mode of living: in a colony
Life span: 15-18 years
Gestation period: 1 month
Offspring: 2-4

WHO?
Marmots are related to squirrels and are rodents. They are brown with a black tail. The marmot is 50 cm long and its tail is 15 cm!

WHAT?
The marmot feeds on grass, green plants and seeds. Before it goes into hibernation, it eats until it is completely full! This will last it through the winter.

WHERE?
Most marmots feel at home in mountainous areas, but some prefer living in the woods. They dig burrows in the ground, where they spend a lot of time.

DID YOU KNOW THAT...
... a marmot makes a special room underground where it can go to the toilet?
... the holes it digs in winter are deeper than the holes in summer?
... a marmot's front teeth are brown-yellow?

Take the test!

1. When a marmot hears a sound outside...
   A.   it stops dead in its tracks
   B.   it quickly runs into its burrow

2. The sound that a marmot makes sounds like...
   A.   whistling
   B.   singing

3. Does a marmot have sharp teeth?
   A.   Yes
   B.   No

Lynx

WHO?

The lynx is a feline predator. It has wide paws, whiskers on both sides of its head, plumes on its ears and a short tail.

WHAT?

Sometimes a lynx walks up to 200 km to find what it wants to eat. It likes eating hares and deer, but it does not turn down rodents either.

WHERE?

Lynx prefer to live in mountainous areas and in woods with coniferous trees. Since it has thick fur, it can endure cold weather well. It loves to sleep in a cave or in the bushes.

DID YOU KNOW THAT...

... a lynx is about the same size as an Alsatian?

... a lynx has excellent hearing?

... the lynx can hear where a sound comes from with the plumes on its ears?

Weight: about 18–25 kg

Colour: yellow-brown, spotted

Mode of living: alone

Life span: 15 years

Gestation period: 10 weeks

Offspring: 1–5

1. Can lynx stalk quietly?

A. Yes

B. No

2. Is a lynx a mammal?

A. Yes

B. No

IA 2A

Mountain goat

WHO?

A mountain goat is white and has black horns. It is a very good climber. Steep mountains or narrow ridges are not an obstacle to it!

WHAT?

Most mountain goats are grass eaters. They live on grass which they find in the mountains, but they also like moss when there is not enough grass.

WHERE?

Mountain goats live in small herds high up in the mountains. Because they can easily climb on narrow mountain ridges, they are often able to escape their enemies.

DID YOU KNOW THAT...

... mountain goats can stand up immediately after birth?
... a mountain goat has a beard?
... a mountain goat has a mane of hair?

Weight: about 40 kg
Colour: white
Mode of living: in a small herd
Life span: 8 years
Gestation period: 5 months
Offspring: 1-2

1. How does a goat keep warm high up in the mountains?

A.   It has thick fur
B.   It moves about a lot

2. Is a goat a ruminant?

A.   Yes
B.   No

3. Does a mountain goat have horns?

A.   Yes
B.   No

Weight: about 1-1.5 kg
Colour: brown, black, white, grey
Mode of living: alone
Life span: 3 years
Gestation period: 30-34 days
Offspring: 4-7 eggs

Owl

WHO?
The owl is a bird. It has a round, flat face with 2 big eyes at the front. The owl has a beak in the shape of a hook and very strong talons on its feet.

WHAT?
An owl sleeps during the day and hunts for food at night. It loves mice. A few hours after it has eaten, it coughs up a pellet with the bones and fur of the mouse.

WHERE?
When an owl is not hunting, it sleeps in a hollow tree, in a building or on the floor. It cannot build its own nest, so it steals the nest of another bird!

DID YOU KNOW THAT...
... an owl cannot move its eyes?
... that is why it turns its head to look in another direction?
... the smallest owl in the world is called the elf owl?

Take the test!

1. Does an owl make a lot of noise when it flies?
A. Yes
B. No

2. An owl's egg is...
A. oval
B. round

3. Do owls have good hearing?
A. Yes
B. No

18/2B/3A

Weight: about 2–3.5 kg
Colour: brown, light grey
Mode of living: alone
Life span: 10–25 years
Gestation period: 4–6 months
Offspring: 5–10

Rattle-snake

WHO?

A rattlesnake is brown to light grey with spots in the shape of a V on its body. When it shakes the tip of its tail, it makes a buzzing, rattling sound. This is to scare off enemies.

WHAT?

A rattlesnake loves to eat lizards, birds and small animals such as rabbits. It opens its mouth wide and swallows its prey whole.

WHERE?

A rattlesnake is a reptile. It lives in warmer areas where the sun can keep it warm. For instance, there are rattlesnakes in the desert, grassy plains and the jungle.

DID YOU KNOW THAT...

... rattlesnakes cannot hear the sound of their own rattle?
... a rattlesnake is very poisonous?
... a rattlesnake sheds its skin several times per year?

Take the test!

1. What are the rattles at the tip of the tail of a snake?

A. Pieces of skin left over from when the snake sheds its skin

B. Nails

2. Does a rattlesnake lay eggs?

A. Yes

B. No

3. Why do rattlesnakes have broad heads?

A. The poison bladders take up a lot of space

B. They have wide tongues

1A/2B/3A

Marten

WHO?

The marten is a slender predator with brown fur. A lot of martens have a white spot near their throats. A marten is a good climber and can easily jump from branch to branch.

WHAT?

A marten is a carnivore. It mostly likes tree animals, such as squirrels and birds, but also hunts mice and rabbits on the ground. It likes insects too, and even juicy fruit.

WHERE?

Martens prefer to live in large forests or woods. They are very agile and have no trouble jumping from tree to tree. They are most active at night.

DID YOU KNOW THAT...

... people used to hunt martens for their fur?
... martens have more than one burrow?
... newborn martens are blind?

Weight: about 1-2 kg
Colour: brown
Mode of living: alone
Life span: 8 years
Gestation period: 9 months
Offspring: 3

1. Does a marten have a tail?
A. Yes
B. No

2. How does a marten show where it is boss?
A. By leaving droppings in that spot
B. By growling

3. Do martens have a good sense of smell?
A. Yes
B. No

1A 2A 3A

Squirrel

WHO?

There are different types of squirrels. A squirrel is a rodent that can be found in many parts of the world. It has sharp, arched nails, with which it can easily climb in trees.

WHAT?

A squirrel likes nuts, acorns and pinecones. It also likes bark, berries and brambles. In autumn, it collects a lot of food to eat during the winter.

WHERE?

A squirrel prefers to live in woods with high coniferous trees. It builds a nest high up in the tree. It balances while climbing or jumping by using its thick tail.

DID YOU KNOW THAT...

... a squirrel does not hibernate?
... a squirrel loses its coat 2 times per year?
... a satisfied squirrel makes a 'ku-u-uk' sound?

Weight: 250-350 g
Colour: red-brown, brown-grey
Mode of living: alone
Life span: 6-7 years
Gestation period: 5-6 weeks
Offspring: 1-6

1. **What shape is a squirrel's nest?**
A.   Square-shaped
B.   Oval-shaped

2. **Where does a squirrel keep its winter stock of food?**
A.   In bird's nests, hollow trees and holes
B.   At the foot of the tree where it has its nest

18/2A

Colour: black, grey, brown
Mode of living: alone or in pairs
Life span: 1-2 years
Offspring: 2-2000

Spider

WHO?

There are about 40,000 types of spiders in the world. All spiders can bite, but fortunately, most are harmless to people.

WHAT?

Each spider can produce silk. Most spiders make a web or a nest, after which they patiently wait until an insect gets caught in it. Then, they will start to eat!

WHERE?

Spiders are found all over the world. The spider species that make webs build them between the branches of trees and bushes. But there are also spiders that hunt under water!

DID YOU KNOW THAT...

... a spider rebuilds its web almost every night?
... 1,500 spiders crawl around in a house on average?
... the tarantula and the Goliath spider are the largest spiders in the world?

Take the test!

1. How many legs does a spider have?
A.   6
B.   8

2. Is a spider an insect?
A.   Yes
B.   No

3. When you take a spider out of your house...
A.   it tries to come back inside
B.   it stays outside

Weight: up to 1 kg
Colour: brown, brown-red, grey
Mode of living: in a knot
Life span: 5 years
Tadpoles become toads: after 3 months
Offspring: 3,000–6,000

Toad

WHO?

Toads are related to frogs. They are bigger and are a brown or grey colour. Their skin is covered in warts. A toad cannot jump high, but instead crawls or hops on the ground.

WHAT?

A toad goes out looking for food at night. It is a real hunter. It prefers insects, such as flies and mosquitoes. It also likes worms and spiders.

WHERE?

Toads mainly live on land. They are happy in woods, dunes and meadows. Tadpoles are born in the water and they grow into toads there!

DID YOU KNOW THAT...

... toads have poor eyesight?
... a toad inflates itself to seem larger and more dangerous?
... a toad starts to wee when it is picked up?

Take the test!

1. A toad hibernates...
A. underground
B. in the bushes

2. Where do toads migrate?
A. Toads migrate to water to lay their eggs
B. Toads migrate to the sunny South, like birds

1A 2A

Woodpecker

WHO?

There are many different kinds of woodpecker. Woodpeckers are birds with a sharp beak that they use to knock on tree trunks. They have a stiff tail to lean on.

WHAT?

A woodpecker likes worms and insects. When it wants to catch a worm, it taps the ground with its beak. When the worm emerges above ground, the woodpecker seizes the opportunity and eats it up!

WHERE?

Woodpeckers live in areas with trees. They also like it when there are open pieces of land nearby. They bore holes in tree trunks to make nests.

DID YOU KNOW THAT...

... woodpeckers are excellent climbers?
... woodpeckers have an undulating flight pattern?
... woodpeckers spend the whole day boring in trees with their beaks?

Colour: black and white, green
Mode of living: in pairs
Life span: 9 years
Gestation period: 10-12 days
Offspring: 6-8 eggs

1. How do woodpeckers talk to each other?
A.   Through whistling
B.   Through knocking

2. Who takes care of the babies after they are born?
A.   Both parents
B.   The baby woodpecker takes care of itself right away

3. The sound a green woodpecker makes...
A.   sounds like a loud laugh
B.   sounds like a loud crying fit

1B/2A/3A

Weight: 60-120 kg
Colour: dark brown
Mode of living: in a sounder
Life span: 8-10 years
Gestation period: 4 months
Offspring: 3-12

Wild boar

WHO?

The wild boar is related to the pig. It has dark, hairy fur. The male is called a boar and the female is called a sow. Their baby is called a piglet.

WHAT?

A wild boar is an omnivore. Acorns, chestnuts, roots, berries and grass are its favourites, but it also eats worms and insects. It roots about in the earth with its snout to find food.

WHERE?

Wild boars need a lot of space. They prefer living in wooded areas. A wild boar is a nocturnal animal. During the day, it rests in a shallow hole in the bushes, preferably in a sunny spot.

DID YOU KNOW THAT...

... boars can swim well?
... boars make a snorting sound like a pig?
... wild boars take mud baths to take care of their skin?

1. What is the group called in which a wild boar lives?

A.   Herd
B.   Sounder

2. Young wild boars have...

A.   dark-brown fur
B.   striped fur

3. A male has...

A.   2 tusks
B.   2 horns

Wild Animals

In jungles, savannas, deserts or mountains, in the air or in the water, in hot or cold areas, wild animals live everywhere. Some love to eat meat and are real hunters; others only eat plants. Find out everything about wild animals in this chapter full of facts and test yourself. How much do you know about wild animals?

Weight: 3-5 tons
Colour: grey
Mode of living: females in a group, males alone
Life span: 70 years
Gestation period: 20-22 months
Offspring: 1

Elephant

WHO?

Elephants are the largest land animals in the world. Everybody recognises them by their long trunks and big ears. A male elephant is called a bull and a female is called a cow. Their baby is called a calf.

WHAT?

Elephants like eating grass and leaves. In order to find food, they sometimes pull entire trees out of the ground with their trunks.

WHERE?

Female elephants live in a family group with their calves in an area with grass and trees. Male elephants live alone. At night, elephants look for a watering hole where they drink, play and wash.

DID YOU KNOW THAT...

... elephants cannot jump?
... elephants can smell each other from 5 km away?
... elephants have an excellent memory?

Take the test!

1. Can an elephant pick up very small trees with its trunk?
A. Yes
B. No

2. An angry elephant...
A. flaps its ears
B. puts its tail in the air

3. An elephant's tooth is as heavy as a...
A. football
B. brick

1A 2A 3B

Bison

WHO?

The bison is related to the cow. It has thick, dark-brown fur and lots of hair on its head, neck, shoulders and forelegs. The bison has a very arched back and a wide head. Both males and females have 2 horns.

WHAT?

A bison has 4 stomachs, like a cow. It is a ruminant and likes to eat grass, leaves, young twigs and the bark of trees. In autumn, it also eats acorns.

WHERE?

Bison live in a large group called a herd. The boss of a herd is an older bison. A bison feels most at home in a wooded environment. It also likes grassy plains where it can graze.

DID YOU KNOW THAT...

... a bison has a hump on its back?

... it stores fat in that hump for periods with little food?

... bison were nearly extinct 100 years ago?

Weight: about 900 kg
Colour: brown
Mode of living: in a herd
Life span: 40 years
Gestation period: 285 days
Offspring: 1

1. **When bison are scared...**
   A. they all run away at the same time
   B. they stop dead in their tracks

2. **A bison weighs as much as...**
   A. 5 grown people
   B. 12 grown people

3. **Is a bison strong?**
   A. Yes
   B. No

Water buffalo

WHO?
Water buffalo are cattle that look like cows. But they are a lot bigger and are a dark colour. Both male and female buffalo have bent horns on their head.

WHAT?
Water buffalo are herbivores. They prefer to eat grass, but they also like the leaves of bushes or plants. Water buffalo usually eat at night.

WHERE?
A water buffalo feels at home in a wooded environment near water. It does not like hot weather. Therefore it stays in the shade or takes a refreshing mud bath to cool down during the day.

DID YOU KNOW THAT...
... water buffalo have poor eyesight and hearing?
... water buffalo have an excellent sense of smell?
... water buffalo each drink at least 30 litres of water per day?

Weight: 750 kg
Colour: brown-black
Mode of living: in a herd
Life span: 20 years
Gestation period: 11-12 months
Offspring: 1

1. Which animal removes insects from a water buffalo's skin?
A.   A monkey
B.   A bird

2. Are water buffalo dangerous?
A.   Yes
B.   No

3.   What is a male buffalo called?
A.   Bull
B.   Buck

1B/2A/3A

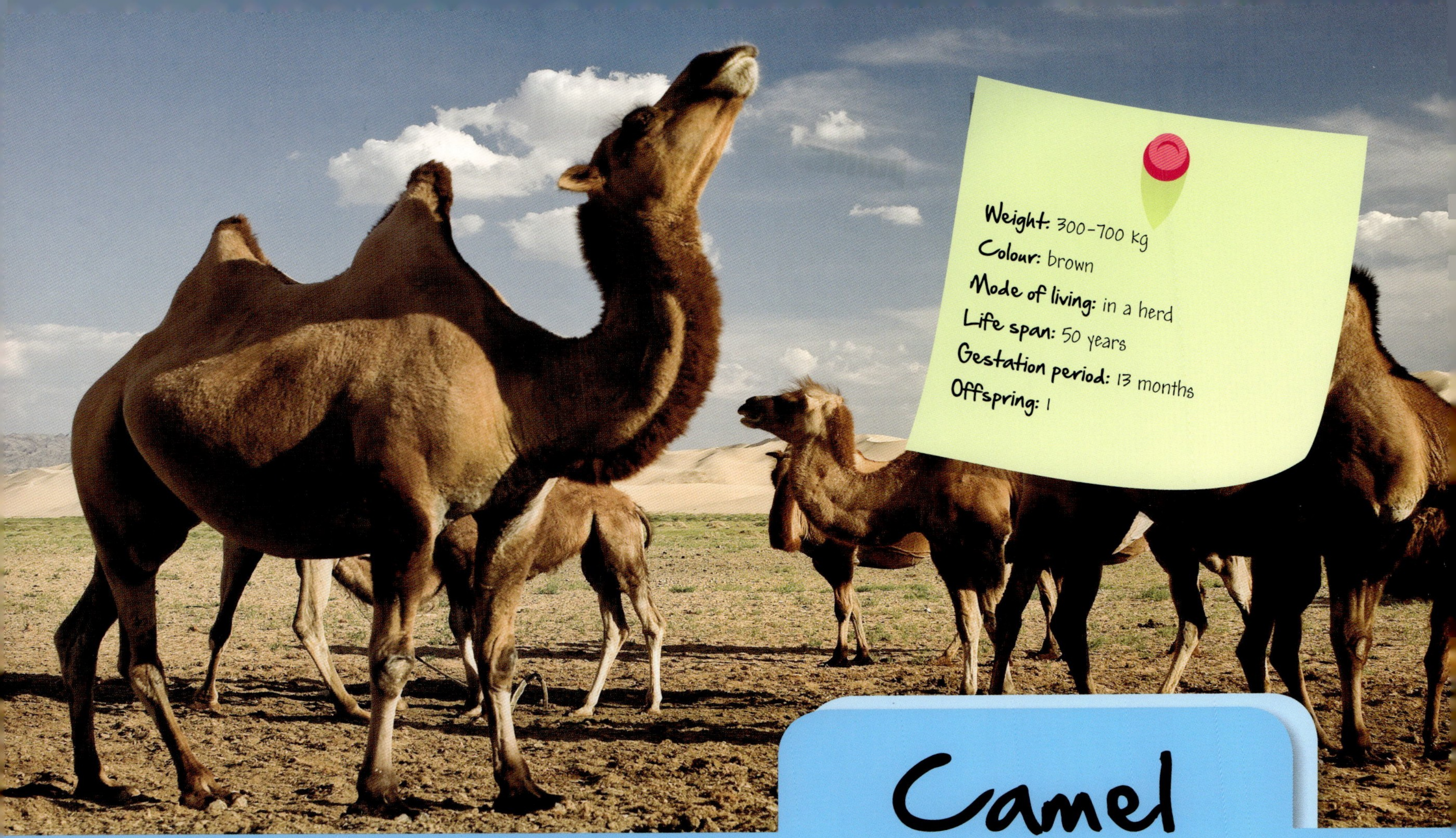

Camel

WHO?

A camel is an animal with 2 humps on its back. It likes both hot and cold weather! In winter, it gets a nice thick fur which it loses in large tufts again in spring.

WHAT?

A camel lives off of whatever it can find in the desert. Sometimes it eats grass, other times it eats branches or leaves. It can go for a long time without water, but when it drinks, it drinks a lot!

WHERE?

Camels live in the deserts. People who travel through the desert often use a camel to transport goods and as a riding animal.

DID YOU KNOW THAT...

... a camel is also called the 'ship of the desert'?

... camels can go without water for weeks?

... the humps on its back disappear when it has nothing to eat?

Take the test!

1. **What is in the 2 humps on the back of a camel?**

A. Fat

B. Water

2. **How does a camel make sure that no sand enters its nose?**

A. It closes its nostrils in a sandstorm

B. It sticks its head between its legs in a sandstorm

1A, 2A

Weight: about 50 kg
Colour: light yellow with black spots
Mode of living: in a small coalition or alone
Life span: 14 years
Gestation period: 90 days
Offspring: 2–5

Cheetah

WHO?

A cheetah is a feline predator. It is the fastest land animal in the world! Its long legs enable it to push off hard. You can recognise cheetahs by their yellowish fur covered in black spots.

WHAT?

Cheetahs hunt early in the morning or early in the evening. They prefer to eat other mammals, such as antelope, gazelle and springbok, but birds are also on their menu.

WHERE?

Cheetahs live in open areas where they can run fast. They feel most at home in places with bushes so that they can hide when stalking prey.

DID YOU KNOW THAT...

... a cheetah is also called a duma?
... young cheetahs do not have spots?
... young cheetahs are better climbers than their parents?

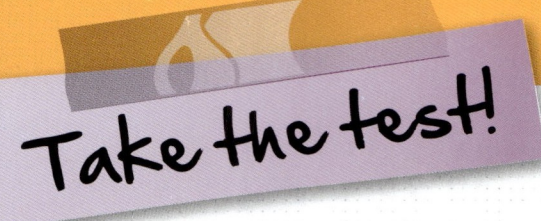

Take the test!

1. How fast can a cheetah run?

A.   100 km per hour

B.   60 km per hour

2. Is a cheetah a mammal?

A.   Yes

B.   No

3. What kind of sound does a cheetah make?

A.   It roars like a lion

B.   It chirps like a bird

Chimpanzee

WHO?

Chimpanzees are anthropoid apes. They are related to humans but have much stronger arms and shoulders and shorter legs. Chimpanzees have long, black hair.

WHAT?

Chimpanzees love fruit. Furthermore, they eat leaves, nuts and bark. They also like small animals, such as insects, and they like birds eggs, too. They use stones and twigs as tools, for example to open nuts or catch ants!

WHERE?

A chimpanzee lives in wooded areas in Africa. It is mostly found on the ground but also climbs trees to find food or to sleep.

DID YOU KNOW THAT...

... a chimpanzee can only have babies once every 4 years?
... chimpanzees are usually right-handed?
... chimpanzees are very clever?

Weight: 45-55 kg
Colour: black
Mode of living: in a small community
Life span: 50 years
Gestation period: 8 months
Offspring: 1

I. Are chimpanzees nocturnal or diurnal animals?

A.   Diurnal
B.   Nocturnal

2. Where does a chimpanzee sleep?

A.   In a tree in a nest it makes itself
B.   On the floor in a hole it makes itself

3. Does a chimpanzee have a tail?

A.   Yes
B.   No

1A 2A 3B

Crocodile

WHO?

Crocodiles are the largest of all reptiles. There are 22 different kinds. They are aquatic animals, but they also enjoy sunbathing on the shore.

WHAT?

Crocodiles love meat! Big or small, hardly any animal is safe from them. They often lie in wait under the water looking like logs. As soon as they spot prey, they come out and attack.

WHERE?

Crocodiles live in warm areas with plenty of water. They need the sun to keep their temperature steady, so that they have enough energy to eat and hunt.

DID YOU KNOW THAT...

... crocodiles already existed at the time of the dinosaurs?
... the largest crocodile is longer than 3 adult humans?
... a crocodile gets new teeth every 2 years?

Weight: 750 kg
Colour: brown, green
Mode of living: usually alone
Life span: 30–60 years
Eggs hatch: after 60–115 days
Offspring: 20–95 eggs

1. Why do the eyes of a crocodile stay above water when a crocodile is swimming?

A.   It does not want water to get into its eyes

B.   It can keep an eye on its surroundings

2. How does a mother crocodile carry her newborn baby from the waterside into the water?

A.   On her back

B.   In her mouth

Weight: 15–30 kg
Colour: light brown with a white tummy
Mode of living: in a herd
Life span: 10–15 years
Gestation period: 170–180 days
Offspring: 1

Gazelle

WHO?

A gazelle is a slender animal with thin legs, a long neck and twisted horns. Gazelles have light brown fur with a white tummy and a black stripe along their sides.

WHAT?

Juicy grass is a gazelle's favourite food. During dry periods, they also like to eat herbs, the leaves of bushes and plants as well as seeds. A gazelle can go for a long time without water: it squeezes water from plants!

WHERE?

A gazelle prefers to live in areas with lots of grass. It can graze there! It lives with other gazelles in a herd. At night, when it gets dark, the herd comes together.

DID YOU KNOW THAT...

... a baby gazelle is born with its eyes open?
... a gazelle can run really fast?
... only a cheetah can catch up with a running gazelle ?

Take the test!

1. How does a male gazelle try to scare an enemy?
A.   By growling
B.   By jumping

2. Why are most gazelles born after the rainy season?
A.   The grass is green and juicy then
B.   They stay dry

3. How do gazelles communicate with each other?
A.   By sounds
B.   By making movements with their body

18/2.N 35

Weight: 100-200 kg
Colour: black
Mode of living: in a troop
Life span: 35-50 years
Gestation period: 9 months
Offspring: 1

Gorilla

WHO?

Gorillas are large anthropoid apes. Gorillas do not have tails and can stand upright, like us. When they walk, they bend over so their hands touch the ground.

WHAT?

Gorillas love leaves, stalks and fruit. The females and young gorillas climb trees to pick ripe fruit. Males cannot climb trees because they are too heavy!

WHERE?

Gorillas live in tropical rain forests among the trees. They can usually be found on the ground. They live in family groups, which consist of a couple of females and their babies. A male is their leader.

DID YOU KNOW THAT...

... male gorillas have a bump on their heads?
... a male gorilla is also called a silverback?
... a gorilla can grow taller than 2 m?

Take the test!

1. Why do they call a male gorilla a silverback?

A.   The hairs on its back are silver-grey

B.   He likes shiny things

2. How long do young gorillas stay with their mother?

A.   Until they are 1 year old

B.   Until they are 3 years old

3. A gorilla pounds its chest...

A.   when it is angry or startled

B.   when it is hungry

1A/2B/3A

Gibbon

Weight: 4-8 kg

Colour: grey, grey-brown, black

Mode of living: in a small family group or in pairs

Life span: 25 years

Gestation period: 7 months

Offspring: 1

WHO?

Gibbons are anthropoid apes. On the ground, they walk upright, just like people. Thanks to its long arms, a gibbon can also move well in trees and swing from branch to branch.

WHAT?

Gibbons mainly eat fruit, which they pick in the trees. But they also like leaves and flowers, and they enjoy a tasty meal of birds eggs and insects!

WHERE?

Gibbons live high up in the trees of the rain forest. They can swing from branch to branch very fast without using their legs. They do not grab the branches, but they use their hands as hooks!

DID YOU KNOW THAT...

... people hunt gibbons to sell them as pets?
... gibbons can sing?
... newborn gibbons always have light fur?

1. What do gibbon couples say to other gibbons when they sing?

A.   We are happy today

B.   This is our territory; stay out of our way

2. Gibbons walk upright, holding their long arms up a bit, because...

A.   they would trip over their hands

B.   they can keep their balance better

1B/2B

Weight: 125-150 kg
Colour: yellow-brown with black spots, black
Mode of living: alone
Life span: 12-20 years
Gestation period: 90-110 days
Offspring: 1-4

Jaguar

WHO?
Jaguars are large and strong felines. They have yellow-brown fur with lots of black spots. A jaguar is a nocturnal animal with excellent night vision.

WHAT?
A jaguar eats animals that live in its environment. Deer are its favourite, but other animals such as birds, frogs, porcupines and fish also have to be careful when there is a jaguar nearby.

WHERE?
Jaguars live in wooded areas. There are also jaguars in open terrains, but only when there are enough places where they can hide while hunting. Jaguars always prefer to stay close to the water.

DID YOU KNOW THAT...
...jaguars can climb well?
...jaguars can also swim well?
...jaguars can catch animals that are 4 times heavier than they are?

1. A jaguar ...
A. roars
B. growls

2. Where does a jaguar eat its prey?
A. In the same place where it caught it
B. In a shelter

Weight: 40-85 kg
Colour: brown, grey
Mode of living: in a pack
Life span: 20 years
Gestation period: 100 days
Offspring: 1-3

Hyena

WHO?

A hyena has a large head with powerful jaws with which it can even crush bones! Since its forelegs are longer than its hind legs, it looks as though it has a slanted back.

WHAT?

Hyenas are real carnivores. They are happy to eat the meat of dead animals they have found, but they also kill animals themselves. They will even eat the bones of their prey! Hyenas mostly hunt at night.

WHERE?

Hyenas live on savannas. These are areas with plenty of grass, so animals are attracted there for food. And it is precisely these animals that are on a hyena's menu!

DID YOU KNOW THAT...

... a baby hyena has black fur?
... baby hyenas are born in a hole?
... hyenas usually hunt in a pack?

Take the test!

1. Who is the leader of a hyena pack?

A.   The male
B.   The female

2. What is the sound called that hyenas make?

A.   Laughing
B.   Howling

3. When a hyena lifts its tail, it is saying...

A.   look out for me
B.   I see prey

1B/2A/3A

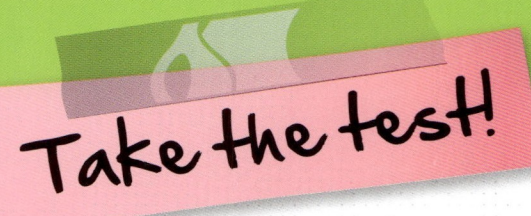

Weight: 150–250 kg
Colour: light brown
Mode of living: in a pride
Life span: 10–14 years
Gestation period: 100 days
Offspring: 2–4

Lion

WHO?

Lions are related to cats. Male lions are larger than females, and you can recognise them by their long manes around their head and shoulders. Most felines live alone, but lions live in a group.

WHAT?

Lions prefer to eat zebras and deer. If zebras are not around, they will simply attack smaller animals. Only when the adult males have eaten their fill are the females and cubs allowed to eat.

WHERE?

A lion lives in the savanna, but for most of the day it will rest in the shadow of a tree. It can let distant relatives know where it is by roaring.

DID YOU KNOW THAT...

... young lions are cared for not just by their own mothers but by other lionesses as well?
... a lion is also called the 'king of the animals'?
... lions see everything in black and white at night?

Take the test!

1. What is the name of the family group of a lion?
A. Gang
B. Pride

2. Who is the best hunter?
A. The male
B. The female

Koala

WHO?
Koalas are marsupials and related to kangaroos. They move slowly and live in the trees. On the ground, they are fairly clumsy.

WHAT?
A koala virtually only eats the leaves of the eucalyptus tree. It skips the young leaves, but it enjoys the older ones. A koala never drinks anything: it squeezes water from leaves!

WHERE?
Koalas are good climbers and they feel at home in the trees. A baby koala lives in its mother's pouch for the first 6 months and then moves to her back.

DID YOU KNOW THAT...
... a koala can swim well?
... a koala eats 4 hours per day and sleeps and lounges for 20 hours?
... a koala does not have a tail?

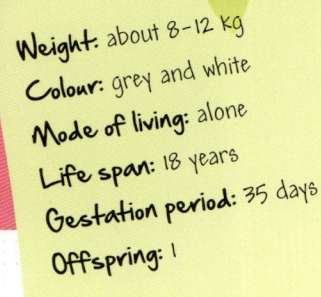

Weight: about 8-12 kg
Colour: grey and white
Mode of living: alone
Life span: 18 years
Gestation period: 35 days
Offspring: 1

1. What is the sound called that a koala makes?
   A. Bellowing
   B. Grawling

2. Is a koala a nocturnal or a diurnal animal?
   A. Nocturnal
   B. Diurnal

3. A koala sleeps...
   A. in a nest
   B. between 2 branches

Panda

Weight: 80-100 kg
Colour: black and white, red
Mode of living: alone
Life span: 15 years
Gestation period: 90-160 days
Offspring: 1-2

WHO?

Pandas are related to bears. A giant panda has a white head with black eyes and black spots around its eyes. But there is also another type, the red panda, which is red!

WHAT?

A panda is a herbivore. It eats grass, fruit and fish, but bamboo shoots are its favourite. It is a big eater and eats for 14 hours a day. It also drinks lots of water.

WHERE?

Pandas live in mountainous areas and in areas with trees. A panda spends most of the day on the ground, but when there is danger it will climb a tree and stay there until it is all clear again!

DID YOU KNOW THAT...

... a baby panda is bald and pink?
... pandas have a good sense of smell?
... pandas have an extra thumb on their front paws?

1. The noise a panda makes sounds...
A.   like a sheep bleating
B.   like a bear roaring

2. A panda...
A.   is a mammal
B.   lays eggs

3. A panda prefers to be...
A.   alone
B.   in a group

1A 2A 3A

Weight: up to 150 kg
Colour: brown, grey
Mode of living: in a herd
Life span: 20 years
Gestation period: 10–11 months
Offspring: 1

Llama

WHO?
Llamas are related to camels. They are used as beasts of burden. Llamas are very strong and can carry heavy loads for people in the mountains. A female llama is called a dam and the male is called a sire.

WHAT?
A llama lives off grass, leaves and bushes, which it finds in the mountains. But it also likes toadstools or moss. A llama can go for days without water.

WHERE?
Llamas are found in different places: they live on grasslands but also in the desert. In the mountains, they feel very much at home. They can even survive at a height of 4,000 m.

DID YOU KNOW THAT...
... a llama is also called a sheep camel?
... a llama can become as big as an adult human?
... a llama sometimes spits at other llamas?

Take the test!

1. Why does a llama spit?
A.   Because it wants to play
B.   Because it wants to be the leader

2. A llama's coat consists of...
A.   wool
B.   feathers

1B/2A

Flamingo

Weight: 15–40 kg
Colour: pink, orange
Mode of living: in a flock
Life span: 20 years
Gestation period: 28 days
Offspring: 1 egg

WHO?

A flamingo is a water bird. It has a long neck, which it can turn in any direction, and pink-orange feathers. You often see it standing on one leg in the water.

WHAT?

A flamingo eats food which it finds in the water. Its beak is a kind of sieve with which it can fish shrimp and crayfish out of the water. Then it can drain the water!

WHERE?

Flamingos live in the sea or in lakes with salt water. They often stand in water with a very muddy bottom. They stand still for most of the day.

DID YOU KNOW THAT...

... a flamingo is pink because it eats pink food?
... it would be almost white without this food?
... a flamingo cleans its feathers for hours per day?

Take the test!

1. A flamingo often stands on one leg, because...

A.   it wants to keep its other leg warm against its tummy

B.   it only has one leg

2. Do flamingos have a good sense of smell?

A.   Yes

B.   No

3. A flamingo lays an egg...

A.   in a nest

B.   under the sand

IA/28/3A

Tiger

WHO?

Tigers are the strongest and largest cats in the world. A tiger has black stripes on its orange-brown fur. Its colouring allows it to blend into the shadows and trees!

WHAT?

A tiger is a predator. It loves meat. It prefers to hunt alone at night to catch zebras and deer, but it will not turn down a monkey once in a while!

WHERE?

Most tigers live in the woods or on grasslands. Some live in warm areas, others are more at home in the cold, but they always live near water!

DID YOU KNOW THAT...

... a tiger mother will hit her baby on the nose when it has to listen?

... a tiger can swim well?

... a tiger is 10 times as strong as a human?

Weight: up to 280 kg
Colour: orange-brown with black stripes
Mode of living: alone
Life span: 15 years
Gestation period: 105 days
Offspring: 2-6

1. Using its whiskers, a tiger...
   A. can feel its way around at night
   B. can swat flies from its nose

2. Baby tigers are born in...
   A. a deep hole
   B. a tree

3. The tiger's biggest enemy is...
   A. wolves
   B. humans

Raccoon

WHO?

Raccoons are related to small bears. You can recognise them by their striking black and white mask on their pointed snout and by their white tail with black rings.

WHAT?

Raccoons are omnivores. They eat meat, such as worms, lobsters, fish and hares, but they also like fruit and corn. They carry food with their forelegs from one place to another.

WHERE?

Raccoons are nocturnal animals. During the day they sleep in a hole underground, in a hollow tree or high up in the tree in an abandoned bird's nest. They prefer to live in woods with water nearby.

DID YOU KNOW THAT...

... a raccoon can feel excellently using its paws?
... a raccoon is a superb climber?
... raccoons can stalk like cats?

Weight: 3-15 kg
Colour: black, white, grey
Mode of living: alone or in a small group
Life span: 16 years
Gestation period: 60-73 days
Offspring: 4-5

1. Can raccoons swim?

A.   Yes
B.   No

2. Raccoon comes from the Native American word arakum; what does the name mean?

A.   It scratches with its hands
B.   It washes with its hands

3. Do raccoons hibernate?

A.   Yes
B.   No

1A 2A 3B

Weight: 200-350 kg
Colour: black and white
Mode of living: in a herd
Life span: 25 years
Gestation period: 1 year
Offspring: 1

Zebra

WHO?

Zebras are related to horses and donkeys, both of which can be tamed. A zebra cannot be tamed and therefore is a wild animal. You can recognise a zebra by its black and white fur.

WHAT?

A zebra is a herbivore. It mainly eats grass but also the leaves of bushes. Zebras eat the whole day long. There is enough grass in the rainy season, but in dry seasons they have to walk far to find food.

WHERE?

Zebras live in herds on open plains and grasslands. A male zebra is the leader of the herd. Each year, the male zebras fight to decide who will be the new leader!

DID YOU KNOW THAT...

... a zebra foal has brown stripes?
... each zebra has a unique stripe pattern?
... zebras sleep standing up?

Take the test!

1. Can a zebra gallop fast?
   A. Yes
   B. No

2. Zebras often seek the companionship of herds of wildebeest or antelope because...
   A. they like company
   B. it is harder for lions to catch them

1A/2B

Weight: 95-800 g
Colour: black and white, red, yellow, etc.
Mode of living: in a flock
Life span: 20 years
Gestation period: 2-3 weeks
Offspring: 2-4 eggs

Toucan

WHO?

There are nearly 40 different types of toucan. A toucan has shiny, black feathers on its back and white or brightly coloured feathers on its chest. Its large, yellow beak sometimes is just as long as the bird itself!

WHAT?

A toucan loves fruit. It uses its enormous beak to pick fruit from branches. When there is no fruit available, it also enjoys insects or spiders or it will ransack a bird's nest.

WHERE?

Toucans live in trees in warm and humid forests. They live in flocks of 12 birds. Each group has its own sleeping place and will move when they are disturbed!

DID YOU KNOW THAT...

... toucans like beak wrestling?
... a male toucan throws grapes at a female toucan he likes?
... a toucan prefers to hop from one branch to another instead of flying?

Take the test!

1. The beak of a toucan...
A.   is very heavy
B.   is very light

2. The beak of a toucan...
A.   is always yellow
B.   can also be another colour

Giant Animals

Are large animals always dangerous or are they usually nice? Can animals with enormous bodies run and climb well, or do they move slowly? Do giant birds lay giant eggs, or do large animals have small babies? Find out everything about the life of giant animals in this beautiful chapter full of facts and test yourself. How much do you know about giant animals?

African elephant

WHO?

The African elephant is the fattest land animal. It has a long trunk, which is very useful for eating and drinking, and large ears. Both males and females have tusks.

WHAT?

The African elephant is a herbivore. It loves plants and leaves. A grown elephant can eat as much as 250 kg of food and drink 300 litres of water every day!

WHERE?

African elephants live on grasslands, the savannas, in Africa. They love taking baths and are often found at large watering holes.

DID YOU KNOW THAT...

... an elephant calf stays with its mother for 10 years?
... people hunt elephants for their tusks?
... the African elephant has poor eyesight but excellent hearing?

Weight: 3,000–6,000 kg
Colour: grey, brown
Mode of living: females in a group, males alone
Life span: 70 years
Gestation period: 20–22 months
Offspring: 1

1. When walking, an elephant always has...

A. 3 legs on the ground
B. 2 legs on the ground

2. Does an elephant have a good sense of smell?

A. Yes
B. No

3. How many hours per day does an African elephant eat?

A. 8 hours
B. 16 hours

Weight: 500–2,000 kg

Colour: yellowish with brown spots

Mode of living: in a herd

Life span: 15–20 years

Gestation period: 14–15 months

Offspring: 1

Giraffe

WHO?

The giraffe is the tallest land animal in the world. It can grow up to 6 m in height! Giraffes have long necks and long legs with which they can run very fast.

WHAT?

A giraffe uses its long, black tongue to grab food from trees: it loves the leaves, buds and branches of the acacia tree. When it drinks, it spreads its front legs wide apart. This way it can reach the water on the ground.

WHERE?

Giraffes live in herds. They are mostly found on the grasslands of Africa. Although a giraffe needs trees in its environment, it does not like to live in dense forests!

DID YOU KNOW THAT...

... a mother giraffe will abandon her child if it cannot walk after one hour?

... male giraffes try to push each other over with their necks?

... they do this to determine who is the leader?

Take the test!

1. The tongue of a giraffe is...

A.   nearly 1 m long

B.   almost 0.5 m long

2. When a baby giraffe is born...

A.   it falls down more than 2 m

B.   mother giraffe gently places it on the ground

1B / 2A

Weight: 3,000 kg
Colour: pink, grey
Mode of living: in a herd
Life span: 7-9 years
Gestation period: 7-8 months
Offspring: 1

Hippopotamus

WHO?

A hippopotamus looks a bit like a horse: it has the same ears and lips and makes a whinnying sound, but it is actually related to the pig! Even though it is a land animal, it spends a lot of time in the water.

WHAT?

Hippos love to graze. They prefer grass to water plants and can therefore often be found in meadows. In order to stay healthy, a hippo has to eat 70 kg of food per day!

WHERE?

Hippos live in Africa in places with lots of water and plants. They like deep water, preferably with reeds, and they like it if it is surrounded by grassland.

DID YOU KNOW THAT...

... a hippo eats at night?
... hippos have poor eyesight at night?
... hippos can scare crocodiles?

Take the test!

1. How does a hippopotamus find its way at night if it cannot see well?

A.   It leaves a trail of poo and this way it can smell how to walk back

B.   It always walks the same route and knows it by heart

2. Can a hippopotamus move fast on land?

A.   Yes

B.   No

1A, 2A

Rhinoceros

WHO?

There are 5 different kinds of rhino. The white rhino is the largest. It has 2 horns on its nose, a big one at the front and a smaller one behind it.

WHAT?

Rhinos are real herbivores. They graze day and night and munch on grass, fruit and the leaves of bushes. The white rhino has wide lips with which it can easily pick grass.

WHERE?

Rhinos live on the African savannas. They feel at home in places with lots of trees and bushes because they provide shelter from the sun and the wind. A rhinoceros also likes to have water nearby.

DID YOU KNOW THAT...

... a white rhino is not white but grey?
... a rhino can drink up to 100 litres of water per day?
... the horn of a rhino sometimes breaks off during fights?

Weight: 1,000–3,600 kg
Colour: grey
Mode of living: in a small herd
Life span: 45 years
Gestation period: 18 months
Offspring: 1

1. Is a rhinoceros born with with horns?

A.   Yes
B.   No

2. How do female rhinos greet each other?

A.   They rub their noses against each other
B.   They rub their bottoms against each other

3. What is another name for the white rhinoceros?

A.   Long-horned rhinoceros
B.   Square-lipped rhinoceros

Dolphin

WHO?

Dolphins are related to whales. They are not fish. They are mammals and they do not lay eggs! Dolphins have to come up for air regularly. There are nearly 30 different types of dolphins.

WHAT?

Dolphins mainly eat fish. They like squid too. When they are not hunting for food, they like to play. They jump in the air, chase each other while diving or swim along with a boat!

WHERE?

Dolphins feel most at home in shallow parts of the sea. They always live in large schools. Sometimes, more than 1,000 dolphins swim together!

DID YOU KNOW THAT...

... the orca is the largest dolphin?
... a dolphin is a very clever animal?
... dolphins are very nosy?

Weight: 40-4,500 kg (depending on the species), regular dolphin: 75 kg
Colour: grey, black, white
Mode of living: in a school
Life span: 35 years
Gestation period: 9 months
Offspring: 1

1. A dolphin breathes through a blowhole...
A.   at the top of its head
B.   at the front of its head

2. Does a dolphin talk with sounds?
A.   Yes
B.   No

3. A newborn dolphin baby eats or drinks...
A.   fish
B.   mother's milk

Weight: 9,000 kg
Colour: black and white
Mode of living: in a group
Life span: 35-50 years
Gestation period: 12-16 months
Offspring: 1

Orca

WHO?

Orcas are the largest type of dolphin in the world. This enormous animal is easy to recognise by its black and white colouring and large dorsal fin which can grow to up to 2 m long!

WHAT?

Orcas hunt in groups. They like fish and sea birds, but they enjoy seals, dolphins and even whales as well!

WHERE?

Orcas live in the middle of the sea but are also found near the coast. Sometimes they live in large groups and sometimes in small ones. The oldest females are the leaders.

DID YOU KNOW THAT...

... an orca is also called a sword whale?
... orcas never sleep?
... orcas never fight each other?

Take the test!

1. Why is an orca also called a sword whale?

A.   Because of its teeth, which are as sharp as a sword

B.   Because of its big, pointed dorsal fin

2. Does an orca have teeth?

A.   Yes

B.   No

3. What is a baby orca called?

A.   A chick

B.   A calf

1B/ 2A/ 3B

Weight: 3,000 kg
Colour: grey-white, yellow, brown
Mode of living: alone or in schools
Life span: 50-100 years

Shark

WHO?

There are many different kinds of sharks. Most are not dangerous to humans. Sharks have existed for 400 million years. Almost all sharks have a mouth full of sharp teeth. The white shark is the largest predatory fish.

WHAT?

Most sharks eat other fish. Large sharks, such as the great white shark, love to eat seals and dolphins. Only the whale shark does not eat large animals, because it prefers plankton.

WHERE?

Sharks live in seas and oceans. Some live in rivers in warm areas. The great white shark feels most at home in cold and deep oceans. It does not like warm water.

DID YOU KNOW THAT...

... the whale shark is the largest fish in the world?

... a shark can smell one drop of blood in 100 million drops of water?

... a shark sheds thousands of teeth throughout its life?

Take the test!

1. Can sharks swim backwards?

A.   Yes

B.   No

2. When a shark stops swimming...

A.   it sinks

B.   it stays in the same place

3. Do sharks have good night vision?

A.   Yes

B.   No

1B/2A/3A

Whale

WHO?

The whale is a mammal that lives in the sea. Its distant relatives had 4 legs! Whales regularly come to the surface to breathe and blow steam high in the air when they exhale.

WHAT?

Whales mostly live off plankton and small fish. They swallow a large amount of water and sieve it, so that only food remains. A baby whale drinks its mother's milk for 7 months, up to 90 litres per day!

WHERE?

A whale lives in colder seas. There are even whales around the poles. Each year, they migrate to warmer areas where they stay for a couple of months. Baby whales are born in warm seawater.

DID YOU KNOW THAT...

... whales explore their surroundings using echoes?
... a baby whale can swim straight away?
... whales can hear through small holes in their head?

Weight: up to 190,000 kg
Colour: grey
Mode of living: in a school
Life span: 85 years
Gestation period: 12–15 months
Offspring: 1

---

1. A whale can...

A. sing
B. stay underwater all day

2. Is a whale a fish?

A. Yes
B. No

3. What are males and female whales called?

A. Bulls and cows
B. Stallions and mares

1A, 2B, 3A

Polar bear

WHO?

Polar bears are related to brown bears. They are very big, strong and dangerous. A polar bear can grow up to 3 m tall! Its light fur makes the polar bear difficult to see in the snow.

WHAT?

Polar bears like meat. They like to eat seals, which they can smell from a great distance. They also eat fish and will tuck into a small whale once in a while, but they do not eat penguins because these live at the South Pole!

WHERE?

Polar bears do not live in groups. They prefer to live alone. They live around the North Pole amongst the snow and ice. When they go looking for food, they sometimes have to walk long distances.

DID YOU KNOW THAT...

... you can tell by the teeth of a polar bear how old it is?
... the tail of a polar bear is smaller than a pencil?
... the skin of a polar bear is black?

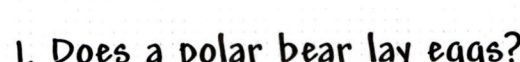

Weight: up to 800 kg
Colour: yellow-white
Mode of living: alone
Life span: 15-18 years
Gestation period: 200-250 days
Offspring: 2

1. Does a polar bear lay eggs?
A.   Yes
B.   No

2. Under water a polar bear...
A.   keeps its eyes open
B.   keeps its eyes shut

3. A polar bear tooth...
A.   becomes thicker each year
B.   falls out each year

1B/2A/3A

Weight: 400 kg
Colour: brown, black
Mode of living: alone
Life span: 30 years
Gestation period: 6-8 months
Offspring: 2

Bear

WHO?

Brown bears are dangerous predators. They live on the land and can run really fast. Young bears can hunt when they are 3 months old! There are 8 different kinds of bear.

WHAT?

A brown bear will eat anything from grass to deer, but it prefers plants, roots and fish. In autumn, they have to eat a lot to become fat so that they do not have to look for food during the winter.

WHERE?

Bears live in many places around the world. They mostly live in wooded and mountainous areas, often near water. In winter, bears will rest in their caves.

DID YOU KNOW THAT...

... a baby bear is born in a cave or hole?
... a bear's claws can become almost 15 cm long?
... bears lose half their body weight during hibernation?

Take the test!

1. When are baby bears born?

A.   In winter

B.   In summer

2. Do bears have a good sense of smell?

A.   Yes

B.   No

1A 2A

Weight: 300-800 kg
Colour: grey-brown, red-brown
Mode of living: in a herd and alone
Life span: 25 years
Gestation period: 8 months
Offspring: 1-2

Moose

WHO?

The moose is the largest of all the species of deer. It can grow even bigger than a horse! Only males have antlers. A female moose is called a cow. The male is called a bull.

WHAT?

A moose's favourite dish is young twigs, bark and leaves. A moose usually lives alone, but in winter it seeks the company of other moose.

WHERE?

A moose feels most at home in humid woods with coniferous trees. It likes to swim and can often be found in the water. In summer, it lives near water, but in the winter it travels to dry areas.

DID YOU KNOW THAT...

... a moose has the heaviest antlers of all deer?
... their antlers can weigh up to 36 kg?
... a mother moose chases away her baby when she has a new baby?

Take the test!

1. A moose...

A. never sheds its antlers

B. sheds its antlers each year

2. A moose comes out especially...

A. when it gets dark

B. in the middle of the day

3. Can a moose swim and dive?

A. Yes

B. No

1B/2A/3A

Kangaroo

WHO?

There are almost 40 different species of kangaroo. The largest is the red giant kangaroo, which is almost as large as a fully-grown person. A newborn kangaroo weighs less than a paperclip and stays in its mother's pouch until it does not fit in it anymore!

WHAT?

A kangaroo is a herbivore and likes to eat grass and leaves. It spends about 10 hours a day eating.

WHERE?

The giant kangaroo lives in dry areas of Australia. It likes to live in groups of sometimes 100 kangaroos! Males will fight each other to decide who the leader is.

DID YOU KNOW THAT...

... kangaroos use their tail as a third hind leg to lean on?

... a giant kangaroo can jump more than 8 m forward?

... a baby kangaroo is called a joey?

Weight: 40-80 kg
Colour: brown, red-brown, grey
Mode of living: in a herd
Life span: 15 years
Gestation period: 35 days
Offspring: 1

1. A kangaroo stamps on the ground with its hind legs...
   A. to warn in case of danger
   B. when it has an itchy leg

2. A baby kangaroo only starts to grow when...
   A. its older brother or sister has left the pouch
   B. when it has left the pouch

1A, 2A

Andean condor

WHO?

Andean condors belong to the vulture family. They are one of the largest flying birds in the world. The Andean condor has black feathers, a white collar and a bald head.

WHAT?

The Andean condor lives off dead animals. It eats mice and rabbits but also deer and even llamas. It sticks its head deep into the skeletons of dead animals and pecks the meat off the bones.

WHERE?

An Andean condor feels at home in the mountains of Latin America, the Andes. It lives at high altitudes and flies long distances in search of food every day.

DID YOU KNOW THAT...

... the Andean condor can blush?
... it pees on its own feet to cool down?
... the Andean condor has a wingspan of 3 m or more?

Weight: 11–15 kg
Colour: black and white
Mode of living: alone or in pairs
Life span: 50 years
Gestation period: 7–9 weeks
Offspring: 1

1. An Andean condor lays its eggs...
A.   in hard to reach cliff faces
B.   in a nest in a tree

2. Male condors and females...
A.   never stay together long
B.   stay together their whole life

3. Is the Andean condor a bird of prey?
A.   Yes
B.   No

Weight: 155 kg
Colour: the male: black and white; the female: brown
Mode of living: in a herd
Life span: 20-30 years
Gestation period: 40 days
Offspring: 10-15 eggs

Ostrich

WHO?

An ostrich is a special bird: it cannot fly! It can run very fast though. When it is running, it can easily cover 2.5 m in a single stride.

WHAT?

An ostrich can grow 2.5 m tall. Its eggs are also big: as big as 24 chicken eggs combined! An ostrich prefers to eat plants and small animals.

WHERE?

Ostriches live on grasslands and are also found in the desert. They live in herds. When an ostrich goes to sleep, it sits down and lays its neck on the ground. The leader will stay awake and watch over its herd.

DID YOU KNOW THAT...

... the ostrich is the largest and heaviest bird in the world?
... it can reach a speed of 70 km per hour?
... an ostrich only has two toes on each foot?

Take the test!

1. Can an ostrich see far?
A.   Yes, they recognise animals from 3 km away
B.   No, they can only recognise an animal from 2 m away

2. Ostriches lay all eggs of their herd...
A.   in 1 nest
B.   in separate nests

iA 2A

Orang-utan

Weight: 40-90 kg
Colour: red-brown
Mode of living: alone or in pairs
Life span: 50 years
Gestation period: 8 months
Offspring: 1

WHO?

Orang-utans belong to the family of anthropoid apes. They have very long arms and strong hands and feet so they can climb trees well.

WHAT?

An orang-utan will find everything it needs in the trees: it loves fruit and likes to eat leaves and insects. When it is thirsty, it drinks rain water from the tree or it will chew some leaves.

WHERE?

Of all anthropoid apes, the orang-utan spends the most time in the trees. Therefore, it lives in wooded areas. At night, it sleeps high up in the trees in a nest, which it has built out of branches.

DID YOU KNOW THAT...

... orang-utan means 'person of the forest'?
... orang-utans are very clever?
... orang-utans make umbrellas out of leaves when it rains heavily?

Take the test!

1. Does an orang-utan have strong teeth?
A. Yes, it can crush nuts with them
B. No, it can only bite through fruit with them

2. Baby orang-utans are born...
A. up in the tree
B. down below in the bushes

3. Orang-utans sleep...
A. always in the same nest
B. in a new nest, which they build every day

Giant panda

WHO?
Giant pandas are related to bears. Newborn babies are still pink, but after a few weeks, they become black and white so you can recognise them as giant pandas.

WHAT?
Bears are omnivores, but a giant panda prefers to eat plants. Its favourite food is bamboo. When there is really nothing else, it will eat the occasional fish, a couple of insects, some flower bulbs or a little grass.

WHERE?
The giant panda can only be found in the wild in China. It lives in the mountains there. The Chinese call the giant panda the cat bear because just like a cat it can climb trees very well! This giant animal prefers to live alone.

DID YOU KNOW THAT...
... a giant panda does not hibernate?
... it likes to rest in a hollow tree?
... the name 'panda' comes from the Nepalese word for 'bamboo eater'?

Weight: 80–100 kg
Colour: black and white
Mode of living: alone
Life span: 15 years
Gestation period: 90–160 days
Offspring: 1–2

1. A newborn giant panda weighs...
A.   as much as 2–3 sandwiches
B.   as much as 2–3 packets of sugar

2. The giant panda uses its tail...
A.   as a brush, to leave its scent on trees
B.   as a sweeping brush to clean the ground before it sits down

Great Dane

WHO?

The Great Dane is one of the biggest dogs in the world. People keep them as pets. Baby Great Danes are called puppies. A Great Dane is also called a Danish Hound.

WHAT?

Great Danes eat a lot. They like meat and dry dog food that is specially made for Great Danes. They also need to drink clean water.

WHERE?

Great Danes can be kept as pets, but they need plenty of space! A Great Dane likes to run and walk outside, but does not like walking in the rain!

DID YOU KNOW THAT...

... Great Danes are among the strongest dogs in the world?

... Great Danes are excellent guard dogs?

... the largest Great Dane is more than 1 m tall?

1. The Great Dane is...

A. an active dog

B. a quiet dog

2. A Great Dane is usually...

A. good with children

B. not good with children

3. Great Danes used to be used as...

A. lap dogs

B. hunting dogs

Weight: 150-250 kg

Colour: light brown

Mode of living: in a pride

Life span: 10-14 years

Gestation period: 100 days

Offspring: 2-4

Lion

WHO?

Lions are huge cats. They have large canine teeth and long claws, which they can withdraw. Lions are strong animals and have agile bodies. A lion uses its tail to keep balanced when running and climbing.

WHAT?

Lions, or actually lionesses, prefer to hunt in the morning when it is not too hot yet. They surround their prey so it cannot escape.

WHERE?

Lions used to live in Africa, Europe and Asia, but today they only live in the wild in Africa. They feel most at home on large grassy plains with trees to rest under.

DID YOU KNOW THAT...

... a lion's roar can be heard from a distance of 9 km?

... a lioness hides her newborn babies in different places so hyenas cannot eat them?

Take the test!

I. A lion sees in black and white at night and during the day...

A. too

B. in colour

2. Is a lion a predator?

A. Yes

B. No

3. Which lion has a long mane around its head?

A. The male

B. The female

1B/2A/3A

Weight: 25–550 kg
Colour: green, brown
Mode of living: alone
Life span: 40 years
Gestation period: 5–7 months
Offspring: 6–50

Giant snake

WHO?

There are many different kinds of snakes. Giant snakes belong to the boa family. The anaconda is a species of giant snake which can grow 8 m long!

WHAT?

Giant snakes especially like to eat birds and small rodents. But sometimes they eat larger animals, such as a boar or a small crocodile. They coil around their prey, suffocate it and eat it.

WHERE?

Giant snakes often live in trees, but some giant snakes are too heavy for the branches and prefer to move about on the ground in the mud or lie in the water.

DID YOU KNOW THAT...

... a giant snake is not poisonous?
... giant snakes are also known as constrictor snakes?
... some anacondas eat each other?

Take the test!

1. The giant snake eats its prey...
A.   whole
B.   in tiny bits

2. The giant snake...
A.   lays eggs
B.   lays ready-made babies

3. Do giant snakes hibernate?
A.   Yes
B.   No

Giant squid

WHO?

The giant squid is the largest of the squid family. It is very strong and lives deep underwater. A giant squid can grow up to 13 m long! Female squid are larger than males.

WHAT?

Giant squid mainly eat smaller fish, but they also hunt other squid. They catch their prey with their arms, pull it to their mouth and eat it.

WHERE?

A giant squid lives deep in the ocean. It likes salt water. Because it lives so deep underneath the water, it is difficult for humans to study it.

DID YOU KNOW THAT...

... giant squid have the largest eyes of all animals?

... they are sometimes as big as a football?

... the giant squid was photographed for the first time in 2006?

Weight: 150–275 kg
Colour: red-brown
Mode of living: alone
Life span: unknown

1. How many arms does a squid have?

A.   6 arms

B.   8 arms

2. Why does a squid squirt ink when it is in danger?

A.   To make sure the enemy does not see or smell

B.   By squirting ink, it can swim away extra fast

3. When a giant squid loses an arm...

A.   a new one does not grow back

B.   a new one grows back

Weight: 300 kg

Colour: green-brown, grey-black

Mode of living: alone

Life span: 150 years

Eggs hatch: after 60-120 days

Offspring: 2-50 eggs

Giant tortoise

WHO?

Giant tortoises have been around for a very long time. There are currently about 10 different species alive. Giant tortoises have shells protecting their backs and tummies. They can grow to 1.5 m long!

WHAT?

Giant tortoises mainly live off grass, leaves, herbs and fruit. They grow the most in the rainy season because there is lots of food to be found. During the rainy season, they eat 3 times as much as in the dry season!

WHERE?

Giant tortoises are mostly found on the islands in the Pacific. For most of the day they lie down to rest in a nice spot in the shade.

DID YOU KNOW THAT...

... female tortoises lay their eggs in a hole under the sand?

... there were giant tortoises 60 million years ago ?

... a giant tortoise can only walk 200 m in 1 hour?

1. Do giant tortoises have a tail?

A.	Yes

B.	No

2. A newborn giant tortoise baby...

A.	digs its way out of the hole in which it is born

B.	is dug out of the hole by its mother

1A/2A

Weight: 750 kg
Colour: brown, green
Mode of living: usually alone
Life span: 30–60 years
Eggs hatch: after 60–115 days
Offspring: 20–95 eggs

Crocodile

WHO?

Crocodiles are reptiles. This strong animal has a mouth full of sharp teeth and a long tail. It always lives close to the water. There are more than 20 different types of crocodile.

WHAT?

Crocodiles are carnivores. A crocodile can swim so quietly that other animals usually do not hear it. It mostly eats fish, insects or frogs, but it also likes larger animals!

WHERE?

Crocodiles are found in warm areas with lots of water. They need the sun to stay warm. Most crocodiles do not like salt water, except the saltwater crocodile.

DID YOU KNOW THAT...

... a baby crocodile squeaks before it crawls out of the egg?

... the mother crocodile takes her young to the water in her mouth?

... a crocodile can go without food for a year, if necessary?

Take the test!

1. Do young crocodiles already have sharp teeth?

A.   Yes

B.   No

2. Of all reptiles, the crocodile...

A.   is the least clever

B.   the cleverest

3. Can crocodiles make a noise?

A.   Yes

B.   No

1A. 1B./3A.

Walrus

WHO?

A walrus is a large mammal with wrinkled skin and a shaggy moustache. Both males and females have tusks, which can become as long as 1 m. They are excellent swimmers and divers.

WHAT?

A walrus finds its food at the bottom of the ocean. It can dive as deep as 80 m. It has 450 whiskers, which it uses to find its way in the dark water. It prefers to eat shellfish, sea urchins and crabs.

WHERE?

A walrus lives on the ice near the North Pole but spends most of the day in the water. Because of its thick layer of fat, which wobbles when it moves, it stays warm on the ice and in the water.

DID YOU KNOW THAT...

... walruses become pink when they lie in the sun?

... a walrus roots about on the bottom of the sea with its nose like a pig?

... walruses can stay underwater longer than 10 minutes?

Take the test!

1. A walrus baby...
   A. is born underwater
   B. is born on the ice

2. When a walrus mother dives into the water...
   A. her baby clings to her neck at the front
   B. her baby clings to her tail on her back

1B/2A

In the Footsteps of
Augustine Henry
and his Chinese plant collectors

Seamus O'Brien

Foreword by Roy Lancaster OBE VMH

AUGUSTIN HENRY.
1929

In the Footsteps of
Augustine Henry
and his Chinese plant collectors

Seamus O'Brien

Foreword by Roy Lancaster OBE VMH

GARDEN · ART · PRESS

ISBN-13: 978-1-87067-373-0

Endpapers: FRONT *Davidia involucrata* var. *vilmoriniana*, one of Augustine Henry's most famous finds; BACK Henry discovered *Koelreuteria elegans* ssp. *formosana* near Bankinsing (now known as Wanchin)

Frontispiece: A portrait of Augustine Henry by Celia Harrison, 1929. In the background are leaves of one of his most famous finds, *Rhododendron augustinii*.

Title page: *Ganoderma lucidum,* an important medicinal mushroom cultivated on a commercial scale in Shennongjia. It is grown on the buried logs of *Quercus variabilis* on a three-year system and sold all over China.

Dedication page: Door (detail), Bamboo Garden, Chengdu, Sichuan Province

Printed in China for Garden Art Press, an imprint of the Antique Collectors' Club Ltd, Woodbridge, Suffolk IP12 4SD

In memory of my brothers

Thomas and Lorcan

In paradisum deducant te Angeli

The Xiang Xi river, with the mountains of Xingshan County to the rear. Once a small stream, this tributary and its valley had been substantially flooded by the Three Gorges dam at the time of our 2004 expedition to Hubei Province.

Contents

Foreword
Roy Lancaster OBE VMH

On an unusually bright and mellow afternoon in November 2007, I found myself in the company of Tony Kirkham, Curator of the Arboretum at the Royal Botanic Gardens, Kew. We were examining, and I was admiring, some of the recent introductions of trees he and his colleagues had made, principally from China, which were now established and, in some instances, already flowering and fruiting. They included several *Sorbus* and *Malus* species, not to mention *Quercus, Lithocarpus, Betula, Pterocarya* and many rare conifers. The light was beginning to fade when Tony pointed out a broad-crowned tree of 11 m (36 ft) or so, which he explained had recently been liberated from the competing growth of an old, densely planted windbreak. It was, he informed me, *Ulmus castaneifolia*, the chestnut-leaved elm, a Chinese species I had neither seen nor even heard of before.

With its large, handsome, multi-veined and toothed, glossy green leaves, *Ulmus castaneifolia* resembled no other elm I knew and I was suitably impressed. I presumed that this was yet another tree recently introduced from a country that has provided gardens of the Western world with more hardy plants of ornamental value than any other. I was mistaken. It appears to have been planted during the 'reign' of that master dendrologist W. J. Bean (1863–1947), who, for 46 years, served Kew, latterly as Curator. During this time, Bean met and corresponded with most of the great gardeners, plant explorers and dendrologists of his day, and none more notable than Augustine Henry, who, it transpires, was the first European to discover *Ulmus castaneifolia*, in China's Sichuan Province in May 1888.

It was yet another reminder to me of that great Irishman, physician, botanist, dendrologist, forester and pioneering plant collector, to name but a few of his activities, who, while working as a Customs official in China in the last two decades of the 19th century, contributed so much to our knowledge and understanding of an immensely rich and fast-disappearing flora. Indeed, it could be argued that Henry's presence in China came in the nick of time, as the 20th century brought a great acceleration in the exploitation of her natural resources and the despoliation, if not destruction, of much of her native forests. Not that he was able to prevent or even delay deforestation, but he at least helped to draw attention to and record what was being threatened

I long ago read, and have never forgotten, the story of how this young man first trained for a medical career and was then persuaded, aged 24, to sign up with the Chinese Imperial Maritime Customs Service, before sailing eventually to a small city called Yichang (then Ichang), one thousand miles from the sea and even further from home, on the shores of one of the world's mightiest rivers, the Yangtze. That he should then, in his spare time and with only a comparatively limited knowledge of medicinal plants, begin searching for and collecting native flora over a vast wild and scattered terrain is something that has never failed to impress and inspire me. Of course, he was by no means the first European to explore for plants in China, but it was the sheer scale of his collecting and his exceptional results in discovering plants new to science that set him apart.

We are told that, in the 15 years he spent in China, he collected and prepared some 158,050 dried specimens, representing more than 6,000 distinct species, of which over 1,726 were new to science. His remains the largest single collection ever made by a plant hunter in China. Small wonder then that Dr Emil Bretschneider, in his *History of European Botanical Discoveries in China*, published in 1898, paid tribute to Henry as 'one of the most successful of the explorers of the Chinese flora, who was lucky enough to collect in an entirely new field, which proved to be extremely rich in novelties'.

Henry also introduced some of these plants by means of seeds and bulbs into Western cultivation, while even more of them were introduced later as seeds, plants or bulbs by the English plant hunter E. H. Wilson, who benefited greatly from Henry's advice and expertise. There are those who feel that Wilson has received more credit than Henry for the discovery and introduction of new Chinese plants into cultivation, the suggestion being that garden history has treated Henry less favourably, but this is simply not true. In China, Henry had a full-time job as a Customs official, collecting dried specimens of plants in his leisure time, mainly for scientific study, whilst Wilson, though he too prepared specimens for the herbarium, was a professional plant hunter, engaged to collect living material for introduction into cultivation, and was employed to do so first by the English nurseryman James Veitch & Sons of Chelsea and Coombe Wood and then for the Arnold Arboretum in Cambridge, Massachusetts.

The two men had different characters and agendas, though, taken together, they were a formidable presence in China, one following the other, each succeeding spectacularly in his own field. Anyone who even imagines that the attention undoubtedly paid by some popular writers to Wilson's exploits might have, in any way, diminished those of Henry should consider Wilson's own tribute to 'the master': 'no one in any age has contributed more to our knowledge of Chinese plants than this scholarly Irishman'.

On a more personal level, as a gardener, I have much to be thankful for Henry's contribution directly or indirectly growing in my own garden of one-third of an acre in Hampshire, England. On a recent tour, I noted the following Chinese plants he either first discovered or introduced – or both: *Itea ilicifolia*, *Saruma henryi*, *Corydalis cheilanthifolia*, *Lilium henryi*, *Mahonia lomariifolia*, *Parthenocissus henryana*, *Rosa chinensis* var. *spontanea*, *Sorbus hemsleyi*, *Buxus henryi*, *Illicium henryi*, *Staphylea holocarpa* var. *rosea*, *Lonicera crassifolia*, *Lonicera calcarata*, *Rubus henryi* var. *bambusarum* and *Deinanthe caerulea*. No, I am not especially a collector of plants with a Henry connection; just ornamental or interesting ones, and, if I may be permitted another, it is the *Davidia involucrata* var. *vilmoriniana* I gave to my neighbour, which created a sensation in May 2009 when its branches were hung with those curious and highly ornamental blooms that attracted Henry when he first found this tree in the mountains of south Wushan County in Sichuan Province on 17 May 1888.

For many years, I was puzzled as to why no comprehensive account of Henry's plant exploits in China had ever been written for general publication. Then, in August 2002, as a member of what is now known as the Royal Horticultural Society's Bursaries Advisory Committee, I found myself discussing an application from a young man working for the National Botanic Gardens, Glasnevin, in Dublin. He proposed leading an expedition to central China, travelling 'in the footsteps of Augustine Henry' with a view to revisiting his old haunts and searching for the plants he first made known to the West. If all should go well, he hoped to write a book. That young man was the present author, Seamus O'Brien. Well, he succeeded with his request, and, over the next four years, he and his colleagues made not one but three expeditions to central and south-west China and Taiwan.

Following the final expedition, Seamus presented the committee with a detailed report; it was also the largest and heaviest it has ever received. To describe it as impressive would not convey the whole of it, and we were in no doubt that the long-awaited book on Henry's plant collecting in China was a realistic possibility.

Congratulations, then, to the author and those colleagues, enthusiasts and plant lovers who shared his dreams, travels and explorations, and those who encouraged and supported him in producing this deserving and ambitious account of Ireland's greatest plant explorer. The book's 13 generously illustrated chapters tell not one but two stories, detailing, on one hand, the travels and discoveries of Augustine Henry and his Chinese plant collectors between 1885 and 1900, and, on the other, the author and his colleagues' experiences in revisiting those hallowed places and reliving the excitement of plant hunting more than a century ago.

Having myself visited a few of those locations and seen some of the plants first discovered or collected by Henry, I can understand the author's feeling of having 'arrived' and I can sense and share his excitement in finding plants first collected in the same location all those years ago by a man he clearly and understandably has huge respect for. We all have our heroes. It makes a potent brew and is well conveyed in a narrative richly peopled with brief but tantalising accounts of some of those characters Henry met in China, such as the English naturalist Antwerp Edgar Pratt, who brought his wife and family with him to Yichang, where Henry was based, leaving them to get on as best they could during his several absences in the mountains as far west as the Tibetan border. Henry persuaded Pratt to take one of his trained plant collectors with him, which worked to their mutual satisfaction. It was on the Tibetan border that Pratt met the French missionary and plant collector Père Jean André Soulié, who was later captured, tortured and put to death by Tibetan monks. At Yichang, Henry also met the German missionary Dr Ernst Faber, the first botanist to climb the plant-rich and sacred Mount Omei in Sichuan Province.

Having spent 18 years there, Henry finally sailed away from China for the last time on 31 December 1900. Botanically, he had made his name and earned his reputation as the greatest living authority on Chinese plants. It was the end of an era. For some people, that would have been quite enough, but not for Henry. He was still relatively young, just 43, with his life ahead of him. He decided on a new direction. Training first as a forester in France, he then spent several years collaborating with the noted English traveller and naturalist Henry J. Elwes on the classic, multi-volumed work *The Trees of Great Britain and Ireland,* published between 1906 and 1913. This saw Henry visiting every country in central and western Europe, as well as the Pacific north-west of America and Canada. Even then he wasn't finished, beginning a new and equally successful career first as Reader of Forestry at Cambridge, and then, aged 56, becoming the first Professor of Forestry at the Royal College of Science in Dublin. He retired 13 years later, in 1926, four years before his death aged 73. These last years, briefly described in the author's final chapter, brings to an end this inspiring and most enjoyable account of Henry's life of trees and plants.

Many tributes have been paid over the years to this kind, gifted, energetic and versatile Irishman whose achievements touched and benefited so many lives. But one of his most enduring legacies, as this book reminds us, can be enjoyed wherever people garden or plant trees.

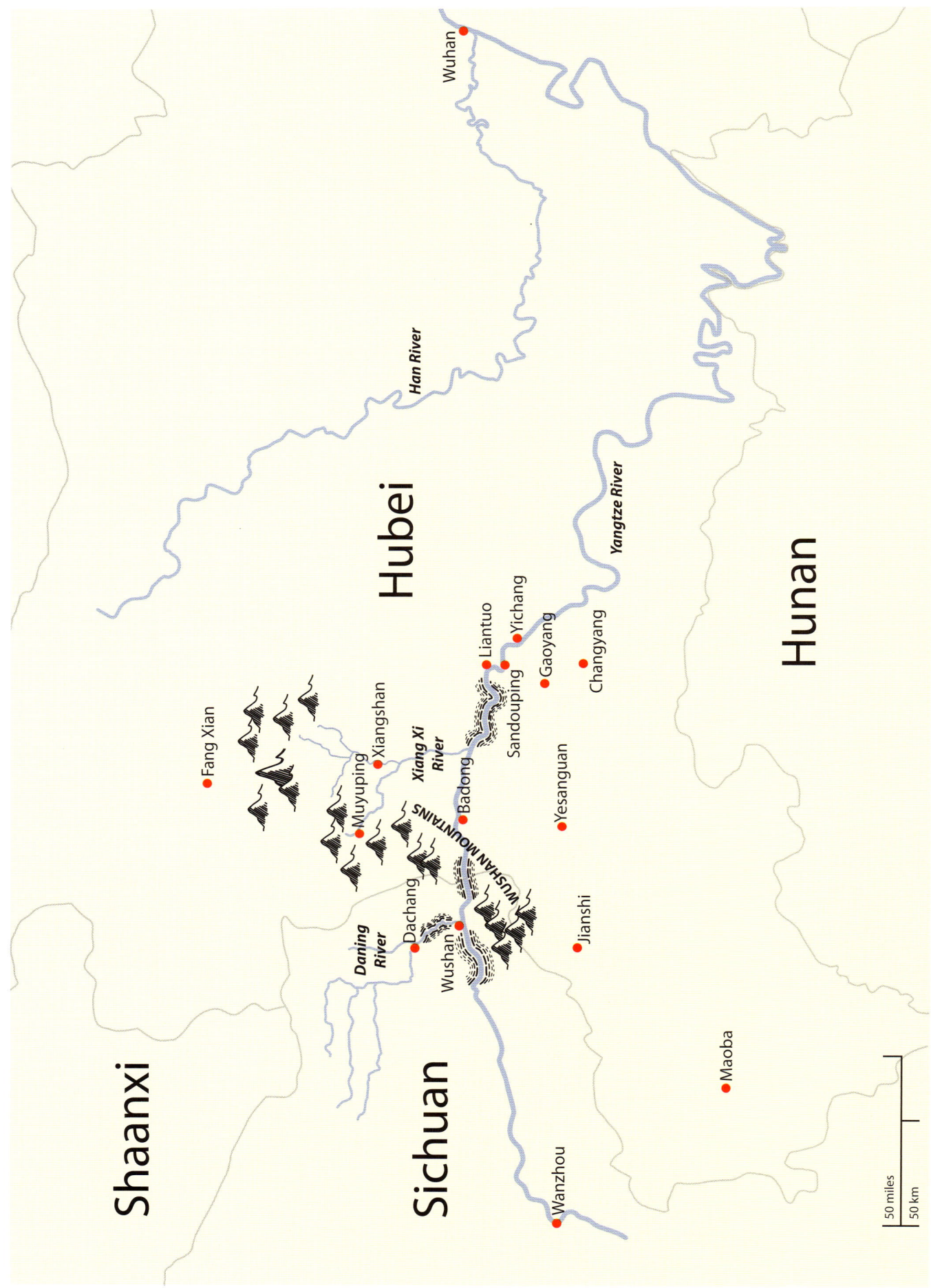

Western
Sichuan

*Min
River*

*Min
River*

● **Chengdu**

*Dadu
River*

● Baoxing

● Kangding

● Ya'an

●Luding

GONGGA SHAN

EMEI SHAN

●Leshan

Emei ●

WA-SHAN

*Min
River*

30 miles

30 km

*Yangtze
River*

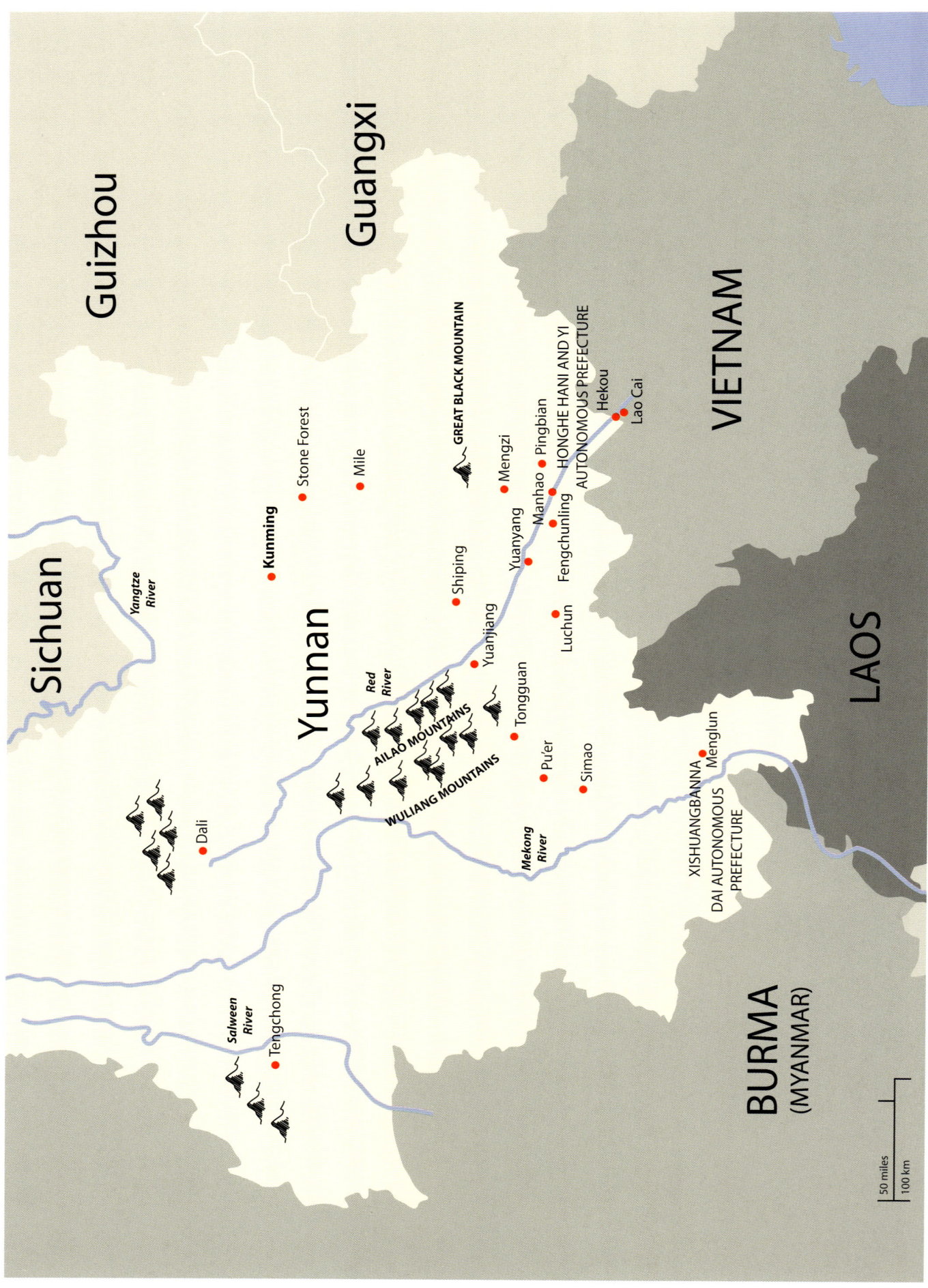

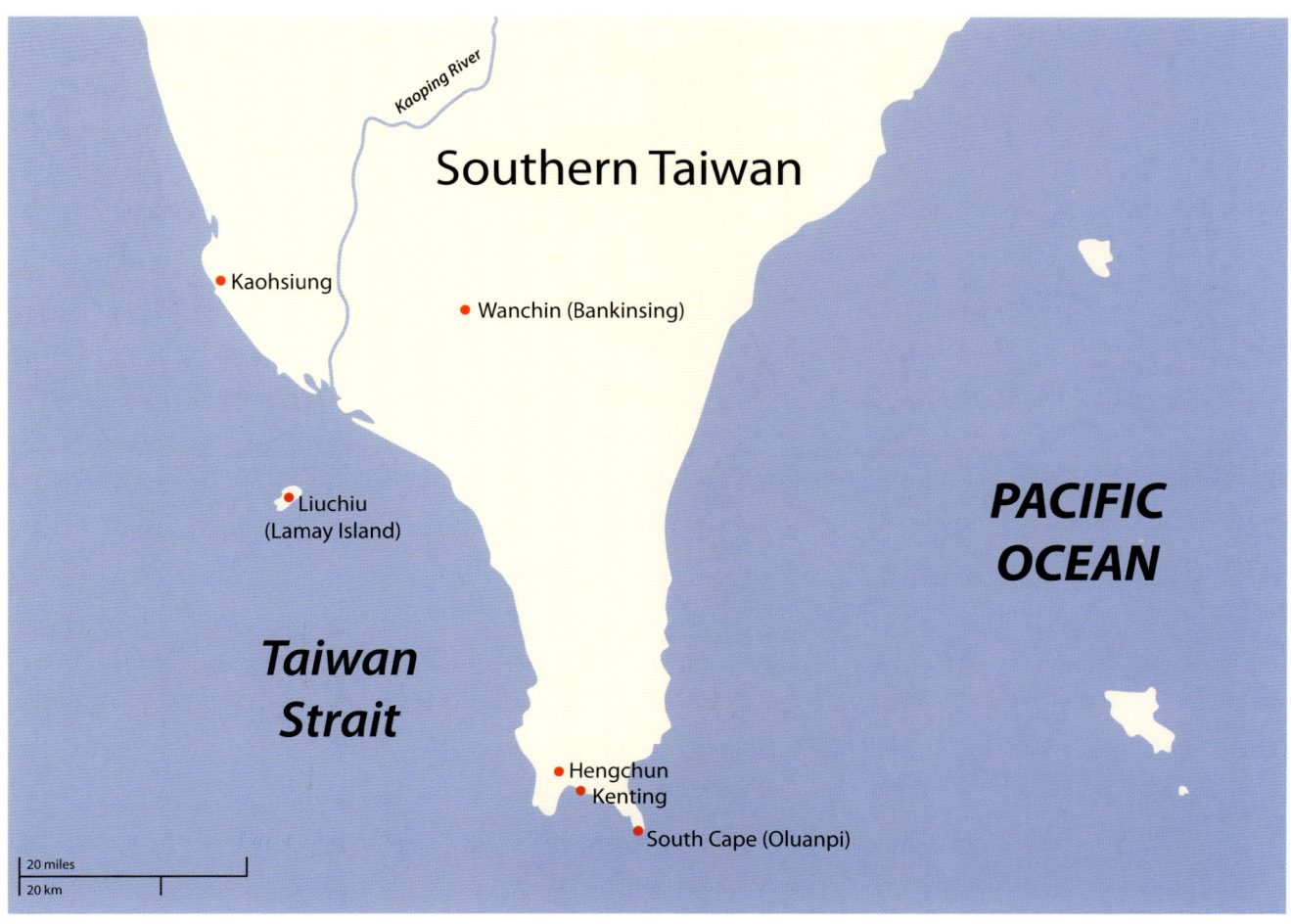

Acknowledgements

It has taken eight years of research and travel to bring this book to a conclusion, and I owe a great deal of gratitude to a number of individuals and organisations. At the National Botanic Gardens in Glasnevin, Ireland, I received valuable help and support from former Directors Donal Synnott and Dr Peter Wyse Jackson, and from Glasnevin's current Director, Dr Matthew Jebb. From the same institution, I would also like to thank the garden's Curator, Paul Maher, and Sarah Ball, Alexandra Caccamo and Colette Edwards from the Library and Archives. The late Grace Pasley, Herbarium Assistant at Glasnevin, quietly carried out a great amount of administrative work during the planning of expeditions and travelled on two of the trips to central China and Taiwan.

At the Royal Botanic Gardens, Kew, in the UK, I am most grateful to James Kay, Fiona Ainsworth and Michele Losse of the Library and Archives. In the USA, I would like to offer my thanks to Emily Ashley of New York Botanical Gardens, Kathleen Fisher of the Strybing Arboretum in San Francisco, California, and Beth Bayley from the Arnold Arboretum, Boston, Massachusetts.

Many thanks to Roy Lancaster OBE VMH, who has been a great supporter of this book and generously penned its foreword. I am especially grateful to Mary Bradshaw, who very kindly read the text and made suggestions; to Roy Briggs, who supplied a photograph of his great-uncle, E. H. Wilson; and to Dr Barbara Phillips, Augustine Henry's grand-niece, who supplied a number of images of Henry in China and at home in Ireland. Kathe Scullion, Henry's great-grand-niece (in Philadelphia, Pennsylvania, USA) sent constant encouragement, as did many of the Henry family in Ireland. Thanks must also go to Bill O'Sullivan for his help in producing accurate, contemporary maps to feature in this book.

Funding for all three expeditions came from a number of sources, and to these sponsors I am most grateful: the Royal Horticultural Society Bursary Fund, the Stanley Smith (UK) Horticultural Trust, the late Valerie Finnis (Lady Scott) and the Merlin Trust, the Michael McCoy Trust, and the National Botanic Gardens, Glasnevin, Trust Fund. Valerie Finnis was a stalwart friend and sponsor over several years, and Marjorie Noel of the RHS Bursary Fund was always extremely helpful.

In China, expert help and support came from the Chinese Academy of Sciences; in particular, from Professor Ding Zhaohua, Professor Chen Chang, Professor Chen Zhonping, Professor Mingxi Jiang, Mr Deng Wenqiang, Miss Wang Qing and Miss Yang Bo of Wuhan Botanical Gardens in Hubei Province. I am also greatly indebted to Professor Wen Liang Chou and Mr Kevin Chen of the Taiwan Forestry Research Institute in Taipei, who organised our travels in southern Taiwan and our permits to collect there. Thanks must also go to Professor Ho-Yih Liu of the Department of Biological Sciences at National Sun Yat-sen University, Kaohsiung, Taiwan, who organised our fieldwork in the Kaohsiung area, and to his student, Burke Chih-Jen Ko, who facilitated our visit to Bankinsing and Ape's Hill. In Yunnan Province, we received valuable help from Professor Guan Kaiyun, Director of Kunming Botanic Gardens, and from Professor Wang Zhong-Lang, who acted as our untiring and very patient guide. I am also enormously grateful to the many forestry officials in various localities of both China and Taiwan who made our visits to forest reserves possible.

To my fellow travellers in China – Jimi Blake, Assumpta Broomfield, Helen Dillon, Paul Gardiner, Stephanie Henry, Matthew Jebb, Paul Maher, Emer O'Reilly, Cathal O'Sullivan, Grace Pasley, Joan Rogers, Elizabeth Ryan and Noeleen Smyth – I cannot think of a better group to have shared this remarkable adventure with. Many thanks for coming along.

And to anyone else who offered assistance to our work in China and the preparation of this book, many thanks. Without you, this story could not have been told.

Friends we met along the way: a group of children on the roadside between Yichang and Badong. Our work collecting seeds and herbarium specimens raised great curiosity among adults and children alike.

Photographic acknowledgements

I am most grateful to the following institutions and individuals for permission to use their images in this book:

Carol Acton: 313, 315, 329 (top right)
Arnold Arboretum of Harvard University, Jamaica Plain, Boston, Massachusetts, USA: 24, 25, 68, 107 (middle right), 204, 213, 322 (top)
Jimi Blake: 94 (bottom), 97 (top), 121 (top), 134
Roy Briggs: 270
Paul Cook, Ness Botanic Gardens, University of Liverpool, UK: 249 (left), 308 (left)
Professor Douglas Fix, Reed College, Portland, Oregon, USA: 197, 200 (right)
Historic Properties, Office of Public Works, Dublin, Ireland: 27, 29, 232, 236, 240, 242 (top and bottom right), 253 (right), 254, 259, 261 (bottom), 263 (top), 271 (right), 274
Chun-Kuei Liao, National Sun Yat-sen University, Kaohsiung, Taiwan: 203 (right)
Darach Lupton: 151

National Agricultural Library, United States Department of Agriculture, Beltsville, Maryland, USA: 29, 101 (top right), 314 (right)
National Botanic Gardens, Glasnevin, Dublin, Ireland: 2, 18, 21 (left), 26, 33 (right), 36, 37, 57, 60, 161, 162, 163 (right), 166, 167, 169, 170, 171, 172 (top left, top right), 178, 180 (top left), 181, 183, 233, 235, 241, 242 (top, middle, bottom left), 244, 253 (left), 262, 263 (bottom), 264, 271, 314 (left), 318, 323, 324 (right), 326, 327 (top and bottom left), 328
National Sun Yat-sen University, Kaohsiung, Taiwan: 228 (top right)
Cathal O'Sullivan: 296 (top), 301 (top left)
Dr Barbara Phillips: 258, 260 (right), 325
Queen's University Belfast, Belfast, Ireland, UK: 20
Royal Botanic Gardens, Kew, Richmond, Surrey, UK: 31, 46 (left), 76 (bottom), 91, 191, 261 (top), 307, 308 (right), 309
Kathe Scullion: 19

NOTE: Every effort has been made to secure permission to reproduce the images reproduced within this book, and we are grateful to the individuals and institutions that have assisted in this task. Any errors or omissions are entirely unintentional, and the details should be addressed to the publisher.

Introduction

Ithink I first heard of Augustine Henry during my student days at the National Botanic Gardens, Glasnevin, in Dublin in the early 1990s. Among the 20,000 or so different plants that grew there were many named after the legendary Irish plant hunter. One of his best-known finds, *Lilium henryi*, grew in great drifts in the herbaceous border and created a dazzling display every summer, while, by the pond, *Emmenopterys henryi*, a great rarity, had formed one of the finest trees in cultivation. In the National Herbarium at Glasnevin, hundreds of his dried specimens from China are preserved alongside those of a later, and perhaps better-known, collector, Ernest Henry ('E. H.') Wilson.

It was in October 1999 that the idea of bringing an exhibit to the Royal Horticultural Society's Chelsea Flower Show was first mooted by the Irish Garden Plant Society. The theme of our exhibit was to be 'Augustine Henry – an Irish plant collector in China' and I was chosen to chair a team to carry out the project and to research the plants Henry had discovered, as we planned to put many of these on display at that famous London show. Little did I know what an enormous task this would prove to be.

Henry's is a remarkable story. The son of an Irish famine emigrant, he left Ireland in 1881 to take a post as medical officer in the Chinese Imperial Maritime Customs Service. His first base was the city of Yichang, an important treaty port at the head of navigation on the Chang Jiang (Yangtze River) in Hubei Province, central China. Yichang lies near the eastern mouth of the famous Sanxia (Three Gorges) region, one of China's most fantastic landscapes. Those mountains and gorges were to become Henry's playground, and he would spend much of his leisure time botanising in the area.

Alongside his medical duties, Henry was responsible for placing levies on the many plant-derived medicinal goods that were shipped down the Yangtze to Yichang from the hinterlands, and it was through this trade that he gained an interest in botany. His problem, however, was that while he could confirm local Chinese names for these plants, it was impossible to get their botanical equivalents. With this in mind, he contacted Sir Joseph Dalton Hooker, then in his final year as Director of the Royal Botanic Gardens, Kew, in the UK. Hooker had travelled widely in the Himalaya and other regions as a young man, and was more than happy to help this obscure Irishman. Through his position at Kew gardens, Hooker played an important role in the development of colonial agriculture, and understood that a person in Henry's position could be very useful to his own work. Indeed, the relationship proved to be a fruitful one: by the time he left China in December 1900, Henry had sent more than 158,000 herbarium specimens to Kew, consisting of around 6,000 species, one-sixth of the entire Chinese flora. Within this vast assemblage were 5 new families, 37 new genera and more than 1,726 new species, subspecies, and varieties.

Augustine Henry constantly wrote to Kew, urging authorities there to send a collector to China before its great tracts of primeval forests were felled. He was not oblivious to the horticultural potential of these plants and informed botanists at Kew of the suitability of the flora of western and central China for cultivation in the gardens of Britain, Ireland, and North America. Funds were not available to employ a collector from Kew, but Sir William Turner Thiselton-Dyer, Hooker's successor at the Royal Botanic Gardens, did manage to convince Sir Harry (James) Veitch, the greatest nurseryman of his day, to send out a professional collector – and the man they chose was the young Kew-trained gardener, E. H. Wilson. Wilson met Henry in China and, later, followed in his footsteps, introducing many of Henry's finest discoveries to cultivation from the Three Gorges region and further afield. Wilson accredited his success in China to the valuable advice given to him by Augustine Henry at the beginning of his plant-hunting career, and to the fact that Henry allowed him to use the native plant collectors whom he had trained at Yichang more than a decade previously.

Augustine Henry was responsible for initiating a golden age in plant exploration in China. Several notable plant hunters – including George Forrest, Frank Kingdon Ward, Frank N. Meyer, William Purdom and Joseph Rock, as well as E. H. 'Chinese' Wilson – travelled to China as a result of Henry's pioneering work there, and, during the early decades of the 20th century, a flood of fantastic new garden plants reached our shores until China once again shut her doors to Western travellers.

It was during our research for the Chelsea exhibit that I first heard of the Three Gorges Dam (Sanxia Daba)

Augustine Henry's best-known find has to be the lily that bears his name. *Lilium henryi* is a glorious plant and has proved to be easy to grow and long lived in Western cultivation. Alas, it is now a rarity in the Three Gorges Reservoir Region where Henry first found it in July 1887.

hydropower project and its implications for the valleys and gorges in the Hubei and Sichuan provinces where Henry and, later, Wilson had collected plants a century before. As we were busy in Ireland preparing for the Chelsea Flower Show, more than 27,000 labourers in central China were working 24 hours a day in three shifts to create the world's largest dam. That same colossal structure was to span almost 2.5 km across the Yangtze and to rise more than 185 m (607 ft – equivalent to a 60-storey building) above the deepest part of the riverbed. The enormous artificial reservoir would submerge more than 200 cities, towns, and villages that lay in its path – and a number of plants endemic to the region faced extinction. The same valleys explored by Henry and Wilson were doomed to a watery grave and time was short. Flooding was due to begin in October 2002, and, once that process began, the gorges would change forever.

Our goal, therefore, was to sail the Three Gorges before flooding began, and, in the autumn of 2001, I contacted the Chinese Academy of Sciences to organise a series of botanical expeditions tracing the routes covered by Augustine Henry in the late 19th century. In May 2002, our Chelsea exhibit won a coveted silver-gilt medal, the second highest accolade awarded by the Royal Horticultural Society; less than four months later, we flew out to China to begin the first of a series of great adventures. Over the course of three further expeditions, we were to retrace the trails of Augustine Henry, his Chinese plant collectors, and also that of 'Chinese' Wilson. Indeed, the last Westerner to explore many of the regions we visited was none other than E. H. Wilson himself.

When Augustine Henry died in 1930, the bulk of his private library – including his Chinese diaries, notebooks and hand-drawn maps – was bequeathed to the National Botanic Gardens, Glasnevin, and it was on this material that I based the routes of our expeditions. Henry wrote little of his travels, but his copious correspondence held at Kew, the Arnold Arboretum (Harvard University, USA) and with Evelyn Gleeson, his life-long friend in Ireland, paints a full picture of his time spent in China. His massive botanical collections have also been published in hundreds of journals over the past century, and, over a period of five years, I have been able to complete an entire catalogue of his 158,000 specimens, listing all of his new discoveries and the regions where he found them. That same catalogue gave us a good idea of the plants and the sort of terrain to expect when visiting these regions.

China has, however, changed enormously since Henry's time there. In his field notes at Kew and Glasnevin, Henry speaks of mountain ranges cloaked with extensive tracts of virgin forest. In the passing of a century, many of these great forests have been felled, and we were saddened to visit these regions and see little more than thickets of regenerating vegetation. On a global scale, we are losing biodiversity at an alarming rate. Henry himself despaired at the rate of deforestation in southern Yunnan Province and accurately predicted that many species would be forced into extinction in 50 years if the process was allowed to continue. He would shudder if he returned there today.

Yet there is hope. Several areas first botanised by Augustine Henry are now national parks and biosphere reserves. Those that come to mind are Shennongjia in Hubei Province, Kenting National Park on the island of Taiwan and the Daweishan range in south-eastern Yunnan Province. These biological hotspots have been saved primarily because they harbour a multitude of plants that are useful to man.

From our travels in China, we raised thousands of seedlings. Many of these are great rarities and have found safe homes in several state-owned gardens around Ireland. The following pages recount Augustine Henry's associations with these plants, his odyssey in the 'Middle Empire' and the story of our travels through the same regions of China more than a century later. Happy reading!

Chapter 1

Famine and farewell
– a new life in China

O ur story begins in Ireland during the bleakest period of its history and concludes in better times. In 1845, Ireland had a population of 8 million people, compared to England, Wales and Scotland's 16 million. This large population was sustained by the potato, an easy-to-grow crop that required little attention, and, during the early 1840s, no fewer than 3 million people depended on this single food source.

On 20 August 1845, Ireland was struck a devastating and disastrous blow when the first signs of potato blight were noticed on plants at the National Botanic Gardens, Glasnevin, near Dublin.[1] The cause of the disease was then unknown, but investigations later proved it to be the result of a minute fungus, *Phytopthora infestans*. This tiny agent turned the crop of 1845 into an evil-smelling, rotten mush and, by August 1846, the entire Irish potato crop had been lost. The consequences were catastrophic. A million people died of starvation and disease,

Humble beginnings: the Henry homestead at Tyanee, County Derry. Built by his grandfather, Augustine Henry spent his childhood years at the house following the death of his mother in 1871. In later years, he would stay there with his brother Tom when on home leave from China.

and the disaster was soon followed by mass emigration of millions more to England, Australia, Canada and the USA.

By 1848, Ireland had lost a quarter of her population, and, in May of the same year, Bernard Henry, an 18-year-old Derry lad, boarded one of the many 'famine ships' destined for a better life in America. The Henrys were farmers of Roman Catholic background and had lived at Tyanee, a townland to the north of Portglenone in County Derry, since about 1650. Bernard Henry arrived in New York on 5 June 1848, having crossed the Atlantic on board the *New Zealand* from Newry in County Down. News had broken, earlier that year, of the discovery of gold in California, and, in 1849, Bernard joined a stampede of other hopeful emigrants to those western goldfields. From his base in New York, young Bernard took a steamer to Central America and crossed the Isthmus of Panama on foot before sailing on to San Francisco, which had been transformed almost overnight from a small, sleepy village into a substantial town. In 1851, gold had also been found in Australia, and, having had little luck in California, Bernard Henry set sail for the goldfields there in 1854. Henry's stay in Australia was a brief one, however. He returned to Ireland a short time later without a fortune.

In 1855, while visiting his sister in Dundee, Scotland, he met a local girl called Mary MacNamee, and later married her. Mary's mother was the daughter of the Provost of Banff, and she had eloped with Mary's father, an army sergeant. Mary Henry was said to have inherited her mother's independence of character. Born a Protestant, at the age of 18 she converted to Catholicism. The Henrys lived on Hillbank Road in central Dundee for a year or so, where Bernard Henry established a grocery shop. In 1856, their daughter Matilda was born and the 2 July 1857 saw the birth of their first son, Augustine.

When he was just a month old, Bernard and Mary Henry brought young Augustine and his sister back to Ireland. There, they settled at Cookstown in County Tyrone, where the family kept a grocery shop and where Bernard Henry became a successful merchant in Ulster's booming flax industry. Augustine was soon followed by four brothers (Edward, Joseph, Thomas and Daniel) and three sisters (Annie, Mary and Agnes). The family had become relatively prosperous and were close knit, though this happy circle was shattered by the death of Mary Henry in 1871 (very soon after giving birth to Daniel), when Augustine was only 14 years old.

The loss of their mother must have been a cruel blow to the Henry children. She was just one of a number of people to touch Augustine Henry's life briefly and die all too early. From then on, Henry and his siblings spent much of their time with their grandmother, Anne, in the rolling countryside of Tyanee in County Derry. There, the young Henrys enjoyed a happy childhood.

Augustine Henry was a brilliant scholar. He gained a place in Queen's College, Galway (now the National University of Ireland, Galway), where he studied natural science and philosophy. In 1877, aged 20, he graduated from Galway with a first-class degree. In the following year, he obtained a Master of Arts postgraduate degree from Queen's College (now Queen's University), Belfast. One of the conditions of the scholarship Henry had gained at Belfast was that the holder must spend a year in one of London's teaching hospitals, and Henry spent the following year doing just that.

At the end of his resources, bored with examinations and not particularly keen on practicing as a physician, Henry returned to Belfast in 1879, where one of his professors at Queen's College told him of a vacancy in the Chinese Imperial Maritime Customs Service under another Irishman, Sir Robert Hart.[2] Hart had returned to Europe to oversee the Chinese exhibit at the third Paris Exhibition (Exposition Universelle), and, while visiting his former College, he let it be known that he was looking to recruit a well-educated man – if possible, one with some knowledge of medicine. Henry's medical qualifications at this time were not sufficient, but he obtained his degree quickly in Edinburgh by taking a special examination at double fees. He was accepted into the Customs Service on 10 August 1881.

The Chinese Customs Service was a remarkable organisation, directed from Beijing (then Peking), yet almost entirely run by Europeans, and at its head was Sir Robert Hart (1835–1911) from Portadown in County Armagh. The history of this organisation is worth recounting since the service was to employ Henry for almost two decades.

Tom Henry (1868–1946) and his wife Catherine. A civil engineer by profession, Tom also farmed the family lands and bore a striking resemblance to his older brother, Augustine.

Born in Portadown, County Armagh, in February 1835, Sir Robert Hart headed the Chinese Imperial Maritime Customs Service for several decades, and, during that period, he recruited many young Irishmen into the organisation – including Augustine Henry, in 1881.

The Chinese Imperial Maritime Customs Service
In 1853, during the Taiping Rebellion (1850–64), Shanghai was taken by a rebel organisation called the Hsiao-tao hui. The rebellion was led by a convert from a missionary station in Guangdong Province who was convinced that he was on a mission from God and professed to be the younger brother of Jesus Christ. His movement attempted to raze Buddhist, Taoist and Confucian temples and idols to the ground, and, during the rebellion, 20 million people died and 12 provinces were devastated. Chaos ensued throughout China, particularly in Shanghai where the Chinese Customs collectors fled their posts and there was a breakdown in the collection of duty for the imperial government. In the absence of these Chinese officials, the European staff who remained collected the customs duties on behalf of the Chinese government. The Qing administration in Beijing not only received the money, but very much more than they would have through their own collectors, who always secretly retained a portion for themselves.

The result was that, when peace was re-established in 1854, the Chinese Customs Service re-opened on the Bund (Waitan) in Shanghai and took a number of these consuls into their service – one of these was Sir Robert Hart. In 1863, the Empress Dowager Cixi appointed Hart Inspector General of the Customs Service. As such, he was the highest-ranking

foreigner employed by the Chinese government, and, over the years, he recruited many young Irishmen into the service. Under Hart, the Customs Service became responsible for domestic customs administration, postal services, harbour management, anti-smuggling operations and for mapping, policing and lighting China's coast and areas along the Yangtze River. The service also organised China's representation at nearly 30 world fairs. By 1895, more than 700 Westerners were employed in this international Civil Service. At this time, the Chinese Customs Service provided half the revenue of the Emperor. The service had stations throughout China, and this allowed its staff the opportunity to travel throughout the country – and to those, like Henry, who were interested in botany, it provided an unrivalled chance to collect plants in the most remote corners of the empire.

China opens her borders to the West
Henry was not the first Irishman to collect plants in China. One of the most remarkable expeditions to China during the 18th century took place between 1792 and 1794. The embassy was sent by King George III to the Emperor Qianlong (Qing Dynasty), one of the most able rulers China has ever known. The ambassador leading the expedition was Lord George Macartney (1737–1806), from Lisanoure in County Antrim. The secretary of the legation was another Irishman, Sir George Leonard Staunton (1737–1801), from Cargin in County Galway. Also travelling in the retinue was Staunton's 11-year-old son, Master George Thomas Staunton, who learned Chinese during the 10-month voyage from Europe.

In August 1793, the embassy reached China, and, a short time later, both Macartney and Staunton met the Emperor at his summer palace at Chengde (then Jehol) near Beijing in Hebei Province. Their route from Beijing to Chengde took about six days and meant having to cross the Great Wall before finally reaching the summer palace. During this meeting, Staunton's son was presented to the Emperor. Both conversed in Chinese and the Emperor was 'so charmed with the converse and elegant manner of this accomplished young gentleman that he took from his girdle his areca-nut purse … and presented it to him in his own hand'.[3]

Two gardeners travelled with the expedition and, alongside Staunton, they managed to gather more than 400 dried specimens and seeds of a small number of plants. Most of this material was collected on the Beijing plain, and, from there, south through the eastern provinces as far as Guangzhou (then Canton) in Guangdong Province.[4] Staunton presented some of these seeds to the Royal Botanic Gardens, Kew, and among the many seedlings raised there was the Macartney rose, *Rosa bracteata*. This lovely rose, with its large, single, cup-shaped white flowers, has grown at the National Botanic Gardens, Glasnevin, for more than 200 years now and was perhaps the most beautiful plant discovered by Staunton. The plume poppy, *Macleaya cordata*, was also introduced to cultivation by the same embassy, and it was to be reintroduced to cultivation by the second Glasnevin expedition to the Three Gorges region exactly 210 years later. George Staunton is commemorated in the climbing genus, *Stauntonia*.

Staunton and Macartney arrived in China at a time when it was virtually impossible for a Westerner to travel far inland. For centuries, China had closed her great bamboo curtain to the outside world and travel in the 'Middle Empire' remained only for a privileged few. Isolated from the Western world, the Chinese were proud of their ancient civilisation and regarded themselves as a highly cultured race and foreigners as barbarians. Seafaring Europeans,

The striking evergreen foliage of the Macartney rose, *Rosa bracteata*, makes a perfect foil for its large, delicately perfumed blooms. On a wall, its thick branches can scramble to 6 m (20 ft).

however, refused to be held back by the Great Wall, and slowly but surely made an entrance. At first, merchants were restricted to limited trade at a few chosen ports. The Portuguese were the first to gain a permanent foothold, in 1557, when permission was granted to them to set up a base at Macau. Over the following century, the British, Dutch and Spanish were equally vociferous in their calls for diplomatic relations and trading rights with China. By 1685, the Emperor Kangxi (Qing Dynasty) opened trade in the port of Guangzhou on a limited basis to foreign merchants, though there were tough terms for those who wanted to trade with China. Foreigners could only live in restricted areas in Guangzhou and had to leave once the trading season ended. Ships began arriving from the British East India Company, and, in 1700, the trading company (then the world's largest commercial organisation) received permission to build a storage warehouse outside the city.

The Opium War and Western influence in China

Initially, trade with Western countries flourished in China's favour. However, British purchases of porcelain, tea and fine silks far outweighed the Chinese purchases of English goods, and merchants looked for a means of balancing the books. The answer was opium. In 1773, the British East India Company began to balance its huge purchases with China by selling Indian opium to the Chinese in return for Mexican silver. Addiction was rapid and dramatic, and silver flowed out of China by the tonne. Realising the folly of this trade, the imperial court dispatched one of its officials, Lin Zexu, to Guangzhou in 1839 to stamp out the illegal traffic once and for all. Lin surrounded the opium warehouses with troops, stopped food supplies and refused to let anyone leave until all stocks of opium had been surrendered. The operation was a great success. After a six-week siege, more than 20,000 chests of opium were confiscated, though the incident was used as a pretext by the British government to

Earl Macartney of Lisanoure. The image represents Macartney's entrance into China, introduced by a mandarin. The three figures between the mandarin and the female representing commerce are soldiers of the Emperor.

21

Many of the French missionaries became outstanding naturalists, none more so than Père Jean Pierre Armand David and Père Jean Marie Delavay. Hundreds of Chinese plants bear their names, and Père David is commemorated in a fine, snake-bark maple, *Acer davidii*.

win support for military action against China. In 1840, British naval forces moved up the coast towards Beijing. The Opium War (1839–42) had begun.

Intimidated by British military threat, the Opium War was eventually ended by a series of unequal treaties forced on the Qing government, opening numerous ports to foreign trade and ceding Hong Kong to Britain 'in perpetuity'. In the space of just half a century, a spate of these treaties opened more than 50 treaty ports to foreign trade, with resident foreign communities in each.

In England, the Horticultural Society (now the Royal Horticultural Society) was one of the first organisations to take advantage of this new opportunity, and, just a year after the Opium War had ended, they employed the Scottish plant hunter Robert Fortune (1812–80) to collect for them in China. The ports open to foreign trade at that time, however, were scattered along the eastern coastal regions, and travel further inland was still strictly forbidden for non-Chinese individuals. Fortune received instructions from the Society to search for yellow camellias, double yellow roses, blue peonies and, perhaps most importantly, various types of

tea. During the next three years, his collecting was carried out in large gardens and nurseries in cities along the coast as far north as Shanghai. Fortune also made two further trips to China for the East India Company, who employed him to collect seeds and plants of the tea plant, *Camellia sinensis*. To carry out this task, Fortune risked death by disguising himself as a native and then made a 322-km (200-mile) journey inland from Ningbo, Zhejiang Province. His mission was successful, and the plants raised from this expedition laid the foundations for India's tea industry. China had finally lost the monopoly of the tea trade.

The continuous opening up of China over the following decades also saw a flood of European missionaries, and two of these, Père Jean Pierre Armand David (1826–1900) and Père Jean Marie Delavay (1834–95), stand supreme in the history of botanical exploration in China. Both travelled extensively in western China, sending back vast quantities of dried specimens to the Natural History Museum in Paris.

Born in Espelette, near Bayonne (France), Armand David arrived in China in 1862, where he was attached to the Mission of the Lazarists at Beijing, and, from there, he explored much of the north of the country. David's most famous expedition began in 1869, when he travelled to Baoxing (then Mupin) County in Sichuan Province and began collecting botanical, geological and zoological specimens. His most remarkable finds included the handkerchief tree, *Davidia involucrata*, and the giant panda *Ailuropoda melanoleuca*.[5]

Perhaps the greatest of the French missionary collectors, though, was Père Delavay from Abondance in Haute-Savoie. Delavay was sent to China by the Société des Missions Étrangères (Society of Foreign Missions) in 1867, where he first served in Guangdong Province in the south-east. In 1881, while on leave in France, Delavay was introduced to the famous French botanist, Adrien René Franchet (1834–1900), who persuaded him to collect for the Paris Muséum National d'Histoire Naturelle. On his return to China, Delavay was designated to a station in north-west Yunnan Province and found himself surrounded by an entirely unknown flora. Between then and 1895, he was to send more than 200,000 herbarium specimens to the Paris museum. Franchet, who worked on the collection, estimated that it contained more than 4,000 species, of which about 1,500 were new to science. His herbarium specimens were remarkable for both their beauty and excellence.[6]

Augustine Henry's arrival in China

At the time of Augustine Henry's arrival in China, virtually nothing was known of the flora of central China and the bulk of the dried specimens in the herbarium at Kew came from the eastern coastal regions. It was presumed that the flora of China

had been thoroughly explored and little remained to be discovered. That opinion was about to be changed!

In the summer of 1881, having gained his medical degree and passed a routine examination for the Customs Service, 24-year-old Henry bade farewell to Ireland and set sail for a new life in China. He first arrived in Hong Kong, then in its heyday of British colonialism. In 1842, the Treaty of Nanking (Nanjing) had ended the Opium War and placed the island of Hong Kong under British control. In a matter of decades, the barren rocky outcrop had been transformed, and, by the time of Henry's arrival in July 1881, it had became one of richest cities in Asia and its deep, wide harbour was one of the busiest ports in the world.

Augustine Henry's stay in Hong Kong was brief. After only two days, he boarded a small coasting steamer and sailed for Shanghai. On approaching the city, it was possible to discern the mud of the Yangtze River discolouring the sea a hundred miles or more from its mouth. The city itself lies not on the Yangtze but on one of its tributaries, the Huangpu River, which is wider than the Thames at Westminster (London) and can handle large, ocean-going vessels. Situated at the centre of China's vast and densely populated eastern coastline, and at the mouth of its most productive river system, the Yangtze, Shanghai had been ideally placed to develop as a major international trading port. The Opium War had opened up

A view of Jade Dragon Snow Mountain (Yulongxue Shan) and the district of nearby Lijiang Town in north-west Yunnan Province. The area was thoroughly explored by Père Delavay during the early 1890s, and his discoveries were later introduced by George Forrest.

several concessions and an international settlement had been established on the banks of the Huangpu River in 1863. Spurred on by massive international investment, Shanghai had rapidly developed into a busy port and an industrial city.

In Shanghai, the young Augustine Henry was trained for the various duties he would soon carry out on behalf of the Customs Service. Office hours were between 10:00 and 16:00 – though he would rise at 05:00 in the morning and head off with his pony outside the foreign settlement. Shanghai was full of graduates from several Irish universities and Henry soon fell in with Shanghai society. The city's social outlet was the Shanghai Club where men met before lunch and dinner. Leisure time was passed playing tennis, racing Mongolian ponies or making evening visits to hear bands play in the public gardens, where a notorious sign near the entrance stated 'No dogs or Chinese allowed'. Henry soon grew bored of this lifestyle, however. A welcome change came in March of 1882, when he was posted to Yichang (then Ichang), a busy treaty port on the Yangtze River in Hubei Province, a then little-known region in central China.

Chapter 2

Upon the *Fairy Raft*
– exploring Yichang

Henry was released from his training in Shanghai on 10 March and departed for Wuhan, Hubei Province's capital city, on the steamer *Kiang-Tung*, reaching the Hankou (Hankow) district of present-day Wuhan some nine days later. Hankou was then one of the busiest ports on the Yangtze River and a major tea distribution centre. The district possessed the finest bund in China, though, like other towns along the river, it was prone to flooding, and travel from house to house had to be carried out by means of *sampans* (flat-bottomed wooden boats). After a brief stay in the city, Henry set off on a smaller craft on the last leg of the journey and Yichang was finally reached at 20:00 on 16 April 1882.

Yichang lies more than 1,100 miles (1,770 km) from Shanghai, and, during the 19th century, it acted as a gateway to China's remote western provinces. The city was an important transhipping port since it lay at the head of steam

A snapshot of the west end of Yichang in March 1904. The photograph was taken by E. H. Wilson from the summit of a nearby peak known to European residents as 'the Dome'. It reveals the city much as Augustine Henry would have known it. A British gunboat lies anchored on the Yangtze, and, at this point, the river is more than a kilometre wide, having just exited the famed Three Gorges region.

navigation on the Yangtze. It is situated on the left bank of the river, not far from the eastern mouth of the famous Three Gorges, at an altitude of only 21 m (70 ft) above sea level. It is at this point, having travelled through thousands of kilometres of rugged mountainous topography, that the Yangtze suddenly descends onto China's eastern plains and sprawls to more than a kilometre wide. The countryside immediately surrounding Yichang is broken into low hills, which are more or less pyramidal in shape. To the east, these hills gradually merge into a great plain that extends all the

way to the east coast. To the north, south and west of the city, they are mere foothills to ranges that rise from 1,500 to 3,050 m (5,000 to 10,000 ft) in height, these spurs being the most easterly extensions of the mighty Himalayan range.

Yichang became a treaty port in April 1877, and continued to be the furthest inland treaty port for many years, since large passenger and merchant vessels were, at that time, unable to navigate the gorges upriver to Chongqing. At Yichang, cargo was unloaded from large boats plying the Yangtze and was re-loaded onto smaller junks running between it and Chongqing. Six steamers regularly traded between Yichang and Wuhan, and the many thousands of native crafts lined up along the banks of the river attested to the city's importance as a trading port.

Yichang was then a walled city, with narrow cobbled streets lined by low traditional buildings with mud walls and tiled roofs. About 30,000 people lived there, of whom a large number made their living from the enormous trade of goods shipped up and down the Yangtze. The principal exports were items of *materia medica* transported down the gorges from Sichuan Province and Tibet (Xizang) and from the mountains north of the city. This trade consisted largely of medicinal rhubarb root, *Rheum officinale*, of which enormous quantities went to Europe, and items such as elk horn and dried centipedes. Other exports included raw silk and musk; there was also a large import trade of Manchester goods, such as cotton, long-cloth, figured prints and velveteen.[1] All of this trade passed through the hands of the Customs Service officials.

The east end of Yichang, showing the Foreign Compound in which Henry once lived to the right-hand side. To the left are the city walls, which were built during the Sui Dynasty (589–618 AD) but demolished during the 1920s.

Fishing was also an important industry, and enormous specimens of the Chinese sturgeon, *Acipenser sinensis*, weighing anything up to 500 kg (1,100 lb), were captured in nets. On the opposite bank of the river was a small village, known to the European residents as 'otter village' because of the fact that the natives had trained otters for fishing. These otters could be seen at any time of day tied up in the bows of sampans and appeared to be quite tame. When the Yangtze was low in winter and early spring, beggars could be seen inhabiting the shallow caves scooped out by the action of the water on the riverbank. There, they just about existed, in a miserable state, skinning and cooking dogs and cats, or anything else they could lay their hands on for food, and they were often treated with terrible cruelty by the richer inhabitants of the city.[2]

A small Foreign Compound had been built near Yichang in 1877 along the river front, south-east of the city walls, to accommodate Western residents. On the opposite side of the Yangtze River to the foreign settlement lay a conspicuously pyramidal-shaped hill known to European residents as 'the Dome' (Moji Shan). This hill was supposed to exert a baneful

The enormous trade of medicinal plants and plant-derived products through Yichang stimulated an interest in botany for Augustine Henry. Rhubarb root was one such product. It was gathered from the mountains of Hubei and Sichuan provinces and, from there, passed through the Three Gorges to Yichang before being traded as far afield as western Europe.

influence over the town, and it was held responsible for Yichang's poverty of local *literati*. It was not until the Taoist Tungshantzu Temple was built on a higher crest behind the town, sufficiently high to overlook the Dome, that this evil influence was counteracted. The same year as the Tungshantzu Temple was completed, a local student passed the provincial examinations with high honours, thus proving the beneficial effects of the building.[3] The temple was said to have been one of the most strikingly conspicuous objects at Yichang, and was richly endowed. Geomancy enters largely into Taoist customs, and, following the principles of *feng shui*, local officials believed that the area along Yichang's riverbank, between the Dome and the Tungshantzu Temple, had good *chi* (or energy), and so it was chosen, in 1877, as the site for the Foreign Compound.

Near the base of the Dome, the European community had a small cemetery, and their greatest difficulty here was preventing the local Chinese residents from desecrating the graves. The Dome was approached through a very picturesque

glen called the 'Monastery Valley', in which there was a temple and cave. The summit of the hill lay at 183 m (600 ft) and allowed panoramic views of the city, the nearby Foreign Compound and the Yangtze River.

The Customs House was based within the compound and would become Augustine Henry's home for the next seven years. Besides the Customs House and the British and German consulates were two missions and buildings belonging to a few European businessmen. The Protestant mission, belonging to the Church of Scotland, was in the charge of the Rev. G. Cockburn, who was the oldest foreign inhabitant of Yichang. His wife was the first European woman to live in the city. The Roman Catholic Franciscan mission was presided over by Bishop Benjamin, and there was also a small convent. Behind the Foreign Compound lay paddy fields and areas in which vegetables and cotton were cultivated. To the rear of these were burial mounds and a number of large ponds.

Yichang was considered a healthy place to live. Summer temperatures often rose to 30 °C (86 °F), while winters were cold and snow lay on the ground. A free ferry service was operated across the river. However, the small foreign community was regarded by locals with suspicion, and often with open hostility. Rumours existed at Yichang that foreigners ate children who disappeared, or used their bodies to prepare precious charms and medicaments.[4]

The Three Gorges and the Yangtze

Above Yichang lie the Three Gorges, one of the most famous landscapes in all of China. For more than 2,000 years, the Yangtze has been a vital trade artery for inland navigation and the means by which products have been transported to and from the less densely populated western provinces. Originating on the Tibetan Plateau, the Yangtze

A view from the Foreign Compound across the Yangtze River to 'the Dome' (Moji Shan). It was a scene to which Henry awoke every morning.

The Wu Gorge (or 'Witch's Gorge') is the second of the famous Three Gorges on the Yangtze River. In the 19th century, the river was the only efficient mode of transportation of goods from the westernmost provinces.

Junks in the Wu Gorge. This photograph, taken by Henry in the late 1880s, shows the common type of craft used to carry goods upriver from Yichang through the gorges.

is the world's third largest river and has a course of 6,380 km (3,964 miles). In contemporary Chinese, it is the Chang Jiang – the Long River or Eternal River. The name used in the West, the Yangtze, means 'Son of the Sea' and is an old name for the river's tidal waters near the East China Sea.

The Three Gorges begin in eastern Sichuan Province, extend along the Yangtze River for 196 km (122 miles), and then cross into Hubei Province before terminating above the city of Yichang. The Yangtze's last great obstacles before reaching Yichang are the famed Three Gorges, one of the great geological wonders of the world. Over millions of years, the river has incised an incredibly deep channel into the folded rocks of the Wushan mountain range in Sichuan Province, forming the first of the gorges: the Qutang Gorge. With peaks soaring to more than 1,220 m (4,000 ft), the gorges have inspired China's most famous landscape artists and moved poets and scholars to reflect on the magnificence of nature.

The shortest and the narrowest of the gorges, the Qutang Gorge extends for 8 km (5 miles) and is known locally as 'the gorge of the bellows', since furious winds from nearby mountains are rapidly funnelled through its cliff walls. Enclosed by peaks that rise more than 1,000 m (3,280 ft) above the river, this gorge is well known for its soaring cliff walls of carboniferous limestone and overhanging precipices. As a consequence, sailing through this spectacular stretch of river has been likened to travelling along an underground cave. In places, the channel of the river is only 50 m (164 ft) wide, and it is said the river at that point is of an appalling depth and that on its floor are the countless remains of sunken vessels. According to E. H. Wilson, soundings were taken by British gunboats in the Three Gorges in 1900, and these gave 63.5 fathoms (116 m, 380 ft) of water depth in two places; at Yichang, the depth was less than 1.8 m (6 ft).[5]

On exiting the Qutang Gorge and entering the confluence of the Daning (Taning) River (a tributary from the northern side), the Yangtze enters the Wu Gorge, named for the nearby town of Wushan. This 'Witch's Gorge' (Wu Xia) is the longest of the Three Gorges, and extends for more than 45 km (28 miles) from the mouth of the Daning River near Wushan in Sichuan Province to beyond the town of Badong in Hubei Province. At this point, the Yangtze follows an erratic zigzag course – and often blindly approaches cliff walls – before turning sharply to flow onwards through some of China's most wonderful scenery. The landscape here is hauntingly beautiful. Cliff faces rise sheer out of the water to more than 610 m (2,000 ft) above the river, and above them soar the massive peaks of the Wushan mountains, with names such as 'Flying Phoenix' and 'Climbing Dragon'. It is through the Wu Gorge that the provincial frontier is crossed before finally meeting with the last great obstacle on the Yangtze, the Xiling (or Yichang) Gorge.

The Xiling Gorge extends for some 66 km (41 miles) from Zigui, a town located in the valley of the Xiang Xi river, to the Nanjin Pass near the Cave of the Three Pilgrims, a few kilometres above Yichang. The scenery there is ruggedly enchanting. Above a coffee-coloured, silt-laden Yangtze rise canyon walls so colossal as to block out the sun's rays, and the river flows often bounded on either side by perpendicular cliffs almost 610 m (2,000 ft) high. In the 19th century, it was this gorge that achieved notoriety for its violent rapids and dangerous shoals that took a heavy toll on vessels and on the crews who worked them.

The main gorge system through which the Yangtze flows is joined by numerous tributaries, which run through glens and ravines of outstanding beauty. These streams almost always fill the floor of the glen and are bounded by massive limestone cliffs 305 m (1,000 ft) or more sheer, on which vegetation is rampant, and, following the wet season, waterfalls are everywhere to be seen. In the 19th century, during the month of September, thousands of tiny lamps

The Wu Gorge in October 2002. The mist-shrouded, time-worn cliffs fall steeply into the depths of the Yangtze below. Evocatively named peaks from the Wushan mountain range soar skyward above these enormous cliff faces and the region's enchanting landscape has inspired poets for centuries. Flooding began a month after this photograph was taken.

towpaths barely 45 cm (18 in.) wide that had been cut into the cliffs 30 m (100 ft) above the river. Should the boats make a sudden outward sheer, and if these hired labourers (referred to historically as 'coolies') lost time in disengaging themselves from the tracking rope, they were very likely to be dragged to their deaths off the cliff face and be swept away in the violent currents of the river below. The Yangtze was at its most dangerous in autumn and winter, when the level of the river was low and when many of the huge granite boulders projected 6 m (20 ft) above the surface. A single rapid of only 200 m (220 yards) could take an entire day to cross, giving some indication of how slow and difficult navigation was in the Three Gorges region during the late 19th century.

Cornell Plant (1866–1921), River Inspector for the Chinese Customs Service in the early 1900s, stated that one junk in ten was badly damaged, and that one in twenty was totally wrecked on each trip. It was common for trackers to fall to their deaths or to break a limb and be left behind by their junks. Accordingly, Yangtze boatmen developed a wealth of rites to be observed in order to ensure a safe passage through the raging waters. At the beginning of a voyage and before entering the gorges, it was the cook's task to light incense, set off firecrackers and to kill a rooster and sprinkle its blood on the bows of the junk. It was necessary, too, to sprinkle rice on the water while negotiating the rapids. Boatmen also had to contend with the ghosts of the drowned, who would gather themselves in a line behind the boat, preparing to board the vessel and cause consternation. The way to shake them lose was to cut quickly in front of another boat, so that the ghosts would lose their grip and attach themselves to the boat behind. It was a game that often left the trailing boat's owner jumping, cursing and shooting off firecrackers to pacify his increased string of ghosts.[6]

Early travellers described the scenery of the gorges as nothing short of magnificent. Instead of the low swampy banks seen about Yichang, the river was confined between mountain peaks and towering precipices. Above the Yangtze, cliff faces soared skywards, and, from them, fell waterfalls 91 to 305 m (300–1,000 ft) high. Enormous caves occurred in places, often full of stalagmites and stalactites. Throughout the gorges, hundreds of brightly painted pagodas had been built on the crags and peaks to prevent flooding (it was believed that floods were caused by dragons, or by evil demons, and that a pagoda could prevent the wealth of a nearby town being swept away in the currents).

The landscape of western Hubei Province was too wild and rugged for the development of agriculture. With a marked absence of mineral deposits, it was consequently under-populated and little was known of the region in the Western world. The vegetation had therefore suffered less at the hands

were floated down the surface of the Yangtze. They extended for several miles and were released a short distance above Yichang. These lights were offerings to the deity for the souls of those who had lost their lives by drowning in the turbulent rapids, and consisted of a cup with a little oil into which a wick was extended. The wicks were made from the pith of the common rush, *Juncus effusus*, which was harvested further up the gorges and in which there was a considerable downriver trade.

Life on board a junk in the Three Gorges was hard, and often entailed dangerous work. The largest of the junks had crews of up to 80 men, and the heaviest work was done by trackers on the riverside who had to haul crafts of several tonnes upriver over fierce rapids and whirlpools. These immense whirlpools caused extraordinary destruction, and, once a junk was caught in their reaches, it was tossed around like a cork. Up to 400 men pulling bamboo ropes in unison across these terrifying obstacles was a common sight in the gorges. Very often, all that these trackers had to work with were recessed

The countryside around Yichang was scattered with temples and monasteries, and Henry was a regular visitor to the 'monastery valley' and the temple on the summit of the Dome. There, he would have seen many garden plants favoured by the Chinese. This photograph, taken in Yichang at the turn of the 20th century by the American plant hunter Frank N. Meyer, shows a very fine tree peony, or Mudan, most likely a *Paeonia rockii* hybrid.

of farmers than in other regions of China. The most luxuriant vegetation was found on the steep cliffs of the Three Gorges and in the many of the side glens that ran off them. A common tree on the hills above the Xiling Gorge was the Chinese vegetable tallow tree *Sapium sebiferum* (Euphorbiaceae), from whose seeds oil and fat were extracted, and from which candles were made. It was a favourite of Henry's, and he asserted that its brilliant autumnal tints painted the same hills gold and amber in the autumn.[7]

In other places, the mountain slopes had been terraced and cultivated, but the resulting harvests often scarcely merited the outlay of labour involved, and, in the late 19th century, extensive tracts of virgin forest still cloaked the higher peaks to the north and south of the Three Gorges. Those same mountain forests were rich in medicinal plants, and the mountain peasants made a good living from harvesting them for sale downriver.

The Dome, Monastery Valley, Glen of the Three Pilgrims
Life was quiet in Yichang in 1882. After work, Henry sometimes played tennis, cards or went shooting, though, by his own admission, he was a wretched shot. He also loved to head off into the countryside on long walks; his diary

reveals that, on 25 May 1882, he was in the hills above Yichang with a colleague hunting for fossils. (E. H. Wilson, who later lived in the region, stated that the dominant fossils around Yichang were those of cycads, and these were found in thin beds of coal.[8]) The same evening as his fossil hunt, Henry took his first Chinese lesson from a local teacher, Mr Teng. The monotony of life in that backwater treaty port was also broken by the arrival of many Western steamers from Wuhan and Shanghai. Henry and some of the other residents from the Foreign Compound often dined on board these ships, catching up on the latest news from the other treaty ports and from home. Henry was also a prolific letter writer, and much of his voluminous correspondence from Yichang survives, particularly his letters to Miss Evelyn Gleeson, his friend in Ireland. Henry had studied with Evelyn's brother, Jim, in Galway, and while a university student he had often stayed in their beautiful home, Benown House, located near Athlone in County Westmeath. By the time Henry was living in Yichang, Evelyn was based in London, where she was studying art, and her brother Jim had joined the Indian Civil Service.

Another favourite weekend destination near Yichang was 'the Dome', a pyramidal-shaped hill, which, as mentioned

The mouth of the San You Dong glen where it meets the Yangtze near the Nanjin Pass above Yichang. This was one of Augustine Henry's favourite retreats, and, on his recommendation, it was later thoroughly explored by E. H. Wilson.

earlier, lay directly opposite the Foreign Compound on the right bank of the Yangtze. His diary for Saturday 14 October 1882 reveals that Henry travelled there with the Acting British Consul, E. L. Allen. They approached the Dome through the Monastery Valley, bringing with them Henry's cook, three sedan chair 'coolies', four carriers and three dogs. The entrance to the Monastery Valley was beautiful; beneath towering cliffs more than 244 m (800 ft) tall were numerous large caves and a Taoist temple. Within one of these caves was a large lake that was held in great veneration by the local people since it had no visible inlet or outlet. Europeans were not allowed to explore it, though Henry was to later collect plants in the mouths of adjoining caves. Beyond the temple and caves, the valley became narrower and narrower, and, near its edge, was a series of waterfalls.

By climbing up a large ridge by the waterfalls, Henry and Allen got their first view of the rear of the Dome. He had the following to say of it in his diary:

The appearance [...] is very impressive – an immense shelf-like structure rising up almost sheer on three sides

– black conglomerate – with just a little bit of vegetation, trees, and a small *joss house* on top. The Dome springs from a basin with steep bushy slopes at [the] bottom [...] We cross the connecting ridge, ascend by zigzag path and reach the summit [...] There is a splendid view of Ichang, the river [...].[9]

Another pastime was boating along the Yangtze on a small craft called the *Fairy Raft*. Sailing upriver from Yichang, one of his favourite destinations was the San You Dong glen (then, San Yu Tung; the Glen of the Three Pilgrims). In 819 AD, three Tang Dynasty poets made an excursion to the glen and, while staying there, they inscribed poems on the walls of a cave. They were later referred to as the three pilgrims, or travellers, and the glen was named after them.

The same glen was located some 10 km (6 miles) above Yichang, near the mouth of the Xiling Gorge. In reality, it was a narrow ravine closed in by massive limestone cliffs that towered more than 152 m (500 ft) high, and the cliffs were home to goral, monkeys, flying squirrels and kingfishers – and also to many cliff-loving plants. A small stream of remarkably clear water wound its way through the floor of the glen, and fishermen could be seen casting nets with great skill near its mouth.

Like the Monastery Valley, there were several caves in the limestone cliffs, and, near the mouth of these caves, grew enormous colonies of the maidenhair fern *Adiantum capillus-veneris.* Huge slabs of stone with ferns attached were quarried from the caves and sold downriver, where they were known as 'Ichang fern-stones' and commanded a ready sale.[10] High up on one of the many limestone cliffs in the glen was a natural cave of great beauty and considerable size, the entrance to which was on the face of a precipice. Inside the cave was a small temple where a Taoist monk had lived for more than 45 years. The temple also had an enormous bell, and the sound of its vibrations echoed from the cave into the depths of the glen beyond.

A further branch of the San You Dong was called the 'Goat Glen' because it was inhabited by a species of wild goat. Given the rugged nature of the locality, these animals must have seemed particularly adapted to their habits. The English naturalist Antwerp Edgar Pratt, who later visited the glen on Henry's recommendation, gave the following impression of the place:

Picture to yourself a deep valley, with the entrance very narrow and steep, widening out here and there into broad, cup-shaped expansions almost surrounded by unscalable precipices, and here and there huge piles of enormous boulders lying in the greatest confusion, a small stream of water running through the centre fed by several rivulets, plants of almost innumerable species, many being of great beauty, growing in every possible place, and some idea may be formed of this exquisite gorge. [...] The whole aspect of these gorges is beautiful in the extreme. Lofty precipices, clear limpid streams, luxuriant vegetation, and charming flowers combine to make it one of the most delightful spots I have ever visited.[11]

The *Fairy Raft* often carried Henry into the Xiling Gorge as far as the small village of Pingshanba (then Pin-shan-pa), where the locals cultivated oranges. At this point, there was a small *Le-kin*, or Customs House station, where native boats were examined. The small hamlet of Liantuo (then Nanto) lay beyond Pingshanba on the left bank of the river, and Henry's first trip there is recorded in his diary entry for 11 November 1883. The following day, he strolled his way from Liantuo to the Chinkang Shan Taoist temple. A heavy blanket of snow lay on the ground and the view of the surrounding countryside was spectacular. To the southeast

Sir Joseph Dalton Hooker is generally regarded as the greatest botanist of Victorian times and one of the most able directors of the Royal Botanic Gardens, Kew. The enthusiastic response Henry received from Hooker encouraged him greatly in his early plant-hunting years.

lay the Yichang pagoda, and it was said one could see five provinces from the temple.[12]

A healthy interest in botany must have developed during these excursions; an entry in his diary for 22 August 1884 mentions 'order *Bentley's Botany*', while another made on 25 November of the same year reads 'crossed river – botanised about Shil-liu-lung'.

Early days as a botanist and plant collector

Augustine Henry's training as a medical doctor would have given him a basic knowledge of botany. An interest in plant identification and botany would also have been further stimulated through his work in the Customs Service. One of his routine duties was to compile lists of plant- and animal-derived products of *materia medica* that regularly passed through the treaty ports. This was no easy matter. While he could locate the common Chinese name of a plant, it was impossible to get its botanical equivalent, and it occurred to him that the only practical means of solving this problem was by forwarding specimens to the Royal Botanic Gardens, Kew. On 20 March 1885, Henry penned a letter to Sir Joseph Dalton Hooker (1817–1911), then in his final year

Two of Thomas Watters' finest discoveries from Yichang. *Rehmannia angulata* was introduced to cultivation by E. H. Wilson and first flowered in Harry Veitch's Coombe Wood Nursery (London) in May 1902. Wilson called it the *feng tang hwa* (honey bee flower) and collected plants in the San You Dong glen above Yichang. *Viburnum utile* makes an upright evergreen shrub more than 2 m (7 ft) tall and bears dense, rounded trusses of blossoms in May.

as Director of Kew. Enclosing seeds of the varnish tree (*Rhus verniciflua*), he penned the following lines:

> I beg to forward you a packet of seeds of the Chinese varnish tree [...] in the hope of their proving interesting. The tree grows in the mountains about here, and also occurs in Chekiang [Zhejiang] and other provinces of China. According to Bretschneider, it is only partially known to botanists. [...] I hope to be able to obtain the flower and leaf this year. I have not seen the tree growing, as I have not made a sufficiently long excursion into the mountains.
>
> A good number of medicines are grown about here, and there seems to be a fair number of interesting plants; and, as this part of China is not very well known to botanists (at any rate, as compared with the south and also the northern and maritime provinces), interesting specimens might be obtained. I know very little of botany and have scarcely any books of reference. However, I should be very glad to collect specimens and forward them to you if you think they would prove useful. In this

case, any hints would be very acceptable [...].

> Note. The seeds ought to succeed if planted in London. The natives say the tree will not grow on the hot plains, but requires a cold climate. The varnish is got by incising the bark. Out of the seeds an oil is expressed which is used in making candles. Other particulars I shall try and ascertain when I get an opportunity of making an excursion into the mountains. Two kinds of primrose are now in bloom here. Two kinds of soap tree also occur here. In the hills, raspberries, strawberries and blackberries are also to be met with.

In April 1885, Henry received a letter from the famous English botanist Henry Fletcher Hance (1827–86), then Vice-Consul at Huangpu (then Whampoa) in Guangdong Province in southeast China. Hance was a leading authority on the flora of China and had helped several botanists and plant collectors in their work there. At the time of his death, just a year after writing to Henry, his private herbarium amounted to 22,437 species.[13] Hance suggested to Henry a number of botanical works to help him in his endeavours,

Primula obconica, a common house plant in Europe and North America. In the glens and gorges above Yichang, it is an abundant wild flower. It was introduced to cultivation by the Veitchian collector, Charles Maries.

including Franchet's two-volume set *Plantae Davidianae ex Sinarum imperio*, the first volume of which had been published in Paris in 1884. In a later letter, Hance advised Henry on how to protect his specimens from the ravages of insect damage and how to properly press, dry and preserve a herbarium specimen. Hance passed on much valuable advice to Henry, including the following very valuable tip: 'I will tell you (what no manual I think does) that so long as a specimen strikes cold to the palm laid on it, it is not sufficiently dry'. The same methods of preserving plants in the field described in this letter are still employed today.

Henry was not the first person to collect plants around Yichang. Thomas Watters (1840–1901) had arrived in Yichang as Acting British Consul in April 1878, and began collecting plants, which he sent to Hance in Guangdong Province and also to the herbarium at Kew. The greatest authority on Buddhism of his time, Watters was described as a quiet, unostentatious gentleman, a genial Irishman with a good sense of humour and one of the ablest and most learned men who ever went to China.[14] He hailed from Newtownards in County Down and Henry had met his sister, Martha, while studying at University College, Galway.[15] Indeed, Henry became a regular visitor to the Watters' home and soon fell in love with the young lady. He proposed marriage to her, but the offer was declined. Despite this, both remained good friends and kept up a lively correspondence during Henry's years in China.

Watters' interest in plants may have stemmed from an appeal from Kew, sent out to British and Irish citizens based in China, for material relating to the economic botany of China. Watters was not to become as prolific a collector as Henry, but he discovered many interesting plants around Yichang. One of the most important of these was *Primula*

obconica, now a common and popular houseplant in Europe and North America. In the gorges above Yichang, it grew on the steep slopes and cliff faces in hundreds of thousands, so much so that the same cliffs became a sheet of colour in early spring. In fact, it was so abundant there that Henry later dismissed it as a weed. Another important find by Watters was the very beautiful *Viburnum utile*, a large evergreen shrub carrying broad corymbs of white, scented flowers in early summer. The stems of this shrub were made into pipe stems by the local peasants, hence the specific epithet *utile* (useful). Thomas Watters' most beautiful find, however, has to be *Rehmannia angulata*, a short-lived perennial similar to our native foxglove (*Digitalis purpurea*) and a common cliff plant in the gorges.

Watters probably advised the English plant hunter Charles Maries (1851–1902) about the best locations to collect plants on his arrival at Yichang in the spring of 1879.

Charles Maries was one of 22 plant hunters employed by Veitch's nursery. He had limited success during his travels in China, though he made many remarkable finds in Japan and Taiwan.

Maries had been employed by the famous British nursery firm Veitch of Chelsea, with instructions to collect plants on their behalf in Japan, Taiwan and China. Maries did not fare well with the locals at Yichang, however. He was often threatened by them and had his baggage robbed on a number of occasions. As James Veitch was later to state, 'Maries had enthusiasm, but lacked "staying" power'.[16] Maries has gone down in botanical history for having narrowly missed discovering one of the richest temperate floras in the world. Ernest Wilson found this incredible:

He found the natives there unfriendly, and, after staying a week, was compelled to return. [...] For some curious reason or other, he concluded that his predecessor, Fortune, had exhausted the floral resources of China,

Rhus verniciflua, the Chinese varnish tree. It occurs both wild and cultivated in the Three Gorges region, and the plant pictured above grows at Glasnevin (Ireland), having been raised from a collection made by E. H. Wilson (W. 123) in the mountains near Yichang in September 1907.

and, most extraordinary of all, his conclusions were accepted! When at Ichang, he could but have gone some three days' journey north, south or west, he would have secured a haul of new plants such as the botanical and horticultural world had never dreamed of. By the irony of fate, it was left for two or three others to discover and obtain what had been almost within his grasp.[17]

Despite having missed being the person to expose the enormous wealth of the flora of central China, Maries did nonetheless manage to introduce a number of plants to cultivation from Yichang and the gorges, including *Primula obconica* (which must have made the Veitch firm a small fortune over the years).

Augustine Henry confined his own collecting work to a 24-km (15-mile) radius of Yichang, with his favourite 'hunting' ground comprising the Dome (Moji Shan), the Glen of the Three Pilgrims, the nearby Goat Glen, Antelope Glen and Pingshanba. The first mention of native plant collectors appears in his diary on 4 May 1885, when his 'coolie' returned with flowers of the varnish tree, *Rhus verniciflua*. Three weeks later, the same collector, Man Yang, 'came up river with plants'. Man Yang was the first of several native collectors Henry would train to collect and dry plants for him. He was based at Badong (then Patung) County, in an ancient city (often also referred to as Badong) situated on the southern bank of the Yangtze River. Located 80 km (50 miles) upriver, the city lay on a steep riverside bank, between the mouths of the Wu and Xiling gorges. In his field notes at Kew, Henry described the countryside around Badong as having high mountain ranges clothed for miles on end with extensive tracts of virgin forest, and with snow laying on the highest peaks over the winter months.

The use of native plant collectors had been pioneered by Sir Joseph Hooker, who trained several Lepcha boys to collect and dry plants when he arrived in Darjeeling (northern India) in 1848.[18] Henry's use of such collectors greatly increased the amount of material gathered and, thus, the scope of his own work. As a full-time employee of the Customs Service, his only chance of getting away to collect plants was at weekends and on holiday time. Though Henry was less than pleased with the standard of Man Yang's early collections, he was later to become one of his best men (though a bit of a mischievous rogue, as we shall later learn).

From this point onwards, Henry's interest in botany rapidly gained momentum, and tennis, shooting and card-playing took up less and less of his time. By this stage, his Chinese was also remarkably good and this must have made his expeditions into the surrounding glens and gorges easier.

Joseph Hooker and the Royal Botanic Gardens, Kew

Back in London, Joseph Hooker must have read Henry's letter from Yichang with great interest. Kew was more than willing to help in any way it could. Ethnobotany had been shaped by imperialistic motives, and Britain, with its expanding empire, needed new raw materials, medicines, fibres, dyes and food sources to transplant to her colonies. Kew was at the centre of all of this distribution, and was eager to exploit whatever economically valuable plant-derived products Henry might find. Henry, as has been established, spoke Chinese fluently, had a smattering of botany through his medical training and could record common Chinese names – and, therefore, would prove to be very useful to Kew.

Hooker himself had travelled widely throughout his life, visiting Antarctica, South America and the Himalaya while still a young man, and making enormous collections of plants and seeds along the way. He is widely regarded as the greatest botanist of the 19th century, and Henry could not have approached a more qualified person from whom to seek advice.

The enthusiastic response from Hooker induced Henry to redouble his efforts. From Kew, Henry also received a pamphlet containing further instructions on how to collect and dry plants, stating the importance of field notes and of labelling and numbering specimens in the field. Henry collected up to ten duplicate sets of specimens; in his letters

The Royal Botanic Gardens, Kew, was a major distribution centre of new plant-derived products during the 19th century. During this period, botanists worked at a frenetic pace to describe previously unknown species of plants, and, in the years following Augustine Henry's arrival in China, a plethora of new plants were sent to Kew.

to Kew, he explained that he would keep one set for himself and that the others would be forwarded to the herbarium there. All he asked in return was that he be sent a list of determinations with the botanical names of his specimens corresponding with each number. By this means, he was able to build up his own correctly labelled herbarium in China and could finally match colloquial Chinese names with Western botanical equivalents.

In a second letter to Joseph Hooker, Henry mentioned his plans to lead an extended expedition into the high mountains to the north of Yichang from where many of the famous plant-derived medicines passing through the Customs Station at Yichang were harvested.[19]

In November 1885, Augustine Henry sent his very first consignment of 1,073 dried specimens and 183 items of fruits and seeds to Kew. For the next 15 years, Kew was to receive a continual flow of material. Each specimen was carefully numbered, stating the region from where it had

China of 1881, a map prepared for the *Index Florae Sinensis*, the first ever flora of China. From the mid 1880s, Augustine Henry's collections dominated its pages and it was his collections that laid the basis of our present knowledge of China's great floral wealth.

been collected, giving details of the plant's habit, habitat, economic uses, date of collection and Chinese name. The collection arrived in London the following spring and caused great excitement when examined by taxonomists. The consignment was a revelation and proved to be rich in new species and varieties. These were not just botanically interesting, but of great beauty and of enormous horticultural potential. At a time when it had been stated that the flora of China was thoroughly known and had little new material to offer, Henry's specimens must have caused quite a stir. In the

Kew archives is a note in the handwriting of Professor Daniel Oliver (1830–1916), Keeper of the Kew Herbarium, declaring: 'This collection is one of the most important which we have ever received from the interior of China'.

Though the French missionaries – in particular, Père David and Père Delavay – had sent enormous collections to the Paris Muséum National d'Histoire Naturelle prior to this time, that institution did not have the same resources as Kew. Its leading botanist, Adrien Franchet, had produced a number of papers on new Chinese plants discovered by the missionaries, but many of the specimens were lost through carelessness, and, as a result of understaffing, the Paris museum team was slow in describing new species. Conversely, Kew was at the centre of a vast empire and, seeing its great potential in enhancing the agricultural production of her colonies, the British parliament had always ensured the gardens were adequately supported.

Material arriving from all parts of the globe was given almost immediate attention by Kew's large staff of very competent botanists and taxonomists.

Henry had begun his collecting at a very opportune time. In the spring of 1886, the Linnean Society of London published its inaugural volume of the *Index Florae Sinensis* (1886–1905), the first ever flora of China. Before this, the only such floras available were Carl Maximowicz's *Index Flora Pekinensis*, which covered the Beijing region, and George Bentham's colonial *Flora Hongkongensis* (1861). Through the three-volume *Index Florae Sinensis*, the Linnean Society aimed to produce an up-to date catalogue of China's flora using material deposited in the herbaria at Kew and the British Museum. The catalogue was undertaken by Francis Blackwell Forbes (1839–1908) of the British Museum and William Botting Hemsley (1843–1924), Assistant Keeper of Kew's Herbarium. It was completed almost 20 years later and, more than any other single collector, Augustine Henry's material was to dominate its pages. Thus, it was Henry's collections, rather than those of the French missionaries, that were to lay the basis for our present knowledge of China's great wealth of plants.

The earliest parts of the catalogue were freely circulated among British and Irish residents in China with the hope of inducing them to assist in the work of collecting specimens. The final catalogue, published by the Linnean Society in 1905, stated:

> Amongst the earlier [foreign collectors in China] was Dr Henry, at the time an officer in the Chinese Imperial Maritime Customs. [...] Henry's collections revealed the existence of a flora of surprising and unexpected richness, and raised problems of geographical distribution of the highest interest.[20]

Augustine Henry's interests were not only confined to plants. As previously noted, one of his favourite hunting grounds was the Antelope Glen, a narrow ravine that led off the Xiling Gorge. Henry described the glen, in one of his letters to Kew, as being 'a wonderful ravine a little inland from the Ichang Gorge, with perpendicular (or nearly so) cliffs rising 1,000 to 1,200 ft – on the ledges of the rocks, a new species of antelope occurs in numbers, hence the name of the glen. This glen I shall work out during the year and I fancy it will yield very interesting specimens'. The new antelope was in fact a shy little mountain goral that stood as high as a sheep and occurred only on precipices within the gorges. The locals called it the *Shan-yang* (mountain goat), and Henry commented that he had often startled them while botanising in the glen.[21] He managed to procure the skin and skull of an adult specimen,

which he sent to the French missionary and naturalist Père Pierre Heude. Heude later described it as a new species, *Kemas henryanus*.[22] Today, it is known as *Nemorhaedus griseus* and is really a southern Chinese species of the common goral. A live specimen was later brought from Yichang by a river-steamer captain to Heude for his small menagerie near Shanghai, and was painted by the French Jesuit, Père Charles Rathouis (1834–1890). The same painting once hung in Henry's study in Dublin and is now in the Glasnevin archives with many of his other Chinese collections.

Shooting wild animals was not in Henry's character, however, and years later he wrote rather nostalgically about his early years of plant hunting in China:

> Before going to China in 1881, I had no training in botany and was quite ignorant of gardening. I always had been fond of walking and of long excursions and cared little for games. Shooting never stirred my blood.

Kemas henryanus (now *Nemorhaedus griseus*) as depicted in a watercolour by Père Charles Rathouis. This little goral was often startled by Henry during his botanical rambles.

I prefer to keep still and listen to the birds and the drowsy hum of the bees. I love to watch the antelope as he lies asleep on the ledge of a cliff far below, the leopard crawling in the dusk over rocks, and the wolf as he trots in the moonlight along the path by the maize field.

[…] After some months in Shanghai, I was appointed in 1882 to Ichang, then at the end of navigation by steam on the Yangtze, a port a thousand miles from the sea. Opposite the town, the great river is already nearly a mile wide, and is beginning its course in the great plain. It has just made its exit, a few miles further up, from the mountains, through which it cuts its way and tumbles along in wild rapids or glides through silent gorges. These mountains and gorges were my playing ground, and I began to collect plants there in 1885. On the sides of the river are countless glens, often narrow as a house, and with vertical walls, a thousand feet or more, reaching to the sky.

Each ravine has some peculiar plant, and this is the feature of western China, the astonishing richness of the flora; each new valley and range yields some new species. When on the march, I always reckoned on meeting a different species of *Rubus* each ten miles of travel, and was never disappointed. Western China is the back of the Himalaya. This great chain presents its steep face as a wall to India; its sloping side descends by successive terraces through Tibet, Yunnan, and Szechuan, to sink at Ichang into the great plain, which is there not a hundred feet above sea level. No such deeply cut-up region exists elsewhere on the earth, hence the diversity of its plants, which are all the more interesting in that most of them can be grown in the open air in Britain.

I ought to explain that my botanising began accidentally; and as I had no previous training or knowledge, it was mainly successful because I was the first comer, a pioneer digger in a glorious gold-field. The first plant which I collected and dried was *Clematis henryi*, a species with large, simple, ovate-acuminate leaves and white waxen flowers which peeps out of the snow in February. Luck has kept with me from the start, and many new genera and hundreds of new species have fallen to my trowel and knife since that day […].[23]

While his father had left the gold-fields of California and Australia empty-handed, Augustine Henry reaped a rich reward from his own gold-fields in the glens and ravines beyond Yichang. His first consignment of just over 1,000 herbarium specimens yielded 120 new species, subspecies, varieties and forms – this at a time when it was thought that China had no new plants to offer. Many of these had been collected by him in the glens and ravines around Yichang, while a substantial proportion had been gathered by Man Yang, his native plant collector based in the mountains above Badong.

New plants from Yichang

These new finds were not only of interest to botanists, but were of outstanding horticultural merit and, when introduced by later plant hunters, they had a profound influence on Western gardens. Take, for example, *Anemone hupehensis*, one of the commonest wild flowers of Hubei Province, where it forms a charming picture when seen growing by thousands in mountain meadows. Henry called it the *yeh-mian-hua*, or 'wild cotton', from the inflated cotton-like seed heads it carries in late autumn. It was first described, in 1909, by the French nurseryman Émile Lemoine (1862–1942) from plants that flowered in his nursery; these had been raised from seeds sent to France by one of the French missionaries. It was one of Augustine Henry's earliest discoveries and is still abundant around Yichang.

Equally common in the damp glens around the city was *Lysimachia henryi*, a very vigorous, handsome perennial with a tufted trailing habit, bearing large yellow flowers in the angles of its crowded leaves. In its native habitat, the plant forms a spreading carpet to about 10 cm (4 in.) tall and roots at nodes as it spreads. Enjoying the same sort of shaded, damp conditions was *Begonia henryi* and the blue-flowered *Campanula* relative, *Adenophora rupincola*.

Henry didn't have to stroll too far to discover new plants. According to his field notes, *Aster henryi* grew on the banks of the Yangtze River at Yichang. *Euphorbia henryi* was common in the glens, where it formed a sturdy, upright

Anemone hupehensis, a common perennial in the mountains of western Hubei Province. Pictured above is an outstanding form collected by the Glasnevin Central China Expedition from near Yichang in October 2002.

Lysimachia henryi is rarely encountered in gardens, which is a great pity. It is a first-class garden plant requiring partial shade and a damp position. Given these conditions, it thrives and requires little further attention.

Viburnum ichangense flowering its heart out outside of the Herbarium building at Glasnevin. Almost 11,000 of Henry's Chinese and forestry herbarium specimens are held in the Glasnevin collections and are regularly used for scientific study.

Parthenocissus henryana is one of Henry's best-known finds and it has become a firm favourite in Western gardens. In the Three Gorges region, it scales the limestone cliffs that rise above the Yangtze River.

spurge to 60 cm (2 ft) tall carrying terminal cymes of lime green flowers. A common perennial on the edge of paddy fields and on cliff faces within the gorges was *Rehmannia henryi*, a beautiful species to about 50 cm (20 in.) tall bearing upright spikes of large, golden-yellow, foxglove-like flowers. It was described in 1909 from Henry's dried herbarium specimens, and from plants raised at Kew from seeds collected in Hubei Province by E. H. Wilson.

One of his lesser-known 1885 discoveries is a fine shrub that bears the name of the city that, for many years, was Henry's home: *Viburnum ichangense* is a deciduous shrub to about 2 m (5 ft) tall and bears slender, branched cymes of small white flowers during May and early June. It produces a showy display every year near the herbarium building at Glasnevin, but is rare in cultivation. On the hills above Yichang grew the blood-red flowered *Buddleja lindleyana* var. *sinuatodentata*. This

remarkably beautiful shrub was later introduced to cultivation by E. H. Wilson in 1908 from western Sichuan Province. According to that great authority on hardy woody plants, William Jackson Bean (1863–1947), it grew for more than half a century at Glasnevin, having been raised from the same Wilson collection (W. 1375).[24] That plant died many years ago and the variety is no longer known in cultivation.

While some of his collections have remained great rarities, others have became commonplace in our gardens. One of Augustine Henry's best-known finds is the vigorous deciduous vine *Parthenocissus henryana*. In the glens and ravines near Yichang, it scaled limestone cliffs by means of adhesive disc-tipped tendrils. This beautiful climber is deservedly popular in gardens on account of its silvery-white and pink variegated digitate foliage, which, like the best of the true Virginia creepers, turns fiery red in autumn.

Roses were abundant in the region, and many of those collected by Henry were previously unknown to science. Cascading its lax stems from the cliff faces in the Xiling Gorge was *Rosa chinensis* f. *spontanea*, the wild ancestor of the Chinese monthly rose. One of the parents of our modern hybrid teas and floribundas, it introduced important characteristics, such as perpetual flowering and fragrance. The wild plant is a rose of elegant habit and singular beauty, carrying solitary, large, red flowers on arching stems.

The diversity of hollies (*Ilex* spp.) in China is astounding; Augustine Henry collected no fewer than 33 different kinds, of which a dozen were new to science. On the crest of glens leading into the Xiling Gorge he found *Ilex centrochinensis*, an evergreen shrub to 3 m (10 ft) tall. Endemic to the provinces of Hubei and Sichuan, the best-known habitats for this species are the Three Gorges region and the nearby 'Metasequoia Valley', where it is found in forested areas and alongside streams and roadsides at 500 to 700 m (1,640 to 2,296 ft) above sea level. It is rare in cultivation.

Rhododendrons find their centre of diversity in the Sino-Himalayan region, and the first to be collected by Augustine Henry – *Rhododendron auriculatum* – was, not very surprisingly, a new species. He found it to be common on precipitous cliffs and in ravines to the west of Yichang. There, it formed small trees to 10 m (33 ft) tall, though it rarely reaches these dimensions in Western gardens. *Rhododendron auriculatum* is one of the latest species to flower. In the months of July and August, it carries umbels of up to 15 large, deliciously scented, funnel-shaped, white flowers. *Rhododendron mariesii*, a low-growing, deciduous, lilac- to rose-coloured azalea was abundant on the cliffs of the Three Gorges. Based on collections made by Maries, Henry and Wilson around Yichang, this species was first found by Robert Fortune in Zhejiang Province and was one of Henry's earliest introductions. He sent seeds to Kew in 1886, and it first flowered there in the Temperate House in April 1907.

Racing its way through trees and cascading its lax stems from the limestone cliffs in the Antelope Glen was *Actinidia callosa* var. *henryi*, a vigorous climber to 7 m (23 ft) tall, bearing white, scented flowers in May followed by ovoid, kiwi-like fruits in autumn. E. H. Wilson recorded it as being common in the mountains to the north and south of Yichang at the turn of the 20th century, and he later collected it on the two sacred Buddhist mountains, Wa Shan and Emei Shan, in western Sichuan Province.[25] *Clematis montana* var. *rubens* made rampant vines, festooning the tallest of trees with its scrambling stems. What a glorious sight it must have made in the glens and gorges above Yichang. In spring, the new foliage is bronze-purple, followed by sheets of large pink flowers. It was introduced to cultivation by E. H. Wilson in 1900 through his employers, Messrs Veitch, who first flowered it three years later. The variety was described from one of these seedlings and no type specimen was ever designated. In Veitch's *Novelties for 1908–9* catalogue, plants were available for two shillings and six pence to seven shillings and six pence each. It was awarded a First Class Certificate when shown at a Royal Horticultural Society Show in 1905 from the Coombe Wood nursery.

Another common climber in the region was *Holboellia coriacea*, a handsome evergreen bearing bold, glossy trifoliate leaves, and it scrambled its way through trees to 6 m (20 ft) tall by means of twining stems. The white male and female flowers are borne in separate corymbs and are delicately flushed purple. These are followed in autumn by fleshy, purple, egg-like fruits. Though discovered by Henry in 1885, it was described from material gathered in Sichuan Province in 1891 by the Norwegian and Austrian plant collectors, Carl Bock (1849–1932) and Arthur von Rosthorn (1862–1945). Henry stated that the fruits were relished by mountain peasants.

Holboellia coriacea, a relatively common climber in the forests of western Hubei Province. Its large, fleshy fruits were eaten by mountain peasants.

Another of his 1885 finds, *Abelia graebneriana*, has remained a great rarity in gardens, which is hard to comprehend since it is both a first-rate ornamental shrub and is not particularly difficult to propagate. I have long admired this species since first seeing the old Wilson plant in the Chinese shrubbery at Glasnevin, where, every summer, it carries masses of pink blossoms with yellow throats.

In many cases, plants that were originally discovered by Augustine Henry were named for other collectors later based in the Three Gorges region. Ernest Wilson, who followed in Henry's footsteps and later introduced his finest discoveries, is a good example. Augustine Henry was the first plant hunter to gather Wilson's balsam *Impatiens ernestii*, and, while it commemorates the English plant hunter, it was described as a new species by Joseph Hooker, based on the collections made by Père Delavay in Yunnan Province during the 1890s, by Henry in 1885, and from material gathered on Emei Shan by Ernst Faber in 1887 (more of Faber later) and Wilson in the first decade of the 20th century. On the banks of streams and by mountain torrents, Henry found *Salix wilsonii*, the most common willow in the mountains of western Hubei Province, where it forms trees to 13 m (43 ft) tall. On the banks of the

The Metasequoia Valley near Maoba in south-western Hubei Province. Many plants share their centre of diversity here and in the nearby Three Gorges region.

Yangtze in the Xiling Gorge, *Lonicera pileata* grew as a low-growing, evergreen, spreading shrub. It is now extremely popular with gardeners and landscape architects as a groundcover plant. The flowers of this species, though insignificant, are sweetly scented and are followed in autumn by striking, violet-coloured fruits.

Members of the true laurel family, Lauraceae, are a dominant feature of the warm-temperate forests in many parts of China. *Lindera fragrans* belongs to this group and was a common shrub in warmer valleys. According to Henry, the leaves of this species were pounded by watermills into powder and used, with the branches and roots of *Platycladus orientalis*, to make incense.[26] *Lindera megaphylla*, on the other hand, formed a large dioecious tree, with a massive trunk and a broad oval crown of erect spreading branches. Henry discovered it growing by a temple at Shih Pai Shan in the Xiling Gorge near Yichang.

The mountainous terrain of Badong lies south of the Yangtze River in the heart of the Three Gorges region. In the 1880s, these mountains were covered in dense primeval forest. Today, only patches of secondary forest remain.

New plants from Badong

The Badong collections were also full of new, exciting discoveries. Badong lay at a far higher altitude than Yichang and the mountains to the north and south of the town still had vast areas of undisturbed virgin forest. The flora, as a consequence, was markedly different from that of Yichang. As Henry pointed out in one of his letters to Kew, snow lay on the mountains for several months of the year and so he reckoned that any plants growing there would be hardy enough to withstand the climate of Britain and Ireland.

Medicinal plants were widely cultivated in Badong County's mountainous region. One of these, *Magnolia officinalis* had been known to Chinese people for centuries, but remained unknown in the West. This beautiful tree is still widely cultivated in Hubei and Sichuan provinces for its bark and flower buds, which make a valuable Chinese medicine. A deciduous tree to 15 m (49 ft) tall, *Magnolia*

officinalis carries foliage similar to the Japanese *Magnolia hypoleuca* and bears large, white, cup-shaped flowers in spring. The Chinese call it the *hou-p'o* tree and the removal of its bark has led to a serious decline of wild populations. According to Wilson, the boiled bark yields an extract that, when taken internally, acts as an aphrodisiac, a cure for coughs and colds, and as a tonic and stimulant during convalescence. A similar extract from the flower buds was called *yu-p'o* and was taken by women to correct irregularities of menstruation. Henry sent seeds to Kew in 1887. These apparently never germinated and so it was later introduced by Wilson in 1900.

Eleutherococcus leucorrhizus, a deciduous shrub in the ivy family (Araliaceae), was used in the same manner. This much-underrated deciduous shrub makes a beautiful sight in autumn when carrying large clusters of fleshy, black fruits. According to Henry, it was called the *wu-chia-p'i* and the bark of the roots was used as a drug.

The bauhinias are a beautiful group of trees, shrubs and climbers with showy, orchid-like flowers and distinctive twin lobed leaves. Henry found several new species during the course of his explorations and the first of these was *Bauhinia hupehana*, a rampant, scandent vine, climbing to 7 m (23 ft) by means of tendrils. The flowers vary from white to pink, and, though pretty, are foul smelling, which may account for its rarity in Western cultivation.

A common woodland perennial in the higher mountains of the region was *Smilacina henryi*, an elegant plant bearing racemes of small, starry, white flowers. The roots of this species were (and continue to be) used in herbal medicine. Also among the first consignment of plants from Badong was *Ligularia wilsoniana*, a plant commonly found by streams and in swampy areas, where it carried stiff spikes of large, golden-yellow, daisy-like flowers above bold, handsome, rounded leaves.

Badong's great tracts of primeval forest were full of novelties. A dominant chestnut there was *Castanea henryi*, which formed trees to 25 m (82 ft) with girths of up to 2.5 m (7 ft). It is extremely slow growing in the British Isles and Ireland, probably as a result of our rather dull, insular summers. Maples abound in this region of central China, and two new types appear in the 1885 Badong collections. *Acer cappadocicum* var. *sinicum* f. *tricaudatum* formed fine trees to 20 m (65 ft) tall, carrying broad, spreading crowns and bearing three lobed leaves. This form is endemic to Hubei Province and its coppery-red new growths are a beautiful sight in spring and early summer. The second maple, *Acer stachyophyllum* ssp. *betulifolium*, bears, as the name suggests, birch-like foliage. It is rare in gardens, and is cultivated at Glasnevin from a Kew–Sichuan collection.

Medicinal plant products for sale on the lower slopes of Emei Shan (Mount Omei) in Sichuan Province. Products for sale include bracket fungi, the stems of *Sargentodoxa cuneata* and *Clematis armandii*. Also on the same stall are the bark and flower buds of *Magnolia officinalis*.

Another interesting find was the Hubei crab apple, *Malus hupehensis*, a tree to 15 m (49 ft) tall that carries myriads of rose-tinted, white flowers in early summer. According to Henry, the foliage of this tree was sun dried at Badong and then exported down the Yangtze to distant cities where it was used as a tea substitute.[27] *Malus hupehensis* is allied to the Siberian crab, *Malus baccata*, and produces its seeds apomictically. Also common on the edge of these woods, and in open countryside amongst rocks, was the white to rose-pink flowered *Rhododendron argyrophyllum* ssp. *hypoglaucum*.

Henry relied on his Badong collector, Man Yang, to supply him with descriptions of what these dried specimens actually looked like in their living state. Man Yang was not always completely honest in giving a correct account and, as a result, the information Henry sent to Kew with specimens was sometimes not at all accurate. Take, for example, *Buddleja albiflora*. From information originally supplied by Man Yang, the Kew botanist W. B. Hemsley described this species as a tree to 9 m (29 ft) tall and bearing white flowers, hence the 'albiflora'. The specific epithet is a complete misnomer. The shrub rarely exceeds 4 m (13 ft) tall and the flowers are lilac in colour!

Perhaps the best known and most widely grown of Henry's 1885 Badong collections is *Viburnum rhytidophyllum*, an upright, evergreen shrub to 5 m (16 ft) tall, carrying large corrugated leaves, the undersides of which are plastered with a thick felt of yellow-grey down. The dull, creamy flowers are of no great beauty, but, in autumn, cymes of red (ripening to black) fruits are a handsome and conspicuous feature. This fine shrub was instantly popular when introduced to cultivation by Ernest Wilson in 1900, on account of its bold foliage and handsome habit.

Neillia sinensis is one of my favourite garden shrubs. I first encountered it many years ago in the beautiful garden on Garinish Island (Ilnacullin), off the coast of County Cork (Ireland). It was a common shrub in thickets around Badong and, in summer, carried slender terminal racemes of rosy-pink flowers. A shrub of elegant habit, the sharply toothed, lobed foliage of this species is distinctly attractive and the brown peeling bark is an added bonus. The genus commemorates the Scottish naturalist, Patrick Neil (1776–1851).

Acer cappadocicum var. *sinicum* f. *tricaudatum*, a young tree at the RHS Garden, Wisley. The newly emerged coppery-red leaves are a beautiful feature of this tree which is endemic to Hubei Province.

Chapter 3

Tracing the seasons through Yichang and Badong

The spring of 1886 saw Augustine Henry busily gathering specimens. He was systematic in his collecting and thoroughly worked each glen and ravine, gathering everything from weeds to flowering trees and shrubs before moving on to a new area. It is little wonder that so few Western botanists revisited these areas after he and later E. H. Wilson had completed their work there, however. The Glen of the Three Pilgrims (San You Dong), for example, proved to be rich in new species, though its rugged landscape of cliffs and crags was not without danger. In his diary, Henry records botanising there with one of his 'coolies' and states: 'Loo Chang fell off a cliff (drunk) and got hurt...'.

This was an isolated incident though. The inhabitants of the gorges were particularly good mountaineers and Henry relied heavily on their climbing skills for the many plants that had evolved to grow on the limestone cliffs that rose above the glens. Anyone who has collected plants around

A view of the Glen of the Three Pilgrims (San You Dong) in October 2004. The floor of the glen was flooded several years ago, following the completion of the first dam on the Yangtze – the Gezhou Dam – which lies a short distance downstream. Beneath these waters, Augustine Henry and his men blazed a trail, and were followed by Antwerp Edgar Pratt and E. H. Wilson.

Yichang in Hubei Province will know what a daunting task this can be. Antwerp Pratt, whom we shall soon meet, was impressed with the agility of the men:

The hill Chinese are exceedingly good mountaineers, and it is most alarming to see them on the face of a cliff nearly perpendicular, finding footholds on ledges only a few inches wide, with a sheer drop of perhaps hundreds of feet beneath them. If a break occurs in the ledge, and there should happen to be any vegetation over their

ABOVE: *Campylotropis macrocarpa*. The unfurling growths are covered in a dense, fawn tomentum, and this show is followed by racemes of lavender, pea-like blossoms. This beautiful deciduous shrub was unknown in Irish gardens prior to our 2004 expedition.

heads, they will not hesitate to seize it with their hands and swing themselves over the gap. It is a thing to be seen before one can thoroughly comprehend it, and I hear, without much surprise, that loss of life by accident was not infrequent among them.[1]

The chief glory of the Glen of the Three Pilgrims was in late winter, when the lilac primrose, *Primula rupestris*, flowered on ledges on the cliffs beneath the cave and temple. According to Henry, these ledges were continuous for almost half a kilometre and the plant appeared to live on pure limestone without any soil, and bore flowers in December and January. The same well-known Yichang plant was, for a long time, confusingly regarded as being the allied *Primula sinensis*.

Despite being undoubtedly hardy and of great beauty, some of Henry's discoveries from the Glen of the Three Pilgrims have never reached cultivation. Few hardy, terrestrial, Chinese orchids are grown in Western gardens, with the exception of the slipper orchids. What a pity! One of the most beautiful orchids in the glen was *Hemipilia henryi*, which was also later collected, by other plant hunters, in both the Sichuan and Yunnan provinces. During the months of July and August, this tough little plant bears racemes of pink to purple-red flowers above a single ovate–cordate leaf.

The Dome (Moji Shan) was frequently visited by Henry during 1886, and that hill also offered up many new plants. Being located across the Yangtze, directly opposite the Foreign Compound, meant it was easily accessible by ferry, and a small, steep track led to a temple on the summit. The Dome was approached through the Monastery Valley, which, at that time, was uncultivated and a number of fine trees grew by the monastery itself, including a magnificent specimen of *Photinia serratifolia*, a beautiful tree both in terms of flower and foliage, though one of the parents of the justifiably berated *Photinia* x *fraseri* 'Red Robin'.

A common plant in the Monastery Valley and on the lower

slopes of Moji Shan was the silver-stemmed *Rubus innominatus* var. *kuntzeanus*, a vigorous shrub to 2 m (6.5 ft) tall. Henry was so impressed with this wonderful new bramble that he sent seeds to Kew that same year, whereupon Hemsley named it for the 19th-century botanist, Dr Otto Kuntze, an expert on this extremely variable and perplexing group.

The schisandras are an interesting group of climbers of ancient lineage, and are closely allied to the magnolias. Henry discovered several during the course of his travels, and the first of these, found in the Monastery Valley, was *Schisandra propinqua* var. *sinensis*. Though the yellow flowers of this variety are by no means showy, good forms have beautifully marbled, narrow, lanceolate leaves. With it grew the pink-purple flowered *Campylotropis macrocarpa*, a lax-habited shrub to 2 m (6.5 ft) tall, and *Photinia davidsoniae*, an evergreen tree that was commonly planted around shrines and temples in the Three Gorges region. Described as a new species many years later by Alfred Rehder (1863–1949) and Ernest Wilson in their monumental *Plantae Wilsonianae* (three volumes, edited by Charles Sprague Sargent), the latter had the species named for Mrs Henry Davidson, a missionary based in Chengdu (Sichuan Province), for the help she gave following an accident that broke his leg in two places in September 1910.

The slopes of Moji Shan were full of good plants, and two of the finest that Henry discovered there that year were *Callicarpa bodinieri* and *Callicarpa bodinieri* var. *giraldii*. Both shrubs are well known and widely grown in Europe and North America on account of their spectacular autumn show of violet-purple fruits and pink-red colour.

Sir William Turner Thiselton-Dyer was director of the Royal Botanic Gardens, Kew, between 1885 and 1905. He was also a life-long friend of Augustine Henry.

Yichang and Liantuo – arrivals and departures

In his diary for Easter Monday, 26 April 1886, Henry recorded the arrival of a steamer from Shanghai with a number of globetrotters on board. The following day, he sailed upriver with the captain of the ship and the group of travellers, and, over the next few days, struck up a great friendship with one of these: Lord Kesteven from Casewick House in Lincolnshire, England. Both regularly set out together for walks in the countryside, and, while Henry botanised, Kesteven shot snipe and woodcock. Later that year, after Kesteven had returned to England, Henry sent him seeds of a holly-like shrub that he had discovered in the glens near Yichang a year previously. It first flowered at Casewick House in 1895 and was one of Henry's earliest introductions.

The plant in question, *Itea ilicifolia*, is an evergreen shrub to 5 m (16 ft) tall with holly-like leaves and which bears long, pendulous, catkin-like racemes of fragrant, greenish-white flowers during the month of August. Because of the holly-like appearance of its foliage, the Yichang tassel bush was known colloquially in the Three Gorges area as *lao shu tz'u*, a name also applied to *Ilex cornuta* and *Ilex centrochinensis*.

In early May, Henry organised a five-day trip upriver through the gorges taking ten 'coolies', two sedan chairs, his Chinese teacher and a cook. He was probably accompanied on this trip by Lord Kesteven. In his baggage were stacks of paper and plant presses, for drying plants, and labels and notebooks in which he recorded his field notes. The sedan chair was an essential travel piece in 19th-century

China, and was a statement of high rank that commanded the respect of local people. His accommodation at night was in temples and in shops, and, though these places were basic and abominably filthy, he rarely complained of such discomforts. In his diary on 5 May, Henry stated the group set out at 07:30 a.m. to descend the Xiling Gorge (Xiling Xia). Their passage through the rapids was uneventful, but one of the places Henry passed during the journey was a small village called Sandouping (then San-tou-p'ing), located 32 km (20 miles) above Yichang. Little did he know that, more than a century later, the world's largest dam would span the width of the Yangtze at this village.

On 23 June 1886, Henry sent a second consignment of plants to Kew. His new contact there was Sir William Thiselton-Dyer (1843–1928), who had succeeded Joseph Hooker

ABOVE, OPPOSITE: The Yichang tassel bush, *Itea ilicifolia*, was one of Augustine Henry's earliest introductions. The tiny creamy-white flowers are sweetly scented.

ABOVE: The tiny hamlet of Liantuo (formerly Nanto) was a base for one of Henry's most successful native plant collectors. Liantuo lies perched on the northern bank of the Yangtze above Yichang and is surrounded by cliffs on all sides. In 1882, Henry gathered fossilised cycads in thin beds of coal here. Three years later, he began collecting plants.

(Thiselton-Dyer's father-in-law) as director. At this time, Henry had a second native plant collector at work at Liantuo (Nanto), a small hamlet nestled among orange groves some 32 km (20 miles) upriver from Yichang. Liantuo was spectacularly located on the north bank of the Yangtze River, within the Xiling Gorge, and its little cluster of houses sat in a muddle with an enormous wall of limestone crags at its back. It faced directly onto the Yangtze and even taller cliffs on the river's opposite bank. According to E. H. Wilson, the same cliffs contained both Cambrian and Ordovician fossils.[2] Henry's Liantuo man concentrated his collecting in the wooded mountains to the north of the hamlet, and, at times, travelled as far north as Fang, a mountainous region then still heavily forested.

Liantuo proved to be a treasure trove of new, exciting, highly garden-worthy plants, and Henry's best find from the region in 1886 has to be the giant lily, *Cardiocrinum giganteum* var. *yunnanense*, a spectacular plant, which, seven years after germinating from a tiny seed, throws up a 2-m (6.5-ft) tall, burgundy-purple flowering stem. The individual funnel-shaped flowers, like the rest of the plant, are gargantuan in scale. Each gloriously scented white flower is striped maroon and up to 25 cm (10 in.) in length, and a dozen are carried 2 m (6.5 ft) above a basal rosette of large, dramatic, heart-shaped, copper-toned leaves. This enormous show costs the giant lily its life, a spectacular finale to an astonishing plant. Before dying, however, it produces plump, upright seed capsules, containing thousands of seeds, and several bulbils form around the

original bulb that will flower just fours years later, as opposed to a seven-year wait from seed. This noble lily was so abundant in the Three Gorges region during the late 19th century that Henry stated its gorgeous turret of flowers could be spied miles away across the valleys.[3]

This Chinese variety differs from the type plant – *Cardiocrinum giganteum*, from the Himalayan region – in its outer morphological features: the dark stems, the bronze spring foliage, the horizontally held flower's habit of opening from the top of the stem downwards, and the shape of the seed capsules. It is also shorter, rarely more than 2 m (6.5 ft) tall. The Himalayan plant, *Cardiocrinum giganteum*, was discovered by Dr Nathaniel Wallich (1786–1854) in Nepal in 1825 and was introduced by means of seeds sent by the Irish collector Colonel Edward Madden to Glasnevin in 1847. *Cardiocrinum giganteum* has a native range extending from Kashmir to as far as Tibet and the Yunnan Province, while Henry's var. *yunnanense* extends from Yunnan (where he later made further collections) to Hubei Province.

The Chinese quince, *Chaenomeles cathayensis*, was common

around Liantuo and Yichang, where it formed an open-branched shrub to 4.5 m (15 ft) tall. Probably the finest of all the fruiting quinces, there is an old wall-trained plant at Glasnevin that, every February, carries clusters of pale-pink flowers on short-spurred growths, followed in autumn by large, deliciously scented, golden yellow fruits to 15 cm (6 in.) long. It grew wild in the Three Gorges region and Wilson observed that it was grown as a hedge plant at Changyang, a county to the south of Yichang in Hubei Province. Though described as a new species from Henry's central Chinese collections, this quince had been introduced to Europe in 1800.

Hemiboea henryi was not just a new species, but also a beautiful new genus. This hardy herbaceous gesneriad was common on the faces of damp cliffs, where it formed dome-shaped plants to about 30 cm (12 in.) high and carried waxy, white, tubular flowers with a yellow splash in the

Chaenomeles cathayensis. The flowers are borne in early spring on short-spurred growths, and these are followed in autumn by large, deliciously fragrant, golden-yellow fruits.

Sarcococca ruscifolia, more commonly known as winter box. It is now a popular plant in European and North American gardens on account of its sweetly scented blossoms.

Cardiocrinum giganteum var. *yunnanense* – an impressive group of plants in fruit at the Royal Botanic Gardens, Kew. The dark stems and plump seed capsules prolong the season of interest long after flowering finishes.

throat. Henry called it the *hsiang-lung-ts'ao* and noted that a decoction of the root with alcohol was used by village doctors to treat cases of snakebite. Wilson later introduced it, though it did not persist for long in cultivation.[4]

Another cliff inhabitant around Liantuo that also proved new to science was the *ai-pai-ts'ai*, or cliff cabbage, *Triaenophora rupestris* (syn. *Rehmannia rupestris*). It too was much esteemed in traditional herbal medicine and, according to Henry, it grew only in the most inaccessible places on the faces of cliffs at Liantuo and within the gorges, where it formed a very striking plant when in flower. He introduced it to cultivation through Kew, where it first flowered in 1888.[5]

The winter boxes, *Sarcococca*, are valuable shrubs and their small white flowers bring a magical scent to the garden in the depths of winter and early spring. Henry discovered no fewer than three new species, and how poorer our Western gardens would be without the finest of these: *Sarcococca ruscifolia*. It was particularly common around Liantuo and in the glens above Yichang. That delightfully scented, late-flowered, mock orange *Philadelphus incanus* was also discovered near Liantuo in the same year.

There is never a time in the Three Gorges region when a plant is not in flower and Henry and his collectors were as busy in mid winter as at any other period of the year. February 1886 saw the discovery of *Camellia cuspidata*, a medium-sized evergreen shrub bearing masses of small ivory-white flowers. The emerging foliage of this species is copper tinted and it is one of the parents of the wonderfully floriferous *Camellia* 'Cornish Snow'.

On the margins of woods and thickets near Liantuo, the Chinese bladdernut, *Staphylea holocarpa*, formed wide-spreading trees to 9 m (30 ft) tall, and its dense, drooping panicles of white flowers were carried on bare wood during April and May. Wilson later introduced it from Badong in 1908 and considered it to be the most beautiful member of the genus. Few who know this species would disagree with him.

Ficus sarmentosa var. *henryi*, a sprawling shrub, preferred more open situations and crept over rocks around Yichang and in the Antelope Glen. Henry sent large consignments of seed to Kew in 1886 and this included a new cucurbit, *Actinostemon glandulosum*. Though little has been written about Chinese ferns in Western botanical literature, they are an abundant group in China's relict flora and Henry discovered dozens of new species while based at Yichang, including the endemic *Colysis henryi* (Polypodiaceae), which he also gathered on the Daweishan mountain range near the Vietnamese border in southern Yunnan Province many years later. Liantuo, as we shall see, would offer up many exciting novelties in the years that followed.

Rhododendron augustinii, one of the real aristocrats of its clan and one of a few species that are perfectly lime tolerant. It was seized upon by plant hybridisers, soon after its introduction, to breed many of the blue hybrids.

New plants from Badong

On the higher mountains above Badong, Henry's native plant collector, Man Yang, made some spectacular discoveries during the 1886 season. The best of these has to be *Rhododendron augustinii*, an evergreen shrub capable of reaching 7 m (23 ft) tall in its native habitat. In its best forms, this is the finest of all the blue-flowered species and has the added bonus of being perfectly lime-tolerant. It is extremely common in western Hubei Province, where it is variable in flower colour, and it first flowered in the collection of Maurice de Vilmorin at the Arboretum National des Barres, France, from seeds sent there by the French missionary and plant collector, Père Paul Guillaume Farges (1844–1912) in 1899. Sent to China in 1867, Farges was stationed in northeast Sichuan Province until 1903, though it was not until 1892 that he began to collect botanical specimens. Before moving south to Chongqing, he sent more than 4,000 specimens to the Paris Muséum National d'Histoire Naturelle. Many of his discoveries were later introduced by E. H. Wilson, though scores of these – including *Abies fargesii*, *Catalpa fargesii*, *Clethra fargesii*, *Cypripedium fargesii* and *Decaisnea fargesii* – were first found by Augustine Henry.

Scattered throughout Badong's great forests were mammoth trees of *Magnolia sprengeri* that towered 20 m (65 ft) overhead.

Deutzia discolor. The plant featured here was raised at Glasnevin in the spring of 1908 from a collection made by E. H. Wilson (W. 570) at Xingshan (Hsingshan), a county north-west of the city of Yichang in Hubei Province.

Eleutherococcus henryi forms a pretty picture indeed when it carries globular clusters of fleshy black fruits. Easy to grow and very long lived, it is a shame that it is so rarely encountered in gardens.

What a sight they must have made there during the month of April, when the large, erect, saucer-shaped blooms lit up those ancient woodlands. *Magnolia sprengeri* is variable in the wild. The flowers, which are fragrant and held in an erect poise, range from purest white to rosy-pink and rose-red. A second new species, the rare, lemon-scented *Magnolia biondii*, formed trees up to 12 m (39 ft). It was a great rarity even in Henry's time and has never become common in cultivation. Though discovered by Henry, it was described from material collected by the Italian missionary Padre Giuseppe Giraldi (1848–1901) in neighbouring Shaanxi (Shensi) Province during the early 1890s.

Sorbus folgneri, one of the finest of the whitebeams, was also common in those woods. It is an exceptionally elegant tree of more or less pendulous habit, and, like the other whitebeams, the leaves are silvery-white beneath. The tree is a beautiful sight when its leaves are caught in the wind. In autumn, it takes on a hue of golden-pink, which forms a brilliant contrast with the silvery undersides.

Corylopsis, that lovely group of spring-flowered shrubs and small trees, is represented by several species in western Hubei Province. *Corylopsis henryi* is the rarest of these; Henry's collector found it once only, and Wilson failed to find it at all during his travels throughout the region.

Vaccinium henryi, on the other hand, was common in oak woods, where it formed evergreen shrubs to 3 m (10 ft) tall. For some unexplained reason, *Viburnum henryi* has remained uncommon in gardens, despite being a first-class shrub. Man Yang found it in upland thickets where it formed large upright evergreen shrubs. It was also one of the many plants we exhibited at the Chelsea Flower Show in May 2002, and I remember well the work involved in forcing it into flower a month early. At Chelsea, it was an instant hit and everyone wanted to know its name and from where it could be bought. It is a beautiful plant in habit, foliage, flower and fruit, and I wouldn't be without its pyramidal panicles of deliciously fragrant flowers in June.

Deutzia discolor also flowered in time for the Chelsea Flower

Spiraea henryi, rare in cultivation, though a first-class plant. The mountain peasants of Hubei Province made tea from its small, rounded leaves.

Show and it too was an 1886 find from Badong. This fine shrub has long grown at Glasnevin, where it is represented by collections made by both Reginald Farrer (1880–1920) and Ernest Wilson. A graceful shrub to about 1.5 m (5 ft) tall, it produces sprays of white or faintly rose-tinted flowers in May and June.

The bridal wreaths are often dismissed by many gardeners, yet such snobbery is often unwarranted. Admittedly, some can be decidedly plain, though this is no reason to neglect the better species, of which *Spiraea henryi* is one of the real aristocrats. One of the charms of this shrub is its lax, arching habit, and it is a glorious sight in June when it produces great masses of small white flowers in rounded corymbs. According to Henry, the leaves were used as a tea substitute in the Three Gorges region, where it was known as the *tsui lan ch'a*. It was introduced by Wilson in 1900, and two of his 1908 collections from Baoxing (W. 1318) and Wa-Shan (W. 1172) in western Sichuan Province grew at Glasnevin in the early 20th century.

Eleutherococcus henryi was common on the cliffs at Badong, and the shrub's root continues to play an important role in Chinese herbal medicine today. The drug extracted from the root

51

Dregea sinensis, a pretty climber for a warm, sunny wall. Wilson introduced it to cultivation in 1907.

Lonicera henryi is a vigorous climber and ideal for training into small trees or across large tree stumps.

Lonicera tragophylla, one of the best of the Chinese honeysuckles. What a pity it is not scented.

bark is said to strengthen the sinews and bones, and it is also used as a very effective anti-inflammatory. Also new was *Atropanthe sinensis*, a robust perennial in the potato family (Solanaceae) that was much valued for the sake of a cardiac drug extracted from it.

Another important medicinal plant from Badong was *Aconitum hemsleyanum*, indisputably the best of the climbing herbaceous monk's hoods. It was common in thickets and glades, where it formed vines to 2.5 m (8 ft) tall carrying rich violet-blue hooded flowers in late autumn. Climbing plants abounded in the forests and thickets, and one of these, the cucumber relative *Thladiantha henryi*, formed large sprawling vines, though it is of interest more to botanists than keen gardeners and horti-culturists. Another cucurbit, *Hemsleya chinensis*, proved to be an

entirely new genus and was named for Henry's friend, the Kew botanist William Botting Hemsley. Like the *Thladiantha*, the tuberous roots of this species are used in herbal medicine; in this case, to treat diarrhoea, dysentery and bronchitis.

While the former are of botanical and medicinal interest, *Lonicera henryi* is a superbly ornamental plant and has become extremely popular in cultivation. This rampant evergreen needs plenty of space and is best grown through a tree. The purplish-red flowers are carried in clusters at the end of shoots in June. It was abundant around Badong in the late 19th century, and is still common there today. *Lonicera tragophylla*, one of largest flowered and perhaps the most glorious of all the climbing honeysuckles, was also found in thickets around Badong (where Henry stated it was rare), and there it rambled its way through trees to 4 m (13 ft). In June and July, this species is at its best when carrying terminal clusters of up to 20 large, golden-yellow, tubular flowers surrounded by an unusual disc-like bract. What a shame it is not scented.

Schisandra henryi twined its stems through surrounding trees and shrubs. The flowers of this species are creamy-white and are followed by pendant spikes of fleshy fruits. Wilson described it as being rare in Hubei Province, and noted that the fruits were eaten by mountain peasants. *Dregea sinensis* has remained rare in cultivation, which is a pity. Though often stated to be tender, it thrives on a wall at Wisley, one of the coldest gardens in England. It is ideally suited to wall culture, or will smother a fence, and reaches about 3 m (10 ft) tall. The white, later pink-flushed flowers resemble those of a *Hoya* and are delightfully scented. The foliage, too, is distinctly handsome and the undersides of its leaves are beautifully grey-felted.

Rubus henryi was also common around Badong, where it made a rampant evergreen scandent shrub and scrambled its way through trees and shrubs to 7 m (23 ft) high. It is a remarkably distinct species, readily distinguished by handsome three-lobed leaves that are covered, on the underside, with a fine white felt. In the Three Gorges region, it is called the *chi-chao-ch'a*, as the leaves were dried and used as a tea substitute in the 19th century. It is more often represented in Western cultivation by *Rubus henryi* var. *bambusarum*, one of Henry's later discoveries from Wushan in Sichuan Province.

ABOVE: *Abelmoschus manihot*, a handsome perennial that is found through warmer regions of China. From the roots of this mallow relative, a mucilage was prepared and used in the production of paper.

1886 collections from around Yichang

The Glen of Three Pilgrims also provided a multitude of new species during the 1886 season, including a new bamboo, *Phyllostachys heteroclada*, a handsome plant to 6 m (20 ft) tall. Bamboo has a multitude of different uses in China, and this species was used for papermaking in the Three Gorges region. The culms were cut into lengths and immersed in pits of water for three months. They were then washed and stacked in layers, each layer being sprayed with lime and water. After two months, the stems were well retted. The fibrous mass was then washed to remove all traces of lime, steamed for 15 days, washed and placed back in the soaking pit. There, it was finally reduced to a fine pulp and was then ready for conversion to paper. A portion of the pulp was placed in troughs with a mucilage prepared from the roots of the mallow relative, *Abelmoschus manihot*. From there, it was placed in bamboo trays with a fine-meshed bottom to allow drainage. The film that collected formed a moist sheet of paper.

In glens not far from Yichang, growing on the edge of woods, Henry discovered another remarkable new genus: *Tupistra chinensis*, a low-growing rhizomatous perennial with strap-like leaves, in the lily-of-the-valley family (Convallariaceae). The roots were, according to Henry, used in treating mouth and throat diseases. The low-growing *Thalictrum ichangense* was common in the Antelope Glen, as was the handsome

nettle relative, *Elatostema ichangense*. Henry also gathered a vast assemblage of grasses from around Yichang, many of which were new, including *Fimbristylis henryi*. This same species was also later collected by a lesser-known Irish plant hunter, the missionary Father John Scallan (1851–1927), in Shaanxi Province during the 1890s. Father Scallan, perhaps better known as Pater Hugo, discovered and introduced the lovely yellow-flowered *Rosa xanthina* f. *hugonis* through Kew, where the original plant still flourishes.

In the rocky glens near Pingshanba (Pin-shan-pa), Henry discovered a new winter sweet, *Chimonanthus nitens*, which he described as a small evergreen shrub bearing creamy-white flowers. It has remained extremely rare in cultivation, though there is quite a good young plant in the Asia section of the San Francisco Botanical Garden (Strybing Arboretum). *Rosa henryi* also grew in the glens around Yichang, where it formed a scandent shrub to 5 m (15 ft) tall and bore enormous umbellate corymbs of up to 15 large, fragrant, white flowers followed by clusters of dull red fruits. This species was later introduced to cultivation by Ernest Wilson in 1907 (as *Rosa gentiliana*) and seedlings

53

In western Hubei Province, *Rosa henryi* is found in thickets and on the edge of woods, where its long stems ramble through surrounding trees and shrubs. Sweetly scented white flowers are carried in May.

from the same seed batch (W. 609) were raised at Glasnevin the following spring.

Henry followed up his June consignment of plants to Kew with the following letter to Thiselton-Dyer:

I have received your letter of March 16th and I am glad that the specimens I sent at the end of last year reached you in good order. I wrote to you a good while ago promising more specimens, but I was unable to get them off till a week ago. I hope you will receive the lot sent now in good time [...].

I enclose a memorandum which gives particulars concerning the present lot. I am making a large collection this summer, and it may not be very long before I send off another lot. I note what you say regarding keeping separate the plants from different localities, and that you desire specimens with fruit attached. I am collecting myself and have two natives at work, one in the mountains to the s.w. and another in a n.w. direction. I hope you will excuse the motley order, the duplication and triplication

of identified plants, and the other inconveniences of my collection. But I am occupied a good deal with official work, and have not as much time as I should like to devote to arranging the collection in a proper manner.

I am very much obliged to you for your kind promise to send me a list of determinations. I have so far been collecting, and have scarcely made any study of the plants in a botanical way. By now I have a good number of helpful books [...] and once started with the names of 300 or 400 plants, I should be able to make head-way in gaining scientific knowledge of the plants of China.

Help given to me now in this way will be advantageous to you hereafter, as I shall be able to make some travels in China bye and bye and with some scientific knowledge I may then secure for you a good deal of additional knowledge of the flora of China.

I am well provided with the best Chinese books on plants, and once the list of scientific names of these two lots (and of my next lot) comes to hand, I shall be able to make a good number of trustworthy identifications, of Chinese names of plants, hitherto unknown or identified erroneously.

I intend to devote a good deal of attention to: 1. economic uses of plants in China; 2. origin of cultivated plants – what light can be thrown on this subject by a study of Chinese botanical works?; 3. compiling an alphabetical list of all Chinese names of plants with their scientific determinations, uses, etc.

These are ambitious schemes but I have plenty of time and intend to proceed slowly and surely. If I could show any results, in all probability, I should receive encouragement and facilities for further work from the Chief of the Service in which I am engaged (Sir Robt. Hart). I shall be very glad, in case you should require any *living* plants, any information on any subject connected with plants or drugs, etc., etc., to try and supply you with what you require. I hope the present lot of plants will reach you in good order and that I shall be able to forward you a bigger case in the course of one or two months.

In mid July, Henry travelled by sedan chair to the Glen of the Three Pilgrims. The river was at its highest level, since it was the rainy season, and there was a great outpouring of water from the glen. After a busy day collecting plants, he spent the night in a houseboat, which was immensely more preferable to staying in one of the local temples or inns. The next day, he and his 'coolies' descended to Yichang in the record time of 33 minutes as the Yangtze was in spate.

In September 1886, Henry made one of his most remarkable finds while botanising in a shallow pond less

Chimonanthus praecox is a relatively common inhabitant of the Three Gorges region, where it is invariably found perched on limestone cliffs. In this habitat, its stems bake in the summer heat in much the same manner as wall-trained plants do in Western gardens.

than a quarter of a mile to the rear of the Foreign Compound at Yichang. The plant in question was a small floating aquatic, similar to the water chestnut *Trapa natans*. *Trapella sinensis* was one of 27 new genera discovered by Augustine Henry in central China between 1885 and 1889 and belonged to an entirely new family, Trapellaceae. It was apparently rare: Henry found it twice only, in the pond mentioned and in a nearby rice field; Wilson always regretted that he was unable to find it, though it was later found near Yichang by another plant hunter, Frank N. Meyer (1875–1918).[6] Around Yichang, *Trapella* was known colloquially as *t'ieh ling chio*, or 'iron trapa', indicating the uselessness of the plant compared to *Trapa*, which is an important crop.

Specimens of this anomalous new aquatic reached the herbarium at Kew in February 1887. Further material was needed, however, to sort out the taxonomy of the plant, and, in July of that year, Henry dispatched specimens preserved in alcohol. This allowed Francis Oliver (Professor Daniel Oliver's son) to give a complete and detailed account of the plant. In the same publication, Oliver 'Junior' went on to state:

> That I am able now to give this monographic account of a plant unknown to science before 1887 speaks of Dr Henry's prompt courtesy in obtaining and dispatching material. No botanist in China in recent times has sent home collections richer in entirely new forms than has Dr Henry, who is now working on the flora of central China, hitherto an almost sealed book.[7]

Spring 1887 – wintry yet auspicious

The spring of 1887 was the coldest at Yichang in more than 30 years, and heavy snow and ice hampered Henry's botanical work. Man Yang, his Badong collector, began to travel further afield, thus bringing back a wider range of plants than before. By this time, Henry had stationed a third man near Changyang, a small town to the southwest of Yichang.

Despite the cold season, Henry's collections were full of showy spring-flowering plants. The common winter sweet, *Chimonanthus praecox*, was frequently met with in the gorges, and its sweet, spicy scent must have pervaded those narrow glens and ravines. In February, he was working his way through the flora of the Antelope Glen, where he found *Mahonia eurybracteata* (syn. *Mahonia confusa*), a small, erect shrub to 1.5 m (5 ft) tall, bearing short racemes of yellow flowers above bluish-green pinnate foliage. It was introduced to cultivation almost a century later by the English plantsman and author, Roy Lancaster.

Ligustrum henryi was abundant in the same glen, where it formed evergreen shrubs to 4 m (13 ft) tall. It is one of the most ornamental of the privets, having a neat habit, and the large pyramidal panicles of small white flowers are deliciously scented. Lilies abounded in the Antelope Glen, including *Lilium leucanthum* var. *centifolium*, a tall species that, under good conditions, may reach 3 m (10 ft) tall and which bears up to 18 scented, white, purple-flushed flowers. Henry not only discovered it, but also introduced it through Kew, where it first flowered in 1891. Reginald Farrer was also impressed with this lovely lily when he stumbled upon it in a small garden in Gansu Province many years later.

Elaeagnus henryi was a relatively common shrub in the glens to the west of Yichang, where it formed scandent shrubs to 5 m tall. Like other members of the genus, *Elaeagnus henryi* bears masses of tiny, inconspicuous though deliciously fragrant flowers, and the salmon-red fruits of this species are a beautiful feature. *Abutilon sinense* was a rarity around Yichang, and it grew there as a cliff plant. Henry discovered it on the towering limestone walls of the Xiling

Mahonia eurybracteata flowering in the garden of Beech Park House near Dublin. The plant featured here was raised from Roy Lancaster's original introduction from Emei Shan in western Sichuan Province.

Illicium henryi, one of a large number of primitive flowering plants found in the mountains to the north of Yichang. Suited best to milder coastal gardens, it is a handsome evergreen shrub of upright habit.

Schisandra sphenanthera, perhaps the most beautiful member of this wonderful genus of climbing shrubs. The plant pictured here grows at Glasnevin, where, every year, the branches are smothered in small, rounded blossoms.

Gorge – the largest of the Three Gorges – where it formed widespreading shrubs to 5 m (16 ft) tall and carried showy, shallowly tubular, golden-yellow blossoms in profusion during the month of March. Wilson later collected it on the cliffs of the Wu Gorge in neighbouring Sichuan Province in 1908, while his contemporary, the Scottish plant hunter George Forrest (1873–1932), had gathered it in north-western Yunnan Province in 1906. Henry stated that it deserved introduction to European gardens, though, to my knowledge, this has never happened.

An interesting late spring find was *Illicium henryi*, a small evergreen tree to about 6 m (20 ft) high. The Illiciums are an interesting part of China's well-preserved relict flora and are closely allied to other primitive flowering plants, such as *Nymphaea* and *Schisandra*. *Illicium henryi* was abundant on the cliffs in the glens above Yichang, where it flowered profusely between April and June. The many-petalled flowers are fragrant and vary from pink to reddish-crimson.

In May of that year, Henry discovered *Schisandra sphenanthera* in the Antelope Glen, near Yichang (Ichang). According to E. H. Wilson, this is the commonest of the Schisandras in central and western China above altitudes of 1,600 m (5,250 ft), and it exhibits considerable variation over that range.[8] I have long admired this beautiful twining climber from the first time I saw an old Wilson plant bloom on the clematis corral at Glasnevin, where, every May without fail, it carries masses of terracotta-coloured flowers.

Another new climber in the Antelope Glen was *Aristolochia heterophylla*, and it, like the *Illicium* and the *Schisandra*, is a palaeo-shrub belonging to the Three Gorges

region's ancient flora. In the Antelope Glen, it scrambled its way through shrubs in thickets to 3 m (10 ft) tall. This rambling shrub is for lovers of the curious. The chocolate- and gold-coloured flowers have the characteristic 'Dutchman's pipe' shape of the group, and, during the late 19th century, the roots were used as an ingredient of traditional medicine. Several species of *Aristolochia* are used medicinally in various parts of the world. Their original use (in Europe) seems to stem from the doctrine of signatures (herbalism). The flowers are reminiscent of the shape of a human foetus in the correct, upright position prior to birth, hence the Greek *aristos* (best) and *lochia* (childbirth). The birthworts are used by many races in both the northern and southern hemispheres. In China, *Aristolochia heterophylla*, *A. fangchi* and *A. kaempferi* continue to be used as ingredients in traditional medicine. On the Indian subcontinent, *A. indica* is used as a contraceptive. In Iran, *A. rotunda* is valued as a tonic, and, in North America, the Virginian snakeroot, *A. serpentaria*, is used as a snakebite remedy.

Peucedanum dielsianum also grew in the Antelope Glen, and, like many other plants in the carrot family (Apiaceae), it was highly valued as a medicinal plant. Henry thought it might be of economic interest and so sent seeds to Kew the following year. These germinated and were later planted out in the herb garden there.

Following a desperately cold start to the year, the months of April, May and June were extraordinarily wet. This, coupled with an infestation of caterpillars and various insects, meant some of Henry's specimens were completely destroyed. Such were the problems faced by 19th-century plant hunters.

1887 – More visitors to Yichang

On 15 April, the steamer *Kiang-tung* made one of its regular journeys from Shanghai, and among her passengers was the German missionary, the Reverend Dr Ernst Faber (1839–1899). An accomplished Sinologist and botanist, Faber was sent to China by the Rhenish Missionary Society in 1865 and began collecting plants in the southeast in 1878. Faber's stay in Yichang was a short one, as he was *en route* to western China on a four-month expedition, but, upon arriving there, he spent his time studying Henry's specimens, and, before he departed the city, Henry managed to persuade him to collect a duplicate set of specimens for the herbarium at Kew.

Faber's travels were to take him further afield from the Three Gorges region to Chongqing and to the city of Leshan on the Min River (Min Jiang), a tributary of the Yangtze, in Sichuan Province. From there, his journey continued to the famous Buddhist mountain of Emei Shan (Mount Omei) near Chengdu (Chengtu) in western Sichuan. Indeed, Faber holds the distinction of being the very first botanist to climb this floristically rich mountain. His collections from these regions were enormous, and those from Emei Shan, in particular, later proved rich in new species. Sending an extra set of his collections to Kew transpired to be a lucky move for Faber, since his own personal collection was later destroyed by a fire in Shanghai.[9]

In August of the same year, a second visitor, with his wife and young family, arrived in Yichang. Antwerp Edgar Pratt, the English naturalist and traveller, was to spend the following three years exploring the upper Yangtze River and the mountains of western Sichuan Province. Accommodation was difficult to come by, however, and, due to the hostility of the locals towards foreigners, staying in Yichang was out of the question. Pratt and his family stayed in the British Consulate in the European settlement for a fortnight before renting a Chinese house. Conditions for travellers in 19th-century China were very basic, though, and Pratt was less than happy with his lodgings:

It really was nothing but an empty barn, with mud walls and a roof of timber and tiles. There was neither ceiling nor partitions, and the floor was of earth. Close to the side was a large cesspool that was replenished daily from the city, and in the evening its contents were used to fertilise a large garden opposite. The continual stirring of its contents made us quite aware of its fragrance, and though none of us suffered in consequence, my Chinese boy got typhoid fever, from which I am glad to say he eventually recovered.[10]

Henry and Pratt struck up an immediate friendship and often took evening walks together through the surrounding countryside. On 19 August, they witnessed an eclipse of the sun at Yichang. In his diary, Henry records that Taoist monks in the Tungshantzu temple to the rear of the Foreign Compound 'beat the bell and drummed vigorously' to the spectacle, no doubt adding to the atmosphere of the occasion.

Henry also took Pratt on a visit to see one of Yichang's most remarkable plants, a gargantuan climber on the opposite bank of the Yangtze. The plant in question was *Mucuna sempervirens*, an evergreen climber in the pea family that had been described as a new species from Henry's collections in 1887. A single plant near Yichang covered half an acre and carried several stems as thick as a

The English explorer Antwerp Edgar Pratt arrived in Yichang in August 1887, and based himself there before moving on to Sichuan Province.

Mucuna sempervirens – this pea relative formed giant vines near Yichang. Augustine Henry introduced it to cultivation through Kew.

Ernst Faber discovered a plethora of new, exciting, garden-worthy plants during his visit to Emei Shan in Sichuan Province. One of these, *Mahonia gracilipes*, was introduced to cultivation in the 1980s. The plant featured here was photographed on Emei Shan by the author in September 2002.

man's waist. This species is very floriferous on old wood and its large, fleshy, red to maroon-purple, evil-smelling flowers are carried in May on the stems, and are rich in nectar and attract a wide variety of insects. The flat seedpods are bean-like and can be almost a metre (3.3 ft) long. This rampant climber can reach 25 m (82 ft) tall, and was introduced to cultivation by Henry in 1888 through Kew, where the original plant grew until recently in the Great Palm House.

Beside this climber grew the soap thorn, *Gleditsia sinensis*, a large tree with pinnate leaves, carrying flat seedpods in autumn. According to Pratt, the pods were the most useful part of the plant, and were gathered, stored and used, without further preparation, in the same way as soap is used. The pods of this tree are rich in saponin and were used in laundry and tanning work and also in herbal medicine. It is still an important medicinal plant in China today. The fruits are currently used to expel roundworm and to treat cases of constipation. The dried spines are also used as a medicine and are administered externally to

patients suffering from scabies and leprosy.

By early September, Antwerp Pratt had had enough of his rough-and-tumble accommodation at Yichang so he hired a native houseboat, with six compartments for himself and his family, and embarked for the Glen of the Three Pilgrims. His native boy, who had just recovered from typhoid, was sent to stay in the temple in the Cave of the Three Pilgrims while Pratt spent his time making daily excursions into the glen collecting insects of every kind. Pratt, like Henry, found the glen to be an enchanting place. He was spellbound by its spectacular scenery and the many beautiful plants that inhabited the cold, grey limestone cliffs. Lilies abounded and attracted several species of butterfly, one of which proved to be a new species.[11]

A few days before Pratt's departure from Yichang, Ernst Faber returned from his travels in western Sichuan Province. Henry must have been delighted to have had two visitors with whom he had much in common staying in Yichang at the same time. It took both Faber and Henry six days to sort Faber's collections from Emei Shan and to extract a set of specimens for Kew.[12] Henry packed up the collection and forwarded it to Kew on 17 September with the following letter to Thiselton-Dyer:

I beg to inform you that I am today sending from Ichang [...] one case of botanical specimens collected by the Rev. Ernst Faber who has been on a trip this summer as far as the famous Mount Omei in Szechuan. Mr Faber has asked me to send off the specimens and to enclose to you a list of the localities; and he will receive as a favour from you a list of determinations of the specimens, 1,200 numbers in all. He would also be glad to receive from you a note acknowledging their safe arrival. His address is Rev. Ernst Faber, Shanghai, China.

These specimens have been sent with [the] idea not only that there will be novelties and interesting plants in them, but that they will also be of service in connexion [*sic.*] with the *Index Florae Sinensis*. And you have said in a letter to me that you are desirous of knowing more about the distribution of plants in China. Very few plants have been, we think, sent to Europe from Szechuan, and, as a good number of these are from the summit of Omei, 11,000 feet altitude, there ought to be some interesting material.

[...] The accompanying list scarcely requires any explanation. In some cases, I have taken the liberty of adding a note in which the fact is mentioned that the same plant also occurs at Ichang and will be sent to you

in my next lot, which will be at the end of the year [...]. A good account of Mount Omei where Mr Faber stayed for some time (his place of residence being for the most part a monastery [at] 3,500 feet altitude) is given in Mr Baber's explorations of Szechuan, published by the Geographical Society. I am sure, speaking my own opinion, that this lot will be very interesting; and think it a piece of good fortune that Mr Faber was able to do so much collecting in the limited time at his disposal for that work. I hope, then, you will write to him on the safe arrival of the collection.

Antwerp Pratt and his family returned from the Glen of the Three Pilgrims later that month. Thiselton-Dyer sent Henry a list of determinations of his last consignment of plants to Kew a few days later. These and subsequent lists for his central Chinese collections are preserved in archives at Glasnevin, while mimeograph copies are housed in the library at Kew.[13]

Badong, Yichang and Liantuo – the 1887 season
Once again, his collections for the 1887 season were rich in new species. Badong supplied an incredible number of novelties, including *Rhus punjabensis* var. *sinica*, a small tree to 12 m (39 ft) tall that was known colloquially in Hubei Province as *hung-fu-yang*. It is rare in gardens, though there is a fine tree near the Temperate House at Kew. Its large pyramidal panicles of fruits are very beautiful in early autumn.

An interesting discovery made by Henry's Changyang collector that year was the *du zhong* (or *tu chung*),

Rhus punjabensis var. *sinica* – rare in Western gardens, though hardy and of obvious horticultural merit. In England, it is cultivated at the Royal Botanic Gardens, Kew, while in Ireland, there is a fine young tree at Tullynally Castle in County Westmeath.

Eucommia ulmoides, a new monotypic genus in its own new family. This dioecious tree is the source of the very valuable Chinese drug *tu-chung* and was mentioned by the Emperor Shennong in his herbal. Both the bark and leaves of *Eucommia* contain large amounts of gutta percha, an elastic-like substance that, when snapped and drawn across, exhibits a silvery sheen of innumerable threads of gum. When heated, they melt and burn with the characteristic smell of rubber.

Eucommia ulmoides was introduced to France by Père Farges in 1890 and seedlings were raised at the Jardin Colonial (Nogent-sur-Marne), in the garden of the Faculty of Medicine and by the nursery of Maurice de Vilmorin near Paris. In November 1897, de Vilmorin presented a

A Chinese 'coolie' with a load of *tu-chung*, the bark of *Eucommia ulmoides*. *Tu-chung* is still a valuable product in China today.

plant to Kew, the first to be cultivated in England. By 1901, the Jardin Colonial was growing experimental plots of *Eucommia* in Vietnam and North Africa. At Glasnevin, two plants were raised from Wilson's 383, from a collection made from a cultivated tree in Badong in April 1908. One of these trees was 4.5 m (15 ft) tall by 1921, and the other was about 2.5 m (8 ft) and bushy. The first tree mentioned still exists in the old Chinese shrubbery and is now about 15 m (49 ft) high.

According to Henry, an enormous trade of *Eucommia* bark existed in late 19th-century China. From the central provinces of Hubei, Sichuan and Shaanxi, *tu chung* was brought to the Hankou (Hankow) area of modern-day Wuhan, and, from that trading port alone, 100 tonnes were exported annually by steamer to other treaty ports. The product commanded a high price, and the Hankow exports reaped £18,000 in 1888 for the Customs Service. Wilson noted that it was taken as a tonic (it has been used in China for more than 2,000 years), a diuretic, an aphrodisiac and a cure for colds. It is also used as a tonic for the liver, to strengthen sinews and bones, to prevent miscarriage and to alleviate significant back pain in pregnant women.

During the course of his travels in China, Henry collected more than 80 distinct species and varieties of *Rubus*, many of which were highly ornamental. Henry reckoned that each new valley or mountain yielded some new species of *Rubus*, and many of these bore fruits of exquisite flavour. One of the finest of these has to be *Rubus ichangensis*, a slender, semi-evergreen, rambling shrub to 7 m (23 ft) long. Wilson, who later introduced this species in 1900, regarded it as one of the finest of Chinese *Rubi* on account of its beautiful and long (30 cm–1 ft) panicles of orange fruits. It thrives in the mild Irish climate and there are good plants at the Glasnevin, Kilmacurragh and Mount Usher gardens.

The pink-flowered *Indigofera ichangensis* was a common shrub in western Hubei Province, particularly on the cliffs of the Xiling Gorge, where it grew with other novelties such as *Philadelphus hupehensis*, *Peucedanum henryi*, *Sindechites henryi* (a new climbing genus in the milkweed family, Apocynaceae) and that very striking vine, *Tetrastigma hemsleyanum*. *Cotoneaster dammeri* was an 1887 discovery from Huangpo Shan, near Changyang, and it has became one of the most popular evergreen groundcover shrubs used in modern landscape design.

An interesting find in the glens above Yichang was the lace-bark pine, *Pinus bungeana*. Originally discovered by the Russian botanist Alexander von Bunge (1803–90) in the grounds of a Buddhist temple near Beijing (Peking) in 1831, it has always been planted in pairs by temples and courtyards and in the tomb enclosures of the imperial

Eucommia ulmoides, here pictured in the Metasequoia Valley in south-western Hubei Province, where it is cultivated on a commercial scale. Endemic to China, *Eucommia* has been found in a fossilised state in European coal deposits.

The aptly named lacebark pine, *Pinus bungeana*, seen here in the arboretum at Kew. Augustine Henry found the first authentic wild populations in Badong.

classes, hence the superstition that, to thrive, they should be planted on the grave of a Manchu prince. *Pinus bungeana* was introduced to cultivation by the Scottish botanist Robert Fortune in 1846 by means of living plants. Augustine Henry's collections were the first records of truly wild trees in China. It is a beautiful small tree with grey-green bark flaking away to create a patchwork of green, purple, yellow, white and brown.

Maddenia wilsonii was rare around Yichang; Henry found it once only, as a 3-m (10-ft) tall, multi-stemmed shrub. Strangely, it grew in the same area as *Sorbus wilsoniana*, both of which were described and named from material later gathered by E. H. Wilson. The evergreen *Clematis quinquefoliata* inhabited thickets and woodland verges, where it scrambled its way to 5 m (16 ft) overhead. Allied to *Clematis armandii*, it differs in having pinnate

leaves and the lateral cymes of small white flowers are produced in autumn.

Henry's most famous discovery must be the lovely lily that bears his name, *Lilium henryi*, which he found near the summit of Moji Shan ('The Dome') in July 1887. He also later collected a few scattered plants on the limestone crags of the Xiling Gorge, and noted that it was common on grassy slopes by cliffs near a Taoist monastery at Pingshanba. According to Wilson, Henry's lily had been virtually eliminated from the type locality by the time of his arrival in 1900. In the wild, it grows to about 1 m (3.3 ft) tall and bears three to four pendant, orange, turban-like flowers. In cultivation, it performs far better and is one of the most glorious of all Asiatic lilies, thriving in alkaline soils and hating a peat-based soil. Ernest Wilson was full of praise for Henry's lily, and, when writing a monograph on the

Corydalis cheilanthifolia, a short-lived perennial, though generous in its self-seeding and capable of tolerating the driest of shade.

group many years later, he penned the following lines:

> It is peculiarly fitting that such a noble addition to our gardens should bear the honoured name of a pioneer who has done so much to acquaint a sceptical world of the rich floral wealth of interior China, Professor Augustine Henry.[14]

Man Yang's collections, too, from Badong were full of new, exciting plants. One of the most beautiful of these has to be *Corydalis cheilanthifolia*, a short-lived perennial to 30 cm (1 ft) tall, bearing rosettes of finely dissected, bronze-toned foliage in winter and early spring, above which it produces upright spikes of golden, spurred flowers. In Badong, its bedfellows included *Acer davidii*, *Angelica henryi*, *Asplenium henryi*, *Dicentra spectabilis*, *Eomecon chionantha*, *Aegopodium henryi*, *Arisaema erubescens* and *Iris tectorum*.

Another common plant on cliffs at Badong in Hubei Province was *Androsace henryi*, a clump-forming perennial bearing large umbels of pure white flowers. It was also later collected in Sichuan Province by the Swedish botanist Harry Smith (1889–1971), by George Forrest in Yunnan Province

and by Frank Kingdon Ward (1885–1958) in Burma. Wilson introduced it through Veitch's Coombe Wood nursery, though it has long been lost to cultivation, which is a great pity. In mountain meadows, Wilson's yarrow, *Achillea wilsoniana* was a common sight. Henry collected it several times, both north and south of the Yangtze.

Ligularia veitchiana was common in marshes in the higher mountains above Badong, and, according to Henry, it was known as *ch'ing ho yeh*. Wilson introduced it many years later, and it was named for his employers. It is still popular in gardens on account of its large, rounded, bold foliage and 2-m (6.5-ft) tall spikes of showy, yellow, daisy-like flowers, which are carried during August and September.

Another Henry discovery/Wilson introduction is *Lithocarpus cleistocarpus*, a wide-spreading evergreen tree to 30 m (98 ft). It was known colloquially as the *chou-ko-li* and its tough wood was much in demand with local carpenters. The largest trees in Great Britain and Ireland grow in Caerhays Castle in Cornwall and are 22 m (72 ft) tall.

The Chinese witch-hazel, *Hamamelis mollis*, was described at Kew from Henry's 1887 Badong collections, but, unknown to botanists there, it had been previously discovered and introduced by Charles Maries (working for the Veitch nurseries) in 1879. It is incredible to think that such a valuable new shrub grew unrecognised for 20 years in their nursery and was merely considered a superior form of *Hamamelis japonica*. The identity of the Veitch plant was corrected by George Nicholson, Curator of Kew, and the company did not begin to propagate it until 1898.

Another exciting discovery from Badong was *Cornus kousa* var. *chinensis*, one of the finest of all the flowering dogwoods. Henry called it the *shih-tsao*, and E. H. Wilson

The Chinese witch-hazel, *Hamamelis mollis*, was described from Augustine Henry's collections, though it had been previously discovered and introduced by Charles Maries.

The sensational *Lilium henryi* towering in the herbaceous border at the National Botanic Gardens, Glasnevin. At Yichang, Henry reported that this lily grew to just one metre tall, yet in British and Irish gardens it reaches almost 3 m (10 ft) in height.

later recorded it as being common around Yichang. Wilson's 223, collected near Yichang in 1907, has formed a fine tree at the western end of the pond at Glasnevin, where it forms a beautiful picture every June when covered in masses of white bracteate flowers, which later age to blush-pink. It was from the parent of the old Glasnevin tree (W. 223) that the variety was described, though Henry had discovered it a good two decades earlier.

Emmenopterys henryi was another remarkable new genus and Henry stated it was known around Changyang and Badong as the *hsiang-kou*. It was common throughout the Three Gorges region where it formed trees to 30 m (98 ft) tall with girths of up to 4 m (13 ft). The specific epithet is very apt and derives from the Greek root forms *emmeno* (lasting) and *pter* (a wing), alluding to the fact that one of the calyx lobes develops into a large, white, leaf-like appendage, adding to the beauty of the tree at flowering time and persisting on the tree to later serve as a sail to distribute the fruits.

Emmenopterys henryi was first introduced to cultivation from Yichang by E. H. Wilson (W. 622) through the Arnold Arboretum in November 1907. A tree at Kew was obtained from this source in 1913, and, six years later, a plant was donated by Kew to Glasnevin, having been propagated from this tree. The Glasnevin tree, once the finest in Europe, has now succumbed to honey-fungus, though it has been propagated and young trees grow at both Glasnevin and its country estate at Kilmacurragh in County Wicklow. Following 90 years of growth at Glasnevin, that old tree is reputed to have flowered only once, during a hot summer in the 1990s, though its annual spring show of newly emerged, bronze-tinted foliage has more than compensated for this shortfall. *Emmenopterys* needs a warmer summer than the insular seasons provided in Great Britain and Ireland, and young plants have begun to flower well in northern California, Washington and near Philadelphia in the USA.[15]

Man Yang was, it seems, not without a sense of humour, and pulled a number of mischievous pranks while collecting for Augustine Henry, including the creation of hoax specimens. The most famous of these has to be one that was later described as a new genus, *Actinotinus sinensis*, by Professor Daniel Oliver. *Actinotinus* was in fact a combination of two plants. By inserting the inflorescence of *Viburnum plicatum* f. *tomentosum* into the terminal bud of a previously unknown horse chestnut, *Aesculus wilsonii*, Man Yang managed to construct a specimen so convincing that it fooled even the most senior taxonomists at Kew. The hoax was only noticed after it had been published, and Henry's field notes mention others, including an *Alangium* with the flowers of a *Lespedeza* inserted. In another case, Hemsley described *Rhododendron*

Late spring sees the emergence of bronze-tinted foliage on *Emmenopterys henryi*. In Hubei Province, flowering commences in June. In cultivation, the tree blooms best where summers are hot and with plenty of sunshine.

OPPOSITE: *Emmenopterys henryi* by the pond at Glasnevin. Following almost 90 years of growth, this tree is said to have flowered once only, though the emerging copper-toned leaves more than compensate for this.

aucubaefolium from the foliage of *Diphniphyllum macropodum* with the flowers of *Rhododendron stamineum*.

Despite his mischievous nature, Henry regarded Man Yang as his best native plant collector and his specimens were of a first-class standard, so much so that E. H. Wilson was to hire him when he arrived in Yichang 13 years later.

It was about this time that Henry began to take an interest in lichens, mosses and liverworts. His first lichen collection, the widespread *Heterodermia speciosa*, was made on the mountain above Badong.

Aesculus wilsonii, the common horse chestnut of central China, where it forms medium-sized trees. Wilson's horse chestnut was used by Henry's native plant collector to create the hoax genus, *Actinotinus*.

Sargent's glory vine, *Sargentodoxa cuneata*. The plant pictured here was donated to Glasnevin by Professor Sargent and, until recent years, was the only known plant in Europe.

Henry's Liantuo man also made several interesting discoveries in 1887, including the rampant climber, *Sargentodoxa cuneata*, the sole member of a new genus in its own new family. Not only that, his collector had inadvertently mixed material of a hitherto unknown climber, *Sinofranchetia chinensis* (another new genus), with it. *Sargentodoxa*, or Sargent's glory vine, is a vigorous, deciduous, twining climber that commemorates Professor Charles Sprague Sargent (1841–1927), the founding father and first director of the Arnold Arboretum of Harvard University. He was also a friend of Augustine Henry.

Sargent's glory vine is extremely rare in cultivation. Wilson introduced it from Changyang in 1907, and, until recently, the only known plant in Europe grew at Glasnevin. That same plant was donated by Sargent in January 1917, having been propagated from the original Wilson introduction at the Arnold Arboretum. It is a climber of exceptional beauty with large, bold, trifoliate leaves, and, in spring, the plant bears long racemes of lime-green flowers over newly emerged foliage. Although stated to be unisexual, the old Glasnevin plant bears both male and female flowers in separate racemes.

On the clefts of cliffs to the north of Liantuo grew *Urophysa henryi* (syn. *Semiaquilegia henryi*), a small, dainty, clump-forming perennial bearing bright blue to pink-white flowers. Sharing the same habitat was the hardy gesneriad *Briggsia speciosa*, a beautiful little perennial with delightfully spotted flowers similar in size and shape to the common foxglove, *Digitalis purpurea*. The same damp cliffs were also home to a new balsam, *Impatiens fissicornis* var. *henryi*.

On the edge of damp woods, *Chrysosplenium macrophyllum* formed extensive colonies by means of its stoloniferous nature. This exciting perennial has only recently come into cultivation and its rosettes of large, 15-cm (6-in.) long leaves have even fooled modern-day plant hunters into believing it was a species of *Bergenia*.[16] Another interesting find from the same region was *Stylophorum lasiocarpum*, which, although cultivated as a medicinal plant, is native to the Three Gorges region. Henry called it the *jen-hsueh-ts'ao*, which signifies 'man's blood herb', from the red juice in the root and stem.[17] It is a pretty little poppy with large, coarsely lobed leaves, and the yellow, four-petalled flowers are followed by long, upright seed capsules.

Winter to Spring, 1888

In February 1888, as a heavy blanket of snow lay on the ground outside, Henry wrote to Thiselton-Dyer at Kew, sending a case of botanical specimens and seeds. In the same letter, Henry suggested that Thiselton-Dyer might send him funding to extend the work of his native plant collectors, whom he paid about 30 shillings a month. He also related that he had finally applied to Sir Robert Hart for six months' leave, stating: 'This leave, if obtained, I shall spend on an extended trip into the mountains, and I thus hope to make a grand collection'.

Henry had hoped that this would be the start of extensive exploration, and, in another rather, secretive letter to Kew, dated April 13th 1888, he revealed the following:

Confidential. From what you say of my collections turning out so rich in novelties, it seems to me that you might make an effort to get me detached to explore, say, south of Ichang to Pakhoi, i.e. parts of Hunan, Kuangsi, Kueichow provinces. Sir Robert Hart has aided formerly many branches of scientific work [...]. It is no use myself applying, because I could not lay sufficient stress on the importance of the work and it might be looked on as a fad of my own. If you thought it proper, you might write to Sir R. Hart, suggesting that I should get leave of absence and permission to work at botanical exploration for, say, a year.

I have no private interest in this matter, save that I should not like to go home without having done all [that] was possible to complete the knowledge of the Chinese flora. Travelling in the interior is rough and unpleasant work, and I should gain nothing in either a pecuniary or health point of view from such work as botanical exploration of the interior. I take a great interest in the work, as it throws light on the Chinese books on botany and *materia medica* the branches [of] which I am primarily interested in.

[...] In writing to Sir R. Hart, you could say that you know I was eager to do what I could in botanical work. I am certain that, if you wrote, he would give me leave of absence to pursue this work, if not to help me to defray expenses. The latter matter I do not care much about. I only wish to have the time (my present trip is my own). Please inform me whether or not you approve of the idea, and, if you do, then it would be well to write to Sir R. Hart at once.

Thiselton-Dyer did send a letter to Hart on 9 June 1888, but it seems Hart was less than sympathetic to the cause and Henry never got to explore the territories he outlined.[16] Instead, he had his own six months of leave in which to explore the Three Gorges region.

On 16 March 1888, Henry wrote a poignant note in his diary: 'Grandma died today'. It must have been hard for him being so far away from Ireland on that occasion. His grandmother had raised him and his young siblings when his mother had passed away in 1871. Now she was gone too.

Below: The poppy relative, *Stylophorum lasiocarpum*, was an important medicinal plant in 19th-century China.

Chapter 4

To the roof of central China

E. H. Wilson's Chinese plant collectors. These men had originally been employed by Augustine Henry and were trained by him to collect plants during the 1880s.

The Customs Service granted Henry leave from 28 March to 15 October 1888. For the first three months, he chose to explore the mountainous regions to the south-west of Yichang; from 20 July, he would travel into the towering mountains to the north-west. He must have been greatly excited at the prospect of organising these expeditions, which he had first mentioned in his letters to Kew more than three years previously.

On the morning of 14 April, several men from Badong arrived at the Foreign Compound in Yichang and made their way to the Customs House residence. Henry had hired them to train as plant collectors – and it was these men that E. H. Wilson would later re-hire when he arrived at Yichang 12 years later. The route chosen by Henry for his three-month, south of the Yangtze expedition was to take

him on a journey south-west to the mountains of Changyang County, continuing west on a parallel course inland to the Yangtze, to Badong and Jianshi County. From that point, he would cross the provincial border into south Wushan County, Chongqing Municipality (then part of Sichuan Province).

Henry already had a native plant collector at work in the Changyang region, and this man, alongside his collectors at Badong and Liantuo, continued to collect in those regions throughout the year and worked independently of his newly trained team.

To the mountains of Changyang

On 16 April, Augustine Henry and his men set off on what, without any doubt, must be the one of the most productive six months of plant hunting ever carried out in China. Also travelling with him as far as Changyang County was Antwerp Pratt, who planned to stay in the region for several months using Henry's native plant collector as a guide. The group set out from Yichang and crossed the Yangtze by ferry to the river's southern bank near the Dome (Moji Shan).

Changyang lay four days away. After two days of travel, the countryside began to rise; rolling hills were replaced with magnificent mountains and valleys, and virgin forest finally appeared. Marco Polo spoke of the mid-Yangtze region being thickly wooded in places, but, by the 19th century, those forests had long since been felled and, in the Three Gorges region, a traveller had to be prepared to travel a considerable distance to reach areas of primeval forest.

Situated in a valley by a wide river, Changyang was nothing more than a tiny market village made up of mud huts. The surrounding scenery was spectacular: Changyang was encircled by a mountainous landscape with deep gorges and valleys, and forest cover extended far into the horizon. The vegetation was starkly different from that at Yichang, and the undisturbed forest contained a rich understorey flora. A single copse of bamboo extended for 1.6 km (1 mile) and the thinly populated region was home to golden pheasants, woodcock, deer, porcupines, wild pigs, tigers and leopards.

The early settlers who farmed this district faced many hardships and dangers from these wild animals. Tigers were very numerous and had been a particular problem in the region since farmers began to clear the forests for cultivation. Though never attacking humans, they often made raids on livestock belonging to the natives, and, according to Antwerp Pratt, tigers were so numerous throughout Changyang that attacks occurred on a daily basis. The remains of domestic ponies and cattle that had been killed by tigers were poisoned by local farmers, with the flesh then invariably devoured on a return trip, which, in turn, proved fatal within a very short space of time. The bones of the tiger were a particularly valuable component in Chinese *materia medica* and so commanded enormous sums. (Though illegal, this trade continues in China today.) Wild boars and

The finest Chinese lacquer is still harvested from the bark of *Rhus verniciflua*. It is commonly cultivated in the Three Gorges region for this purpose, and this tree was photographed in forests at Badong, which lies to the west of Changyang in Hubei Province.

pigs also caused extensive damage during their night-time visits to maize fields, their work being carried out when the crop was ripe enough for harvest.

Apart from livestock and maize, these farmers also raised fields of opium poppies, *Papaver somniferum*, which were harvested and used to barter for goods in the surrounding villages. The locals also cultivated *Rhus verniciflua*, the varnish tree, of which Henry had sent seeds to Hooker with his very first letter to Kew. It had performed poorly on the sun-scorched hillsides around Yichang, but, in the higher mountains of the Three Gorges region, it grew very well. In early summer, 'v'-shaped incisions were made in the trunk and limbs, and, at the end of this, a mussel shell was

ABOVE: A densely forested peak in the heart of Changyang County. Much of the region's forest cover was felled during the 1950s, though vast areas of secondary forest have regenerated with a rich surrounding flora.

inserted, into which the sap flowed. Every morning, the contents of these shells were emptied into a wooden bucket, and bleeding of the tree continued for about a fortnight. The sap of *Rhus verniciflua* is a major irritant (being closely related to the American poison ivy) and collectors often suffered from severe rashes. The collected sap was used as a high-class varnish, and, with walnuts and opium, it was the principal item used in Changyang to barter for other goods.

For the next month or so, Henry and Pratt stayed in a small, mud-walled, thatched cabin belonging to Henry's Changyang collector. This little house was located in the mountains above the village in the middle of dense forest: an excellent base for the two collectors. *Cornus wilsoniana* was discovered by Henry at this time. It was rare in Hubei Province even then, but, by streams and rivers in Changyang, it formed dome-shaped trees to 10 m (33 ft) tall. *Euonymus hupehensis* formed trees of similar dimensions, and, evidently, this was also quite rare; Henry found it once only, and it was later introduced to cultivation by George Forrest from Yunnan Province. One of his trees (F. 8496) has formed a 9-m (29-ft) tall tree at the Royal Botanic Garden, Edinburgh.

One of the most abundant climbers in those ancient forests was *Holboellia angustifolia* Fargesii Group, a scrambling shrub to 6 m (20 ft) tall. According to Wilson, it is a variable plant in the wild, where it occurs at higher elevations than Henry's other discovery, the allied *Holboellia coriacea*.[1] This is one of many plants discovered by Henry and named from collections later made by Père Farges during the early 1890s in neighbouring Sichuan Province. On the humus-rich forest floor, *Calanthe henryi*, a hardy terrestrial orchid with long, bold, pleated foliage, formed extensive colonies.

Augustine Henry wrote little about this trip. In fact, his diary is completely blank for the duration of the entire six-month expedition. He was far too preoccupied, no doubt, with his botanical work to devote time to writing up a journal of any kind, and so it falls again to his travelling companion, Antwerp Pratt, to give us an idea of the sort of countryside they encountered:

> In May and June, the cuckoo may be heard, reminding one of home, and the air is loaded with the fragrance of the honeysuckle. Azaleas grow to a height of from 12 to 14 feet, and are covered with pink blossoms. There is also a very fine *Clematis* running over rocks. Higher up in the forests, rhododendrons are found growing luxuriantly, and in many fine, large, white, fragrant blossoms. Towards the north, the country is much broken; range after range could be seen on a clear day from my mud house. Looking to the west, the spurs are covered with dense forest, and I remember on one particular moonlit night the black forest standing out against the horizon, the loneliness, isolation and wildness of the scene were most impressive.[2]

Though Henry spent only a month in Changyang County, Pratt stayed until the end of September, when increasingly cold, wet weather convinced him to return to the relative comforts of Yichang. Before departing, he set off on one last journey into the mountains to the south of his cabin:

> I decided, before going, to make an excursion over the summit of the range and into the valley beyond. When I got to the ridge, I saw the country to the southward was much more open, there being no forest; the surface was also more cultivated, and there were no more mountain ranges near, but it was much cut up by deep ravines and watercourses, which were rich in beautiful plants, flowers and ferns. It is no exaggeration to say that it is quite possible to talk to a man across one of these ravines when it would perhaps take two days' journey to reach him, so deep and precipitous are they and dangerous to traverse.[3]

Augustine Henry stayed for only four weeks in Changyang before heading further west. He left behind his native plant collector in the company of Antwerp Pratt, and he continued to gather specimens until the end of the year. This included *Celtis julianae*, a common tree by the sides of streams, and the shrubby *Rostrinucula sinense* (Lamiaceae), which was abundant on cliffs there.

From Changyang, Henry and his men continued west, making collections in the tea-growing district of Changleping (then Changlo), where he discovered *Sorbus hemsleyi*, a fine whitebeam with typically brilliant silvery-white felting on the undersides of the leaves. It has always remained rare in cultivation, though it is found in larger collections, such as Glasnevin and at Ness Botanic Gardens in Cheshire.

A view of the mountainous countryside above the town of Badong. When Augustine Henry and his men crossed these mountains in the spring of 1888, the region was covered with dense primeval forest.

Into the mountains of Badong

From Changleping, Henry and his men ventured further into neighbouring Badong County. There, Henry met Man Yang, his Badong collector, who most likely advised him on suitable locations for collection work and where the highest mountains were located.

Badong's county seat (commonly known as Badong, also) was, as it still is, the westernmost town in Hubei Province; at the time of Augustine Henry's visit in 1888, it was a muddle of mud-walled houses strewn across the steep bank of the Yangtze. In ancient times, this busy river port was situated on the north side of the Yangtze and belonged to the state of Ba. During the Song dynasty (960–1279 AD), the town was relocated to the southern bank, and there it occupied a beautiful location not far from the eastern mouth of the Wu Gorge. A long steep flight of hundreds of steps ascended the riverbank to the town, and labourers, pitch black with coal dust, were a common sight as they loaded and unloaded baskets of locally mined coal from junks.

Just a few miles inland, to the south of the town, were

several ranges of lofty mountains rising in places to more than 2,133 m (7,000 ft). In his field notes at Kew, Henry described this upland area as being covered with extensive tracts of virgin forest, and, in winter, the highest peaks were covered with snow for months on end. Over the previous three years, Man Yang had made many remarkable finds in this district, and no doubt Henry enjoyed the prospect of seeing those mountains and their rich flora for himself.

Despite Man Yang's earlier efforts, there remained many new plants still to be discovered in those now long-felled

Stewartia sinensis in the Shennongjia National Nature Reserve (part of UNESCO's International Man and Biosphere Reserve Network) in northwest Hubei Province. The peeling bark is one of this tree's most attractive features.

forests. Flowering trees were abundant; especially cherries, and Henry and his men were in time to catch the spectacular show put on by *Prunus litigiosa*, by then carrying a mass of small, pinkish-white blossoms. Other new cherries from Badong included *Prunus wildeniana* and the white-flowered *Prunus pilosiuscula*. An interesting member of this group, but by no means new to science, was *Prunus serrulata* var. *spontanea*, the hill cherry, a native of China, Korea and Japan. This is the national tree of Japan, where it is widely planted around temples and shrines. Henry's collections were the first record of the variety occurring wild in China, and it was introduced to cultivation by Wilson from Hubei Province in 1900. It is a beautiful sight in spring, when masses of its white, pink-tinged flowers peep through copper-coloured emerging foliage.

Above altitudes of 1,300 m (4,265 ft), *Pinus tabulaeformis* var. *henryi* formed woods of handsome, flat-topped trees to 27 m (88 ft) tall. A new beech, *Fagus longiopetiolata*, made fine trees to 16 m (52 ft) tall with girths of up to 2 m (6.5 ft). Another new find was *Stewartia sinensis*, one of the most beautiful trees from western Hubei Province, where it forms medium-sized trees to 10 m (33 ft) tall. The fragrant, white, camellia-like, cup-shaped blossoms of this species are carried in the leaf axils in late summer, and, while they are pretty, it is really grown for its sandstone-coloured bark, which peels and flakes to become a wonderful mottle of maroon, purple and brown. The autumn colour, too, can be brilliant, with foliage assuming wonderful fiery red tints. Augustine Henry called it the *ma-liu-kuang* and stated it was common in mountain forest at Badong,[4] though Ernest Wilson, writing some 22 years later, said it was rare in western Hubei Province.[5]

Two new maples were also discovered by Henry during the course of his explorations in Badong. The first and the finest of these was *Acer oliverianum*, a small tree with five-lobed leaves similar to those of *Acer palmatum*, and, like the latter, it produces wonderful autumnal hues of purple, red and orange. Wilson introduced it during his first expedition to China for Veitch in 1901, and George Forrest also encountered it in north-west Yunnan Province in May 1925. The specific epithet commemorates Professor Daniel Oliver of Kew. Henry's original type specimen was destroyed in Berlin during the Second World War. *Acer cappadocicum* var. *sinicum* was an interesting find, and is essentially a five-lobed Chinese variant of the Himalayan form. The young, coppery-red growths are striking, as are the clusters of bright red fruits in autumn.

Through these trees grew a number of new climbing plants, including *Rubus flagelliflorus*, a graceful, climbing, evergreen shrub with white, felted stems and small,

Rhododendron praevernum bringing early colour to the woodland garden at Glasnevin, where it generally opens its first blooms in mid February.

decurved prickles. According to Henry, it was called the *pao-ku*, and the black fruits had a good flavour. It was introduced to cultivation by E. H. Wilson in 1901, and, in their *Novelties for 1908–9* nursery catalogue, Messrs Veitch were selling plants for three shillings and six pence each.

Between altitudes of 1,600 to 2,133 m (5,250–7,000 ft), rhododendrons became a conspicuous part of the flora. *Rhododendron praevernum* was one of the earliest to flower at Badong, and, in early spring, its many umbels of white, pink-tinged, bell-shaped flowers must have lit up those dark primeval woods. Perhaps even more beautiful was the *yeh-p'i-pa*, or *Rhododendron houlstonii*, a shrub to 4 m (13 ft) tall bearing trusses of large rosy-pink flowers. This fine shrub commemorates Mr G. Houlston of the Chinese Imperial Maritime Customs Service at Yichang, a friend of E. H. Wilson.

Aucuba chinensis f. *angustifolia* formed dichotomously branched shrubs to 3 m (10 ft) tall bearing long, extremely narrow lance-shaped leaves. Among its bedfellows was *Euonymus sanguineus*, a large, dome-shaped shrub bearing purple-flushed spring growths, followed, in autumn, by large red, yellow-coated fruits and beautiful scarlet autumn colour. Near it grew another new species that has become better known in

cultivation: *Euonymus myrianthus*, a large, evergreen, slow-growing shrub. In early winter, this fine shrub is at its best when the four-lobed fruits ripen and split to reveal scarlet-orange seeds within.

Philadelphus sericanthus was common on the higher mountains above Badong. One of the latest of the mock oranges to bloom, it was introduced to cultivation by Père Farges, who sent seeds to Messrs Vilmorin in 1897. It is endemic to Hubei and Sichuan provinces, and the centre of its range is the region immediately around the Wu Gorge.

Berberis henryana was also discovered at this time, and it has long been one of my favourite plants. For some strange reason, this wonderful shrub has always remained in obscurity. It is rarely mentioned in literature – even then getting, at most, a scant mention – and it is currently unavailable from nurseries. This has to be one of the most glorious of all the barberries, and it never fails to produce masses of short, pendant racemes of lemon-yellow blossoms in early summer.

73

Berberis henryana, Henry's barberry, is rare in Western gardens, though it deserves to be better known and more widely grown.

Arisaema sikokianum var. *henryanum*, still a common plant where woodland has persisted in the Three Gorges region.

The forest floor was also a rich source of interesting new plants. *Chrysosplenium henryi* grew as a stoloniferous perennial to 20 cm (8 in.) tall and sported lime-green flowers in terminal cymes surrounded by large leafy bracts. Enjoying a similar habitat was *Paeonia obovata* var. *willmottiae*. This well-known peony was later described from plants growing in the garden of plant-hunter's patron Ellen Willmott (1858–1934), having been raised from seeds collected in Hubei Province by E. H. Wilson.

New plants continue to be found in Henry's herbarium collection to this day, and one of these, first described in 1999 from Henry's 1888 Badong collections, is the *kuei-chiu*,[6] or *Podophyllum versipelle* ssp. *boreale*, a dramatic perennial with bold, lobed, peltate leaves borne on a long petiole arising directly from a fleshy underground rhizome. The curious, burgundy-coloured flowers are carried in clusters from the underside of the leaf petiole, thus protecting the flowers from extremes in weather at pollination time. According to Henry, it formed extensive colonies beneath the shade of montane woodland. Such colonies are clonal and are a result of adventitious root buds.[7]

Other beautiful woodlanders included *Paris fargesii*, which was described from material later collected in Sichuan Province by the French naturalist Père Paul Farges. Henry's cobra lily, *Arisaema sikokianum* var. *henryanum*, is probably the most sinister-looking of all the aroids from western Hubei Province. It is a spectacular plant when in flower, and bears a purple-black hooded spathe, striped white along its lower half. In the dense shade of the forest interior, *Hymenophyllum henryi*, a delicate filmy fern, draped its delicate fronds across rocks and tree trunks.

Another fine Badong plant that bears Henry's name is the green slipper orchid, *Cypripedium henryi*. In Hubei Province, this species inhabits deciduous woodland and scrubby slopes and grassland at the verge of forests. It is also one of the easiest of the slipper orchids to grow. In the meadows were many new perennials, including *Geranium franchetii*, *Pedicularis filicifolia*, *Meehania henryi*, *Scrophularia henryi* and the geum-like *Coluria henryi*.

At night, Henry found accommodation in local inns and temples, and, on 29 June, he wrote a letter to William Thiselton-Dyer from the Pao-an Temple, a Taoist shrine in

Lithocarpus henryi, seen here in the Hillier Arboretum in Hampshire. In the woods of western Hubei and Sichuan provinces, it forms medium-sized, domed-shaped trees.

Henry's slipper orchid, *Cypripedium henryi*, is distributed across much of western and central China. It is seen here flowering in time for our exhibit at the RHS Chelsea Flower Show in May 2002.

Liriodendron chinense, the Chinese tulip tree. A genus once thought to be endemic to eastern North America, it was from Augustine Henry's specimens that the Chinese tree was described as a new species.

the Badong mountains. In the coming years, he often stayed in such temples and used their altars to sort specimens and as a desk on which to write up his notes. This was in no way disrespectful. Though born into the Catholic faith, Henry remained a life-long atheist, but always treated other people's beliefs with due respect.

American counterparts in Jianshi County

From the great mountain ranges above the county seat of Badong, Augustine Henry and his men continued their travels to the mountains of Jianshi (then Chienshih) County, which lay some 80 km (50 miles) to the south-west. Jianshi was a small, isolated, impoverished settlement and copper was mined in the area. Though the mountains were not quite as high as those in Badong, the flora was equally rich and Henry immediately set to work on collecting. This must have been a remarkably enjoyable time for him, considering the isolation of the region, the wonderfully rugged terrain, the wealth of the flora and the enormous volumes of dried specimens, many of which would later prove new to science.

The forests at Jianshi consisted of a rich assemblage of deciduous and evergreen trees. One of the most dominant of these was *Lithocarpus henryi*, a magnificent evergreen tree to 16 m (52 ft) tall bearing long, shining, leathery lanceolate leaves. Wilson introduced it in 1901, through Messrs Veitch, and one of his collections (W. 775) still grows at the Kilmacurragh Botanical Gardens in Ireland.

Another interesting find from that district was the Chinese tulip tree, *Liriodendron chinense*, a member of a genus previously only known from eastern North America. Henry was not the first person to discover this species, though his were the first complete specimens on which the new species could be based. The Chinese tulip tree was first collected in 1875 by Dr George Shearer on the Lushan mountain in neighbouring Jiangxi Province. Shearer's specimen was without flower or fruit and was mistakenly presumed to be a naturalised tree of the American *Liriodendron tulipifera*. Again, in 1878, the Veitchian collector, Charles Maries sent specimens from the same region. His collections came from an immature shoot and neither the leaves or fruits were fully developed. With the

Sycopsis sinensis. The plant featured here is the original Wilson introduction from 1901 that grows at the National Botanic Gardens, Glasnevin.

Rubus lasiostylus. Its ghostly white stems make a wonderful addition to any winter garden. Henry found it in Badong in May 1888 and introduced it through Kew in 1889.

arrival of Henry's Jianshi specimens, botanists could finally distinguished the Chinese tree from its New World cousin. Henry called it the *wo-chang-ch'iu*, or 'goose-foot', an apt name that refers to the shape of the leaves.[8]

Until the discovery of *Nyssa sinensis* at Jianshi, this genus was also thought to be endemic to North America. It was rare even then, in western Hubei Province, and occasionally formed trees to 20 m (66 ft) tall. Only one seedling was ever raised from Wilson's 1902 introduction, and it has never become common in gardens. It is a magnificent tree in all respects. The young emerging leaves and shoots are red and are clothed with pale grey silky hairs, and the scarlet and red tones of autumn colour are brilliant and spectacular.

Economic plants were always of great interest to Henry, and he regularly sent back samples of plant-derived products to the economic botany collections at Kew. On a forested ridge in Jianshi County, he gathered material from a tree locally known as *tuan-shu*. He was particularly interested in this tree because the sandals in which he did his climbing were made from the fibres of its inner bark. At Kew, it was later determined to be a new species of linden

or lime; duplicate specimens were sent to Vienna, where an expert on the group named it *Tilia tuan*. Henry sent samples of these linden sandals to Kew in 1890, and, for many years now, they have been on display in the museum building opposite the Great Palm House.

In Jianshi, Henry discovered a number of plants that were described from collections later made by Père Paul Farges,

The linden sandal sent to Kew by Henry in 1890. Made from the inner bark of *Tilia tuan*, it was in a pair of these sandals that he did his climbing while plant hunting in 1888.

ABOVE: *Dicentra macrantha*, this rare woodlander was introduced to cultivation in the spring of 1889 when botanists at Kew removed seeds from Henry's Jianshi County specimens.

including *Carpinus chinensis*, *Lilium fargesii*, *Actinidia melanandra* and *Paulownia fargesii*. Farges' foxglove tree grew on steep cliffs with the more common *Paulownia tomentosa*, which Henry always claimed to be his favourite flowering tree.

At lower altitudes, *Meliosma henryi* formed large evergreen trees. This species is sometimes planted by temples in China today. *Prunus dielsiana*, a charming deciduous cherry, was another of Henry's Jianshi finds. It is rare in gardens, which is a pity, since it puts on such a fabulous spring show of white or pale pink flowers. The mahogany-red bark of the trunk and branches is also a beautiful feature, especially in the depths of winter.

Near streams, in ravines and at altitudes of up to 1,300 m (4,265 ft), the witch-hazel relative *Sycopsis sinensis* was common and formed small, erect, evergreen trees to more than 6 m (20 ft) tall. Wilson introduced it in 1901, and there is a fine tree at the west end of the pond at Glasnevin that originates from this source. Every spring, without fail, it produces thousands of clusters of small yellow flowers borne without petals but consisting of yellow and red anthered stamens, securely wrapped in black-brown scales.

Another spring favourite, *Corylopsis sinensis*, shared a similar habitat at Jianshi, and, at the time of Henry's visit, it carried masses of pendant racemes of fragrant, primrose-yellow flowers. With it grew *Styrax dasyantha*, a small tree bearing slender racemes of small, white, bell-shaped flowers in July.

Rubus lasiostylus was common in open glades and thickets, and there it formed an erect deciduous shrub to 1.5 m (5 ft) tall with biennial stems covered in a blue-white waxy bloom. Henry gathered seeds of this species a few months later, while trekking in mountains to the north of the Yangtze, and sent them to Kew, where plants flowered for the first time in the summer of 1894. It is a beautiful shrub for the winter garden, and, upon returning to Ireland many years, later Henry planted this ghostly white-stemmed bramble in his Dublin garden.

Rambling their way through trees and shrubs were a number of new climbers, too, including the yellow-flowered *Schisandra pubescens*, a remarkable species bearing 20-cm (8-in.) long spikes of orange-red fruits in autumn. Other new climbers included *Jasminum urophyllum* var. *wilsonii* and *Rosa helenae*, a gloriously vigorous rambling rose. At Glasnevin, it is trained though an 8-m (26-ft) tall tree of *Ilex aquifolium* and, in early summer, it is covered in wide corymbs of fragrant white flowers. The specific epithet, by the way, commemorates Ernest Wilson's wife, Ellen.

Of perennials, *Dicentra macrantha* has to be the finest of the Jianshi discoveries. Henry described finding it in a dark wood where a few specimens grew with *Podophyllum versipelle* ssp. *boreale* and *Caulophyllum robustum*. Seeds were taken from his herbarium specimens at Kew in April 1889, and it was by this means that the plant came into cultivation. The narrow, creamy-yellow flowers are carried in short racemes in May over coarsely toothed, pale green foliage. Lovers of the curious will grow it, but it is by no means easy to please and may often be damaged by wind or late frosts.

Dipteronia sinensis, a new genus related to the maples. From Acer, it differs in its pinnate leaves and disc-like seeds.

Acer henryi, E. H. Wilson's original 1903 introduction, seen here flowering in the arboretum at Glasnevin. Its amber autumn colour is equally spectacular.

North-west to Wushan

From Jianshi, Henry and his expedition team travelled north-west and crossed the provincial border into south Wushan County, Sichuan Province. The landscape here was broken by the Wushan mountain range and consisted of jagged mountain peaks, cliffs and deep ravines. The countryside was sparsely populated and, as a result, extensive tracts of forest remained on the higher mountain slopes.

By the time of Henry's arrival in south Wushan, it was May: optimum flowering time in the Three Gorges region. The forests and surrounding thickets were a riot of colour, and one of the prettiest small trees there was *Amelanchier sinica*, then draped from head to toe in a dense gown of small, snowy-white flowers. Among his earliest finds there were three new species of elm: *Ulmus bergmanniana*, *Ulmus castaneifolia* and *Ulmus wilsoniana*. The latter formed trees to 25 m (82 ft) tall with dark-grey fissured bark and a slender, narrow crown. Wilson introduced this fine tree from Fang Xian (Fang County, Hubei Province) in 1910 by means of graft wood.

Again, several new maples appear in Henry's collections from this region, the best of which must be *Acer henryi*, a small tree to about 10 m (33 ft) tall. I have long admired this tree since first meeting with the old Wilson–Veitch tree in the arboretum at Glasnevin. Though now well over a century old, Henry's maple never fails to lift the spirits in early summer, when its slender pendulous flowers emerge, just as the beautifully tinted coppery-red trifoliate leaves unfold. In autumn, the same foliage takes on a brilliant red hue.

One of Henry's most remarkable finds from south Wushan was *Dipteronia sinensis*, a small tree with long pinnate leaves that later proved to be a new genus in the maple family. From the maples, it differs by having seeds that are surrounded by a circular membrane. The large clusters of these elm-like seeds, which turn red in autumn, are a handsome feature of this rare tree.

Of the many new endemic genera discovered in central China by Henry, *Poliothyrsis sinensis* is one of the most beautiful and least known in cultivation. In its native habitat, it forms a deciduous tree to 13 m (43 ft) tall, and, in late summer, it carries conical panicles of fragrant, creamy-yellow flowers. It is extremely rare in gardens, though in the old Chinese shrubbery at Glasnevin there is a superb 9-m (29-ft) tall tree raised from seeds collected by Wilson in the San You Dong glen near Yichang in 1907. There is also a fine young tree near the Great Palm House at Kew that flowers heavily every year.

Other exciting new trees from the area included *Castanopsis fargesii*, *Prunus velutina*, the silvery-rose flowered *Cercis racemosa*, *Malus yunnanensis* var. *veitchii*, *Enkianthus serrulatus*, *Styrax hemsleyanus*, *Sorbus keissleri* and *Cornus chinensis*. The latter was introduced from Assam (north-eastern India) many years later by Captain Frank Kingdon Ward.

The most famous of all Henry's discoveries from south Wushan County was made on 17 May 1888, near the small village of Mahuanggou (then Ma-huang-po). He was riding his pony through a river valley when he spotted a single, spectacular tree flowering near the base of a large cliff. As he was later to relate, the scene was one of the strangest sights he ever witnessed in China. It seemed as though the branches had been draped in thousands of ghostly-white handkerchiefs.

ABOVE, BELOW: A young tree of *Poliothyrsis sinensis* giving a fine display at the Royal Botanic Gardens, Kew. The tree is a great rarity in Western gardens.

Henry had stumbled across *Davidia*, the handkerchief tree, a genus found by Père Armand David near Baoxing (Sichuan Province) in 1869. Most authorities state that it was the type species – i.e., *Davidia involucrata* – that Henry collected, but this is quite incorrect. He had discovered a new variety, the glabrous-leaved *Davidia involucrata* var. *vilmoriniana*.[9] In *Plantae Wilsonianae*, E. H. Wilson explicitly states: '*Davidia involucrata* var. *vilmoriniana* was first discovered in Wushan Hsien, eastern Szech'uan, by A. Henry in 1888'.[10] The tree impressed Henry so much that he sent his native plant collectors back to the region that autumn to collect seeds for Kew. These were duly dispatched, though curious botanists there had them pickled and the variety was not introduced until Père Farges sent seeds to Paris in 1897. Little did Henry know that that single tree was to initiate the greatest era of plant introductions from western and central China, and it was later to become the sole quest of E. H. Wilson's first expedition to China.

Ilex intermedia was an interesting find. This small tree is endemic to the *Metasequoia* area (Lichuan Xian, or Lichuan County); south Wushan County lies close to the border of the fossil tree's territory. *Rosa rubus* was everywhere abundant and formed large scandent bushes that scrambled through the surrounding trees. Its fragrant, creamy-white flowers are held in dense clusters, and the bark of this species continues to be used in China for extracting tannin. Like many of Henry's finest discoveries, it was introduced by Wilson from Hubei Province – and was later reintroduced by Farrer from Gansu Province. Other new roses collected from south Wushan included *Rosa sertata*, a very graceful, lax-habited bush to 2.5 m (8 ft) high, bearing rich, rose-pink blossoms. *Rosa banksiopsis* was very common in thickets of low-growing shrubs, and its upright reddish-purple stems were remarkably free from prickles. Its blossoms varied from pink to red and it was described as a new species many years later from a plant in Ellen Willmott's garden. It is stated to be not known in cultivation,[11] though this is quite untrue: there is an old plant on the Vine Border Wall at Glasnevin. Two months later, when travelling in Xingshan County, a region to the north of Yichang, Henry discovered the closely allied, rose red- to pink-flowered *Rosa saturata*, and it too was described from Miss Willmott's garden. Miss Willmott grew many of Henry's discoveries in the early 20th century, and they became good friends on his return from China.

Viburnum erubescens var. *gracilipes* was also common in the region, and its panicles of fragrant, white, pink-tinged flowers almost smothered the foliage beneath. Forrest later collected this variety in Yunnan Province, and, many decades later, it was found by the British plant hunters Frank Ludlow (1885–1972) and George Sherriff (1898–1967) in the mountains of Bhutan.[12]

Salix fargesii, one of the largest leaved of all willows, is another fine Henry discovery, and, in its native habitat, it varies from being a 3-m (10-ft) tall shrub or it may assume a procumbent habit and reach no more than 60 cm (2 ft) tall. The latter form would certainly be popular if ever introduced to cultivation.

Cotoneaster henryanus formed large evergreen shrubs with a graceful pendulous habit. The long narrow leaves of this species are one of its best features, as are the clusters of crimson fruits in autumn. Frank Kingdon Ward was fond of the species, too, and, in his wonderfully titled book, *Berried Treasure*, he had much to say about its panicles of fiery berries, and went further to recommend growing several together in a great mass.[13]

South Wushan also yielded a fine new birthwort, *Aristolochia chrysops*. Lovers of the curious and rare will grow this in their gardens, and the specific epithet, *chrysops*, meaning 'with a golden face', is aptly suited to this lovely climber. The pendulous golden-yellow and purple flowers have been compared to a curled tobacco pipe. More than a century after he visited south Wushan County, a new climbing genus, *Sichuania alterniloba* (Asclepiadaceae), was discovered in Henry's Kew collections from this area. *Sichuania* is endemic to China and, so far, is only known from Sichuan Province.

The steep limestone cliffs offered up many new plants, too. One of these was the tiny lilac-flowered *Primula nutaniflora*. Decades later, while living in Dublin, Henry received a letter from Reginald Farrer that was addressed, quite simply, from 'The Valley of the Rocks and Wolves, Chinese Thibet'. Farrer was looking for the exact location of this lovely little primrose in the hope of introducing it. (That same letter is preserved in the Henry archives at Glasnevin.) With it grew other cliff inhabitants, such as the tiny *Viola henryi* and an entirely new genus, the lovely perennial gesneriad *Ancylostemon saxatilis*.

While Henry and his men travelled west, a number of his native plant collectors remained stationed in Changyang, Badong, Jianshi, Zigui (then Kuei) and Liantuo in Hubei Province. His Liantuo man made a number of interesting finds, including Henry's bamboo, *Phyllostachys henryi*, and *Iris henryi*, a charming species with narrow, strap-like leaves, bearing blue- or violet-coloured flowers to 2.5 cm (1 in.) across during the month of May. Two flowers per stem are carried and the lower parts of the fall and standard petals are mottled yellow. Another Liantuo discovery was that beautiful herbaceous *Hydrangea* relative, *Deinanthe caerulea*. The generic name stems from the Greek *deinos*, meaning 'wondrous', and *anthos*, 'flower' – enough to make any keen gardener want to grow it. This exquisite, violet blue-flowered perennial is a joy in summer; the shy pendant flowers need to be lifted to be seen, in the same manner as the spring-

The glabrous-leaved handkerchief tree, *Davidia involucrata* var. *vilmoriniana*, one of Augustine Henry's most famous finds. The tree carried thousands of blossom-like bracts during his brief visit to south Wushan County on 17 May 1888.

LEFT: *Salix fargesii*. With its large, handsome leaves, swollen mahogany-red buds and dark, chocolate-brown stems, it has to be one of the best of all the willows.

ABOVE: *Aristolochia chrysops*, a curious climbing birthwort. This photograph is of an old plant at Glasnevin that was obtained from Messrs Veitch in 1914.

flowered hellebores. It is a plant of singular beauty, and, given a shaded location and relatively rich, moist soil, it is easy to grow, bulks up quickly and is long lived.

By 29 June, Henry and his men were sailing down the gorges towards Yichang. The first part of his expedition was over and it was time to deposit his collections within the safety of the Foreign Compound and prepare for the second part of the expedition, which would take him to the mountain ranges north of the Yangtze. He could report to Thiselton-Dyer: 'I have had a most enjoyable trip amongst a most amiable people, and have accumulated a good deal of material concerning agriculture, folklore, customs, etc'.[14]

One of the most gorgeous of all woodlanders, *Deinanthe caerulea* has always remained a plant for connoisseurs, though, given partial shade and rich, moisture-retentive soil, it is easy to grow and long lived.

Acer franchetii wild in the Shennongjia Reserve, a short distance to the west of Xingshan, where Henry found it in July 1888. It is a handsome maple with three-lobed leaves and can reach 10 m (33 ft) tall.

Tilia henryana. E. H. Wilson later found Henry's linden on the *T'an-shu-ya*, or lime-tree pass. The leaves emerge copper-flushed.

North of the Yangtze: Xingshan County

If Henry considered that his first trip had been a great success, then the latter part of his leave was to eclipse that three-month expedition. Having called on a number of his collectors stationed in different areas throughout the Three Gorges region, he returned to Yichang on 14 July, where a letter awaited him stating that he had obtained a further three months' leave, until 15 October. His plan was to travel in a north-westerly direction through the counties of Xingshan (then Hsingshan) and Fang, and to continue across north Badong into north Wushan in Sichuan Province before returning to Yichang, by way of the Yangtze, through the Three Gorges.

A further grant of £15 from Kew enabled him to send two of his men back to continue collecting in Jianshi and south Wushan so specimens of the most interesting plants from those regions could be sent to Kew both in flower and fruit. Henry laid particular emphasis with his collectors on gathering ripe fruits of the handkerchief tree. Having carefully nailed up his specimens in boxes in the Foreign Compound, he departed for Xingshan (he had rested for only six days at Yichang before setting out again).

His route took him directly north through Tunghu, a district of Yichang (itself a prefecture-level city). There, he discovered *Ormosia henryi*, a small tree in the pea family, which is now extremely rare in its native habitat. From Tunghu, the trail continued on to Baokang (then Paokang) before finally crossing into the rugged mountainous scenery of Fang County.

Close to the towns and villages, Henry and his native plant collectors passed terraced paddy fields of rice. Farming families were busy tending to crops of peas, neat rows of *pak choi*, sweet potatoes and groves of oranges, pears and plums. At higher altitudes, maize and common potatoes were grown, and, above that level, they were forced to scale steep mountain slopes with razor-like ridges. Cultivation of crops in those upland regions was impossible and so enormous areas of dense forests remained.

Xingshan is a large county to the north-west of Yichang, with a county town of the same name (in the 19th century), and it was through there that Henry travelled before making his way to the higher mountains to the north. Xingshan town was then one of the poorest settlements in all of Hubei Province, and consisted of a few hundred houses, most of which were in a ruinous state. Little business was carried on, and thick-bottomed boats plied the Xiang Xi river (a tributary of the Yangtze) between the town and the Xiling Gorge.[15]

Henry and his team immediately set to work exploring the region. The local flora was markedly different from that he had just traversed to the south of the Yangtze, and again new species abounded. The three-lobed *Acer franchetii* was particularly common and grew as a small tree to 6 m (20 ft) high.

A more interesting find, however, was *Tilia henryana*, the largest of all the lime trees from western and central China, and without a doubt the most beautiful. Ernest Wilson later found it on the mountains between Yichang and Xingshan at a place called *T'an-shu-ya* ('the lime tree pass'). The same pass was named for a gigantic specimen of Henry's lime, which Wilson recorded as being 24 m (80 ft) tall and 8 m (27 ft) in girth.[16] In spring, the unfolding, heavily toothed leaves of this tree are covered with a silvery-white tomentum and emerge bronze before finally maturing to green. The finest trees in Europe grow at Birr Castle in the Irish midlands; these were raised by Michael Parsons, 6th Earl of Rosse, from seeds sent from Lushan Botanic Gardens in 1938.

In ravines and valleys, by the side of mountain streams, *Sinowilsonia henryi* formed multi-stemmed bushes or small trees to 8 m (27 ft tall). This monotypic genus commemorates the closely linked work of 'Chinese' Wilson, who introduced it, and Augustine Henry, who discovered it. *Sinowilsonia* is of botanical interest only; the terminal pendulous racemes of green, petal-less flowers offer little attraction in the garden, though the golden autumn colour carried on the witch-hazel-like foliage can be very beautiful.

Callicarpa japonica var. *angustata* was abundant in thickets above 1,500 m (4,920 ft). What a sight it must have made on those mountainsides in the autumn of 1888: the violet-coloured fruits of this variety are crowded in great clusters amid fiery, pink-purple autumn colour.

Many medicines were cultivated on the mountains above Xingshan, especially *tang-shen*, a beautiful herbaceous climber in the bellflower family (Campanulaceae) whose fleshy roots were credited with tonic and aphrodisiac properties and were used as a substitute for the very costly ginseng. From the old Hankow (Hankou) district of modern-day Wuhan city alone, more than 500 tons of roots were exported annually. It was named at Kew, by Professor Oliver, as *Codonopsis tangshen* and was introduced to cultivation by Henry from this same expedition. It is a charming species, with soft, olive-green, bell-shaped flowers that are strongly net-veined and spotted purple within.

Smilax scobinicaulis was another common climber on the

Codonopsis tangshen, a hardy herbaceous climber and the source of the important Chinese drug *tang-shen*.

Sinowilsonia henryi, seen here at Wuhan Botanical Gardens in eastern Hubei Province. This monotypic genus first flowered in the Arnold Arboretum in 1923. It is extremely rare in Hubei Province nowadays.

Callicarpa japonica var. *angustata*, another Xingshan discovery. One of the best, though least known, of this colourful group of autumn-berried shrubs, it gives a fantastic autumn show at Glasnevin every year without fail.

cliffs around Xingshan, and there it formed 4-m (13-ft) tall, prickly, deciduous vines with handsome heart-shaped leaves. This species attaches itself to nearby trees and shrubs by means of short tendrils, and several of Wilson's 1907 seed collections of this species were raised at Glasnevin the following spring, including W. 680 from the type locality at Xingshan.

83

To the roof of central China: Fang and Shennongjia

From Xingshan, Henry and his men travelled northwards to the small town of Fang (Fang Hsien), which lay at an altitude of 2,134 m (7,000 ft) and was surrounded by soaring mountain peaks attaining altitudes of up to 2,895 m (9,500 ft). The town had little to offer in the way of interest to the traveller and was surrounded by narrow moorland valleys clothed with grass and bounded by steep hillsides covered with thickets.[17]

The topography of the region must have made it tough going. This district lies in the heart of the Daba Shan mountain range that extends from nearby Shaanxi Province and is a never-ending series of razor-backed ridges separated by narrow valleys, deep chasms and high mountain passes. This enormous expanse of highlands and mountains forms the watershed between the Han and Yangtze rivers. The travellers' route to Fang took them across the wild, rugged landscape of Shennongjia (then Sheng-neng-chia). An area of savage grandeur, Shennongjia has the highest and most spectacular mountain peaks in all of central China. Commonly called 'the roof of central China', this heavily forested district has mountain peaks that soar well over 3,048 m (10,000 ft).

In a letter to Kew,[18] Henry noted that, in places, the forests had been felled for the cultivation of opium poppies and potatoes, but E. H. Wilson, who crossed the region with his native plant collectors many years later, related that nature had taken her revenge about 1890, when potato blight devastated the region causing a great exodus of all the inhabitants. Wilson trekked through Fang and Shennongjia in May 1907, during his first expedition for the Arnold Arboretum, and there is no doubt that he too was left in awe of this wild, desolate wilderness:

The crest of the saddle I made 9,500 feet altitude, and from this point we obtained a fine view of the series of bare, savagely jagged peaks from which the range (Sheng-nèng-chia) takes its name. The highest peaks probably exceed 11,000 feet altitude, and the lower slopes are forested [...] Animal life is remarkable for its absence, and hardly a bird was to be seen. The solitude which reigned in this remote, inaccessible region was broken only by the noise of rushing water and the low whining of the wind amongst the tree-tops. In shady places, blocks of ice still remained and, about the head of the pass, the grass was only beginning to show green.[19]

Henry, however, recorded seeing wild cattle, white-maned antelope, two types of bear, boars, monkeys, several species of pheasant and badgers. No foreigner, not even the Roman Catholic missionaries, had been to the region before him. Henry was popular with the local inhabitants

and being fluent in Chinese was obviously a great advantage. He wrote very little of this part of his trip, despite it being the most extensive and probably the most exciting plant-hunting expedition he had or would ever carry out. He did, however, issue a brief account of his trip to Xingshan, Fang and Shennongjia in an article he published in William Robinson's *The Garden*:

The coolies whom I employed to collect in the distant mountains brought me so many plants unknown in the immediate neighbourhood of Ichang that I made up my mind to take a long trip. I obtained six months' leave of absence, and from April to October, 1888, I wandered amongst the high mountains of the interior, south-west and north-west of Ichang. I twice reached the province of Szechwan, and returned eventually down the hundreds of miles of wild scenery of the gorges and rapids. I hardly enjoyed this trip which only took ten hours of actual sailing time, as the river was in high flood. I was in a small boat, with twenty of my men and a precious freight of a dozen or more boxes of dried plants, and I knew the slightest accident, a wrong turn of the sweep, might involve the loss of these boxes. The trip was, even to me, a revelation, especially in its northern half, when I reached the grand chain which separates the Yangtze and the Han river basins. There the mountains rose to 10,000 feet altitude, and were clothed in their upper parts (from 7,000 to 10,000 feet) with great coniferous forests, made up of various species of *Abies* and *Tsuga*. The average height of the trees was two hundred feet, with trunks of about four feet in diameter, straight as needles, the upper branches often broken by the weight of the winter snows. In the depths of these forests scarcely a ray of light could penetrate, and there was a thick growth of small bamboos, rendering progress impossible. Here and there were great tracts covered by huge birch trees, the species being *Betula utilis* Don. Its bark is distinctly red, and it grows to an immense size. I had a good opportunity of judging, as I once came across about two acres of these trees, which had been blown down by some tornado not long before. Their roots had been torn up out of the ground by the fierce wind and lay on the ground like ships in a dockyard. Another birch, *Betula fargesii*, with blackish bark, occurs at high levels.

On the summit of the mountains, at 9,000 to 10,000 feet, copses of rose trees are met with, often a mile or more long. I did not see these in flower, only in fruit, and so missed a glorious sight. This species is *Rosa sericea* Lindley. It is quite erect, forming a tall shrub or small tree. On the

grassy parts of these high ranges numerous herbs were to be seen, turning the mountain meadows into flower gardens. I remember of these the many beautiful gentians and swertias and the numerous species of *Saussurea* with captivating foliage. *Saussurea henryi* Hemsley, which occurs on the very high cliffs, is pretty indeed.

[…] It would be impossible to name all the trees of the mixed forest; many of my specimens are as yet undetermined. Of well-known genera, *Quercus*, *Carpinus*, *Fraxinus* and *Acer* have numerous species. There is a new beech and five kinds of linden, four of these being new species. It was in the sandals made of their bark that I used to do my climbing. Some of the new genera are worth noticing, e.g. *Dipteronia*, a very common tree, which is the only close ally of the maple known; it differs from *Acer* in having pinnate leaves and fruits which are winged all around the margin. *Tetracentron* is very remarkable; it has short lateral branches on which are borne a leaf and an inflorescence of many small flowers. This tree grows to an enormous size and is very widely distributed in China.[20]

Tetracentron sinense, a deciduous tree to 30 m (98 ft) tall, was a new genus and the only member of an ancient

A hazy day on the upper, forested slopes of Shennongjia, the tallest mountains in central China. Augustine Henry was the first Westerner to visit the region and he was followed, nine years later, by E. H. Wilson. At this altitude, the forests are dominated by *Abies fargesii*. Note the dead culms of *Sinarundinaria nitida*. This bamboo had also flowered prior to Henry's visit in the autumn of 1888.

and highly interesting family, Tetracentraceae. This tree is not only of botanical interest, however. In the forests of central and western China, the only other broadleaf to surpass it in size is another relict, *Cercidophyllum japonicum* var. *sinense*. The heart-shaped, slenderly pointed foliage is red-tinted in spring. There are several young *Tetracentron* trees at Glasnevin, though it grows with greater vigour in the deep, acidic soils of Kilmacurragh in County Wicklow.

The red-barked birch Henry mentioned was not the Himalayan *Betula utilis*, but a new species, *Betula albosinensis*. This fine tree was described from material later collected by Père Paul Farges in 1891. The trees Henry discovered in Shennongjia were up to 26 m (85 ft) tall and with girths of 3.5 m (13 ft) across. The bright orange bark peels in thin strips to reveal a creamy undersurface, and it is by far one of the most ornamental of the birches. The second birch (with 'blackish bark') was not *Betula fargesii*,

Rosa sericea ssp. *omeiensis* was described from Ernst Faber's 1887 Emei Shan collections and from those made by Henry in Shennongjia in 1888.

Betula albo-sinensis, photographed in the Shennongjia National Nature Reserve (International Man and Biosphere Reserve Network) in September 2004. Augustine Henry discovered it in the same area 116 years earlier.

Sorbus koehneana, one of the best of the rowans from central China. It was introduced to cultivation by E. H. Wilson, but has never become common in gardens.

but *Betula delavayi*,[21] a small, slender tree to 12 m (39 ft) high. Franchet based this species on a specimen collected by Père Delavay in western Sichuan Province on 24 May 1889; Henry had discovered the tree some nine months previously.

The enormous *Abies* he discovered was *Abies fargesii*, and it still crowns the tallest mountains of the region. The rose mentioned was also new: *Rosa sericea* ssp. *omeiensis* was described from Faber's 1887 Emei Shan collections and Henry's Shennongjia material. Commonly known as the Mount Omei rose, it is widespread across much of central and western China and Bhutan. The flowers vary from pure white to creamy white.

Two new species of spruce also occurred in the region. *Picea brachytyla*, one of the most stately of all the Chinese spruces, formed round-headed trees to 27 m (88 ft) tall with slender upcurved branches and drooping branchlets. *Picea wilsonii* formed shapely, pyramidal trees of similar stature with short, dense, horizontally spreading branches. The single specimen

collected by Henry was sterile (without cones), but it was later described from more complete material collected by Wilson.

Other new trees included the Chinese yew, *Taxus chinensis*. In his *The Trees of Great Britain and Ireland* series, which he compiled with Henry John Elwes (1846–1922), Henry noted that this tree was rare in the mountains of Hubei and Sichuan provinces, and that it grew there on wooded cliffs between 1,800 m (5,905 ft) and 2,500 m (8,202 ft). The largest tree he encountered was 6 m (20 ft) tall with a girth of 2.4 m (8 ft), and it was called the *kuan-yin-sha* ('the fir of the goddess of mercy').

Sorbus koehneana was common in thickets at similar altitudes and formed small trees bearing clusters of porcelain-white fruits. One of the least known of the rowans, this species is easy to grow, even thriving in the shallow, gravel soil of the arboretum at Glasnevin.

No fewer than two new species of beech were found by

Fagus engleriana. Flowering occurs just as the leaves unfurl in spring. In Hubei Province, it forms trees up to 23 m (75 ft) tall.

Discovered by Augustine Henry, the rosy-purple *Rhododendron sutchuenense* was described from collections later made by the French missionary, Père Paul Farges in 1891. E. H. Wilson introduced it in 1900, and it first flowered ten years later when only 60 cm (2 ft) tall.

Saruma henryi flowering in the woodland garden at Glasnevin. Augustine Henry introduced it to cultivation in 1889, though it did not persist for long and it was not reintroduced again until 1980.

Henry near Fang. *Fagus engleriana* grew by streams, where it formed small, multi-stemmed trees. In gardens, it is rare but is worth growing for its wonderful spring show of silk-like, newly emerged foliage. *Fagus lucida* grew as a medium-sized tree with a broad, rounded crown, and, alongside *Fagus engleriana*, it often formed pure woods.

Other new trees included the snake-bark maple, *Acer maximowiczii*, a new ash, *Fraxinus platypoda*, the rather widespread, nine-lobed *Acer flabellatum* and *Malus kansuensis* f. *calva*, a beautiful little crab apple carrying large corymbs of snow-white blossoms in May, followed by scarlet, egg-shaped fruits in the autumn. *Ilex fargesii* formed small evergreen trees to 14 m (46 ft) tall, sporting distinctive, long, narrow, opaque leaves. This holly is exceptionally rare in cultivation, and, as previously stated, it is one of dozens of plants named for Père Paul Farges, but first discovered by Augustine Henry – in this case, three years previous to Farges' Sichuan collections.

New garden-worthy shrubs abounded on those mountain slopes, and one of the best of these was *Syringa reflexa*, a magnificent lilac bearing densely packed, pendulous, pyramidal panicles of purplish-pink blossoms to 25 cm (10 in.) long in mid summer. How unfortunate that it is not scented. *Rhododendron sutchuenense* was common beneath the canopy of oak woods, where it grew in the company of bamboo.

The residents of this rural mountainous region made a good living from the sale of medicinal plants. These were gathered from the surrounding forests, but were also cultivated on a large scale. One of these, *Saruma henryi*, proved to be a new monotypic genus. Regarded to be among the most primitive members of the birthwort family, the generic epithet, *Saruma*, is an anagram of the closely related *Asarum*. *Saruma* bears petals, unlike *Asarum*, on which they are absent or vestigial within a cup-like calyx.[22] *Saruma henryi* is a distinguished woodland perennial to

87

45 cm (1.5 ft) tall. Its heart-shaped leaves are extremely handsome and emerge purple-flushed in early spring. In gardens, *Saruma* carries a succession of butter-yellow flowers for nearly six months of the year. Henry introduced it to cultivation in 1889[23], but it seems it did not persist for long in European gardens until it was reintroduced by the Sino-American expedition to Hubei Province in 1980, and again in 1981 by the Japanese plant hunter Mikinori Ogisu from Wuhan Botanical Institute. In the wilds of central China, *Saruma henryi* is used to treat stomach ailments, and the newly emerged shoots are boiled and eaten as greens. It is also the sole larval food for *Luehdorfia longicaudata*, a colourful butterfly much valued by collectors.[24] It is extremely rare in gardens, where it thrives under the same

The roots of *dang-gui*, *Angelica sinensis*, photographed in the Derentang pharmacy in Chengdu, Sichuan Province.

It was medicinal plants such as *Angelica sinensis* and *Astragalus henryi* (pictured) that stimulated Augustine Henry's interest in botany.

conditions enjoyed by *Cardiocrinum*, *Meconopsis* and *Podophyllum*, for example. *Saruma henryi* is a charming plant and deserves to be more widely known and grown.

Another discovery from Fang was *Angelica sinensis*, the roots of which are the source of *tang-kui* (or *dang-gui*). This drug is widely available in western and central China, and is also available in health stores in Dublin and other European cities. The roots are used as a tonic, and are also used to treat cases of abdominal pain and traumatic injuries. In a similar case, the roots of *Astragalus henryi* proved to be the source of the important drug *hoan-ch'i*.

On exposed cliff faces grew a host of new ornamental plants like *Codonopsis henryi*, *Delphinium henryi*, *Notopterygium forbesii* (an important medicinal plant and a new genus in the Apiaceae), *Impatiens henryi*, *Calamagrostis henryi* and the pretty little *Geranium henryi*.

Another equally exciting find was *Meconopsis oliveriana*, a gorgeous Asiatic poppy to 90 cm (3 ft) tall carrying solitary, golden-yellow blossoms from May to July. Allied to *Meconopsis chelidoniifolia*, this species has never reached cultivation. Efforts were made at Kew, in May 1889, to raise seeds collected from Henry's herbarium specimens, but this proved unsuccessful. Though less colourful, lichens abounded, and Henry even managed to discover a new species: *Sticta henryana*.

From Fang, Henry and his men made an arduous trek to the rugged Shennongjia region, boasting the highest mountains in all of central China. This was to be the toughest part of the entire six months of travel, but it proved well worth the effort, both in terms of collections and the spectacular scenery. It was a wild, savage landscape and its great forests had survived the woodsman's axe.

The views were spectacular in all directions from the summit of the tallest mountain. A new bamboo, *Sinarundinaria nitida*, formed extensive colonies on these high peaks, and Henry recorded travelling through an enormous area of dead canes. (Like other bamboos, this species dies after flowering.) He had been informed that, three years before his visit, it had flowered all over the province and had produced seeds, which had been gathered by local mountain people and utilised as food in the same manner as rice. *Sinarundinaria nitida* was raised at Kew from seeds sent from St Petersburg; these had been collected in neighbouring northern Sichuan Province by the Russian explorer and naturalist, Grigori Potanin (1835–1920) in 1889.

Of new sub-alpine plants, one of the prettiest and most abundant was the tiny gentian relative, *Lomatogonium bellum*. This dainty little species is also native to Tibet, where it was collected by Sir Francis Younghusband (1863–1942) and later again by Frank Ludlow and George Sherriff.

From Shennongjia, Henry and his 20 native plant collectors crossed into the portion of Badong County that lay north of the

Yangtze. In north Badong, he discovered a fine new variety of butterfly bush, *Buddleja davidii* var. *magnifica*. It was common in that region by the sides of streams and bore enormous panicles of violet-purple flowers with a deep orange eye. This aptly named variety was later put to good use in Europe to breed many of the cultivars we enjoy in our gardens today.

North Wushan and back through the gorges to Yichang
From north Badong, the trail continued into north Wushan County, thus completing a full circuit through the Three Gorges region, both north and south of the Yangtze. North Wushan, like its southerly counterpart, was extremely rich in new plants. *Sorbus caloneura* and *Sorbus zahlbruckneri* were common on the edge of forests, where they formed small trees, while Henry's hornbeam, *Carpinus henryana*, and an elegant new maple, *Acer sinense* var. *concolor*, formed dominant forest trees. In the same forests, Henry and his men discovered a new species of fungus, *Lenzites sinensis*.

One of the most exciting discoveries from this region was *Pentapanax henryi*, a large, dichotomously branched, cliff-side shrub, or a small tree, carrying large, bold pinnate leaves. This fantastic foliage plant was one of the stars of our exhibit at the 2002 Chelsea Flower Show, and the same Chelsea plant has proved hardy on the Chinese Slope at Glasnevin, where it produces a very exotic effect. Other good garden shrubs growing in north Wushan County included the well-known

ABOVE: *Buddleja davidii* var. *magnifica*, the finest variety of the common butterfly bush. It was discovered by Augustine Henry in north Badong and was later introduced by Wilson. In Europe, it was seized upon by hybridisers to create many fine new cultivars.

Sarcococca humilis, *Abelia umbellata* and *Pittosporum henryi*.

The pink-flowered *Astragalus wushanicus*, a cliff dweller, bears the name of this region, as does the small stitchwort, *Stellaria wushanensis*. By far the most beautiful of all plants discovered by Augustine Henry in north Wushan was the gentian relative, *Megacodon venosum*, a stately perennial bearing bold, pleated foliage and carrying 1.5-m (5-ft) tall spikes of large, creamy-white, trumpet-shaped flowers, spotted green in their centres.

Reginald Farrer, who had a good eye for new garden-worthy plants, also enquired from Henry about the location of this plant in the hope of introducing it to cultivation. Farrer was one of a number of later plant hunters who envied Augustine Henry's achievements in the field. The fact that he was normally based in little-known and relatively unexplored regions of China meant that a huge proportion of the specimens Henry collected were new to science. Farrer looked upon the golden era that Henry had opened with a little jealousy, and so must have been unaware of the hardships he often endured. On a journey from

Pentapanax henryi, a large shrub to 4 m (13 ft) with bold, pinnate leaves. It has proved perfectly hardy at Glasnevin.

his base in Gansu Province, Farrer sailed through the Three Gorges and reminisced about Henry's early days there and the many discoveries he had made:

> I could not help envying early collectors, the fame they acquired so comfortably and easily, boating up the Yang-dz [*sic*] and mooring here and there, and exploring (often vicariously) these pleasant ravines and chines. And in those far-off golden days too, when everything that every coolie brought home to you, basking over a book in your boat, was either a new species or a new genus: till you could not step ashore into a back-yard without the merest hideous little weed there being a novelty.[25]

Henry might not have agreed. He was a prolific collector and worked hard to reach his goals. From those six months of travel, he and 24 of his native plant collectors gathered more than 27,300 herbarium specimens. Anyone who has had to deal with pressing and drying herbarium specimens in the field can guess at the enormous effort it must have taken to ensure these were properly tagged, recorded and preserved before reaching a permanent base at Yichang. And so it was that, from the town of Wushan, Henry and his men, along with several crates of dried plant specimens bound for Kew, set sail through the gorges, at the end of what must count as one of the most productive plant-hunting expeditions ever carried out in China.

Waiting on his return to Yichang were 50 copies of the recently published *Chinese Names of Plants*, Henry's first botanical publication. This pioneering paper appeared as a 50-page supplement in the *Journal of the China Branch of Royal Asiatic Society*. In it, Henry attempted to organise the enormous muddle of Chinese plant nomenclature. It was a very useful work, giving the colloquial Chinese names of important medicinal plants followed by their Latin equivalents, and he also went on to discuss the uses to which they were put. The publication must have been warmly welcomed by other botanists similarly struggling to systematise Chinese plant names. Henry sent copies to those interested in the botany of China, including Ernst Faber and the well-known Latvian botanist and Sinologist, Emil Bretschneider (1833–1901).

The days that followed were spent sorting out his collections for Kew, and two of his collectors, Meng and Jao, returned with further material that they had collected over the previous three months from the districts south of the Yangtze that Henry had explored earlier that year.

On 17 February 1889, Augustine Henry received a blow: he was notified of a transfer from Yichang to the large tropical island of Hainan (Hainan Dao) off the southern coast of China.

The opinionated author Reginald Farrer. In April 1914, Farrer wrote to Henry (then living in Dublin) from Gansu looking for the location of plants discovered by Henry in south Wushan during his 1888 expedition.

He must have been gravely disappointed; he had ambitious plans to send his collectors to a number of new localities in Hubei and Sichuan provinces. Those plans were now in ruins.

The entry to his diary for 2 March 1889 reads: 'I had no sleep'. He departed from Yichang at 06:00 a.m. the same morning and reached Shanghai six days later. It was a difficult parting. Henry had made many friends at Yichang, both Chinese and European, and it must have been a wrench to part from his native plant collectors, the men who had served him so faithfully over the past number of years. As he walked towards a waiting steamer, the Chinese staff of the Customs Service lit a double row of fireworks along his path to the river and he was presented with a great bouquet of *Primula rupestris* from the ledges beneath the Cave of the Three Pilgrims in the San You Dong glen.[26] It was a very fitting gift, though the parting was a sad one indeed. He was never to return to Yichang.

Chapter 5

A pilgrimage to Yichang

The Great Palm House at the National Botanic Gardens, Glasnevin, in Dublin. Established in 1795 by the Royal Dublin Society, Glasnevin cultivates more than 20,000 different plants, and this enormous collection is maintained through expeditions to various parts of the world each year. China is a particularly close link.

Preparations for the first 'Henry expedition' began far from home. It was July 2001, and I was in the Tibetan capital of Lhasa having lunch with the English plant hunter Keith Rushforth by the Jokhang Temple in the shadow of the mighty Potala Palace. It was our last day in Tibet before flying back to Nepal, and we had spent the previous weeks trekking through wooded valleys full of giant Himalayan lilies and alpine meadows strewn with irises, primulas and blue Himalayan poppies. Our memorable mid-summer expedition coincided with the Indian monsoon, however, and we had been thoroughly drenched.

Not content with having just completed one expedition, though, we began to plan another. Our conversation was fixed on the subject of the Three Gorges Dam (Changjiang Sanxia Daba) project in Hubei Province, China. I had first

learned of the dam's construction in the autumn of 1999, when, back at the National Botanic Gardens, Glasnevin, a meeting was held to discuss a proposal about bringing an exhibit based on Augustine Henry's pioneering botanical work in China to the RHS Chelsea Flower Show. The dam across the Yangtze was nearing completion, and its floodwaters would soon drown many of the glens and low-lying areas where Augustine Henry and, later, Ernest Wilson made their most notable finds. I was determined,

therefore, to visit the Three Gorges region – and see it as the great plant hunters knew it – before the rising currents of Yangtze River changed it forever.

Back in Lhasa, we put together a three-week itinerary that would bring our group from Emei Shan in Sichuan Province (where we retraced Antwerp Pratt's 1889 route) down the Yangtze River and through the Three Gorges to Yichang in Hubei Province. This expedition was carried out during September and October 2002, and the areas visited were north Wushan in Sichuan and south Badong and Yichang in Hubei.

One expedition, however, was not going to allow enough time to visit all of Henry's former haunts in Hubei and Sichuan provinces, and so we returned a second time, in the autumn of 2004, to travel through Changyang, north Badong, Xingshan, Shennongjia and the hillsides overlooking the city of Yichang. The following chapter is based on those two expeditions.

The Glasnevin Central China Expedition

Back in Ireland, the expeditions were organised through a series of emails to the Chinese Academy of Sciences and Professor Ding Zhaohua from Wuhan Botanical Garden in eastern Hubei Province. It took many months to iron out an agreement between both sides, and to obtain permits that allowed our group to collect material in the Three Gorges region. The aim of the Glasnevin Central China

Kilmacurragh Botanic Gardens, Glasnevin's country estate in rural County Wicklow. The seat of the Acton family for 300 years, successive directors from Glasnevin have been involved in the garden's development since the 1850s. Following decades of decline, it was purchased for Glasnevin by the Irish State in 1996 and a major replanting programme is now underway.

Expedition was to collect seeds and herbarium specimens for the National Botanic Gardens, Glasnevin, and for her sister garden, Kilmacurragh Botanic Gardens in County Wicklow. All this work was carried out in collaboration with botanists and horticulturists from Wuhan, who travelled with us through Hubei and Sichuan provinces.

In Glasnevin's 207-year history, this was the very first plant-hunting expedition to China to have been organised directly from the garden. Indeed, it had been a busy and exhausting year. Our Henry exhibit at the 2002 RHS Chelsea Flower Show, London, in May had won a coveted silver-gilt medal, the second highest accolade awarded by the Royal Horticultural Society. The same exhibit had also received a lot of press attention in Ireland, and the *Irish Times* had mentioned our plans to retrace Henry's footsteps in the area then due to be flooded by the Yangtze. The article was spotted by Gallivanting Media, a film production company that was keen to make a documentary about our travels. A few weeks later, I met Fiona O'Dwyer and Fergus

The author with HRH The Duke of Edinburgh at the Henry exhibit during the Gala Evening of the RHS Chelsea Flower Show in May 2002.

Tighe and, having heard their plans and viewed some past productions, agreed to their travelling with us.

At that time, I was also compiling *Plantae Henryanae*, a catalogue of the 158,000 herbarium specimens collected by Henry in China. This gave us a very good idea of what he and his native plant collectors gathered throughout his various bases in the Three Gorges region – and, so, what we could expect to encounter. The prospect of visiting and plant hunting in Sichuan and western Hubei provinces was thrilling. Central China, while well explored in the late 19th and early 20th centuries, has seen relatively little botanical exploration in recent decades – unlike the more westerly provinces, which have been inundated by visitors since China reopened her doors to foreign travel during the 1980s. Having previously visited regions made famous by other great plant hunters, such as Delavay, Forrest, Rock and Kingdon Ward, it was time to retrace the trail of a fellow countryman. From Dublin, our group of ten enthusiastic botanists and horticulturists departed for China, thus beginning a great Irish adventure.

Hubei – a biological hot spot in the heart of China

The mountainous terrain of western Hubei is one of China's richest provinces in terms of botanical diversity and has attracted the attention of Western botanists and horticulturists since the late 19th century. The province derives its name from '*Hu*', or lake, and '*bei*', meaning north, referring to the fact that Hubei lies north of Lake Dongting, China's largest freshwater lake, and covers an area of 187,400 km² (72,355 square miles). With a population in excess of 64 million people, Hubei is located along the middle reaches of the Yangtze River.

The province may be very easily divided into two distinct regions. To the east of Yichang lies a low plain with many lakes, and it is here that the greater part of Hubei's agricultural production takes place. Wuhan, the provincial capital, lies at the confluence of the Han and Yangtze rivers on the Jiangshan Plain, which reaches its lowest level at just 23 m (75 ft) above sea level. In contrast, to the west of Yichang, the province takes on a rugged mountainous aspect, with peaks soaring to 3,105 m (10,187 ft) in the Shennongjia area.

Hubei Province experiences four well demarcated seasons, and belongs to the East Asian subtropical monsoon climate district, though its varied topography gives rise to several localised microclimates. Spring is generally cloudy, with rain and frequent temperature fluctuations. In early summer, precipitation is heavy with an associated high humidity; by late summer, conditions are drier and the climate is generally hot. In autumn, the eastern plains experience cool, crisp temperatures while precipitation is mostly experienced in the mountains to the west. Winters are cold, with less precipitation. The average yearly temperature is 15–17 °C (59–63 °F) in most parts of the province. The warmest month is July, when the average temperature is 27–29 °C (81–84 °F). Wuhan is one of the warmest cities in China, and summer temperatures there can exceed 40 °C (104 °F). The coldest month is January, when temperatures average 2–4 °C

During our 2002 expedition to China, a film crew travelled with us making a documentary about Henry and the fate of the Three Gorges.

The Fenjingya Nature Reserve in Shennongjia Forestry District, with *Sorbus discolor* (syn. *S. hupehensis*) in the foreground. These mountains harbour one of the richest floras in China.

The fossil tree, *Metasequoia glyptostroboides*, is perhaps Hubei's best-known gift to gardeners. Pictured here is the original 'type' tree visited by our group in 2002.

(36–39 °F). An absolute minimum of −17.3 °C (0.86 °F) was recorded at Wuhan on 31 January 1969.

The flora of Hubei Province is one of the richest and most diverse in all of China in which warm-temperate and temperate elements predominate, though subtropical elements are obvious at low altitudes. To botanists, the flora of Hubei is full of interest; the province marks the juncture of the Sino-Himalayan and Sino-Japanese floras, with an associated complex floral composition. To horticulturists, this same flora is a rich source of many beautiful garden plants. By present calculations, Hubei is home to 3,816 species and 242 varieties of vascular plants belonging to 1,165 genera. Of these, 182 species represent pteridophytes (ferns), 37 species and 5 varieties are gymnosperms and 3,579 species and 237 varieties represent the angiosperms or flowering plants. Among rare and endangered plants, 47 species from the Three Gorges region are under national protection.

In Hubei, like many other provinces in China, the flora is characterised by distinctive vertical zoning. Evergreen broadleaved forest (generally dominated by members of the Lauraceae) may be found at altitudes beneath 1,300 m

(4,265 ft); mixed evergreen and deciduous broadleaved forests dominate the mountain slopes between 1,300 to 2,200 m (4,265 − 7,218 ft); while, on the highest mountain peaks, above 3,048 m (10,000 ft), mixed deciduous and coniferous forests give way to bamboo, scrub and sub-alpine meadow.

Hubei's flora preserves a wealth of plants that exist only as fossils in other parts of the northern hemisphere. The fact that the region escaped the effects of Quaternary glaciation accounts for the survival of many relict plants there today. Perhaps the best known of these 'living fossils' are *Ginkgo* and *Metasequoia* from the Mesozoic.[1]

Thirty-six species of flowering plants are endemic to the Three Gorges area. Eleven of these were discovered by Augustine Henry, and they include the following: *Allium henryi*, *Angelica henryi*, *Aster limosus*, *Cacalia begoniaefolia*, *Chrysosplenium lanuginosum* var. *ciliatum*, *Hydrocotyle dielsiana*, *Megacodon venosum*, *Peucedanum henryi*, *Pilea rubriflora*, *Pimpinella renifolia* and *Saussurea decurrens*.[2] *Peucedanum henryi* was introduced to cultivation by the 2004 Glasnevin Central China Expedition from Xingshan and first flowered at Kilmacurragh in September 2007.

Adiantum reniforme var. *sinense*, one of the casualties of the Three Gorges dam project. This pretty little fern once grew on the banks of the Yangtze near Wanxian. It has now been submerged and is officially extinct in the wild.

A Great Wall across the Yangtze

In recent years, the Three Gorges have attracted worldwide attention because of the construction of the Three Gorges Dam at the small town of Sandouping, some 40 km (25 miles) upriver from the existing Gezhouba Dam near Yichang in Hubei Province. Sun Yat-sen (1866–1925), the founder of modern China, is credited with having first proposed the idea of a hydroelectric dam in the Three Gorges in 1919. Following a series of devastating floods along the Yangtze during the mid 1950s, Chairman Mao Zedong (1893–1976) ordered feasibility studies for damming the river. Work finally began on the project in 1994 and, following its completion in 2009, a 2,335-m (7,660-ft) wide, 185-m (607-ft) high wall (the equivalent of a 60-storey building) now spans the Yangtze to contain the world's largest artificial reservoir with a storage capacity of 40 billion m³. Twenty-six of the world's largest turbines will harness more power than 18 nuclear power plants, enough to supply one-ninth of all China's energy needs. More than 27,000 people, working 24 hours a day in three shifts, have toiled on this gargantuan dam, and it is not since the construction of the Great Wall of China, more than 2,000 years ago, that China has embarked on such an ambitious project. Now completed, the dam forms an artificial lake that sprawls more than 560 km (350 miles) in length.

The statistics are enormous. One of the largest civil engineering projects in history, the dam is estimated to have cost $24 billion to construct, and 1.9 million people have had to be relocated; $10 billion of the final costs were put towards the relocation programme, the largest peacetime relocation in history. Half of the people moved are farmers, and 303,525 ha (750,000 acres) of rich agricultural land has been taken out of production to create the 650-km² (251-miles²) lake. By 2009, a staggering 137 cities, towns and villages had been moved from the riverside, and some of these have been completely relocated.[3]

The dam will bring great benefits to this rather outlying region of China. Two five-stage locks (the largest ever built) on the northern side of the dam will raise deep draft vessels almost 150 m (492 ft) to the new reservoir and allow ocean-going ships to travel 2,400 km (1,491 miles) inland to Chongqing, while a ship lift will serve smaller vessels. Navigation will be made easier and annual flooding can finally be controlled (during the 20th century, the Yangtze claimed the lives of more than 300,000 people).

Critics have warned of silt and pollution (80 per cent of

The relocation of farmers to mountainous areas due to flooding has placed additional pressures on the few remaining tracts of forest in the Three Gorges region. This house, surrounded by rows of vegetables and maize, was being built in Badong.

Chinese cities have no sewage treatment plants), earthquakes, embezzlement and lack of compensation for residents. Environmental groups warn of the chemical poisoning of the river from submerged factories that will leak industrial toxins such as methylmercury, arsenic and cyanide. The Environmental Impact Statement for the dam project makes scant reference to the local flora and fauna. The Three Gorges region has a remarkably rich flora of some 2,859 species, 26 subspecies and 14 varieties of flowering plants. Of these, 47 species are listed as rare and endangered and 36 are endemic. Three endemics have become extinct in the wild due to flooding and the destruction of their habitats. These include *Adiantum reniforme* var. *sinense*, a tiny maidenhair fern that grew in a small area above the banks of the Yangtze near Wanxian City, *Myricaria laxiflora*, a fluviatile shrub that once grew on the banks and cliffs of the river just above flood level around Badong and Wushan, and *Chuanminshen violaceum*, an important medicinal plant in the carrot family (Apiaceae) that occupies a small site near the hamlet of Liantuo near Yichang. Though not growing within the reservoir area, its habitat has been severely affected by the dam's construction.

It is estimated that the dam project will have affected approximately 550 plant species, and riverside populations of *Buddleja lindleyana*, *Distylium racemosum*, *Bauhinia brachycarpa*, *Buxus microphylla* var. *sinica*, *Buxus harlandii*, *Securinega suffruticosa*, *Hibiscus syriacus*, *Cotinus coggygria* var. *glaucophylla* and *Geum aleppicum* all face mass

Central China possesses huge deposits of high-sulphur coal. Hydro-electricity generated by harnessing the currents of the Yangtze will massively reduce the amount burned.

Sailing through the Wu Gorge in October 2002. A city (one of many) has been razed to the ground while a new city emerges on higher ground. Much of this work was carried out by hand and without the aid of heavy machinery.

submergence, particularly in the regions near Badong and along the south bank of the Yangtze near Wushan. The Chinese river dolphin is now officially extinct in the wild, and the migratory Chinese sturgeon and the Yangtze alligator are also threatened with a similar fate since their natural breeding grounds lie beyond the dam walls.

Families – including some that have tilled the same patch of land since the Ming Dynasty – will inevitably lose out on the redistribution of land, and many have been forced to farm poorer soils in upland areas. Each displaced family will receive land, or an apartment, plus financial compensation of, on average, $1,200. In those mountainous areas, once-barren hilltops have been terraced with dry-stone walls to create hundreds of sweet potato plots, though this does not bring in the same income as tangerines, the most valuable riverside crop in the Three Gorges region. This relocation has also placed additional pressures on the few remaining forested areas. Whatever the arguments may be, the fact remains that the Three Gorges region will change forever –

and many of the low-lying areas visited by early plant hunters will be lost beneath a new reservoir.

On the other hand, the dam will bring great benefits. China depends heavily on its enormous deposits of high-sulphur coal for three-quarters of its electricity needs. As a result, its air is among the most polluted in the world. The country's carbon dioxide emissions pose a huge threat to global warming, and a quarter of all deaths in China are due to pulmonary disease. The dam will dramatically reduce China's dependency on fossil fuels. Catastrophic floods will become a thing of the past and hydro-electrical power will reduce the consumption of millions of tonnes of coal, thus reducing smog. Navigation upriver from Yichang has always been hampered by unfavourable conditions, but the new lake will widen shipping lanes, create a constant water level and remove the threat posed by dangerous obstacles such as submerged rocks and sand bars. The Chinese Government believes that, ultimately, the benefits justify the massive spending, environmental damage and the human displacement involved.

The Wu Gorge in October 2002, just weeks before flooding commenced. Cruise ships more than five storeys high are dwarfed by soaring limestone cliffs and the murky waters of the Yangtze race onwards towards the plains beyond Yichang.

Through China's Three Gorges

In late September 2002, we boarded a large riverboat packed to capacity with hundreds of people who were making their way to Yichang for the annual Moon Festival. Sailing with us were Professor Ding Zhaohua, Professor Chen Chang and a number of other staff members from Wuhan Botanical Garden. Our journey began on the quays of the busy riverside city of Wanxian (Wanxian Prefecture, now Wanzhou District in Chongqing Municipality). Traditionally referred to as 'the gateway to Sichuan', Wanxian was a hub of transportation and communication along the Yangtze between eastern Sichuan and western Hubei provinces. The city was living on borrowed time, however, and faced the heaviest burden of resettlement. More than 571,000 people, half of the town's population, were in the process of moving to higher levels. A third of the 2,000-year-old city – embracing 11.6 km² (7 miles²), including 900 factories and 597 km (370 miles) of roads – would be fully submerged by 2009. In the entire Three Gorges flood area, 1,208

archaeological sites faced certain inundation. More than 300 of these were in Wanxian – sites dating from the Ming Dynasty to 50,000-year-old Stone Age tombs. Many families resisted the move, and Wanxian proved to be a hotbed of trouble nearing the completion of the dam, with several protesters receiving prison terms for organising blockades and for taking their stories to foreign journalists.

Walking through the city's streets, signs of displacement were everywhere. Riverside homes were in the process of being demolished and teams of men and women were busily salvaging bricks, timber and roof tiles to build new homes at higher levels. Most of this work was carried out without the aid of machinery. To compensate for all of this disturbance, the city was going to be connected by a rail and riverside highway that would also link Chengdu and Shanghai. An international airport capable of handling jumbo jets was built on a mountain top to the south of the Yangtze River, and linking it to the city necessitated the construction of one of the world's longest single-arch bridges.[4] This region of

ABOVE, BELOW: The massive Three Gorges dam, the largest dam in the world, spanning the third largest river on the planet. By 2009, flooding of the Three Gorges region had been completed, creating an artificial lake so vast that it can be seen from space. Almost two million people have been relocated.

cliffs were artificial caves with coffins. These are the burial places of the ancient Ba people, an unstudied race whose history will be obliterated by the rising waters of the reservoir.

For thousands of years, all trade and communication in the Three Gorge region depended on the waterway. It was not until the early Qing Dynasty (1644–1912) that a solution was found by constructing plank roads high up on the cliff faces. Mile after mile of these amazing thoroughfares run through the most inaccessible areas of the gorges and consist of piles driven into the cliff faces and covered with flagstones or timber. A sedan chair carried by six people could easily negotiate these roads, but the loss of life during their construction must have been appallingly high. Alas, many of the ancient plank roads will also disappear beneath the rising levels of the Yangtze. Beyond the Qutang Gorge, the river widens, the racing currents of the Yangtze slow to a less frantic pace, and the cliffs are replaced by gentle slopes clothed by orange groves.

From the town of Wushan (Chongqing Municipality), our party departed on another large riverboat, and, from there, we sailed for a day through the Wu Gorge and the Xiling Gorge before finally reaching Yichang. All about were signs of change. On the slopes above riverside orange groves, plaques proclaimed the new 175-m (574-ft) high level of the Yangtze. These plaques were like portents of doom; everything below them would be flooded when the Yangtze rose to its new, final height in 2009. Daubed in red paint on many of the surrounding buildings was the Chinese character '*chai*', which means 'demolish'. The contrast between new and old was startling; entire cities, towns and villages were being razed to the ground, and, above the 175-m level, newly built cities were emerging. It was as though all the riverside communities had been bombed into oblivion, and it made a sinister and ghostly sight.

The Yangtze acted as a busy highway, as hundreds of Mississippi-style boats, barges, sampans, junks and pleasure crafts plied their trade between Chongqing and Yichang. Some had perhaps even travelled as far afield as Shanghai. The mist had finally cleared, allowing fine views of time-worn cliffs and towering mountain peaks. Nothing had prepared us for the spectacular scenery that lay ahead, though. Unlike the narrow course of the Qutang Gorge, here, the Yangtze River, while still confined by cliffs, widens significantly in the final two gorges, and the enormous

China is enormously rich in coal, salt and natural gas, and these new links would help distribute these and other products throughout the country and further afield.

Dawn was breaking as we entered the Qutang Gorge (the smallest of the Three Gorges) in Fengjie County (Fengjie Xian), Chongqing Municipality, and our rusty old ship slowly sailed between mist-shrouded, copper-toned cliffs. The enormous towering cliff walls seemed like two gigantic gates through which the furious Yangtze pushed forward at a relentless pace. Towering peaks and grotesque crags framed the sky above, and it was indeed an exciting entry to 'Henry country'.

This spectacular stretch of river features the Three Gorge's fastest currents and had notoriously claimed the lives of hundreds of 'coolies' (hired labourers) and trackers before blasting was carried out on the riverbed to remove obstacles during the 1950s. High on the cliff faces were the remains of recessed towpaths where those unfortunate men had carried out their dangerous and arduous work. Also visible on the riverboat we sailed on seemed minuscule in comparison. It was exciting to be just hours away from Yichang, yet it was sad to reflect on the fact that we would be the very last botanical expedition to sail the Three Gorges before flooding began, just a few weeks later. Some of the greatest plant hunters of all time had sailed these same waters, and at least we would see the region as they had known it.

The sun was rising over the cliffs as we sailed into the Wu Gorge, and we spent most of that day on deck, gazing onto the soaring limestone cliffs, peaks and caves, trying to guess (with the aid of binoculars) what grew on the cliff walls and along the tributaries and narrow glens. Finally, we reached Sandouping – and the site of the Three Gorges Dam. Suddenly, the scale of the project was put in place: the side of a mountain had been sliced away and an enormous concrete wall, stretching across one of the greatest rivers on this planet, was nearing completion. From our viewpoint, the most enormous earth-moving machinery looked like mere toys and construction workers looked like scattering ants.

We sailed the gorges twice; first in 2002, shortly before the final section of dam was put in place, and again two years later, when a significant rise in the level of the river was obvious and, when by the dam itself, an embryonic artificial reservoir was taking shape. On the spill side of the dam, three gigantic overflows were in operation, and from these jetted enormous volumes of water: an incredible sight.

Frank Meyer's words, 'I am now on *Terra Sancta*', came into mind as we arrived that evening on the docks at Yichang ('Ichang' in Meyer's day); even as contemporary plant hunters, it did feel as though we had reached a holy land. It was strange yet exhilarating to stroll through the city that was once home to Augustine Henry, Charles Maries, Thomas Watters and E. H. Wilson – and, as if by fate, we arrived in Yichang on the very evening before the last surviving European-style building belonging to the Foreign Compound was demolished.

One of the Chinese members of our party, Professor Chen, had lived in Yichang for more than 15 years and knew where the remains of the old Foreign Compound could be found. Its location was just as Henry and Wilson had described; directly across the Yangtze from the pyramidal-shaped hill known to European residents as 'the Dome' (Moji Shan). We were in awe. Early the following morning, armed with cameras, we made a daylight visit to the house, before being finally ushered out by the local police. A short time later, the old building was gone, the last trace of a Foreign Compound that had sprung up more than 140 years before, when a treaty port was established at Yichang. It was curious that we arrived at such an opportune time, and it added a wonderful story for the film crew who accompanied us. It was from an adjacent building

in the 1880s that Henry had dispatched tens of thousands of specimens to Kew, and I couldn't help but wonder how he'd have felt had he known that a botanical party from Glasnevin, Dublin, would be the last Europeans to see what remained of the old Compound. But China is in a new age: the era of the 'treaty port' is an embarrassing part of her history now best forgotten, and such buildings are of little value in that rapidly developing country.

We found Yichang a pleasant place. Plant hunters from past to recent times claimed it to be a dreary, mundane city with no redeeming features. During the last decade, it has seen massive redevelopment and a new city of well-planned parks and modern squares has replaced the old. In Henry's time, Yichang was home to about 30,000 souls; today, there are more than two million people living there. The Three Gorges Dam project has turned the city into a boomtown.

Producing tofu from soybeans in a courtyard in Yichang. Frank Meyer, who took this photograph in the early 20th century, regarded Yichang as '*terra sancta*' – as did our group, more than nine decades later.

The last remaining house from the Foreign Compound in the east end of Yichang. The building was demolished shortly after this photograph was taken and nothing now remains of Augustine Henry's base at Yichang.

A view of the Nanjin Pass and the mouth of the Xiling Gorge from the Glen of the Three Pilgrims, near Yichang. A rich assemblage of plants still clings to the inaccessible limestone cliffs.

The Glen of the Three Pilgrims, the hills around Yichang
Just 10 km (6 miles) northwest of Yichang is the Glen of the Three Pilgrims. In 819 AD, three Tang Dynasty poets – Bai Zhuyi (Bai Juyi), his brother Bai Xingjian and Yuan Zhen – arrived in Yichang and visited this scenic spot, which inspired them to carve poems onto a cave wall. They were afterwards known as 'the first three pilgrims', and the cave is referred to as 'San You Dong' ('Three Travellers' Cave'). During the Song Dynasty (960–1279 AD), the well-known literary family of Su – a father and his two sons – visited San You Dong while travelling to Beijing to take the imperial examinations, and they also carved poems on the walls of the cave. In China, they are known as 'the second three pilgrims', and, over the centuries, other visiting literati have left their own verses behind, too.

It was Sunday, 3 October 2004 when we made the short drive from Yichang to the Glen of the Three Pilgrims. It was the time of the Moon Festival and the whole week was a national holiday in China; consequently, everywhere around Yichang, including the glen, was packed with local tourists.

The entrance to the glen afforded spectacular views of the Nanjin Pass and the mouth of the Xiling (Yichang) Gorge. Good garden plants, both familiar and rare, grew near this entrance area, including *Wisteria sinensis* and the crape myrtle, *Lagerstroemia indica*. Around Yichang, the crape myrtle forms deciduous trees to about 9 m (29 ft) tall, and, in July, August and September, it bears flowers varying from pink to deep red. The bark on mature trees is an attractive smooth grey. Despite the specific epithet coined by Linnaeus, it is native to China and Korea, and, in

Statues of the three famous Tang Dynasty poets in the cave (San You Dong) of the Glen of the Three Pilgrims.

The Glen of the Three Pilgrims in October 2004. Boats now sail across trails that Henry, Pratt and Wilson trod over a century before. The cave is on the cliffs to the right.

A Taoist temple with a fine young specimen of the sago palm, *Cycas revoluta*, in the San You Dong Glen. Many temples and shrines adorned the higher crags overlooking the glen and the Xiling Gorge; such religious sites are often good places to find rare plants.

One of Henry's earliest discoveries, *Corydalis saxicola*, pictured here in the Glen of the Three Pilgrims. Henry found it on rocky ledges in the Xiling Gorge in 1885. The specific epithet, *saxicola* – meaning 'a grower among rocks' – is very apt. The flowers are yellow.

Henry's time, the crape myrtle (or *tzu ching*) occurred both wild and cultivated in the area around the Three Gorges. It was widely planted in gardens and around temples, where selected forms with white and pink to carmine coloured blossoms were common. The genus commemorates the Swedish merchant and naturalist Magnus von Lagerström (1696–1759), who was responsible for the acquisition of the type material and the introduction of this species from China. Lagerström's position as Director of the Swedish East India Company allowed him to acquire herbarium specimens from China, which he sent with living plants to the Uppsala University Botanic Garden in Sweden.

Further into the Glen of the Three Pilgrims, one of Augustine Henry's discoveries, *Corydalis saxicola* (syn. *C. thalictrifolia*), clung to a rock face. According to Henry, this species was known as the *ai-huang-lien* (or the *yanhuang lian*) and was a common plant on the ledges of

103

The tung oil tree, *Aleurites fordii*, seen here growing wild in the hills above Yichang. The large seeds are the source of a valuable oil used in varnishes and paints.

Hydrangea aspera ssp. *strigosa*, pictured here in a damp glen west of Yichang.

cliffs in the gorges, where it carried conspicuous yellow flowers in spring. The large woody rhizomes of this species were used as a drug (as a substitute for *huang-lien*, or *Coptis chinensis*, hence the Chinese name *ai-huang-lien* or 'cliff coptis'), and, in the gorges, it flowered in March and April. *Corydalis saxicola* was introduced to cultivation by E. H. Wilson while collecting for Messrs Veitch. Writing in the *Gardeners' Chronicle*, Frederick William Burbidge (another Veitch collector) noted that it was cultivated with other rarities in the enclosed fruit garden at Glasnevin at the beginning of the 20th century. Henry also grew it in his greenhouse in Ranelagh, in the south Dublin suburbs, during the 1920s, where it flowered throughout the winter months.

Moving deeper into the glen, we ascended a narrow track set on the edge of a sheer cliff overlooking its floor. This area was flooded to such an extent that small ferries could navigate the same route taken on foot by E. H. Wilson and his men to the nearby city of Xingshan 94 years previously. This flooding was not as a result of the gigantic Three Gorges Dam project, however, but of the smaller, yet still enormous, Gezhou Dam, which lies a few kilometres downstream. Continuing on, we soon reached the cave from which the Glen of the Three Pilgrims takes its name, and, to the rear of the cave, were three fine marble statues of those scholarly visitors. Nearby were the shattered remains of older statues (victims, no doubt, of the 'Great Proletarian Cultural Revolution'), while countless poems lined the walls of the cave. Henry, Wilson and Pratt were all regular visitors to this glen and its famous cave, and it gave us a great sense of excitement to here retrace their route.

Passing the cave, the glen opened up and the hills and peaks were crowned with fine Taoist shrines and temples overlooking the Xiling Gorge. In the largest of these temples, traditional music was played, and in the courtyards grew many colourful plants, including potted specimens of *Cycas revoluta* and a rose very close to *Rosa* x *odorata* 'Old Blush'. Nearby, *Koelreuteria bipinnata* was in flower and also carried masses of inflated, salmon-pink, bladder-like

fruits. *Bauhinia brachycarpa* formed lax shrubs to about 3 m (10 ft) tall and *Crataegus hupehensis* carried a heavy crop of large, edible fruits. These fruits are made into confectionery in some parts of Hubei Province.

From the Glen of the Three Pilgrims, we drove into the low hills above Yichang to study what little remained of the area's natural vegetation. *Aleurites fordii* (syn. *Vernicia fordii*), the tung oil tree, was common in this region, both as a wild and cultivated plant. This small tree bears seed capsules the size of a small apple, and, from the seeds, 'wood-oil' is extracted. In the late 19th century, it was used extensively for caulking, painting, varnishing and preserving woodwork. The best sort of Chinese ink used in traditional calligraphy was made from soot obtained by burning this oil. Central China was the chief area of production, and, from there, enormous quantities were exported. Wilson stated that it was abundant in the Yangtze valley in the region from Yichang to Chongqing, but was best seen around the Three Gorges and in the mountains above them at an altitude of about 800 m (2,625 ft). It is a beautiful

Loropetalum chinense, a common shrub in the warmer parts of China. It was introduced by Charles Maries in 1880.

sight, when, during the month of April, it bears myriads of white blossoms stained pink and yellow. Tung oil is still produced in great quantities in China (it was once a relatively important commercial crop in the USA). Teak oil, sold in Europe and the USA for fine furniture, windows and doors is usually made from refined tung oil.

Extensive plantations of mandarin oranges (*Citrus reticulata*) covered the hills in places, and, at the edge of these, *Hydrangea aspera* ssp. *strigosa* formed fine shrubs to about 3 m (10 ft) tall. One of my favourite Chinese shrubs, *Loropetalum chinense*, was abundant on the sun-baked hillsides and trailing through them were vines of *Ampelopsis aconitifolia*, *Maclura cochinchinensis* and *Clematis otophora*. Native to China, Laos and one region of Japan, *Loropetalum chinense* is a wiry, evergreen shrub to 1.5 m (5 ft) tall and produces spidery, white flowers in February and March, much like those of the closely related witch-hazels. It was introduced to cultivation by Charles Maries in 1880 and grows reasonably well in the mildest parts of Britain and Ireland. The genus is monotypic and numerous cultivars have been selected in China from the red-pink flowered *Loropetalum chinense* f. *rubrum*.

However, I think the plant that we Glasnevin people will forever associate with Yichang is *Saccharum arundinaceum*, a showy and vigorous grass forming immense clumps of luxuriant foliage and bearing spectacular plumes of pink flowers on 3-m (10-ft) tall stems. It is particularly abundant around Yichang and consequently I always link this plant with that famous place. Yichang's pink plume grass is best seen in its homeland, however. Seedlings raised in Ireland grew well and formed plenty of foliage, but sulked and

The silvery-pink plumes of *Saccharum arundinaceum*, one of the commonest plants on the sun-baked hillsides above Yichang.

Asarum maximum, the *ma-ti-hsiang* (or horse-hoof) fragrance plant. The curious flowers are fly pollinated and hidden beneath a crown of beautifully variegated foliage.

steadfastly refused to flower because of lack of sunshine. Our rather insular climate does not suit this sun-loving plant, but it might be worth a trial in the Mediterranean regions of the world.

In the shady, damper glens above Yichang, we found several exciting plants, the most memorable moment being when we stumbled across a wild ginger discovered by Henry in the same glens in 1887. *Asarum maximum* has been described by the American plant hunter and explorer Daniel J. Hinkley as the most stunning member of this fascinating genus, and I thoroughly agree. The glossy, leathery, heart-shaped leaves of this wonderful wild ginger are variably splashed and marbled giving a handsome, variegated effect, and the white, velvety, succulent flowers are beautifully edged with a broad black edge blossom.

Henry called it the *ma-ti-hsiang*, or 'horse-hoof fragrance', and stated the root was used in herbal medicine. He introduced it to cultivation through the Royal Botanic Gardens, Kew, where it first flowered in 1895.

Moji Shan, known to Henry and Wilson as 'the Dome'. Seen here shrouded by industrial smog, this photograph of the hill was taken opposite the last remaining house in the old Foreign Compound – and this is the view to which Henry awoke every morning. The Monastery Valley lies to the left.

'The Dome' and a fine view across Yichang

The following day, we crossed the Yangtze at Yichang and made our way towards the pyramidal-shaped hill that overlooks the city. Known to Henry, Wilson and other early European residents as 'the Dome', the hill is officially called Moji Shan.

We began our ascent from the Monastery Glen. Since Henry's plant-hunting days, the vegetation of the glen has been stripped to make way for groves of mandarin oranges. Like the Glen of the Three Pilgrims, Moji Shan is a popular destination with locals from Yichang. Many of these had been out since early morning and the hillside was thronged with visitors. A long, steep flight of steps led our way up the slopes through a formal avenue of *Juniperus formosana* and *Ligustrum lucidum*. Near the base, *Kalopanax septemlobus* grew as a young 3-m (10-ft) tall tree. This widespread species is distributed from Russia, across China and into Korea. In the wild, it forms a large deciduous tree to 30 m (98 ft) tall, and has reached 14 m (46 ft) in cultivation. The branches of this tree are armed with large yellow prickles and the handsome palmate leaves are up to 35 cm (14 in.) across. It was introduced to Western gardens by the Russian botanist Carl Maximowicz (1827–91) in 1865.

Along our route, we spotted trees of *Platycarya strobilacea* and *Paulownia fortunei*. The former is an interesting member of the walnut family with pinnate leaves and forms a small tree to about 15 m (49 ft) tall. It is known colloquially in Hubei Province as *huan-hsiang-shu*, and, according to both Henry and Ernest Wilson, the fruits were used to make a black dye for cotton goods. This interesting deciduous tree bears cone-like fruits and is extremely rare in gardens. The original introduction by Fortune from eastern China in 1845 was not reliably hardy; those sent by Wilson from Yichang in 1907 proved to better suit British and Irish gardens. Young trees at the Kilmacurragh Botanic Gardens raised from seeds collected on Moji Shan have grown with relative vigour, and appear to be perfectly hardy and remain semi-evergreen, perhaps because of the garden's mild, coastal climate. The genus was once much more widespread, and has been found as fossil specimens in London clay deposits.

Paulownia fortunei also grew as a street tree on the quays at Yichang, and, on the lower slopes of Moji Shan, young trees formed entire groves, which must make a glorious sight when in bloom. The fragrant flowers of Fortune's foxglove tree are lavender-purple on the exterior, while, inside, they are creamy white and heavily spotted dark purple on the interior.

The widespread climbing fern *Lygodium japonicum* scaled its way through surrounding bushes, including a fine 2.5-m (8-ft) tall shrub of the bitter orange, *Poncirus*

ABOVE: The west end of Yichang from the summit of Moji Shan in October 2004. Industrial smog envelops the city and the Yangtze spills out from the gorges to sprawl over a kilometre wide. The city is now high-rise, though boats still line the Bund as they did when Wilson took his photograph from the same spot in March 1908 (right).

trifoliata. Native to Korea and northern China, this citrus relative is naturalised in central China, where it is often used as a stock onto which various types of citrus fruits are grafted. In gardens, it forms a medium-sized, viciously armed, deciduous shrub and should be more widely planted. There is a beautiful old plant in the rock garden at Glasnevin that has acquired an elegant, gnarled, domed shape with the help of a century or so of judicious pruning. In spring, it bears hundreds of large, white, sweetly scented, orange blossom-like flowers on naked stems, and these are followed, in autumn, by small yellow fruits that look just like oranges.

The wild form of Lady Bank's rose, *Rosa banksiae* var. *normalis,* carried masses of small globular fruits, and we were delighted to stumble across it. The wild Banksian rose was first found in China by Père Delavay on 30 April 1885, and Henry found it a year later in the Three Gorges region. This rose is the ancestral stock of the double yellow *Rosa banksiae* 'Lutea', a beautiful early flowered climber that is popular in old Irish walled gardens.

The bitter orange, *Poncirus trifoliate,* is naturalised around Yichang. It is popular in British and Irish gardens because of its small, orange-like fruits.

107

From Glasnevin, I had brought with me a copy of a photograph of Yichang taken by E. H. Wilson from Moji Shan in March 1908. Reaching the site upon which there had once stood a fine temple (destroyed during the Cultural Revolution), it became obvious that we were standing on the very spot where Wilson had taken his photograph 96 years before our visit.

Yichang was much changed and a blanket of smog meant our photographs were not quite as clear as Wilson's. From our vantage point, we could see the new multistorey building that had replaced the old European-style building in the Foreign Compound that had been demolished during our visit two years previously. We made our way down Moji Shan that evening, overflowing with enthusiasm. The last Western plant hunter to collect on the hill before us was E. H. Wilson himself, and we had stood in his (and Henry's) very footsteps.

Three Gorges Botanical Garden

While based in Yichang in October 2002, our Chinese counterparts from Wuhan took us to visit the nearby Three Gorges Botanical Garden, one of two satellite gardens belonging to Wuhan Botanical Garden. Near the entrance, field trials of forestry, horticultural and fruit crops were being carried out. Among these trials were new Chinese cultivars of *Cotinus coggygria* (common wild in the gorges), *Cercidophyllum japonicum*, *Carya cathayensis* and various species of *Cinnamomum* and *Magnolia*.

A large area was set aside for *Actinidia chinensis* trials. This close relative of the kiwi fruit (*Actinidia deliciosa*) has been much improved as a result of extensive breeding programmes at Wuhan Botanical Garden. In his *Notes on Economic Botany of China*, Augustine Henry wrote:

Actinidia chinensis [...] the *yang-t'ao* [...] a very large climbing shrub with white conspicuous flowers and fruits about the size of a plum, which can be made into a good jam with a guava-jelly kind of flavour. The fruit might be much improved by cultivation'.[5]

Wuhan has done just that with *Actinidia chinensis*. The fruits we saw, and later sampled, were the size of large apples and were far superior to those of *Actinidia deliciosa* imported into Europe from New Zealand. It comes as a surprise to many to learn that the kiwi fruit is not, in fact, a New Zealand native but a Chinese endemic. *Actinidia* has its centre of diversity in Hubei Province and the world's largest genetic collection is maintained at Wuhan.

Though these exotic fruit trials were fascinating, our interests lay more in the 200-ha. (494-acre) reserve of native forest, and this area gave some respite from the intense heat experienced out in the open. Little low-lying warm-temperate woodland survives in this part of Hubei today and so it was a good opportunity to see the sort of terrain that was familiar to the early plant hunters.

One of the most striking plants near the woodland entrance was the kudzu vine, *Pueraria lobata*, a rampant tuberous rooted climber to 10 m (33 ft) tall with large trifoliate leaves and tightly packed racemes of intense purple pea-like flowers. Common at low altitudes in Hubei, it is known as *ko t'eng*. During the 19th century, this plant furnished *ko-pou* fibre, which was manufactured into a fabric used for underclothing in summer, and as a slow-burning fuse for explosives. Due to the costly and primitive process of preparation, the manufacture of the fabric declined. From the thickened rootstock (the tubers can weigh up to 30 kg), starch was once prepared as a food, though it was only used during famine times by peasants. In places, it is still cultivated as a source of starch for thickening soup, etc.

The kudzu vine has been used in Chinese herbal medicine since ancient times as a remedy against colds and flu, muscle ache, dysentery, hypertension and migraine. The kudzu vine also contains a compound that reduces the cravings of alcohol addiction. Scientists at Harvard University have investigated extracts of the vine (which has been used in China since 200 AD to suppress the desire for alcohol) and have confirmed its effectiveness. The chemical has been synthesised and is still under trial. It is naturalised in the south-east of the USA, where it was introduced for cattle forage and where it has become a pest. The costs of removing this rampant climber (which runs over entire houses, barns and telephone wires) are enormous, setting a good example for the care needed when introducing alien plants to a new locality.

The Chusan palm, *Trachycarpus fortunei*, was common beneath a woodland canopy of *Cinnamomum camphora*, *Pinus massoniana*, *Photinia serratifolia*, *Quercus dentata* and *Quercus variabilis*, and, alongside the Chinese parasol tree, *Firmiana simplex*, it gave an exotic flavour to the area. Another common woodlander was *Phyllostachys pubescens*, an enormous bamboo that is commonly used for scaffolding purposes in China. Other trees included *Juniperus sabina* var. *chinensis*, the wild Chinese persimmon, *Diospyros kaki* var. *sylvestris*, *Lindera megaphylla* and *Lindera glauca*. The finest and most interesting tree within the reserve had to be *Aesculus wilsonii*, a magnificent horse-chestnut first found in south Wushan by Augustine Henry and later introduced by Ernest Wilson. Beneath Wilson's horse-chestnut, *Alangium chinense* formed thickets.

The Three Gorges Botanical Garden is located near the Xiling Gorge above Yichang, and acts as a satellite of Wuhan Botanical Garden on the eastern plains of Hubei Province.

Liantuo

From the Three Gorges Botanical Garden we made a brief visit to the tiny village of Liantuo, once known as Nanto. This was the village to which Henry often sailed on the *Fairy Raft*, and it was where many fabulous new garden plants, such as *Sarcococca ruscifolia* and *Sarema henryi*, were found. Liantuo is spectacularly located near the terminus of the Xiling Gorge, opposite a massive craggy cliff that soars above the Yangtze and is called 'the Three Swords of Nanto'.

The village itself is overshadowed by another jagged peak to its rear, and it was north of this peak that Henry's native plant collector gathered many of the herbarium specimens that, today, are housed in Kew, Edinburgh, Glasnevin, Harvard, Calcutta and Hong Kong.

It was time to leave this historic place and travel further afield.

Retracing the 1888 route – south of the Yangtze

Sailing the gorges and plant hunting around Yichang was an easy and enjoyable task, but we also needed to venture further afield and follow the trail of Henry's 1888 expedition, thus taking us deep into the remote mountains that lie north and south of the Yangtze. These regions have been little visited by Westerners since the days of Henry and Wilson, and we had scant information on the present state of the area's vegetation. Luckily, we could fall back on the database of Henry's collections from the Three Gorges region, though we knew that many of the forested areas there must have been long since felled. We felt privileged to have been allowed to collect in this part of western Hubei Province; Kew had an interest in the region, but had never gained permits to collect there.

Our previous visit to Changyang, in late October 2002, had been a brief one. We had just completed our travels through the gorges, and it was there that we began the enormous task of dividing thousands of herbarium specimens and seed packs between Glasnevin and Wuhan, a chore that took us into the early hours of the morning.

We returned to Changyang in October 2004, and our route from Yichang brought us past the small town of Gaoyang in a rural mountainous district. The main business of this town appeared to be the production of *penjing*, better known in the West as 'bonsai'. The Chinese art of *penjing* (which means 'potted scenery') has been practiced for more than 2,000 years, and became particularly popular with Taoist monks. Taoism is a religion of nature. Its followers

Spectacular mountainous countryside seen from the summit of Tianthu Shan near Changyang. The silvery plumes of *Miscanthus sinensis* may be seen to the left. The last Western plant hunter to collect in this region before our 2004 visit was E. H. Wilson.

believe that everything in nature, whether a mountain, tree or stream, contains its own spirit and that miniature examples possess it in concentrated form. A contorted, gnarled shape was thought to represent the bodies of those in the world beyond mortality, where they attained great age. Out of these beliefs, the art of *penjing* emerged. A few hundred years after its birth in China, *penjing* became popular in Japan. The Chinese word for a pot plant is *penzai*; the same characters are pronounced '*bonsai*' by the Japanese.[6]

Several different styles were practiced in this little town; some plants were superbly trained as solitary trees, while other containers had entire groves, with large rocks adding beautifully to the miniature landscapes. The examples we saw had been produced by digging old, gnarled, stunted plants from the local mountains. These were then cut hard back and some of the resultant shoots had been trained and retrained for a number of years before being potted into their shallow earthenware and terracotta containers. The most popular subjects used in Gaoyang were *Mahonia bealei*, *Distylium racemosum*, *Adina rubella*, *Ginkgo biloba*, *Ilex pernyi* and a heavily fruited persimmon, *Diospyros*

armata. The latter was discovered by Henry near Liantuo in 1888 and was introduced by Wilson 16 years later. Wilson described it as a very rare tree and knew it from only one or two localities in Hubei.

By riversides, *Pterocarya hupehensis* made 10-m (33-ft) tall trees, and, beside it, we collected seeds from the globular fruiting clusters of *Camptotheca acuminata*; Henry himself had collected this tree in Changyang. *Camptotheca* is known as the 'happy tree' or 'cancer tree'. It is a handsome deciduous tree of rapid growth and can reach about 25 m (82 ft) high, with recorded girths of up to 2 m (6.5 ft). It is found throughout western and central China, though, like Henry's persimmon, Wilson recorded it as being rare in Hubei Province. The genus was discovered by Père Armand David on the Lushan (Mount Lu) range in Jiangxi Province in 1868. In traditional Chinese herbal medicine, the fruits of this species are used to treat patients suffering from cancer of the digestive tract and leukaemia. The active compound, which shows such promise in treating cancer, is camptothecine, and cultivars with higher yields of this compound are being developed. Indigenous to China, it is

110

A *penjing* (literally, 'potted scenery') production area in the small town of Gaoyang. The specimens being trained here are *Adina rubella*, a common shrub found on the banks of the Yangtze and its numerous tributaries.

now commercially grown as a crop plant in India, Japan and the USA. The parts originally used in China were the stem, bark and seeds, but it is now mainly the young leaves, and trees are clipped for repeated harvests. In China, the *xi shu*, or 'happy tree', has also been used for centuries to treat colds and diseases of the spleen, liver, stomach and gall bladder.

Debregeasia longifolia was abundant along the approach road to Changyang, as was *Celastrus angulatus*, a vigorous climber that cascaded its long wiry stems from roadside cliff faces, and, at that stage, its large, yellow, fruiting capsules had split open to reveal bright orange seeds within. From our Changyang collections, a particularly fine form of

Actinidia rubricaulis, with beautifully marbled, purple-brown splashed foliage, was raised at Glasnevir and now grows at her sister garden at Kilmacurragh.

'Gem of gems' was how one of our travelling companions, Assumpta Broomfield, described *Campanumoea javanica* var. *japonica* after finding it in a nearby roadside thicket. This herbaceous climber scrambled its way through surrounding bushes to about 1.5 m (5 ft) high, and carried masses of small, cream-coloured, bell-shaped flowers, each with a purple splash in the throat. Gem of gems, indeed. We collected plenty of seeds and a voucher specimen, and continued our foray for good garden plants.

'Gem of Gems', *Campanumoea javanica* var. *japonica*, an herbaceous climber that was common in thickets along the approach road to Changyang.

Camptotheca acuminata, the 'cancer tree'. The tree's chemical compound, camptothecine, has proved effective in the treatment of leukaemia.

Macleaya cordata, the plume poppy, wild on a cliff face at Changyang. The true plant is rare in cultivation.

In the mountains above Changyang

Changyang is situated on the banks of the Qingjiang (a tributary of the Yangtze), and, on the night of our arrival, we crossed the river in a tiny boat to a restaurant on the opposite side. Changyang is by no means a pretty town, but it did make a lovely picture by night as the lights of the town reflected across the river. Once again, the Glasnevin Central China Expedition made history by being the first Western botanical party to collect plants in Changyang since E. H. Wilson last visited there in 1907. Local forestry officials had arranged for us to visit Tianthu Shan, a reserve in the mountains that was reached after a 40-minute drive. The town itself was a grotty little place and our hosts from Wuhan Botanical Garden were far from impressed with the local hotel arrangements. I wondered if they have ever forgiven me for bringing them to such a godforsaken place.

Changyang was well worth the visit, however. The countryside surrounding the town was stunning, and I will always remember it as one of the most beautiful places I have been to in Hubei Province. We were surprised to see how well its flora had survived despite its relative proximity to Yichang. It took Henry and his men four days to reach Changyang in the spring of 1888; it took us modern travellers less than two hours. Changyang was just as Antwerp Pratt described it. Massive mountain peaks soared above spectacular steep-sided valleys, and the flora was considerably different from that of Yichang.

The original forest cover on Tianthu Shan had been felled several decades earlier, probably during Mao Zedong's 'Great Leap Forward' of the late 1950s and early 1960s, though regeneration had been good and we found this area of secondary forest to be species rich with many fine woodland plants.

Near the base of the mountain, we stumbled upon one of Henry's finest discoveries: *Rhododendron auriculatum*. It grows well in Irish gardens, especially at Kilmacurragh, where Wilson's original 1901 introduction has formed a 10-m (33-ft) tall tree and bears richly scented white flowers with a pink flush. Wilson stated that, in western Hubei, forms of this species occasionally bore rosy-red flowers, and, to my knowledge, this form is not in cultivation. Our collections were made in October, so, obviously, no flower colour was seen, and, since this fine rhododendron takes 10 to 15 years to flower from seed, it will be a long wait to see if our Changyang plants are the rare red form.

With it grew the Chinese tulip tree *Liriodendron chinense*, *Acer davidii*, *Diospyros lotus*, *Taxus chinensis* and *Pinus tabulaeformis*, the Chinese red pine, a beautiful flat-headed tree that is depicted on Willow pattern (or 'Blue Willow') china. *Cornus kousa* var. *chinensis* was abundant on

Glasnevin's plant propagator, Joan Rogers, with *Lilium brownii* in hand. Dozens of seedlings were raised at Glasnevin, Dublin, and these flowered at Kilmacurragh Botanic Gardens in Kilbride, County Wicklow, two years later (below).

Henry's cobra lily, *Arisaema sikokianum* var. *henryanum*, wild on the forest floor at Changyang. There, it grew with a host of other woodlanders.

The fleshy seed capsule of *Zingiber moiga*. The stems of this species are widely used in Chinese cuisine and we regularly had it with our meals while travelling north of the Yangtze.

the steep mountain slopes, and appeared to be a pioneer species that had quickly colonised recently disturbed forest. On Tianthu Shan, it formed perfectly symmetrical trees to 7 m (23 ft) tall, though, much to our disappointment, the fruits had been stripped by birds.

Macleaya cordata, the plume poppy, was also rather common in open glades and at the base of cliffs. On those lonely mountains above Changyang, the large plume-like seed heads made a wonderful rattle when caught on a breeze. The true *Macleaya cordata* is a rare plant in gardens, often being represented by an impostor, *Macleaya* x *kewensis*. Seedlings from our visit to Changyang now grow in the 19th-century Double Borders at Kilmacurragh, and, in autumn, when its stems rattle in the wind, I'm momentarily transported back to the mountains of central China.

On a cliff near the plume poppy, *Crataegus cuneata* formed 60-cm (2-ft) tall shrubs, all laden with fleshy, orange-red berries. Henry called this species the *hou-chua-tzu*. It is also native to Japan and has always remained very rare in cultivation, so we collected a good supply of seeds, which later germinated very well. Another cliff inhabitant was *Rhododendron simsii*, a widespread shrub in China, and it still carried a few salmon-pink flowers at the time of our visit. *Kerria japonica* also grew there, and it was interesting to meet this common spring-flowered shrub in its wild habitat. It has been grown for centuries in Japan, though, despite its specific epithet, it is not native there. Two pretty annual balsams also grew nearby; one with large yellow blossoms, the other pink-purple. Both remain to be keyed out (*Impatiens* are a taxonomic nightmare). We collected a large batch of seeds from both to be grown in the Order Beds in front of Glasnevin's newly restored Great Palm House.

Two species of elder grew in the reserve: the first, *Sambucus williamsii*, made 3-m (10-ft) tall shrubs; the second, *Sambucus chinensis*, was an altogether more refined plant, and, by roadsides on Tianthu Shan, it grew as a low-spreading sub-shrub to about a metre (3.3 ft) tall and carried large, flat corymbs of small, orange fruits. *Sambucus chinensis* is currently used in Chinese herbal medicine as a diuretic and as a painkiller to treat cases of traumatic injury.

In thickets, the arching stems of *Weigelia japonica* var. *sinica* had taken on an autumnal hue of deepest claret, and running though it was *Dioscorea zingiberensis*, a climbing yam discovered by Henry near Yichang in 1885. On the summit of a massive cliff, we found a single plant of the musk lily, *Lilium brownii*, bearing three plump seed capsules. Known as the *peh-ho* in China, where it is much esteemed as a table delicacy, this beautiful lily does not reach more than 1 m (3.3 ft) high and produces two or three large, fragrant, nodding flowers in midsummer.

Woodland plants are very much in vogue at the moment, and the forests on Tianthu Shan contained scores of suitable candidates. I had flowered *Arisaema sikokianum* var. *henryanum*, an astonishing and exquisitely beautiful cobra lily, earlier that summer and so I was delighted to find it in its wild habitat. Nearby grew the closely allied *Arisaema sikokianum* var. *serratum*. Both carried spikes of fleshy red berries containing masses of seeds, which germinated readily and I grow both of these varieties against a north-facing wall near my house in the courtyard at Kilmacurragh.

Changyang proved to be rich in good garden plants. One of these, the annual *Gentiana rubicunda*, was first found by Père Armand David near Baoxing in western Sichuan Province in May 1869. It was later recollected by both Delavay and Henry.

Another exciting find was a yet-to-be-identified variety of *Paris polyphylla* (below).

Cardiocrinum giganteum var. *yunnanense* carried several seed capsules, each containing hundreds of thin, disk-like seeds, though even more exciting was a fruiting plant of *Zingiber mioga*, a hardy ginger that we had met (and eaten) earlier in the mountains to the north of Yichang. A yet-to-be-identified variety of *Paris polyphylla* had set a small cluster of fleshy orange berries, and these were surrounded by a collar of purple-black bracts. *Asparagus cochinchinensis* carried feathery, plume-like growths to 60 cm (2 ft) tall. *Disporum cantoniense*, another beautiful perennial woodlander, was also common beneath the woodland canopy, and carried clusters of pendulous, fleshy, black fruits. *Skimmia japonica* ssp. *reevesiana* completed this sylvan scene, and the small shrubs we met were smothered with crimson-red fruits.

In open sunny glades, several plants of the sky-blue flowered *Aconitum henryi* sprang from cliff faces. *Gentiana rubicunda* grew as a flat prostrate perennial and bore tubular pink-lavender flowers. *Aster brachyphyllus* also tumbled from the cliffs, and carried pendulous sprays of blue, Michaelmas daisy-like blossoms in a double rank along the length of its stems.

Pushing further on and gaining altitude, we continued to climb a steep mountain ridge. The dominant tree on this ridge was *Sassafras tzumu*, and there it formed trees to 15 m (49 ft) high, all with fiery-red autumn colour. Henry stated it was abundant in the woods near Yichang, where it was known as *tzu mu*, hence the specific epithet. The Chinese sassafras was named from specimens collected by Henry's native plant collector in Badong, though it had been discovered by the Irish Chinese Imperial Maritime Customs Service official William Hancock (1847–1914) near Ningbo in eastern Zhejiang Province in May 1877, and was rediscovered, two years later, by Charles Maries in the Yangtze Valley. In *The Trees of Great Britain and Ireland*, Henry stated that Wilson's 1900 introduction had formed handsome, vigorous trees of about 3 m (10 ft) tall

at Veitch's Coombe Wood nursery by 1908.

Prior to the collections made by Hancock, Henry and Maries, *Sassafras* was thought to be monotypic and peculiar to the flora of the eastern USA. A third species, *Sassafras randaiense*, has since been found in Taiwan and is cultivated at Mount Usher Gardens in County Wicklow, Ireland. According to Bretschneider, *Sassafras tzumu* is the *t'ze* tree of the Chinese classics and was much valued by the ancient Chinese for its timber. It is a highly ornamental tree with two-lobed leaves, and the bark on old trees is longitudinally fissured. Copious amounts of yellow flowers appear on the tree in early April, before the leaves unfold, and, in autumn, the foliage turns orange and red. Beneath the Chinese sassafras, we found several bushes of *Salix fargesii* with gorgeous chestnut-brown stems and large red winter buds half hidden by large lance-shaped leaves.

Perhaps our most important find on Tianthu Shan was *Campylotropis macrocarpa*, a low-sprawling shrub of about a metre (3.3 ft) tall. Henry collected this species on a roadside in the Monastery Glen near Moji Shan in June 1886. Seedlings from our Changyang collections were raised at Glasnevin in the spring of 2005, and the shrub proved to be rare in cultivation (and new to Irish gardens). *Campylotropis macrocarpa* flowered for the very first time in Ireland at Kilmacurragh Botanic Gardens in August 2007. The short racemes of pink-lavender, pea-like flowers are handsome, though the silky, fawn-coloured young growth and emerging trifoliate leaves are the main attractions of this rare shrub.

Our visit to Changyang was brief though rewarding. How I wish we had allocated more time to the region, but our itinerary was a busy one. Changyang had been a revelation and I can recommend it to future plant hunters travelling in China.

From Changyang County, our journey continued west to Badong County, which we reached in October 2002 from our base at Yichang.

ABOVE: *Lonicera gynochlamydea* was a common shrub on the roadside cliff faces between Yichang and Badong. There, its stems were decked with masses of spectacular red fruits.

Adventures in Badong

It was late September 2002 when we followed a winding mountain road from our base at Yichang to the town of Badong. Eager to stop and collect whenever and wherever possible, we were delighted to meet a traffic jam midway through our journey, and our team scattered into the surrounding hillsides to see what novelties grew there. The occupants of hundreds of stationary trucks and cars gazed on with mild curiosity as we climbed the roadside cliffs to collect specimens and seeds. *Celastrus orbiculatus* cascaded its long, sinuous stems from the rock faces, and its large seed capsules had split open to reveal scarlet seeds held in the yellow inner lining. *Rosa multiflora* var. *cathayensis* is perhaps the most abundant rose in the Three Gorges region, where its massively rampant branches scramble through even the largest of trees. In gardens, it needs plenty of space and is best grown through trees or allowed to cover a steep bank. Some of our seedlings from the 2002 expedition flowered within three years at Glasnevin, and their arching stems were smothered with small corymbs of large, fragrant, snow-white blossoms.

Schisandra propinqua var. *sinensis* twined its way through a riverside plant of *Salix hypoleuca*, and the plant we saw bore pendulous spikes of yellow fruits, though these are generally red. In gardens, this species is rare and is grown on account of its foliage, which, in good forms, is wonderfully marbled with grey-green splashes. At Glasnevin, dozens of seedlings were raised, and the finest forms were retained to be grown at Kilmacurragh. The evergreen *Clematis uncinata* is a handsome plant with large compound leaves; in Badong, it sprawled its way across the roadside and carried large cymes of silky seed heads. *Clematis argentilucida* was altogether a more boisterous plant and ran rampantly through nearby pine trees.

Not everyone would like to grow *Paederia scandens* var. *tomentosa* in their gardens, though I have to confess I find its small, silvery-white, purple-throated flowers very beautiful, and, in any case, we were also looking out for potential candidates for the Order Beds at Glasnevin. The problem with this strong-growing climber is that every part of it stinks to the high heavens, though its unusual flowers and rich, amber-orange autumn colour more than compensate for this. *Lespedeza davidii*, a 1.5-m (5-ft) tall shrub, was also common there, and carried dense clusters of small, rosy-pink and white, pea-like flowers above its small trifoliate leaves.

Stunted bushes of *Lonicera gynochlamydea* sprang from the cliffs and were absolutely laden with masses of translucent red fruits. Discovered by Henry's Badong collector, it has always been very rare in gardens. Back in Ireland, plants from this seed collection grow with great vigour, and, in May, it is a pretty sight when branches are wreathed in small, white, pink-tinged blossoms, which are carried in pairs in the leaf axils. With it grew *Cotoneaster gracilis*, a small upright bush bearing wine-red fruits.

Other cliff inhabitants along this stretch of road included *Calamagrostis pseudophragmites*, a handsome clump-forming grass with dense, bold, flower spikes, *Thalictrum laxum* and *Swertia punicea*, an annual to 80 cm (31 in.) with black, star-like flowers. *Philadelphus sericanthus* also grew nearby, inviting a dangerous scramble to collect seeds, and

The sacred bamboo, *Nandina domestica*, grows wild in the Three Gorges region and, according to Henry, it was cultivated in temple gardens at Yichang in the late 19th century.

through it scrambled a wild vine, *Vitis quinquangularis*. The latter was one of the finest climbers we brought back from our travels, on account of the leaf undersides, which are covered in a dense, vividly-white felt, and, in autumn, it bears 15-cm (6-in.) long bunches of blue, grape-like fruits.

In more hospitable areas, and by the edge of woods, grew the Chinese weeping cypress, *Cupressus funebris*, a handsome tree to 20 m (66 ft) tall, though the trees we saw were no more than 10 m (33 ft) high. It was first noticed by members of Lord Macartney's embassy to China, in 1793, in the Vale of the Tombs, where it was planted around graves, and was introduced by Robert Fortune in 1849. Henry stated this tree was planted around shrines and temples in the Three Gorges region, and it provided a home to Reeve's pheasant, one of the most beautiful birds from the Yichang area. It is not completely hardy in cultivation and the largest specimen in Britain and Ireland grows at Kilmacurragh Botanic Gardens.

Common in roadside thickets was the loquat, *Eriobotrya japonica*, and the Chinese vegetable tallow tree, *Sapium sebiferum*, which was by then assuming autumnal shades of amber and gold. Other notable plants in this area included *Callicarpa*

bodinieri var. *giraldii*, then smothered in pale violet fruit, and the *t'ien chu* (or 'heavenly bamboo') *Nandina domestica*, an evergreen unbranched shrub to 2 m (6.5 ft) and bearing doubly and trebly pinnate leaves to 45 cm (1.5 ft) long, which are red on emergence. The small white flowers are borne in large erect panicles, and these are followed, in autumn, by dense clusters of bright red fruits. Native to central China, it has been cultivated in Japan for centuries, from where it was introduced in 1804.

Eupatorium chinensis was one of the most beautiful perennials that grew along the roadside and at the edge of woods and thickets. A perfect candidate for any herbaceous border, it has a stiff upright habit to about 1.5 m (5 ft) and bears loose corymbs of white, pink-tinged flowers on purple stems. It grew in colourful mix with *Ptheirospermum japonicum* and *Caesalpinia decapetala*, a thorny, climbing shrub to 3 m (10 ft) tall with billowing masses of bold pinnate foliage and racemes of striking yellow and red-spotted exotic-looking blossoms.

Our most important collection during this brief stop was *Hypericum longistylum*, a low-growing, dome-shaped bush with, as its name implies, long, whiskery, well-developed styles. Discovered by Henry near Yichang in 1885, the seeds we collected that day allowed its introduction to Western cultivation.

117

OPPOSITE: *Emmenopterys henryi*, a 250-year-old specimen – and one of only two remaining trees in Badong County, the type locality where Henry found it in 1887.

Emmenopterys henryi retains an extended season of interest long after its pyramidal clusters of large, white flowers wither and fade. The pink-tinged, wing-like bracts attached to the seed capsules give the tree the appearance of still being in flower when seen from a distance.

Rare trees in the mountains above Badong

The town of Badong was a fairly dull, soulless place. At the time of our arrival, much of the lower-lying parts had been torn down and a new city was being built 3 km (2 miles) upriver. The old town has, by now, disappeared and lies in a watery grave.

The following morning, we were given a noisy police escort into the mountainous countryside. Our party raised much attention as we left the city with police sirens roaring. It later emerged we were being interviewed by representatives from Badong television and our pursuits made primetime news that night!

The city officials had heard of our plan to retrace Henry's route through their territory (Badong is a county town, also known as Xinling Zhen) and were amazingly helpful during our visit to the region. We were brought high into the mountains to see a remarkable 250-year-old tree of *Emmenopterys henryi*. Once common in Hubei and Sichuan, it is now one of the rarest components of the flora of those provinces. The old tree we saw was about 15 m (49 ft) tall with a girth of 2.8 m (9 ft). Despite a large hollow to the left-hand side of the trunk, the tree still showed vigour and its spreading branches were laden with large, flat corymbs. These corymbs carried up to 50 seed capsules. Attached to these were large, pink-tinged, wing-like bracts that obviously serve as parachutes to aid seed distribution. Though flowering had long since finished, these persistent bracts gave the impression that the tree was in full bloom.

Ernest Wilson described *Emmenopterys* as one of the most strikingly beautiful trees of the Chinese forests, stating that it was known colloquially in Hubei and Sichuan as *hsiang-kou-shu* and that it was common in moist forests. Badong is the type locality for *Emmenopterys*, and, in all of Badong County, only two trees remain. Having read of the enormous tracts of virgin forest in the mountains above Badong in Henry's field notes at Kew, I had rather foolishly expected much of this to remain; the hills had been mercilessly stripped of those great forests, and only occasional relicts, such as the *Emmenopterys*,

remained. The immense forests that Henry wrote of a century before have long since been cleared for agriculture, and the low germination rate of *Emmenopterys* seeds limits its ability to recolonise cleared areas.[7] Because of their great rarity, the two remaining trees at Badong are under the protection of the Badong County Deputy (perhaps this was the reason for our police escort), though we were allowed to collect seeds and herbarium specimens. There have been few reintroductions of *Emmenopterys* from the wild, and we were pleased to have seeds to bring back to Ireland.

Sargentodoxa cuneata sprawling its way through young trees of *Quercus fabri*. We met this vine in 2002 at Badong, and again, in 2004, at Changyang. Much to our frustration, seeds were not visible on either occasion.

Grace Pasley, Matthew Jebb and Helen Dillon are pictured here with their Chinese counterparts pressing herbarium specimens on the road between Yichang and Badong in October 2002.

Another great rarity that grew in thickets nearby was Sargent's glory vine, *Sargentodoxa cuneata*. In the wilds of Badong, its vigorous stems clambered through young trees of *Quercus fabri*. The autumn colour on these vines was magnificent. Its large trifoliate leaves had turned deep claret, and, although we could find no fruits, we were able to collect several good herbarium specimens that now lie alongside Henry's original specimen in the National Herbarium at Glasnevin. Its stems are an important component of Chinese herbal medicine, and, earlier on the trip, we had purchased its dried stems from a vendor of herbal medicines on the lower slopes of Emei Shan.

Other good climbers in this area included the beautifully scented *Clematis urophylla*, *Lonicera henryi*, *Tetrastigma hemsleyanum*, *Vitis sinocinerea*, *Schisandra sphenanthera* and the climbing gentian *Tripterospermum discoideum*, a really

beautiful perennial to about 1.5 m (5 ft) tall, bearing pendant, violet-blue, bell-shaped flowers in the axils of its leaves. We found *Celastrus hindsii* only once. According to Augustine Henry, the fruits of this rampant climber were eaten by wild antelopes in the Three Gorges region. *Actinidia chinensis* sprawled its way through surrounding trees, and, to our delight, the vines we found were covered in fruits. Ernest Wilson stated that these were known throughout the Yangtze valley as 'the Ichang gooseberry', and he introduced it to cultivation in 1900. Seedlings raised from our Badong collections grow in the new Chinese garden at Kilmacurragh, where they are being trained into mature oaks. Hopefully, there will be both male and female clones among these young plants to ensure a good crop of juicy Chinese gooseberries.

Early October had brought rich autumn colour to many trees and shrubs on those mountains. The foliage of *Pyrus pyrifolia* had assumed fiery scarlet tints and trees carried masses of small, rounded, brown fruits. The Chinese varnish tree, *Rhus verniciflua*, also grew there, and the 'v'-shaped incisions on its trunk indicated that sap had been extracted earlier that summer. The large pinnate leaves of the 'wax tree', *Rhus succedanea*, had, by then, turned a glowing red. This deciduous tree was once cultivated in Japan for vegetable wax, or tallow, which was extracted from the fruits to make candles until it was replaced by American and Russian petroleum.

Another fine fruiting tree on the hills above Badong was *Diospyros lotus*, a hardy persimmon whose orange-shaped fruits ripen to yellow before finally becoming a bloomy purplish-black. Other trees on the hillsides included the Chinese chestnut, *Castanea mollissima*, *Alnus trabeculosa*, *Cunninghamia lanceolata* and *Tetradium ruticarpum*, a small tree of about 3 m (10 ft) tall with large pinnate leaves and enormous corymbs of red and black, highly aromatic fruits. In China, where most plants have a use in herbal medicine, these fruits are used as a drug to alleviate pain and to stop vomiting.

It was on the mountains above Badong that Henry's native plant collector found *Populus lasiocarpa* in 1887, so we were delighted to encounter several trees on a very cold, mist-shrouded mountain slope where it formed medium-sized trees with a broad pyramidal crown. To my mind, this is the most ornamental of all the cottonwoods. The broad heart-shaped leaves can be as much as 30 cm (12 in.) long,

The author, collecting specimens from a thicket in Badong. The large, parasol-shaped bush in the top right-hand corner of the photograph is *Aralia echinocaulis*. In the background, packing a herbarium press, is Noeleen Smyth. Shortly after this photograph was taken, we gathered seeds of this new, viciously armed *Aralia*, thereby introducing it to cultivation.

and it is best grown as an isolated specimen on a lawn, thus, unhindered by other competing trees, it can assume its broad, pyramidal habit. Augustine Henry knew it as the *ta-yeh-p'ao*, and observed that ladles were made from its timber.

Lindera communis, another of Henry's many discoveries, formed small evergreen trees and carried blackish-purple fruits. According to Wilson, it abounded on the cliffs and in the gorges near Yichang, and, in the late 19th century, its branches and leaves were cut and thoroughly tied into bundles. They were then pounded into a powder in a stamping mill driven by hydro power, and the powder was then treated with a glutinous rice-water to make it adhesive, and, finally, made into incense sticks. These sticks, which were known to foreigners as 'joss-sticks', were used in enormous quantities at religious ceremonies.

Of the hollies, one of the most beautiful we saw was *Ilex pedunculosa*. In this part of rural Badong, where native forests faced repeated felling, it grew to no more than 3 m (10 ft), though it is capable of much more. It is a handsome evergreen with glossy, wavy-edged leaves and bright red fruits. New to cultivation was *Aralia echinocaulis*, a 5-m (16-ft) tall tree with enormous bipinnate leaves and huge panicles of glossy black fruits. Every last part of this new *Aralia*

Decaisnea fargesii. Around Badong, it formed large, gangly shrubs, draped with large clusters of blue, bean-like pods. It is a common shrub in the damp woods of western Hubei, Sichuan and parts of Yunnan provinces.

Pyracantha creno-serrata, a common firethorn in central China. On dry, rocky, sun-baked slopes around Badong, it was abundant; there, its branches were weighed down by small, orange, pear-shaped fruits.

Spiraea japonica var. *fortunei* flowering in the Chinese garden at Glasnevin. This plant was raised from our 2002 collections from the mountains above Badong.

is heavily armed with vicious spines, and it has attracted much attention and admiration since its introduction from Badong.

Stachyurus are a much-neglected group of spring-flowered shrubs. I can never understand why a plant that puts on such a marvellous display at this bleak time of year should be so under utilised. Flowering before the emergence of foliage, the small yellow blossoms are held in tightly packed pendulous racemes. The great English plantsman E. A. Bowles (1865–1954) very aptly compared the catkin-like flowers to 'pretty hanging tails like threaded cowslips'. At Badong, we met with the unaccountably rare *Stachyurus yunnanensis* (syn. *S. oblongifolius*), a 3-m (10-ft) tall, wide-spreading shrub that grew in a shallow ravine and carried short clusters of seeds in the axils of leaves. With it grew *Decaisnea fargesii*, a large upright shrub to 7 m (23 ft) bearing long, blue, broad bean-like seedpods.

Augustine Henry made his collections of the 'rice-paper plant', *Tetrapanax papyrifera*, in Badong – as did our group 117 years later. In China, this bold foliage plant is called the *t'ung-ts'ao*, which literally means 'facilitates urination', giving a clue to its use in traditional herbal medicine. The stems of *Tetrapanax* are filled with a white pith once used in the production of rice paper, which was widely used by Chinese artists.

Another good garden shrub in this ravine was *Coriaria sinica*, a medium-sized shrub with beautifully arching branches on which short racemes of tiny red flowers are borne on naked wood in early spring. Seedlings raised from our Badong collections flowered just two years later and have grown with great vigour at Glasnevin and in the Chinese Garden at Kilmacurragh. *Spiraea japonica* var. *fortunei* formed low, mound-shaped bushes and, even at that late stage, plants still carried flat corymbs of small pink blossoms.

Viburnum betulifolium giving a spectacular show at Badong. Discovered in Gansu Province by the Russian explorer Grigori Nikolaevich Potanin on 10 July 1885, this species was introduced to cultivation by E. H. Wilson in 1901.

Pyracantha crenato-serrata (now *P. fortuneana*) was common on rock outcrops at the edge of cultivated areas, where it formed upright evergreen bushes of about 2 m (6.5 ft) high and carried tightly packed clusters of bright red berries. This popular firethorn was first found by Thomas Watters near Yichang in the spring of 1879, and was introduced by the French missionary Père Ducloux (1865–1945) through Maurice de Vilmorin's garden at des Barres, near Paris, in 1906. In England, some plants derive from seeds collected by Reginald Farrer in Gansu Province in 1914. It is a useful winter-interest plant since birds do not seem to be attracted to its fruits, and our Badong plants form an effective hedge to the rear of my house at Kilmacurragh.

Rhamnus hemsleyanus, a densely branched shrub of 4 m (13 ft), carried masses of dull black berries clustered along its stems. It was first found by Henry in nearby Jianshi in May 1888, and Wilson later collected it on Emei Shan and at Baoxing in western Sichuan Province. Other good berrying shrubs included *Ilex pernyi*, *Stranvaesia davidiana*, *Rhamnus leptophyllus*, *Photinia villosa* var. *sinica*, *Viburnum oliganthum* and *Cotoneaster dielsianus*, whose long, arching branches were draped with small, scarlet, pear-shaped fruits. The best of these 'berried

treasures', however, had to be *Viburnum betutifolium*, a common species in western and central China, where it forms one of the most glorious sights in autumn. In thickets and on the fringes of woods around Badong, the plants have

Noeleen Smyth gets to grips with ever-mounting herbarium specimens in Badong County as local children look on. Our work generated much attention in these rural parts.

Common plants at Badong. CLOCKWISE: *Rubus henryi* var. *bambusarum* (seen here scrambling through a fence at Glasnevin); *Lysimachia barystachys*, an altogether better plant than the similar and more widely grown *Lysimachia clethroides*, *Clerodendrum trichotomum*, the blue fruits of which are surrounded by a persistent crimson calyx; *Aconitum carmichaelii* commemorates Dr J. R. Carmichael of the London Mission Society. According to Augustine Henry, large quantities of the tuberous roots of this monk's-hood were shipped down the gorges and used medicinally.

saw were weighed down with heavy clusters of bright red, translucent berries. In China, the bark fibre of this magnificent shrub is used to make ropes and paper.

Several different species of *Rubus* grew on the hills above Badong. One of the most admirable was *Rubus pacificus*, an evergreen scandent shrub of about a metre (3.3 ft) tall with bold, heart-shaped foliage and delicious yellow fruits carried along its slim, gracefully arching branches. Even better again was *Rubus henryi* var. *bambusarum*, whose long scandent stems ran across large boulders and into nearby trees. It is one of the commonest brambles in the Three Gorges region, and is one of the most ornamental. Unlike the type, i.e. *Rubus henryi*, whose leaves are three-lobed, the foliage of *Rubus henryi* var. *bambusarum* consists of three very narrow, lance-shaped leaflets, and these are plastered with a fine white felt on the underside.

The viciously armed *Zanthoxylum armatum* (syn. *Z. planispinum*) also grew in this area and formed a wide spreading bush of about 4 m (13 ft). Henry knew it as the *kou hua chiao* and stated that it was common on the plains in hedges, and that it was very often planted on graves. In my estimation, this is the finest of all the hardy zanthoxylums, and, at Kilmacurragh, it retains its foliage right up to the end of January. It is for its exotic-looking pinnate leaves that this species is generally grown. These are composed of five stalkless leaflets and the main petiole carries a broad conspicuous wing along its length. The leaflets increase in size towards the end of the leaf; the terminal one is up to twice as long as the others, and all leaflets bear large, pinkish-red pairs of spines on the upper- and undersides. In autumn, it carries great clusters of small red fruits. Native to much of East Asia, in Nepal, toothbrushes are made from the branches of this shrub and the fruits are used to relieve toothache and to stupefy fish.

Ferns were common in shaded gullies and on the edge of woods. *Matteuccia orientalis* was one of the most handsome of these and carried its fronds in the typical shuttlecock fashion. The five-fingered maidenhair fern, *Adiantum pedatum*, is common over much of East Asia and North America and is popular in European gardens on account of its gracefully curving, circular fronds that carry finely dissected foliage on finger-like stems to one side of the rachis. Enjoying the same conditions were perennials such as *Epimedium saggittatum* (mentioned in Chinese herbals as an aphrodisiac for sheep!), *Aconitum carmichaelii*, *Changium smyrnioides*, *Hosta ventricosa*, *Houttuynia cordata* and *Lysimachia barystachys*. The latter is a fine garden plant, similar to the more widely grown *L. clethroides*, though it is taller growing and bears longer flower spikes that bloom over a far longer period.

Magnolia officinalis, the *hon-po*, was commonly cultivated around hamlets and villages near Yesanguan Town.

Yesanguan and Langping

From the hills above Badong town, we travelled further south towards Yesanguan, a small town near Jianshi where Augustine Henry made many remarkable finds in May 1888. Yesanguan lay deep in one of the most rural mountainous districts of south Badong County, though its flora, too, had been seriously plundered and all that remained were occasional copses of secondary vegetation and roadside thickets.

These, however, still harboured many interesting plants and the area was certainly worth a visit. Vegetation also still clung to mountain summits and to exposed ridges, and it was on a steep ridge between Yesanguan and Langping (in Changyang County) that we found the extremely rare *Sorbus wilsoniana*, an 8-m (26-ft) tall tree with large, red, sticky buds and rounded clusters of small orange-red fruits. First found by Henry, Wilson collected this fine rowan in Badong in May 1901, and found it again in 1907 near Yichang and in woods near Changyang. He introduced it to cultivation through Ellen Willmott's garden at Warley Place (now a nature reserve) soon afterwards, though that tree died without being propagated and it was not reintroduced to Western gardens until 1985, when seeds were obtained from

ABOVE: The Chinese blackberry lily, *Belamcanda chinensis*. Its rhizomes are used in traditional Chinese herbal medicine to treat throat disorders.

Hunan Province through the Shanghai Botanical Garden annual seed list.[8] Trees now in English gardens all derive from this source, and our collections, the first to be gathered in Badong since Wilson collected it there just over a century previously, now grow in the arboretum at Kilmacurragh. Wilson's rowan is closely allied to *Sorbus sargentiana* from western Sichuan Province, though the latter is perhaps better regarded as a subspecies of it. *Sorbus keissleri* also grew on the same ridge, and there it formed a 9-m (30-ft) tall tree sporting clusters of green, orange-shaped fruits. This handsome whitebeam was found by Henry in south Wushan, and was introduced by Wilson from Sichuan in 1904. It was reintroduced from Yunnan Province by George Forrest in 1931.

Other trees on this ridge included *Carpinus fargesiana*, *Clethra delavayi*, *Myrsine semiserrata*, *Pterocarya stenoptera* and *Cornus macrophylla*. The latter is found scattered across the Himalaya and much of China and Japan. By villages, *Magnolia officinalis* was cultivated for its medicinal bark, and, by the roadside, enormous piles of *tu-chung*, the bark of *Eucommia ulmoides* awaited transportation down the Yangtze. *Celastrus glaucophyllus* was a common climber around Yesanguan, where it scrambled through the trees to 15 m (49 ft) overhead. Discovered by Augustine Henry in Mengzi County, Yunnan Province, in 1896, it was rediscovered by Ernest Wilson on Emei Shan in May 1904 and was introduced by him from nearby Baoxing County, in western Sichuan Province, in October 1908.

Beneath the woodland canopy grew numerous shade-loving perennials – and two interesting parasites. The first of these, *Xylanche himalaica*, was known only from the Himalayan region until it was found on the summit of Emei Shan by Ernst Faber in 1887. It was later re-collected in the mountains above Fang by Henry in the autumn of 1888. The plant we found carried a 20-cm (8-in.) tall spike of pinkish-white flowers and was completely lacking in green colouration. In its native habitat, the host plant for this species is *Rhododendron*. The second parasite, *Monotropa uniflora*, was a plant of similar stature and was also devoid of any green tissue. This curious little perennial carries a single, nodding, pink blossom at the end of its short stems, though, by the time of our visit, this had long since faded and the plant had set prodigious quantities of seeds.

In more open sunny situations, we found the blackberry lily, *Belamcanda chinensis*, an iris relative with long, strap-like leaves. At the end of slim zigzag stems, this colourful, though short-lived, perennial carries salmon-coloured blossoms that are heavily splashed with orange-red blotches. On maturity, the seedpods split open to reveal beautiful clusters of jet-black seeds, hence the common name.

Another fine woodlander was *Polygonatum cyrtonema*. This species was based on material gathered by Père Farges in Sichuan Province in 1892, though it had been found by Henry near Yichang in the spring of 1887. It grew alongside *Angelica polymorpha*, *Cardiocrinum giganteum* var. *yunnanense*, *Lysimachia clethroides*, *Ophiopogon japonicus*, *Tiarella polyphylla* and *Tricyrtis maculata*.

Giant ginkgoes at Bai Sha

Not far from Yesanguan lies the tiny village of Bai Sha, a charming clutter of mud-built, two-storey farmhouses and outhouses full of oxen, fowl and pigs. Our purpose in travelling to Bai Sha was to see a venerable 1,000-year-old maidenhair tree, *Ginkgo biloba*. The ginkgo grew on limestone pavement – similar to the Burren in County Clare, Ireland – and was surrounded, on one side, by houses and, to the rear, by maize fields. The tree stood more than 30 m (100 ft) tall and its main trunk had half decayed, though the tree still showed signs of vigour and had produced several other trunks from lignotubers either side of the original trunk. We were told it produced 250 kg (550 lbs) of fruit each year. The maidenhair tree is known as *peh-k'o* in China, where its seeds, after being roasted, are esteemed as a dessert nut or are added to stews.

Gardeners and dendrologists the world over owe much to religious orders for the introduction and preservation of many trees. In China, where every available patch of land is devoted to agriculture, a vast number of trees would have become extinct long ago were it not for the efforts of Buddhist and Taoist priests. The most noteworthy example of this benevolent preservation is the maidenhair tree.

Ginkgo is a relict of a very ancient flora, and was once common across Europe and North America. Fossil remains dating from the Jurassic period have been found in these regions, and it was during the Cretaceous period that the maidenhair tree reached its maximum diversity of at least 11 species. Due to geological cataclysms, only one species was left (*Ginkgo adiantoides*) in the Tertiary period, and it was as recent as 2.5 million years ago that *Ginkgo* disappeared from the European fossil record. Trees are now extremely rare in the wild and the maidenhair tree is listed in the International Union for Conservation of Nature and Natural Resources (IUCN) Red List of endangered plants. *Ginkgo biloba* can live for as long as 3,500 years, and trees are amazingly tough and adaptable. Having evolved before leaf-eating insects, the tree is never damaged by them, and, in August 1945, when an atomic bomb was dropped on Hiroshima, maidenhair trees growing near the epicentre rebudded after the blast, without any major deformation, while adjacent temples were blown away.

An old farmer at Bai Sha, resting by his mud-built house. We were given a great welcome by the villagers.

Paleobotanists believed the maidenhair tree to be extinct for millions of years, until trees were found in Japan by Engelbert Kaempfer (1651–1716) in 1691. The maidenhair tree had been brought from China thousands of years

Bai Sha, a traditional farming village in rural Badong. The maize crop had been harvested at the time of our visit.

The maize crop had been harvested prior to our visit, and cobs were being cleaned for winter storage. Maize is a major crop in the higher valleys of the Three Gorges region.

Late autumn at Bai Sha in Badong County. The little village lies high above the Three Gorges and will be unaffected by flooding.

before, and had been cultivated around Buddhist temples. From Japan, it was introduced to European gardens in 1730. At the Royal Botanic Gardens, Kew, a tree planted in 1762 still flourishes, though *Ginkgo biloba* is generally short lived in Western cultivation, when compared to the ancient giants of its homeland. Female trees are rare in gardens, probably as a result of their rather repulsive smelling fruits, though an effort should be made to seek them out.

Whether the maidenhair tree still exists truly wild in China is a matter of debate. Some experts believe it does grow wild in two small mountainous areas on the border of Zhejiang and Anhui provinces and in Hubei, Sichuan and Guizhou provinces. The maidenhair tree is thought to be more closely related to the cycads than to true conifers, since ginkgoes and cycads are the only living, seed-producing plants that have motile, or free-swimming, sperm. Green algae also form an endosymbiotic relationship with cells in the ginkgo embryo, and the endosperm is uniquely photosynthetic. *Ginkgo biloba* is the sole living link between the lower and higher plants, between ferns and conifers.

Ginkgoes have a relatively primitive vascular system and the bilobed leaves exhibit dichotomous venation (the veins

Old trees of *Ginkgo biloba* can carry hundreds of kilos of fruit. We raised several seedlings from this tree.

Ginkgo biloba, a 1,000-year-old tree at Bai Sha. Whether these trees are wild or relicts of cultivation is a matter of great debate.

continuously divide into twos, a feature unique to the maidenhair tree. Extract of ginkgo shows promising results in treating Alzheimer's disease, and the tree has played a crucial role in Chinese herbal medicine for centuries. Studies have shown that good extracts will improve blood circulation and memory, prevent blood clotting, benefit asthma, coughs, bladder irritability, blennorrhoea and chilblains. The tree is dioecious, and male trees usually assume a slim, columnar habit while female trees generally have wide-spreading crowns. Seedlings raised from the ancient giants at Bai Sha have been planted out into their permanent positions on the 'Fossil Lawn' at Kilmacurragh, where they nestle with wollemi pines, monkey-puzzles,

dawn redwoods and other living fossils.

We were led through fields to another younger, yet more spectacular maidenhair tree. Along the way, we stopped to collect seeds from a particularly handsome specimen of the Chusan palm, *Trachycarpus fortunei*. While seed collecting was an easy procedure, making a pressed herbarium specimen was another matter, though, after much reducing, we managed to press a fairly respectable example. Sprawling its way across the ground near the Chusan palm was *Clematis lasiandra*, which bore small, slatey-purple, bell-shaped blossoms in axillary cymes. In thickets at the edge of maize fields, we found the spine-covered *Paliurus hemsleyanus*, and it grew alongside *Koelreuteria paniculata* and *Quercus variabilis.* The latter is a common oak at low altitudes in Hubei and in southern Yunnan, and was introduced to Western gardens by Robert Fortune from Beijing in 1861. In Hubei, its tough, durable wood was once much esteemed for boat building. The cups of the acorns were used to dye silk yarn black and the bark of the tree was used by peasants to roof their houses. Young saplings were felled by mountain farmers, and, on them, they cultivated the edible fungus, *Himeola polytricha.* It is a handsome oak with large chestnut-like leaves and beautiful corky bark.

The second ginkgo made a breathtaking sight. The rest of our group had made it to the tree before us, and, from our vantage point on the brow of a low hill, they pretty much put this 800-year-old giant into scale. It was a better specimen than the first, 1,000-year-old tree, and slightly taller, probably about 35 m (115 ft), and its butter-yellow autumnal foliage was further enhanced by the low glow of early October sunlight.

Beneath that venerable ginkgo, we met an old farmer whose family, generation after generation, have been this tree's dynastic guardians. It was hard to imagine that one family could till the same patch of land for such a lengthy period, never mind protect a tree from birth to old age over eight centuries. We were humbled. The farmer was a nice old fellow and we got on well. I envied his idyllic home in this remote corner of western Hubei, far from the hustle and bustle of modern life and the worries that go with it. I wondered had he even heard of the giant dam on the Yangtze, but then those high hills will never be affected by the river's rising waters.

Before we left, he dug me some tubers of *Amorphophallus rivieri* that he grew between rows of maize beside the old ginkgo tree. *Amorphophallus* is commonly cultivated in Hubei and Sichuan provinces, from where its edible tubers are exported to Japan. That same tuber flowered in the Alpine House at Glasnevin the following

Members of the 2002 Glasnevin Central China Expedition in the bole of Bai Sha's ancient *Ginkgo biloba*. Back row, left to right: Matthew Jebb, Grace Pasley, Paul Maher, Jimi Blake, Professor Ding Zhaohua (Wuhan Botanical Gardens), Seamus O'Brien (author, expedition leader). Front row: Assumpta Broomfield, Noeleen Smyth and Helen Dillon.

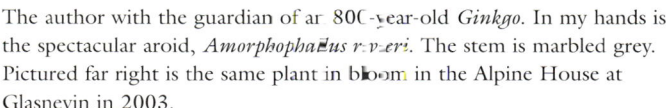

The author with the guardian of an 800-year-old *Ginkgo*. In my hands is the spectacular aroid, *Amorphophallus riveri*. The stem is marbled grey. Pictured far right is the same plant in bloom in the Alpine House at Glasnevin in 2003.

summer, and its large, deep-purple flower spathe received much attention from visitors. 'Devil's tongue' is one of its common names, and, having seen its exotic flower, one can see why this sinister-looking bloom deserves such a moniker.

A small distance from the village, we climbed a rather dry hillside, which seemed bereft of any interesting plants – until we found weedy clumps of the yellow-flowered *Chrysanthemum indicum*. It is hard to believe that this humble little plant is the ancestor of the florist's chrysanthemum, and it made a curious and interesting find.

We were sorry to leave Bai Sha. Like many other villages we passed through, we were given the very warmest of welcomes. Our travels south of the Yangtze were completed, though, and it was time to return to Wuhan Botanical Garden to sign agreements and divide herbarium specimens and seeds between the Chinese and Irish teams.

Water gardening at Wuhan. Trees of *Taxodium distichum* var. *imbricatum* stand with their feet in a shallow lake surrounded by various species of *Nymphaea*.

Back to Wuhan Botanical Garden

China now has more than 100 botanic gardens, all of which are involved in the conservation and preservation of the nation's rich floral diversity. One of the most important of these is Wuhan Botanical Garden, which is located in a beautiful lakeside setting on the edge of China's fifth largest city and the capital of Hubei Province. Situated in the heart of China at the confluence of the Han and Yangtze rivers, Wuhan is a conglomeration of what were once the independent cities of Hankou, Hanyang and Wuchang. Hankou was barely a village until the Treaty of Nanking (1842) opened it to foreign trade, and, with the construction of a railway line from Beijing in the 1920s, it became the first major industrial centre in the interior of China. Today, with a population of more than three million, the city of Wuhan is an important terminal for Yangtze ferries travelling between Chongqing and Shanghai.

China's first botanic gardens were established in the early 20th century. The Chinese Academy of Sciences is responsible for the management of 12 of China's leading botanic gardens. These lie in varying climatic extremes and cover a land area of more than 3,000 ha (7,413 acres). Wuhan Botanical Garden was founded in 1956, and, half a century later, it maintains a collection of more than 7,000 species in an area of some 70 ha (173 acres). As part of the garden's expansion policy, it is due to double in size by 2012. Within the collection is the world's largest genetic pool of *Actinidia* species and cultivars and East Asia's most comprehensive collection of aquatic plants. Wuhan has two satellite gardens: the Three Gorges Botanical Garden near Yichang and the Rare and Endangered Plant Transition Site in Huangpi District.[9] Wuhan is a major research garden with an extensive library and herbarium. In the herbarium, we were able to inspect specimens from the 1980 Sino-American Expedition, the last major botanical expedition to the Three Gorges region involving a Western team before the arrival of our parties in 2002 and 2004.

Water gardening is big at Wuhan. More than 4 ha (10 acres) of man-made rivers and ponds host more than 160 sacred lotus (*Nelumbo nucifera*) cultivars, including Wuhan's own *Nelumbo* 'Ogha', a hybrid bred in the gardens in 1965 by crossing *Nelumbo* 'Chinese Ancient', which had been raised from

A lake and pavilion at Wuhan Botanical Garden. Wuhan cultivates the largest collection of aquatic plants in Asia.

Wuhan Botanical Garden on the eastern plains of Hubei Province. The gardens are administered by the Chinese Academy of Sciences.

The Fujian cypress, *Fokienia hodginsii*, a rare conifer from south-east China. This genus was first described by Augustine Henry and H. H. Thomas in 1911.

Chinese seed unearthed when it was 1,000 years old, with 'Ohga' grown from 2,000-year-old seed unearthed in Japan.

Medicinal plants have played a crucial role in China since ancient times, and the medicinal garden at Wuhan contained many familiar plants and introduced to us their roles in traditional Chinese medicine. More than 800 species are cultivated on a 2.5-ha (6-acre) plot, making it one of the largest medicinal gardens in China. In the centre of this area is a statue of the famous Chinese herbalist, Li Shizen (1518–93).

The most fascinating area to explore was the rare and endangered plant section, where we were introduced to many unfamiliar trees. More than 130 protected species are grown there, and one of the most intriguing of these was *Sinojackia xylocarpa*, a small deciduous tree related to *Styrax*. *Sinojackia* was described by the famous Chinese botanist Dr H. H. Hu in 1925 from a single tree found near Nanjing (Jiangsu Province). A short time afterwards, the same tree was felled to make way for a new road, and, for a while, it was thought the genus had become extinct until a new colony was discovered on the Pukow Hills on the opposite side of the Yangtze River from Nanjing.

Magnolia ernestii is restricted to the mountainous areas of the Hubei–Sichuan border, and uncontrolled logging and habitat clearance have caused a considerable decline in wild populations. Southern China is the world centre of diversity and distribution of *Magnolia* species, many of which are threatened because of exploitation and habitat destruction. The magnolia family is of exceptional evolutionary interest, and, like the maidenhair tree, it is part of China's relict flora. Magnolias occurred throughout the northern hemisphere in the late Cretaceous and Tertiary periods, and, today, it has a disjunct distribution in Asia, from eastern India to New Guinea, and in the Americas, from eastern North America to Brazil.[10]

Other threatened species included *Zenia insignis* and *Eurycormbus cavaleriei*, both monotypic genera that are endemic to China. *Ormosia henryi*, a small tree that even Ernest Wilson stated was rare in Hubei Province in the early 20th century, has had its population further reduced. In Henry's day, it grew around Yichang, but massive demand for its light yellow wood, so popular for carving, has led to its near extinction. Plants well known in European gardens and represented here included *Cercidophyllum japonicum* var. *sinense*, *Davidia involucrata* and *Liriodendron chinense*.

The garden is not just a functional one; it has many attractive ornamental features, including glasshouse displays, a tree peony garden with more than 200 cultivars, a shaded fern garden and an extensive bamboo garden. In the arboretum are good specimens of the rare pine relative, *Cathaya argyrophylla*, *Glyptostrobus pensilis*, *Fokienia hodginsii* and *Cephalotaxus oliveri*. Most remarkable of all, however, were the many submerged groves of *Taxodium distichum* var. *imbricatum* that formed small forests in the middle of a shallow lake.

North of the Yangtze – Shennongjia Biosphere Reserve
Located in north-west Hubei Province, Shennongjia Forest District is the last remaining area of primeval forest in central China. The reserve was created, in 1970, from parts of the existing counties of Badong, Xingshan and Fang, and covers an area of 3,250 km^2 (1,255 miles^2).[11] Shennongjia Biosphere Reserve is located in the south-western part of Shennongjia Forest District and was recognised by the United Nations Scientific and Cultural Organisation (UNESCO) as one of the world's biosphere preservation zones in 1990.

Known as 'the roof of central China', this area is characterised by interlocking mountain peaks, cliffs and well-developed valleys, due to the effects of the Himalayan uplift. Shennongjia forms a transitional region from the towering Sino-Himalaya to the west and the plains of eastern China. The enormous variation of geographical and environmental conditions in the reserve has given rise to numerous complicated ecosystems.

Our 2002 expedition members pictured at the entrance to Wuhan Botanical Garden.

The Wuming Peak ('peak with no name') is the highest mountain in central China. Seen here in autumn splendour, dark trees of *Abies fargesii* have reached the tree line, above which is scrub and sub-alpine meadow.

The mountains of Shennongjia are an extension of the south-eastern Daba range (Daba Shan) and have an average elevation of 1,800 m (5,905 ft), with six peaks above 3,000 m (9,842 ft). The tallest mountain, the Wuming Peak, is 3,105 m (10,187 ft) above sea level, while the lowest point is met at Laijiahepingkou, which is a mere 420 m (1,378 ft) above sea level.[12]

The climate of this remote region varies according to altitude, from subtropical and warm temperate on the valley floors to cold temperate on mountain summits. Because of the high, steep mountains and deeply incised valleys, microclimates also vary greatly. At higher altitudes, especially in the regions of *Abies fargesii* and *Sorbus discolor* (syn. *S. hupehensis*) forest, conditions tend to be foggy, with much rain in summer and autumn and very cold, with snow, in winter. At lower altitudes, there are distinct dry and wet seasons, with a greater range of temperatures. The coldest month is January, when temperatures average 2.3 °C (36 °F); July is the warmest, with an average of 13 °C (55 °F). Shennongjia lies in the path of monsoons moving north, and

Sorbus discolor, one of the best of the rowans. It is native to the northern provinces of China, as well as to Hubei Province – in Shennongjia, it covers the highest peaks.

Shennongjia Forestry District lost much of its forest cover between 1962 and 1980. The lower-lying slopes are now cultivated, and, in the warmer valleys, tea (*Camellia sinensis*) is widely grown.

annual precipitation can be as much as 1,093 mm (43 in.).

Prior to 1962, Shennongjia's primeval forest cover was practically untouched. Between then and 1982, the region became an important logging area. This caused serious destruction to biological resources, in particular to populations of *Abies chensiensis*, which had been distributed over a large area, but is nowadays reduced to a few small stands. During their visit, the American team from the 1980 Sino-American Expedition to Shennongjia observed the region's flora being changed at an alarming rate. Below 1,800 m (5,905 ft), virgin forest had been badly plundered for timber, or to provide cropland, leading to serious soil erosion problems. From our observations in September 2004, it is true to say that the only remaining tracts of virgin forest lie at high altitude, though there are large areas of recovering secondary forests with a rich and varied flora. The present forest cover is 68.5 per cent. With the completion of the Three Gorges Dam, it is now considered vital to protect Shennongjia's forest cover to reduce silt deposits in the new reservoir.

The name 'Shennongjia' comes from an ancient Chinese story about Shennong, the famous Emperor who invented traditional medicine. Legend has it that the Emperor rested here while travelling in search of medicinal plants.

Shennongjia is one of China's most important botanical reserves, harbouring 2,638 species and intraspecific taxa, of which 1,886 are medicinal plants. More than 55 per cent of Hubei's protected plants (almost 9 per cent of China's total) are found there, and 42 species are endemic to Shennongjia. Seventy species of animals under State protection are found in this upland region, including the endangered golden monkey, *Rhinopithecus roxellanae*. In 1980, only 500 golden monkeys survived in Shennongjia. By 1998, that figure had risen to 760. Local lore has it that the region's ancient forests are home to a Chinese 'Bigfoot' or '*Yeren*' (from the Chinese '*ye*', for savage, and '*ren*' for person), a tall, red-haired creature, thus adding to the appeal and allure of the place.

This mountainous landscape has been likened to a Noah's ark of relict plants. The influence of the Quaternary glacier on the reserve was so small that the area became a refuge of Tertiary flora. This allowed several relict genera to survive there when glacial activity was prevalent in other parts of the world. Plants were able to migrate south during the Pleistocene and returned when the climate warmed at the end of the last period of glaciation. Shennongjia has thus preserved an array of living fossils, and ancient relicts conserved there include *Bretschneidera*, *Cercidophyllum*, *Davidia*, *Eucommia*, *Emmenopterys* and *Tetracentron*.

The paper mulberry, *Broussonetia papyrifera*. Its globular, orange-red fruits (above) are an attractive feature, though it is better known as a foliage plant, with very heavily lobed leaves on some trees (below).

Buddleja lindleyana. In China, it is called the *tsui yu ts'ao*, or 'fish stupefying herb', since its crushed flowers, when thrown into water, will stupefy fish. Lindley's butterfly bush has a quiet charm matched by few other species in this colourful genus.

On Sunday, 25 September 2004, our group departed from Wuhan and drove for a day to Muyuping, a small village in Shennongjia Forest District. It was autumn and harvest time in Hubei Province, and, in the fields, the rice crop had been gathered and sheaves of straw were laid out in tidy, uniform rows to dry. Farmers were busy ploughing with oxen, and trees of the Chinese persimmon, *Diospyros kaki*, were absolutely laden with bright orange fruits. *Nelumbo nucifera*, the sacred lotus, is cultivated in flooded fields on a massive scale in eastern Hubei for its edible tubers and seeds. What a sight it made: acre after acre of dinner plate-sized leaves crowned by handsome, upright seed capsules.

The *kou shu*, or paper mulberry, *Broussonetia papyrifera* was a common roadside tree. Almost a weedy species in many parts of China, the paper mulberry has the ability to reproduce by means of suckers from its roots and can soon form extensive colonies. It is a handsome tree, however, with leaves lobed to varying degrees, and it carries attractive globular, orange-red fruits, typical of the mulberry family. At

Yichang, in the late 19th century, the bark of the paper mulberry was used for making string and paper. Paper making in China dates from the dawn of Christianity. Previous to this period, silk and cloth provided the medium on which to write, and, before this, the early annals were recorded on bamboo. Paper money first originated in Sichuan Province during the reign of the first emperor of the Sung Dynasty (960 AD)

Lunch was near the small village of Wudu in Yichang County, not far from the city of Yichang. We were excited at the prospect of beginning our collecting work and departed immediately after lunch on a brief foray to see what grew in the area. I was surprised at just how many good plants could be found on the side of the road, but then this is Hubei, home to one of the richest floras in all of China. What a pleasant surprise it was to find *Buddleja lindleyana*, a graceful butterfly bush, named after one of the early members of the Royal Horticultural Society by Robert Fortune (then employed by the Society). Lindley's butterfly bush grew on a steep roadside bank with *Anemone*

Pennisetum alopecuroides, one of the most abundant grasses along the roadsides approaching Yichang, seen here wild in the Three Gorges (Sanxia) Botanical Garden, Yunnan Province.

hupehensis, Conyza canadensis and masses of the very elegant *Pennisetum alopecuroides.*

Polygonum perfoliatum, a wiry annual climber, scaled its way through the surrounding herbage and was decked with distinctive, turquoise-blue fruits and viciously armed foliage. By the Wudu River grew another gem: *Lobelia seguinii*, a handsome perennial carrying pale blue flowers in spikes at the end of branchlets. The closely related *Adenophora hunanensis*, a perennial to 40 cm (16 in.) tall, carried upright spikes of blue, bell-shaped flowers and proved to be a common plant throughout our travels in Hubei Province. *Humulus scandens* is a common hop in this part of the world, almost on a weed-like scale, but worth collecting nonetheless.

Almost immediately after departing from Yichang, we left the great eastern plain of Hubei behind us and entered the mountainous terrain of western Hubei. Following the course of the Xiang Xi River, our route continued on past the city of Xingshan to our base at Muyuping (Muyu). The landscape suddenly loomed above us as we entered a land of soaring peaks, towering cliffs, waterfalls and rivers. We were amazed to see that the dam on the Yangtze had affected this far-flung region, too: the floodwaters of the Yangtze had invaded the course of the Xiang Xi, and much of the local farmland and many of the surrounding villages were abandoned and submerged.

We arrived in Muyuping late that evening, tired from a long day's drive. What a spectacular location for a village. It reminded me of a scene from the Austrian Alps. Muyuping was completely encircled by steep, cone-like peaks, all crowned with virgin forest. Excitement kicked in; we were to be the first Irish botanical party to cross these slopes since Augustine Henry. I couldn't wait!

Shennongjia Biosphere Reserve: Fenjingya

We divided our time in Shennongjia between three reserves, and, with us, had travelled Professor Mingxi Jiang, a senior research scientist from Wuhan Botanical Garden and an expert on the Shennongjia area. The professor brought us to his favourite parts of the reserve, and to where the most interesting plants could be found. His great love for the area was evident, and it was also clear to see how absorbed he was with the world of plants. We were blessed; not only was Mingxi a superb and knowledgeable guide, but a thoroughly likeable and jovial character, and the Chinese and Irish teams got on very well together indeed.

The following morning, having rested after the long journey from Wuhan, we drove to the Fenjingya Nature Reserve on the summit of Shennongjia's tallest peak. Our drive that Sunday morning brought us to the edge of extensive belts of *Abies fargesii*, dark, sombre, narrowly columnar trees, and these were enlivened by extensive tracts of *Sorbus discolor*, then in wonderful autumnal shades of burgundy and amber. *Sorbus discolor* is one of the very best of the rowans – and my favourite species. On Shennongjia's steep slopes, it made small trees to about 4 m (13 ft) tall and carried clusters of pearly, white fruits. Enormous areas of *Sinarundinaria nitida* had flowered about a decade previous to our visit, and the landscape was broken by extensive thickets of dead bamboo, giving a hazy, almost ghostly effect.

Acer franchetii appeared from time to time; by then, its foliage was butter-yellow. Discovered in this same general area by Henry in the autumn of 1888, this maple commemorates Adrien Franchet (1834–1900), the famous French botanist who described the collections of David and

Thickets of the red-flowered *Rhododendron oreodoxa*. In the foreground are dead clumps of *Sinarundinaria nitida*.

Delavay. On the edge of *Abies fargesii* forest grew extensive colonies of *Rhododendron oreodoxa*. One of the best of the early flowered species, a plant grows in the Mill Field at Glasnevin, where, every February without fail, it puts on a brave and colourful show with its rounded trusses of large red flowers. *Rhododendron oreodoxa* should be top of the list on any serious rhododendron grower's guide. At Shennongjia, it must make a beautiful sight in spring, with a dark background of *Abies fargesii* and a carpet of snow at its feet. Other rhododendrons that grew nearby were *Rhododendron augustinii* and the white-flowered *Rhododendron micranthum*.

Rosa sericea ssp. *omeiensis* was also common at this altitude, and it was nice to stumble across it in the same area as Henry had made his collections 114 years previously. Above the tree line, we met with numerous Henry plants, many of which have yet to reach cultivation. The most exciting of these had to be *Allium henryi*, an aristocratic little onion to about 15 cm (6 in.) tall, bearing masses of globular heads of small blue flowers on delicate pendant stems. *Allium henryi* absolutely smothered the highest peaks, transforming damp, mossy outcrops into a sea of blue. What

a stir it would create if ever introduced to Western gardens.

With Henry's onion grew a number of other diminutive flowering plants, including *Chrysanthemum indicum* var. *aromaticum*, a much more compact and floriferous plant than the species itself. Endemic to Shennongjia, its cheery golden-yellow blooms made a beautiful contrast with the cool blue flowers of *Allium henryi*. One of Henry's earliest discoveries, the perennial *Adenophora capillaris* was common on damp cliffs and its lax, 60-cm (2-ft) long pendulous stems were covered in tiny, bell-shaped, light blue flowers. This was also my first encounter with *Hypericum japonicum*; at this altitude, it formed tiny, cushion-like plants with dainty yellow blooms that could have been mistaken, at a distance, for a species of *Saxifraga*. *Sedum major* made a colourful show on damp rocky outcrops by the forest's edge. A small perennial to about 10 cm (4 in.) tall, it transformed and illuminated the area with sheets of pretty pink blooms.

Thistles can be handsome and garden-worthy plants, and two species discovered by Augustine Henry also grew in this reserve. The most interesting of these had to be *Cirsium henryi*, a biennial to a metre (3.3 ft) tall with a

Allium henryi. Endemic to Shennongjia, this aristocratic little onion has yet to reach cultivation. We found it to be common on the rocky crags of Shennongjia's highest peaks. Alas, our collection permits did not allow us to collect material in this reserve.

beautiful, very decorative, lace-like calyx. The perennial *Cirsium fargesii* also caught our attention on account of its bold, spiny foliage, and, while not quite as spectacular as *Cirsium henryi*, it is still a plant of obvious horticultural potential. This trip allowed us to introduce both plants to

cultivation. *Cirsium henryi* first flowered outside of China in the Order Beds at Glasnevin in the autumn of 2005, while *Cirsium fargesii* blossomed the following year.

Viburnums were plentiful, and, once again, the best of these for autumn show was *Viburnum betulifolium*. *Viburnum*

Cirsium henryi, a beautiful biennial thistle. Note the lace-like, very decorative calyx. We introduced it to cultivation, from nearby Xingshan, and it first flowered outside of China in the Order Beds at Glasnevin, Dublin, in the summer of 2006.

Hypericum japonicum, a dwarf annual species with a wide area of distribution, from Nepal to as far afield as New Zealand.

Sedum major, a shade-loving stonecrop. On damp boulders by the edge of woodland, it provided a great splash of colour. Henry discovered it near Liantuo in 1886.

Chrysanthemum indicum var. *aromaticum*, another of Shennongjia's many endemic plants. Since its discovery, it has been put to use in the perfume industry, and may be used in future Chrysanthemum breeding programmes.

rhytidophyllum was also quite common, and, near the summit, were scattered plants of *Viburnum erubescens* var. *prattii*, a great rarity that was originally discovered by Antwerp Pratt on the mountain slopes above Kangding in western Sichuan Province. Other good garden plants in this reserve included *Clerodendrum trichotomum* var. *fargesii*, *Rhus chinensis*, *Cacalia tangutica*, the charming winter-flowered *Lonicera standishii* var. *lancifolia*, *Triosetum hirsutum*, *Anaphalis margaritacea* and *Rodgersia aesculifolia*. According to Henry, the latter was referred to in Chinese herbals as the *kuei-teng-ch'ing*, or 'devil's lamp-stand', and was known colloquially in Hubei Province as *lao-she-p'an*, or 'old serpent's dish'; he also stated that the rhizomes were the source of a drug.

A nearby mountain meadow must have made a spectacular sight earlier that summer. In the long grass, we spied dozens of stems of *Veratrum album*, masses of *Geranium sibericum* and *Saussurea veitchiana*. The latter was first flowered in cultivation by Sir Frederick Moore at Glasnevin, having been raised from seeds collected by E. H. Wilson.

The lower slopes of the reserve were cleared for

The Chinese box, *Buxus microphylla* var. *sinica*, seen here in a mist-shrouded ravine near the summit of the Wuming Peak (Wuming Shan) in Shennongjia Forest District.

cultivation during the 1960s, though much of the forest cover has regenerated and a large range of plants has returned to the secondary forests. In the low-lying valleys, tea is grown on the south-facing slopes. The mountain people of this area lead a simple, almost primitive way of life, and, being far from any town or village, they have learned to rely on the surrounding forests for their needs. We met one old lady donning a fine shawl made locally from the stem fibre of the Chusan palm, *Trachycarpus fortunei*.

In a large, open, sunny glade, we met with another little-known inhabitant of these mountains. Described as a new species in 1985, *Dipsacus asperoides* is a beautiful teasel to about 1.5 m (5 ft) high, and, in Shennongjia, it grew in a meadow with *Melilotus indicus* and *Sanguisorba officinalis*. It towered above all of its meadow companions and carried clusters of small, honey-coloured seed heads. The mountain inhabitants of Shennongjia use this plant to treat kidney disorders.

Not far from the teasel, on the forest's edge, we stumbled upon *Spiraea myrtilloides*, which even at that late stage was still carrying flat corymbs of pink blossoms. Originally described by Alfred Rehder in 1913 from a collection made by E. H. Wilson in western Sichuan Province in 1908, Augustine Henry had discovered it in Xingshan some two decades previously. Beside it grew two Wilson plants; the first, *Spiraea veitchii*, formed tall arching shrubs to about 3 m (10 ft) tall. The second, *Crataegus wilsonii*, an altogether more desirable plant, made small trees to about 4 m (13 ft) tall and bore a heavy crop of large, red succulent fruits.

Not far from Wilson's hawthorn, *Vitis betulifolium* scrambled through fine fruiting trees of *Euptelea pleiosperma*, *Malus hupehensis* and *Malus kansuensis*. The latter was by then laden with a heavy crop of golden yellow fruits. On the forest floor, *Polygonatum verticillatum*, a tall, stately Solomon's seal, carried pendant clusters of scarlet berries.

Dipsacus asperoides, a handsome, small-flowered teasel that is common in meadows and glades in the Shennongjia Nature Reserve.

A peasant lady on the lower slopes of Shennongjia. The shawl around her shoulders is made from the stem fibre of the Chusan palm, *Trachycarpus fortunei*.

Crataegus wilsonii, a small shrubby tree to about 7 m (23 ft) tall. Wilson introduced it, through the Arnold Arboretum, in September 1907 from nearby Fang County (Fang Xian).

Patrinia angustifolia. This short-lived perennial was discovered by Augustine Henry in the Monastery Valley, near Yichang, in July 1886. Behind it is another Henry discovery, *Vernonia mntcienensis*.

Dipsacus asper, a beautifully scented perennial and the best of the small-flowered teasels. Previous to Henry's collections, it was only known from the Khasia Hills in eastern India. Butterflies and bees love it.

The cucumber relative, *Trichosanthes kirilowii*. Several species of *Trichosanthes* grow in central China, and many are used in traditional Chinese medicine.

Shennongjia Biosphere Reserve: Qianjiaping

From the Wuming Peak, we moved to the Qianjiaping Nature Reserve to study an area of broad-leaved forest. A few conifers were also present, however, including *Taxus chinensis* and *Torreya fargesii*, both of which were discovered by Henry during his north of the Yangtze expedition in the autumn of 1888. An interesting find was *Hydrangea longipes*, this species was first described in Paris from material gathered in Baoxing by Armand David in April 1869. By coincidence, it was described once again from Henry's collections at Kew in 1887 using the very same specific epithet.

On the forest's edge, *Vernonia martienensis*, an upright perennial to 1.5 m (5 ft), sported panicles of pink-purple pincushion-like blooms. *Patrinia angustifolia* was also common in this area, and carried its beautiful lime-green flowers in horizontal corymb-like panicles up to a metre (3.3 ft) tall. This stunning species has much potential as a border perennial, though it is rare in gardens, and, as far as I am aware, it was unknown in cultivation prior to our 2004 collections from neighbouring Xingshan. We had first met with *Dipsacus asper* in the mountains above Badong in 2002, so it

was a pleasant surprise to find it north of the Yangtze. In my opinion, *Dipsacus asper* is the best of the small-flowered teasels and it bears masses of white, sweetly scented blossoms in late summer and autumn. Watch it, though: like all the teasels, it has colonial ambitions! At its feet grew *Silene fortunei*, an elegant lax-stemmed perennial with pink, raggedly petalled flowers. *Silene fortunei* is a widespread species in China, and is one of many plants to commemorate Robert Fortune.

Climbers, too, were plentiful in those ancient forests. A handsome perennial cucurbit, *Trichosanthes kirilowii* carried bright-red fleshy fruits, and we found it to be a common vine throughout our travels north of the Yangtze. *Akebia quinata*, a climbing shrub I first met with during my student days at Powerscourt Gardens in County Wicklow, Ireland, made rampant lianas. *Cocculus orbiculatus* carried a heavy crop of blue fruits, and the capsules of *Celastrus angulatus* had split to reveal orange seeds within. The Chinese ivy, *Hedera nepalensis* var. *sinensis*, was in full bloom, supplying bees from nearby hives with valuable late nectar. The well-known *Parthenocissus tricuspidata* is a widespread climber in China, Korea and Japan, and, in the

143

Native to China, Taiwan and Japan, *Silene fortunei* was discovered by Sir George Staunton when travelling on Lord Macartney's embassy to the Emperor of China in 1793. Robert Fortune later collected it on the archipelago of Zhousan (Chusan).

Aconitum hemsleyanum, the best of the climbing monk's-hoods. We were delighted to find a thicket full of its flowering stems.

forests at Shennongjia, it scaled high into the tallest trees. On the forest floor, *Senecio scandens* gave a great show of yellow blossoms and straggled its way through the nearest shrubs. *Rubus ichangensis*, one of Henry's better-known discoveries, carried grape-like clusters of small orange fruits.

By riversides, the woods were chiefly composed of *Emmenopterys henryi*, *Corylus chinensis*, *Carpinus fargesii*, *Quercus oxyodon*, *Fagus engleriana*, *Diospyros lotus* and *Davidia involucrata*. Another rare tree in this area was *Tapiscia sinensis*, a monotypic genus discovered by Henry and now endangered in the wild. The pinnate leaves of this tree bear a resemblance to *Pistacia*, and the generic name *Tapiscia* is an anagram of the latter.

Across a large stream from the *Tapiscia*, we noticed a clearing and in it was an entire thicket draped with vivid blue flowers. Eager to get a closer look, the braver members of our group did a balancing act (some crawled on all fours) across a log bridge constructed from a fallen *Tapiscia* – and made it to the other side. To our surprise and delight, the plant was *Aconitum hemsleyanum*, the *ch'uan-wu-tu*, a climbing herbaceous perennial with large, showy, rich blue flowers. On the edge

Tapiscia sinensis, a large tree to 30 m (98 ft) tall. It is a great rarity in western Hubei Province.

Expedition member Assumpta Broomfield couldn't conceal her excitement on finding *Aconitum hemsleyanum*, even getting down on all fours to crawl across a log bridge hewn from *Tapiscia sinensis* to reach this wonderful monk's-hood.

of a forest already packed with exciting plants, this scrambling monk's-hood gave such a show that it would have got gold at any Chelsea show. This fantastic perennial was named in honour of Henry's friend at Kew, William Botting Hemsley.

We were thrilled to find *Acer henryi* in its native habitat; in Shennongjia, it formed spreading trees to about 7 m (23 ft) tall. The form we encountered had a serrated leaf edge and had turned a wonderful purple-red shade with the onset of autumn. *Clerodendrum bungei* carried large, flat, terminal corymbs of rosy-red, fragrant flowers, and, near it, two aroids grew side by side. The first, *Arisaema erubescens*, had lost all its foliage, but a fat, fleshy fruit spike remained on the ground. Beside it, a fine clump of *Pinellia ternata* was in full bloom. According to Henry, a drug was made from the tubers of this plant and it was administered to stop vomiting. In the same region, farmers cultivated crops by the river's edge, and one of these was *Aconitum sinomontanum*, a giant monkshood of about 3 m (10 ft) tall, grown for the sake of its medicinal tubers. *Zingiber mioga* was also grown by these mountain folk, and, as we were later to discover, it is the perfect antidote to too much fatty bacon and homemade Chinese rice wine. Vegetables, by necessity, were home grown, and in one riverside patch were neat rows of *pak choi*, beans, Chinese cabbage, lettuce, peppers and Chinese chives. The abundant *Iris japonica* bullied its way back from the riverbank, seemingly determined to conquer back its old territory. If only we had weeds like this in the West. Oh, to have a vegetable garden in Shennongjia!

The aptly named 'fool's strawberry', *Duchesnia indica*, is a widespread perennial in this part of Asia. It may not be the most exciting plant in the world, but it always makes a good talking point with children and the horticulturally uninitiated. It is also a good plant for dry shade, where its aggressive manner is better controlled.

Viburnum propinquum formed dense bushes to about 2 m (6.5 ft) tall. There are several good plants at Glasnevin, including an old, rather shapely shrub in the rock garden. There, it is grown on account of its handsome evergreen foliage and compact habit; certainly not for its rather nondescript, unexciting flowers. Having seen many *Viburnum* species in the wild, I am convinced that we should grow them not only for their flowers, but, equally, for their autumn fruits, and the only way to achieve this with most species is to grow several clones together. I was completely taken with *Viburnum propinquum* and its magical show of luminous blue fruits, and would encourage large-garden owners to follow this instruction. *Viburnum propinquum* was discovered by Augustine Henry in the Antelope Glen near Yichang in 1887.

Acer henryi, a form with serrated leaves. Henry's maple is rare in cultivation, being found only in botanical collections. It is one of the best of the Asiatic maples, assuming wonderful autumnal hues.

Clerodendrum bungei, a small suckering shrub to 1.5 m (5 ft) tall. It is best suited to the milder counties of Britain and Ireland, where its stems are not cut down by frost.

Shennongjia Biosphere Reserve: Tianzhuqiao

Our final visit while based in Shennongjia was to the Tianzhuqiao Nature Reserve. The very first tree we were to see that morning grew near the entrance, and the sight of it stunned us all to silence. We stood on top of a massive ravine, and, raising its head above it, was a colossal, 45-m (148-ft) tall, 1,000-year-old *Emmenopterys henryi*. It was hard to imagine that this tree began its life just as the Vikings were establishing the city of Dublin. We were left in awe, humbled at the sight of this ancient monument, the same way as a visitor to the Californian redwoods might be. Near the reserve's entrance was a small garden displaying some of the trees found inside. One of the first trees we met with was *Neocinnamomum fargesii*, a handsome evergreen tree belonging to the laurel family.

Further into the reserve, a massive old tree of *Ginkgo biloba* grew by the base of a sheer cliff and carried a heavy crop of golden-yellow, egg-like fruits. Even more impressive was a gargantuan specimen of *Keteleeria davidiana* said to be 1,200 years old. We estimated its height to be 35 m (115 ft), and measured its girth, which was 7.3 m (24 ft) at breast height. Near the *Keteleeria*, a slope had been cleared (of virgin forest) to make way for an impressive flight of steps, and, at the summit, was a sculpture of Shennongjia's *Yeren*, or 'wild man'. We soon entered the forest cover by an enormous cascading waterfall (the rainy season was just over and waterfalls crashed and tumbled over many of the cliffs we passed) and climbed our way over it by means of a boardwalk and several flights of steps.

On an enormous mossy boulder, at the summit of the waterfall, grew the sensational *Lilium henryi*, and to see this wonderful lily in its wild native habitat made our trip to Hubei Province more than worthwhile. It could not have grown in a more stunning location: perched on a boulder in the middle of a thundering waterfall and surrounded by towering peaks all clad with ancient forests, the sort of stuff that would have been familiar to the great plant hunters. The plant we saw was a mere metre (3.3 ft) tall and carried three seed capsules. In Helen Dillon's Dublin garden, it towers to about 2 m (6.5 ft) and carries a myriad of blooms. But then Helen gardens next door to the house in which Augustine Henry once lived, and, as she often explains to visitors, the reason it does so well with her is because his benevolent spirit peers over the garden wall from time to time!

On the damp, shaded cliffs, the hardy gesneriad *Corallodiscus cordatulus* formed handsome rosettes. What a show it must give in early summer. Enjoying the same habitat were *Cyrtomium fortunei*, *Kinostemon ornatum*, *Woodwardia unigemmata*, *Chloranthus henryi* and the rather evil-smelling *Boenhaussenia albiflora*. *Saxifraga giraldiana* var. *hupehensis* also scaled the damp cliffs, as did the more familiar *Saxifraga stolonifera*.

Illicium henryi was abundant in this area and formed shrubs with a stiff, upright habit. The ivy relative *Nothopanax davidii* was also common, especially by streamsides. *Aucuba chinensis* made wide-spreading shrubs to about 2 m (6.5 ft) tall. The plants we saw had a speckled variegation. Near it grew *Mahonia bealei*, another favourite in cultivation on account of its deliciously scented racemes of yellow flowers. The pittosporums are a popular group of trees and shrubs, and are well suited to the milder coastal regions of Britain and Ireland. We tend to grow species from Australia and New Zealand, but the Chinese species have much to offer, including magnificent scent. In this reserve, *Pittosporum illicioides* formed shrubs of about 2 m (6.5 ft) high, and we later collected a batch of good, viable seeds in nearby Xingshan.

Other good shrubs here included *Elaeagnus lanceolata*, *Hypericum przwalskii*, *Zanthoxylum ailsianum*, the very aptly named *Lindera megaphylla* and *Daphne tangutica* var. *wilsonii*.

Another plant in the reserve that bore Wilson's name was *Cinnamomum wilsonii*. This small, evergreen, aromatic tree was in fact one of Augustine Henry's earliest discoveries. He stated that its bark was used locally as a medicine. With Wilson's camphor tree grew *Acer flabellatum*, *Quercus glauca* and *Meliosma flexuosa*. These gave support for climbers such as *Actinidia arguta*, the very rampant *Akebia trifoliata*, *Clematis montana*, *Rosa cymosa* and *Trachelospermum jasminoides*.

By a small hamlet, we spotted the wild Moutan, *Paeonia suffruticosa* ssp. *spontanea*, a tree peony that has spawned a league of cultivars in China. Nearby grew extensive drifts of *Miscanthus sinensis*, and these merged with groves of the Chusan palm, *Trachycarpus fortunei*, and *Phyllostachys bambusoides*, a tall and very graceful bamboo to about 8 m (26 ft) tall. On exposed sunny cliffs, *Cotinus coggygria* var. *pubescens* was assuming a flame-like autumnal hue. We had been spoiled; Shennongjia was simply wonderful, but it was time to move east to Xingshan.

Miss Wang Qing, who manages the medicinal garden at Wuhan Botanical Gardens, in a colourful patch of *Aconitum sinomontanum*. Henry collected it in nearby Jianshi in the autumn of 1888.

Aconitum sinomontanum is, as the name implies, native to the mountains of China. This beautiful plant bears enormous, tightly packed racemes of hooded blue flowers.

Wild Man, a dramatic sculpture of Shennongjia's Yeren (or Yeti).

Keteleeria davidiana, a 1,200-year-old specimen in the Tianzhuqiao Nature Reserve (part of the Shennongjia Biosphere Reserve). Augustine Henry introduced this rare conifer to cultivation through Kew in 1888.

Breathtakingly beautiful: the mountains of Xingshan and the Xiang Xi river, near its confluence with the Yangtze.

To the mountains of Xingshan

Like E. H. Wilson, we found the old Xingshan city to be a dull and lifeless place. Less a city than an aged gathering of filthy factories and dilapidated houses. One of those monstrous factories belched out massive plumes of choking, noxious smoke and had killed every tree and shrub on the mountain behind. Xingshan was practically abandoned at the time of our visit. Many of the lower-lying areas had been inundated by the flood waters of the Yangtze, and a new city (Gufu Town) had been built nearby to replace the original.

Over the previous number of years, 31,000 inhabitants of the old city had been moved to Gufu Town to start a new life, and the old city of Xingshan will have been completely submerged by 2009. The new town was like a scene from Lego Land and its residents were obviously proud of it. However garish it appeared to us, it was a lot better than the monstrosity they had left behind.

That night, we hosted yet another official dinner with the local forestry officials. Every new reserve meant wining and dining these officials, making formal speeches and toasting future Sino-Irish ventures. I soon began to master my after-dinner speeches, and, in the beginning, I actually enjoyed them, if only a little less Chinese rice wine had been poured! The speeches and the after effects of the local liquor, however, were worth the trouble. All these local foresters were very helpful and were delighted that we took such an interest in their region of China. We spent three days in Xingshan, and, like Shennongjia, I look back on my time there as one of the most exciting and productive trips I've ever carried out in China.

Xingshan, too, was a land of high peaks and deep valleys, and it still had relatively good forest cover, although almost all of this was secondary growth. Nevertheless, an interesting and diverse flora remained. The first reserve we visited was Hann Shao Shan, a mountain that lay about half an hour's drive from the new city. The lower slopes were heavily cultivated, mainly with crops such as tea and tobacco; by hamlets, *tu chung*, *Eucommia ulmoides*, and *hou-p'o*, *Magnolia officinalis*, were widely grown.

In these same little hamlets grew beautiful cultivars of *Rosa chinensis* and *Rosa* x *odorata*, and these were much more refined and dignified plants than the mongrel hybrid teas of the West. We collected some seeds from one of these cultivars and were very surprised when, a few years later, a seedling sported clusters of loosely packed, gloriously scented, magenta-pink blossoms bearing subtle white stripes. Good garden roses are rarely raised from seeds randomly collected from an existing cultivar, and a name has yet to be given to this distinct and very lovely rose. I propose to name it *Rosa* 'Grace Pasley' after the late Grace Pasley (1956–2007). For more than 30 years, Grace

Rosa 'Grace Pasley', the original plant flowering for the very first time at Glasnevin. Raised from our Xingshan collections, it created great excitement when it first bloomed in the summer of 2008. It has a wonderful scent.

worked as an herbarium assistant at Glasnevin and travelled on two of the three 'Henry expeditions' to China, where she took charge of pressing and drying thousands of herbarium specimens. This vibrant Chinese rose has an old-fashioned charm about it, and its name carries on that of a much-missed colleague and fellow traveller in China.

At the base of the reserve, the woods were chiefly composed of *Rhus verniciflua*, *Pyrus pyrifolia*, *Pinus armandii*, *Pinus massoniana* and *Castanea seguinii*. *Castanea seguinii* is a relatively common tree in western Hubei Province, where it is often cultivated for its edible fruits, which are far superior to those of the more commonly grown *Castanea mollissima*. On many of the chestnuts grew the semi-parasitic *Loranthus setchuenensis*. The undersides of the leaves of this species are plastered with velvety fawn-coloured hairs. It was first found near Yichang by Henry in 1885, and he stated its host trees were oak, elm, crab and mulberry.

Towards the edge of the chestnut woods were several bushes of *Euonymus alatus*, then sporting rich scarlet autumn colour. In China, the woody 'wings' on the stems of *Euonymus alatus* are used as a painkiller. Beside it, *Elaeagnus difficilis* grew to about 2 m (6.5 ft). An early flowered species, it was already carrying masses of small, creamy-white flowers.

In its native habitat, *Ilex pernyi* makes a small tree to 8 m (26 ft) tall. Discovered in 1858 by the French missionary Père Paul-Hubert Perny, this species is endemic to China and was introduced to cultivation by E. H. Wilson in 1900. In Veitch's 1908 nursery catalogue, plants were available for the staggering sum of 21 shillings.

Ilex pernyi is probably the commonest holly in western Hubei Province, and plants here made handsome upright bushes to about 5 m (16 ft) tall. A shrub of dense habit, the plants we saw were laden with lustrous red berries. Introduced to cultivation by Wilson, this species performs well in British and Irish gardens and deserves to be better known. Twining its way through the holly was *Lonicera henryi*. Its luminous purple-black fruits made a beautiful contrast with the red berries of the holly, and what a good idea it would be to reproduce this combination in a garden situation. Another good plant for autumn berries was *Symplocos paniculatus*, a small tree that gave a stunning show of electric-blue berries.

I was delighted to find a small clearing full of the delicate flowering stems of the beautiful little gentian relative, *Halenia elliptica* var. *grandiflora*. We had first encountered this *Aquilegia* look-alike in Badong, in 2002, where it was by no means common, but, on the mountainous slopes of Xingshan, it made a colourful show and grew in great numbers. *Codonopsis lanceolata* scrambled its way through the dense herbage; it is a pretty plant, both in terms of flower and its large distinctive seed capsules.

In the same clearing, *Quercus spinosa* formed small shrubs to 1.5 m (5 ft) tall, and these were furnished with small,

spiny, puckered leaves. In damp, boggy areas, *Ligularia dentata* gave a good, albeit late, display of golden-yellow blooms. A good collection of bryophytes was also gathered during our travels through Xingshan, and it was interesting to collect *Leptogium menziesii* f. *uliginosum*, a lichen that grew on a damp, shady bank. Augustine Henry also made his collections in the same district in the autumn of 1888.

Aralia chinensis formed a small, sparsely branched tree to about 6 m (20 ft) tall, and carried huge quantities of small black seeds, much to our delight. In Chinese herbal medicine, the spine-covered stems of this tree are used as a diuretic, to promote blood circulation and as a painkiller.

I think the plant I will always associate with Xingshan is the stately and very beautiful *Saussurea populifolia*, and it was there that Henry discovered it during his north of the Yangtze tour. He described it as being common on mountain summits, and that statement still holds true today. It is a beautiful biennial or short-lived perennial to about 1.2 m (4 ft) tall, and, in autumn, it carries bold, artichoke-like blossoms. Another common Henry plant on these mountains was *Cotoneaster horizontalis* var. *perpusilla*, a prostrate shrub that was common on rocky ridges. By the roadside, our Chinese counterparts dug up the Chinese

Saussurea populifolia, a handsome biennial that was common on the higher peaks of Xingshan Xian (Xingshan County), Hubei Province. Henry discovered it in nearby Shennongjia in 1888.

Halenia elliptica var. *grandiflora*, a beautiful upright annual, which, in autumn, carries long-spurred, violet-blue flowers with white centres.

Clematis lasiandra, here photographed at Bai Sha near Badong. Flower colour varies on different plants, from white to violet-purple, rosy-purple or slatey-purple.

helleborine *Epipactis mairei* for the medicinal garden at Wuhan. This widespread orchid was first found by Henry in July 1885, and was based on collections made by the French missionary Edouard Ernest Maire (1848–1932) near Kunming, Yunnan Province, in the early 20th century.

The same day, we stopped for lunch in Henji Town, a very poor, dilapidated little village lined with street trees of *Cryptomeria japonica* var. *sinensis*. Having eaten, we took a brief stroll to the outskirts of the village to see what plants grew in the area. In a small roadside waste area, no more than 10 m (33 ft) long and 2 m (6.5 ft) wide, we gathered *Clematis lasiandra*, *Kerria japonica*, *Macleaya cordata*, *Buddleja davidii*, *Cynanchum officinale*, *Cucubaiis baccifer* and Chinese madder, *Cuscuta chinensis* Foreigners rarely travel through this upland region and the villagers took a great interest in our activities.

We had planned to climb a wooded hillside behind the village, and made our way through fields in that direction. The best plant in those fields was *Phytolacca acinosa*, the Indian pokeweed, a perennial to about 1.5 m (5 ft) – and an obvious weed to local farmers. One man's weed is

another is another man's precious ornament, however, and we were keen to collect seeds from one small population with pendulous spikes of fleshy black berries.

As soon as we had collected the pokeweed seeds, the heavens opened and, within minutes, we were thoroughly soaked and still running for cover in a huge open field. We were a fairly sorrowful-looking sight by the time we made it back to the bus with our Chinese companions, where a fellow traveller, Assumpta Broomfield, was waiting with an armful of towels she had just purchased in a nearby shop. Hooray for Assumpta!

It was a silent drive back to our base at Gufu Town. Everyone's clothes were stuck to them and the windows had fogged up. Bored, I wiped the bus window and, gazing onto the hillsides, it was as though snow had fallen. Stop the bus! While the rest of our party slept, a small group of us crept up the slope to investigate, and I cannot describe a more delightful scene. The whole hillside was smothered with small bushes of the white-flowered *Abelia chinensis*, and an incredible, sweet scent lingered in the warm, humid mountain air. We were like rats, soaked to the skin, and yet I can still see

153

Celosia argentea GCCE 610, blooming with other amaranth relatives in the Order Beds in front of the Great Palm House at Glasnevin, Dublin, in the summer of 2005.

The parent plant in the wilds of Xingshan County.

the look of delight on my companions' faces when we discovered where that wonderful perfume was coming from.

Beneath the *Abelia* grew prostrate shrubs of *Ficus tikoua*, a plant I had last seen by the banks of the Yangtze in north-west Yunnan Province in 1996. The nearby woods were dominated by the large-leaved *Quercus aliena*, and, on its verge, grew *Hydrangea glabripes*, *Myrsine africana*, *Vitex negundo* and *Mallotus apelta*. The latter is an exotic-looking shrub in the spurge family (Euphorbiaceae) with large three-lobed leaves. Previously unknown in Irish gardens, plants raised from our Xingshan collections are proving hardy at Kilmacurragh, and flowered there for the first time in July 2008.

Ilex cornuta was also common on the hillsides. The seed oil of this holly has been used in China in the manufacture of soap and a dye and gum are extracted from its bark. Near the holly, the lilac purple-flowered *Lespedeza formosa* made beautiful arching shrubs to 80 cm (31 in.) high, and, not far from it, Grace Pasley's eagle eyes spotted the gorgeous *Celosia argentea*, a bushy annual with upright spikes of silvery-white, pink-tipped plumes of small, densely packed flowers.

Our final day in Xingshan was spent in the Dragon Gate River Forest Park. What a great name for a nature reserve that was absolutely jammed with an incredible range of rare and wonderful plants. If dragons do live there, then what a spectacular landscape of great gorges, towering mountains, cliffs, caves, gushing streams and waterfalls they have to call their home!

The damp cliff faces in the reserve soared hundreds of feet overhead and were host to a diverse range of trees, shrubs, perennials and ferns. *Asarum pulchellum* formed extensive colonies wherever humus had gathered along the ledges of cliffs, and its round, heart-shaped leaves made a fine contrast with neighbouring plants of *Adiantum pedatum*, *Mahonia bealei* and *Aucuba chinensis*.

Cotoneaster henryanus was by no means common, and, on the same cliffs, it grew as 2 m (6.5 ft) tall bushes with a beautifully lax pendulous habit. This species has remained rare in gardens, and plants labelled as such are usually forms of *Cotoneaster salicifolius*. The most abundant plant on the cliffs had to be the Yichang tassel bush, *Itea ilicifolia*, and it grew in hundreds – an incredible sight. This lovely shrub is one of my favourite garden plants, especially in the month of August, when it carries masses of scented, lime-green blossoms held in long, pendulous, catkin-like racemes.

Another of Henry's plants was the wonderfully marbled *Parthenocissus henryana*, and it shared the same cliff space with *Cupressus funebris*, *Stachyurus chinensis*, *Nothopanax davidii*, *Trachelospermum jasminoides* and *Buddleja officinalis*. *Paulownia fargesii* also inhabits this mountain range, and, by the roadsides, it formed dome-shaped trees to 10 m (33 ft) tall. Discovered by Henry in June 1888, it has never become common in gardens, and it was good, therefore, to have been able to secure wild-sourced material for Glasnevin and Kilmacurragh.

By a riverside, *Sarcococca ruscifolia* made low, compact shrubs and carried a good crop of large, fleshy, red berries. *Holboellia coriacea* scaled its way through tall trees and shrubs and had produced a few purple, egg-shaped fruits. Known colloquially, in the Three Gorges region, as the *pa-yueh-cha*, it is a vigorous evergreen climber to 7 m (23 ft) tall, and hikes its way through its host by means of twining stems. Corymbs of white, purple-tinged flowers are carried in late spring, and these are followed, in autumn, by the fleshy purple fruits just described.

The nearby Red Dragon Reserve is a small part of Dragon Gate River Forest Park, and this area was crammed full of rarities. We entered the reserve by crossing a mossy, hump-backed, moon bridge and one of the very first plants we were to meet was the Yichang lemon, *Citrus cavaleriei*. The Yichang lemon is a very distinctive species, on account of its winged petioles. These wings are as broad as the leaf blades, giving the appearance of a double leaf, and, in the glens and hills above Yichang, it makes a tree of some 10 m

(33 ft) tall. Henry found it in the Antelope Glen in October 1887, and it was also cultivated near the city for its coarse lemon-like fruits. It grows further north and at higher altitudes than any other citrus fruit, and, as a consequence, is hardy in Britain and Ireland. In Ireland, it grows vigorously at Glanleam on Valentia Island, County Kerry.

At the base of a cliff, another Henry plant, *Osmanthus armatus*, formed groves to about 5 m (16 ft) tall. *Quercus glauca* was a common oak in these woods. Sometimes known as the 'bamboo oak', it makes a handsome evergreen tree to 20 m (56 ft) tall with a dense, rounded crown. Its timber, according to Henry, was very hard and was used to make carrying poles. Growing with it was *Quercus myrsinifolia*, another evergreen species that is widely

Citrus cavaleriei (syn. *C. ichangensis*), a hardy lemon tree from western Hubei Province. We found it wild in Xingshan County, and later collected a good supply of seeds in eastern Hubei. Note the inflated petiole, which gives the appearance of a double leaf.

Dawn breaks over Wushan. In the background is the entrance to the Wu Gorge, the second of the Three Gorges along the Yangtze River. It was just south of here that Henry discovered *Davidia involucrata* var. *vilmoriniana*, and, in 1914, Reginald Farrer planned to stop here to collect two of Henry's discoveries, *Megacodon venosum* and the dainty *Primula nutaniflora*.

distributed across China, Laos, Korea and Japan. Noted for its slender and elegant foliage, this species often exceeds the 25 m (82 ft) guide height when cultivated around shrines and in the grounds of temples.

Phoebe zhennan, a rare member of the laurel family also grew there. A protected tree in China, I had only ever read of it before and so it was good to meet it first hand. Another rare tree, *Pteroceltis tatarinowii* (a member of the elm family), grew as a single isolated tree near a fine, 2-m (6.5-ft) tall bush of *Pittosporum adaphniphylloides*. I first met with this species in the walled garden at Malahide Castle, near Dublin, many years ago, where it was covered with clusters of creamy-white, deliciously scented flowers. We were also rather pleased to be able to collect material of *Polygala wattersii*, a small, yellow-flowered shrub of about a metre (3.3 ft) tall. It was discovered by the Irish diplomat and part-time plant hunter Thomas Watters in April 1880. Above it grew *Ilex purpurea*, a widespread holly in China, though the most abundant shrub in the reserve was Henry's privet, *Ligustrum henryi*.

The views near the summit of the reserve were spectacular. Range after range of mountain peaks, all heavily forested; waterfalls crashed and tumbled onto the valley floor. The mountains of Xingshan are formed of limestone, and we

had seen a number of karst features during our travels, though nothing prepared us for what lay ahead. Passing through a small opening in the hillside, we entered an eerie world of stalagmites and stalactites, all artificially lit in a range of colours. Our jaws dropped on entering the central cavern, a subterranean chamber on an enormous scale, where, over many millennia, stalagmites and stalactites had merged to create the most phantasmal forms. It was like standing in a great cathedral, long hidden from the world outside. What a fantastic way to complete our travels in Xingshan.

The following day, we boarded a small ferry and sailed from Xingshan down the Xiang Xi River. Just below the city of Badong, we joined the Yangtze and sailed our way eastwards through the spectacular Xiling Gorge to Yichang.

North Wushan and the Lesser Three Gorges

It was an early morning in September 2002 when we arrived in the town of Wushan in Chongqing Municipality (eastern Sichuan Province). We had spent the previous week trekking up the slopes of Emei Shan, another of China's great biological hotspots and we had also made a brief visit to the little village of Maoba (formerly Modaoqi) in Hubei Province to pay our respects to the original 'type' tree of *Metasequoia*

Towering cliffs and turquoise waters in the Lesser Three Gorges (along the Daning River). As of the end of 2009, this landscape was submerged beneath an enormous artificial reservoir.

Native to Burma, China and Japan, the bulbous *Lycoris aurea* was in full bloom on the steep inaccessible cliffs of the Lesser Three Gorges during our visit.

glyptostroboides, the 'fossil tree' or dawn redwood.

Like Yichang, Wushan was much visited by the early plant hunters. Ernest Wilson made enormous collections there, and it was in the mountains to the south of the town that Augustine Henry discovered the glabrous-leaved handkerchief tree, *Davidia involucrata* var. *vilmoriniana*. Our travels took us through north Wushan County along the lower reaches of the Daning River (a tributary of the Yangtze) through the Lesser Three Gorges.

The Longmen Gorge, Bawu Gorge and the Dicui Gorge between Wushan and the ancient town of Dachang may not boast the same austere majesty of their counterparts, the famous Three Gorges on the Yangtze, but we found it a rewarding trip. Extending over a 50-km (31-mile) stretch of river, the crystal-clear, fast-flowing waters of the river are enclosed by soaring sheer cliffs, so tall in places that they almost block out views of the skies above.

At the town of Wushan, we hired a small flat-bottomed boat and sailed our way against the current of the Daning River towards Dachang town. Along the banks of the river, we spotted troupes of chattering monkeys leaping from branch to branch at the edge of dense forest. Wilson mentioned he never saw the monkeys reputed to inhabit the

gorges; during his time at Yichang, the stone-throwing antics of these little animals at passing boats were used by Chinese officials as a reason why foreign steamships could not ply their trade between Yichang and Chongqing!

The grey limestone cliffs were speckled with many flowering stems of the golden-yellow, nerine-like *Lycoris aurea*, a pretty, bulbous plant that seemed to grow from solid rock. Our boatman struggled to get his vessel over the shallow rapids, and I could only imagine how difficult passage must have been through this region during the 19th century. *Distylium chinensis* and *Adina rubella*, two evergreen fluviatile shrubs, were abundant on the lower cliffs by the water's edge. *Pterocarya stenoptera* made fine trees above lush thickets of *Arundo donax*, and, higher up the cliffs, *Lindera fragrans* was common, alongside *Vitex negundo* and *Berchemia polyphylla* var. *leioclada*. Discovered by Augustine Henry in 1885, this variety was based on a collection made by Wilson in July 1907. Henry stated it was known colloquially in the gorges as *lu-mi-k'o-tzu*, and that the leaves were used as a tea substitute.

The plank road along the Daning River is the oldest surviving plank road of its kind in China. From the mouth of the Longmen Gorge, it runs high above the water's edge

Professor Ding Zhaohua of Wuhan Botanical Gardens, now Vice Director of South China Botanical Gardens, was our untiring guide through the Three Gorges region. He was very familiar with Augustine Henry's travels in Hubei and Sichuan provinces.

LEFT: Racing against the currents of the Daning River. Our plant collecting was limited to a few accessible hillsides and valleys. High up in these cliffs we spotted hanging coffins, all that remains of the ancient Ba civilisation.

along the cliffs for more than 100 li (a unit equal to about half a kilometre), and it served as a vital highway between the Qin, Ba and Chu kingdoms in ancient times. Like the Qutang Gorge on the Yangtze, 'hanging coffins' are another feature of the gorges. We were able to spot many of these coffins with the aid of binoculars, though how the ancient Ba people placed these coffins so high up in the cliff-side crevices and caves is still unknown. Their ways may now never be known; the Three Lesser Gorges is the last place historians can study the Ba, and the same region contains many irreplaceable historical sites, some dating back as far as 4,000 years.

Collecting plants along these cliffs was out of the question, but we did find one point at which to disembark and followed a steep walkway overlooking the gorge to a wooded hillside, where we collected *Gymnosporia variabilis*, a rare relative of the European spindle bush that was first found in the Xiling (Yichang) Gorge by Charles Maries in

1879, and was introduced by him through his employers, Messrs Veitch. Clambering through the trees were several climbers, including *Sinomenium acutum*, *Rosa laevigata* and *Vitis flexuosa*; the latter was, by then, covered in small bunches of maroon, grape-like fruits. While we were busily collecting, we met a small group of hill people with hand-woven baskets full of recently collected medicinal plants. Both of our groups were eager to see what the other had collected, and these quiet mountain folk took great interest in our plant presses and the specimens in them.

At the terminus of the Lesser Three Gorges is the ancient town of Dachang. Founded in Taichang County in 265 AD (during the Jin Dynasty), it is one of the best-preserved ancient towns in the Three Gorges region, and was, at one time, the capital of Sichuan Province. Like many other communities in the area, Dachang would have been submerged by the Yangtze in 2009, but the town's important place in history and valuable relics have been

Ginkgo biloba, an ancient tree at the village of Bai Sha in rural Badong County. It was from the fruits pictured above that we raised several seedlings, and these now grow at the Kilmacurragh Botanic Gardens in County Wicklow.

saved by an ambitious scheme that has moved the entire place to a higher location.

Despite being exhausted on the day, following a long journey from Emei Shan, we enjoyed a spectacular boat trip up the turquoise waters of the Daning River. It is sad,

though, that this wonderful landscape has now been lost forever, following its recent inundation by the floodwaters of the Yangtze River. Those fast-running turquoise waters have now been replaced by a placid reservoir that has risen high along the gorges' towering canyon walls.

Chapter 6

To the snows of Tibet with Antwerp Pratt

As Augustine Henry settled into his new post on China's tropical Hainan Island (Hainan Dao), his colleague Antwerp Pratt was busily organising an expedition to the Tibetan frontier. His route had been partly chosen by Henry based on the itineraries of other explorers. One of these was Edward Colborne Baber (1843–90), a member of the British Consular Service. Baber was the first foreigner to climb both Emei Shan and Wa-shan in Sichuan Province, in the summer of 1877, and reports of his explorations were widely read at the time. Henry's colleague Ernst Faber was, as previously stated, the first botanist to climb Emei Shan, and, during a fortnight's stay there, he discovered 70 new species and a number of new genera. In 1869, at Baoxing (also in Sichuan), the famous French missionary and naturalist Père Jean Pierre Armand David (1826–1900)

Emei Shan is said to have one of the most spectacular sunrises in all China. We were more than impressed as we stood on the summit before dawn, when a glowing sun rose in the distance and the skies transformed into an amber inferno.

made notable finds, including the handkerchief tree, *Davidia involucrata*, and the giant panda, *Ailuropoda melanoleucus*.[1] Outside of the work of those travellers, little was known of the natural history of western Sichuan.

The purpose of Pratt's visit to the region was to collect entomological material, but, at Yichang, Henry managed to persuade him to bring along his Changyang collector to gather botanical specimens for Kew.[2] Henry's man was to make two separate and very different collections: one for Antwerp Pratt and a second set for Augustine Henry.

160

The English explorer Antwerp Pratt here photographed in 1889. Pratt dressed in traditional Chinese clothes to distract attention from himself and to avoid being attacked by anti-foreign Sichuanese people.

Pratt's boat anchored on the Yangtze at Yichang in March 1889. The boat was constructed locally and varnished with the sap of *Rhus verniciflua*.

The notorious 'Sin-tan' rapid, one of the most dangerous obstacles to navigation on the middle reaches of the Yangtze during the 19th century. In spring, the river was at its lowest level, exposing enormous boulders and creating whirlpools.

In March 1889, Pratt began an earnest start on preparations for an extended expedition from Yichang. His journey would take him through the Three Gorges and up the Min River (a tributary of the Yangtze) to the city of Leshan (then Kia ting fu). He needed a boat suitable for the purpose and with sufficient room within to safely store his collections. While moored at Leshan, the boat would also serve as a base while he explored the hinterlands.

It soon became apparent that such a craft was not available at Yichang, and so he commissioned a local shipbuilder to construct a boat strong enough to withstand the rapids of the Three Gorges. The boat was coated with vegetable varnish produced from the sap of *Rhus verniciflua*, and, once the craft was completed, Pratt's next consideration was to obtain a captain and crew.

This was accomplished through the Yichang Customs Service, and the ship's captain stayed with Pratt for the next two years, proving himself to be an able navigator and taking the boat safely through many dangerous stretches of the Yangtze and Min rivers. The crew consisted of eight boatmen and eight trackers. The latter were engaged in the unenviable task of hauling the boat across rapids and whirlpools from narrow cliff-side tracks hundreds of feet above the river. The crew were also joined by Pratt's cook–interpreter, his German assistant and a boy, making it 21 hands on board.

The boat was then loaded with equipment essential to the expedition, including 70 butterfly nets for distribution among native collectors, bundles of paper for pressing and drying botanical specimens, papers for Lepidoptera (moths, butterflies, etc.) and a good supply of tins for Coleoptera (the order to which ladybirds and beetles belong).

1889 – through the Gorges to Sichuan and Tibet
On 26 March 1889, Pratt and his team finally departed Yichang. The steamer *Kiang-Tang* was anchored in the river, and, as Pratt's boat passed her, the captain 'saluted' with a blast of the steam whistle. That same steamer had carried Augustine Henry from his first base in Shanghai to Hubei Province seven years previously. Yichang soon disappeared into the distance and an adventure had begun.

A pontoon opposite the Foreign Compound at Yichang. The steamer on the Yangtze is the *Kiang-Tung*, the ship that brought Augustine Henry to Yichang in April 1882. The hill to the rear is Moji Shan, known to Henry and Pratt as 'the Dome'.

Antwerp Pratt's description of sailing through the gorges differs little from the horror stories told by his contemporary travellers. Extra trackers needed to be hired and it took 15 men to haul the small boat over rapids of the Xiling Gorge. On the second day of their journey, the wreck of a large houseboat swept passed them, and, that evening, a junk was smashed on the rapids. Travel that day was also aggravated by a sandstorm that raged for hours, covering the boat with fine sand that penetrated everywhere. One of his trackers had cut his thumb severely, through careless handling of a bamboo rope, and had cut muscles all around down to the bone. Pratt had no choice but to land him and find a new tracker.

Four days after leaving Yichang, the notorious Sin-tan rapid was reached. The most fearsome of all the obstacles in the Three Gorges, its violent currents had smashed innumerable junks and sent many a sailor to a watery grave. Thirty men struggled on the towropes, and, even then, progress was in inches. Though the rapid was only 200 m (220 yards) long, the ascent took several hours, giving some idea of the violence of the currents. Shipping was big business in the gorges, and, near any large rapid, a village was always found. The inhabitants made their living by hauling junks across the raging currents, and from making and selling bamboo ropes. They lived in bamboo-framed huts that could easily be moved, depending on the height of the Yangtze, and always lived close to the water.

Pratt's was the first European-owned boat to make the ascent through the gorges. However, knowing, from former experience, the feeling of residents towards foreigners, he took special care in having her secured at night. Two anchors were laid out and a watch was kept all night to guard against treachery. The locals, it seemed, would have had no hesitation in cutting the boat and its crew adrift and sending them down the rapids to their deaths.[3]

By 1 April, the city of Badong was reached, and, two days later, the boat entered the sparsely populated Wu Gorge (Wu Xia). Progress through this stretch of the river was swift, since there were no rapids of any great consequence to be found, and, just a day later, they entered the final, Qutang Gorge (Qutang Xia). Here, the boat almost came to serious grief when it got caught on a rapid and its bamboo towrope was swept away. A passing junk and its crew were asked for assistance, but refused to help a 'foreign devil' out of a dangerous situation. Pratt's boat was then driven into a whirlpool and forced downriver for a considerable distance, causing a vexatious delay.

Limestone cliffs soared 610 m (2000 ft) over the river, and, high up on one of the cliff faces, a new road was being constructed and 'coolies' could be seen suspended on plank scaffolds, drilling holes for explosives. Beyond the gorges, the river calmed, and Pratt anchored for the night at the city of Wanxian, opposite two large pagodas. Wanxian lay halfway between Yichang and Chongqing, and Pratt described the city as a most picturesque place. By then, it was mid April and the large orange groves nearby were in full flower and the air was laden with their perfume. The first botanical specimens were gathered near the city and were dried for later identification at Kew.

Upriver from Wanxian, the land soon levelled out and, on sandbanks by the river's edge, men could be seen panning for gold. The currents were calm along this stretch of river, and the little boat made good progress. The countryside was cultivated, and cereals, pulses, fruit and opium poppies were grown in quantity. The district was well populated and the inhabitants seemed pretty prosperous.

On 21 April, Pratt reached the city of Chongqing (then Chung-king). On landing, a sedan chair was hired, as it was dangerous for Europeans to walk the streets of many Chinese cities at that time. Chongqing was a large and important city, being the principal trade centre for the provinces of Sichuan and neighbouring Yunnan, and hundreds of junks traded from the city as far down river as Yichang. While based in Chongqing, Pratt stayed with a

ABOVE: Boats on the Min River below the city of Leshan. In the background are densely forested sandstone cliffs.

LEFT: *Rubus cockburnianus*, one of the finest Chinese brambles. It was discovered in the mountains of western Sichuan Province by Antwerp Pratt, and named for Augustine Henry's friend, Mr H. Cockburn of the British Consular Service in Chongqing.

friend of Henry's, Mr H. Cockburn, a member of the British Consular Service.

Three years later, when Pratt's collections were being published, the Kew botanist William Botting Hemsley named two of Pratt's finest discoveries after Cockburn. The best known of these is *Rubus cockburnianus*, a striking bramble with tall, purple, arching stems covered with a waxy, brilliant white bloom in winter. The second, *Primula cockburniana*, is also relatively well known in cultivation, and is a handsome candelabra type carrying whorls of pretty orange-red flowers. Both were found in the mountains above Kangding.

But we are getting ahead of ourselves. Pratt found Chongqing to be a disagreeable place and his stay there was relatively short. The boat's crew were changed before departure, since local Chongqing men would be better acquainted with the upper reaches of the Yangtze. Pratt's next destination was Leshan, a small city on the edge of the Chengdu Plain. In late April, he departed from Chongqing and bade goodbye to his European friends, the last Westerners he was to see for a very long time. The countryside along this stretch of the river was broken into low ravines and valleys, and the scenery impressed him greatly. The voyage was not without incident, however; passing a small riverside town, a crowd of people came to the bank of the river and stoned his

boat, crying out 'kill the foreign devils'. The threatening attitude of the local village inhabitants meant it was impossible to collect plants along long stretches of the Yangtze. A little further upriver, the body of a man swept past them, a poor tracker who had been dragged into the river, and still with a tracking belt of twisted bamboo around his waist.

Vast fields of poppies were passed, all grown for the production of opium. The warm-temperate climate also allowed the cultivation of tobacco on a large scale, of which two sorts were grown: *Nicotiana rustica* and *Nicotiana tobacum*. Tobacco – or *yen*, as it is known in the Three Gorges region – was introduced to China about the same time as maize (*c.*1530 AD).

A Giant Buddha at Leshan and the ascent of Wa-shan

In early May, Pratt and his team finally reached the confluence of the Yangtze and Min rivers. The principal trade in this region of Sichuan Province was with other cities in neighbouring Yunnan Province, and of great interest to Pratt were the enormous bales of the skins of wild beasts, such as bears, leopards, tigers, deer, badgers and wolves. An imperial army had also been based in the region by the emperor to try to subdue the Yi (then known as the Lolos), an ethnic group who maintained a more or less independent kingdom nearby.

It took 70 'coolies' to haul Pratt's boat up the rapids of the lower Min River, and it was there that he first saw the use of fishing cormorants. Bamboo rafts were scattered along the river, and each fisherman had about six birds, all perfectly trained and capable of bringing in a large catch for their masters each day.

On 14 May 1889, the team reached the city of Leshan, then a major centre in the trade of silk, timber, and insect wax.[4] Leshan lay on the confluence of three major rivers – the Min, the Dadu and the Qingy – and the boat was anchored near the city. It didn't take long, however, for the boat to be showered with stones by an angry mob, and, to

A boat on the Min River near its confluence with the Dadu and Qingyi rivers.

A houseboat anchored on the banks of the smoggy, modern city of Leshan, now home to more than six million people. The street trees in the background are *Metasequoia glyptostroboides*.

Leshan's colossal 71-m (233-ft) tall Great Buddha. Far taller than Pratt's estimate of 48 m (150 ft), it has seen major restoration in recent years.

avoid being massacred, Pratt had the boat set adrift and moored a mile beneath the city. To disguise himself, he had his head shaved and dressed in Chinese clothes, including an artificial ponytail, which was secured inside his cap. From then on, little attention was paid to him.

The nearby low hills were densely forested with trees of *Pinus massoniana* and Henry's Changyang collector was sent out with two other men to gather botanical and entomological specimens. On the opposite bank of the river to where Pratt's boat was anchored were cliffs of red sandstone, and, above them, in the pine-covered hillsides, were scattered temples containing gilt images. Most impressive of all these images was a colossal image of Buddha cut out of the sandstone. Pratt reckoned the statue was at least 48 m (150 ft) high, and it was seated with its hands on its knees. Small trees had taken root on the huge Buddha, and its head was overgrown with creepers, which Pratt believed would utterly destroy the work over the course of time.

A few days after Pratt's arrival at Leshan, the *Tao-tai* (one of the city leaders) boarded his boat with a staff of about 15 attendants. To the English traveller's amusement, he was informed that the locals believed that he had an infernal machine on board, and that his intention was to destroy the city. Pratt finally managed to persuade the group that his object was to collect birds, butterflies and plants – and his goal was not the ultimate destruction of Leshan.

Satisfied by this explanation, the *Tao-tai* was then vexed by Pratt's route, and asked him not to proceed to the distant mountain of Wa-shan since a guard could not be provided, and asked instead that the route be changed to go in the direction of the large city of Chengdu, the provincial capital of Sichuan. Pratt refused, stating his destination was Wa-shan, and that he would go there with or without permission. The *Tao-tai* left in a foul temper having made little progress with Pratt, who was later not only allowed to travel on, but was supplied with two armed guards to accompany him as far as Emei Shan. Wa-shan was a sister mountain to the sacred Emei Shan and lay 129 km (80 miles) south-west of Leshan. Its bulk was visible from the summit of Emei Shan and it resembled a huge Noah's ark, perched high above the clouds.

He was later to learn that the *Tao-tai*'s reluctance to allow him to travel the route he had chosen arose from the fact that it passed close to the border of the Yi (Lolo), the independent ethnic group previously mentioned, and with whom the Chinese Government were in a constant state of war and had never been able to subdue. The old leader feared that Pratt and his men would be taken prisoner in one of their raids, and that he would be held responsible.

On 19 May, having obtained 30 porters to carry his equipment overland, Pratt departed for Wa-shan, where he intended to stay for the summer, before returning by river to Yichang that autumn to send his collections back to Europe. The expedition's route crossed China's great rice-basket, the Chengdu Plain, one of the most fertile and productive areas of farmland in all of China. The region was well irrigated by enormous waterwheels equipped with bamboo cups. So fertile was the area and so benign was the climate that three crops of rice were produced in a single year.

Taro, *Colocasia esculenta* var. *antiquorum* was also widely grown on the plain for its massive, edible, nutty-flavoured tubers. Its bold, luxuriant foliage gave an exotic feel to the intensely cultivated fields. Taro is an ancient crop that originated about 7,000 years ago. It is no longer found in the wild, but may have come from the wet, rice-growing regions of India. More than 200 cultivars have been selected over the past 2 000 years, and, over that period, the plant has been almost exclusively propagated by vegetative means. Taro requires the same growing conditions as rice, and will grow in soil too wet for the sweet potato.

Colourful fields of *Carthamus tinctorius* – a thistle-like annual bearing handsome orange flowers above toothed, prickly leaves – were grown in the region for the production of safflower, a deep orange pigment much esteemed in the dyeing of costly silks. It is thought that the safflower was originally domesticated in the eastern Mediterranean region (the earliest archaeological records are from Mesopotamia) though, today, it is only known in cultivation. *Canna indica*, the Indian shot and a native of the neotropics, was also widely grown for its fleshy, edible rhizomes.

One of the commonest trees on the Chengdu Plain was a species of alder. It was planted on the margins of paddy fields and around farmsteads, where it provided shelter and fuel. Specimens were gathered by the Changyang collector, and these were incorporated into Augustine Henry's herbarium, from which it was described, a decade later, as a new species: *Alnus cremastogyne*. On trees of *Fraxinus chinensis*, Pratt reported seeing large clumps of the epiphytic *Dendrobium nobile*, a beautiful orchid still widely used in traditional herbal medicine.

The town of Emei was reached that evening. The group was only a few miles away from the famous Buddhist

ABOVE, BELOW: *Dendrobium nobile*, an epiphytic orchid with stiff, erect, cane-like pseudobulbs. Native from India to Thailand and China, the colour of its scented flowers varies from white to rosy purple. Its stems are commonly used in herbal medicine and as an insecticide.

mountain of Emei Shan, which they would ascend twice the following year. On their march to Wa-shan, Pratt and his men passed scores of Chinese 'coolies' carrying baskets containing the eggs of a scale insect. The production of insect white wax, from which candles were made, constituted a huge industry in 19th-century China, particularly in western Sichuan Province. Two host plants were employed in farming the scale insect, *Ericerus pela*. Eggs were laid (each female is capable of laying up to 15,000 eggs) on the stems of trees of the Chinese privet, *Ligustrum lucidum*, growing in the valley of the Anning River in southern Sichuan, and, in late April, they were removed and carried over 200 miles to the production areas in western Sichuan.

This monumental task was achieved by hundreds of porters who were employed to carry the larvae with all possible speed to the growing areas. The journey was undertaken by night with the aid of lanterns, lest the larvae hatch in the heat of day. The 'coolies', or porters, travelled 40 miles a day, and, by aid of relay, the 200-mile journey by foot over the mountains was carried out over a six-day period. The route brought the porters through the then independent country of the Yi, who permitted them to cross the state (an area the size of Wales) on payment of duty.[5]

Having reached the production centres in Sichuan, the larvae were placed on heavily pollarded trees of the Chinese ash, *Fraxinus chinensis*, where they immediately hatched and began to deposit wax. In China, the insect's natural predator is the ladybird (referred to by the Chinese as '*la gho*', or

'wax-dog'). At the end of August, branches holding the insects were heavily infested with wax. The branches were then cut off and the wax removed in vats of boiling water. The finished product was later used to coat pills, make candles, polish furniture and to impart a gloss to silk. The wax produced was said to be superior to ordinary European wax of the time. Since the candles had to be shipped down the Yangtze, through the rapids and whirlpools of the Three Gorges, the expense incurred meant the finished product was used by the wealthy upper classes only.

By late May, Pratt and his team safely crossed the borders of the independent Yi country, and he was to see their stone-built tower houses on the opposite bank of the river. From there on, the route became difficult and dangerous. The road disappeared, to be replaced by a narrow track across a steep precipice, and one wrong step would send him or his men on a fatal fall. Below them, as they crawled in single file along a narrow track, could be seen the river tearing along its rocky bed hundreds of feet below. In that wild landscape, the river formed the boundary between the Chinese Empire and the independent Yi kingdom.

On 26 May, Pratt and his men reached an old French mission house run by Père Joseph Martin. Martin had not seen a Westerner since Baber travelled the region 11 years previously, and he provided Pratt with accommodation at the mission. The old missionary lived in a nearby village, where he kept a pretty garden full of familiar European flowers, such as Sweet Williams, the seeds of which had been

May 1889: Antwerp Pratt and his Chinese plant collectors resting in the Mission House at the base of Wa-Shan.

Wa-shan, in a photograph taken by E. H. Wilson during his visit to the region in September 1908. The mountain can be seen as a succession of tiered cliffs with a strange, very flat summit.

sent from France. Behind the mission house could be seen the towering bulk of Wa-shan. It was still a little early and too cold to collect butterflies, but the hills surrounding Wa-shan were rich in plants and Pratt and his men immediately set to work on gathering and drying specimens. The area was thinly populated and the cultivation of maize and potatoes had been introduced by the French missionaries. The countryside was rugged and thickly forested, and tigers, leopards, bears and antelope abounded.

In early June, Pratt and his men began to ascend Wa-shan and found the southern slopes densely covered in virgin forest. Further up the mountain, they encountered huge icicles hanging from projections on the cliffs. Many of these, according to Pratt, were as large as a church steeple, and, where they had fallen, they had brought down tonnes of earth and rock in front of them, leaving huge semicircular cavities beneath where they had been suspended.

The mountain was remarkably square in appearance and its four sides were more or less perpendicular. The upper storey was formed by a series of 15 61-m (200-ft) tall precipices layered one above another until they eventually reached a peculiarly flat summit, which was slightly higher than that of Emei Shan. Viewed from the near distance, Wa-shan could be seen to consist of successive tiers of vertical limestone cliffs culminating on the summit as a marshy plateau half a mile across and forming what Baber called 'the most charming natural park in the world'. Wa-shan, like Emei Shan, was one of China's five holy mountains, and on the summit was a temple built of local fir.[6] On Wa-shan, Pratt continued to employ 30 men to collect material for him and placed the team under the supervision of Augustine Henry's botanical collector from Changyang.

Wa-shan inevitably offered many new and exciting plants, and it was from material collected by the Changyang man, which was later incorporated into Augustine Henry's collections, that *Rhododendron insigne* was described as a new species. In this region, it grew to 6 m (20 ft) tall, and, despite it being so late in the season, plants still carried large trusses of rosy-pink bell-shaped flowers. One of Pratt's most remarkable finds on the mountain was *Cladrastis sinensis*, a medium-sized tree in the pea family, bearing large branched panicles of white to rosy-pink fragrant flowers in summer.

It was on the densely forested slopes of Wa-shan that Pratt's native collectors gathered material of *Ribes henryi*.

167

These pressed, dried specimens were also later incorporated into Henry's herbarium, and were named in his honour nine years later. *Ribes henryi* was inadvertently introduced to cultivation by E. H. Wilson in 1908, when seeds of *Sinowilsonia henryi* were sown at the Royal Botanic Garden, Edinburgh. From this seed batch, a stray seedling of *Ribes henryi* mysteriously appeared. The Edinburgh plant proved to be male and flowered for the first time in the spring of 1912. Edward Janczewski (1846–1918), the monographer of *Ribes*, who described the closely allied *Ribes laurifolium*, raised a single seedling of *Ribes henryi* in a case that almost parallels the Edinburgh plant. A single plant came up among seedlings of the aforementioned *Ribes laurifolium*. This was female and produced fruits by crossing with *Ribes laurifolium*. This seedling undoubtedly was raised with seeds of *Ribes laurifolium* (Wilson 817), gathered on Wa-shan in September 1908. It is a very handsome small shrub, and Augustine Henry grew it in his Dublin garden during the 1920s.

Sorbus scalaris was also described from a Wa-shan collection found in Augustine Henry's herbarium. A handsome, small, spreading tree, its foliage turns brilliant orange-red in autumn, when it also usually carries a heavy crop of bright-red fruits. In the wild, this species is confined to an area south of Baoxing to Wa-shan.[7]

Several roses were gathered on the mountain, including *Rosa davidii*, an erect, open shrub with loose corymbs of up to a dozen bright-pink flowers. In Sichuan, it seems to be restricted to Wa-shan and the region around Baoxing, where it was originally found by Armand David in 1869.

In the surrounding forests, the curious birthwort *Aristolochia moupinensis* scrambled its way through thickets. E. H. Wilson later visited Wa-shan on a number of occasions, and, from there, introduced the *Aristolochia* through Messrs Veitch in 1903. Wilson made a return trip to Wa-shan in October 1908, and it was from this expedition that he introduced *Rhododendron insigne* through the Arnold Arboretum.[8] He was greatly impressed by the mountain, and its extremely rich flora, and had the following to say of his time there:

I have climbed and botanised on many mountains in different parts of China, some much higher than this, but none have I found richer in cool-temperate plants, and more especially flowering shrubs. Altogether, with its rich flora, peculiar fauna, its singular geological formation, and its magnificent park on the summit, Wa-shan has many claims on the attention of the naturalist.[9]

Having completed his initial exploration of the mountain, Pratt made a change from his original plan of basing himself on Wa-shan for the summer, and decided to make an advance to the city of Kangding (then Ta chien lu) on the Tibetan borderlands. In his absence, he placed Henry's Changyang man in charge of the large team of native plant collectors. Pratt was more than pleased with this collector, and wrote to Henry giving him an update on the progress of his work:

I took your man along with me as far as Wa-shan, and, being a most interesting flora, I left him there during our absence at Ta chien lu, and on my return I found he had made a very nice collection (not large but in good order) and I think most of them will prove new.[10]

A party of porters was then engaged to carry vital food and equipment to Kangding; each porter carried up to 57 kg (126 lb) across ravines and rocky mountain passes as high as 2,675 m (8,778 ft). It was early July, and rhododendrons and several species of *Hydrangea* were in flower. Near the town of Luding, a sweeping view of the landscape opened in front of them from one of the many high passes. The panorama of a single, densely forested ravine several miles across greatly impressed the English traveller. The view, with clouds rolling into the ravine beneath, presented a remarkable spectacle. Despite the magnificent scenery, though, Pratt was appalled by the state of the local inns he was forced to stay in by night. The following comments give some idea of the discomforts he faced:

In justice to the town I might here say that if we had gone a little further we might have had more decent accommodation, for though I had some idea of what a dirty place a Chinese inn might be, this one for filth, discomfort, and the quantity of vermin that it contained was entitled to take the cake. My room was small and with no window, a lamp having to be used in the day time. The walls were black with slime, and in spite of being very tired I could get but little rest during the night, my unfortunate body being invaded by hosts of vermin of all sorts. I left this at an early hour the next morning, being only too glad to get away. During my travels, I have been forced to take refuge in some curiously dirty places, but this inn will remain fixed in my mind as containing the most varied collection of the most disagreeable things I have ever met with at one time.[11]

Pratt's journey followed the course of the Dadu River (then the Tung River), at that season a thick roaring torrent full of huge boulders and whirlpools. The road his team followed was a mere groove cut into a precipice 1,000 feet

The mist-shrouded mountains above Kangding. Antwerp Pratt had reached a chilly 4,120 m (13,520 ft) when this photograph was taken.

above the river. One false step would send the travellers into the torrents of the river beneath.

One of the commonest plants in the valley of the Dadu River was the gorgeous *Rosa brunonii*, the Himalayan musk rose, whose rampant stems scrambled their way through trees to 10 m (33 ft) and were laden with broad corymbs of richly fragrant, snow-white blossoms.

At the town of Luding (then Lu-ting-chiao), Pratt encountered the iron-chain suspension bridge for which the town is famous even today. Luding lies on both banks of the Dadu River, and the construction of the bridge was ordered by the Emperor Qing Kangxi in 1705 to serve as an important link along the Sichuan–Tibet road. The bridge was about 110 m (150 yards) long and spanned the river 46 m (150 ft) below. A narrow footway was formed by unfastened wooden boards, and Pratt was heartily laughed at by the locals when crossing, since the oscillation was so great and there was no handrail on the bridge. The English explorer was violently swung like a pendulum above the raging torrents of the Dadu River.

A long and gruelling journey continued by the course of the river, and, along this route, they met a great deal of traffic, mainly traders bringing tobacco, salt and tea to Kangding, from the southern, warmer parts of Sichuan

Province, and hides, musk, deer antlers and herbal medicines being carried south from Kangding, where they had been gathered in the hinterlands. In the low-lying valleys, *Opuntia stricta*, a prickly-pear cactus from the southern USA and South America, had naturalised itself, having been originally introduced to the region for its edible fruits. Good peaches, apricots and apples were also grown in the warm, low-lying valleys, and sent to the markets at Kangding.

Approaching the city, the scenery was magnificent. Views through massive ravines disclosed snow-capped mountains, below which were forests of dark fir and pine, and successive zones of vegetation scaling the mountainsides could be distinctly traced. Pratt recorded the altitudinal sequence of the flora, beneath the snow line was alpine grassland, followed in rotation by fir and pine forest, rhododendrons and broad-leaved evergreen trees, leading to sub-tropical plants in the low-lying valleys. He also noted that the vegetation was more Tibetan in character than Chinese. His observations were correct: the flora of the Kangding region is heavily influenced by Himalayan elements. His knowledge of the Chinese flora and vegetation types was by then relatively good, despite his having arrived at Yichang a short time before with no great interest in botany.

Kangding, a view of the city from the south. Nestled below towering mountains, the city marks the edge of China and the beginning of an historically Tibetan region. For centuries, it has been a trading centre between the two nationalities. The city is bisected by the Kangding River, a tributary of the Dadu River, which it joins near Luding.

Kangding – gateway to Tibet

Perched at 2,620 m (8,595 ft), Kangding was the gateway to Tibet. The harsh, rugged countryside around it was Tibetan in character, and the district was ruled by native chieftains.[12] The city nestled amid majestic scenery, and, to the south-west, the mighty peak of Gongga Shan soared to a staggering 7,556 m (24,789 ft). On entering the city gates of Kangding, Pratt found the streets crowded by a strange gathering of ethnic groups, with a mixture of all the nations of Asia, and Tibetans predominating.

It was there that Antwerp Pratt met another group of French missionaries, including the famous plant collector, Père Jean André Soulié (1858–1905). Born in Saint Juéry, Aveyron, Soulié been stationed at Kangding since 1886. During his time in western China, he collected more than 7,000 herbarium specimens, and introduced a number of plants to cultivation through the Muséum National d'Histoire Naturelle (Natural History Museum) in Paris, most notably the very beautiful *Rosa soulieana*.

These missionaries gave Pratt and his men a great deal of help during their stay, since they spoke both Tibetan and Chinese and were liked by many of the locals. They were extremely cautious of the local lamas, however, who bore

them no good will. Little were they to know that poor Soulié was to be later tortured and shot by lamas at Yaragong, on the Yangtze, in 1905 – a sad end for a caring missionary and outstanding plant collector. Antwerp Pratt appreciated the tough lives these missionaries faced, and all the collectors he trained at Kangding were Christians, brought up from childhood by the bishop and his fathers. Pratt's camera was the first ever in the region, and the missionaries were delighted to have photographs to send home to their families in France.

Kangding was an irregular, sprawling city with houses of all sizes and narrow streets paved with large flat stones. The city lay on the high road between Beijing (then Peking) and Lhasa, and government messengers could sometimes be seen passing through, having made a long journey from the Imperial City.

The inn Pratt used at Kangding was unusually clean and had a stable yard for horses and yaks. In the centre of the yard was a wooden pole, from which strings of Tibetan prayer flags were draped and fluttered in the wind. Lamas, dressed in scarlet cloaks and with shaven heads, strolled the streets and a large monastery lay outside the city. Sky funerals were practiced in the region: when a lama died, his body was carried to a lofty plain where his flesh was cut off the bones, and the

August 1889: Antwerp Pratt with the French plant collector Père Jean André Soulié. Their tent is pitched in the mountains to the north of Kangding at an altitude of 3,353 m (11,000 ft).

bones were crushed and mixed with flour. Both were then fed to the vultures, and the body was thus disposed of. Antwerp Pratt and his men were in the heart of Buddhist country.

Large caravans passed through Kangding, mainly Tibetans who used horses and yak–cow crosses to carry enormous loads across the difficult mountain passes. The Tibetan drivers of these caravans were wild-looking men and wore rawhide boots and loose, brown, woollen coats. Enormous quantities of brick tea came into Kangding from Ya-an (then Ya-chou Fu). According to Pratt the loads carried by porters were enormous and ran to more than 136 kg (300 lb). Each slab of tea weighed up to 7 kg (15 lb), and the entire load was carried on a wooden frame with two rope loops through which the arms were passed. A T-stick was always carried, and, while resting, the weight of the load was taken by the top of the stick. At Kangding, these huge slabs of tea were cut up into 'bricks' and were then packed in hide to be taken by the caravans to all parts of Tibet, as the chief ingredient of Tibetan butter tea. Some of these caravans travelled an amazing 2,400 km (1,500 miles) from Kangding to trading towns to the west of Lhasa, and could be on the road for a full six months. Indian rupees and Russian roubles were recognised currency in 19th-century Kangding

In late July, Pratt was in the mountains to the west of Kangding, collecting plants just beneath the snow line. The mountains soared to enormous elevations, and his lodgings were in a stone-built hut in the valley beneath. On the woodland floor was a rich understorey layer of showy plants such as *Lyonia ovalifolia*, an elegant evergreen shrub bearing racemes of small, white, bell-shaped, *Pieris*-like flowers. The Sino-Himalayan *Enkianthus deflexus* meets its most easterly range in Sichuan Province, and is one of the commonest and most beautiful shrubs in that region. It is rare in cultivation, which is puzzling since it is the largest-flowered species in the genus and its flame-coloured autumn hue is a thrilling sight. Through the trees raced immense vines of *Clematis montana* var. *grandiflora*, with stems as thick as a man's wrist. *Deutzia longifolia*, a common shrub around Kangding, was by then a mass of starry white blooms. With it grew a new species of mock orange, *Philadelphus subcanus*, then a mass of snow-white, sweetly fragrant, bell-shaped flowers.

Another remarkable find from this region was *Sinojackia henryi*; not just a new species, but the specimens gathered were the first ever collections of a new genus. This small rare tree has never been introduced to cultivation, which is

171

Père Jean André Soulié seen here with his Christian converts. In the late 19th century, more than 2,500 Roman Catholic missionaries were based in China. Of these, the French produced a number of outstanding naturalists, such as Bodinier, Cavalerie, David, Delavay, Ducloux, Farges, d'Incarville, Perny and Soulié, for example.

ABOVE: E. H. Wilson's photograph of 'coolies' carrying brick tea for the Kangding market shows the enormous loads these porters bore, often over very long distances.

BELOW: *Cypripedium tibeticum*, seen here on the Tra La in south-east Tibet. This stunning lady's slipper orchid was described from Antwerp Pratt's Kangding collections, and from those of Sir George King in Sikkim (India).

a pity and a loss to Western gardens. In its native habitat in western Sichuan, *Sinojackia henryi* produces short racemes of delicate, white, styrax-like flowers in early summer.

On the edge of woodland and in alpine grassland grew one of Pratt's finest discoveries, the regal Tibetan slipper orchid, *Cypripedium tibeticum*. One of the glories of the Himalaya and western China, this beautiful little orchid can form large colonies in undisturbed habitats, and each plant carries large, solitary, pouch-shaped, dark-purple flowers above bold pleated foliage. Though his expertise may have been in entomology, Pratt's interest in botany must have been greatly enthused having been surrounded by such a remarkably rich and beautiful flora.

Other meadow inhabitants from the same group included *Cypripedium flavum*, a lemon-yellow-flowered species evocatively referred to by Reginald Farrer as 'Proud Margaret' since it bears its large flowers on stiff, erect stems. Also forming small colonies beneath the shade of tall firs and rhododendrons was the purple-flowered *Cypripedium*

172

The wild, single-flowered form of the burr rose, *Rosa roxburghii* f. *normalis*. The delicate rose-pink blossoms are pleasantly scented.

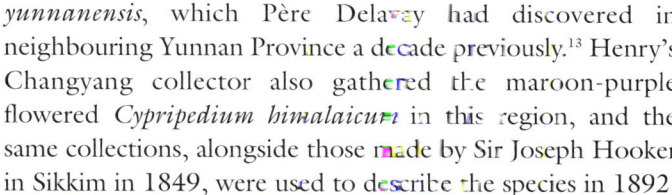

Rosa moyesii, gorgeous in blossom, though equally ornamental when carrying its autumn fruits.

In autumn, the burr rose produces large, spiny, apple-like fruits, as seen here on plants at the Royal Botanic Gardens, Kew.

yunnanensis, which Père Delavay had discovered in neighbouring Yunnan Province a decade previously.[13] Henry's Changyang collector also gathered the maroon-purple flowered *Cypripedium himalaicum* in this region, and the same collections, alongside those made by Sir Joseph Hooker in Sikkim in 1849, were used to describe the species in 1892.

The alpine meadows presented a rich kaleidoscopic array of colour, and *Anemone rivularis* grew in tens of thousands. This beautiful perennial occupies a large native range from the Himalaya of northern India to mountains of south-west China. There, it is one of the chief glories of alpine meadows, producing umbels of small white flowers stained blue beneath. With it grew *Anemone hupehensis*, *Delphinium potaninii*, *Caltha scaposa*, *Pedicularis superba*, *Trollius ranunculoides* and *Delphinium pachycentrum*, the latter two being new to science.

In August, at his wit's end with the filth of his lodgings, Pratt bought an embroidered Tibetan tent and moved to an altitude of 3,350 m (10,990 ft). The scenery was magnificent and the snow line above him commenced at 4,870 m (16,000 ft). The country was well wooded, and he made rich collections over the following weeks.

One of the most abundant trees in the area was the Tibetan hazel, *Corylus tibetica*, a very distinctive species bearing large, decorative, burr-like husks. On the verge of these woods, the first nodding golden-yellow flowers had appeared on *Clematis tangutica* ssp. *obtusiuscula*. Other new species collected by Pratt in this mountainous region included *Malus prattii*, a handsome crab bearing small yellow or red egg-shaped fruits. On the same slopes grew *Betula utilis* var. *prattii*, whose orange-brown trunks must have been a conspicuous feature in those dark woods.

Roses were common in the surrounding thickets, and Pratt's best-known discovery – the incomparably beautiful *Rosa moyesii* – was abundant on the edges of woods, in shades varying from pink to the more familiar intense blood-red. It is now a deservedly popular garden plant, offering a liberal summer display of blossoms followed by large, bright crimson, flagon-shaped fruits in September. *Rosa prattii* was also common on rocky, sun-scorched slopes, where it formed large bushes bearing deep rose-pink flowers, followed in succession by scarlet, bottle-shaped fruits. The aptly named 'burr rose', *Rosa roxburghii* f. *normalis*, was also common, though at lower altitudes than the former and it was particularly abundant in semi-arid river valleys. Around

Kangding and the Chengdu Plain, it was commonly used as an effective hedge plant. Though the fragrant, shell-pink flowers of this form are pretty and it has attractive peeling bark, it is generally grown for its large, spiny, apple-like fruits.

Pratt's collections make a mouth-watering read, and

Sorbus prattii, a beautiful rowan with pearly-white fruits. It was introduced to cultivation by E. H. Wilson in October 1910.

Hydrangea heteromalla, seen here on Zibenshan in Yunnan's Salween (Nu Jiang)–Mekong (Lancang Jiang) divide. It is a widespread species, found across much of the Himalaya and China.

those from Kangding, in particular, were full of highly garden-worthy plants. One of his finest discoveries, though the least known in cultivation, is a rowan that bears his name: *Sorbus prattii*, a small attractive tree bearing lax clusters of pearly white fruits in autumn. In thickets, *Clematis rehderiana* scrambled its way through trees and shrubs, sporting primrose-yellow bell-shaped flowers, scented of cowslips. *Hydrangea heteromalla* formed small trees to 8 m (26 ft) and bearing wide corymbs of small white flowers bordered by large ray-florets.

In the same woods grew *Salix moupinensis*, a handsome willow carrying large, bold, glabrous leaves. With it grew *Hypericum hookerianum*, *Polygala arillata*, *Sambucus adnata* and the curious *Helwingia japonica*, a strange shrub of botanical interest, bearing tiny unisexual flowers on the midribs of the upper surface of the leaves. Native to Japan and China, it is rarely grown outside of large collections, which is a shame, since its foliage and its growth habit are so elegant.

The going was tough for Pratt and his men, however. The countryside was divided by deep canyons, and landslides and avalanches made trekking a dangerous occupation. Père Soulié joined Pratt in mid August and both men enjoyed the rare opportunity of collecting together on those high altitude slopes. On mossy boulders, well above the tree line, grew the tiny *Gaultheria trichophylla*, a charming little shrublet by then covered with masses of large, deep-blue, fleshy fruits. Above it, on open moorland, grew *Cassiope selaginoides*, a small shrublet bearing pendant, bell-shaped, white flowers. In the Himalaya and parts of western China, this species covers enormous tracts of alpine moorland, in the same way as heather, *Calluna vulgaris*, covers a similar habitat in Britain and Ireland.

Just beneath the snow line, the travellers encountered one of the most beautiful of all Himalayan alpines, the dainty lavender-blue-flowered *Cyananthus incanus*, a small prostrate perennial in the campanula family. Easy to grow under alpine-house conditions, it occupies a large geographical range, from central Nepal to western China.

Soon, however, it was time to leave

Cyananthus incanus, a pretty little alpine distributed from the mountains of central Nepal to south-west China. Pictured here on the Doshong La near the Tibet–Bhutan border.

Kangding and make the long journey back to Yichang, and so Pratt said goodbye to the Bishop and the French Fathers and made his way first to Wa-shan, where he recalled his collectors to look over their collections. They had done marvellously well, and he had every reason to be pleased with their exertions.

With 24 opium-addicted porters, Pratt made his return to Leshan by sampan, and found his own boat safe and undamaged, despite the fact that the city had just witnessed the worst floods in a century. In a single night, the river had risen 15 m (50 ft) and had entered the city gates, destroying houses and property of all kinds. That night, the cries of flood victims could be heard throughout the city and hundreds of boats and sampans were dashed to pieces – the loss of life was appalling. Somehow, Pratt's vessel survived.

During his absence from Leshan, the most extraordinary stories circulated in the city about Pratt's travels. It was said that he was kidnapping children and then making chemicals out of their eyes for his camera. The old story of his 'infernal machine' that was set on the destruction of the city was also revived. Such was the strength of anti-Western sentiment during that period in China.

Pratt reached Yichang in mid September, after an adventurous sailing down the Yangtze. The floods at Leshan had continued down the river and the Yangtze had risen to sweep villages and houses away from its course. In the gorges, he reported that his boat looked like a mere toy in a stream. Enormous waterfalls swept over the cliffs, making a picturesque and atmospheric approach to Yichang through the gorges. Pratt anchored his boat off the Foreign Compound; he was as good as home.

175

The Shanjue Temple is one of the many temples and nunneries scattered across Emei Shan. The large tree to the left is *Cryptomeria japonica* var. *sinensis*.

A densely forested ravine on Emei Shan. This sacred mountain is home to more than 3,200 species of flowering plants, of which more than 200 are endemic.

The Shenshen cliffs near Emei Shan's summit fall for more than one mile sheer. E. H. Wilson described this view as 'a never to be forgotten scene'.

1890 – a spring reconnaissance on Emei Shan

Having spent the winter at Yichang, Antwerp Pratt gathered his men for a return expedition to western Sichuan Province. On 18 February 1890, he departed the city determined to get to Kangding in time for a spring collection of plants, mammals and insects. The Yangtze was at its lowest at that time of year, and snow lay on the steep hills to the rear of Yichang.

By late March, Pratt and his team had reached the confluence of the Min and Yangtze rivers. The contrast could not have been greater; the Min, with its strikingly clear waters, against that of the silt-laden, muddy Yangtze. The current was strong, however, and once again extra trackers had to be hired to ascend the lower Min River to Leshan.

On 10 April, the group departed Leshan and slept that night in the small town of Emei (then Omei-hsien). Above the little town towered the mighty bulk of Emei Shan – or 'Mount Omei', as it is also known – the holiest mountain in all of China. Sacred to Buddhists, its great bulk soars like an island above the Chengdu Plain, and, in the late 19th century, the mountain's one hundred or so monasteries

housed thousands of monks. Emei Shan was a place of pilgrimage and tens of thousands of devout visitors made it to the mountain each year, travelling from monastery to monastery until finally reaching the Golden Summit Temple at 3,099 m (10,167 ft).

Emei Shan had been protected for centuries by the monks, and the only time trees were felled was when a temple had to be rebuilt, or when firewood was needed by the monasteries, but for no other purpose. It was unlikely, therefore, that holy Emei Shan would ever be denuded of its great forests. No life was ever taken on the mountain, and Pratt almost found himself in serious trouble for shooting below the temples. Emei town supplied the monks living on Emei Shan with food and other provisions before winter set in and roads up the mountain became blocked with snow and ice. Henry's friend Ernst Faber had climbed the mountain three years previously, and reported it to be a rich field for the collector. Pratt therefore planned a spring and autumn trip to Emei Shan that year.

The following day, he and his men climbed a long series of stone steps to the Wannian Monastery, '*Wannian*'

Faber's fir, *Abies fabri*, seen here on the summit of Emei Shan, where it had been discovered by Ernst Faber in 1887.

Rhododendron strigillosum. Native to western Sichuan Province, where it is rare, this beautiful species was discovered by Père Armand David in 1869, and was introduced by Wilson in 1904.

meaning 'the temple of 10,000 years'. Wannian was the oldest surviving of all sacred Emei Shan's temples, and was reconstructed in the 9th century. The temple was full of many fine images, including an enormous clay and gilt statue of Buddha. Pratt also mentions having seen the famous statue of the Bodhisattva Puxian (the protector and patron saint of the mountain) seated on an 8.5-m (28-ft) tall, white, six-tusked elephant, cast in copper and bronze in the 8th century. By the temple were enormous incense bowls. One hundred such temples and monasteries were scattered across the slopes of Emei Shan, and the entire mountain was church property.

Outside the temples were stalls selling herbal medicines, crystals from Wa-shan and carved walking sticks to ease the steep ascent and to take away as a memento. Wannian was surrounded by immense forests, and the road to it afforded magnificent views of vast ravines and mountain slopes clothed by dark forests of *Abies fabri*. On the higher reaches of the mountain were small trees of the striking and very beautiful *Rhododendron strigillosum*, a rare species in western Sichuan Province, where it is known only from Baoxing, Emei Shan and Wa-shan. In the shelter of Emei Shan's ancient fir forests, its brilliant crimson, bell-shaped flowers must have made a magnificent sight and created a great impression on Pratt.

Primula ovalifolia was common on Emei Shan's mid-

forested slopes, where it grew by waterfalls and streams, on shaded vertical cliffs and in moist woods. It was in full flower during Pratt's visit and had carpeted the ground with colour as soon as the snows had begun to melt. It is a remarkably beautiful plant, with deep violet-purple (approaching blue) flowers, and was introduced by means of living plants by Wilson in 1901. It was probably on Emei Shan that Pratt made his collections of *Rhododendron concinnum*, where it had been discovered two years previously by Faber. A common species in western Sichuan, this handsome shrub carries masses of purple, funnel-shaped flowers in broad terminal trusses in April and May.

The temples were clean and Pratt found the monks extremely civil. For a small sum of money, pilgrims and visitors could sleep in the monasteries, and Pratt stayed in the Wannian Monastery that night. He put four of his native plant collectors to work on the forested slopes around the monastery, and was surprised to meet a Tibetan family he knew from Kangding on a pilgrimage to the mountain. The following morning, from the 'temple of 10,000 years', Pratt started for the summit. His route

Rhododendron concinnum, a widespread shrub in Sichuan Province. It was discovered on Emei Shan by Ernst Faber in 1887.

177

followed a steep, winding road, then covered in snow and ice, and he reached the bitterly cold peak late that evening.

The Golden Summit Temple, one of the mountain's most famous and elaborate structures, was then a mass of ruins, having been destroyed by lightning in 1819. The temple had been located on the edge of what Pratt reckoned was the highest precipice in the world, a sheer cliff face that fell 1.6 km (1 mile) into the forests beneath. A steady stream of pilgrims made it to the summit, and the monks told tales of tigers carrying off visitors who were never heard of again. (It was thought that only wicked men, though, were so taken.)

The morning of 13 April 1890 was beautifully clear, and magnificent views could be obtained from the summit. To the south-west, the great bulk of Wa-shan soared above the cloud cover, while, to the north-west, the peaks above Kangding pierced the sky. Range after range projected into the distance, forming a magnificent spectacle.

A French prince arrives at Kangding

From Emei Shan, Pratt and his men continued on to Kangding by way of Ya-an (then Ya-chow), a busy market town that traded in brick tea and tobacco. The heat of the low-lying river valleys was stifling – too much so, in fact, for Pratt's Tibetan dog, 'Ja-ma', who was carried through the region on a sedan chair. At higher levels, the flora was interesting and his botanical collectors were set to work.

Kangding was finally reached on 27 April. In early May, Pratt and nine of his men left the city through its south gate determined to visit the snow-clad mountains to the south-east of the city. Not far from the gates, at an altitude of 1,220 m (4,000 ft), was a ravine covered in dwarf pink azaleas, anemones and many sub-alpine flowers. Between that level and 3,658 m (12,000 ft), rhododendrons grew in great variety, some with stems more than 30 cm (1 ft) in diameter.

Among the rhododendrons grew the most spectacular primulas, including the gorgeous *Primula blinii*, a

August 1890: Pratt's view of the summit of Emei Shan capped by several monastic buildings, below which fall the Shenshen cliffs.

ABOVE: Looking west from the summit of Emei Shan towards the mountains above Kangding. Silhouetted against a dense, fleecy cumulus are large trees of *Abies fabri*. In the far distance is the snow-capped Gongga Shan (Mount Gongga).

RIGHT: *Rhododendron lutescens*, a commonly found species in western Sichuan and north-east Yunnan provinces, where it grows in thickets and on the margins of woods. It is the most beautiful yellow-flowered member of the Triflorum series.

widespread species in western Sichuan and neighbouring Yunnan provinces, where it grows on forested mountain slopes, on cliffs and in meadows between 3,200 to 4,200 m. It was introduced to cultivation by George Forrest in 1915.

The tent was pitched at 3,810 m (12,500 ft) and the group's fuel was supplied with logs of the largest species of *Rhododendron*. A good fire needed to be kept up as, that night, there was a severe frost and a heavy fall of snow.

Pratt was a mere two hours' walk from the line of perpetual snow and glaciers; there was not a house to be seen for miles. *Rhododendron lutescens* was common on the mountains above Kangding and its primrose-coloured blossoms must have lit up these dark, sombre, forested slopes. In its native habitat, it forms small trees to 6 m (20 ft) tall, and it is most likely that it was this species that Pratt and his men were forced to fell for firewood.

Père Soulié arrived two days later, and the campsite was fixed at a chilly 4,288 m (14,070 ft). The location was beautiful: a large, deep lake surrounded on three sides by precipices many hundreds of feet high and filled by a waterfall on its southern end. On its northern end were poles strewn with Tibetan prayer flags.

Where these two Europeans could collect was determined by the local king, whose palace lay a few miles outside the city. Pratt eventually met the elderly king, dressed in fine Tibetan robes. He was practically independent of Imperial China, apart from the occasional tribute to the Emperor in Peking. It was while collecting in this area with Père Soulié that *Rhododendron prattii* was discovered by both men at the margins of fir forest.

179

Kangding, a street leading to the south gate. Though on the Tibetan borderlands, the city is classically Chinese in its architecture.

Tsuga chinensis, the Chinese hemlock, seen here in the Pinetum at the RHS Garden, Wisley (England). In central and western China, it forms trees to 30 m (98 ft) tall. Discovered by Père David near Baoxing in Sichuan Province, it was introduced to cultivation from Hubei Province by E. H. Wilson in 1902. Wilson stated it was commonly made into roofing shingles in Hubei.

Described by Franchet some five years later, it is a large shrub with white, bell-shaped flowers and leathery leaves coated, on their undersides, with a fawn-brown indumentum.

A few days later, Pratt and Soulié returned to Kangding. On entering the city by the south gate, the men witnessed the heads of five Tibetan bandits suspended in bamboo cages. The frontier, it seemed, was in an unsettled state, and, after they had been exhibited at Kangding, the heads would be sent on to Chengdu as a warning to other outlaws in the region.

From Kangding, Pratt dispatched his German assistant with six porters to the independent principality of Baoxing (then Mupin), where Père Armand David had discovered the handkerchief tree, *Davidia involucrata*, just 11 years previously. Baoxing was a ten-day journey to the north-east of Kangding, and little was known about it.

In the meantime, rich pickings were to be found in the mountains around Kangding. It was mid May and the place

was alive with colour. Pitching his tent at the head of a valley, he could see miles of rhododendrons with blossoms of every conceivable shade forming a never-ending sea of colour. Even high up in the trees of the Chinese hemlock, *Tsuga chinensis*, were epiphytic shrubs of the rare *Rhododendron dendrocharis*, bearing pairs of bright, rosy-red flowers in the upper leaf axils of their stems. The specific epithet, *dendrocharis*, means 'tree adorning' and aptly describes the habit of this plant. It has recently been introduced to cultivation. Another epiphyte on trees and on humus-clad rocks and cliffs was *Vaccinium moupinensis*, a dwarf evergreen shrub bearing racemes of urn-shaped, chocolate-red flowers. It was discovered by Père Armand David in Baoxing in July 1869, and was introduced to cultivation by E. H. Wilson from the same locality in 1909.

In marshy ground at 3,048 m (10,000 ft), Henry's Changyang plant collector was to discover one of the most

Père Soulié with Pratt's native plant collectors, seen here camped at 4,288 m (14,070 ft) in the mountains above Kangding. One of these native collectors may be Augustine Henry's man from Changyang. *Ja-ma*, Pratt's Tibetan dog, is seated beside Soulié.

gloriously beautiful of all Chinese perennials, *Primula pulverulenta*, the largest of all the candelabra primulas and probably the easiest of the group to grow. Native to western Sichuan Province, it is especially abundant around Kangding, where it grows in marshes and by streams in semi-shade at altitudes above 2,000 m (6,560 ft). The original Kangding collections were later incorporated into Henry's herbarium, and were described, from his specimens, in the *Gardeners' Chronicle* some 15 years later.

Although little known or grown in cultivation, *Berberis prattii* is one of Pratt's best finds from the Kangding area. It has grown at Glasnevin since it was first raised from Wilson's 1908 introduction from Kangding. Though its flowers are not in any way showy, it puts on a fiery display of autumn colour, and the stunning crimson fruits are not much sought after by birds and hang on the shrub well into February.

In the woods, fir and pine trees were festooned with metre-long strands of *Usnea longissima*, a beautiful and abundant lichen still common over many parts of western China. The woods were full of wild blackcurrants, raspberries, gooseberries and strawberries, and these were often eaten by Pratt and his men during their travels.

Peeping from the snow on a mountain pass at 3,900 m (12,800 ft) were many beautiful alpines, and the locals made a good living collecting rare medicinal plants on those high slopes. The principal exports from the region were the roots of *Rheum officinale* and the bulbs of *Fritillaria*

Pratt's photo of the Gongga Shan range with glaciers at an altitude of 3,900 m (12,800 ft).

ABOVE: *Usnea longissima*, a common lichen in the forests of Sichuan and Yunnan provinces. Its long stems are often mistaken for Spanish moss (*Tillandsia usneoides*). In that part of China, it gives the woods a haunted feel.

BELOW: *Berberis prattii*, a great rarity in cultivation. It was introduced by Wilson from western Sichuan Province and the best forms, such as the plant pictured here at Glasnevin, are marvellous in the winter garden, since birds are not attracted to the fruits of this species.

cirrhosa, which were used to prepare a tonic. Pratt encountered these medicinal plant collectors at altitudes as high as 4,630 m (15,200 ft) while collecting wild onions and various species of lily.

The weather was damp, however, and in order to preserve his specimens Pratt set his men to building a log hut on the mountain, in the same style as a North American log cabin. He called it his 'celestial cottage'. Once completed, a fire was kept burning in it night and day, and, from then on, the piles of rapidly accumulating botanical specimens were dried without problems.

By June, snow lay thick on the ground, frosting over the blooms of rhododendrons. The snowstorm continued for days, and one of Pratt's porters heard, from the medicine plant gatherers, that there was a foreigner residing in the area and that the weather was attributed to his presence! The cold weather soon abated, however, and Pratt placed Augustine Henry's Changyang plant collector in charge of a team to gather botanical specimens by day and to collect moths by night.

Primula pulverulenta, a fine candelabra type with a dusty grey bloom along its flowering stems.

The French explorer and naturalist Prince Henri d'Orléans. His Asian travels yielded several new plants, including *Rhododendron principis* and *Rodgersia aesculifolia* var. *henricii*.

On 24 June, Pratt was back in Kangding, and was excited to hear the news that another European explorer had arrived in town and had taken quarters in the same inn as he was based. The renowned French naturalist Prince Henri d'Orléans (1867–1901) was a great-grandson of the last French king, Louis-Philippe. The young prince had hoped to join the French army in 1887, but discovered that legislation had been passed in 1886 against members of the families of Orléans and Bonaparte, many of whom were forbidden to enter or live in France. With no future in the army, and having to avoid the political scene, Prince Henri turned his attention to travel, and, during his short life of 33 years, he accomplished much and travelled widely. He is also the only plant hunter known to have fought a duel.

In 1887, aged just 19, his father, the Duc de Chartres, sent him tiger hunting in Nepal, thus igniting a lifelong passion for travel and natural history, and he was later to quote, 'he who has drunk the cup of travel will wish to drink and drink again and drink for always'. Two years later, his father found him a

place on an expedition led by Gabriel Bonvalot, and the explorers set out from Paris in July 1889, when the prince was just 21 years old.[14] His route took him across Siberia, over the Tian Shan, through Chinese Turkestan and, from there, to Tibet, where they glimpsed the capital Lhasa, then forbidden for Westerners to enter. Two years later, aged 23, the young French prince reached the Chinese–Tibetan frontier. Kangding had rarely seen such a gathering of Europeans, let alone so many naturalists, who were destined to be forever recorded in the annals of botanical exploration in China.

The following evening, Pratt had dinner with the French prince and Père Soulié. The conversation no doubt was centred on the natural history of the region and the collections each had made over the previous months. From Kangding, Prince Henri d'Orléans continued his journey south through Yunnan Province and eventually reached Hanoi in Vietnam, then a French colony. Pratt took charge of the prince's collections in Sichuan Province and later brought them as far as Shanghai.

More than 22,000 stone steps lead devout pilgrims to the summit of Emei Shan. During our visit, in September 2002, we cheated, driving midway up the mountain and taking a cable car on the higher slopes. Plant hunting is always easier on a downhill descent!

Sorbus setschwanensis, seen here on the upper slopes of Emei Shan, where it grows in woods with *Abies fabri*.

An autumn journey to Emei Shan

In August 1890, Pratt returned to Emei Shan to see how the collectors he had stationed there for the spring and summer seasons had fared during his absence. Once again, he stayed in the Wannian Monastery and ascended the mountain for a second time that year. A never-ending stone staircase led him past richly forested gorges, and numerous streams coursed their way down the mountainside. The principal time for pilgrimages was autumn, when the harvest had been taken in and the monasteries were therefore full of devout travellers.

Pratt remained on the summit of Emei Shan for ten days, during which time the weather was mostly wet and windy. Occasionally, the weather cleared, allowing spectacular views of the clouds far below. When they struck the base of the mile-deep precipice, the clouds would roll up and envelop the summit in mist.

On two occasions, he was to see the famous 'Glory of Buddha' from the edge of the precipice. This extraordinary

phenomenon is caused by the reflection of the sun on the upper surface of the clouds beneath and gives the appearance of a golden disc surrounded by radiating bars in the colours of the rainbow. They are constantly moving, sparkling and changing colour, giving a remarkable appearance. The 'Glory of Buddha' was held in great respect by Buddhists, and pilgrims travelled a considerable distance to see it. Some, according to Pratt, became so overcome by religious fervour on seeing it that they threw themselves over the cliffs and their bodies fell onto an inaccessible spur in the forests a mile below. E. H. Wilson, who later visited Emei Shan, stated that he had met pilgrims who had walked all the way from Shanghai, some 3,200 km (2,000 miles) away. Tibetans and Nepalese people even made the journey.[15]

Further collections were made on Emei Shan at this time, most notably a new species of rowan, *Sorbus setschwanensis*, which was described several years later from a specimen in Augustine Henry's herbarium. On Emei Shan, it formed small trees, by then clothed in a fiery scarlet cloak of autumn foliage from which bunches of snow-white fruits peered.

Pratt's German assistant had also just arrived back from Baoxing, and the summer had been very profitably spent there. The expedition was returning to Yichang with a remarkable collection of specimens from a little-known region of western China. The botanical collections were divided into two lots: one that Pratt would later sell to Kew, and a second set for Augustine Henry. Both sets contained very different plants. Perhaps Henry's Changyang plant collector sorted the specimens so that Henry would not receive herbarium sheets similar to material in his Hubei collections.

By mid August, Antwerp Pratt and his team departed from Emei Shan and made their way back to the boat at Leshan. In caves in the red sandstone cliffs there, he discovered a new species of bat, *Hipposideros prattii*.[16] Commonly known as 'Pratt's round-leaf bat', this little mammal is also found in Burma, Vietnam, Thailand, and Malaysia, but is nowadays very rare and is listed in the IUCN Red List of Threatened Species.

Though our visit to Emei Shan was 112 years after Pratt's, little has changed, and the mountain has one of the best-preserved floras in all of China, thanks to Buddhist monks based there. Pictured here is Noeleen Smyth busily preparing specimens of *Staphylea bumalda* for pressing on the steps below the Xianfeng monastery. The walking stick in front of her is made from a local bamboo, *Chimonobambusa tumidisinoda*.

At Leshan, his native plant collectors converged from the many localities he had based them throughout western Sichuan Province. He was delighted with the year's collections, but found he had to hire a large sampan alongside his own boat to carry his material down the Yangtze, and another boat for the collections he had taken charge of for Prince Henri d'Orléans. From Leshan, the small flotilla – carrying a large and valuable collection of botanical, geological, entomological and zoological specimens – travelled as far as Chongqing, where Pratt took the opportunity to call on Henry's friend Mr Cockburn and a number of English missionaries domiciled in the region.

From there, the journey continued down the Three

Gorges. The river was high and Pratt and his team were forced to remain at the city of Wushan for a day, due to the strength of whirlpools in the Wushan Gorge. Pratt's boat was tossed like a cork in the Xiling Gorge, but he made it safely with his men to Yichang on 25 September 1890. There, he sold his boat, repacked his collections and boarded a steamer to Shanghai, where he deposited Prince Henri d'Orléans' collections with French missionaries based in the city.

During his stay in Shanghai, Pratt found accommodation in the Shanghai Club, then a great favourite with expatriates. By late October, he was home with his family in England after a three-year absence. His dried plant collections contained more than 500 species, of which more than 150 were new to science.[17] The set sent to Augustine Henry also contained a plethora of new species and two new genera; it had been a marvellous and entirely worthwhile adventure. His book *To the Snows of Tibet Through China* was published in 1892 with 33 photographs, the first images many European readers were to see of western Hubei and Sichuan provinces.

The book was published to great acclaim, and Pratt sent a copy to his friend Augustine Henry, who was then based at Kew. That same copy is now in the rare book room at Glasnevin, and it is from that copy that I have been able to summarise Pratt's adventure and the important part played by Henry and his native plant collector from Changyang. Antwerp Pratt, who had originally set out to only collect zoological collections, owed much of his success to Henry, who not only supplied a well-trained collector but also suggested a suitable route. No doubt the two collectors had much to talk about on the English explorer's return to London.

More than 200 plants are endemic to Emei Shan, and perhaps the best known of these is the 'Mount Omei balsam', *Impatiens omeiana*. We found it to be abundant there, and no doubt Antwerp Pratt encountered it, too.

Chapter 7

A transfer to Hainan

Pandanus odoratissimus, a shrubby, much-branched screw pine that is widely distributed along the tropical coasts of the Indo-Malaysia region to Australia and Polynesia. Augustine Henry collected it near Kiungchow in northern Hainan in 1889, and found it a few years later at Kaohsiung in southern Taiwan.

Augustine Henry spent 17 March 1889 – Saint Patrick's Day – in Hong Kong, where he called on Charles Ford (1844–1927), the first Superintendent of Hong Kong Botanic Gardens. It was on that visit he gave Ford bulbs of *Lilium henryi*, instructing him to send half of the batch to Kew. Thus, one of the most beautiful of all the Asiatic lilies was introduced to cultivation. *Lilium henryi* flowered at Kew in August of that year, causing a sensation.

Two days later, Henry boarded the steamer *Soochow* and reached Haikou the following day. Haikou is Hainan Province's capital city and lies on the northern coastline of Hainan Island, at the mouth of the Nandu River. The port had become a centre for international trade after the area was opened to foreign ships under the Treaty of Tianjin (1858) in 1876, and it handled the island's commerce with the mainland.

Despite its beautiful stretches of palm-lined beaches and its tropical jungles, Hainan was a backwater of the Chinese Empire; it was one of the poorest regions in the country and a miserable place of exile for banished officials from the Forbidden City.[1] At that time, the island was an unhealthy place to live: diseases such as cholera were rife and omnipresent swarms of mosquitoes carried malaria.

In the centre of the island, along the Limulingshan mountain range, lived three large aboriginal groups: the Li, Hui (or Huizu) and Miao (Miáo) people. The range was

Nelumbo nucifera, the sacred lotus, has Buddhist and Hindu associations and is a symbol of eternal life. It is cultivated on a massive scale in many parts of China, since most of the plant is edible. Seen here at the Jardin des Plantes (Muséum National d'Histoire Naturelle) in Paris.

covered in dense tropical forests, and their mud-walled, thatched huts were found in rainforest clearings. The Li were the first ethnic group to inhabit the island. Li women wore bright, colourful costumes and had a custom of tattooing their bodies from the age of 12. The Miao were widely spread across southern China, northern Vietnam, Laos and Thailand, and Henry would meet the group again a few years later in southern Yunnan Province. They migrated to Hainan during the Ming Dynasty (1368–1644) and most lived in the mountainous centre of the island. The origins of the Hui, Hainan's third ethnic group, are less well recorded. It is thought that they may be descendants of ancient Persians who came to do business with the Chinese. They continue to follow Islam, write Arabic and use an Islamic calendar.

Henry soon settled into the day-to-day work of his new position. In late May, he received specimens from Yichang that had been gathered by one of his native plant collectors in the mountains above Fang, in northern Hubei Province. Evidently, he was still keen to maintain a link with his collectors in central China, despite being located so far away himself.

Typhoons swept Hainan between May and October,

battering the island's luxuriant cover of lush tropical rainforest. Henry's diary for the period shows that he immediately set to work collecting specimens. The flora of Hainan, as could be expected, was markedly different to that of central China. Many of the plants found along the seashores were widespread species found throughout the tropics. Though little explored, Hainan could hardly be called a new field. Père Delavay visited the island in 1878 and collected a number of plants near Qiongshan, in the north, including the Alexandrian laurel *Calophyllum inophyllum*. Four years later, the Reverend B. C. Henry of the American Presbyterian Board of Foreign Missions visited the region and travelled to the central mountainous areas (on foot), where he met with the Li people. The American Henry had also previously explored large areas of neighbouring Guangdong (Kwangtung) Province, and his best-known find – and one that is sometimes credited to his Irish namesake – is the lilac-flowered *Rhododendron henryi*.[2] A climber in the milkweed family, *Tylophora augustiniana* (syn. *Henrya augustiniana*), which Augustine Henry first found at Yichang in 1887, was later named to commemorate both the American and Irish plant hunters.

The sea hibiscus, *Hibiscus tiliaceus*, seen here on Lantau Island near Hong Kong. A handsome littoral tree of pantropic distribution, the flowers emerge bright yellow with a maroon eye and change colour as the day progresses. Photo taken 10:00 a.m.

Plant hunting around Haikou

Augustine Henry wrote very little of his botanical work in Hainan. However, having recently catalogued his collections, it is a little easier to gauge a better idea of how and where he spent his time there. Most of his specimens were gathered within a 16-km (10-mile) radius of Haikou. Five kilometres (3 miles) south of Haikou lay the town of Qiongshan (then Kiungchow or Qiongzhou), and this area became one of his favourite hunting grounds, especially the countryside around the Qiongshan pagoda. In the centre of the island, missionaries managed to find him two native plant collectors whom he trained to gather specimens near the towns of Danzhou (then Nodoa) and Lingmen.

Henry's collections were not just restricted to wild, ornamental plants. He was aware that Kew was on a constant search for new economic plants to transplant to other corners of the empire. In the past, he had sent many samples of little-known plant products from central China to Kew, and he took a keen interest in the crops grown around his new post. Outside the city of Haikou, the fields were full of strange tropical fruits, vegetables and spices, such as guava, custard apples, papayas, mung beans, jack beans, sweet Chinese yams and henna.

The smooth loofah or dish-cloth gourd, *Luffa cylindrica*, made rampant vines in the fields around Haikou. A vigorous annual found throughout tropical Asia, and probably native to India, it is thought to have been introduced to China during the Tang Dynasty (618–907 AD). The fibrous inner tissues of the fruits are used in the USA for absorbing oil from water, and are also put to good use as shock absorbers. In Asia, the fibre is used to stuff pillows and saddles, and also as an effective back scrub.

By 14:30 p.m., the sea hibiscus has changed the colour of its petals from yellow to orange-yellow.

Not far from Qiongshan were fields of the sacred lotus *Nelumbo nucifera*, which has been cultivated in China for more than 14,000 years. In many regions of China, plants are grown by millions in flooded fields and make a spectacular show in summer, when a succession of fragrant, rose-pink flowers soar on slender stalks above the large, dark-green, peltate leaves. All parts of the lotus are useful. The young leaves are either eaten raw or cooked, or are used to wrap small portions of food before cooking. The seeds, which are embedded in a large flat-topped receptacle, are roasted and eaten, and the long, elongated tubers are edible and a common part of Chinese cuisine. The magnificent sky-blue-flowered water lily, *Nymphaea stellata*, was common in ponds around Qiongshan, and, on the boggy margins, Henry was to collect the carnivorous sundew *Drosera indica*, a widespread species of the Old World tropics.

Along the seashore grew great carpets of the beach morning glory *Ipomoea pes-caprae*, a pantropic, semi-

The final photo, taken at 19:00 p.m., shows a total transformation in flower colour over a nine-hour period. The flowers will have fallen from the tree by the same night.

succulent perennial bearing pale-purple funnel-shaped flowers. A common seaside tree was the sea hibiscus, *Hibiscus tiliaceus*, a pantropic tree of rapid growth reaching about 10 m (33 ft) tall. The attractive flowers are held in terminal panicles and are carried all year round. Individual flowers emerge light yellow with a maroon eye and gradually change to deep orange before falling from the tree the following evening. Polynesians use the lightweight wood of this tree for the outriggers of their canoes, the flowers as a laxative and the bark is used to manufacture a fine fibre for dance skirts used in religious festivals.[3]

Dense forests lay beyond the cultivated plains, and one of the most interesting trees that grew there was the sea mango, *Cerbera manghas*, a tropical tree to about 10 m (33 ft) tall that is native to the coastal regions of Polynesia, westwards to south-east Asia and the eastern shores of Africa. The delightfully fragrant white blooms are carried almost all year around, and are followed by highly toxic, oily, rounded fruits. The tree's poisonous nature is mirrored in the generic epithet *Cerbera*, which is derived from 'Cerberus', the name of a three-headed dog from Greek mythology that guarded the entrance to Hades, the underworld. The fruits are lightweight and waterproof and are distributed on ocean currents.

The endemic *Lithocarpus naiadarum* – a tall, evergreen, oak relative – dominated the forests in places. Though familiar to those of us in more temperate climes as a houseplant, *Ficus benjamina* formed massive trees to 30 m (98 ft) tall. Beneath the forest canopy lay an exotic world of palms, lianas and bold aroids. Most impressive were the many trees of the Burmese fishtail palm, *Caryota mitis*, a handsome species distributed from Burma to Java and the Philippines. Through the trees ran vines of *Passiflora moluccana* var. *teysmanniana* and the starry white-flowered *Clematis meyeniana* var. *granulata*. The latter was described several years later from Henry's collections. Epiphytic orchids, such as the pale-rose-flowered *Dendrobium loddigesii* and the robust, monopodial, pink- and red-flowered *Renanthera coccinea*, clung to the trunks and branches of trees. On the forest floor, Henry found numerous new exotics, including the handsome aroid *Alocasia hainanica* and the ginger relative *Alpinia hainanensis*.

Plants from the mountainous interior

Further inland, towards the mountainous centre of the island, American missionaries had based themselves in the small towns of Danzhou and Lingmen. With their help, Henry managed to recruit Li plant collectors.[4] The central mountainous part of the island supported an interesting flora, and it was in the mountains above the town of Danzhou that Henry's native plant collector discovered *Ilex*

Clerodendranthus spicatus. This beautiful member of the mint family is widely distributed from India to the Philippines.

hainanensis, a small evergreen tree to 5 m (16 ft) tall. This holly is also distributed across the southern provinces of mainland China.

Further inland, in the mountains above Lingmen, grew the Siamese ginger, *Alpinia galanga*, whose rhizomes, when freshly cut, are used to flavour foods and curries. Distributed from the Himalaya to Java, Borneo and the Philippines, Marco Polo noted, in the 13th century that this species was grown in southern China, and exports were brought to Europe through India to the Red Sea and along the Mesopotamian trade routes. It is used to dye wool yellow, and is apparently effective in stimulating the appetite of sick elephants.

Lingmen had an interesting flora, and the rise in altitude on the mountains brought about a change to the local vegetation. On the lower slopes grew *Clerodendranthus spicatus*, a widespread tropical perennial in the mint family that is distributed across tropical India to the Philippines. Though hardly known or grown in Western cultivation, it is an exquisitely beautiful plant bearing densely crowded spikes of long-stamened white flowers.

At higher altitudes grew *Rubus playfairianus*, a bramble that Henry had previously collected in the Antelope Glen near Yichang. A rambling shrub with slender, whip-like, dark-green stems, the habit of this shrub is very graceful, and, while its foliage is distinctly handsome, its flowers are horticulturally insignificant. It was discovered by the Irish diplomat George M. H. Playfair (a friend of Henry's) in Guangdong Province and was later introduced to cultivation from Yichang, Hubei Province, by E. H. Wilson in 1907. In Hainan's tropical forests, Playfair's bramble grew beneath fine trees of the Chinese sweet gum, *Liquidamber formosana*.

The move to the tropics was having a malevolent effect on Henry's health, however, and entries to his diary for early July record headaches and fever. He was battling pernicious malaria. A few days later, after a stay of less than four months, he left Hainan Island and sailed to Hong Kong to convalesce. Hainan could never compare to Hubei. Its flora did nothing to stimulate Henry's enthusiasm and he left the island emotionally and physically drained. Hainan would remain forever like a stain on his memory. It must have been a bitter parting, and Henry was glad to see the back of the place. In a letter to Kew, written from Hong Kong, he vented his frustration, and it is clear to see how glad he was to escape the island:

> I can scarcely bear to speak of Hainan. I suffered from heat, home-sickness, got very ill, and the last blow has been the death of a dear friend from cholera on Sunday last. It is a perfect inferno.[5]

In Hong Kong, Charles Ford broke the news to Henry of the trick perpetrated by his Badong plant collector, Man Yang, and the embarrassment caused to Professor Oliver in naming the new hoax genus, *Actinotinus sinensis*.[6] It was news Henry could have done without, and he failed to see any humour in the prank.

Sir Robert Hart granted Henry two years' leave in early August, and, a few weeks later, he boarded the rather appropriately named *Gaelic* and set sail to Japan. Yokohama was reached on 31 August, and, the following day, he travelled to Tokyo to visit the renowned Japanese botanist Jinzo Matsumura (1856–1928).

On 18 September, Augustine Henry reached San Francisco, his first time visiting America and seeing the city to which his father had travelled while the Great Famine had raged throughout his native Ireland. An overland route brought him across the USA to Chicago, where he visited an uncle, and, in early October, he was in Canada, where he made a brief visit to Toronto. On 8 October 1889, Henry boarded the *Wyoming* and set sail to Ireland. At 09:00 a.m. on 17 October, he spotted the Skelligs, a spectacular island group off the rugged coastline of County Kerry, and, a short time later, the steamer landed in the busy harbour of Cobh (then Queenstown) in County Cork.[7] It had been nine years since he'd last seen home, and how his heart must have raced at the prospect of seeing family and friends again.

Henry corresponded with Père Delavay while at home in Ireland recuperating from illness. In November 1889, Delavay sent him a consignment of *Pedicularis* species. One of those species probably included *Pedicularis siphonantha* var. *delavayi*, seen here in the Shangri La Alpine Botanic Gardens in north-west Yunnan Province.

Kew's senior herbarium staff, and the very men who described Augustine Henry's Chinese collections. Seated left to right are John Gilbert Baker, a noted fern expert; William Botting Hemsley, who named most of Henry's newly discovered species; Otto Stapf, then an assistant in the herbarium; and, finally, Professor Daniel Oliver, Keeper of the Herbarium. Henry received an enormous welcome from this group during his first ever visit to Kew in November 1889.

Ireland, Kew, and a new love found

At home in Ireland, Henry kept up his usual voluminous correspondence with colleagues in China. He was keen to keep in contact with those involved in plant hunting, and, in December, he received a letter from William Richard Carles (1848–1929) of the British Consular Service in China. Carles collected in eastern China and Korea (Corea), and it was while travelling in North Korea between 1883 and 1885 that he discovered *Viburnum carlesii*, one of the most sweetly fragrant of all shrubs and one of the most beautiful of all *Viburnum* species. It is also one of the parents of the very popular *Viburnum* x *burkwoodii*. In November, Henry received a letter from Père Delavay, then still busily collecting in north-west Yunnan Province. The two men had corresponded for some time, and, later that month, Delavay sent a consignment of *Pedicularis* to Henry's father's home in Tyanee.

After a brief stay in Ireland, Henry made his way to London. He was keen to meet William Thiselton-Dyer,

Director of the Royal Botanic Gardens, and to see Kew for himself. The fifteenth of November must have been a tremendous day for Henry, because it was then that he finally met the botanists with whom he had been corresponding over the years and who had described many of the new species he had discovered. He was given a warm greeting by Thiselton-Dyer, and, in the herbarium, he met the botanists John Gilbert Baker (1834–1920), who had described most of his ferns. William Botting Hemsley (1843–1924), who was still busily compiling the first flora of

191

China through the *Index Florae Sinensis*, Professor Daniel Oliver (1830–1916), Keeper of the Kew Herbarium, and Dr Otto Stapf (1857–1933), then an assistant in the herbarium.

During this visit, Henry also met Charles Baron Clarke (1832–1906), a former superintendent of the Royal Botanic Garden, Calcutta. On retiring from the Indian Civil Service in 1887, Clarke had settled at Kew and continued his research into Indian botany. This included assisting Joseph Dalton Hooker in compiling the monumental, multi-volume *Flora of British India*. An expert on sedges and grasses, Clarke was to describe many of Henry's new grasses over the years, and, following this initial meeting, the men remained life-long friends.

The plants that Henry had sent back to Kew had almost overwhelmed botanists there as they rushed to have his material included in the new flora of China, and descriptions of his new plants appeared in a plethora of botanical journals, raising great interest in both Europe and North America. Henry spent the day with Thiselton-Dyer visiting the various departments at Kew, and was surprised by the enthusiastic greetings he received from senior staff there. His botanical work in central China had made him a celebrity. He had become a famous plant hunter, and was renowned not only in the botanical circles of Britain and Ireland, but in North America, too.

That evening, Kew threw a welcoming party for Henry, inviting the most famous figures in English botany and horticulture. Among the guests was Sir Harry Veitch

Neoclassical elegance, Shanghai's Bund by night. The second building to the right is the Shanghai Customs House. It was in a gothic-style building on the site of the present Customs House that Augustine Henry trained for the Customs Service. He lived here with his first wife Caroline in 1891, and they often strolled the Bund together.

(1840–1924), head of the largest, most influential nursery in Europe. Over five generations of family ownership, the firm had dispatched 22 plant hunters to the Americas, Australia, India, Japan, China and the South Seas. Henry's success in China had been closely followed and admired by the Veitch family, and it was his efforts that had alerted the nursery to the horticultural potential of the plants from central and western China.[8]

By mid December, Henry had based himself in London and spent the following 18 months in the herbarium at Kew. During that time, he worked not only on his own specimens, but also on those of other collectors based in China. As if by chance, Antwerp Pratt's collections from western Sichuan Province arrived in England during Henry's first visit to Kew, and he helped sort to the specimens and translated notes on the plants that had been written in Chinese by his Changyang plant collector. During his time at Kew, Henry learned botany remarkably quickly, and his studies would later be of great benefit to him when he teamed up with Henry Elwes to write about trees.

Not all his time was spent working, however. His friend

Evelyn Gleeson was then also based in London, where she worked in a studio called Ludovici's. The following summer, Henry holidayed with the Gleeson family in Ireland at their home, Benown House, a charming Georgian property surrounded by a wooded estate on the shores of Lough Ree.[9]

It was there that Augustine Henry met and fell in love with Caroline Orridge, a friend of Evelyn's who was also studying at Ludovici's. Caroline was the daughter of a London jeweller. She was a talented artist and Henry found in her an honest, genuine soul. It was a match made in heaven and they married on 20 June, 1891, two weeks after the death of Henry's father. Shortly after their brief honeymoon in France, the couple set sail for China – and it was there and then that the fairytale ended. Caroline had tuberculosis and was hospitalised upon her arrival in Ho Chi Minh City (then Saigon). By the time they reached Shanghai, she was a semi-invalid.[10]

A return to Shanghai

Augustine and Caroline Henry arrived in Shanghai in March 1891. Caroline was still extremely ill and made little progress during her time there. In Shanghai, they rented an apartment on the Bund, Shanghai's fashionable waterfront along the Huangpu River. Caroline's frail condition meant that the couple rarely had an opportunity to socialise with other expatriates. It pained Henry to see his wife so cut off from her work as an artist and from the pleasures of society. Caroline's only escape was through occasional strolls with Augustine along the Bund, where they could watch large shipping vessels plying their trade along that stretch of river, or to take a rickshaw through the streets.

Among the first people Henry met on his arrival there were the English explorers Captain H. Bower and Dr W. G. Thorold, who had just returned from an expedition to Tibet.[11] Both men had explored more than 1,287 km (800 miles) of mountainous countryside never before touched by either European or Asiatic explorers. One-hundred-and-fifteen species of flowering plants were collected, many of which were new including the remarkable *Saussurea tridactyla*, which was collected at a staggering altitude of 5,791 m (19,000 ft). No flowering plant had previously been collected at so high a level.[12]

Saussurea tridactyla is one of the most curiously beautiful plants of high Himalayan passes in Nepal and Tibet. There, it is generally found just beneath the line of perpetual snow on unstable screes and it is only the most energetic explorers that manage to see it in its native haunts. Living in such an inhospitable habitat, this alpine has evolved to cope with tough conditions. At a glance, the

Saussurea tridactyla, one of the most curious alpines from the Himalaya. A dense mat of cotton-like hairs protects the plant from winter cold. Pictured here on the Showa La in south-east Tibet.

plant looks like a white ball of cotton wool, due to a dense coating of white woolly hairs that acts as a thermal blanket to the foliage beneath. Bower and Thorold's collections were originally destined for the herbarium at Calcutta, but, on Henry's recommendation, a set was sent to Kew to be included in the new flora of China.

In November of the same year, Henry was paid a visit by the American explorer W. Woodville Rockhill, who had mounted an expedition to Tibet in 1888 and was about to embark on another when he called on Henry in 1891.[13] Henry, it seems, knew just about everyone involved in Chinese botanical exploration, and, in a letter to Thiselton-Dyer, he described Rockhill as:

[A] very nice fellow, and is a good friend of mine [...]. His prospected course of travel is a secret. I enlisted his sympathies in plant-collecting, and he intends to do his best to make a collection, which he promises to send me, so that it may be forwarded to you'.[14]

It must have been disappointing for Henry to see these plant hunters come and go when his own career was at a standstill. The immediate vicinity of Shanghai was not a good collecting area, and, in any case, he would have nowhere to store his specimens since the Customs Service was in the process of building a new Customs House on the Bund.

Instead, he concentrated his energies on the study of ethnobotany, and it was during this time that he wrote *Notes on Economic Botany of China*, which was published by the Presbyterian Mission Press in Shanghai two years later. The booklet contained information on plants of economic importance in China, giving their Chinese and Latin names,

and an opening invitation to 'missionaries and others living in the interior' to collect plant specimens and plant-derived products for Kew. Only 100 copies were ever published, and one of these was later sent by Henry to David Fairchild (1869–1954) of the United States Department of Agriculture (USDA). Fairchild headed the Office of Foreign Seed and Plant Introductions, and was so impressed with the publication that he later had it reprinted. Henry's permission was never sought, but, apparently, he was flattered rather than angered by having his booklet pirated. The booklet would have been much larger but for the fact that Caroline was so ill while he was working on the manuscript.[15]

There was little by way of improvement in Caroline's health during their stay in Shanghai, nor did her spirits lift. It was a difficult time for them both, and Henry's letters to Kew for this period make sad reading. In one letter to Thiselton-Dyer, he relayed that 'We have had a hard time of it'.[16]

In January 1892, he met the English diplomat and explorer Alexander Hosie (1853–1925), who was based, as Acting British Consul, in Tamsui (Danshui), a busy port in north-east Taiwan. Hosie had explored much of western China between 1882 and 1884, and had made a special study of Chinese insect wax in the vicinity of Emei Shan for Kew.[17]

In April of the same year, Augustine and Caroline went on a ten-day trip on a revenue cruiser amongst the rocky islets that extended from the mouth of the Yangtze to Ningbo (Zhejiang Province). Caroline's health was slowly improving, and, during working hours, Henry spent his time inspecting local lighthouses (one of his Customs duties). Although the season was early, he managed to collect some specimens, and reported that one island he visited had dense woods of *Camellia japonica* and *Cinnamomum camphora*.

By midsummer, Caroline was very ill. Augustine hoped a dry, warm climate might suit her frail condition better, and, in early July, they travelled to Japan together. Caroline spent the summer and autumn in a little mountain village near Kobe. For a short time, she improved and even found time to collect specimens, such as the foxglove relative *Melampyrum japonicum*, which she gathered near Arima.[18]

In September 1892, Henry wrote to Kew from

194

Shanghai, informing Thiselton-Dyer that Ernst Faber's house had burned to the ground only a week previously, and that the greater part of his botanical collections had been destroyed. What luck, then, that Henry had earlier persuaded him to send a duplicate set to Kew.

Caroline sailed back to Shanghai later that month, though the climate of Japan had done little to improve her condition. In a letter to Thiselton-Dyer, written shortly after her return to Shanghai, Henry stated he had applied to Sir Robert Hart for a transfer to southern Taiwan. Another cold Shanghai winter would, he feared, have a devastating effect on his wife's health.

In October, he met a fellow Irishman, William Hancock (1847–1914), who also worked for the Chinese Imperial Maritime Customs Service. Hancock was a keen botanical collector and had been based in China since 1874; during that time, he collected plants in the east of the country and on the islands of Hainan and Taiwan. He was on the point of departure for the Customs station at Mengzi in southern Yunnan Province in October 1892. In his letter to Kew, Henry wrote of Hancock: 'He has a splendid opportunity to collect. I tried to stir him up'.[15]

Henry seemed to enjoy his last weeks in Shanghai; the whole foreign community was full of life and energy'. He spoke of the many sporting events: tandem racing, the regatta, yachting, house-boating, shooting, horse racing and a great cricket match against Hong Kong 'that smashed that little colony'. Happy and jovial letters indeed, no doubt due to the fact that Caroline was back in his life once again.

BELOW: *Notes on Economic Botany of China*. Written by Augustine Henry while he was based in Shanghai, we brought it with us to Chengdu in Sichuan Province in 2002, and, using it we bought a number of Chinese herbal medicines, including *tang-shen* (*Codonopsis tangshen*), seen on the scales. To the left is *hoan-ch'i*, (*Astragalus henryi*), and, to the right, *dang gui* (*Angelica sinensis*).

Chapter 8

To the tropics of Taiwan

ABOVE: Traditional fishing boats moored in a sheltered cove at the base of Ape's Hill (Wanshoushan) near Kaohsiung in southern Taiwan. Ape's Hill was one of Augustine Henry's favourite hunting grounds

The Henrys arrived on the island of Taiwan on 18 November 1892. Their new home was located in the Foreign Compound at Kaohsiung (Gaoxiong; or, at that time, Takow or Takao), which was then a small town of 3,000 people on the south-west of the island.

In 1517, the first Europeans, a band of Portuguese navigators, landed on the island's shores and were so taken with its spectacular scenery, rugged peaks and luxuriant vegetation that they called it '*Ilha Formosa*', or 'beautiful island'. Thus, for many centuries, Taiwan was known to European explorers as 'Formosa'. Since the Ming Dynasty (15th century), the Chinese have called it 'Taiwan', or 'terraced bay', referring to the natural terraces of this mountainous island. In October 1863, permission was granted, by the Qing Court, to establish offices for the

Customs Service in Kaohsiung. The harbour opened as a treaty port in 1864, following the signing of the Tianjin Treaty. This busy shipping area consisted of a large, very deep lagoon, several kilometres in length, and was skirted along its shores with well-developed mangrove swamps.[1]

The small European community comprised the staff from the British Consulate and the Chinese Imperial Maritime Customs Service. Kaohsiung was an exceptionally beautiful place to live, so long as one was prepared to accept the occasional typhoon or earthquake, and Henry was full of hope that Caroline might recuperate during her stay

196

there. The place was said to possess a healthy, moderate, tropical climate, and was thought to be specifically curative to those suffering from tuberculosis.[2] The town lay on the edge of a broad, fertile plain and tropical crops, such as sugarcane, sweet potato, turmeric, mango, ground nuts, betel nuts and pineapples, were widely grown.

Taiwan could be considered as two distinct regions: the west consisted of a broad, low-lying, alluvial plain, interspersed with shallow creeks and rivers, and, though heavily cultivated, few roads existed; to the east lay an entirely upland region, made up of great mountain masses that ran the length of the island, the tallest of these being Yushan (Mount Morrison), or 'Jade Mountain'. At 3,997 m (13,113 ft), this soaring, snow-clad peak is the tallest mountain lying between the Himalaya and the Sierra Nevada in western North America.

The area surrounding Kaohsiung town proved very interesting to Henry. Nearby, on the northern extremity of the harbour, lay Ape's Hill, a beautiful, densely forested spot, covered with luxuriant tropical forests across most of its slopes. Not far from the Foreign Compound, on the shores of the harbour, were large mangroves, while, to the west, lay an intensively cultivated plain. Henry immediately wrote to Kew, full of enthusiasm. He was eager to begin collecting again.

ABOVE: A late 19th-century view of Kaohsiung (Takow) from Ape's Hill. The cluster of buildings nearest to the shore is the Foreign Compound where Augustine and Caroline Henry lived during the early 1890s. The palm on the brow of Ape's Hill is *Phoenix hanceana*.

Botanical collectors in Taiwan

At this time, the island of Taiwan had scarcely been explored. The first plant hunter to reach its shores was Robert Fortune, who spent a day at the northern town of Danshui (Tamsui) in April 1854. Thirty years later, Charles Ford of Hong Kong Botanic Gardens also made collections on the north of the island. He was followed in turn by Robert Swinhoe (1836–77), one of the most successful of the 19th-century explorers to visit Taiwan. Swinhoe concentrated his attention on zoological specimens, but, between 1861 and 1866, he also collected more than 200 species of plants in Tamsui and on Ape's Hill.

Swinhoe was also responsible for the visits of two Kew collectors to Taiwan. Charles Wilford (d.1893) made collections along the east coast in the summer of 1858, though it seems as a plant hunter he was terribly lazy and did little but exasperate Sir William Hooker, who was less

Podophyllum pleianthum. The dried stem and rhizome of this beautiful woodland perennial are currently used in Chinese herbal medicine to treat cases of traumatic injury and snakebite.

The Chinese parasol tree, *Firmiana simplex.* According to Henry, Taiwanese aborigines made cloth from the inner bark fibres of this tree.

than pleased with the results of his expedition to Taiwan:

> My surprise & astonishment I need not say daily increases that we hear nothing from you & receive nothing from you. Your last letter was your unfinished journal about Formosa [...] Since that, not a parcel, not a seed, not a word [...] Yet you continue to draw bills, without giving us any notice or any account whatever how this money is spent.[3]

Hooker lost no time in dismissing Wilford, and replaced him, six years later, with a young Kew gardener, Richard Oldham (1837–64), who left England with instructions to avoid his predecessor, who was then still based in the Far East. Oldham proved to be an excellent collector and worked mainly along the east coast, though he died of dysentery a few months after his journey to Taiwan, aged just 26.

The Kew collectors were followed by three Irishmen: George Playfair, Thomas Watters and William Hancock. Playfair was twice based in Taiwan, first in 1877 and again in 1888–89, while serving as Acting Consul at Tainan, in

the south-west of the island. He made an admirable collection of more than 400 species, chiefly on Ape's Hill and on the plains around Kaohsiung.[4]

William Hancock spent a year in Danshui (Tamsui), between 1881 and 1882, and, during that time, he managed to carry out a journey into the higher mountains of the district, where he mounted an expedition to visit the aboriginal tribes of the region. Hancock, it seems, was consumed with the Victorian passion for ferns, and he made a rich harvest of the group while based in Taiwan, many of which were new to science. During his lifetime, Hancock also collected in many parts of China, Japan, Sumatra, Java, Jamaica, Guatemala and Mexico.

Thomas Watters was based with the British Consular Service near Tamsui, and collected plants in that region from 1881 to 1883. One of his best-known finds in Taiwan was *Podophyllum pleianthum,* which he introduced to Kew by means of living plants in March 1883.[5]

Augustine Henry was next on the scene; during 1893 and 1894, he and his native plant collectors gathered more than 23,000 herbarium specimens, mainly from the south of the

island. In 1896, Henry produced the first flora of Taiwan, based not only on his own collections, but also on material gathered by previous plant hunters. It was the most important of his early scientific papers and was published as 'A list of plants from Formosa' in the *Journal of the Asiatic Society of Japan*. It makes interesting reading, even today. In the opening pages, Henry acknowledged that half of the island was still unexplored and that many more species remained to be discovered. In his flora, he included 1,429 plants, consisting of 1,283 flowering plants. 131 ferns and 15 fern allies. Of these, he excluded 81 plants that only occurred in cultivation and 20 naturalised plants. He placed the then-known flora of Taiwan at 1,328 species and intraspecific taxa.[6]

Ethnobotany was another of Henry's interests, and throughout his flora of Taiwan are references to many plant-derived products used by local inhabitants. He noted that the aboriginal people of southern Taiwan made cloth from the stem fibre of native plants, such as *Alpinia zerumbet*, *Boehmeria nivea* and *Firmiana simplex*, while game bags were also manufactured from the inner bark fibre of *Morus australis*.

In another case, aboriginal hunters made their bows from the wood of the endemic *Viburnum luzonicum* var. *formosanum*, and, at Bankinsing (also known as Wanluan or Wanchin) in modern-day Pingtung County, villagers blackened their teeth by rubbing them with the flower buds of *Pisonia aculeata*, a pantropic, scandent, prickly shrub that grows in open forest and along seashores in southern Taiwan.

ABOVE: Rice has been cultivated in Asia for at least 7,000 years, and is generally grown in low-lying valleys and plains. In the most favoured areas of China – for example, the Chengdu Plain in Sichuan Province – up to three crops a year are harvested. This lady, a member of the Bai ethnic group, was photographed between Dali and Lijiang in north-west Yunnan Province.

Kaohsiung Plain's tropical crops, mangroves, exotic trees

New tropical crops were of great interest to Kew, and Henry gathered specimens of many of the vegetables and fruits grown in southern Taiwan. Rice (*Oryza sativa*) was an important crop on the plains, though it is surprising that, throughout his extensive travels in China, Henry only once gathered specimens of rice, and that material came from the Kaohsiung Plain. Rice is the world's most important food crop, and an estimated 1.7 billion people depend on it for daily sustenance. It has been cultivated in Asia for at least 7,000 years, and, in China, as in many other parts of Asia, it is grown in paddy fields. The still water in these fields prevents the growth of terrestrial weeds, and rots the plant material left behind after harvesting.

Glycine max also appears in Henry's collections from the Kaohsiung Plain. Better known in the West as 'soy' or 'soja bean', this ancient Chinese crop is thought to have been first grown in the eastern part of northern China in the 11th century BC. In China, soybeans are referred to as 'poor man's meat' or 'cow without bones', indicating the important

ABOVE: A view of the Kaohsiung Lagoon, with Ape's Hill and the village of Takow. The Love River can be seen to the right.

LEFT: Fossilised coral at the base of Ape's Hill, with the Kaohsiung Lagoon in the background.

nutritional role that this legume plays. There are more than 2,500 cultivars known today. The germinated seedlings are 'bean sprouts', and are a popular stir-fry ingredient. Soybean was introduced to the West by French missionaries, and it is considered by experts to be one of the plants that will feed the planet's ever-growing population in the future.

Henry also collected *Amaranthus tricolor* at Yichang (Hubei Province), Hainan and in Taiwan. Grown as an ornamental plant in the West, many amaranths are an important food source in China, and *Amaranthus tricolor* has been used as a vegetable in south-east Asia since ancient times. Known as 'Chinese spinach' on the Shanghai markets, the young shoots and leaves are eaten in the same manner as spinach, and the fruits resemble grains in flavour. Like soybean, this species has been hailed as a valuable crop for the escalating population of our planet, since it will grow, even flourish, in arid and saline areas, producing a nutritious harvest from otherwise useless land.

Turmeric, *Curcuma longa*, was another important crop in 19th-century Taiwan. Turmeric is a stemless, ginger-like perennial with handsome yellow and white flowers carried in oblong spikes. It is an ancient cultigen thought to have originated in India, and is one of the most widely grown spices in the tropics. The fleshy rhizomes are bright orange-yellow inside and the flesh was used to provide a yellow vegetable dye used with costly silks, wool and cotton. Turmeric is an anti-inflammatory and has a cholesterol-lowering effect. It has long been used as a natural antibiotic agent and modern studies on animals have shown that turmeric can prevent or inhibit the development of certain cancer cells. As a culinary spice, it is well-known, and, after being peeled and grated, the rhizomes form the basis of curry powder.

Though well known today, many of the crop plants that

Augustine Henry sent to Kew were obscure or completely unknown in the West at that time. With these specimens, he sent notes on their cultivation and uses. He also sent seeds from time to time, and these were trialled at Kew before being sent for distribution to other tropical regions of the world.

Within view of the Foreign Compound, on the edge of the lagoon were the best-developed mangrove swamps in Taiwan. Asian mangrove forests tend to be richer in species than their New World counterparts, and Henry used to visit those hot, steamy, odorous forests once a month in the hope of finding interesting specimens. Nothing new appeared from those brackish swamps, but the forests themselves were fascinating, especially the fine trees of *Bruguiera gymnorrhiza*, a native of tropical Africa and south-east Asia. In the lagoon at Kaohsiung, its large massively buttressed trunks rose directly from several metres of saline water. Many of these mangrove trees are well adapted to littoral life, and their fruits can float on ocean currents for thousands of miles before germinating on distant shores. *Lumnitzera racemosa* uses the same mode of seed dispersal, and this adaptation has allowed it to colonise shores from tropical Africa, across Asia to Australia.

One of the most widely distributed of all tropical climbers is the pea relative *Entada phaseoloides*, which Henry collected at South Cape (currently known as Oluanpi on the Hengchun Peninsula, Pingtung County) in southern Taiwan, and again, a few years later, near Mengzi in southern Yunnan Province. The enormous pods of this remarkable climber are up to 120 cm (4 ft) long, and, according to Henry, the seeds could be commonly found on the shores of southern Taiwan, just as they were occasionally found on the west coast of Ireland, having

drifted from the West Indies.[7] In recent years, a collection of these 'drift seeds' have been gathered off Ireland's west coast, and were germinated with relative ease at the National Botanic Gardens, Glasnevin.

A little further inland, on the edge of the town, grew the guest tree, *Kleinhovia hospita*, a monotypic species native to the tropics of the Old World. Linnaeus gave this spectacular flowering tree the specific epithet '*hospita*' because of its many resident guests, such as epiphytic flowering angiosperms, ferns, mosses, lizards and snakes. In Malaya, the poisonous leaves are used as an insecticide and to eradicate head lice.[8]

To the west of Kaohsiung, the Love River (Ai He) and a number of small creeks bisected the plain before terminating in the harbour. On their banks grew a handsome new endemic willow, *Salix kusanoi*, a small tree bearing reddish-brown branches and bold sword-shaped leaves. Other new endemics from the same area included the ginger *Zingiber oligophyllum*, a perennial with pseudostems to 60 cm (2 ft) tall, and a curious perennial birthwort, *Aristolochia cucurbitifolia*, whose scrambling stems sported cucumber-like foliage.

Ape's Hill – a new hunting ground

The most interesting place to find plants near Kaohsiung was on Ape's Hill, a 354-m (1,161-ft) high bluff on the northern extremity of the harbour. Ape's Hill rose from the sea as cliffs of limestone, and also contained huge debris slides of fossilised coral that had been uplifted from the ocean floor about 100,000 years previously. European settlers had named the hill after its most famous residents, a large colony of Formosan rock macaques, *Macaca cyclopis*.

The western slopes of Ape's Hill were heavily forested with a rich assemblage of exotic, tropical trees, and, near the summit, was a wide plain where the forests thinned out into scrubland and rough pasture, which included a new grass, *Digitaria henryi*. Henry was an early riser, and often spent a few hours collecting on the hill before returning to his office to continue with his official duties.

Many of the trees that grew on Ape's Hill were well-known, widespread species found throughout the Old World tropics, but were of great interest nonetheless. Take, for example, *Crataeva religiosa*, the sacred garlic pear, a strikingly beautiful, deciduous, flowering tree that can be found in forests from tropical Africa to Australia and the Pacific Islands. Typical of the family to which it belongs (Capparidaceae), the blooms are spectacular, with creamy,

Phoenix hanceana, one of the most abundant palms on Ape's Hill. Its fruits are edible.

TOP: *Ficus pumila*. According to Henry, an excellent jelly was made from the fruits of this fig. He collected it in Hubei Province, Hainan and Taiwan. E. H. Wilson stated it was common around Yichang.

BOTTOM: *Akebia longiracemosa*. Discovered by Henry on Ape's Hill, it has since been found in southern mainland China.

four-petalled flowers and long, whiskery, purple stamens. The petals deepen to an orange hue as they age and are garlic scented. The fruits are about the size of a tennis ball and dangle on long stalks. Inside is a mass of fleshy, poisonous pulp, in which horseshoe-shaped seeds are embedded. *Crataeva religiosa* is held sacred in India and is traditionally planted around tombs and temples.

The most abundant tree on Ape's Hill was a small palm, *Phoenix hanceana*. It clothed an entire face of the hill overlooking the sea, giving the area a very exotic look. This species is tolerant of baking heat and drought, and was thus perfectly adapted to the harsh, xerophytic conditions it encountered on Ape's Hill's vast sheets of fossilised coral. Henry stated that the fruits of this palm were edible, and that it was known colloquially as the '*kuang-lang*' or '*k'eng-lang*'.

Another very common forest inhabitant was *Acacia confusa*, an evergreen tree to 15 m (49 ft) tall and with trunks of up to a metre (3.3 ft) across. In spring, it provided a dazzling floral display across the hillside with its golden-yellow, globe-shaped blossoms. At that time, the tough and durable wood of this tree was used in the construction of junk-frames, rudders and for the shafts of sugar mills. The acacia tended to grow in drier areas, especially on ridges and outcrops of fossilised coral and limestone, and this habitat

was also shared by a number of giant banyans (*Ficus* spp.).

Vines were rampant, with one of the most gorgeous being the well-known *Hoya carnosa*, a succulent climber with a wide distribution from India to China. *Hiptage benghalensis* is also widespread in the Asian tropics, and, on Ape's Hill, it formed giant lianas to over 30 m (98 ft) in length. It is often cultivated in the tropics for its deliciously fragrant white flowers. *Ficus pumila* was also quite common and formed prostrate evergreen shrubs on rocks and on the trunks of surrounding trees. It is a relatively common shrub in the warmer provinces of China and also extends into northern Indochina and Japan.

Henry discovered a number of new vines on Ape's Hill, and the most impressive of these has to be *Akebia longiracemosa*. He found it in flower there on 12 May 1893, and it formed a large climber with broad, five-foliate leaves and long peduncles of purple-brown flowers. It has recently been introduced to cultivation, and has proved perfectly hardy at Glasnevin. Other new vines included *Erycibe henryi* (Convolvulaceae), a scandent shrub that is native to southern China, Taiwan and Japan, and *Celastrus kusanoi*, a rampant liana capable of scrambling its way to 18 m (59 ft) through nearby trees.

The sweetly scented *Ligustrum pricei* was another of

Henry's snake palm, *Amorphophallus henryi*; here, a cultivated plant in the Tropical Pit House at Glasnevin. The stems are beautifully mottled.

Amorphophallus hirtus, seen here on the lower slopes of Ape's Hill. The inflorescence is followed, in autumn, by spikes of handsome blue berries.

Henry's discoveries from Ape's Hill. Endemic to Taiwan, this handsome evergreen grows in broadleaved forest below 1,800 m (5,905 ft) and was introduced to cultivation by E. H. Wilson in 1918. *Hypericum geminiflorum* was also common in more open, sunny areas. Hemsley named this species just two years after Henry discovered it on Ape's Hill, and chose the rather fitting specific epithet '*geminiflorum*', which means having twinned flowers. The buttercup-yellow blossoms of this species are carried in pairs in the axils of leaves on slender pendulous stems. The overall habit of this shrub is elegant and graceful; Henry obviously liked it – he sent seeds to Kew in February 1893.

Alas, both Kew and Paris, the two main centres to which European missionaries, plant hunters and travellers sent their seed collections from China, had bad reputations when it came to germinating seeds sent from the Orient. Gardeners at Kew were hopelessly unsuccessful with many of the large seed consignments Henry sent and managed to kill what would have otherwise been exciting new introductions. The 'Kew Inwards' book, which recorded the fate of Henry's donations from China, makes a depressing read; he might have had better luck with a commercial nurseryman such as Harry Veitch. Indeed, in the late 19th century, commercial nurseries were more successful in this area than many of the large botanic gardens, and the French missionaries soon learned to send

their seeds not to the Paris museum, but to leading nurseries such as those headed by Messrs Chenault, Lemoine and Vilmorin.

Taxonomy, on the other hand, was where Kew excelled, and botanists lost no time in identifying Henry's Taiwan collections, with a number from Ape's Hill causing particular excitement. Among these were two striking aroids that grew beneath the dense, lush, forest canopy that cloaked most of Ape's Hill. *Amorphophallus* is an exciting genus restricted to the Old World tropics, and many of its members don spectacular if not curious blooms. Henry discovered two species; the first of these, *Amorphophallus henryi*, formed a tuberous perennial to 60 cm (2 ft) tall. He later stated it was the most peculiar of all the new plants he discovered on Ape's Hill, and that its villainous, reddish-purple, bristle-covered spadix was such a gruesome sight that dogs took fright! Dense spikes of blue fruits followed the inflorescence in autumn.

The second species, *Amorphophallus hirtus*, was a giant in comparison. On Ape's Hill, this species has been recorded as growing to 2.8 m (9 ft) tall, and its giant, pink-purple inflorescence lasts only three to six days. In that period of time, it throws out a repulsive odour that is irresistibly attractive to pollinating beetles. Like *Amorphophallus henryi*, it is endemic to Taiwan, where it is restricted to the southern side of the island.

Headhunters in Bankinsing

In the late 19th century, the western alluvial plain of Taiwan was inhabited by Chinese farmers who had migrated across the Taiwan Strait (Formosa Strait) from the nearby province of Fujian (Fuchien). Few inland roads existed and travel was carried out by boats along the coastal towns. The eastern mountainous side of the island was still inhabited by communities of headhunting aborigines, and the Chinese lived in fear of these warring tribes. From his house in Kaohsiung, Henry could see their campfires by night.

About 48 km (30 miles) to the east of Kaohsiung lay the tiny rural hamlet of Bankinsing. This little settlement lay in the foothills of the massive central range of mountains that bisects the island, and, at that time, it was surrounded by extensive tracts of primeval tropical rainforest. It was also the only safe trading post between the Chinese and the local

Plant hunting in Taiwan was by no means a safe occupation in late 19th- and early 20th-century Taiwan. This photograph, taken by E. H. Wilson during his visit to the island in 1918, portrays a head-hunter with his trophy.

headhunting tribes, and, as such, was an important centre of trade. A Spanish Catholic mission had been established at Bankinsing, and a church was built there in 1865.

Many years later, having returned to Europe, Henry was persuaded by the opinionated Irish gardening journalist, William Robinson, to write an account of his years in China. It makes wonderful reading for the armchair explorer, and that first visit to Bankinsing seems to have remained as vivid as ever in Henry's memory. Though some of the language used is not entirely appropriate by today's standards, it does nonetheless paint a clear picture of the dangers faced by his native plant collectors in this remote part of Taiwan:

After returning to China from my first home leave, I spent some time in Shanghai; but had subsequently two years in Formosa, 1893 and 1894. I collected there 2,000 numbers, and made some interesting trips into the mountains, which are inhabited by savages of Malay origin. Never shall I forget my first sight there of savages – one morning that I visited the neutral ground whither they came armed to barter with the Chinese. They were a band of forty, led by two chiefs, the younger of whom wore a coronet of boar's teeth. A few women accompanied them; wild creatures, dressed for the occasion in longish robes. I noticed that they were tattooed transversely across the wrists. The men were longitudinally tattooed on the wrists, and wore only an apron. Their hair hung down unkempt in wild disorder, and their rolling eyes were never steady for a moment. Dwarf in stature, they scarce looked like human beings, and the old Spanish priest of the mission, where I had stayed the night before, assured me that for all practical purposes they had no souls. They warred continually with the Chinese of the plain, chiefly to decorate their huts with skulls of the latter, and no young savage was allowed to wed until he had brought home one skull. It was impossible for me to enter their territory here, and a slight excursion, which I made up a ravine for two or three miles into the mountains, was most uncomfortable, as my Chinese coolies were in abject terror. I succeeded later in penetrating savage territory from the South Cape, much to the south of the tribe just referred to.[9]

With the help of the old Spanish missionary, Henry managed to persuade a local Bankinsing man to collect for him, and he later proved to be the best of all Henry's Taiwanese plant collectors. (Henry's only complaint was that he would not venture far into the mountains for fear of losing his head!) He also had a collector based at Chiayi (Kagee, Kagi; historically, Tirosen) in the centre of the

island, though his services, due to lack of interest in his work, were soon discontinued.

Not all of Henry's meetings with Taiwan's aboriginal groups were a success, however. Once, he was captured by one of the more hostile tribes, but saved himself by putting on his scarlet doctor's gown and mortarboard. The natives were so impressed by the sight that they fell down on their faces, thinking he was a god.[10] Despite the dangers he faced in those early days, though, Henry persisted in his plans of hiring local plant collectors, and of personally mounting botanical expeditions into the mountainous interior.

Not surprisingly, the mountains that surrounded Bankinsing contained scores of new and interesting plants. One of these was a vigorous perennial grass that was grown in forest clearings as a food crop by a local headhunting tribe. From Henry's collections, it was described as a new species, *Eccoilopus formosanus*, and he also sent seeds to Kew in the hope that it would be put on trial as a new cereal crop.

The tropical forests at Bankinsing also contained many fine new trees, such as the evergreen *Litsea hayatae*, *Castanopsis formosana* (the wood of which was popularly used for making carts), *Celtis formosana* and the endemic *Turpinia formosana*. The latter was based on material gathered by Henry's native plant collector at Bankinsing, and from a specimen later collected by E. H. Wilson in

ABOVE: *Koelreuteria elegans* ssp. *formosana*; a fruiting tree in the grounds of the National Sun Yat-sen University at the base of Ape's Hill, Kaohsiung. Henry discovered the tree near Bankinsing (Pingtung County) in 1894.

central Taiwan in 1918. Another very common tree from this district was *Koelreuteria elegans* ssp. *formosana* (syn. *Koelreuteria henryi*), a handsome plant bearing large, bold, pinnate leaves and carrying masses of spectacular, rose-coloured, bladder-like, inflated seed capsules in autumn. It was introduced to Kew by means of seeds in 1976 and has proved remarkably hardy there.

The camphor tree, *Cinnamomum camphora*, was abundant in this district. Native to tropical Asia and Malaysia, Henry had also previously collected it near Yichang in 1885. At Bankinsing, it formed tall, aromatic evergreen trees to more than 50 m (164 ft) tall, with massive trunks and wide-spreading canopies supporting a dense mass of foliage. According to Henry, it was rare in Hubei Province (where it reaches its western limit of distribution) and of little commercial importance. In Taiwan, however, it was abundant in submontane forests, and there its massive trunk was often clothed with epiphytes, especially ferns, such as *Asplenium nidus*, and orchids, such as *Vanilla albida*.

205

The camphor tree has been known in China since ancient times for its excellent wood, and the enormous tracts of camphor tree forest throughout Taiwan set the base for a lucrative new industry. By the early 20th century, the island held the monopoly on the Asian camphor trade. The timber is distilled to yield an essential oil used to treat colds, influenza, fever, pneumonia and diarrhoea. It is also used in the manufacture of incense, disinfectants and celluloid, and, in the past, to make smokeless gunpowder. Old-fashioned mothballs were also made from camphor. The camphor tree is hardy in the milder coastal counties of Britain and Ireland, and there is a fine, 15-m (49-ft) tall specimen at Glanleam House on Valentia Island in County Kerry, Ireland.

Lianas abounded around Bankinsing and scrambled their ways to great heights throughout the surrounding forests. The most remarkable of these had to be *Calamus quiquesetinervius*, a monstrously vigorous climbing rattan palm with stems reaching no less than 70 m (230 ft) long. Beneath the canopy of all these forest trees lay an enormous variety of shrubs, some previously known to science, but also many that proved to be exciting new finds. One of these, *Osmanthus matsumuranus*, formed large evergreen bushes to more than 20 m (65 ft) high. It was later found to have a much wider range of distribution, from Khasia in India to southern China and Indochina. In Taiwan, this species is distributed in broad-leaved forest, where it was first found by Henry in 1893.

The endemic *Camellia nokoensis* was another exciting discovery from this region, and it formed very graceful evergreen shrubs of slender habit, and bore small, white, cup-shaped flowers enclosing a central boss of golden-yellow stamens. This species has a beautiful charm about it and dignity that is lacking in many of the larger, modern camellia cultivars. *Itea parviflora* grew nearby, and, while not quite as beautiful as Henry's earlier find, *Itea ilicifolia* from Yichang, it proved to be an interesting new endemic species.

Deutzia pulchra was an interesting find, and, while previously known from the Philippines, the Bankinsing plants proved to be a new record for this species in Taiwan. A shrub of real aristocratic bearing, its white or occasionally pink-flushed flowers appear in early summer and have been likened to drooping spikes of lily-of-the-valley. It was introduced to cultivation from Taiwan by E. H. Wilson in 1918, and was first flowered by the Marquess of Headfort at Headfort House near Kells in County Meath, Ireland, four years later. On the forest floor grew a new ginger, *Zingiber pleiostachyum*. This species is known only from Henry's original specimens. Two collections were made for Kew and it has never been seen in the wild since then.

The lighthouse at South Cape

In February, while inspecting lighthouses as part of his routine duties, Henry spent two days in the company of the Koalut tribe at South Cape on the southern tip of Taiwan island. The group had recently relinquished its headhunting ways, but, only two decades previously, had slaughtered an entire ship's crew when the vessel had come to grief on rocks nearby. The incident was reported in many European newspapers, including the *Illustrated London News*:

An American merchant barque, the *Rover*, was wrecked on the 13th March, on a small island to the south of Formosa [...] and the master, Captain Hand, with his wife, the second mate, and three Chinamen of the crew, made their way in one of the boats to the shore of Formosa. They lay down on the beach and were attacked in their sleep by the savages of that country, who murdered them all, it is believed, except one of the Chinamen: he alone escaped to tell the tale.

Mr Corral, the British Consul at Takow [...] having been informed of the outrage [...] went at once to the place, where they found the remains of the broken boat and saw a few natives at a distance. Next morning, three of the ship's boats, well manned and armed [...] pulled ashore, having onboard a Chinese acquainted with the savage tongue, and carrying presents of spirits, blankets, and cloth as a ransom for any survivors. No sooner, however, were one or two of the party on shore than a sharp cross-fire from muskets was opened from two visible points, accompanied with a shower of arrows. The enemy being invisible and unapproachable, it was deemed advisable to withdraw, and orders were accordingly given. Though the mission had been intended for a peaceful one, yet, knowing the blood-thirsty nature of these savages of Formosa, Captain Broad had directed the cutter to lie about thirty yards offshore.[11]

As a result of the massacre of the crew of the *Rover*, the Customs Service had a lighthouse erected, and it was while inspecting the same lighthouse that Augustine and Caroline Henry first met this tribe. Seizing a rare opportunity, Henry hired the tribal chief and put him to work collecting plants in the tropical rainforests that surrounded the lighthouse at South Cape. This district lay 96 km (60 miles) to the south of Kaohsiung, and his native plant collector was supervised by a European lighthouse keeper.

On another occasion, Henry managed to venture further inland (to present-day Kenting National Park on the Hengchun Peninsula, Pingtung County) and brought presents to another local tribe, to reward them for rescuing

a shipwrecked crew, and provided a feast on behalf of the Customs Service, followed by dancing and celebrations. Henry had the ability to win the affections of many people, no matter what their class, rank or background. He had fallen in love with Taiwan, its landscape and its people, and wrote with great affection about the region:

> I have heard the lark sing high over the grassy downs in south Formosa and my heart throbbed with glee. Often seated on the mountain top, gazing through the lattice made by the thick growth of the small bamboos, I saw far off the square fields of man in the valley and wished that he had never spoiled the planet.[12]

Southern Taiwan was an unspoiled tropical paradise, and the coastal scenery at South Cape, where the lighthouse was located, was particularly beautiful. The tropical forests that surrounded the lighthouse proved to be rich in exotic, flowering trees. One of the showiest of these was the orange jessamine, or Chinese box, *Murraya paniculata*, a small evergreen tree bearing cymes of fragrant, white, orange blossom-like flowers throughout the year. Native to tropical Asia and Australia, it is widely distributed in Taiwan and Henry stated that its wood was used by aboriginal tribes for making tobacco pipes. The genus commemorates Johann

ABOVE: A view of South Cape from the region's famous lighthouse. The hills in the distance are part of what is now Kenting National Park. Augustine Henry hired a tribal chief from a group of head-hunters to collect plants for him at this, the most southern point of Taiwan.

Andreas Murray (1740–91), a Swedish pupil of Linnaeus.

Magnolia compressa soared to heights of 20m (65 ft) or more, and carried small, white, goblet-shaped blooms in spring. The trunks of this species can be a metre (3.3 ft) in diameter, and it is a rather valuable timber tree in Taiwan.[13] *Elaeocarpus sylvestris* formed medium-sized evergreen trees with long, striking, lance-shaped leaves that emerge copper toned. In Taiwan, Henry stated the genus was known as the '*shih-nan*', and its timber was of such value that the Customs Service put it on display at the 1889 World Fair (Exposition Universelle) in Paris.

These trees played host to enormous colonies of tropical epiphytic orchids, and Henry considered the white-flowered *Phalaenopsis aphrodite* to be the most striking of all these. This species was abundant in lowland tropical forest in Taiwan in the late 19th century, but is now very rare, both there and in the Philippines.

Rhododendron simsii grew on the edge of forests and in

207

Murraya paniculata, variously known as the orange jasmine, mock orange or Burmese boxwood. In Java, the sweetly scented blossoms are used in the manufacture of perfume.

Elaeocarpus sylvestris, a handsome tree bearing copper-toned foliage in spring and summer. It has only recently entered Western cultivation and has proved perfectly hardy at Glasnevin.

open glades. It is one of the most widespread of Chinese rhododendrons and Henry collected it in Hubei Province, Taiwan and later in southern Yunnan Province. In its native habitat, it forms an evergreen shrub up to 3 m (10 ft) tall and carries terminal clusters of up to six blossoms in shades of red and, occasionally, orange. Kingdon Ward compared the flowering of this shrub to 'the glow from an active volcano at night'. According to E. H. Wilson, it was abundant in the Yangtze valley during the early 20th century, so much so that, in places, whole hillsides in May were red with its flowers. It is one of the parents of the indoor azalea, used as a pot plant at Christmas.

Rhododendron oldhamii occupied the same habitat and formed much-branched shrubs, to 4 m (13 ft) high, and bore terminal clusters of orange-red flowers, stained pink on the upper lobe. Endemic to Taiwan, it is more common on the northern part of the island, where it was discovered by Richard Oldham in 1864; it was introduced to cultivation by Charles Maries through Messrs Veitch in 1878. It was reintroduced by E. H. Wilson in 1918, and is suited only to the mildest, most sheltered gardens of Britain and Ireland (USDA zone 9).

Lilium formosanum was common throughout the island, and it made a pretty picture in the tropical grasslands by the coast at South Cape. Endemic to Taiwan, this delightful little lily carries several nodding, deliciously fragrant, white, funnel-shaped flowers, which are striped wine-red on the outside. According to E. H. Wilson, it was common in the north of the island, but was much less frequent on the coral formations in the south where Henry obtained his material. Wilson missed collecting this lovely lily during his brief visit to the island, and it was from Henry's collections that he based his description of the species in his seminal work, *The Lilies of Eastern Asia*. It was discovered in June 1858 by Charles Wilford in northern Taiwan, and was introduced by Charles Maries in 1880. *Lilium formosanum* is easy to grow and will bloom within six months from seed.

South Cape also proved to be particularly rich in new plants. A common woodland inhabitant of the region was *Eriobotrya deflexa*, a medium-sized evergreen tree found throughout broad-leaved forests at low altitudes in Taiwan. Endemic to that island, Henry called it the '*k'o* tree' and it was first grown outdoors in Europe at Dunloe Castle in County Kerry, Ireland, where it was planted by the English plantsman and explorer, Roy Lancaster. In 2002, it formed part of our Henry exhibit at the RHS Chelsea Flower Show, and, at the time, it carried masses of bold, newly emerged, copper-tinted foliage, which is one of the charming features of this species.

The camellia relative *Schima superba* var. *kankoensis* formed huge evergreen trees, and it later proved to be endemic to southern Taiwan. In late spring, this variety carries small, creamy-white flowers with a central mass of golden-yellow stamens. In later years, Henry was to learn that a high proportion of his collections were new endemics and of extremely limited distribution. Take, for example, the pea relative *Millettia pulchra* var. *microphylla*, a shrub or small tree with short pinnate leaves, and the evergreen oak relative, *Pasania formosana*. Both are only found along a tiny coastal strip of the Hengchun Peninsula that surrounds the lighthouse. In a similar case, the evergreen *Magnolia kachirachirai* shares a limited area of distribution in the South Cape region, and there it forms trees to 17m (56 ft) tall and bears small, white, cup-shaped blossoms in early summer. Henry's native plant collector found this rare tree in 1894, and it was described from material later gathered by Japanese botanists.

On the opposite extreme, some of these new trees, such as *Wendlandia formosana*, a small, semi-deciduous tree in the coffee family (Rubiaceae), were later found to be widely distributed in the Old World tropics; in this case, from Indo-Malaysia, southern China and the Ryukyus to northern Australia. It is a seashore tree in Taiwan. Other new tree species from this region included *Astronia formosana*, *Beilschmiedia erythrophloia*, *Lindera akoensis*, *Lithocarpus amygdalifolius*, *Lithocarpus brevicaudata*,

The epiphytic orchid *Phalaenopsis aphrodite* was commonly found on trees in southern Taiwan a century ago. It is now extremely rare, due to overcollecting.

The gorgeous *Lilium formosanum,* seen here in a bulb frame at Glasnevin. In cultivation, it is often grown in a cool alpine house, where its wonderfully scented, funnel-shaped blooms fill the surrounding air with its exquisite perfume.

Rhododendron simsii, distributed from Burma in the west to Hong Kong in the east. It was introduced to cultivation in 1808 by the East India Company.

The cartwheel tree, *Trochodendron aralioides*. The name stems from the Greek '*trochos*', a wheel, and '*dendron*', a tree. The spreading stamens of the green flowers look superficially like a wheel.

Reevesia formosana, *Syzygium formosanum* and the evergreen *Acer albopurpurascens*, whose leaf undersides are beautifully white-purplish, hence the specific epithet.

Perhaps Henry's most interesting discovery from this region was *Amentotaxus formosana*, a small, rare coniferous tree belonging to the monogeneric family Amentotaxaceae. The genus *Amentotaxus* consists of four species, all of which are found in south-east Asia and are closely allied to the plum yews, *Cephalotaxus*. Taiwan's species forms a thinly branched tree to about 10m (33 ft) tall, and the undersides of leaves bear two brilliant silver stomatal bands.

Vines were abundant, choking the forests in places and making exploration difficult. Some of these were new, and one of the prettiest was *Capparis sikkimensis* subsp. *formosana*, a climber to 6 m (20 ft) tall with stems up to 30 cm (1 ft) thick. *Capparis* are an exotic bunch of showy trees, shrubs and climbers restricted to subtropical and tropical regions of the Old World. Henry's new subspecies was particularly beautiful and carried subumbels of up to 20 small, white flowers with long, whiskery, pink stamens projecting over three times the length of the petals.

Henry had also earlier found *Capparis micrantha* var. *henryi* near Bankinsing, where it formed shrubs to 2 m (6.5 ft) and carried tiny white flowers, often before the emergence of leaves. This species was later found by other collectors in Burma, Thailand and Indochina to Malaysia. During his brief visit to the South Cape in 1918, Wilson also collected it.

Several new orchids were described from material gathered in this region. *Phreatia formosana* was abundant as an epiphyte on trees, and carried dense spikes of tiny white flowers. Others, such as the pale green-flowered *Habenaria polytricha* and the spectacular red-and-green-flowered *Liparis henryi*, grew as terrestrials on the forest floor.

In July 1893, Henry wrote to Kew telling Thiselton-Dyer about an earthquake that struck the southern part of Taiwan, and this was followed by a typhoon that was so strong that rain was forced underneath the roof tiles of his house. The dry tropical climate at Kaohsiung had done little to alleviate Caroline's suffering, and it was at this stage that a decision was made to send her to Colorado, USA, where it was said the climate was better for those suffering from lung complaints and tuberculosis.

On 15 August 1893, Henry spent a day on Lamay Island ('Golden Lion Island'; now Liuchiu Island, or Xiao Liuqiu), which lay about 64 km (40 miles) off the coast of Kaohsiung, and, while there, he made a small collection of plants. No new species were described from his Lamay collections, but it did contain some interesting plants, such as the Indian string bush, *Wikstroemia indica*, which, according to George Playfair, was used for making paper and blankets in Guangxi Province at the time. Fishing was the island's main industry, and it was a peaceful place with secluded coves, sandy beaches and extensive coral reefs. Lamay must have had some curiosity value for Henry, since it had been named after an Irish island (Lambay) in Dublin Bay.

Henry had set his sights on a much more exciting adventure, however. His aim was to mount an expedition into the snow-clad mountains that ran the length of the centre of the island, where he was sure many new plants, including conifers, could be found. He also wrote to Kew of his hopes to explore Orchid Island (Lanyu), then known as Botel Tobago. Orchid Island lay 48 km (30 miles) east off the coast of South Cape, and had two peaks, the higher of which reached 522 m (1,712 ft). The landscape was volcanic and the place was inhabited by aborigines from the Yami (Tao) tribe, who lived in caves.

Mallotus japonicus, native to southern China, Taiwan and Japan; pictured here at the Royal Botanic Gardens, Kew.

More plants from the north of the island

In 1893, Henry engaged Hosea Morse (1855–1934), who was based at Tamsui in the north of Taiwan, to gather specimens. Morse, like Henry, was an officer in the Customs Service and was keen to get the correct botanical names of plants that supplied products such as drugs, fibres and dyes. At Henry's expense, Morse hired a local man to collect plants in the northern camphor district, in the mountains near Tamsui. These specimens and items of *materia medica* were incorporated into Henry's herbarium, and were later sent to Kew.

Not all of the specimens sent from Tamsui were terrestrial plants. Seaweed constituted a valuable industry in 19th-

The toad lily, *Tricyrtis formosana*. In Taiwan, it grows in damp forest, exposed fields and roadsides. There, it spreads by means of vigorous stolons, often forming large colonies. The easiest and the best of all the toad lilies in cultivation.

211

century Taiwan, and huge amounts were harvested off the northern coast and sent to the mainland. Perhaps the most important of these was *Gelidium amansii*. Agar is extracted predominantly from this red algae, and different species of *Gelidium* yield agars with varying properties. These same properties make it an unsurpassed microbiological and tissue culture medium. It is also used in bakery products, to keep them moist, and to clarify wines, juices and vinegars. Other important seaweeds exported from the region for culinary uses included *Onikusa pristoides* and *Enteromorpha intestinalis*.

The mountain flora of the Tamsui area was very different from that of the southern regions and Henry's native plant collector began to send some very interesting plants, many already known to botanists, but also quite a few new species. *Trochodendron aralioides* formed pure stands in those northern forests. Native to Taiwan, Japan and Korea, this evergreen tree is monotypic and is of an ancient lineage with many primordial features. The structure of its wood, for example, resembles that of the conifers, and several fossil genera have been referred to Trochodendraceae, suggesting a much wider distribution for the family in the past. The tree has a handsome, columnar habit and the leathery, shallowly toothed, apple-green leaves are spirally arranged in dense groups, and terminal racemes of vivid green blooms are carried in early summer. Another plant previously known to science but of interest because of its disjunct distribution was *Campylotropis giraldii*, a deciduous shrub to 2 m (6.5 ft) bearing dense panicles of deep purple, pea-like flowers. Native to central and northern China, its distribution in Taiwan is of great interest to those studying plant distribution and evolution.

Mallotus japonicus, a small tree in the spurge family (Euphorbiaceae), was common at low altitude in the Tamsui area. Though the flowers of this species are by no means showy, the large bold leaves are distinctly handsome, and forms from Japan have proved hardy, though slow growing, in cultivation.

The fabulous toad lily, *Tricyrtis formosana*, also grew in the same woods, and Henry later gathered it himself at South Cape. It is a rather common perennial in Taiwan, where it is distributed throughout the island and is endemic. The Formosan toad lily was discovered by the Kew collector Richard Oldham in 1864, and, in recent years, has became very popular on account of its spectacular autumn show of upward-facing, star-shaped, pinkish-white, purple-spotted flowers, which are carried in terminal cymes.

Alnus henryi was discovered by Henry's Tamsui collector on 26 September 1893 growing on the banks of a creek.[14] Little is known of this autumn-flowered species, though it was introduced to cultivation in 1992 by Mark Flanagan and Tony Kirkham, and grows at Wakehurst Place, Kew's annexe in rural Sussex (England).

New hope – Caroline departs for Colorado

In January 1894, Caroline Henry left Taiwan for the USA. Augustine travelled with her as far as Hong Kong, where they were joined by his sister, Mary, who planned to travel with Caroline to Colorado. Mary Henry was a trained nurse, and, by this time, Caroline's condition had became so chronic that she needed regular medical attention. Augustine Henry's health was none the better; during their voyage to Hong Kong, the malaria he had contracted while based in Hainan came back to haunt him. It must have been a miserable parting for them both.

In May of the same year, he wrote to Professor Charles Sargent (1841–1927), the famous American dendrologist and founding director of the Arnold Arboretum. In the same letter, he explained to Sargent that he planned to resign from the Customs Service and join his wife in Colorado. Because of this, he would be forced to sell his private herbarium and he was giving Sargent first choice. This offer must have been extremely tempting to Sargent, who had a keen interest in the flora of Asia. Henry's herbarium at that time contained Ernst Faber's plants from Emei Shan, estimated to be about 700 species, and a set of his own central China specimens, consisting of about 1,000 species, much of which were type specimens of new genera and species. It also contained dried specimens of about 1,500 species from Manchuria and eastern China as well as 2,000 herbarium sheets from Taiwan. Since Kew had a full set, Henry was keen to see the remainder go to American institutions, and Harvard was to get first choice.[15]

The Customs Service granted Henry one year's leave in July, to be taken from 1 November 1894. He wrote to Kew of his eagerness to join Caroline in Colorado, and of his hopes for her recovery. If she improved by the end of the year, he planned to return to China; if not, he would settle in America.

In the meantime, war had broken out between China and Japan over Korea. China suffered a humiliating defeat, and, shortly afterwards, Henry was informed by Sir Robert Hart that the Japanese planned to attack Taiwan and that he was to leave. Henry saw the event as an opportunity to travel to Colorado earlier than expected, but his plans were not to be fulfilled. As fate would have it, he would never see Caroline again. On 25 September, while he was on the point of departing Taiwan for the USA, he received a telegram from Mary Henry informing him that Caroline had died of a pulmonary haemorrhage in Denver.[16] He was devastated.

Even while in exile in Colorado, however, Caroline had managed to find the strength and time to gather specimens, and these, alongside her Japanese plants, are preserved in the Kew Herbarium.[17] Caroline Henry is commemorated in two plants that were discovered by Augustine Henry in southern Yunnan Province in the late 1890s. The first of these, *Lithocarpus carolinae*, is an evergreen oak relative capable of reaching 18 m (59 ft), and is endemic to southern Yunnan. The second, of which very little is known, is also a Yunnan endemic, and is presently known as *Primula henryi* (syn. *Carolinella henryi*). This deciduous perennial bears two to three heart-shaped leaves to about 18 cm (7 in.) long and these arise from a stout rhizome. In early summer, the plant produces a 20-cm (8-in.) long flower spike bearing up to 20 blossoms.

Primula henryi is an invalid name for the Yunnan plant, since the specific epithet has been used earlier for an entirely different plant. *Primula* x *henryi* was first published in the *Gardeners' Chronicle* in 1881 for a plant raised by Mr Anderson Henry as a *Primula denticulata* cross, made in the late 1870s, and, therefore, the Chinese *Primula henryi* must be considered a homonym. In coining a new name, I propose *Primula carolinehenryi* (*see* note opposite), thus commemorating Caroline Henry, as was the original intention. Alas, it is thought that Caroline Henry's primrose from Yunnan may now be extinct. It has only ever been found once, and, like Caroline, it may now be no more than a memory.

From Taiwan, Augustine Henry returned to Europe and, from there, made his way immediately to Denver, where he was consoled by his sister Mary. His final letter from Taiwan was to Sargent, and, in it, he promised to collect specimens for the Arnold Arboretum on his return to China. He closed the letter emotionally:

I am trying to be busy and occupied as I have been visited by so dreadful a loss – so much more bitter as I was on the point of starting out to join my wife when I received the fatal telegram. I am now going to Denver, when it is too late…'.[18]

While in the USA, Henry made his first visit to the Arnold Arboretum and finally met Charles Sargent and his staff in person. He later sold a reduced number of specimens to Professor Sargent, and these were distributed to the principal herbaria of the USA. From Boston, Henry returned to Europe in February 1894, and made his way to London, where he stayed with Caroline's sister and her husband. The past few months had been horrendous, and he was very upset upon arrival in London. Wishing to keep busy and to take his mind off the loss of Caroline, he began working in the Kew Herbarium under Hemsley's supervision.

NOTE: *Primula carolinehenryi* O'Brien nom. nov. Syn. *Carolinella henryi* Hemsley in Hooker's *Ic. Pl.* t. 2726. (1902) *Primula henryi* (Hemsley) Pax in Engler's *Pflanzenr.* IV. 236: 47. (1905) A. Henry 10,735 (type of *Carolinella henryi* Hemsley, type of *Primula carolinehenryi* O'Brien) non *Primula* x *henryi* Hort in *Gard. Chron.* n. ser. 15: 404. (1881)

Professor Charles Sprague Sargent, the founding director of the Arnold Arboretum of Harvard University. Henry visited Sargent in the autumn of 1894, following the death of his first wife, Caroline.

Chapter 9

To Taiwan by way of Shanghai and Hong Kong

Augustine Henry was thrice based in Shanghai, and, since that city was also part of his odyssey in China, we decided to make a brief visit there, too, in October 2004. Shanghai, of course, is a much-changed place to that which Henry knew, but it still has many stark reminders of its treaty port past, and a Customs House still dominates the Bund.

Dubbed the 'Paris of the East' and the 'Pearl of the Orient', Shanghai has become one of China's wealthiest cities. Its citizens are the most affluent in mainland China, and, with only 1 per cent of the country's population, Shanghai generates 5 per cent of the nation's output and 25 per cent of its total trade. 'Paris of the East' is a particularly apt sobriquet for this modern, bright, trendy city, and, given its current rate of growth and prosperity, Shanghai will soon stand once again with Paris and New York as one of the great cities of the world.

The Pudong district of Shanghai by night, an exciting city of lights and a symbol of China's new-found confidence and wealth. A country village in 1990, today it is the heart of Shanghai's money-making machine, with some of the tallest buildings in Asia. It presents a wonderfully striking contrast to the Bund.

We were left in awe of this metropolis, where 21st-century skyscrapers merge effortlessly with 19th- and early 20th-century colonial buildings. The Bund, Shanghai's elegant colonial waterfront, made a wonderfully stark contrast with the space-age Pudong New Area district that it overlooks. Visiting the Bund was like seeing the Eiffel Tower for the very first time. The most elegant waterfront in all of Asia, the Bund, more than any other group of colonial buildings, has came to epitomise Shanghai's treaty port history.

Most of the buildings that line the Bund incorporate

214

The Hong Kong orchid tree, *Bauhinia* x *blakeana* 'Sir Henry Blake', seen here in the village of Mui Wo on Lantau Island.

One of the parents of the Hong Kong orchid tree is *Bauhinia variegata*, pictured here on Ape's Hill in southern Taiwan. It is often grown by Buddhist monks in China and the Himalaya.

The cone-like Lantau Peak rises 933 m (3,086 ft) above sea level. Lantau is the largest of Hong Kong's outlying islands and still possesses a rural charm.

neo-classical themes, and the sight of this 2-km (1.2-mile) sweep of historic buildings is nothing short of magnificent, particularly when the facades are floodlit by night. Arguably, the finest building is the regal Shanghai Pudong Development Bank, with its graceful domed crown and amber marble columns. Alongside is the Customs House, one of the few commercial buildings in Shanghai to have the same role throughout the 20th century. Built in 1925, it replaced the gothic castle-like building in which Augustine Henry received his training for the Customs Service.

In an effort to overcome the legacy left by the colonial powers, China has built Pudong, a futuristic, sub-provincial city on the opposite river bank to the Bund. Pudong could not be more of a contrast. A modern city of neon-lit skyscrapers, including some of Asia's tallest buildings, it has one of the most exciting skylines in the world.

Alas, our stay in Shanghai was a brief one and we grudgingly left the comforts of the city behind us. It was time to leave the mainland and head for the tropical rainforests of southern Taiwan.

Hong Kong, Kowloon and Lantau Island

To reach Taiwan meant first flying to Hong Kong, and we made a brief stop there before continuing our travels. There is nowhere in the world quite like Hong Kong, and, after years of colonial influence, it is more like a Western principality than an administrative region of China. The general image of Hong Kong is one of crammed, high-rise buildings and people going about their hectic lifestyles. That image is only partly true; the outlying islands off Hong Kong make a peaceful escape from the city itself.

The largest and most beautiful of these is Lantau (Lantou), which has a land area twice that of Hong Kong

215

Island, yet supports a population of only 25,000 people. Lantau means 'broken head' in Cantonese, and the island is dominated by the cone-like bulk of Lantau Peak, which rises 933 m (3,060 ft) above sea level.

The island is a sleepy little place, with narrow back roads and with lush tropical vegetation spread across its hilly terrain. After a rather busy three weeks in Hubei Province and three days in Shanghai, it was wonderful to disappear into this quiet hideaway. The village of Mui Wo (Meiwo) on Lantau's southern coast overlooks the stunningly beautiful, island-stippled Silver Mine Bay, and it proved to be an ideal base for exploring the Hong Kong group of islands.

Mui Wo sits on a sheltered strand, lined with trees of *Casuarina equisetifolia* and *Barringtonia asiatica*, both littoral species well able to withstand saline conditions. In the centre of the village were a few flowering trees of the very striking Hong Kong orchid tree, *Bauhinia* x *blakeana* 'Sir Henry Blake',[1] a small tree whose name commemorates Sir Henry and Lady Edith Blake. Henry Blake was governor of Hong Kong between 1897 and 1903 and hailed from County Limerick in Ireland.

The Hong Kong orchid tree is a hybrid between two superbly ornamental species: *Bauhinia purpurea* and *Bauhinia variegata*. The original cross was discovered in the ruins of a house on the seashore at Guangzhou (Canton, Kwangchow), Guangdong Province, from where it was propagated by Roman Catholic missionaries before it made its way to Hong Kong Botanic Gardens. In 1965, *Bauhinia* x *blakeana* 'Sir Henry Blake' was chosen as the city flower of Hong Kong,

ABOVE: Offering gifts to Lantau's giant seated Buddha. The island's famous statue is situated in the heart of Lantau's mountainous central spine. To the rear of these bronze statues are fine specimens of the Norfolk Island pine, *Araucaria heterophylla*. BELOW: At 24 m (79 ft), the main statue is the world's largest outdoor bronze statue of a seated Buddha.

and its exotic blooms appear on several of the city's coins.

From Mui Wo, we travelled past the spectacularly blue Shek Pik Reservoir on the western slopes of Lantau Peak to the island's best-known attraction, the Po Lin Monastery (Baolian Chansi). This brightly painted complex is home to a large congregation of Buddhist monks and nuns, though people come here to see the world's largest outdoor bronze statue of a seated Buddha.

The rich colours painted on the walls of the Po Lin Monastery provided a perfect background for the coral hibiscus, *Hibiscus schizopetalus*. An evergreen shrub to 4 m (13 ft) tall, it is popular throughout the tropics.

Part of our reason for travelling here was to see trees of *Camellia crapnelliana*, an exciting plant that formed groves on Lantau's lower slopes, and its distinctive rust-coloured bark and enormous white flowers made it instantly recognisable.

We reached the Po Lin Monastery in time to catch a large procession of monks and nuns assembling in an inner courtyard. The walls of this area were painted a rich red and made a stunning background for large shrubs of *Hibiscus schizopetalus*, the coral hibiscus from Kenya, Tanzania and northern Mozambique. The specific epithet of this exquisite plant is derived from the Greek '*schizo*', to divide, and '*petalus*', referring, of course, to the much-divided petals.

Hong Kong was as busy as ever during our stay. The *Rainbow Warrior*, the famous flagship belonging to Greenpeace, was docked in Victoria Harbour, and the city has changed little since being handed over to China. It seemed strange to stroll along streets carrying Irish names such as 'Hennessy Road' and 'Connaught Street'. We stayed on Robinson Road, just a few minutes' walk from Hong Kong Botanic Gardens, where, on Saint Patrick's Day 1889, Henry gave Charles Ford bulbs of *Lilium henryi* for Kew. Taiwan beckoned, however, and so from a garden surrounded by skyscrapers we headed off on yet another journey.

Camellia crapnelliana, a small tree with wonderful cinnamon-coloured bark. Seen here in Hong Kong Botanic Gardens.

Messerschmidia argentea, pictured here on Shadao Shell Beach near South Cape, with the azure-blue Taiwan Strait in the background. Its fruits float on ocean currents and can germinate on beaches thousands of miles from the parent plant.

Taiwan, natural conditions

Lying between the Asian continent and the Philippines, the island of Taiwan is about two-thirds the size of Ireland. Just 394 km (245 miles) along its longest axis and 140 km (87 miles) at its widest point, the island is also bisected by the Tropic of Cancer.

Taiwan is located on the fringe of the continental shelf of Asia. This is limited to a belt of islands, which, in fact, are a group of submerged mountain ranges consisting of the Japanese Archipelago and the Taiwan–Liu-kiu (Ryukyu, Nansei) islands. This island chain is situated along a region of instability in the earth's crust known as the Pacific 'rim of fire', and Taiwan is located on its western edge, where the Philippine tectonic plate collides with the Eurasian landmass, thus forming a steep mountain chain.[2] Earthquakes are also a common occurrence in Taiwan. The shallow Taiwan Strait separates the island from the Eurasian landmass, and Taiwan lies only 144 km (90 miles) from the province of Fujian on the Chinese mainland.[3] To the east, the Pacific Ocean sinks to enormous depths not far off the coast.[4]

Due to its mountainous topography, the island encompasses a climatic range from tropical, in the extreme coastal south, to sub-arctic on the tallest peaks of the central range. In the south, particularly around South Cape (now Oluanpi or Eluanbi), the climate is tropical; there is no marked winter season, and flowers may be seen there in profusion at Christmas. Kaohsiung, on the west coast, is also well within the tropics, though there is a decided winter with a halt to growth of vegetation. The mean annual temperature at Kaohsiung is 24 °C (75 °F), while, along the South Cape, that figure is 25 °C (77 °F). Summer heat at the South Cape is relieved by the southern monsoons.

Taiwan is situated in the Pacific monsoon zone. In winter, much rain falls over northern and eastern parts, but has little effect in the south. The south-eastern monsoon affects the southern regions from May to September. The island lies in the track of severe tropical cyclones, known in Asia as typhoons. In summer and early autumn, typhoons sweep the entire island bringing violent winds and tremendous rainfall. Thus, the south-western part of the island (the region visited by the 2004 Glasnevin Taiwan Expedition) has a distinct wet and dry season. South-west Taiwan receives an annual rainfall of up to 1,810 mm (71 in.). Only 11 per cent of this falls from September to April; as a consequence, the region is subjected to winter drought.[5] Due to shallow soils and raised coral reef, xeric conditions prevail for considerable periods of time in coastal areas in the south, and plants are often stunted with sclerophyllous leaves.

Current calculations place the island's flora at more than 4,000 species and infraspecific taxa of vascular plants. Pantropical elements – that is, plants widely distributed in both the Old and New World topics – amounts to 1.5 per cent of the island's flora; examples include *Dodonea viscosa*, *Hibiscus tiliaceus*, *Sida acuta* and *Sophora tomentosa*. Widely distributed Old World or palaeotropical elements amount to 6 per cent; for example, *Barringtonia asiatica*, *Heritiera littoralis* and *Terminalia catappa*. Species endemism is more strongly expressed in Taiwan's temperate herbaceous flora than its woody flora, and the ratio of endemic plants is approximately 20 per cent.

Taiwan's strongest floristic relationship is with southern and eastern mainland China, Hainan and northern Vietnam.

South Cape clearly has associations with the Philippine flora, and species belonging to both the Philippine and Taiwanese flora include *Acacia confusa*, *Deutzia pulchra* and *Ehretia resinosa*. The flora of South Cape consists of lowland, coastal, tropical rainforest. Along the coast, the vegetation is similar to that of most of the Old World tropics. A little further inland, the foothills are covered with dense tropical rainforest. Though Henry labelled his collections 'South Cape', his native plant collector also gathered material further inland, in what is now Kenting National Park.

In spite of its large population and rapid industrialisation, Taiwan's forest cover stands at 52 per cent, this being one of the most extensive areas of primeval forest in eastern Asia. Five national parks occupy 8.5 per cent of the island's land area. The first of these to be established was Kenting National Park, which came into being as recently as 1984.

Collecting specimens for the National Botanic Gardens, Glasnevin, in the tropics of southern Taiwan. Left to right: a local forestry official from Kenting National Park; the author; Kevin Chen from the Taiwan Forestry Research Institute in Taipei; Joan Rogers. In my hands are herbarium specimens about to be pressed; these include *Barringtonia asiatica* and *Pandanus odoratissimus*.

Epipremnum pinnatum, a tropical climbing aroid, seen here on a tree of *Barringtonia asiatica* at Banana Bay Coastal Forest.

Tropical rainforest and grassy downs at South Cape

The flight from Hong Kong to Kaohsiung was a short one, and, on arrival, we were met in the airport by Kevin Chen, an assistant of Professor Wen Liang Chou, our contact from the Taiwan Forestry Research Institute in Taipei. We immediately departed the city and took a bus south along the scenic coastal route to the small village of Kenting on the Hengchun Peninsula (Pingtung County) in the extreme south of Taiwan.

This part of the island is Taiwan's banana belt, a region favourable to tropical agriculture, and rice, sugar cane, banana and betel nut plantations cover the plains. Huge Buddhist and Taoist temples rise above these plantations. Our drive followed the coast, past blue seas and long, white, sandy beaches. Tropical trees were still in bloom, and it all combined to create a very exotic feel. Our base for the next few days was Kenting, a popular tourist resort. Despite the fact that it was late October, the place was still relatively busy and a festive atmosphere pervaded.

The following morning, local forestry officials drove us to the Banana Bay Coastal Forest Reserve between Kenting and South Cape. The forests there grew on uplifted fossilised coral, and were almost wholly formed by *Barringtonia asiatica*, a handsome tree with large, coarse, leathery leaves. Native to the tropics of the Old World, the fruits of this species are dispersed on ocean currents. *Hernandia nymphifolia* was less common, and formed trees to about 15 m (49 ft) tall with large, heart-shaped leaves. Climbing by

The tropical forests of southern Taiwan have been invaded over the past two centuries or so by several alien species. Seen here is *Stachytarpheta jamaicensis* from the New World tropics.

ABOVE: *Scaevola sericea*, a pantropic tree whose fruits are dispersed on ocean currents. Its tough leathery leaves are well adapted to the xeric conditions that prevail in this coastal part of Taiwan.

means of aerial roots over coral formation and into the trees above was *Epipremnum pinnatum*, an exotic liana with large, exotic, fenestrated leaves. Widely distributed in Australasia, it is common in subtropical and tropical forests in China.

On the forest floor, we found another widespread species that grows outdoors in a handful of Irish gardens. *Microsorium scolopendrium* is a small xerophytic fern with pinnate fronds to about 30 cm (1 ft) long, and has thick fleshy rhizomes with which it climbs and crawls over its support. It grows at Glanleam, a large Victorian garden on Valentia Island, off Ireland's County Kerry coast. The garden there was developed by Sir Peter Fitzgerald (1808–80), the 19th Knight of Kerry and a great plantsman, who, in an almost frost-free climate, trialled numerous rare plants on the borderline of hardiness. At Glanleam, this evergreen fern

scales a large rock and continues its way into a native holly. The Taiwanese plant crept across fossilised coral and climbed further into a *Barringtonia*. Obviously, the Knight of Kerry knew how his plants liked to grow in their native habitats.

Nearby, the blue snakeweed, *Stachytarpheta jamaicensis*, a handsome perennial to a metre (3.3 ft) tall, carried spikes of small blue flowers. Native to tropical America, it is now widely naturalised in the Old World tropics. The blue snakeweed grew alongside another perennial, the pink-flowered *Peristrophe roxburghiana*. Both plants are obviously well adapted to the xeric conditions that prevail in this region during the dry season.

Leaving the woods, we climbed our way across vast sheets of fossilised coral and stopped for a while on a boardwalk, from where we were able to observe the wind- and salt-burned vegetation of the outer perimeter of the forest. Plants here have to be tough to withstand the fierce force of the Pacific Ocean, and, prime amongst these, was *Scaevola sericea*, a small tree or shrub with large, glossy, corrugated leaves. Native to the tropical shores that surround the Indian and Pacific Ocean, it is a coastal plant in Taiwan and one of the most common shrubs on beaches there.

Sophora tomentosa also grew on the fossilised coral formations, and reached no more than a metre (3.3 ft) tall. Cosmopolitan in the tropics, we found it to be common on Taiwan's southern shores, where it carried masses of bright yellow, pea-like blossoms. Though it is generally found as a small tree, *Pemphis acidula* was reduced to being a small shrub because of the harsh growing conditions. It is

The 'beach morning glory', or 'railroad vine', *Ipomoea pes-caprae* sp. *brasiliensis*, a prostrate semi-succulent perennial. Its wandering stems can reach to more than 40 m (131 ft) long. The funnel-shape flowers vary from pink to dark purple.

The lighthouse at South Cape. Built by the Customs Service following the massacre of the crew of the *Rover*, it was visited by Augustine and Caroline Henry in February 1893.

Diospyros discolor, an evergreen persimmon that was common in the forests surrounding the lighthouse at South Cape.

frequently encountered on the south coast of Taiwan, and is widely dispersed along tropical coasts of the Old World.

From Banana Bay, we took a short drive down the coast to Shadao Shell Beach, a beautiful stretch of coast with azure blue waters fringed by kilometres of sublime white beaches. On these beaches grew a number of interesting exotic plants, including the wonderful beach morning glory, *Ipomoea pes-caprae* ssp. *brasiliensis*, a vigorous, semi-succulent perennial forming large, flat mats of foliage and bearing tubular, lilac-purple flowers. There was also a fig, *Ficus tinctoria*, a prostrate shrub reaching no more than 2.5 cm (1 in.) tall, though, in more sheltered areas above the beach, it reached shrub-like dimensions, and its leaves became far larger.

The most beautiful plant at Shadao Shell Beach had to be *Messerschmidia argentea*, a fantastic domed-shaped shrub belonging to the borage family, with silvery, silky, tomentose foliage. Like many of the other seashore plants in this part of Taiwan, the fruits of this species are well adapted for widespread distribution on ocean currents, and it is found across much of tropical Asia, Australia and Polynesia.

Our journey continued on to South Cape on Taiwan's southernmost tip. South Cape was every bit as beautiful as Augustine Henry described it, and, on arrival there, I couldn't help but recall the story of how his heart throbbed with glee on hearing a lark sing over the area's tropical

grassy downs. We arrived there 110 years after he heard that little bird sing, and, like him, we were captivated by the region's lush, green hills, sweeping coastline and tropical forests. While the aboriginal population has disappeared, the lighthouse still remains and its newly whitewashed walls gleamed in their tropical surrounds. On hearing of our reason for visiting South Cape, the lighthouse keeper allowed us access to the building, and so we scaled our way up a spiral staircase to the top of the tower. The building was immaculately kept inside and still had all of its Victorian fittings, just as Augustine Henry would have known it.

Standing on the upper deck, we had a 360-degree view of the peninsula. A tropical breeze blew over us, and, facing onto the broad expanse of the Pacific Ocean, it was difficult to imagine that the next point of land south of us was the Philippines, or that, to the east, lay America. Henry before us had stood on this very spot and, like us, had enjoyed the view of blue seas and sweeping stretches of coral beach. South Cape was indeed a tropical paradise.

The forests surrounding the lighthouse were full of all sorts of exotic tropical plants and, having visited the lighthouse, we immediately resumed our work of pressing plants and collecting seeds. Herbarium specimens had to be pressed almost immediately, since the heat at South Cape, even at this late stage of the year, was intense and specimens wilted within minutes. Not far from the lighthouse grew a fine clump of the ginger relative *Alpinia zerumbet*. This particular plant seemed interesting because of its upright fruiting spikes (rather than a pendulous spike, which is the norm); the plant we found was most likely a natural hybrid. Sprawling its way across the ground in front of the alpinia was a naturalised amaranth relative, *Alternanthera bettzickiana*, a mat-forming perennial from Brazil carrying small, silvery-white flowers.

The forest cover at South Cape consisted mainly of *Terminalia catappa*, a small tree with remarkably large oval leaves. This species is common along the shores of the Old World tropics since its fruits, like those of so many other trees and shrubs in South Cape's forests, are dispersed on ocean currents. *Ehretia resinosa* was another common tree, and, as

The South American passion flower *Passiflora foetida* var. *hispida*, an invasive weed in many parts of the Old World tropics. We collected both white and pink-purple flowered forms.

Flagellaria indica, a paleotropical rhizomatous liana capable of reaching 15 m (49 ft) high. In Thailand and Malaysia, its stems are used to make baskets.

previously stated, it is part of the Philippine element in southern Taiwan's flora. It was discovered by Robert Swinhoe near Kaohsiung in 1865, and was also later collected on Ape's Hill by E. H. Wilson. Another fine tree that is native to both the Philippines and Taiwan is the evergreen persimmon *Diospyros discolor*. In the forests at South Cape, it towered 7 m (23 ft) overhead and bore handsome lanceolate leaves to 30 cm (1 ft) long with silvery-grey undersides.

Closer to the seashore, we entered a forest of screw pines, *Pandanus odoratissimus*, another common plant along the tropical shores of Asia. Numerous lianas scaled their way through the coastal jungle, and the most exotic of these was *Flagellaria indica*, a 15-m (49-ft) tall vine, climbing with the aid of spiral leaf-tendrils. This species is widely distributed across tropical Africa, Asia and Australia, and is particularly abundant in dense coastal forest in Taiwan. Other common climbers in this jungle included *Malaisia scandens*, *Paederia scandens*, *Ampelopsis brevipedunculata* var. *hancei*, *Tetrastigma formosana* and the widespread climbing fern, *Lygodium japonicum*, which we had met at Yichang only weeks before. *Guettarda speciosa*, a small tree with enormous obovate leaves, made a fine contrast with *Premna obtusifolia*, a medium-sized shrub with large, shiny, leathery leaves and small corymbs of white flowers.

Our attention was also drawn to a number of handsome garden escapes. The tropics fare far worse than temperate regions when it comes to invasive alien plants and Taiwan has its fair share. Two South American passion flowers were common in more open, exposed areas where they generally clung to coral formations: *Passiflora suberosa* scrambled its way to about 2 m (6.5 ft) high and carried tiny, maroon-brown fruits; *Passiflora foetida* var. *hispida* was an altogether more ornamental plant, with a curious green lacy calyx. *Leucaena leucocephala*, a 7-m (23-ft) tall tree with albizia-like foliage and globular heads of white mimosa-like flowers, is another alien species that has invaded the flora of southern Taiwan. Native to the southern USA, it was introduced by early Dutch settlers as a fertiliser crop, but it is now widely naturalised and abundant.

We were also well warned about the nettle tree, *Dendrocnide meyeniana*. The unfortunate local who happens to be stung by it uses the foliage of a spectacular aroid, *Alocasia odora*, as an antidote in the same way as the leaves of the common dock, *Rumex crispus*, are used to treat stings from the nettle *Urtica dioica* in Europe.

Fine foliage plants were abundant in South Cape's tropical jungles. Those that come to mind include *Melanolepis multiglandulosa*, a large shrub or small tree with enormous, three-lobed leaves more than a metre (3.3 ft) in length, and we were equally impressed with the sail-like foliage of another spurge family member, *Macaranga tanarius*. The latter was a very striking plant, though we were stopped in our tracks by the large, bold, heart-shaped leaves of the Alexandrian laurel *Calophyllum inophyllum*, and we collected plenty of seeds from it for Glasnevin's newly restored Great Palm House. Native to the coasts and islands of the Indian Ocean, much of Asia and Australia, its name derives from the Greek 'kalos', or 'beautiful', and 'phyllon', a 'leaf'. Palms, of course, were abundant in such a benign climate, and the most common of these was *Phoenix hanceana*, a small tree to about 4 m (13 ft) tall. By the palm grew a low bush of *Ficus superba* var. *japonica* and *Pittosporum pentandrum*, a 3-m (10-ft) tall, dome-shape shrub, then heavily laden with orange seed capsules.

223

Native to Taiwan and the Philippines, the leaves of *Dendrocnide meyeniana* are covered with minute hairs, which sting violently. Henry knew it as the '*yao-jen-kon*'.

Alocasia odora, a giant aroid that is native to the tropical forests of the Himalaya, China and the Philippines. Its huge bold leaves act as a perfect antidote to the stinging leaves of the nettle tree, *Dendrocnide meyeniana*.

Macaranga tanarius is often grown as a shade tree in tropical parts of Taiwan. It is a pioneer species that quickly colonises clearings in tropical rainforest.

Pittosporum pentandrum, here carrying a large crop of rounded, orange fruits. Native to southern Taiwan and the Philippines, it forms a small tree.

Abutilon indicum, a pretty sub-shrub to about 1.5 m (5 ft) tall. Henry collected it several times in Taiwan and at Mengzi and Simao in southern Yunnan Province.

Aglaia formosana, a medium-sized evergreen tree with silvery branchlets. In Taiwan, it is found only on the Hengchun Peninsula that surrounds the lighthouse at South Cape.

Clerodendrum paniculatum f. *albiflorum*, the rare white pagoda flower, seen here wild at Kenting National Park.

The common pagoda flower, *Clerodendrum paniculatum*, pictured on Ape's Hill.

Chloris barbata, a common grass in tropical south-east Asia, which Henry collected near Kaohsiung.

In a field above the lighthouse, farmers were busy making hay and it seemed a little strange to stand in a hayfield full of round bales on the edge of tropical rainforest. The headlands were full of *Miscanthus floridulus*, a coarse-looking plant in comparison to the better-known *Miscanthus sinensis*, but worth collecting nonetheless. In thickets by the edge of the same hayfield grew a number of interesting plants, including *Abutilon indicum* and *Sida rhombifolia*, both really only weeds, but handsome plants in their own right.

Trees in this thicket included *Scolopia oldhami* and *Aglaia formosana*, both of which are native to Taiwan and the Philippines. The *Aglaia* is a particularly beautiful tree with silvery-bronze pinnate foliage, and, in Taiwan, it is found only along the seashore of the Hengchun Peninsula – and it was discovered there by Henry in 1893.

From the coastal forests of South Cape, we travelled inland to nearby Kenting National Park. On the edge of tropical rainforest grew many colourful shrubs, and the most flamboyant of these was *Clerodendrum paniculatum* f. *albiflorum*, a bush to 1.5 m (5 ft) tall. The type – *Clerodendrum paniculatum*, commonly known as the 'pagoda flower' because of the tiered arrangement of the flowers in a panicle – is a widespread species

in south-east Asia, and carries upright panicles of fiery-orange flowers. We later collected it on Ape's Hill near Kaohsiung. The form *albiflorum* is a stunningly beautiful plant with pure white flowers, and we gathered a good batch of seeds for introduction through Glasnevin. The white pagoda flower grew alongside *Vitex quinata*, a 4-m (13-ft) tall bush, then a billowing mass of small, lilac-blue blossoms. Through it climbed two species of *Pueraria*. The first, *Pueraria lobata* ssp. *thomsonii*, scaled its way to about 3 m (10 ft) and carried axillary racemes of light blue blossoms. The second, *Pueraria montana*, twined its way to a similar height, and bore densely packed racemes of pink-purple flowers while the undersides of its large trifoliate leaves were beautifully coated in a lining of short silvery hairs.

Another climber that grew nearby was the curiously beautiful bitter gourd, *Momordica charantia*, a slender, annual, palaeotropical vine carrying yellow vanilla-scented flowers followed by multi-ribbed, warty, orange-red fruits, which are dehiscent at maturity and burst into a star-like configuration. The grassy downs approaching the forests were full of *Chloris barbata*, a showy grass bearing digitate flower spikes. Widely spread in south-east Asia, it is considered by some experts to be truly native to tropical America.

Left: Henry's 'grassy downs' of south 'Formosa', an area between South Cape and Kenting National Park.

Below: The large buttressed trunk of *Heritiera littoralis*, seen here on fossilised coral in Kenting National Park.

Kenting National Park

Kenting National Park covers a total area of 32,631 ha (80,628 acres). Of this, 17,731 ha (43,811 acres) is land, while the remainder consists of a marine reserve. The primary features of the park include tropical coastal rainforest, marine ecosystems, uplifted coral reef, waterfowl and migratory birds. Located on the southern tip of Taiwan, Kenting National Park lies on the Hengchun Peninsula with the Pacific Ocean to the east, the Taiwan Strait to the west and the Luzon Strait (Bashi Channel) to the south.

The Hengchun Peninsula sits on the confluence of fault lines and tectonic plates. The result is a landscape that has been pushed, pulled and twisted into its present complex form. The Hengchun Rift Valley runs north to south and cuts the National Park into eastern and western sections. The principal geological feature in the western section is raised coral beds, with mountains in the north and gently rolling hills (Henry's 'grassy downs') in the south. The eastern section comprises uplifted coral beds and limestone.

Kenting is the only national park in Taiwan to include undersea areas. These waters are home to substantial reefs built up by countless generations of coral over thousands of years. Both types of coral – hermatypic (constructive) and ahermatypic (non-constructive) – can be found in the region's warm coastal waters. Hermatypic corals tend to live close to the ocean surface, since they need ample light to thrive; ahermatypic corals live in deeper, darker waters. To date, 236 species of coral have been identified from Kenting's marine reserve.

Our collections from Kenting National Park were made in the nature reserve belonging to Hong Chuaw Tropical Botanic Garden. The reserve and botanic gardens were established during the Japanese occupation and consist of a considerable area of tropical rainforest. Monkeys made a noisy and rapid exit as we drove into the reserve, and one of the first trees we met was the seashore persimmon, *Diospyros maritima*, a large, multi-branched tree with green fruits to about 2.5 cm (1 in.) across. While chopping these fruits to make a herbarium specimen, I soon learned that I should handle any further such strange fruits with care. My hands were stained brown-green for three weeks because of the juice of these wild persimmons!

The reserve proved to be an exciting, exotic jungle, with giant lianas, climbing bamboo, palms, bananas and enormous banyans, all growing happily on a floor of 100,000-year-old fossilised coral. *Musa basjoo* var. *formosana* was an abundant banana, with great paddle-like leaves to more than 3 m (10 ft) long. *Koelreuteria elegans* ssp. *formosana* (syn. *Koelreuteria henryi*) was also common and formed trees to about 15 m (49 ft) tall.

One of the most impressive trees in those forests was the Chinese banyan, *Ficus macrocarpa*, a large evergreen tree with wide-spreading branches from which hundreds of pendulous aerial roots descended and rooted into the ground below, thus acting as a prop for the same branches to spread out even further. By this means, the Chinese banyan is capable of colonising a considerable area of ground.

Heritiera littoralis was another giant in this area of rainforest and the lower trunks of trees were massively buttressed. It is common along the tropical shores of Taiwan, and its curious, boat-shaped fruits are dispersed by seawater. On the shaded forest floor grew *Amischotolype hispida*, a stout perennial with creeping stems and small white flowers in a dense thyrse. Through it scrambled the Japanese pepper *Piper kadsura*, a scandent shrub climbing by means of aerial roots.

The old church at Bankinsing, Takow and Ape's Hill

From our base at Kenting, we drove back up the coast to Kaohsiung, where we were met by Professor Ho-Yih Liu from the Department of Biological Sciences at the National Sun Yat-sen University. We stayed in accommodation on the university campus that night, and it must have the most spectacular location of any university worldwide. Our rooms had panoramic views of one of the busiest seaports in the world, and, from our base, we could see the old town of Takow where Augustine and Caroline Henry once lived. To the right was the massive bulk of Ape's Hill (Wanshoushan).

The following morning, we travelled to the old town of Takow (now a suburb of Kaohsiung municipality called Chi-hou), and also visited a little lighthouse that lies on a rocky bluff above the town. From there, we strolled along the edge of the lagoon where once there were thriving mangrove forests. Though generally poor in species diversity, Henry found the mangroves interesting, and his herbarium collections contain a good representation of these forests, which finally disappeared in the early 1970s. He collected *Bruguiera gymnorrhiza*, a tree that was common along the edge of the lagoon in the late 19th century. It is now locally extinct in Taiwan and no longer part of the island's flora.

The following day, we set off with Professor Liu and one of his postgraduate students and drove east to the village of

ABOVE: A Spanish mission was established at Bankinsing (Wanjin) in 1861, and, eight years later, the present church was built in the Spanish fortress style. Augustine Henry stayed at this mission several times during 1893 and 1894, and his native plant collector gathered specimens on the mountains that can be seen behind the church.

Bankinsing. After much searching and several wrong turns, we eventually found the place, hidden away in the middle of a vast betel nut and banana plantation. At the end of the main street was a 19th-century, Spanish-style church. Having passed numerous Buddhist and Taoist monasteries along the way, it seemed strange to stumble across a Roman Catholic village in this remote part of Taiwan. Perhaps the disparaging Spanish missionary with whom Henry had stayed a century before had discovered a few souls among the local 'savages', after all.

Nowadays, Taiwan's indigenous population accounts for only 2 per cent of the island's population. These native Taiwanese belong to the Austronesian ethnic group, members of which live in a vast area extending from Madagascar in the west to Hawaii and the Easter Islands in the east, and New Zealand in the south to Taiwan in the north. There are ten aboriginal tribes in present-day Taiwan, each with their own distinct customs and dress styles, although these communities are slowly being assimilated into mainstream contemporary culture.

The former British Consulate, now an upmarket restaurant. Established by Robert Swinhoe in 1865, it became a base for visiting naturalists. It is all that remains today of the Foreign Compound at Kaohsiung.

RIGHT: Robert Swinhoe was one of the earliest naturalists to visit Taiwan. Of particular interest to him was the large colony of Formosan rock macaques on Ape's Hill.

Bankinsing was a lovely, quiet, peaceful place, and the local head-hunters have long since given up their ways. The missionary church is the oldest Catholic church in Taiwan, and was made a *basilica* during the late 1990s by Pope John Paul II. There was a great sense of history to our visit; Henry himself had stayed there, and it was at Bankinsing that he had his first encounter with indigenous peoples. To the rear of the church rose mountains on which he secured specimens for study at Kew. Our time was running short in Taiwan, however, and so we returned to Kaohsiung to explore Ape's Hill.

Before Henry's arrival in Taiwan, Kaohsiung had been home to another important explorer and naturalist, Robert Swinhoe, the first British Vice-Consul at Formosa (Taiwan). Born in Calcutta in September 1836, Swinhoe arrived in southern China in 1854, when he was only 18 years old. He lived a brief, albeit highly noteworthy, life and is best remembered for his work on the ornithology of Taiwan.

Swinhoe's first visit to Taiwan was in March 1856. His second trip was made aboard the British warship, HMS *Inflexible* in June 1858. The object of this expedition was to search for two Englishmen who were believed to have been kidnapped by aborigines. The ship completed a circumnavigation of the island, and, in the course of this trip, Swinhoe was able to collect a large number of plant and animal specimens.

The lighthouse above Chi-hou (formerly Takow). Augustine and Caroline Henry lived on a coastal plain below.

ABOVE: Ape's Hill, with the city of Kaohsiung to the right. It is remarkable that an area of such amazing biodiversity has remained intact next to Taiwan's second largest city. Ape's Hill owes its salvation to its strategic military location, and it is only in recent years that the public have had access.

RIGHT: Ape's Hill, photographed from the suburb of Kaohsiung formerly known as Takow. Along its base is the campus of the National Sun Yat-sen University. In the foreground is a sheet of *Ipomoea pes-caprae* ssp. *brasiliensis*.

In August 1863, Swinhoe was sent to Takow with instructions to establish a British Consulate. We made two visits to the former British Consulate, a beautiful, red brick building on the side of a hilltop overlooking Hsitzu Bay and Ape's Hill. Built in 1865, it was the first foreign consulate in Taiwan, and is the oldest Western-style building on the island. Featuring a façade of archways with balconies, it was designed by American architects and its layout is in feet and inches. From its galleries, we enjoyed unobstructed views of Ape's Hill framed by the building's beautifully proportioned, Romanesque arches.

Takow was renamed Kaohsiung by the Japanese during the 1920s, and, nowadays, it is the second largest city in Taiwan, with a population of more than 1.5 million. Kaohsiung's seaport is the fourth largest container port in the world, behind Rotterdam, Singapore and Hong Kong. To the north of the harbour lay our next port of call, Ape's Hill.

Ape's Hill – or Wanshoushan, as it is better known – has survived remarkably well due to its strategic military position. The Japanese banned entry to the area during their 50-year rule, and the Taiwanese army still maintain a base there. Military restrictions were eased a few years ago, and 1,200 ha (2,965 acres) of Ape's Hill were re-opened to the public as a nature park. Ape's Hill's most famous residents are its large colonies of Formosan rock macaques, first recorded there by Robert Swinhoe. This species is known by

229

An abundant understorey palm was *Arenga tremula*.

The Formosan rock macaque, *Macaca cyclopis*, wild on Ape's Hill. We learned to keep our distance, having previously met with thieving, mischievous macaques on Emei Shan in Sichuan Province.

OPPOSITE: *Ficus macrocarpa*, a common banyan on Ape's Hill, where its fruits are eaten and dispersed by the Formosan rock macaque. *Ficus benjamina*, more often seen as a houseplant in the West, make equally large trees.

its dark grey fur and large cheek pouches, used to carry food while foraging. The Formosan rock macaque consumes fruit, leaves, berries, seeds, insects and small vertebrate animals. Its tail is not prehensile, and is, therefore, of no assistance to the animal while climbing trees. Since the opening up of Ape's Hill, however, these macaques have changed their lifestyles; many have become overweight, and some have even been diagnosed with diabetes and hypertension, due to the many visitors indulging them with all kinds of snacks. Some have become spoiled and have learned to beg for food; many even aggressively snatch food from visitors. Local conservationists attribute the problem to the government's over-development of the area through the addition of pavilions, park benches and pathways to the hill.[6]

The region of Ape's Hill we visited was well served by a maze of boardwalks that ran across a large part of the hill. It is remarkable that a reserve as rich in biodiversity as this has survived on the very edge of a major city. Ape's Hill was certainly beautiful, and a perfect place to spend our last day collecting in Taiwan. Many species of *Ficus* grow on limestone and coral formations on Ape's Hill and are well

adapted to this habitat. The roots of these trees can secure an especially strong grip on coral due to a highly specialised mechanism whereby they produce an acidic secretion that partially dissolves the soluble stone, thus allowing the roots to further penetrate the rock.

On Ape's Hill, the fruits of various species are dispersed by birds and macaques, and some of these, including *Ficus benjamina* and *Ficus macrocarpa*, form very large banyans.

Ape's Hill is also the type locality of *Amorphophallus henryi*, which we found several times and of which we pressed several good fruiting specimens. *Arenga tremula* was abundant as an understorey, shade-loving palm, and we gathered a good supply of seeds for Glasnevin's palm collection.

Several climbers scaled their way through low trees and shrubs, the prettiest being the butterfly pea, *Clitoria ternatea*, a trailing herbaceous vine to 3 m (10 ft) high with glorious sky-blue, pea-like blooms. *Clematis formosana* sported small white flowers in lateral cymes; this species is endemic to Taiwan and was discovered by the Irish plant collector George M. H. Playfair in 1888. *Mussaenda pubescens* scrambled its way through surrounding trees and carried dense cymes of small, tubular, yellow flowers with large, showy, white, leaf-like bracts attached.

Our final day in Taiwan was spent exploring the many trails that led to the summit of Ape's Hill. Before departing, I gave a lecture to postgraduate students at the Sun Yat-sen University on Augustine Henry's adventures in China. It seemed strange to deliver a talk about this great Victorian plant hunter at the base of the very hill on which he once collected. Taiwan had been a great adventure – but Yunnan beckoned.

Chapter 10

To the wilds of Yunnan

A Hani man at his loom in the mountains to the south of the Red River in southern Yunnan Province. Henry's photograph, taken in the late 1890s, depicts the traditional Hani thatched huts of woven bamboo. His pony can be seen to the left.

Henry returned to China in January 1895, and was stationed for a short time in Shanghai. The city was developing rapidly as another new treaty had made way for enormous extensions to the foreign factories. The expatriate community enjoyed a boisterous social life, too; balls were a nightly affair, except on Sundays, and there were hunting and shooting trips in the countryside. For Augustine Henry, however, Caroline's death still weighed heavily, and he was very much out of tune with Shanghai's party atmosphere. Memories of happier times with Caroline depressed him and life in China would be lonely without her. He poured his heart out to Evelyn Gleeson:

I find great difficulty in picking up the threads. Every walk on the Bund vividly recalls to me all those with Caroline; and I grieve for myself. She is so different from the others; how interesting she made life. All the Chinese shops where she used to buy little odds and ends, how commonplace and stupid they seem. I have no pleasure in looking at anything.[1]

He had lost interest in life, he was homesick and saw Shanghai in a new light; everything there reminded him of Caroline's struggle to survive. He blamed himself for her death and wished he had made the decision to move from China sooner:

Caroline's illness was to me a constant terror; and I suffered so continuously. There was much in it that I never told or can tell. I was so foolish. I think I might have saved her life had I fought more strenuously and taken the risk of leaving China earlier [...] She made life to me so interesting. She taught me the wonderful strength of a true and loving nature; and her peculiar genius brightened up and illuminated everything [...] At times I forgot all this, when shattered by illness, her mind gone away and she was a poor sick child [... How different Shanghai now looks to me, the place so paltry in its meanness of life, in its absence of ideals.[2]

In April, Henry leased a house, and, in an attempt to 'escape the blues', he shared it with two colleagues from the Customs Service, one of whom he had previously worked with in Taiwan. People were kind to him, and he became very friendly with Arthur von Rosthorn, an Austrian official who had joined the Customs Service in 1883. He often strolled the Bund with von Rosthorn and his young wife, Paula. A noted scholar of Chinese literature, von Rosthorn had previously been stationed in Sichuan Province, where he had hired native plant collectors to gather specimens for him during 1891 and 1892. A number of new species were described from his collections, including *Celastrus rosthornianus*, *Holboellia coriacea*, *Macropanax rosthornii*, *Mahonia polydonta*, *Osmanthus armatus*, *Rhus punjabensis* var. *sinica* and *Vitis betulifolia*, for example, though all of these had been previously discovered by Henry in the Three Gorges region during the 1880s.

Henry also knew Sir Thomas Hanbury, a wealthy Quaker who created La Mortola, one of the most celebrated gardens on the Italian Riviera. Hanbury was a great benefactor of gardening, and, in 1903, he purchased land at Wisley, in Surrey, and presented it to the Royal Horticultural Society to replace their old Chiswick garden. Hanbury's son was based in Shanghai at this time; Henry saw a good deal of him and held him in the same high regard as he held his father.

A transfer to Mengzi

In May 1896, Augustine Henry left Shanghai having received a new post at Mengzi (then Mengtze) in Yunnan Province in south-western China. He was replacing William Hancock, who was transferring to Guangdong Province in eastern China. Yunnan was the most varied of all China's provinces, with terrain ranging from low-lying tropical rainforest, in the south, to soaring snow-capped peaks on the Tibetan frontier in the north-west. Regarded as a backwater by most Chinese citizens, it did not become

A view of the market place in Mengzi as sketched by a travelling companion of Prince Henri d'Orléans during his visit there in February 1895.

Chinese territory until 1252, and, even then, wasn't fully integrated into the empire until 1658. This allowed the survival of a great diversity of ethnic groups and the preservation of vast areas of forest cover.

Little was known about the botany of the region in the closing years of the 19th century. Plant collecting did not begin until 1868, when an English medical officer and naturalist, John Anderson, gathered specimens near Tengchong on the Burmese border. French collectors led the way over the next few decades, with the arrival of Père Jean Marie Delavay in 1882. He was followed, in turn, by Père Paul Viall (1886) and Prince Henri d'Orléans (1890, 1894). In 1894, William Hancock made large collections around Mengzi County. These comprised about 150 species of flowering plants and 120 ferns, most of which were new to science. Henry was familiar with the exploits of these men and looked forward to the opportunities his new base would provide.

In Hong Kong, he joined an American couple, the Spinneys, who had also worked with him in the Customs Service in Taiwan and who were also moving to Mengzi. From the hustle and bustle of Hong Kong, the small party

ABOVE: A silt-laden Red River makes its way through tropical forests and steep hillsides to the north-west of Hekou. Both Augustine Henry and Ernest Wilson sailed this stretch of river, in the late 19th century, from Lao Cai in present-day Vietnam to reach Mengzi and Simao.

sailed to Haikou on Hainan Island, where Henry had been stationed in 1889. Many memories, not exactly pleasant, came back to haunt him. From Hainan, their journey continued on to Haiphong in Vietnam (then part of French Indochina), where they rested for three days before boarding a river steamer up the Red River to Hanoi. The small frontier town of Lao Cai was finally reached by means of a number of small launches on the 12 June.

The last 130-km (80-mile) stretch of the Red River through Vietnam was full of treacherous rapids, and it must have brought back memories of the Three Gorges to Henry. The river well deserved its name; it was stained a rusty-red hue by the enormous quantities of red clay that had washed into it from hillsides in Yunnan Province. The countryside around was mountainous, with hills rising from 304 to 1,310 m (1,000 to 4,300 ft), and wild bananas, laden with small and inedible fruits, luxuriated along the banks of the river, as did palms. It was a lonely stretch of river, with occasional groups of indigenous peoples – though, here and there, were a few French colonial stations, and Henry and his party got on very well with the soldiers based there.

From Lao Cai, a fleet of nine junks brought Augustine Henry, the Spinneys and their Chinese staff with 300 items of baggage across the border into southern Yunnan Province. The following seven days were spent negotiating and tracking a further 130 km (80 miles) of rapids as the river coursed its way through lonely, but lovely, scenery.

The hills became lower and were densely clad with jungle, and, in places, tropical grasses some 4.5 m (15 ft) tall covered the hills. Their boatmen were all opium smokers and had formerly been pirates. Yunnan, as Henry stated in a letter to Kew, was a great opium-producing province.

From that point, an arduous journey began. At the small village of Manhao – a nasty, disease-ridden place – 200 mules were waiting to take the group and their baggage across 64 km (40 miles) of mountain. Henry had come to expect rough and tough conditions when travelling in rural China, but this journey surpassed all his previous experiences and expectations. The caravan was a large and imposing one, and, to reach its destination, mountain passes over 2,134 m (7,000 ft) had to be crossed. By night, accommodation was found in ragged inns and in huts with earthen floors – though, despite these discomforts, Henry enjoyed himself, and even managed to collect plants along the way. For the final three days, he and his companions travelled on the backs of mules, and, at 20:00 p.m. on 21 June 1896, they eventually crossed over the mountains to Mengzi. Previous isolation was nothing compared to this.

Mengzi was a pleasant frontier city of about 11,000 souls, and lay on a large, elevated plain 32 km (20 miles) long by 19 km (12 miles) broad at an altitude of 1,372 m (4,500 ft) above sea level. The plain, which was completely encircled by mountains, was highly cultivated with crops such as rice and sweet potato, and fruits, such as lemons, guavas and pomegranates. About half a mile (0.8 km) outside of the city was the European settlement of just about a dozen people, and this consisted of a missionary, the staff of the French Consul and five Customs Service officials. A large very ornate pagoda was situated nearby, and this and the Foreign Compound overlooked a small lake. Several temples were to be found around Mengzi, and, by one of these, Henry found a gigantic tree of *Cryptomeria japonica* var. *sinensis* with a girth of 5.5 m (18 ft). The Chinese called it the 'kung ch'io sung', or 'peacock pine', and evidently there had been a temple on the site for several hundred years.

Mengzi proved to be a perfect base for Augustine Henry. The place had an agreeable Mediterranean climate, and Henry reckoned that he would be happy to live there for three or four years.[3] The warm, dry climate would have been perfect for Caroline's ailments – but such considerations were now in the past. Mengzi would help Henry overcome the terrible guilt and regrets of Caroline's death, though. Life went on, as did his botanical work.

In February 1895, Prince Henri d'Orléans visited Mengzi, during the course of his second expedition to China, and stayed in the French Consulate. The Prince planned to explore the upper courses of the Mekong (Lancang Jiang), Salween (Nu Jiang) and Irrawaddy rivers, completing his journey in India. His description of Mengzi is interesting, since it was penned only a year before Augustine Henry arrived there:

The first part of our route was a steady ascent, from 510 to 6,150 feet. The mules climbed sturdily in single file, urged by the shouts and imprecations of the drivers [...] It took two days and a half to reach Mongtse [*sic*], sleeping each night in the corners of inn stables. On the way we passed a strange series of isolated hills, like

BELOW: Mengzi's marketplace, February 1895. Oxen rest by their carts, having hauled baskets of fruit and vegetables in from the surrounding Mengzi plain. Mengzi was one of the busiest market towns in south-east Yunnan Province.

Items for inspection in front of the Customs House at Mengzi during the late 1890s. Mengzi was a busy trading place; large quantities of tin were mined to the south of the town and enormous quantities of yarn also passed through this isolated Customs post.

detached sugar-loaves, and christened them the Cone Chain [...] Although only at an altitude of 6,175 feet, we received the impression of high summits [...] Before us lay the great plain of Mongtse. For two hours we continued at a round pace through cultivated fields [...] until we checked our beasts beneath the walls of Mongtse, in front of a spacious white building used as the French Consulate [...].

Mongtse contains about 11,000 inhabitants [...] The people, accustomed to the going and coming of whites, appear indifferent to our proceedings, although the most extravagant reports had been spread about our arrival. It was said a king's son [...] was coming to Mongtse with a thousand men. I was used to such legends.

Every week on market day the streets present an interesting spectacle. At the entrance, outside the rampart, long strings of carrier oxen stood waiting behind the straw-wrapped bales of yarn or sheet tin for the customs-house inspection. Crowds of country folk thronged the gate, the Poula [the Pula or Bulang] element predominating. The women of this race, with rounded faces sheltering under linen bonnets somewhat resembling those of the little Sisters of the Poor, crouched beside baskets of vegetables. The men wore small open vests and a blue turban, round which they twisted their pigtails.

[...] Besides the consular and mission staff, we found very agreeable society at the customs-house. The superintendent was a Mr Carl, a connection of Sir Robert Hart, and well qualified to give me interesting commercial statistics [...] The grounds of the customs-house adjoined those of the consulate [...] Although verandahs are common, one need scarcely seek shelter from the sun; the climate of Mongtse is splendid; except in the two rainy months, it is almost always fine. The plain is healthy for Europeans. The natives have to fear plague, which is endemic, and seems to haunt certain localities of Yunnan without cause. The sickness generally comes in summer and sometimes claims four thousand or five thousand victims. First to be attacked are the rats, which may then be seen scampering in the streets, jumping and writhing as if mad. Then comes the turn of the cats. It is as if the poison rose from the ground, and, mounting, infected in succession all it met [...] Europeans are seldom included in its ravages.

[...] There are many pretty walks in the neighbourhood; in the mountains, you may find silver pheasants and hares, while the rice fields of the plain teem with water-fowl and white herons. The Chinese protect the latter birds; they say they carry the souls of the dead to heaven; and upon their tombs in their religious designs they give a symbolic significance to the heron analogous to that we give to the dove.[4]

On the day of his arrival, Henry's assistant, a young Englishman called Fred Carey, shot a panther just 50 yards outside the Foreign Compound. Mengzi was surrounded by wild countryside and the higher mountains surrounding the city were home to many aboriginal tribes.

Henry wrote to Thiselton-Dyer, his letter full of questions. Should he aim to make a vast collection like he did in Hubei? Should he continue to make ten sets of every number collected? Would it be more practical to confine his work to small collections of only interesting plants? Would he send bulbs and seeds in quantity? What about other fields of scientific inquiry; perhaps a study of the languages of the many aboriginal tribes might be worthwhile?[5] After such a long break from plant hunting, he was anxious to get back to his botanical work.

Sophora davidii. Native to central and western China, it is abundant on dry, barren hillsides. Henry introduced it to cultivation through the Royal Botanic Gardens, Kew, in 1897.

New plants from the Mengzi area

At Mengzi, he met William Hancock, who gave him valuable advice on the flora of the area and a list of suitable locations where he could find interesting plants. Despite the work carried out by Hancock in the region, Henry believed that there was still a great field left for him. His hunch was correct: Hancock's obsession with ferns meant that he had overlooked many of the flowering plants from the area, including one of the most obvious trees on the Mengzi plain, *Albizia bracteata*, one of Henry's earliest discoveries from Yunnan Province. Occasional thickets of native vegetation survived on the plain, and in one of these Henry found *Passiflora henryi*, a beautiful passion flower that later proved to be endemic to Yunnan. He went on to discover two further species in the area: *Passiflora cupiformis*, which grew in woods at about 1,800 m (5,900 ft), and *Passiflora wilsonii*, a handsome evergreen climber to 5 m (16 ft) tall and bearing beautifully sculpted, bell-shaped leaves. In southern Yunnan, a subgroup of the Hani people use this vine as an ingredient in traditional herbal medicine to treat cases of rheumatism and malaria.

The local flora was alien to Henry and he scarcely recognised a familiar plant, apart from the blue-flowered *Sophora davidii*, which was common on the Mengzi plain. He collected seeds of this spiny shrub later that autumn and sent them to Kew. Plants were raised there the following spring, and it was by this means that it first reached cultivation. Henry was keen to introduce garden-worthy plants and wrote to Thiselton-Dyer asking him to contact George Nicholson (1847–1908), Curator of Kew, for directions on how to pack bulbs and seeds [6]

In July 1896, Henry came in contact with Pierre Bons D'Anty (1859–1916), the French Consul at Simao (then Szemao), a city in the extreme south-west of Yunnan Province near what is now the Laos border. Bons D'Anty had an interest in botany, and it was during a visit to the French Consulate at Mengzi that he struck up a friendship with Henry. During this meeting, Augustine Henry managed to persuade him to collect plants around Simao and in a district to the south of Simao called Xishuangbanna, where extensive tracts of undisturbed tropical rainforest remained. Bons D'Anty sent regular consignments over the following two years, and, in return, Henry identified the plants for him. In all, Henry received more than 500 specimens from Simao, giving him a basic knowledge of the flora of the region.[7] These specimens were later incorporated into Augustine Henry's herbarium and were sent to Kew. Some were new, such as *Craibiodendron henryi*, a rare member of the heath family (Ericaceae) that produces beautiful, copper-flushed growths throughout the growing season. A Customs Service was established in Simao in the autumn of the same year and this would later open up further opportunities for collecting.

Henry's first plant-hunting adventures were carried out on the rather barren-looking grassy hills that lay to the south of the Mengzi plain. Despite their appearance, these hills were home to an astonishing number of plants, especially orchids and lilies. The latter were abundant in long grass, particularly *Lilium bakerianum* var. *delavayi*, which Delavay had discovered on the Cangshan mountain range above Dali in north-west Yunnan Province in 1888. With it grew the allied *Lilium bakerianum* var. *rubrum*, the eastern-most variety of Baker's lily. This lovely variety was found by William Hancock on the Mengzi hills in 1895.

Orchids were also common around Mengzi, and a number of terrestrial species from the same rocky mountainsides were new. Amongst these was the lithophytic, yellow-flowered *Liparis yunnanensis*. Others included *Eulophia yunnanensis*, *Habenaria yunnanensis* and *Brachycorythis henryi*. Henry claimed the latter was a rare plant around Mengzi, though it has subsequently been found in Burma and Thailand.

It was not just exotic orchids that provided a splash of colour on the grassy slopes. The blue-flowered spikes of *Delphinium umbrosum* were a common sight, and *Veratrum mengtzeanum*, highly rated both in terms of flower and foliage, was one of the most beautiful perennials on the hillsides. This rare species is endemic to China and distributed in the Guizhou and Yunnan provinces. *Pimpinella kingdon-wardii*, a short-lived perennial bearing broad umbels of small white blossoms, was another common inhabitant. It was rediscovered, many years later, by the English plant hunter, Captain Frank Kingdon Ward, for whom it is named. Another namesake, *Gerbera delavayi* var. *henryi*, grew in the most exposed, barren parts of the mountains, where generally it formed great drifts.

In clefts on damp limestone cliffs, Henry found the very charming *Saxifraga mengtziana*. This plant is one of ten species belonging to the Irregulares section, a group

The 'drumstick primula', *Primula denticulata*. Distributed from Afghanistan to China, this hardy perennial over-winters by means of plump, fireproof, swollen buds.

Père Francois Ducloux (1864–1945) near Kunming in August 1899, two years after Henry found it. The second, *Roscoea praecox* was discovered by William Hancock at Mengzi and its orchid-like flowers may be purple, violet or white. In its native habitat, it is found along the banks of streams, in meadows and on limestone cliffs. Both species are highly ornamental plants and are endemic to Yunnan. The genus *Roscoea* celebrates William Roscoe (1753–1831), one of the founders of Liverpool Botanic Gardens, who grew a number of species that had been sent to him by Dr Nathaniel Wallich (1786–1854) of the Royal Botanic Gardens, Calcutta. *Roscoea* is found in the Himalaya from Kashmir to south-east Tibet, and, from there, into Yunnan and Sichuan provinces.

The mountains around Mengzi were often exposed to wild grass fires, and a number of plants had evolved ways to survive these, including a small perennial, *Crepis phoenix*. This species was based on material gathered near Mengzi by William Hancock and Augustine Henry, and, from near Kunming, by Père Ducloux. Six of the eight specimens sent to Kew by these collectors had apparently sprung up after the older stems had been destroyed by fire, hence the specific epithet 'phoenix'. Another local plant, *Primula denticulata*, dodged fire damage by retreating into swollen, onion-like, winter buds. The closely allied *Primula pseudodenticulata* was another of Henry's discoveries. This species looks like a small form of *P. denticulata*, but lacks the persistent bud scales and is sometimes stoloniferous. In China, it grows in damp meadows in Sichuan and Yunnan provinces, and the flower colour varies from rose to lavender.

On the Mengzi plain, the most striking plant was *Antiotrema dunnianum* (syn. *Henryettana mirabilis*), an upright perennial to 30 cm (1 ft) that produces masses of blue-purple flowers from March to July. Discovered by his predecessor, William Hancock, this borage relative was so common on the plain that Henry and his European companions mistook large colonies of it for a pond or small lake in the distance. Small ponds did exist on the edges of rice fields on the Mengzi plain, and, in these, grew Henry's pipewort, *Eriocaulon henryanum*, a subtropical perennial aquatic.

distributed through China, Japan and Korea, with the best-known species in the group being the well-known *Saxifraga fortunei* and *Saxifraga stolonifera*. The name 'Irregulares' reflects the asymmetric flowers of the group. This unusual floral arrangement is said to aid the wind-dispersal of seeds. Henry's *Saxifraga mengtziana* was introduced to cultivation during the 1990s, and is said to be the most beautiful member of the section, though, coming from a subtropical region of China, it needs winter protection. The shaded side of damp cliffs hosted many other beautiful flowering plants, particularly rosette-forming gesneriads such as *Petrocosmea minor* and the golden-yellow *Oreocharis aurea*.

Two species of *Roscoea* grew on the mountains, both of which were new. *Roscoea debilis*, a bluish-purple-flowered species, grew in open grassland and was described from collections made by the French missionary and plant collector

ABOVE: *Hypericum beanii*, another of Augustine Henry's earliest discoveries from Yunnan Province. The plant pictured here is seen flowering in time for our RHS Chelsea Flower Show exhibit in May 2002.

The forests beyond Mengzi

In his own time, after office hours, Henry reckoned he could collect up to 40 species in an evening. Weekend trips were energetic; he set off on extended trips every Sunday, leaving Mengzi as early as 05:00 a.m. and not returning until 20:00 p.m. that night. The countryside immediately around Mengzi was bare of trees and large rivers, but a trek of two to four days in any direction led to immense tracts of virgin forest.

These great forests, needless to say, were rich in new plants. *Acer flabellatum* var. *yunnanense* was a common woodland component on mountain slopes at altitudes of 2,600 m (8,530 ft). Allied to the Himalayan *Acer campbellii*, this variety is confined to Yunnan Province and Burma, and the leaves are sharply serrulate. A 12-m (39-ft) tall tree raised from seeds collected by George Forrest (F. 9509) still grows in the Trewithen Gardens in Cornwall (England).

Prunus henryi, a large shrub or small tree to 9 m (29 ft) tall, carried a cloak of white blossoms in springtime. Forrest also later collected this Yunnan endemic (F. 16,232) in the Mekong valley, in February 1918. Forrest is generally credited with the discovery of *Gordonia chrysandra*, though this small evergreen tree had been found 15 years earlier by Henry. In its native habitat, it bears creamy-white, fragrant, camelia-like flowers during the winter months. Other new trees included *Toona ciliata* var. *yunnanensis*, a subtropical tree to 30 m (98 ft) tall, *Millettia velutina*, *Prunus wilsonii* (later found by

Wilson at Xingshan in Hubei Province) and a new bladder nut, *Staphylea holocarpa* var. *rosea*, a small spreading tree bearing pendulous clusters of soft pink blossoms followed by bronze-toned emerging foliage. Wilson introduced the latter from Hubei through the Arnold Arboretum of Harvard University (Boston, Massachusetts, USA) in the spring of 1908.

Bretschneidera sinensis was one of Henry's most important discoveries from the Mengzi area in 1896. A very beautiful deciduous tree to 20 m (66 ft) tall, it bears large pinnate leaves and loose terminal racemes of fleshy pink, bell-shaped flowers in April and May. It was named in 1901 to commemorate Emil Bretschneider, who had died the same year. *Bretschneidera* was an exciting find. Not only was it superbly ornamental, but it also proved to be a new genus in an entirely new plant family – yet another missing link in plant evolution. This tree is extremely rare in the wild, and is a nationally protected species in China.

In the mountains to the east of Mengzi, Henry found *Dipteronia dyeriana*, a small tree to 4 m (13 ft) tall. Henry described and named it as a new species himself in the *Gardeners' Chronicle* in 1903, and chose it to commemorate

LEFT: One of Augustine Henry's native plant collectors (perhaps Old Ho) in pine wood with a fine plant of *Lobelia seguinii* f. *longisepala* soaring skywards to the right. Rarely encountered in cultivation, this is one of the most exciting of all Chinese perennials.

his old friend William Thiselton-Dyer, who was known to his closest colleagues simply as 'Dyer'. Like *Bretschneidera*, this tree is endangered in its native habitat, and Henry only ever found it once.

Other interesting discoveries included two members of the witch-hazel family. The first of these, *Distyliopsis laurifolia*, belongs to a small genus of trees that are widely distributed across south-east Asia. *Distyliopsis laurifolia* is a particularly attractive evergreen tree, and is closely allied to *Sycopsis*. The second, *Rhodoleia parvipetala*, is a handsome tree varying from 10 to 30 m (33 to 98 ft) tall and bears striking crimson blossoms from December to April.

At low altitudes, members of the laurel family dominated the forest composition, and one of these, *Phoebe forrestii*, formed enormous trees. This species is endemic to China and has a limited range of distribution across Yunnan Province as well as south-east Tibet. Another Henry discovery was the closely allied *Actinodaphne forrestii*, a medium-sized evergreen tree to 15 m (49 ft) tall. The oak relative *Cyclobalanopsis augustinii* was relatively common in the forests around Mengzi, where it was generally encountered as a moderate-sized evergreen tree. George Forrest and Joseph Rock both later collected it on the Yunnan (China)–Burma border, and it grew for a short time at Caerhays Castle in Cornwall, England.

Beneath the canopy of forests to the south of Mengzi *Daphniphyllum longeracemosum* grew as a large shrub or a small columnar tree bearing bold, striking, rhododendron-like foliage. In the same woods, *Clematis fulvicoma*, a remarkably beautiful climber, scaled its way to 10 m (33 ft) high and carried a summer display of dark violet flowers almost 6 cm (2 in.) across. Other new shrubs included *Hypericum beanii*, a small, rounded bush with gracefully arching branches producing large, slightly pendulous flowers in great profusion. Augustine Henry also introduced this plant through Kew, in 1898, and, for many years, it was taken to be an improved form of *Hypericum patulum*, which it soon

replaced in popularity. It was not until 1970 that it was finally described as a new species, and was named to commemorate William Jackson Bean, who was curator of Kew between 1922 and 1929.

The violet-blue-flowered *Strobilanthes austinii* (Henry was known to his closest friends as 'Austin') was a common understorey shrub in the forests near Mengzi at similar low altitudes. With it grew *Blumea henryi* and *Phyllagathis tetandra*, a beautiful little shrub to about a metre (3.3 ft) tall that bears cymes of up to 30 lavender-pink blossoms on branch tips. *Rhododendron emarginatum* inhabited the lower forested slopes of mountains to the south-west of Mengzi, and there it formed epiphytic shrubs to 2 m (6.5 ft) tall, bearing yellow, campanulate blossoms in the axils of leaves. This rare vireya rhododendron was recently introduced from Lao Cai Province in northern Vietnam.

On the edge of thickets, *Osteomeles schwerinae* grew as a medium-sized shrub bearing branching corymbs of white flowers above short pinnate leaves. Although described from Augustine Henry's Mengzi collections, W. J. Bean stated it had been raised at the Jardin des Plantes in Paris from seeds sent there by Père Delavay in 1888.

Daphne acutiloba, an evergreen shrub to 2 m (6.5 ft) tall, was common on shaded cliffs. Introduced to cultivation by E. H. Wilson in 1907, it is relatively rare in gardens, probably because its white flowers, though pretty, are unscented. Another daphne relative that grew on the barren, exposed hills above Mengzi was *Stellera chamaejasme* var. *chrysantha*, a long-lived sub-shrub with a thick woody crown bearing numerous unbranched stems to 40 cm (16 in.) tall. The inflorescence comprises up to 50 small yellow blossoms held in a globular head. One of the most beautiful of all Chinese plants, it is much more abundant in north-west Yunnan Province, particularly in the region of Shangri La (Zhongdian), where flowering plants dominate the sub-alpine plains in late autumn.

Indigofera henryi was another common shrub on the exposed, rocky mountains above the Mengzi plain. The pink-purple-flowered *Indigofera mengtziana* also grew in wooded glens near Mengzi, where its bedfellows included the white-flowered *Camellia henryana*, *Grewia henryi*, *Euonymus mengtseanus*, *Mahonia hypoleuca* and *Philadelphus henryi*, a delightfully scented mock orange to about 3 m (10 ft) tall.

In its native Yunnan Province and Guangxi Zhuang

ABOVE: The famous Austrian botanical explorer Heinrich von Handel-Mazzetti, seen here with his native plant collectors in the Salween valley in western Yunnan Province.

Autonomous Region, the white-flowered *Hoya mengtzeensis* may be epiphytic or epilithic, and is generally seen cascading from large rocks and cliff faces. An interesting new climber from Mengzi was the milkweed relative *Ceropegia dolichophylla*, a scandent plant to about 50 cm (20 in.) tall and bearing deep-purplish maroon and green flowers. According to George Forrest, who later found it on the Cangshan range above Dali, the fleshy roots of this species were eaten by hill tribes living in that region. Other new climbers from Mengzi included *Tetrastigma henryi* (a massively rampant vine), *Embelia henryi*, *Holboellia parviflora*, *Actinidia rudis* and *Jasminum urophyllum*.

Poranopsis sinensis, a large climber, scrambled its way over large rock outcrops, and Henry found it laden with masses of small white tubular flowers. It was also later collected by the Austrian botanist and plant collector, Heinrich von Handel-Mazzetti near Kunming in March 1914. Handel-Mazzetti (1882–1940) was a great admirer of Augustine Henry's work, and visited Mengzi in 1915 – although he later declared that he 'did not wish to waste time in the vicinity of Mengzi – territory which had been thoroughly explored by Henry'.[8] This is true of many of the areas that Henry visited in Yunnan; so thorough was the work that he and his native plant collectors carried out that later plant hunters bypassed regions such as Mengzi and Simao.

One of the most striking perennials from the Mengzi area was *Lobelia seguinii* f. *longisepala*, a giant plant, more than 3 m (10 ft) tall, with a huge basal rosette of long lanceolate leaves. Like the exotic echiums from the Canary Islands, this superb plant makes a desperate rush skywards at flowering time, producing fleshy-pink or light blue, spidery blossoms along horizontal lateral branchlets. Favouring the same damp, humus-rich conditions as the giant lobelia was the yellow-flowered *Impatiens mengtszeana*.

Ethnic groups of southern Yunnan Province. These photographs were published by Augustine Henry in his paper 'The Lolos and other Tribes of Western China'.

ABOVE: A traditional Yi village of thatched houses surrounded by broad-leaved, subtropical forest.

ABOVE LEFT: A Hani man with two women. The Hani continue to be a conspicuous group in southern Yunnan.

LEFT: More than any other group, it was the Yi peoples that fascinated Augustine Henry most. This group is pictured at the village of Iwu, near the present-day Laos border.

BELOW LEFT: A ceremonial Yi dance.

BELOW: A Yi idol, a worship-stone at the base of a 'Dragon Tree'. A pig or fowl was sacrificed by the village shaman to this idol twice a year to ward off demons and other evil beings.

Ethnic groups in the mountains near Mengzi

One of the most astonishing features of Yunnan Province was the extraordinary diversity of its human inhabitants. Besides the Han Chinese, themselves immigrants, there were 25 distinct ethnic groups. The high mountainous topography, dense forests and deeply cut river valleys had resulted in isolated communities with enormous cultural divides. The physical character of the landscape had been favourable to the preservation of these communities.

In late July, Henry managed to get away for five days to 'Great Black Mountain' (a range to the north of Mengzi), where he and his men climbed through dense forests to more than 2,743 m (9,000 ft). This was his first chance to get into the higher mountain ranges, and it was while trekking the forests of the region that he had his first encounter with a number of indigenous peoples. He was particularly taken with the Miáo group, who were not in the least frightened by his visit. The Miáo were a pleasant people and Henry thought the group had a trait of gentle manners that could be found amongst the poor peasant folk at home in Ireland. They were small in stature, and wore hempen garments, grown and spun by themselves, and dyed into a multitude of festive colours. The Miáo are animists and ancestor worshippers, and continue to live in neighbouring Laos, Vietnam and Thailand, where a subgroup are known as the Hmong people.

Another interesting ethnic group were the Bulang (Blang), or Pula, who are allied to the Yi (or Nuosu). Henry first met the group on the upper slopes of Great Black Mountain, and they also had a second stronghold near the town of Yuanjiang, which lay to the west. The Bulang were of diminutive stature, and Henry recorded meeting them as follows:

I found one village, isolated in the mountains, north of Mengtse, where the women scarcely exceeded 4½ feet, the men 4¾ feet high, all well-formed people. The inhabitants, who rushed from the fields to see me, were very gay, laughing boisterously, and behaving in an unguarded hilarious way. Their dress is in crude colours of green, blue and red. They worship a tree near the village; and are fond of dancing, music and alcohol. When the Pula come into the Chinese towns, they become silent, reserved and timid. Filing homewards along the mountains in large parties, dressed in gaily coloured garments, these little people are a pretty sight. The Chinese, who are the conquering race in Yunnan, look upon the Pula and Lolos with some dread, as they credit them with powers of witchcraft. It struck me that in Yunnan one can now observe a similar state of things to what may have existed in Britain and Ireland when a primitive population, driven into the mountain wilds and woods by their conquerors, and displaying

similar characteristics of elusiveness and uncanniness, may have given rise to fairy legends. The pigmies of Yunnan are probably a pure race, and their speaking a Lolo dialect is due perhaps to the fact that the Lolos, a conquering race, coming from the north, have impressed their language on the Pulas [...][10]

A small population of about 90,000 Bulang continue to live in the mountainous regions of Yunnan Province. There, they live in small village communities on the verges of forests, and farm at altitudes between 1,524 to 2,438 m (5,000 to 8,000 ft). Their houses are generally constructed of bamboo, and livestock are kept on the ground floor while families live on the first floor. One distinguishing feature of this group is the men's practice of tattooing their limbs and torso. Bulang women chew betel nuts, which temporarily dyes their gums, mouth and lips an orange-brown colour.

At the base of the same mountain range, Henry met with a third group, the Yi. The Yunnan Yi originated in the Daliangshan (or Liangshan) mountains in southern Sichuan Province, where they maintained an independent kingdom the size of Wales.[11] Over the centuries, many migrated south to Yunnan Province, where they established subgroups with starkly different dress. The Yi call themselves the 'Nuosu' (the Black People), though Henry and his contemporaries knew them as the 'Lolos', a derogatory term used by the Han Chinese.

The Yi evolved an aristocratic society based on clans, each clan belonging to a caste, and these formed the basis of a slave society. This system existed as recently as 1959, when some 700,000 slaves were liberated by communist forces. The Black Yi, or Nuosu (from the colour of their clothing), formed the aristocratic, land-owning part of this society. The White Yi, the serfs, formed 50 per cent of the population, but did not enjoy the same freedom of movement as the former group. The lowest classes had no rights whatsoever, and were freely bought and sold as slaves.[12]

Unlike the Miáo, the Yi were a tall, dark-complexioned race with an air of nobility, and could be distinguished from the Han Chinese by their aquiline noses. The men wore black turbans and sheepskin cloaks with tassels. Women were more colourful, wearing red, black, and yellow embroidered waistcoats. According to Henry, the Yi were tormented by all sorts of demons and evil beings, and these needed to be exorcised from time to time, so shamans were an important part of their culture. The Yi had one idol, which was a stone pillar about 30 cm (1 ft) high. This was placed at the base of a 'Dragon Tree', the tree of worship, to which a pig or fowl was sacrificed twice a year. The tree was supposed to be the seat of a dragon that protected the village, and belonged to no particular species: it could be any large tree. The Yi also

The Yao were another group Henry encountered during his travels. Expert hunters, they cultivated medicinal and dye crops in forest clearings.

had the legend of a deluge, sent to punish wicked people. One man, called Du-mu, and his four sons were saved in the hollowed-out log of a *Pieris* tree, and, in this, they also saved otters, ducks and many other creatures. Du-mu was worshipped as the ancestor of the Yi people.

Few people today can decipher the Yi's religious and historical texts, which are written in their own, 13th-century script. This unique mode of writing is pictographic in origin, and, through it, their religious rituals, books of genealogy, songs and beliefs have been handed down from generation to generation. Henry wrote a dictionary of their language (now in the British Museum) and had hoped to write a book on the group, just as he planned to publish a tome on his botanical activities in China. Neither project ever materialised (probably as a result of another great publication he would produce on his return to Europe).

In August 1896, Henry sent his 'coolie', Ho, on a botanical excursion for 15 days into the wild mountains above the town of Fengchunling, which lay to the south of the Red River. This district was home to a hill tribe called the Yao, who nowadays are mainly distributed in isolated villages south of Simao and in Xishuangbanna. Henry also met the group near the Papien River a few years later. He stated that they were expert hunters and always lived in mountain villages. There, using primitive 'slash and burn' techniques, they grew *Panax pseudoginseng* var. *notoginseng* for the production of the famous Chinese drug *san ch'i*. They also grew a species of *Strobilanthes* from which they extracted indigo and made paper from bamboo.[13] Fred Carey, Henry's assistant at Mengzi, stated they were nomadic in their habits, staying only two or three years in one place. Along with cultivating medicinal plants for sale to the Chinese, they hunted the now rare Asian elephant for ivory and tigers for their bones. Both products are, today, banned by the Convention on International Trade in Endangered Species (CITES), but retain an important place in Chinese pharmacopoeia.

New plants from Great Black Mountain

About 32 km (20 miles) to the north of Mengzi lay Great Black Mountain, a range that reached an altitude of about 2,743 m (9,000 ft). At its base was a small village called Dazhuang (then Tachuang), which was inhabited by a few families belonging to a Yi tribe. The area had first been botanised by William Hancock, and he, no doubt, encouraged Henry to visit and collect there. By the late 19th century, the plains that surrounded Great Black Mountain had long since been cleared for the cultivation of rice, though the mountain itself had fared considerably better, and forests still clung to its slopes.

New species continue to be found in Augustine Henry's Yunnan collections. In 1999, the Chinese botanist R. C. Fang described *Gaultheria longibracteolata* from material gathered by Henry, in 1896, on Great Black Mountain and on Kuanyin Shan near Kunming. Henry's specimens of this evergreen shrub lay unrecognised, for more than a century, in herbaria from Hong Kong to Boston, though it is now known to be native to Yunnan Province and Thailand.

The most striking plant he found on this little-known mountain has to be *Rhododendron sinofalconeri*. Henry stated that it was confined to the summit, and there it formed trees to 6 m (20 ft) tall, with bold foliage plastered with a rusty-brown indumentum beneath. In spring, these trees were literally smothered with large umbels of bell-shaped, primrose-yellow blossoms. This superbly ornamental tree was somehow missed by Hancock, but greatly impressed Henry when he visited the region in the spring of 1897. A Chinese counterpart of the Himalayan *Rhododendron falconeri*, this species has only recently been introduced to cultivation by British plant hunter Keith Rushforth, and has performed well in sheltered gardens in Britain and Ireland.

The discovery of *Rhododendron pachypodum* is generally credited to George Forrest, though Henry had previously found it near the summit of Great Black Mountain. One of the most beautiful of all Chinese rhododendrons, under good growing conditions it forms a bush to about 2 m (6.5 ft) tall, and, in late spring, bears clusters of two to three large, fragrant, white, sometimes rose-flushed blossoms. Forrest introduced it, many years later, from the Cangshan mountain range near Dali, though it is tender and restricted to the mildest gardens of Britain and Ireland.

Rhododendron irroratum ssp. *pogonostylum* grew on the mountain's mid-forested slopes, and there formed trees to about 6 m (20 ft) tall. This subspecies is native to south-west China and Vietnam and has only recently been introduced to Western gardens. It is a beautiful plant, carrying terminal racemose umbels of pink or red, tubular bell-shaped blossoms in April and May.

Another Henry discovery–Forrest introduction is *Viburnum calvum*, an evergreen shrub to about 1.5 m (5 ft) tall that is closely allied to *Viburnum propinquum*. The creamy-white flowers of this species are carried in rounded terminal corymbs, and are followed, in autumn, by striking blue-black fruits.

On the lower slopes of Great Black Mountain, Henry found *Cotoneaster harrovianus*, a gracefully arching evergreen shrub of about 3 m (10 ft) tall with a loose spreading habit. This is one of the heaviest flowered of all cotoneasters, and the berries ripen to red in December, giving a good late winter show. It was introduced to cultivation by E. H. Wilson, in November 1899, from the mountains to the south-west of Mengzi. Wilson described it in the *Gardeners' Chronicle* many years later, and chose to name it for George Harrow, the manager of Veitch's Coombe Wood nursery. Another new shrub from the same forests included the rare Chinese pheasant berry, *Leycesteria sinensis*, which has yet to reach Western gardens.

Clematis montana var. *wilsonii* was a common climber on the mountainside. This variety was described from a cultivated plant, raised from a collection made by E. H. Wilson in western Sichuan Province in October 1904. It differs from the typical *Clematis montana* in its later flowering period (July and August), and the flowers are larger and are scented.

In damp thickets and in forest glades, *Sambucus henryana*, a suckering sub-shrub to about 1.5 m (5 ft) tall, carried broad, flat-topped, umbel-like corymbs of fleshy, orange-red berries. Growing on cliffs near the summit of the mountain was the perennial gesneriad *Didymocarpus mengtze*. This beautiful little plant is endemic to Yunnan Province, and is known only from the Mengzi County (Mengzi Xian) region.

Pleione yunnanensis occurred occasionally in grassy glades at the edge of the forest. One of the most beautiful members of the genus, this species was based on collections made in the Mengzi region by Augustine Henry and William Hancock during the 1890s, and was introduced to cultivation, almost a century later, by the English plant hunter Roy Lancaster. This lovely orchid carries solitary flowers with widely spreading, lilac-pink segments and dark purple markings on the labellum. Lancaster rather aptly likens the shape of the flower to a starfish.[14] In China, the flask-shaped pseudobulbs are used in traditional herbal medicine.

A second later-flowered species, *Pleione grandiflora*, was also discovered by Henry on Great Black Mountain.

Great Black Mountain, as seen by our group in September 2005. Only tiny fragments of the original forest cover remain.

Pleione yunnanensis was discovered by William Hancock on Great Black Mountain in 1894, and Henry collected it there again in 1897.

LEFT: The Stone Forests, one of Yunnan's most fanciful landscapes. First appearances are deceptive; the Stone Forest supports a rich and very interesting surrounding flora.

OPPOSITE: *Mahonia lomariifolia*. One of the best of all the mahonias, it thrives in Irish gardens, where it forms small trees. Seen here at Hunter's Hotel, County Wicklow.

North to Mile, Lunan and the Stone Forest

In November 1896, Henry sent his new native plant collector, Ho, to Mile, a small town that lay 160 km (100 miles) to the north of Mengzi, and just over 100 km (62 miles) south-east of the provincial capital, Kunming. Henry's hand-drawn map of collecting localities also indicates the small, nearby market town of Lunan, a stronghold of the Sani subgroup of the Yi people. Lunan derives its name from the Yi language; '*Lunai*' is from '*Lu*', which means 'stone', and '*Nai*', or 'black', thus meaning 'the place covered in black stones'. This alludes to the famous nearby karst landscape, known as the Stone Forest, which was also visited by Ho.

The Stone Forest gained its name from a massive maze of limestone pillars, some up to 30 m (98 ft) tall. An ocean existed in the area during the Permian period, some 270 million years ago, and, as the waters retreated, they left a limestone seabed exposed to the elements. Over countless millennia, rainfall shaped and eroded almost 12 km^2 (4.6 miles^2) of karst landscape into what is now the Stone Forest. The result is a strange and fanciful labyrinth of cold, grey pinnacles, peaks, crags, caves, waterfalls and pools. From a distance, the sculpted landscape looks like an eerie colony of petrified trees. Henry's were the first botanical specimens to be gathered from this part of Yunnan, and it was also the most northerly point in the province from which he acquired material.

From the Mile area, Henry sent seeds of a fine pine to

246

Kew and to the Arnold Arboretum. The same pine also grew over four graves on a mountain overlooking the Mengzi plain, and Henry reckoned it would be hardy enough to grow in England. The tree proved to be *Pinus armandii*, which had been discovered by Armand David in 1873 in Shaanxi Province, and was introduced to cultivation by Paul Farges, who sent seeds to Maurice de Vilmorin at des Barres in 1895.

Henry's seeds germinated at Kew in the spring of 1897, and, by 1910, these were between 3 and 5 m tall and were said to be the finest specimens in Europe. One of his trees still grows in the Kew arboretum. The seeds of *Pinus armandii* are edible when roasted, and it is known in China as the '*peh-sung*', or 'white pine'. Other new trees from the region included *Carpinus pubescens* and *Osmanthus henryi*. In his field notes, Henry described the latter as a 6-m (20-ft) tall tree bearing small white blossoms.

Of shrubs, the best-known discovery from Mile has to be *Mahonia lomariifolia*, one of the most striking of all the mahonias, and a species that thrives remarkably well in Irish coastal gardens and in the milder counties of the UK. In gardens, it makes a large shrub with erect branches, and from the summits of these branches are carried whorl-like arrangements of long leaves composed of anything up to 19 pairs of leaflets. The overall effect of the foliage is very exotic, and the erect racemes of deep-yellow, fragrant flowers

are an added bonus in the depths of winter. If you had only one mahonia to bring to your 'desert island', then this is the one to grow. *Mahonia lomariifolia* was introduced to cultivation by Major Lawrence Johnson of Hidcote Manor from Tengchong in north-west Yunnan Province in 1931. In its native habitat, it can reach 10 to 13 m (33 to 43 ft) tall.

I find it strange that the *Lespedeza* relatives, *Campylotropis*, are so rare in gardens. They are well represented in the Chinese flora, and are particularly common in the western areas of Yunnan Province and Tibet. The timing of Western expeditions may have a lot to do with this. Most botanical groups visit China in late September/early October – optimum seed-collecting time, though this is when most species of *Campylotropis* are just coming into bloom. What a show they put on. In most cases, the branches are heavily laden with masses of pink, lavender or purple flowers carried in dense terminal racemes, which are generally gathered at the tips of branches. Two of the finest and most prolific flowered species are Mile plants. These are the rather aptly named *Campylotropis grandiflora* and *Campylotropis latifolia*. The latter is endemic to the province.

Many of Henry's Yunnan plants have never reached Western gardens, though those from Mile, Lunan and the Stone Forest should prove relatively hardy in Great Britain, Ireland and milder parts of the Pacific north-west coast of America (USDA zone 9). *Leptodermis glomerata* might

ABOVE: *Camellia sinensis*, one of China's most important crop plants. Augustine Henry's native plant collector found wild trees in the mountains south of the Red River.

prove to be a pretty addition to gardens within this climatic zone. At Mile, this charming little plant grew in mountain forest, where it made small shrubs of no more than 60 cm (2 ft) tall and bore masses of tubular, dark red flowers.

The gentian family is well represented in Yunnan, more so as one travels farther into the north-west of the province. One such group, the swertias, are among the most beautiful members of the clan. *Swertia yunnanensis*, a Mile plant, is endemic to China, and is distributed through the provinces of Yunnan, Sichuan and Guizhou. Ferns were also abundant. At Mile, Ho found *Neocheiropteris henryi* – not just a new species, but an entirely new genus.

New plants from south of the Red River

Ho, Henry's new plant collector, proved to be extremely good at his job, and his collections from the regions south of the Red River were full of interest. The lofty mountains there were covered in thick forests of immense trees, and Henry had gathered a number of plants there when he first sailed up the Red River in May 1896. At the tiny riverside village of Hsinkei, near the Vietnamese border, for example, he discovered *Ixora yunnanensis*, a small evergreen shrub bearing cymes of large, four-petalled, tubular, white flowers.

Sending Ho back to this area proved to be very worthwhile. His most important discovery was wild tea,

Camellia sinensis. The plant he found, a 10-m (33-ft) tall tree, grew in virgin forest on a hillside that lay south of the Red River from Manmei, at an altitude of 2,300 m (7,545 ft). The nearest tea-growing district was Pu'er, a subtropical region that lay 320 km (200 miles) to the east, and the spontaneity of the Manmei plant was therefore beyond dispute. Previous to this time, it was believed that the tea plant was actually native to northern India, and that it had been introduced to China.[15] The discovery of an ancestral population of one of the most important crop plants in the world must have excited botanists in Europe and North America. Also from Manmei was *Polypodium manmeiense*, a small fern that has subsequently been found in Burma and Indochina, and a new holly, *Ilex manneiensis*, an evergreen tree to about 9 m (29 ft) tall. The Manmei holly is endemic to Yunnan.

It is interesting to see how plants and their uses stimulated Augustine Henry's interest. In a letter to Thiselton-Dyer, he mentions that Ho brought him back some specimens of a curious *Lysimachia*, the leaves of which had a delicate but strong fragrance. The Chinese used this plant for scenting hair-oil, and Henry offered to send seeds – the plant had obvious commercial potential. This scented loosestrife, *Lysimachia lancifolia*, was described from material collected many years later, in Thailand, by another prolific yet obscure Irish collector, Arthur Kerr (1877–1942), who did for the flora of Thailand what Augustine Henry did for the flora of China. In a similar case, the yellow-flowered *Pittosporum kerrii*, a small evergreen tree to 12 m (39 ft) tall, was described from specimens gathered in Thailand by Kerr in June 1921, having previously been found by Henry near Mengzi in September 1896.

Letters from Liverpool

Winter at Mengzi was delightful. Scarcely a cloud lined the sky and the season resembled a good Irish summer. Sundays were spent plant hunting on the grassy hill tops and in wooded valleys beyond Mengzi. These trips kept Henry sane. Letters from home and from England took weeks to arrive, and life, in reality, was very monotonous. Provisions took forever to arrive, and, when they did, they were often damaged. In January 1897, Henry's stores were running short. His shoes were worn and new ones had not arrived. He was smoking his last tin of tobacco and hadn't the least idea where a camera he'd ordered months before had gotten to.

Begonia cathayana raised by Bulley from Augustine Henry's Mengzi's collections. Pictured here at Kunming Botanic Gardens.

Rhododendrons in mountain forest in southern Yunnan Province, one of Augustine Henry's many images from south-west China.

Arthur Kilpin Bulley, the Liverpool cotton broker who turned nurseryman. Bulley began to correspond with Augustine Henry towards the end of 1896.

One letter that must have stirred his spirits, though, arrived in November 1896 from a Liverpool cotton broker, Arthur Kilpin Bulley (1861–1942). Bulley was a shrewd businessman and would go to any lengths to acquire new, garden-worthy plants. In his letter, he told Henry he wanted to introduce all sorts of beautiful plants for the cottages of the poor.[16] Bulley was an enthusiastic socialist. He had amassed a large fortune, and once asserted, 'I have made more money than the heart of man can desire, and I want to do something with it'.[17] He was an eccentric figure in class-ridden Victorian England, and believed he had a duty to better conditions for the working classes. Bulley found it shameful that so few people in the industrialised cities of England had gardens to enjoy.

Many socialists of that era saw gardens as therapeutic centres for children from the slums, and, in his electioneering campaigns, Bulley used lantern slides to promote the idea. He opened his own garden to the public, free of charge, and when he finally opened a nursery, he sold seeds for a penny a pack so that the poor could grow flowers in pots and in window-boxes.[18]

249

Bulley's good nature and social conscience appealed to Augustine Henry, and early the next year he sent him a cigar-box containing 85 different kinds of seeds gathered in the mountains near Mengzi. Bulley was delighted; all the seed packs were labelled and carefully numbered, and he shared duplicate seeds with Kew. It was from this seed consignment that *Begonia cathayana* was introduced to cultivation. This beautiful foliage plant flowered for the first time at Bulley's garden in Cheshire, England, and at Kew, where it was painted and published in *Curtis's Botanical Magazine* a number of years later.

Henry wished he had nothing else to do but botanise, and he hoped one day to rival Delavay's 3,000 species from north-west Yunnan.[19] He met with many of Delavay's discoveries in the mountains around Mengzi, most notably *Rhododendron arboreum* ssp. *delavayi*, a medium-sized tree carrying round, compact trusses of red blossoms in early spring. He also stumbled upon the well-known *Thalictrum delavayi*, one of the finest hardy perennials from China.

On the Daweishan range near Vietnam
In December 1896, Henry sent his native plant collector to the Daweishan range in Pingbian County, a region that lay 64 km (40 miles) to the south-east of Mengzi. Henry had carried out a brief collecting foray there while travelling up the Red River to Mengzi when he first reached Yunnan, and

was so impressed with the region that he thought it worthwhile to send back Ho to carry out further exploration.

The Daweishan range lies between Pingbian and Hekou counties, south of which is Lao Cai in Vietnam. The range occupies about 25,000 ha (97 miles²) and its highest peak rises to 2,363 m (7,750 ft), while its lowest point is a mere 76 m (250 ft) above sea level. As a result, the landscape is composed of deep, 'v'-shaped valleys. The range is exposed to the warm, moist Pacific monsoon along the Red River, and the underlying rock type is limestone. Augustine Henry was the first Western plant hunter to explore this mountainous region, and he described it as being full of immense trees and with lots of big game, such as bears, wild pigs, red deer, musk deer and panthers.

Something that struck Henry here was how persistent the Chinese had been in deforesting their country. Along the Red River in northern Vietnam, he noted that the hillsides were still covered by extensive tracts of tropical forest, but, the moment one entered Yunnan Province, the forests disappeared and were replaced with mere thickets and grassy

Itoa orientalis is a relative newcomer to Western gardens, and is best suited to the mildest coastal regions of Great Britain and Ireland. It is seen here at Earlscliffe in Howth, County Dublin.

LEFT: *Buddleja forrestii* flowering its heart out at the Royal Botanic Gardens, Kew. It was once known as *Buddleja henryi*.

hills. Elephants still roamed forests on the Vietnamese border; these animals needed large forests to live in, and, therefore, the district, with its great tracts of virgin forest, was an ideal place to send his botanical collector.

Henry also made several trips to the region himself, and made a rich harvest of new, exciting plants. One of his earliest discoveries from the Daweishan range was *Buddleja forrestii*, a deciduous bush to 3 m (10 ft) tall, bearing large, lance-shaped leaves up to 30 cm (1 ft) long. The discovery of this vigorous butterfly bush has long been credited to George Forrest, who introduced it to gardens in 1903. It is a charming species and is very variable across its native south-west China. The scented flowers were described by Forrest as 'grey and maroon', 'reddish maroon', 'soft lavender rose' and 'pale mauve, almost white', indicating a considerable range of colours throughout its habitat.

Illicium burmanicum was another interesting find. E. H. Wilson named this species from material collected many years later by Joseph Rock in nearby Burma, hence the

specific epithet. Henry described the specimen he found as a 6-m (20-ft) tall tree with spidery, greenish-yellow blossoms. *Craibiodendron yunnanense*, a rare pieris relative, formed small bushy trees up to 7 m (23 ft) tall, and, like pieris, it sports striking, reddish-bronze new growths. This beautiful tree was described from collections later made by the French missionary Edouard Ernest Maire (1848–1932), who made a large collection of herbarium specimens in the Kunming region between 1905 and 1916.

Another new tree from the Daweishan range was the little-known *Itoa orientalis*, a new endemic genus named in honour of Dr Keisuke Ito, a pioneer in the modern botany of Japan, and for his grandson, Dr Tokutaro Ito. Keisuke Ito was a friend and pupil of Philipp Franz von Siebold (1796–1866), another well-known scholar of the Japanese flora. *Itoa orientalis* is one of the most exciting plant introductions of recent years, and thrives well in the warmest, most-sheltered gardens of Britain and Ireland. There, its giant, lush, bold foliage gives an almost

Augustine Henry's garden in Ranelagh, in the south-side suburbs of Dublin. Seen scaling the back wall of the house is a vine of *Actinidia henryi*.

subtropical feel, and associates well with other exotics.

Rhododendron tutcherae grew at slightly lower altitudes, where it formed 13-m (43-ft) tall trees. In late spring, this species carries pairs of funnel-shaped, violet flowers in the axils of the uppermost leaves. It is native to southern Yunnan Province and Vietnam, and, as far as I am aware, it has never been introduced to cultivation. Though common in parts of south-east Yunnan, further collections of *Rhododendron tutcherae* were not made until the tree was rediscovered by the Chinese botanist C. A. Wu in 1962. *Rhododendron mengtszense* also grew on the same slopes, and, like the former, it is unknown in Western cultivation, though there is a good plant at Kunming Botanical Gardens. Endemic to south-east Yunnan, this species is generally encountered as a 6-m (20-ft) tall tree, and carries umbels of small, purple-red, bell-shaped blooms in late spring.

Helicia are an exotic group of flowering trees and shrubs in the protea family, and several Chinese species were described from Henry's collections. The finest of these must be *Helicia grandis*, an evergreen tree to 10 m (33 ft) and bearing racemes of rust-coloured flowers. Other new trees from the region included *Sterculia henryi*, the witch-hazel relative, *Altingia yunnanensis*, *Rhamnus henryi* and, perhaps most notably, *Huodendron biaristatum*, a new

genus in the styrax family. Native to Yunnan Province, Burma and Indochina, in early summer, this species bears clusters of snow-white, bell-shaped flowers with reflexed petals. Recently introduced to cultivation, the foliage of this small tree emerges a striking copper colour and the stems have beautifully peeling mahogany-brown bark. This lovely, though rare, tree commemorates the famous Chinese botanist, Professor H. H. Hu.

Several climbers were named from the Pingbian collections, the finest of which was *Actinidia henryi*, a vigorous plant with slightly ribbed young shoots covered with prominent reddish bristles. Small white flowers are produced in the axils of leaves in early summer, and these are followed by small, cylindrical, kiwi-like fruits in autumn. This once-popular climber was later introduced by E. H. Wilson, through the Arnold Arboretum, and Alice and Augustine Henry grew it in their Dublin garden during the early decades of the 20th century. *Microtropis henryi*, a rampant climber, was common throughout the range, and, at lower altitudes, the slender, spiny stems of Henry's rattan palm, *Calamus henryanus*, rambled through surrounding trees.

Yunnan is the centre of distribution for Asian bamboo, and, to date, more than 170 species have been named from the province. In evergreen, broad-leaved forest, at an altitude of 2,300 m (7,550 ft), Henry's native plant collector found *Leptocanna chinense*, a new genus of primitive bamboo. Endemic to Yunnan, the generic name derives from the Greek '*Lepto*', meaning 'thin', and '*canna*', a 'cane', alluding to the very thin culm wall. In Yunnan, this bamboo is popularly used for weaving, and at least one ethnic group uses it to make *gao-sheng*, a rocket used in celebration festivals.

Several orchids were also named from the region, including *Hancockia uniflora*, a new genus named for

A woman collecting firewood (one of Augustine Henry's photographs from the Mengzi region).

253

LEFT: Terraced paddy fields carved by the Hani people at Yuanyang, one of a few dozen images surviving from Augustine Henry's Chinese photographic collection. The Hani are famed throughout China for their hillside rice terraces in this region of Yunnan Province.

BOTTOM LEFT: A father and son by their lime kiln. In front of them lies a bundle of timber for the furnace, while, to the left, lies a heap of the finished product.

BOTTOM RIGHT: Women of the Bulang, or Pula, ethnic group harvesting rice north of Mengzi in the late 1890s. Sheltered from the baking sun by linen bonnets, Henry first met this group on 'Great Black Mountain' in 1896, and at Yuanjiang to the south-west. The Han Chinese credited the Bulang with witchcraft and looked upon them with some dread.

another Irish customs official, William Hancock. Ferns abounded. From the Mengzi region alone, Henry gathered more than 250 species, the great majority of which were new. Few of these have reached the gardens of Europe or North America, though *Polystichum yunnanense* grows at Glasnevin. By far the most important fern discovery from the Daweishan range was the primitive *Archangiopteris henryi*, a large archaic fern that somehow managed to survive from the earliest of times. The discovery of this

'living fossil' can be compared to that of the fossil tree, *Metasequoia glyptostroboides*, or the Australian wollemi pine, *Wollemia nobilis*. Though it may have lived with the dinosaurs, the discovery of this humble, though handsome, fern did not receive wide publicity.

After only six months, the collections gathered by Augustine Henry and his native plant collector had reached enormous proportions. In a room in the Customs residence were more than 10,000 specimen, representing approximately 1,000 species.[20]

Trekking across the Ailao Shan range

At the end of January 1897, Henry set off on a 15-day journey into the mountainous territory of a tribal chief who lived south of Mengzi, near the Red River. For the trip, he bought two ponies from French missionaries, though, because it was the Chinese New Year, it was hard to find men to collect plants. From the Foreign Compound, he departed with his two new ponies, four pack-mules, his dog 'Jack', his hard-working collector 'Old Ho', a 'coolie' and a boy. The previous September, he had a tent made for such trips. The local villages were appallingly filthy, much worse than those of the hill Chinese in Hubei Province, and his tent was an essential travel item rather than a luxury.

Henry spent his time in the Ailao Shan, a great mountain range separating the Red River and Black River basins. In a hand-drawn, 19th-century map outlining his collecting areas, he clearly marks the principal regions as being the mountains that surrounded the towns of Marhao (which is on the Red River), Fengchunling and Yuanyang. The mountains in this region rose to between 8,000 and 10,000 ft (2,440 to 3,050 m).

Yuanyang was a Hani stronghold, and lay high in the mountains to the south-west. The Hani peoples are of Tibetan descent, and are famous throughout China for their steep, hillside rice terraces and for their great variety of colourful traditional costumes. Like the Yi, this group hold rituals to worship a village dragon tree. The position of chief, who conducts village religious activities, is hereditary. Male sorcerers, called *Beimas*, recite prayers to exorcise devils. Female sorcerers are called *Nimas*, and serve as witch doctors. Modern Christian missionaries have had few converts within this group, and thus have exerted little influence. The Hani, like other ethnic groups in China, have a superb knowledge of medicinal plants and their uses.

In bamboo forest in the mountains near Yuanyang, Henry collected the very lovely *Clematis yunnanensis*, a plant that Père Delavay had previously discovered in December 1884. This beautiful, evergreen, bushy climber flowers between October and December, bearing lateral cymes of up to seven, white, bell-shaped blossoms. In its native western China, *Clematis yunnanensis* grows on forest margins and in scrub between 1,600 to 3,000 m (5,250m to 9,850 ft). It has only recently reached cultivation.

The area was ruled over by two hereditary chiefs, brothers, who treated Henry with the greatest kindness, and afforded him a military reception. Henry celebrated the Chinese New Year with them, and the villagers dressed colourfully for the occasion. Diversity was not only restricted to plants. In a state of no more than 32 km² (12 miles²), ruled over by the brothers, he met no fewer than seven distinct ethnic groups, each with

very different physiognomy, languages, dress and customs.

Henry collected short vocabularies of their languages, and found the Yi system of writing still in daily use.[21] With this new-found friendship, Henry hoped to get a Yi scholar to teach him their language and writing. Only one other person had made such a study: Père Paul Viall (1855–1917), the French missionary, ethnologist and plant collector for whom *Primula viallii* is named. In a letter to Evelyn Gleeson, Henry complained bitterly that Viall was 'reserved and mysterious on the subject and wants the whole field to himself'.[22]

Henry correctly theorised that it was isolation that brought about such diversity in that part of China. Isolation caused by Yunnan's multitudinous ranges and valleys had played a great part in the invention of new species of plants, and the development and preservation of individual tribes.

The highest mountains on the Ailao Shan rose to 3,050 m (10,000 ft) in places, and the slopes were densely wooded with large trees of enormous girths to near the summit. Beyond that point, they were replaced by thick bamboo jungle, so that the range, though very long, could only be crossed at a number of points. The area was sparsely populated and gold was mined near Fengchunling.

It was winter, but a number of interesting trees and shrubs were in flower. One of these, *Rhododendron spanotrichum*, was an exciting new find in the mountains above Fengchunling, and there it formed small trees to 6 m (20 ft) tall, covered with lax umbels of crimson blossoms with dark blotches at their bases. This species has only been found once in the wild, and is unknown in cultivation. With it grew with the white flowered *Camellia henryana*, *Euonymus forbesiana*, *Styrax macranthus* and the aptly named *Symplocos spectabilis*.

On the slopes above Fengchunling, the evergreen witch-hazel relative *Rhodoleia henryi* formed 15-m (49-ft) tall trees. This is a particularly attractive species, bearing clusters of five to eight nodding, crimson flowers in March and April. It is endemic to Yunnan, where it grows in evergreen broad-leaved forest in the south-east of the province. At lower altitudes, trees of the evergreen *Caryodaphnopsis henryi* clung to the slopes.

Another new tree collected on this trip was *Stewartia pteropetiolata*. Thought to be a new genus when first studied at Kew, the tree was named *Hartia sinensis* at Augustine Henry's request, in honour of Sir Robert Hart. Three decades later, it was reduced to the status of *Stewartia* and given its present binomial. *Stewartia pteropetiolata* was introduced to cultivation by George Forrest from Tengchong, in western Yunnan, and is rare in cultivation.

The aptly named, red-stemmed *Actinidia rubricaulis* was another discovery from Fengchunling. This kiwi relative is extremely rare in cultivation, although there is an old, wall-

ABOVE: Virgin forest on the Daweishan range near the border with Vietnam. On the forest floor is a rich under-canopy layer, including acres of lush ginger lilies in a range of species. Such was the pristine environment visited by Augustine Henry, though much of this forest cover was to be stripped over the following century, particularly during the 1950s, when Mao Zhedong's 'Great Leap Forward' necessitated the felling of enormous tracts of forest all over China.

trained plant near the nursery at Glasnevin in Ireland, and it has been reintroduced, in recent years, by Bleddyn and Sue Wynn-Jones of Crûg Farm Plants in Wales.

Primula partschiana grew on shaded banks beneath trees near the summit of a mountain to the south of Manmei. A deciduous perennial, it carries 20-cm (8-in.) long spikes of up to 15 rose-coloured flowers. Little is known of this species. It has been collected only once ever, and may now be extinct.

From the mountains, Henry and his team descended into the hot, steamy valley of the Red River. One of the most striking trees there was *Dolichandrone caudafelina*, a bizarre-looking tropical tree that carried seedpods 60 to 90 cm (2 to 3 ft) long with a dense covering of thick brown hairs, exactly like the tail of a cat.

From this trip, Henry sent a parcel of epiphytic orchids to Evelyn Gleeson in Ireland asking that half of these be forwarded to A. K. Bulley. These arrived safely and in good condition and Gleeson was still growing many of them several years later.

Plant hunting with 'Jack'; seedlings at Kew

By May 1897, Henry was left quite alone in his quarters at Mengzi, as staff from there had been transferred to oversee the opening of a new Customs Station at Hekou, a small village that lay on the Chinese side of what is now the Vietnamese border. Hekou was an unpleasant, malaria-ridden place, full of opium smokers, gamblers, pirates and armed robbers. The women were little better. Henry described them, rather politely, to Evelyn Gleeson as small-footed with painted faces – Chinese dames, of sorts! Outside the village were several ethnic groups, mostly farmers; decent folk, but the staff of the Imperial Customs Service hated the place.

May was the month when rice was transplanted in the paddy fields on the Mengzi plain, and gangs of Yi women and girls would stand in fields of still water; all day up to their knees in water, often with a child on their back and a large umbrella in one hand. Aboriginal women in southern Yunnan Province did almost all the agricultural work within their communities, except for ploughing and harrowing.[23]

At the end of May, Henry's long-awaited camera finally arrived. The tin lining had two holes in it and the box was flooded with water. It looked ruined. He took it to pieces, however, cleaned it and glued it back together again. Miraculously, it worked, and produced many of the fine black-and-white images that appear in this book. About this time, he hired a man from a Yi tribe who lived in the mountains south of the Red River. Henry employed him in the Customs residence and trained him as a servant. This was the first time a native from any of Yunnan's ethnic groups had been employed by a foreigner, and Henry took the opportunity to study his language.

In June 1897, he was off once again, with his dog 'Jack' and his pony. Plant hunting in Yunnan Province had its dangers, and Henry related these in letters to Kew. These letters proved so fascinating that Thiselton-Dyer had them published in *Kew Bulletin*. It is a great pity that Henry never published an account of his travels in China. He wrote well, yet left just a few brief articles on his adventures there:

I find, when I go with my pony into the woods, that the wild animals seem less frightened, so I get good glimpses occasionally of deer, weasels, small black ones and large flying ones, of partridges, pheasants, snakes, etc. But the other day I saw bigger game; I was in a deep ravine, with the pony and dog left behind on the side of the hill above. I heard loud and angry barking. I clambered up, and through the trees soon discerned a great spot of orange; it loomed so large I thought it must be a tiger. Further up, I saw a beautiful leopard taking a quiet look at the pony. Loud I hallowed – no sign of the dog; the leopard skulked off over the hill. Sorrowfully I rode off, making much melancholy reflection over poor 'Jack', the dog. To my astonishment, I found him lying waiting for me near the foot of the hill, in an open space where he could look all around. He had been mauled, but not severely, by claws and teeth, but in some mysterious way had escaped out of the leopard's clutch [...] After such a terrible encounter, the dog immediately was in excellent spirits, and had quite forgotten his danger. Curiously enough, the pony wasn't a bit frightened either.[24]

The summer of 1897 was an extremely wet one, hampering Henry's botanical work, while the plague, an annual occurrence at Mengzi, raged through the city. On wet days, he confined himself to a room in the Customs residence set aside for his dried collections, and there he continued the laborious task of labelling and numbering thousands of

Another of Augustine Henry's gifts to gardeners, *Lilium sulphureum* is seen here blooming in the woodland garden at Glasnevin (Ireland). Discovered by Delavay in north-west Yunnan Province in July 1888, Henry sent seeds of this fine lily to Kew in 1897, and plants first bloomed there just two years later. According to Henry, it was common on the hills around Mengzi, and, while visiting Henry in November 1899, E. H. Wilson dug 50 or so bulbs, sending them back to his employer, Messrs Veitch of Chelsea.

specimens. It was not all dull, though. His visits to the tribes continued; he got on well with these people, who were to him reminiscent of Irish peasant folk in their bright graceful manners, in their separate religion from their Chinese conquerors and, alas, in their poverty. In December, he was a guest at a Yi wedding and enjoyed the feast that followed.

That same month, he sent a consignment of seeds to Kew, and it seems staff there were successful in germinating most of these. A. K. Bulley was still in great favour, and Henry requested that duplicate seeds be sent from Kew to his address in Liverpool. Forty-five species were raised in the temperate pits at Kew, including six species of *Begonia* (three of these new introductions were *Begonia augustinei*, *B. hemsleyana* and *B. sinensis*) and *Rodgersia pinnata*. The latter had been discovered by Père Delavay near Dali in north-west Yunnan Province a few years previously.

Another plant raised from this consignment was *Lilium sulphureum*, a lovely plant with pale yellow, green-striped, trumpet-shaped blooms. It was also discovered by Delavay in July 1888 in north-west Yunnan Province, and one of Henry's seedlings flowered for the first time in cultivation at Kew in 1899.

Unfortunately, these seedlings were confused with *Lilium leucanthum* (another Henry introduction) and were figured in *Curtis's Botanical Magazine* as such. The error was not corrected until 1912. *Lilium sulphureum* is a beautiful plant and has grown at Glasnevin since the 1920s. It is an adaptable lily, enjoying a warm, south-facing aspect or an open, well-sheltered glade area in a woodland setting.

Chapter 11

A transfer to Simao

In January 1898, Augustine Henry received a telegram from Beijing appointing him to the Customs Station at Simao (then Szemao), a city that lay to the south-west of Mengzi, near to what is now the Laos border. Henry was pleased with his latest posting and the prospect of fresh territory to explore. He already had plans to send Ho to Xishuangbanna, an area of extensive tropical rainforest to the south of the city.

The collections he had received from the French Consul Bons D'Anty were from that region, and had given him a good preliminary knowledge of the flora of the district. The mountains surrounding Simao were home to many different ethnic groups, too, so Henry had good reason to look forward to his transfer. Before leaving Mengzi, he dispatched 32 crates of plants containing 25,110 specimens (about 2,000 species), all destined for distribution to Kew,

By the time of his transfer to the Customs Station at Simao, Augustine Henry was Acting Chief Commissioner and was accorded the status of mandarin. Pictured here is one of his military escorts in southern Yunnan Province, perhaps the same escort that travelled with him to his new post at Simao.

Edinburgh, Berlin, St Petersburg, Calcutta, Hong Kong, the Arnold Arboretum, New York and Missouri. He also forwarded a consignment of seeds that included a new discovery, the famous medicinal plant *san ch'i* (*Panax pseudoginseng* var. *notoginseng*). It was cultivated in the mountains in the same manner as true ginseng (*Panax ginseng*) and was used as a tonic to treat patients suffering from serious wounds. He also included several duplicate packs of *san ch'i* seeds for distribution to the Royal Botanic

ABOVE: The Chang Lo-Ping suspension bridge crossing a great ravine across the Ho-Ma River east of Simao in Yunnan Province. Two 'coolies' (hired labourers) bear Henry's sedan chair. Though this was an important travel item for foreigners in 19th-century China, Henry preferred to travel on horseback or on foot.

Garden, Edinburgh, the National Botanic Gardens, Glasnevin, in Dublin, and to Thomas Hanbury at La Mortola on the Italian Riviera.

On the morning of 27 January 1898, the caravan set out for Simao, reaching the city 18 days later. Henry rode all the way, more or less leading the party, which, in China, presented a picture of affluence. His small caravan consisted of 30 mules, 2 ponies, 4 servants, his botanical collector, Ho and the latter's wife. His muleteers were capable and good-natured men, and the leading mules were decorated with colourful flags. Their journey took them over immense mountain ranges and precipitous ravines, all covered with extensive forest, and, in places, they were forced to cross great rivers by fords, pontoon, and suspension bridges. Temples and pagodas crowned the peaks, adding a great charm to the landscape.

The aboriginal peoples were, however, the most striking feature of the journey. Chinese farmers occupied small tracts of good land in the high-lying valleys, but the larger part of the population was made up of numerous ethnic groups.

On the north side of the Red River, the Yi were predominant, while, on a large plain near the city of Yuanjiang, the land was cultivated by the Dai. Henry was lucky enough to arrive there on a festival day. The women had dressed colourfully for the occasion and their elaborate costumes made them look like butterflies from afar.[1] In the valley of the Babian (Papien) River, he met with a party of five Yao hunters dressed in brightly coloured costumes and with handsome guns of native workmanship.

From Mengzi, Henry and his contingent trekked their way to the town of Yuanjiang (then Yuan Chiang), where they crossed a suspension bridge over the Red River.

259

A young tree of *Keteleeria evelyniana* on the Western Hills (Xi Shan) near Kunming, Yunnan Province. This rare conifer commemorates Evelyn Gleeson, Augustine Henry's friend from Dundrum in Dublin, Ireland.

Augustine Henry, aged 41, in the courtyard of the Customs quarters at Simao. In his hand is an Irish blackthorn walking stick.

Yuanjiang had an interesting flora, and it was there that he found the rare conifer *Keteleeria evelyniana*. On the lower slopes of mountains outside the town, he collected material from five or six trees. The tree was named in 1903, at Henry's request, for his life-long friend in Ireland, Evelyn Gleeson. In its native habitat, *Keteleeria evelyniana* can grow to 40 m (130 ft) tall (though it is generally seen half that height) and has since been found in Laos and Vietnam. *Hibiscus yunnanensis* was another discovery from Yuanjiang, though it was to be almost six decades before it was described from Henry's 1898 collections.

From Yuanjiang, the caravan continued on to the small town of Tongguan (then Talang), where gold and salt were mined. Just outside the town grew fine trees of *Calocedrus macrolepis*, a beautiful, medium-sized tree with elegant, fan-like sprays of flattened branchlets. This remarkable conifer, which can reach 35 m (115 ft) in its native territory, was discovered in May 1868 by Dr John Anderson while travelling through Yunnan Province on Sir Edward Bosc Sladen's expedition from India. In Yunnan, it is often planted in the courtyards of temple enclosures.

It was also near Tongguan that Henry found *Clerodendrum henryi*. This colourful shrub has since proved to be endemic to Yunnan. With it grew *Micholitzia obcordata*, a climber in the milkweed family (Asclepiadaceae) with fleshy white, hoya-like flowers. This species was later described, in 1909, from a plant cultivated under glass at Glasnevin, Ireland, that had been raised from seeds collected by Wilhelm Micholitz (1854–1932) in India.

From Tongguan, Henry and his retinue made their way to the great tea-growing district of Pu'er, which lay a few miles to the north of their final destination. The roads were busy, and, along the way, they continuously met caravans of tea, silk and cotton. Henry was addressed as 'Your Excellency' for the duration of the journey, and was given a great reception when he finally reached the city of Simao.

Simao was pleasantly situated on a hill in the centre of a small plain, and was surrounded by wooded mountains that rose in places to 1,830 m (6,000 ft). It did not suffer from plague as Mengzi did, but malaria was a problem in the region towards the Mekong River. Two ancient trade routes ran through the town: the tea-horse road and the southern Silk Route. The region surrounding Simao was, and still is, a great tea-growing district. It is the source of the famous Pu'er tea, and Tibetan caravans travelled to Simao twice a year to buy this tea, which is the main ingredient of Tibetan 'butter tea'. Mighty caravans passed through the city from time to time, though trade there was quiet in comparison to Mengzi, and Henry described the place as a sort of no man's land and being of no great importance.

Henry's predecessor, P. A. Carl, was on the point of departure. Carl was Irish-American and a cousin of Sir Robert Hart. The Customs quarters comprised a remodelled Chinese inn, with low doorways and windows of paper instead of glass. Henry occupied the rooms facing the street and market square. Below his room was a little courtyard with some potted plants on two raised stone terraces. At Simao, he had five servants, including a Yi pundit whom he had picked up during his journey from Mengzi.

Opposite his quarters were those of his assistants, Carey and Williams. Behind there was a larger courtyard with stables, kitchens and servants' quarters. Carl had left the place very well stocked with all sorts of Western luxuries. If Mengzi seemed a quiet place to live, then Simao was isolated in the extreme; the foreign community consisted of just five Europeans. Simao, Henry told Thiselton-Dyer, was the end of China. Isolation brought depression for a time, though, once he became thoroughly immersed in his botanical work, his spirits lifted.

The Latvian botanical explorer and historian Emil Bretschneider published a number of important works relating to the botany of China.

In March 1898, Henry was contacted by the Latvian botanist and explorer Emil Bretschneider. Bretschneider was nearing the completion of his classic, two-volumed *History of European Botanical Discoveries in China*, and devoted a large portion of the second volume to Augustine Henry's pursuits in China. Henry gave him a great deal of information on the whereabouts of other European plant hunters in China and their discoveries. This work remains unrivalled, even to this day, as the most accurate and comprehensive reference of the botanical exploration of China during the 18th and 19th centuries.

Then, as now, Simao and Xishuangbanna were strongholds of the Dai peoples, an ethnic group that first emerged in the Yangtze valley 2,000 years ago, and were driven south by the Mongol invasion in the 13th century. This group was impervious to pernicious malarial fever, then prevalent in the river valleys of southern Yunnan Province and so deadly to all other groups. This allowed them to settle the mosquito-infested, low-lying plains and valleys, where many other ethnic groups immediately succumbed. The Dai are Hinayana Buddhists, although, despite these beliefs, the group retains vestiges of primitive religions, in that they believe in natural spirits and worship several gods. Young Dai boys were raised in temples, where they served as priests.

One of Augustine Henry's servants in the courtyard of the Customs quarters at Simao. On the raised stone terrace are colourful potted plants.

Plant hunting around Simao

The flora of Simao was very different from that of Mengzi, despite the fact that both places were in much the same latitude and altitude. The mountains around Simao were less precipitously cut, and there was a great deal of forest at no great distance from the city. The forests were not as rich in species as those at Mengzi, and were dominated, at low altitudes, by evergreen members of the laurel family, such as *Actinodaphne henryi*, *Lindera tonkinensis* and *Litsea pierrei* var. *szemaois* (the latter is endemic to the Simao region). There was also a marked absence of ferns and herbaceous plants, though the tropical forests abounded in lianas and colourful epiphytic orchids. At Mengzi, limestone was the prevailing rock type (limestone generally supports a rich local flora), whereas Simao lay on red sandstone, and that may have partly accounted for its poorer flora.

Needless to say, the forests and hills that surrounded Simao were full of novelties. *Carpinus londoniana* was relatively common. This tree, which is also native to Burma and Indochina, was later collected in the same locality by the Austrian–American plant hunter Joseph Rock (1884–1962), when he visited Simao in 1922. Evergreen oak relatives dominated the woods in places. The finest of these was *Cyclobalanopsis rex*. The specific epithet 'rex', meaning 'king', is not over-used on this magnificent tree. The enormous leaves of this species give it a distinctly exotic look, and it ranks as one of the most beautiful of all the Asian oaks. *Eriobotrya henryi*, the *zhai ye pi ba*, grew as a

ABOVE: A view of Simao in 1895. The sketch, by one of Prince Henri d'Orléans' travelling companions, shows Simao as a typical Chinese city of its time, with paved streets lined by one- and two-storey wooden shops and houses.

small evergreen tree to about 7 m (23 ft) tall. *Photinia glomerata* was also common in the same forests, where it made medium-sized, wide-spreading evergreen trees. In cultivation, it is rather tender and does not reach the same dimensions of its wild counterparts, though the newly emerged, bright red growths are a handsome feature.

Syzygium forrestii was relatively common in hot, humid, low-lying valleys, and Henry described the trees he found as being between 6 to 12 m (20 to 40 ft) tall, and these carried masses of small, creamy-yellow flowers. Endemic to Yunnan Province, it was later rediscovered by George Forrest, for whom it is named. Several more species grew around Simao, including two other endemics: *Syzygium szemaoense* and *Syzygium augustinii*. Further new trees included *Schefflera chinense*, *Schefflera macrophyllum* (a fantastic foliage plant now growing in a few British and Irish gardens), *Toona ciliata* var. *henryi*, the white-flowered *Chionanthus henryanus*, *Lithocarpus fordianus* and *Ostodes katherinae*, a member of the spurge family (Euphorbiaceae) bearing many-flowered racemes of white, staminate flowers in April and May.

Two new magnolias also grew in the region. The first of these, *Magnolia fordiana* var. *forrestii* (syn. *Manglietia*

262

forrestii), is an evergreen species to 20 m (66 ft) tall carrying small, fleshy white, fragrant flowers to 10 cm (4 in.) across in June. This elegant tree is distributed through the provinces of Yunnan and Guangxi, where it is found in evergreen broad-leaved forest. Alas, it has become rare in China since it was first found by Henry. It was in a forested ravine just 13 km (8 miles) south of Simao that Henry found the evergreen *Magnolia henryi*, a small tree to 7 m (23 ft) tall with large, leathery, oblong leaves to 60 cm (2 ft) long. In May, the fragrant, saucer-shaped, thick, fleshy white blossoms appear on the end of stems. Henry only ever saw one tree, and, today, as a result of extensive clearance, only 50 subpopulations are known, and it has been recently evaluated as being critically endangered in its native Yunnan Province.

Acer wilsonii was another Simao discovery. This lovely maple was later rediscovered in Hubei Province by E. H. Wilson, for whom it is named. Wilson's maple is rare in cultivation, which is a pity. The three-lobed leaves emerge bright shrimp-pink and its slow growth rate makes it an ideal candidate for smaller gardens. The largest tree in Britain and Ireland grows at Birr Castle in County Offaly; planted by the 6th Earl of Rosse, it now measures 10 m (33 ft) tall.

Numerous lianas scrambled their way through the trees, including the creamy white-flowered *Schisandra henryi* ssp. *yunnanensis*. This climber has been introduced to cultivation in recent years and has proved perfectly hardy at Glasnevin in Ireland. Epiphytic orchids (a favourite with Henry) abounded on the trunks and branches of tropical trees. Some were new, such as *Chiloschista yunnanensis*, *Dendrobium stenoglossum* and the fragrant, yellow-flowered *Dendrobium henryi*. Orchids were not the only epiphytes. *Hoya pandurata* also clung to the trunks of trees, and its cascading stems hosted showy, fleshy white flowers. The shrubby gesneriad *Aeschynanthus humilis* adopted a similar habit.

Henry must have been fond of *Indigofera caudate*, a graceful shrub with copper-coloured young shoots and white, pea-like flowers arranged in very long, tail-like racemes. He introduced it to cultivation though the Royal Botanic Gardens, Kew, in 1899. In the same consignment were seeds of *Desmodium amethystinum*, a lax-habited plant to about 1.5 m (5 ft) high. It flowered after just two years of growth at Kew, where it produced great panicles of amethyst-coloured blossoms. Other new shrubs from Simao included the violet-flowered *Vitex henryi*, the closely related *Premna szemaoensis*, *Clerodendrum colebrookianum* var. *henryanum*, the shade-loving *Psychotria henryi* and *Camellia mairei* var. *velutina*, another of Yunnan Province's many endemics.

While several of Augustine Henry's discoveries were later collected in neighbouring provinces or adjacent countries, others were found to have an extremely limited

A large fig (*Ficus* sp.) at Simao, an image captured by Augustine Henry with his 'Ross twin lens', a box camera popular in the 1880s and 1890s.

range of distribution. Take, for example, *Alstonia henryi*, a low-growing evergreen shrub bearing cymes of small white flowers. This tropical species is endemic to southern Yunnan, and known only from the type locality at Simao. The herbaceous *Thalictrum simaoense* shares the same limited pattern of distribution. In mountain forest to the west of Simao, Henry found *Clematis ranunculoides* var. *pterantha*. This variety can grow either as a low, busy shrub or as a low-scrambling climber, if provided with support. It is a beautiful little plant bearing small, pale rose-coloured, bell-shaped flowers with reflexed sepals, and its range of distribution is restricted to Pu'er Xian, a few miles north of Simao. In some, very extreme cases, a number of Yunnanese plants have been found to be endemic to a single valley.

On the other hand, some of Henry's finds were later found to be more widespread. Take, for example, the ginger

South Gate Street, the principal business thoroughfare of Simao. The photograph was taken by F. W. Carey, Henry's assistant at Simao.

relative, *Alpinia blepharocalyx*, it has subsequently been found across southern China, India, Bangladesh, Burma, Thailand, Laos and Vietnam.

Henry's best-known discovery from Simao must be *Primula wilsonii*, a beautiful candelabra type bearing whorls of small, tubular, purple blossoms in early summer. It is grown in great drifts in the bog beds by the serpentine pond at Glasnevin, where it creates a spectacular show every year and seems to be less prone to attack from vine weevil than other allied species. In meadows on the mountains to the west of Simao, Henry found *Pimpinella rockii*, a vigorous perennial with finely dissected foliage bearing umbels of small white flowers. It was rediscovered, many years later, by Joseph Rock, for whom it was named.

Primula wilsonii was discovered by Augustine Henry in the summer of 1898; Wilson introduced it the following year, and it first flowered in the rock garden at Kew in 1902.

The tropical rainforests of Xishuangbanna

In April, Henry sent his young English assistant, Fred Carey, on a 20-day trip south of Simao to Xishuangbanna (then the Chinese Shan States), a region in the extreme south of Yunnan Province, next to the present-day borders of Burma and Laos. The name is a Sinicised rendering of the original Thai, *Sip Song Panna*, referring to the 12 rice-growing districts. This hugely fertile region lay just south of the Tropic of Cancer, and was plagued by malaria and cholera. To the Chinese, who quickly succumbed to both ailments, it was known as the 'Land of Lethal Vapours'. It was malaria that kept the majority Chinese ethnic group in 'China proper', and had prevented them from conquering the tropical areas inhabited by aboriginal groups on the southern fringes of Yunnan. For this reason, China had little influence in this far-flung part of her empire over the centuries, and it resembled parts of Thailand in its people and architecture.

Xishuangbanna was principally inhabited by the Dai, but also by several other ethnic groups, such as the Aini (a subgroup of the Hani), Bulang, Jinuo ('slash-and-burn' farmers), Lahu, Miáo and the Wa, a group of fierce warriors who continued to headhunt as recently as the 1970s. A world fair (Exposition Universelle) was to be held in Paris in 1900, and one of the duties of the Customs Service was to ensure China's representation. Carey spent his time visiting as many of the aboriginal groups as possible, and returned with a collection of colourful Hani costumes, ethnic crafts and art, Yi books and manuscripts, musical instruments and various different types of tea.

Henry's native plant collector, Ho, also visited the region soon afterwards, and made many interesting finds. Xishuangbanna's extensive tracts of primeval tropical rainforest had been little affected by the Chinese, though Dai settlers had used elephants to clear the low-lying jungles for the cultivation of rice. The remaining large tracts of tropical jungle were home to wild oxen, Asiatic elephants, gibbons, golden-haired monkeys, brilliantly coloured bantams, leopards, mongoose, flying squirrels and boa constrictors. Almost a third of China's bird life lived within its confines. It was in Xishuangbanna's tropical rainforests that Ho found *Capparis yunnanensis*, a spectacular evergreen climber with exotic, showy blossoms.

That region of Yunnan Province enjoyed a tropical monsoon climate similar to that of northern Laos and Burma. Like Simao, the region had distinct wet and dry seasons. The wet season occurred between June and August, when it rained almost every day. From September to February, there was less rainfall, but thick fogs descended in the late evening and didn't lift until late the next morning, creating seas of clouds that lingered in the low-lying valleys. Spectacular and frequent thunderstorms raged through the region between May and August, and, for variety of plant life, Xishuangbanna was extraordinarily rich. The Mekong River (or Lancang Jiang) meandered its way through the region, and was navigable for most of its 320-km (199-mile) stretch through the province. Originating as an ice-fed stream on the Tibetan plateau, the Mekong is the third longest river in China and is the world's twelfth largest.

Back at Simao, the rainy season began in June, bringing oppressive, muggy, damp heat, and it rained every day, torrentially at times, making Henry's work of drying specimens a difficult chore. He looked forward to the rainless winter season. Once the sun rose in the mornings, the cicadas created such a racket that it was nearly impossible to hear anything else.

In July, news came that his salary was to be doubled: £1,000 a year, an extraordinarily good wage in 1898. At Simao, Henry was Acting Chief Commissioner of Customs and was accorded the status of mandarin (a high-ranking official). Being in charge left him little time for collecting, though, except on Sundays, but his native plant collector Ho was hard working and made good progress. By mid September, the weather improved and blue skies returned once again over Simao. This latter part of the year proved to be much more interesting for plants, and there were as many plants in flower in winter as there were in spring. In just ten months, Henry could report to Professor Sargent that he and his native plant collector had gathered 11,000 herbarium specimens from the mountains around Simao. Ho was the finest of all the Chinese plant collectors he had employed over the years, and the richness of Henry's Simao collections was due in large measure to that old man's hard work.

In a letter to Kew written that November, Henry mentioned that the Customs Service planned to open a new base at Tengchong (then Tengyueh), a city to the north of Simao, located in high mountains near the border with Burma. There was a chance that he could be transferred there, thus providing further opportunities. These hopes never materialised, but he was instrumental in having the Scottish plant hunter George Forrest sent there a few years later.

In the New Year of 1899, Thiselton-Dyer was knighted for his services to botany and horticulture. Henry was delighted for his old friend and felt the honour was well deserved. He sent Thiselton-Dyer a long letter of congratulations; 'More power to you, as we say in Ireland', he wrote![2]

A Dai woman by her house in Xishuangbanna, Yunnan Province. The photograph was probably taken by Henry's assistant, Fred Carey, who travelled to the region to secure items for the Exposition Universelle in Paris.

'Send a professional collector to China'

The flora of Yunnan Province proved so remarkable that Henry wrote to Kew, urging Thiselton-Dyer to devote more attention to the exploration and scientific investigation of the Chinese flora. He complained of how China had been left in the cold, and of how Africa always got the lion's share as regards botany. Much more work needed to be carried out; western and central China, Henry claimed, were evidently the centre of diversity of a great number of genera distributed across Asia and into Europe.

Henry was nearing the end of his stay in China and hoped that a full-time professional collector would be sent out to carry on his work and to introduce many of the plants he had discovered. He wrote to Thiselton-Dyer stating that he doubted that many of his specimens would be collected for another 50 years. He constantly urged authorities at Kew to consider the wealth of ornamental plants that could potentially grace the gardens of the West.

The handkerchief tree at south Wushan in Sichuan Province still remained a vivid memory. He wrote to Kew:

Why *Davidia* is worth any amount of money. I only saw one tree of it, but doubtless there are others in the district. *Davidia* is wonderful [...] fruits of it for introduction would be worth taking an immensity of trouble.[3]

Henry pressed the case that a full-time plant collector

ABOVE: 'Don't waste time – send a collector to China' was Henry's advice. Yunnan Province was still little known; Delavay had explored a small region around Dali and Lijiang, and Henry had covered areas further south. Pictured here is Delavay country: the Jade Dragon Snow Mountain (Yulongxue Shan) range, near Lijiang, framed by ancient trees of *Rhododendron roxieanum* and mammoth trees of the Himalayan hemlock, *Tsuga dumosa*.

could be in the field at all seasons, and, therefore, could identify the plant in flower, gather voucher herbarium specimens and return to collect seeds at a later stage. He was a part-time collector, and his day job allowed little time to travel the great distances needed to harvest seeds. As time went on, his letters became more determined:

I would suggest, so great is the variety and beauty of the Chinese flora, and so fit are the plants for the European climate, that an effort ought to be made to send out a small expedition, the funds, e.g. being provided by a syndicate of, say, a horticulturist, a private gentleman or two, &c. I estimate £1,000 would cover the expenses for two years [...] The locality I would suggest is the mountain range separating Szechwan from Shensi; or thereabouts, the expedition starting from Ichang in April and covering two seasons.

A person like me, with daily official work, can do little or nothing. We live in towns, in the midst of cultivation, and the distances to get to the hunting grounds are enormous, and, when we do get there, we are half worn out [...] My own plant collecting, since I have been here, is enormous, but at such an expenditure of muscular force! It would be strictly paralleled by that of a bank clerk in London who made excursions on Sundays all over

England, and two or three times a year made hurried trips to the Carpathians and the Pyrenees. The bank-clerk would really in such a way expend less energy [...][4]

My trip in the mountains north of Ichang showed the possibilities of central China; and this trip was, as it were, a mere scratch of an exploration. Hundreds of such trips can be made in Szechwan, Hupeh, Kweichow, Shensi; and you may quote this opinion to people who wish to fit out the seed-collecting expedition.[5]

Henry also sent several appeals across the Atlantic to Professor Sargent in Boston, urging him to send out a collector before the forests were cleared. In February, he made a trip on official business for 14 days and travelled west of Simao, crossing the Mekong River. He was shocked by the rate of deforestation and appealed to Sargent to send out an expedition before it was too late. He was having little success in persuading Kew to mount an expedition to China, but perhaps Sargent and the Arnold Arboretum could raise the funds needed. He wrote to the Professor as follows:

The country was dreadfully barren – totally deforested; and all this done by a few wretched settlers, as the population was scarcely five to a square mile. I really appeal to you and others to get up some expedition to western China, to explore botanically and to collect seeds, bulbs, etc. The work of destruction of the forests is going on rapidly, as the Chinese are displacing the aborigines and, wherever the Chinese go, forests disappear. In 50 years, many plants will be extinct, I am sure.

Such an expedition need not be costly, as travelling in China is cheap. I would of course give advice and hints if such an expedition is thought of. The results to arboriculture and horticulture would be very great, as western China is the richest floral district in the world. Now is the time. All W. China plants will grow in the U.S., in some State at least; what won't grow in Maine will grow in California.[6]

Sargent had an insatiable appetite for new woody Asian plants, and was enthusiastic about organising such an expedition. He occasionally received seeds and plants through part-time collectors and commercial nurseries, though quantities were limited and what he really needed was a substantial, regular supply of wild-sourced material to stock the fledgling Arnold Arboretum.

In spite of the work carried out by David, Delavay, Faber, Fortune and Henry, the floral riches of China were far from exhausted. Henry reminded Sargent that whole provinces remained unexplored, and these would surely yield an abundance of new material. Even in the late 1890s, Yunnan Province was little explored. Delavay had worked only a small area near Dali and Lijiang, and the region west of the Mekong was totally unexplored. Henry had wanted to send his collector to the Mekong district west of Simao, but this area was inhabited by the Kawas, a group of head hunters. The low-lying valleys that had to be traversed to reach this district were also rife with malaria, and most Chinese people who went there died of the disease.

Sadly, it was malaria that caused the death of Old Ho, Henry's hard-working Chinese plant collector, in April 1899. Henry despaired at the loss of such an exceptional person. He was fond of the old man, and wrote to Evelyn Gleeson:

He was most honest and hard working and his end was so sad. He died on the roadside while trying to get

back. His comrades left the body, tried to get the village to take it in, but the villagers refused, so they came on here. I sent out a party who brought the body in and he is now grandly coffined (which is the only serious question in China) and tomorrow being a lucky day he will be buried. It is impossible to replace this honest man.[7]

Thiselton-Dyer was also informed of Ho's death. Henry described him to his friend at Kew as an honest, even conscientious Chinese individual, who worked intelligently and with zeal. Nearly all the best finds from Yunnan Province could be attributed to him. Ho is commemorated by *Schefflera hoi*, a small tree with bold, exotic, digitate leaves from the mountains to the south of the Red River.

But life went on as usual. Letters passed between Henry and Sargent, all on the subject of organising a botanical expedition to China. Henry suggested routes, salaries and contacts in China. Western Sichuan Province would be excellent ground, he told Sargent, and north-west Yunnan Province, though well worked by Delavay, would be rich in plants suited to cultivation in northern Europe and North America.

Sargent had hoped that Henry could lead the expedition himself and that the Customs Service would grant him leave to do so, but this was out of the question. Sir Robert Hart had placed him in out-of-the-way postings, such as Mengzi and Simao with the idea that he could carry on his botanical work there, and Henry believed that Hart considered that, in doing this, he had done quite enough. The Customs Service was understaffed, owing to the opening of several new ports in China, and, in any case, Henry had had enough of China and was looking forward to returning home to Ireland.

Schefflera hoi commemorates Augustine Henry's finest Chinese plant collector, 'Old Ho'. Endemic to China, it is distributed in Yunnan Province and south-east Tibet.

Little did Henry know that when he discovered the glabrous-leaved handkerchief tree, *Davidia involucrata* var. *vilmoriniana*, in May 1888, it would later initiate a golden era of plant hunting in China.

E. H. Wilson en route to China

In May 1899, Henry received a letter from Thiselton-Dyer informing him that the nursery firm Messrs Veitch of Chelsea were sending out a professional collector. While Kew did not have the resources to mount an expedition to China, they were successful in persuading the firm's boss, Sir Harry Veitch (1840–1924), to carry out the scheme as a commercial venture.

After many years of persistent persuasion, Henry's efforts had paid off. He was delighted to hear the news. The man they chose was Ernest Henry Wilson (1876–1930), a 23-year-old gardener from Kew. Wilson grew up under modest circumstances in Gloucestershire, England, and worked as a nursery lad for Messrs Hewitt in Birmingham, and, by virtue of his excellent performance there, gained a position as

gardener at Birmingham Botanical Gardens at the tender age of 16. In 1897, he moved to Kew, where he stood out as an exceptional plantsman with great potential. In November 1898, Wilson moved to the Veitch nursery grounds at Coombe Wood near Kingston-upon-Thames in Surrey, and spent the following six months training and preparing for China under the firm's top nurseryman, George Harrow. He also spent a considerable period studying Augustine Henry's specimens in the Kew Herbarium.[8]

Wilson was directed to visit Augustine Henry in Yunnan Province, and to get as much information and advice on travel and exploration in central and western China as was possible. The young plant hunter was given the following, rather cryptic instructions from his employers on signing a three-year contract in March 1899:

> The object of the journey is to collect a quantity of seeds of a plant, the name of which is known to us. This is the object – do not dissipate time, energy, or money on anything else. In furtherance of this, you will first endeavour to visit Dr. A. Henry at Szemao, Yunnan, and obtain from him precise data as to the habitat of this particular plant and information on the flora of central China in general.[9]

The plant in question was *Davidia*, the elusive handkerchief tree that Henry had stumbled upon in south Wushan more than a decade previously.

The Boxer Rebellion

In 1899, the French were planning to construct a railway to connect Hanoi (then the capital of French Indochina) with Kunming in Yunnan Province. The project stirred up ill feeling. The Chinese, who opposed the idea, had had enough of foreign interference in their country. The Imperial government was weak, and further encroachments by European nations made it weaker still. Henry's sympathies were with China. He wished that Western powers would make an honest effort to strengthen China's position. The Chinese, for their part, could see nothing in European nations but the conqueror and the spoiler – and with reason.[10]

Events came to a head in 1899 and 1900. Ordinary Chinese people had had enough of the embarrassing encroachments made on their country by foreign nations. Following the humiliating Sino-Japanese war of 1894–5, a secret Chinese organisation, the 'Society of Righteous and Harmonious Fists' (nicknamed the 'Boxers' by European and American residents), was formed with the prime objective of driving all foreigners out of China, especially the missionaries. The Empress Dowager Cixi and her government cast a blind eye on the movement and showed sympathy by abstaining from any interference with it. The organisation was founded in Shandong Province in eastern coastal China in 1898, when Germans claimed a sphere of influence and aggravated the inhabitants. In retaliation, the 'Boxers' murdered two German missionaries and terrorised other foreign nationals. Their banners read 'by Imperial command, exterminate the Christian religion', and 'kill the foreign devils' became a common street cry. The movement spread like wildfire throughout the other provinces, and it was a dangerous time for any Westerner to travel through China. Fanatically anti-foreign, the Boxers saw 1900 as the dawn of a new age and believed themselves invincible to the bullets of foreign forces.

In June, there was a rebellion at Mengzi and the Foreign Compound was attacked by a mob in the dead of night. Anti-foreign sentiments were rising throughout China, and the Customs House and French Consulate were looted and set on fire. The European and American Customs staff escaped in their nightclothes, and were pursued by a howling mob. It was with great difficulty that they found safety in the city. Two Chinese servants were not so lucky and were burned to death. Little damage was done to the French Consulate, but the Customs House was completely destroyed. It was under the pretext of being members of the Boxer organisation that a group of rebels attacked, but Henry suspected the raid on Mengzi was not politically motivated. Southern Yunnan lay close to the frontier, and the mountains along those borderlands were a refuge for all sorts of hardened bandits and outlaws. The villains were a gang of bloodthirsty criminals who had fled to the hills, eluding the Chinese authorities for weeks. Henry did not fear any further reprisals, though he kept a revolver close by at all times.

He was also glad that no parts of his collections were stored at Mengzi. If they had been, the lot would have gone up in flames. Yet he was worried about his Simao collections: 15,480 specimens lay in storage, and it was too risky to dispatch them through Mengzi, as the approach roads were far from safe and very little post was getting through at the time.

In mid September, the perpetrators of the Mengzi riots were captured and decapitated. A few made their escape, and the ringleader hid in a village in the depths of the mountains near Simao. A party of 300 soldiers finally tracked him down and killed him. His head was brought back to Simao as a trophy and hung in a cage on the market square opposite Henry's house, alongside those of two other rebels. Wilson encountered an equally grim scene on his arrival at Mengzi. Suspended from the branches of a tree to the rear of the ruins of the Customs House were wooden cages containing the heads of five of the rioters. He later met a posse of soldiers bringing in another gruesome-looking head, and this was suspended with the others as a warning against further possible rioting against Western residents.

E. H. Wilson arrives in Simao

Simao, thankfully, remained peaceful, and Henry continued his Sunday outings to the mountains. All the collection work was carried out by him alone since the death of Ho, and it was difficult. The summer of 1899 was the wettest in 30 years. The rain came down in torrents, and this continued almost without end for two months. In mid August, E. H. Wilson reached Lao Cai in northern Vietnam, and was waiting there for the arrival of Mr G. J. Litton, Simao's new British Consul, with whom he would travel to Simao. Wilson, very fortunately, arrived at Lao Cai just as the rebellion broke out at Mengzi; had he been a week earlier, he would most likely have been killed by the insurgents.

The young plant hunter finally reached Simao on the evening of 24 September 1899, and rode into the city with Henry's assistants, Messrs Carey and Williams. Wilson later wrote that he thought the city was 'the most God-forsaken place imaginable', and marvelled that Henry could live out a life there with the company of only five other Europeans.[11] It was Sunday and Henry was away botarising in the mountains as usual, but he returned early in the evening and gave Wilson a hearty Irish welcome. Over the next few days, Henry divulged his vast store of knowledge on the flora of China, and, from his notebooks, furnished the young Englishman with the exact locality of the handkerchief tree. Henry also gave Wilson the names of the native plant collectors he had trained and employed during the 1880s and advised him to hire them for any future expeditions in Hubei and Sichuan provinces. James Veitch, who was then managing the nursery firm with his uncle, Sir Harry Veitch, later wrote:

The object of sending a traveller to central China was to obtain seed of species likely to prove hardy in Great Britain, and living representatives of certain plants only known to exist from dried specimens in the herbaria of various European countries.

Wilson sailed from Liverpool in April 1899. Travelling by way of America, he visited Professor Sargent, the well-known authority on ligneous plants at Boston, and consulted him respecting the trees and shrubs likely to be found in China. The desired information obtained, Wilson proceeded, and arrived at Hong Kong on June 3rd 1899.

Before leaving for the interior it was considered advisable that Wilson should consult Dr Henry and benefit by his unrivalled knowledge of the Chinese flora [...] Szemao was reached on September 24th, and a cordial welcome from Dr Henry awaited the young traveller.

That gentleman freely imparted important information regarding the plants Wilson was in search

In 1899, the young English plant hunter Ernest Henry Wilson (1876–1930) visited Henry at Simao to enquire about the location of the handkerchief tree that Henry had found at south Wushan in Sichuan Province 11 years previously. This portrait of Wilson was taken shortly before his departure to China at the age of 23.

ABOVE: A Buddhist temple near Simao, photographed by Henry's assistant, Fred Carey. The temple contained a large gilt Burmese Buddha.

RIGHT: A Dai couple near Simao during the late 1890s. The Dai stronghold in Yunnan Province is the Simao area and Xishuangbanna to the south

of, and the ways and means of reaching them. The information was valuable, as the district Wilson was instructed to explore was practically a closed book to all but a few, amongst whom was Dr Henry.[12]

For his part, Henry was glad that someone else was going to carry on the work in China that had been on his shoulders for many years. Wilson got on very well with the Chinese people, an important point if he was going to succeed as a professional plant hunter. Henry predicted he would do very well in China. He was agreeable and there was a field for a man like him for a lifetime.

Meanwhile, Professor Sargent still tried every way he could think of to entice Henry into leading an expedition to China for the Arnold Arboretum, though Henry still refused to take the job. Sargent was disappointed; Henry would have been a perfect choice. He had years of experience in the field, had an excellent knowledge of botany and was fluent in Chinese. Soon after declining Sargent's offer, Henry wrote of Wilson's arrival in Yunnan Province. He assured the professor (who was still determined to send a collector to China) that a knowledge of Chinese was not by any means essential to a Western plant hunter in China:

I am sure Mr Wilson will do very excellent work in the way of collecting seeds, bulbs, etc., but of course he will have very little time for preparing dried specimens. He is really at little disadvantage on account of his

ignorance of Chinese […] No expensive interpreter is required, an ordinary 'boy' will do. What is wanted is a man with commonsense, tact and especially good temper […] If Mr Wilson were not employed by Veitch's for seed-collecting, etc., I think he would do very well – as he gets on well with the Chinese and is very keen to do as much collecting as possible.

In support of my contention, I may adduce Fortune, who didn't speak Chinese and yet got on very well. Pratt, the naturalist, who visited Ichang and went as far as the frontier of Tibet also did very well […] The collecting botanist does not want to ascertain facts from the people – only he wants to get to the forests and mountains.

I regret that I do not see my way to thinking of your proposals in the light of accepting them. But I do not feel by declining, that I am really depriving you of the great field of investigating the Chinese flora. You will be sure to find a man. I trust that you will do so, and that you will have many years to live to devote yourself to the flora of China. It is by far the most interesting one on the globe – and, to an American, must appeal even more than to a European as China in some many ways, [with] its great rivers, mountains, climate, etc., seems to be a counterpart of the United States.[13]

For several years, Kew staff had been pestering Henry for cycads for their living collection, and, in forests near Simao, he had stumbled across a population of *Cycas siamensis*, a

Hypericum augustinii. Discovered in 1899 by Henry near Shiping in southern Yunnan Province, this species was not described until 1970, yet it was long established in Irish gardens at this time.

short, palm-like tree carrying whorls of pinnate leaves almost 1.5 m (5 ft) across. In 1882, Henry had collected fossilised cycads in a layer of coal in the hills above Yichang, and now, 17 years later, he was collecting living plants for Kew. With Wilson's help, he dug several plants; half of the batch went to Thiselton-Dyer, for display in the Great Palm House at Kew, while the rest were sent to Messrs Veitch. Before leaving Simao, Wilson also gathered a good quantity of seeds of *Primula wilsonii*. This wonderful plant first flowered in the rock garden at Kew in 1902, and was the very first of Wilson's introductions to bear his name. He was so fond of this species that when his first and only child was born, in May 1906, he named her Muriel Primrose.

Soon after Wilson's arrival, Henry received a telegram stating that he was to take charge of the Customs Service at Mengzi. Henry and Wilson departed from Simao on 16 October, and, needless to say, both men were eager to collect plants along the way. At Tongguan, Wilson found seeds on several trees of *Calocedrus macrolepis*, and it was by this means that it reached cultivation. Due to its tender nature, this interesting conifer has remained rare in Western gardens, and seems to thrive only in the mildest coastal districts of Great Britain and Ireland. It was during this brief visit to Tongguan, on 20 October 1899, that Henry found *Lithocarpus carolinae*, the tree that commemorates his first wife.

From Tongguan, the party rode on to Yuanjiang. Again, time was made to stop and collect, and this must have been a great opportunity for Wilson to learn many of the techniques involved in plant collecting. In 1993, the

Chinese botanist and clematis expert W. T. Wang described *Clematis yuanjiangensis* from a specimen gathered during this trip. This beautiful climber is allied to the better-known *Clematis ranunculoides*, but carries larger flowers with widely spreading pinkish sepals.

The lakeside town of Shiping was the group's next stopover, and it was there that Henry found *Hypericum augustinii*, a charming shrub of about 90 cm (3 ft) tall bearing masses of large, golden-yellow, saucer-shaped blooms. How this species came into cultivation is a mystery; it was already well established in Irish gardens before it was formally described as a new species in 1970. Other discoveries from Yuanjiang were the pink-flowered *Campylotropis henryi* and two camellias, *Camellia stuartiana* and *Camellia skogiana*.

Rebuilding the ruins at Mengzi

Augustine Henry and Ernest Wilson finally reached Mengzi on the evening of 2 November. Back at the Foreign Compound, the Customs buildings lay in a charred heap. Henry, Wilson and the other travellers in the party were forced to camp out among the ruins, and slept under armed guard on a veranda surrounded by enormous cases of botanical specimens, baggage and stores. Henry's first task was to oversee the rebuilding of the Customs quarters, and he set about planning a new house and office building immediately.

Henry brought with him two native plant collectors from Simao whom he had trained to replace Old Ho. Plant hunting resumed around Mengzi immediately, and Henry persuaded Wilson to stay 10 days or so to collect seeds. One of Henry's earliest collections from the area was *Magnolia delavayi*, an evergreen tree bearing large, solitary, ivory-white flowers between April and June. It was discovered by Père Delavay in May 1886, and Henry led Wilson to a number of seed-bearing trees. One of the seedlings raised from this same Mengzi collection first flowered at Kew in 1908.

In oak woods to the south-east of Mengzi, Wilson bagged a lot of tropical epiphytic orchids, including the lovely *Dendrobium bellulatum*, which Henry had previously discovered on the Daweishan mountain range. Wilson was also successful in introducing the double yellow-flowered *Jasminum mesnyi*, *Gleditsia japonica* var. *delavayi* and the greenish-yellow-flowered *Lilium primulinum* var. *ochraceum* from Mengzi.

Wilson remained forever grateful to the older, more experienced plant hunter, and, over the following years, always gave Henry credit for the help that laid the foundations for his own brilliant career. In 1913, he published *A Naturalist in Western China*, the story of his four expeditions through China, and, in the opening pages, he had the following to say:

The opportunity to travel and study the natural history of China I owe to the business enterprise of the house of Veitch, the famous nurserymen of Chelsea, to whom I was recommended by Sir William T. Thiselton-Dyer, at the instigation of Mr. W. Watson, the present Curator of that establishment [...] In my wanderings in China I have been singularly fortunate. The Chinese treated me always with kindly courtesy and respect. I was in the interior [of] China during the Boxer outbreak and the Russo-Japanese war, and visited places shortly before or after anti-foreign riots, but never experienced any incivility meriting the name.

At the commencement of my travels in China, Mr Augustine Henry [...] imparted to me much sound advice, which I did my utmost to follow. To this gentleman and to the devoted services of my Chinese collectors must be largely attributed the results of my work in China.[14]

Ernest Wilson paid Augustine Henry the ultimate tribute when he penned that 'no one in any age has contributed more to the knowledge of Chinese plants than this scholarly Irishman'.[15] Wilson went on to state that Sir Harry Veitch had studied Henry's specimens of the

ABOVE: Many of the oldest trees of *Magnolia delavayi* in British and Irish gardens were raised from Wilson's original introduction from Mengzi. It has proved remarkably hardy in Western gardens, despite coming from such a warm region of China.

Jasminum mesnyi, one of several plants introduced by E. H. Wilson during his brief visit to Mengzi.

handkerchief tree at Kew, and had then decided to employ a collector to contact Henry for its specific location, with a view to introducing it to cultivation.

While Wilson honestly and openly credited Henry for drawing Veitch's attention to China, this was not the case with a less-than-thankful James Veitch, who wanted the credit for Wilson's success to lie solely on his shoulders. He was annoyed that Wilson had publicly acknowledged Henry's role in attracting the firm to China:

You are, however, wrong on one little point, but I do not wish it publicly contradicted. It was not Henry's specimens which drew our attention to China. When I was in Japan in '91, '92 & '93 I was quite aware there was a very rich field, and so was Sargent, with whom I was with some time in Japan.

In fact, I wrote home here to my chief [Sir Harry Veitch] to know whether I might not go [...] but my chief promptly sat on it, I did not go, and the matter was dropped.

For years, I had been pressing the matter, and though Henry's work gave a fillip to my wishes, the expedition was long determined on in my own mind, before Henry appeared on the scene.[16]

James Veitch (1869–1907) was acting like nothing better than the proverbial 'dog in the manger'. It is true that he had written to his uncle Harry from Japan (he had also enlisted Sargent to do the same) seeking permission to travel on to central China, but the elder Veitch replied to his wandering nephew telling him that he needed to stay at home for a while to gain the more practical aspects of running a nursery. Chinese plants might prove to be a commercial success, but that would be a task for another collector. James Veitch

BELOW: Crossing a river in southern Yunnan Province during the late 1890s. Sedan chairs were a necessary travel item during this period, commanding immediate respect from local inhabitants in rural areas.

ABOVE: *Rhododendron excellens* flowering in the Curvilinear Range of glass-houses at Glasnevin, Dublin. The specific epithet '*excellens*', meaning 'superb', is not lost on this lovely species. In China, it is distributed in the western provinces of Yunnan and Guizhou provinces. It is also native to Vietnam.

always regretted the opportunity he lost, and was obviously annoyed that it was Henry and Wilson, not him, that would share the fame of exploring and exposing the great wealth of the flora of central and western China.

Veitch Junior had forgotten that Henry's specimens had reached Kew long before he travelled to Japan with Charles Sargent, and he had also forgotten that one of Veitch's own collectors, Charles Maries, had been there earlier, and had invented the myth that the flora of China had few new plants to offer. That view was accepted until the arrival of Henry's 1885 specimens at Kew. James Veitch had grudgingly gained great benefit from Henry's work, and he and Wilson had actually visited the Kew Herbarium and studied Henry's specimens from central China, as can be seen from his instructions to E. H. Wilson:

[…] It is especially the trees, shrubs and herbaceous plants of the mountain ranges around Ichang and those we saw together in the herbarium, Kew [that] we are anxious to get hold of.[17] The real object of your three-year trip lies before you, i.e. to obtain, during the next two summers and autumns, plants, but more especially seeds of the flora

in the mountain ranges around Ichang, keeping especially in view those you and I know from the Kew specimens are likely to be especially fine and of commercial value.[18]

Veitch was suffering from neurosyphilis at the time of writing, which he may have contracted during his travels in Japan. The affliction brought about his death in 1907, aged just 39. He manifested many of the classic symptoms of the disease, and was said to be fiery and excitable. At times, he brought his own nursery staff close to revolt.[19] Whatever the cause, though, he was not willing to share Wilson's and the firm's success with Henry.

From Mengzi, Wilson departed with Henry's Simao specimens and returned to Hong Kong for the Christmas holidays, which he spent with an old friend from Kew. Before leaving the colony, he dispatched his collections to Messrs

Veitch, and those belonging to Henry to Kew. From Hong Kong, he made his way to Shanghai, and, from there, took a steamer up the Yangtze River to Yichang, where he would spend the next three years collecting seeds from hundreds of plants discovered by Henry more than a decade earlier.

While Wilson travelled to Yichang, Henry put the two native plant collectors he had brought from Simao to work. Life at Mengzi was not as easy as before; relations with the Chinese people were strained, and the most harrowing stories abounded. In February 1900, news arrived at Mengzi that Mr Litton, the British Consul at Simao, had been seriously injured in a shooting near the border with Burma – perhaps killed. The reports of Litton's demise were unfounded, however. He later took the post of British Consul at Tengchong, near the Burmese border. There, in 1904, he befriended the great Scottish plant hunter George Forrest. By a strange twist of fate, Litton did die on the frontier, albeit in 1906, and lies buried alongside Forrest in the mountains above Tengchong.

In April 1900, Henry received a letter from Wilson announcing his safe arrival in Yichang and his future travel plans. News also came through of the death of the great French botanist Adrien Franchet of the Paris museum. Thiselton-Dyer told Henry that, with his passing, there would be little progress in French botany. Père Armand David died the same year, in Paris, and Henry was now the only person alive who had actually seen the handkerchief tree in its wild habitat. While based in Simao, he sketched a tract of countryside the size of New York state, pinpointing the exact location of a single tree for E. H. Wilson. Thiselton-Dyer sent extracts of Henry's letters concerning E. H. Wilson to Sir Harry Veitch. The old nurseryman was delighted with the praise Henry lavished on his young employee, the last of 22 professional plant hunters employed by the firm, and, without question, the greatest of all of them.[20]

In May, Henry put a new collector to work in the mountains to the south of the Red River. He now had three men gathering specimens. In the mountains south of Manmei, one of these men found *Rhododendron excellens*, a sparsely branched, often epiphytic shrub of about 3.5 m (12 ft) tall and bearing clusters of three to four large, funnel-shaped, creamy-white flowers. This native plant collector only ever made a single collection of this magnificent plant, and, for a century, this was the only representation of the species in Western herbaria. *Rhododendron excellens* is extremely rare in the wild, and has only recently been introduced to cultivation.

As head of his Customs post, Henry had little time for botany and he resented the additional responsibilities placed on him. The new buildings were progressing well; the Customs office was a single-storey structure, completed in the classical Chinese style with upturned eaves and painted in the imperial colours. For the Customs residence, Henry chose to build a less-than-modest, European-style, three-storey house with handsome Romanesque arches along the ground floor. Some luxuries were worthwhile.

Trouble at Mengzi – and a hasty retreat to Hekou

With the completion of these buildings, Henry resumed his Sunday trips into the mountains and was joined in his travels by the French Consul. If it were not for anti-foreign feeling, he would have been contented enough at Mengzi. In June, relations between the French and the Chinese had reached a critical state and military preparations were being made on both sides. That same month, mission houses in Kunming were looted and burned. Soon after, the Empress Dowager issued a declaration of war against the foreign powers in the hope that the Boxers would finally drive them out of China. The Qing army held back while foreign nationals (including Sir Robert Hart) were surrounded in the foreign legation compound in Beijing.

In August, combined Japanese, Russian, British, American and French forces of 20,000 soldiers defeated the Boxers and bombarded the Forbidden City. More than 200 foreigners were killed in the incident. The Empress and her court fled to the city of Xi'an and foreign forces levied a massive indemnity on her government. Though foreign forces preserved the dynasty with the Empress Dowager Cixi as ruler, she had finally brought about the end of 2,000 years of Imperial rule in China. Just 11 years later, the Qing dynasty collapsed and the 5-year-old Emperor Puyi lost his throne to a new republic.

A guard was kept on the Customs House every night. Unlike the situation at Beijing, the Chinese authorities at Mengzi were doing their best to protect the small European population. Henry was determined to stay until he got orders from Sir Robert Hart to leave, though, if the staff of the French Consulate left before them, the situation would become very dangerous indeed. Another quandary was that, if the French did leave, the populace at Mengzi would consider war inevitable and attack them on their way to the border town of Lao Cai.

Communications with Beijing had been cut off. Sir Robert Hart and his staff were surrounded by Boxer Forces in the Foreign Compound, leaving the responsibility of five European staff solely in Henry's hands. Events in Beijing were desperate; it had never been more dangerous to be a Westerner in China, and Henry had his specimens packed up in case of a hasty retreat. By mid July, the affair became so critical that Henry and his staff withdrew and made a perilous journey to the Customs station at Hekou. Almost

ABOVE: *Neolitsea sericea*. This rare member of the laurel family forms a beautiful picture each spring, when young, fawn-coloured growths emerge. It was the very last plant collected by Augustine Henry in China.

all of Yunnan's European population had left the province. In Wuhan, a young missionary lady, whom Henry knew, had been put to death in the most horrible manner.

In August, at his wit's end, Henry sent a letter of resignation to Sir Robert Hart. He had had enough of the Customs Service, the Boxer Rebellion and China; he yearned for the green fields of home. In December, he received news that his resignation had not been accepted, but he was being granted leave on half pay for two years. Henry had no intentions of ever returning to China, however, and, in December, he packed up his possessions and left for Shanghai.

It was on an island in the Yangtze delta that he made his very last collection in China: *Neolitsea sericea*, a rare and beautiful member of the laurel family. It was fitting that Henry's last collection was made at the mouth of the Yangtze; his very first had been made, 15 years earlier, near its banks at Yichang. In Yunnan Province, he and his native plant collectors gathered a staggering 48,910 specimens, bringing his overall collections from China to a grand total of 158,050 specimens. This comprised more than 6,000 distinct species, the largest single collection ever made in China, and included 5 new families, 37 new genera, 1,338 new species, 338 new varieties, 30 new subspecies and 20 new forms – a total of 1,726 discoveries.

On 31 December 1900, Henry left China, never to return – thus ending one of the greatest chapters in the botanical exploration of that country.

Chapter 12

End of an odyssey – Yunnan Province

Women threshing rice near Great Black Mountain (Dahei Shan) in September 2005. Rice is an important crop in southern Yunnan Province and it thrives in the region's mild, damp climate.

Yunnan is situated in south-west China and borders Burma to the west and Laos and Vietnam to the south. The province covers an area of some 394,000 km² (152,123 miles²) and has a population of more than 43 million people. Although accounting for only 4 per cent of China's land area, Yunnan is home to more than 15,000 species of higher plants – about 50 per cent of the total Chinese flora.[1] This rich diversity is represented in tropical, subtropical, temperate and alpine habitats. The terrain has an average altitude of about 2,000 m (6,562 ft), and, in the north-west, the Meili Snow Mountain (Meili Xue Shan) range rises to a staggering 6,740 m (22,112 ft), while the lowest point, a mere 72 m (249 ft) above sea level, occurs on the banks of the Red River near Hekou County.[2] The landscape sinks from north-west to south-east until the river valley lowlands

and tropical plains are met south of Simao District (formerly Cuiyun District), Pu'er Prefecture.

Because of the many complex landforms and altitudinal differences, the region experiences several climatic types. Yunnan's climate is also affected by two monsoon seasons – the South Asian and Indian monsoons – and, under their influence, there are distinct wet and dry seasons. From October to May, warm, dry winds from western Asia result in the dry season. In May, the south-west Indian monsoon and the south-east Asian monsoon bring large amounts of precipitation and the rainy season begins.

ABOVE: The topography of western Yunnan Province is divided by several major river systems, giving rise to massive valleys, wide divides and high ridges. Isolation caused as a result of this terrain has given rise to the evolution of a high number of endemic species and the preservation of several minority ethnic groups. Seen here is the Yangtze in the north-west of the province.

The province borders Tibet in the extreme north-west, but the rest of its northern border is shared with western Sichuan Province. In the latter province, rain and clouds predominate; supposedly, when a Nanzhao prince from Dali visited the Tang court, he told the emperor that his land was south of the rainy weather. The emperor then dubbed the region 'Yunnan', or 'south of the clouds'.[3]

Augustine Henry's collections from southern Yunnan Province were made in several climatic zones. In Hekou, near the Vietnamese border, and in Xishuangbanna, to the east, plants grow in the northern tropical zone. This area is frost free; during the coldest month, temperatures average 15 °C (59 °F) and annual precipitation can reach 1,800 mm (71 in.). Temperature and precipitation, however, vary greatly throughout the province. The annual mean temperature of the Red River valley in central Yunnan is 24 °C (75 °F), while, in Deqin County, in the mountainous north-west, that figure is 4.7 °C (40 °F). Central Yunnan has a mild, temperate climate, and the provincial capital, Kunming, is often called the 'city of eternal spring'. Southern parts of the province bordering with neighbouring south-east Asian countries enjoy a tropical climate, while, on the other extreme, the mountainous north-west can be bitterly cold, and glaciers cover the highest peaks.

The tropics were of limited interest to Augustine Henry. He concentrated his efforts in the southern subtropical zone of the Ailao Mountains (Ailao Shan) and in their foothills, particularly around Mengzi and to the south-east as far as the Daweishan range. Within this zone are higher peaks, which support a large range of warm-temperate plants that occasionally experienced light frosts, and it was this vegetation type that interested Henry most.

Yunnan is home to a staggering number of endemic plants, due to the complexity of its landscape and the continuously rising Tibetan Plateau, which has had a very obvious effect on plant evolution. At the end of the Tertiary and the beginning of the Quaternary periods, continental drift caused the collision of the Indian plate with the Eurasian plate, leading to the Himalayan uplift and the rise of the Tibetan Plateau. The Hengduan Mountains (Hengduan Shanmai) system rose in the north-western part of the province, blocking the advance of glaciation from the north. The ice ages of the Quaternary period had little effect on the flora of Yunnan, and, thus, the province acted

ABOVE: A farm near Mile. Agriculture is a highly intensive business in China, and farms there resemble market gardens of the West. This part of Yunnan Province has a benign climate, and crops may be grown all year around.

as a shelter for many archaic plant groups, particularly ferns. One of the most interesting of these, *Archangiopteris henryi* (a 'living fossil'), was found by Henry's native plant collector near the Vietnamese border.

The flora of Yunnan is complex in its composition, and combines elements from arctic, temperate, subtropical and tropical zones. The regions of Xishuangbanna and Simao in the south-west are tropical, and the flora of these areas is similar to that of Burma, Laos and Thailand. The Daweishan mountain range in Pingbian County is part of a major centre of endemism in south-east Yunnan, and is floristically associated with neighbouring Guangxi Province and Vietnam to the south. The Daweishan range is particularly rich in endemic plants and archaic floristic elements.[4]

The province is irrigated by several major river systems, including the Yangtze, which takes two great hairpin bends in Lijiang County in the north-west and continues its way on an easterly route to Shanghai. The other major rivers – the Red River, the Mekong and the Salween – flow in a parallel north–south direction through massive river valleys less than 100 kilometres apart, and continue their routes through the Indochina peninsula before terminating in the Indian Ocean and the South China Sea.

Adventures in Yunnan – Mile, the Stone Forest, Mengzi

I was a little apprehensive as we made our way towards the departure lounge in Bangkok airport in September 2005. We had arranged to meet Professor Guan Kaiyun, Director of Kunming Botanic Gardens, there, as he was taking the same flight as our group to China. Guan was returning from a conference in Europe. The last time we had met was nine years previously, and I was afraid we would not recognise each other. My fears were unfounded and he was soon introduced to the rest of the group. A few hours later, we were flying over the tropical rainforests of northern Thailand.

On arrival in Kunming, we were greeted by Professor Wang Zhong-lang, who was to be our interpreter and guide over the following three weeks. After an overnight stay in Kunming city, we made our way south-east towards the counties of Lunan and Mile. It was in Lunan that Henry's native plant collector pressed specimens of one of Père Delavay's discoveries, the short-lived, purple-flowered *Corydalis taliensis*. This humble little perennial was named for Tali (now Dali), an historic city in north-west Yunnan Province that was home for many years to both Jean Marie Delavay and George Forrest.

Delavay also discovered *Pistacia weinmanniifolia*, a tree to 20 m (66 ft) tall and bearing glossy pinnate leaves that are bright red on emergence. This tree is common in Yunnan; Henry's native plant collector found it in the Stone Forest (Shilin) in Lunan County (now Shilin Yi Autonomous County), and Henry himself gathered it on

ABOVE: Limestone pillars soar above the surrounding vegetation in the Stone Forest near Lunan. This karst landscape supports a rich and varied local flora. The pyramidal conifers in the background are *Cupressus duclouxiana*.

the Mengzi plain and in the mountains to the west of Simao, near the Burmese border. Over a century later, it is still abundant in the Stone Forest.

Because of its proximity to Kunming, the Stone Forest is popular with tourists, and the place swarmed with Chinese backpackers on the morning of our arrival. To escape the masses, we made our way deeper into a labyrinth of stone pinnacles, and spent most of that day exploring the surrounding flora. The towering stone pillars supported a large number of climbing shrubs, and the most impressive of these had to be massively rampant plants of *Rosa banksiae* var. *normalis*, the wild Banksian rose which is common across much of western and central China. Though long out of flower, *Trachelospermum*

Pistacia weinmanniifolia, a common shrub or small tree in the Stone Forest (Shilin) in Shilin Yi Autonomous County. The pinnate leaves are red on emergence.

Corydalis taliensis, discovered by Delavay near Dali (then Tali) in April 1887; Henry's native plant collector found it again in Lunan County (now Shilin County) nine years later.

As a modern ethnic group, the Yi people may be further categorised into various branches. Pictured here are members of the Sani subgroup, who inhabit the region around Lunan County and the nearby town of Lunan. The traditional costumes are very colourful, but are rarely worn by men today.

Domed-shaped trees of *Albizia mollis* rising above limestone pillars.

A colourful spider in the Stone Forest.

RIGHT: A farmer herding his oxen along a rural trail between Mile and Lunan.

bodinieri proved to be one of the most exciting plants we saw that day. Vigorous plants completely swallowed 20-m (66-ft) tall stone pillars, and were laden with narrow, runner bean-like seedpods up to 25 cm (10 in.) long. Other climbers included *Cuscuta chinensis*, *Sageretia thea*, *Ficus sarmentosa*, *Millettia reticulata*, *Hedera nepalensis* var. *sinensis* (then in flower), *Zanthoxylum cuspidatum*, *Pueraria lobata* and various species of *Dioscorea* and *Ipomoea*.

On the cliff faces, beneath fine trees of *Sapindus delavayi*, were several plants of *Arisaema erubescens*, by then weighed down by heavy spikes of fleshy red seeds. The loquat *Eriobotrya japonica* grew among the stone pillars with other trees, such as *Machilus yunnanensis*, *Malus halliana* and *Celtis biondii*. The latter was discovered by Augustine Henry on the summit of Moji Shan, near Yichang, in February 1887, and, in the Stone Forest, it formed medium-sized trees of a more or less pyramidal habit with long, beautifully pendulous branches. Nearby, the Chinese tallow tree, *Sapium sebiferum*, was sporting the first signs of amber-orange autumn colour.

The most dominant tree in the Stone Forest was *Cupressus duclouxiana*, a beautifully columnar tree with a habit similar to the Italian cypress, *Cupressus sempervirens* 'Stricta'. It is endangered in its native habitat, and old growth trees are extremely rare and mostly restricted to the deep gorges of the great rivers of north-west Yunnan. *Cupressus duclouxiana* was discovered near Kunming by Père Delavay in January 1890, and was named for Père Francois Ducloux, who gathered it in the same area 15 years later. It is tender in Great Britain and Ireland and succeeds best in sheltered coastal gardens.

In the shelter of enormous limestone grykes (or grikes),

Trachelospermum bodinieri is one of the most beautiful climbers in the Stone Forest. The long, bean-like pods are a conspicuous feature in autumn.

283

Left: *Cannabis sativa*. Chinese people were the first ethnic group to cultivate hemp, and it was from hemp that the first true paper was manufactured in China.

Left: *Hibiscus indicus*, a widespread species in southern China. It is common in the Stone Forest.

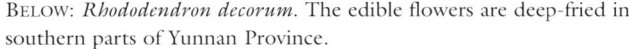

Below: *Rhododendron decorum*. The edible flowers are deep-fried in southern parts of Yunnan Province.

The former French Consulate at Mengzi. Prince Henri d'Orléans stayed here while visiting Mengzi in 1895. It overlooks the lake and the Customs House.

蒙自关历任税务司名录			
姓　　名	国　籍	任　职　时　间	
哈巴安（A. P. HAPPER. JUN）	美国	1889——1893	
柯尔乐（P. A. CARL）	美国	1893——1896	
韩威礼（W. HANCOCK）	英国	1896年	
司必立（W. F. SPINNEY）	美国	1896——1899	
韩尔礼（A. OHENRY）	美国	1899——1900	
狄大顺（O. TIBERO）	意大利	1900——1903	
聂务满（J NUMANN）	德国	1903——1905	

Mengzi's 'Heavenly Emperor' pagoda framed by the brick-red flowers of *Hibiscus rosa-sinensis*. In the background are the bare, rocky mountains that encircle the Mengzi plain.

A wall chart displayed in the Mengzi Customs House. Listed are former Chief Commissioners of Customs. Two Irish names appear; those of William Hancock and Augustine Henry.

Albizia mollis formed spreading, flat-topped trees to about 8 m (26 ft) tall. Beneath it grew *Cannabis sativa*, a common weed in this part of Yunnan. It grew in an unruly thicket with *Hibiscus indicus, Urena lobata, Sida rhombifolia, Commelina communis, Geranium nepalense* var. *thunbergii, Pteris cretica, Amorphophallus rivieri* and wild sugar cane, *Saccharum spontaneum*. After a lunch of *Rhododendron decorum* blossoms (deep-fried in batter), we headed south past Mile to the ancient town of Mengzi, Henry's best-known base in Yunnan.

Pink- and white-flowered *Cosmos bipinnatus*, a Mexican annual now widely naturalised in Yunnan, lined the verges of the motorway to Mengzi, giving a spectacular show. Arriving in Mengzi more than a century after Henry had been based there, we had no idea of the state of preservation of the surrounding vegetation, or what we might possibly see of interest in the town. Few Western botanical expeditions pass that way, preferring instead to head for the temperate forests and alpine slopes further north. Little information was available on the region, apart from brief notes by earlier collectors such as Augustine Henry, Heinrich von Handel-Mazzetti and Ernest Wilson. We did, however, have a complete list of Henry's collections from southern Yunnan Province, which proved to be of great assistance, as did his hand-drawn map indicating the areas where he and his native plant collectors carried out their work.

Mengzi took us by surprise. We were in for a treat, and

I look back on the town as one of the most beautiful places in western China. Dominating the centre of Mengzi was a large lake, and, on its edge, reflecting in the still waters, was a brightly painted classical pagoda. This scene was beautifully framed by an avenue of bright red-flowered trees of *Hibiscus rosa-sinensis*. Mengzi has an idyllic Mediterranean climate, and lies on the edge of a highly cultivated plain surrounded by bare, rocky mountains.

The greatest surprise of all was when we located the old Customs House in which Augustine Henry once worked – and saw his name, and that of William Hancock, included on a list of former staff on a wall plaque inside the building. The Customs House and enclosure we visited was built under Henry's supervision, after the previous building was burned by rioters in June 1899. It was in the same enclosure in September 1899 that E. H. Wilson was greeted by the sight of a wooden cage containing the heads of five of those rioters.

The present Customs House is classically Chinese in style, and sits near the edge of the lake facing the former French Consulate, a beautiful, recently restored, European-style building painted a wonderful ochre-brown colour. Mengzi's street trees included an exotic mix of native and foreign species, such as *Euptelea pleiosperma, Bombax ceiba, Salix babylonica, Ficus elastica, Phoenix canariensis, Caryota urens, Jacaranda mimosifolia* and *Thevetia peruviana*, the yellow oleander from tropical South America.

ABOVE: The Customs House at Mengzi. This building dates from 1899, when it was constructed under Augustine Henry's supervision, following the destruction of the previous building during riots by local rebels.

LEFT: The entrance door to the 'Heavenly Emperor' pagoda at Mengzi, a wonderful example of classical Chinese architecture.

BELOW: A plan of the Customs Service residence at Mengzi. Built at the same time as the present Customs House, Augustine Henry lived in it until abandoning his post in July 1900 during the Boxer Rebellion.

ELEVATION

An old lady grazing her ox on the Mengzi plain. This rural, agrarian area of China exudes a charm now lost in the industrialised eastern provinces.

ABOVE, BELOW: A scene from the Mengzi marketplace in September 2005; everything from medicinal herbs, spices and exotic fruits grown locally on the Mengzi Plain.

Hani girls leaving the marketplace at Mengzi. The Hani are arguably the most colourful of all of Yunnan Province's ethnic groups.

Pomegranates, chestnuts, beans and hen's eggs neatly presented at the Mengzi market.

Great Black Mountain

Mengzi acted as a central base from which we explored the surrounding mountains. One of the first places we visited was Great Black Mountain (in Chinese, the range is called Dahei Shan), which is located a short drive north. We made our way there as the first Western botanical expedition to do so since Henry and Hancock.

There was an element of excitement as we approached Great Black Mountain; it would be interesting to see how the local flora had fared in the passing of a century. The surrounding paddy fields on the plains were a hive of activity, as farmers were busily harvesting and threshing rice, and we were delighted to stumble across a Yi village on the mountainside. Though extremely poor, the little village of Dubi charmed us all, and consisted of mud-walled houses with unpaved streets. Pigs and hens foraged along the main street and tobacco leaves had been draped over wooden fencing to dry in the sun. Dubi was totally untouched by commercialism, and it was as though the place was frozen in time. On our approach, we met oxen drawing carts past orchards full of ripe, bright-orange Chinese persimmons. We were given a great welcome by the villagers.

In the distance, we could hear the chanting of children and so located the local primary school, a small, two-roomed shack near the edge of the village. In that tiny

ABOVE: Dahei Shan (or 'Great Black Mountain', as it was known to Hancock and Henry). In the foreground are harvested rice paddies. Much of the mountain's flora has been stripped, though thickets of interesting plants remain.

A Yi woman with her ox and cart in the little village of Dubi on Great Black Mountain.

ABOVE, BELOW: At Dubi, we stumbled across a little, two-roomed primary school attended by Yi children. Though extremely poor, these youngsters appeared happy. We later sent them a large package of copybooks, colouring books and pencils from Kunming.

A lateral flower spike of *Lobelia seguinii*. Flower colour varies from white, to pink and light blue.

ABOVE: *Oxyspora paniculata*, pictured here both in flower and in fruit. It was one of the prettiest shrubs on Great Black Mountain.

school, we found two classrooms full of delightful little Yi children whose enormous eyes filled with fear on catching their first ever glimpse of Western visitors. This might also have been said of the two teachers, who, once over the initial shock, welcomed us into their tiny staff room and brewed us a pot of green tea over an open fire. The children soon warmed to us, and, before we left, their teachers managed to coax them into singing a traditional Yi song. As we departed to make our way up the mountain, we were given a parting gift of walnuts and the entire village came out to bid us farewell. There are few places in China left as unspoiled as Dubi, and that little village was one of the highlights of our visit to the Mengzi region.

The lower slopes of the mountain were covered by extensive thickets of *Dodonea viscosa*, a pioneering pantropical shrub that is hardy in the milder coastal areas of Great Britain and Ireland. At higher altitudes, *Lobelia seguinii* became a familiar sight by the trackside, where,

from a huge, basal, echium-like rosette, rose a 4.5-m (15-ft) tall spike covered in light-blue spidery flowers.

Much of the mountain's vegetation had been stripped, but thickets of interesting plants remained. Our route took us past a steep slope rich in garden-worthy plants, such as *Abelmoschus moschatus*, *Clerodendrum bungei*, *Thalictrum fortunei*, *Gordonia chrysandra*, *Lyonia ovalifolia*, *Osteomeles anthyllidifolia* and large flowering bushes of *Leucosceptrum canum*, one of the few members of the mint family (Lamiaceae) that does not have square stems. *Alnus nepalensis*, an autumn-flowered alder, gave

Pinus yunnanensis, the common pine of Yunnan Province. A handsome species with long exotic needles usually borne in threes.

a great show and its long, golden-yellow catkins were a colourful and cheery sight. A common shrub on Great Black Mountain was *Oxyspora paniculata*, a dome-shaped evergreen bearing pendulous panicles of small pink blossoms. Of more interest to our group was *Craibiodendron henryi*, a small tree to 10 m (33 ft) tall carrying salmon-coloured new growths.

Craibiodendron henryi, a small tree in the heath family (Ericaceae), whose new growths are flushed salmon-red. It was common in thickets on Great Black Mountain, where it grew with young trees of *Pinus yunnanensis*.

The camellia relative *Gordonia chrysandra*, pictured here on Great Black Mountain. Henry discovered it near Mengzi.

A Buddhist temple on the heavily forested slopes of the Daweishan range in Pingbian Miao Autonomous County (Pingbian County).

South to the Daweishan range in Pingbian County

The following day, we crossed the fertile Mengzi plain and travelled south past plantations of pomegranates, then laden in fruit. Our destination was the Daweishan range where Augustine Henry and his native plant collectors made some of their most remarkable finds. The Daweishan is a major centre of plant endemism in eastern Yunnan Province; to date, 3,994 species have been catalogued from the region, making it one of the most biodiverse areas in all of China.[5] The influence of the Pacific monsoon has also allowed a rich fern layer to evolve, and, at time of writing, 272 species have been recorded there. The reserve also harbours a wealth of rare, endangered and relict plants; 50 plants from this mountain range are listed in China's national list of rare and endangered plant species. Twenty-five mammals and twenty-eight birds from the region are also under national protection, including the black-crested gibbon, the clouded leopard and green peafowl.

Enormous areas of southern Yunnan were deforested during the 20th century, though the Daweishan range has changed little since Henry and his men visited there, and so it gave a very good indication of the sort of terrain they encountered. Because of its enormous biodiversity, the range was listed as a no-felling zone by the Yunnan Provincial Department of Forestry in 1956, and it became a nature conservation zone covering some 154 km² (59 miles²) in 1986. Pingbian and the adjacent Hekou County are home to both the Hani and Miáo ethnic groups.

Pingbian is a plantsman's dream come true, and we found a myriad of wonderful plants there. A rope bridge suspended 30 m (100 ft) above the forest floor gave us a unique vantage point from which to study the forest. On the upper slopes, the forest canopy was dominated by *Lithocarpus pachylepis*, massive trees that towered 50 m (164 ft) overhead. Native to China (south-east Yunnan Province and the Guangxi region) and Vietnam, the large fruits of this handsome tree were scattered on the ground far beneath us. In their boughs grew high-rise, aerial

Suspended high on a rope bridge, we obtained superb views into a forest canopy dominated by the oak relative *Lithocarpus pachylepis*.

gardens full of epiphytic *Aeschynanthus buxifolius* and various species of *Rhododendron* and *Vaccinium*. We had also arrived in time to see great swathes of the glorious *Pleione praecox* in full flower on moss-laden branches and on boulders on the woodland edge.

Beneath the trees were acres of lush *Hedychium yunnanensis*, giving a brilliant show alongside the wonderfully scented *Luculia pinceana*. Tree ferns were abundant; the Sino-Himalayan *Cyathea spinulosa* is just one of a number of species found there, and it grew alongside another relict plant, *Schefflera delavayi*, a fantastic foliage plant with palmate leaves more than 2 m (6.5 ft) long. This exotic fellow gave the forests a prehistoric look, and, alongside the many tree ferns, one almost expected dinosaurs to emerge from beneath the canopy. Another plant in the same family (Araliaceae) that was common there was *Trevesia palmata*, a small, dichotomously branched tree with similarly bold, lush palmate leaves clustered in dense whorls at the end of branches. It is cultivated at the Strybing Arboretum in San Francisco, and should prove hardy in the milder gardens of Great Britain and Ireland.

ABOVE: We found the epiphytic autumn-flowered *Pleione praecox* on moss-covered boulders and high in the boughs of trees. It is one of the most exciting plants on the Daweishan range.

LEFT: *Cyathea spinulosa*, a handsome tree fern that forms part of Daweishan's remarkable relict flora. It is also native to the Himalaya.

BELOW LEFT: *Luculia pinceana*, an evergreen shrub to 2 m (6.5 ft) tall, bearing cymes of white or pink, tubular, intensely fragrant flowers in autumn. Native to India, the Himalaya, China and Vietnam, Henry collected this beautiful shrub here on the Daweishan range in 1896.

Begonias grew with great luxuriance on damp rock faces. Some of these, such as the plant pictured here, were of great horticultural potential. China still has much to offer to our Western gardens.

Schefflera delavayi, discovered by Père Delavay near Dali in September 1889. Henry rediscovered it near Mengzi in 1896, and E. H. Wilson found it again in low-lying valleys in western Sichuan Province in October 1910. In western China, it forms a sparsely branched tree to 8 m (26 ft) tall bearing enormous palmate leaves. It is rare in gardens, but worthy of trial in the mildest coastal counties of Great Britain and Ireland.

Trevesia palmata, a little branched tree to 8 m (26 ft) tall; it gave an exotic air to the forests on the Daweishan range.

Rhododendron arboreum ssp. *delavayi* towered to 14 m (46 ft) overhead, and the groves we saw must have been several centuries old. This fine tree first flowered in cultivation at Kilmacurragh Botanic Gardens in 1904, from a plant sent to Thomas Acton from Kew, and they, in turn, had received plants from Messrs Vilmorin near Paris. Vilmorin's plants were raised from seeds collected by Père Delavay on the Cangshan range – west of Dali, in north-west Yunnan Province – in the autumn of 1883, and his old plant continues to flourish near the Monk's Walk at Kilmacurragh. (In fact, it is in bloom as I write.) On the Daweishan's richly forested slopes, it jostled with other good garden plants, such as *Rubus lineatus*, *Acer cappadocicum*, *Pileostegia viburnoides*, *Actinidia callosa* (which made enormous, 40-m (131-ft) tall vines), *Saurauia nepaulensis* (what an addition this would make in our milder, coastal gardens), *Buddleja yunnanensis* and the witch-hazel relatives *Rhodoleia championii* and *Exbucklandia populnea*.

293

ABOVE: Our group at the frontier town of Hekou. Across the Red River is Lao Cai in Vietnam. In the photograph are, as follows: Seamus O'Brien, Elizabeth Ryan, Paul Gardiner, Assumpta Broomfield and Cathal O'Sullivan.

ABOVE LEFT: *Neocheiropteris palmatopedata*, pictured here on the Daweishan range. Discovered by Augustine Henry in 1896, this fern proved to be a new genus and species.

BELOW LEFT: *Rubus lineatus*. The undersides of leaves are covered with a shining, silky, silvery down. It is occasionally grown in British and Irish gardens.

OPPOSITE: A lush bank of ferns on the Daweishan's mid-forested slopes. The Himalayan monsoon has allowed a large range to thrive here.

Our exploration of the Daweishan range was, alas, a brief one – far too brief and, hopefully, we will return there in the not too distant future. Next, our journey took us further south, where the mountains gave way to rolling hillsides and forests disappeared to be replaced by tapioca, sisal, pineapples, bananas, tea and rubber, all of which formed extensive plantations. Our route took us parallel to the colonial Kunming–Hanoi narrow-gauge railway, built, it is said, to extend French influence into China from her Indochina colonies. It was this railway, more than anything else, that caused such an enormous wave of anti-foreign sentiment and fuelled the Boxer Rebellion in Yunnan. The main physical obstacle in the development of this railway was surmounting the steep ascent from the Red River to the Yunnan plateau. The death rate, during construction, due to fatigue and malaria was appalling: in a single year, more than 5,000 labourers lost their lives.

Hekou was where Henry transferred the Mengzi Customs in June 1900, and he made a number of collections there and across the border in northern Vietnam. Nowadays, Hekou is a busy trading post between the Vietnamese and Chinese. Separated only by the Red River, the gap between the wealth of these two nationalities is astounding. China has made enormous strides in recent years and its economy is booming. Vietnam, on the other hand, has not shared the same rate of progress. A large bridge connects Hekou to Lao Cai, across the border, and that evening we watched a continuous queue of Vietnamese women pushing enormous carts of various goods on modified bicycles across the border – life for some communities is not always easy.

A Vietnamese lady carting goods across the border. A simple concrete bridge across the Red River is all that marks the international boundary between China and neighbouring Vietnam.

ABOVE: Yuanyang lies high in the mist-shrouded southern Ailao Shan range of mountains, and is a major stronghold of the Hani people. Augustine Henry visited this region in January 1897.

Calotropis gigantea was a common shrub in the baking heat of the Red River valley.

Rice terraces and ginger lilies – Yuanyang

Following the course of the Red River, we made our way west towards Yuanyang County, a stronghold of the Hani people and a region still famous for its hillside rice terraces. The flora of the Red River valley is tropical, but we had little time to investigate the area as Yuanyang lay a good day's drive away. By the roadside, tall plants of the scarlet ginger lily *Hedychium coccineum* gave a riotous display with large terminal spikes of fiery orange blossoms. It grew alongside the closely related *Costus speciosus*, an exotic perennial with curious, corkscrew-like stems and with leaves spirally arranged on reed-like stems. At the end of these stems were carried large, shallowly funnel-shaped, white blossoms with yellow-orange centres. Another Red River valley plant that deserves special mention is *Calotropis gigantea*, a bushy shrub to 1.5 m (5 ft) tall bearing large cymes of fleshy white blossoms, which are flushed purple-pink towards the extremity of the petals.

The contrast between Yuanyang County and the baking heat of the Red River valley could not have been greater. The town of Yuanyang (Xinjie, Old Yuanyang) is located north-west of Fengchunling District and lies at a relatively high altitude in the southern Ailao Shan mountains. We arrived late that evening, as a cloud layer enveloped the

ABOVE: A spectacular series of hillside rice terraces. The Yuanyang Hani are famous throughout China for their terracing. By the time of our visit, ginger lilies gave a riotous display on the banks of the higher terraces. (Compare this with Augustine Henry's photograph in Chapter 10 of this book.)

town in a thick, chilly mist. Having donned our fleeces and several layers of heavy clothing, we set out to explore this little-visited mountainous settlement.

We had earlier met a Hani subgroup in the marketplace at Mengzi, and, at Yuanyang, these people were equally conspicuous with their colourfully embroidered, hand-woven costumes. The women of this region still proudly wear their bright traditional garments on a daily basis, though the men, as with most other ethnic groups in Yunnan, have dropped this practice.

One of the most interesting trees around Yuanyang was *Docynia delavayi*, an evergreen tree to 10 m (33 ft) tall. This handsome pear relative was discovered in Yunnan by Père Delavay and is also native to the provinces of Sichuan and Guizhou. E. H. Wilson observed that it was abundant in Yunnan, and that the fresh fruits, known as *tao yi*, were used to ripen persimmons. The fruits of each were arranged in alternate layers in large jars and covered with rice husks. In ten hours, the persimmons were bletted and ready for eating. To the Hani of southern Yunnan, it is the '*qkaqpyuq*', and the bark, leaves and kernels are used by this group to treat diarrhoea and gastroenteritis, and are also applied externally for cuts, sprains and fractures. It was introduced to France in 1890, and first flowered in the UK at the RHS Garden, Wisley, in 1938.

The highest hillsides in this region were forested with the Chinese fir, *Cunninghamia lanceolata*. On the edge of these woods, and on the banks of surrounding rice terraces, grew hundreds of *Hedychium coronarium*, with occasional plants of *Hedychium forrestii* and the scented, yellow-flowered

Hedychium coccineum, one of a number of exotic ginger lilies we encountered during our travels.

297

The most exotic of all Yuanyang's ginger lilies was *Hedychium forrestii*, named for the Scottish plant hunter, George Forrest. It is relatively hardy in cultivation.

Several species of ginger lily were in bloom during our visit to Yuanyang. The most abundant of these was *Hedychium coronarium*. It grew on the edge of rice terraces in hundreds.

We spotted only a single flowering plant of the very lovely *Hedychium chrysoleucum*, on the edge of a glade of *Cunninghamia lanceolata*.

LEFT: The blue shamrock pea, *Parochetus communis*, a prostrate, clover-like perennial grew in rough grass beneath the ginger lilies at Yuanyang. Distributed through Africa and Asia to Java, it is grown in alpine pans at Glasnevin in Ireland and makes an admirable display in a cool Alpine House.

ABOVE: *Schizomussaenda dehiscens*. Augustine Henry found it at Mengzi and Simao. The Hani use it as a traditional medicine to treat cases of bronchitis and laryngitis.

LEFT: *Arundina graminifolia*, the Chinese bamboo orchid, a graceful terrestrial species to 1.5 m (5 ft) tall with grass-like foliage.

Hedychium chrysoleucum. In meadows, the blue pea *Parochetus communis* grew alongside the beautiful little *Torenia violacea*. Yuanyang is famous throughout China for its hillside rice terraces, which have been carved into the landscape by the Hani. These form an amazing and breathtaking part of the surrounding topography. In places, the terraces had just been flooded and planted with the winter rice crop.

From Yuanyang, we travelled south to Luchun County in the Honghe Hani and Yi Autonomous Prefecture. In the mountains grew a handsome Saint John's wort, *Hypericum henryi* ssp. *hancockii*, a prolifically flowered shrub that commemorates the Armagh man, William Hancock. With it grew *Callicarpa bodinieri*, by then covered in masses of tiny violet-coloured berries. Orchids were plentiful, and, in glades beneath deafening colonies of cicadas, the Chinese bamboo orchid *Arundina graminifolia* carried dozens of exotic pink and white blossoms above tall, grass-like foliage. This widespread orchid is distributed from the Himalaya, across Burma, China, Indochina and Malaysia.

Schizomussaenda dehiscens formed a small evergreen tree to 3 m (10 ft) tall, and, at the time of our visit, it bore terminal cymes of tubular golden-yellow flowers surrounded by large, white, leaf-like bracts. *Debregeasia longifolia* is common over much of China; in this region, bushes carried hundreds of pendulous flowering tassels. Another abundant shrub, *Leycesteria gracilis* was a weedy plant lacking the grace and charm of the better-known *Leycesteria formosa*.

Debregeasia longifolia, a common shrub in western China and an obvious member of the nettle family.

The tropical rainforests of Xishuangbanna

On 30 September, after an exhausting all-day drive, we finally reached the tropical rainforests of Xishuangbanna Dai Autonomous Prefecture in Yunnan's deep south. Xishuangbanna is home to the Dai nationality, an ethnic group that has strong ties to other groups in northern Thailand. It is a region of luxuriant tropical rainforest, abundant flora and fauna and charming minority ethnic cultures. Covering less than 0.2 per cent of China's total land area, Xishuangbanna is home to more than 4,000 species of higher plants, and is an oasis on the otherwise desert belt of the Tropic of Cancer.[6]

The tropical rainforests of south-east Asia are one of three major blocks of tropical rainforest on the globe; the others are the forests of Central and South America and those of the Congo Basin in Africa. The tropical rainforests of south-east Asia cover some 250 million hectares (975,000 miles[2]) and are distributed across south-western India, Sri Lanka, Burma, Xishuangbanna in southern China, Hainan, the extreme southern tip of Taiwan, Indochina, the Philippines, Malaysia and Indonesia to Papua New Guinea.

Xishuangbanna lies sandwiched between Burma and Laos, and is drained by the Mekong and its many tributaries. 'Banna', as it is popularly known, is an enormously fertile region and produces quinine, camphor, coffee, cocoa, rubber and fruits, such as bananas, pineapples, mangoes, plantain and cashew. Located on the southern side of the Hengduan

ABOVE: Tropical rainforest in Xishuangbanna, with wild bananas framed by a massively buttressed tree of *Bombax ceiba*, the red silk cotton tree. Tropical rainforest is the oldest ecosystem on this planet, and Xishuangbanna is the most northerly occurring in the world.

Mountains, Xishuangbanna is sheltered by the Ailao and Wuliang Shan mountains to the north, and they allow thick fogs to build up in the rainy monsoon season. It is thanks to this geological incident that Banna possesses the environmental conditions that sustain the most northerly tropical rainforests in the world, a habitat at its latitudinal and altitudinal limits. Many areas of the globe near the Tropic of Cancer are covered by deserts, but Xishuangbanna, which is located at the same latitude, has avoided this fate.

Mainland China's only tropical rainforest is contained within five large nature reserves that cover 12 per cent of Xishuangbanna Dai Autonomous Prefecture. Tropical rainforests are the oldest and most fragile ecosystems on earth. Some 70 per cent of the world's tropical rainforests are said to have disappeared, due to human activities and climate change, and Xishuangbanna's forest cover fell from 60 per cent, in 1960, to just 34 per cent, in 1995. Following millions of years of evolution, tropical rainforests build up their own specific microclimates. Once the forest cover is removed, a drier climate is created, which, in many cases, will not allow the regeneration of tropical forest. This situation

A Dai village in Xishuangbanna; its architecture reflects that of nearby Thailand.

Young Dai monks playing cards in a Buddhist temple in southern Xishuangbanna.

can be seen in the savanna–forest boundary in tropical Africa.

Xishuangbanna has a typical tropical monsoon climate, with an annual mean temperature of 22 °C (72 °F), and annual precipitation may be as high as 1,556 mm (61 in.), of which more than 80 per cent falls during the rainy season between May and the end of October. The dry season lasts from November to the end of April, but is partly compensated for by damp fogs that descend over the entire region.

Despite being rather fragmented, these forests are still an important habitat. The region is home to 762 animal species, many of which, such as the Asian elephant, wild ox, tiger, leopard, red panda and the white-cheeked gibbon, are under state protection. Despite the intervention of CITES, China still faces the problem of dealing with illegal cross-border trade of wildlife products from tropical rainforest regions between Burma, Vietnam, Laos and Cambodia. These include tiger claw pendants, trophies such as elephant tusks, tiger skins or tropical orchids and other medicinal plants.

The Asian elephant, whose ancestors originated in Africa, once ranged from modern Iraq to the Yellow River in China, but, nowadays, is restricted to a region from India to Vietnam. Asian elephants are threatened more by habitat destruction than by poaching. Clearing of tropical forests for agriculture has cut off traditional seasonal movements, and has created conflicts between elephants and farmers. Elephant numbers in southern Yunnan Province dropped to about 150 in 1970. Today, due to conservation work, it is estimated that there are 16 to 18 herds, or about 170 to 180 wild elephants, roaming the mountain valleys, forests, and grasslands of Xishuangbanna. Three drifting herds of 24 elephants have been reported as far north as Simao, Pu'er Prefecture. However, some of these are not reproducing, since a disruption in the ecological corridor they once used to reach Simao means females have no contact with bull elephants. The Xishuangbanna herds account for 80 per cent of China's wild elephant population.

An amazing 700 species of butterfly inhabit the forests and tropical grasslands of the region, accounting for 70 per cent of China's total. Fourteen aboriginal groups call the area their home. These ethnic minority populations all have a long history of living harmoniously with the surrounding forests and possess a rich knowledge on biodiversity utilisation. These abundant resources vary from timber and firewood to wild vegetables, wild fruits, herbal medicines, fibres, rattan, oils, waxes, tannins and game. Human interaction with the surrounding forests includes shifting cultivation (still practiced by Hani, Yao and Yi hill tribes) and religiously motivated protection of designated forest areas and of certain individual species.

The Dai are by far the largest group, accounting for 35 per cent of the local population. They have engaged in agriculture for more than 2,000 years. The local Dai philosophy reveres nature, and certain areas are designated as 'holy hills' and are retained in a semi-natural state, effectively acting as small, traditional, nature reserves. The 'holy hill' forests of the Dai are considered to be the homes of gods, and this can be traced back to their ancient polytheistic beliefs before the arrival of Buddhism in the middle of the Tang Dynasty. Both religions are sympathetic to the conservation of plants. Violence against plants and animals on these holy hills risks divine punishment. More than 250 hills are distributed throughout tropical Xishuangbanna, protecting an estimated 1,500 ha (3,700 acres). Their diversity is said to be as high as that in government reserves, and they contain Red List species such as *Homalium laoticum* and *Magnolia henryi*.

Xishuangbanna Tropical Botanic Garden and Simao

Our base for the next few days was Menglun, a small town near the Laos border. There, we stayed in the Xishuangbanna Tropical Botanic Garden, which is administered by the Chinese Academy of Sciences. The garden lies on an island on the Luosuo River (a branch of the Mekong), and was established by the famous Chinese botanist, the late Professor Cai Xitao in 1959.

Over the past 50 years, this garden has played an important role in the research of tropical botany, forest ecology, conservation and public education. Spanning an area of some 900 ha (2,224 acres), the garden houses a living collection of 10,000 tropical and subtropical plants, the richest plant collection in all of China, and it also contains an area of primary tropical rainforest.

It is strange that what is probably the best botanic garden in China should be located in one of the most remote corners of the country. The collection was impressive: well maintained and labelled, and the entire garden was beautifully planted and laid out. Our hotel was located in the centre of the garden, with a large swimming pool surrounded by palm trees such as *Roystonea regia*, *Caryota urens* and an enormous traveller's palm, *Ravenalia madagascariensis*. Plant exploration at its leisurely best, we thought – I found myself questioning why there was no swimming pool at Glasnevin!

ABOVE: Xishuangbanna Tropical Botanic Garden is one of the finest properties administered by the Chinese Academy of Sciences, and has the largest plant collection of any garden in China. In the pool are the large floating pads of the South American *Victoria cruziana*.

The gardens gave a good introduction to what we were likely to see in the surrounding tropical rainforest over the following days. My notebook was soon crammed with the names of unfamiliar trees and shrubs. I was particularly impressed with the collection of ginger relatives (Zingiberaceae), which grew beneath a canopy of exotic trees such as *Litsea dillenifolia*, a 15-m (49-ft) tall tree with narrow lanceolate leaves to 60 cm (2 ft) long. The endemic *Vatica xishuangbannaensis* also formed fine trees, and other gargantuan rainforest trees included *Anthocephalus chinensis*, *Pometia tomentosa* and the spectacular *Erythrina macrosperma*.

The orchid collection was equally remarkable, and flourished outdoors beneath the forest canopy in benign conditions. The most beautiful of these orchids were the many flowering plants of the scented, orange-yellow, epiphytic *Dendrobium chrysanthum*, whose pendulous floral sprays lit up the dark, humid rainforest.

Our group beneath an enormous rainforest tree of *Bombax ceiba*, in the reserve belonging to Xishuangbanna Tropical Botanic Garden.

What an exotic setting. The giant Amazonian waterlily, *Victoria cruziana*, flourished outside in a garden pool and performed every bit as well as the cosseted plants at Kew and Glasnevin. Exotics such as *Crinum asiaticum* var. *sinicum*, *Alpinia purpurea*, *Clerodendrum japonicum* and *Heliconia psittacorum* sported bold, brash colours, the likes of which are only found in the tropics.

In the tropical rainforest reserve near the gardens, we spent a magical day in unspoilt primeval rainforest. The forest canopy provided a welcome relief from the intense baking heat in the open, and, yet again, we were left in awe and humbled by ancient, enormous tropical trees such as *Shorea chinensis* and the massively buttressed trunks of *Pterospermum menglunense*. Most impressive of all had to be the colossal trees of *Bombax ceiba*, the red cotton tree that Henry collected in nearby Simao. In spring, this tree presents a magnificent sight when it is covered with masses of short-lived, waxy, red flowers. It is native from India to Malaysia and the from the Philippines south to Australia. The flowers are used in Chinese herbal medicine while the fruit capsule furnishes a type of cotton, which, in 19th-century China, was used for stuffing pillows. In Burma, the flowers are relished as a kind of vegetable curry.

Rambling their way through these towering giants were massive vines with stems as thick as a man's waist. What a rich and exotic assemblage: screw pines (*Pandanus furcatus*), strangler figs, wild bananas and giant lianas. My

BELOW: The bat plant, *Tacca chantrieri*, was common on the edge of the rainforest, and was one of the most exciting plants we were to encounter in Xishuangbanna. Augustine Henry collected this spectacular perennial near Simao.

ABOVE: *Dendrobium chrysanthum*, a spectacular epiphytic orchid that was common on the trunks of trees, from where it lit up the dark, gloomy rainforest.

favourite plant from Xishuangbanna, however, had to be *Tacca chantrieri* – the 'devil flower', 'bat plant' or 'cat's whiskers' – a spectacular perennial carrying a terminal inflorescence of purple-black tubular flowers held within a rather sinister-looking, black, hood-like bract. Distributed in Cambodia, Laos, Thailand, Vietnam and southern China, we found the 'bat plant' abundant on the forest edge. In China, it is known as 'tiger's paws' because of the flower's slender, pendulous, whisker-like bracteoles. The poisonous rhizomes are used in traditional Chinese herbal medicine. The Hani people of Xishuangbanna call this plant the '*beepavqnav*', and use the roots, leaves and stems to treat cases of dysentery, indigestion, hepatitis and lung infections.

Xishuangbanna is famous for its abundance of medicinal plants, and this is one of the reasons why the region is protected from the forester's axe. Ethnobotanists have come to realise that ethnic groups and aboriginal races possess an uncanny ability to recognise diversity, even within a single species. Characteristics that cannot be distinguished by trained botanists are very often used by forests dwellers to differentiate local variants, strains, races and ecotypes of edible and medicinal plants.[7] These ecotypes are extremely local strains with important characteristics, such as resistance to cold and disease, tolerance of drought or they may be variants that mature at different times during the growing season. These characteristics may prove highly desirable in future breeding programmes. Ethnobotanists from Kunming and Menglun have spent many years documenting which plants are important to Yunnan's ethnic groups, and have sifted through immense repositories of folk beliefs for plants that may serve the needs of China's massive population. Not before time – on a worldwide scale, it is thought that the current rate of destruction of biological and cultural diversity, particularly in the tropical regions, will rob us of the accumulated wisdom of a thousand years in a single generation. Therefore, it is vital that regions with such amazing biodiversity, such as Shennongjia, the Daweishan range and Xishuangbanna, have their populations of wild fibre, edible and medicinal plants preserved, thus conserving important plant populations with as large a genetic pool as possible.

From the tropical rainforests of Xishuangbanna, we drove north to Simao, the historic city, where, on 24 September 1899, 23-year-old Ernest Henry Wilson arrived to obtain details of the location of the elusive handkerchief tree from Augustine Henry. One-hundred-and-six years later, following three magical trips that brought us across much of China, we finally achieved our goal of retracing Augustine Henry's footsteps in China. Simao was our very last destination, and, just as Reginald Farrer's 'rainbow bridge' set at Yichang, so did ours at Simao, as we stood on a hillside overlooking this modern, uninspiring yet historic town.

Below us lay the town in which Henry had once lived, and from where Ernest Wilson had launched his brilliant plant-hunting career in China. Little did that young Englishman know of the adventures that lay ahead of him, or the fame it would bring his way. Few botanical parties come this way, even today, and it was a fitting end to our journey. Our travels in Augustine Henry's footsteps were finally over – what an adventure.

BELOW: Simao lies on an elevated plain and is completely surrounded by mountains. Though little visited by Western botanists and horticulturists, it remains one of the most famous cities in the history of European botanical exploration in China. It was at Simao that our travels in Henry's footsteps ended and we reached our 'rainbow bridge'.

Chapter 13

Henry the forester

Henry's journey home from Shanghai took him to an equally exotic location – India. His sister Mary, who had travelled with Caroline to Colorado, had planned to arrive there in early March with her husband Stewart Crum, who was returning from the Boer War in South Africa.

Henry arrived in Sri Lanka in early February and initially based himself on a tea plantation near Kandy. While waiting for Mary, he spent most of his time exploring the higher mountains, where, very naturally, he took time to study the local flora. The aspect of the vegetation was like that of Simao. Many of the genera – for example, *Gordonia*, *Symplocos* and *Vaccinium* – he recognised immediately, but of course the species differed. He visited Sri Pada (Adam's Peak), a lofty, 2,243-m (7,359-ft) high, cone-shaped mountain located in the southern reaches of the central

Larch and lodgepole pine on Turlough Hill in the windswept Wicklow Mountains of south-east Ireland. Augustine Henry advocated the use of fast-growing foreign conifers such as these. In Ireland, he is remembered as the 'founding father of Irish forestry'.

highlands. The mountain's name, Sri Pada, is derived from Sanskrit and roughly translates as 'the sacred foot'. This refers to a famous footprint embedded in rock on the summit, which, according to traditional lore, is that of Buddha. Other traditions assert it belongs to Adam, who left it on the mountain by his first entrance to the world. However the print appeared, the mountain was, and still is, revered by Buddhists, Hindus and, to a lesser extent, by Jews, Muslims and Christians.

Like Emei Shan in China, Sri Pada was a place of pilgrimage, and the summit could only be reached on foot by following a

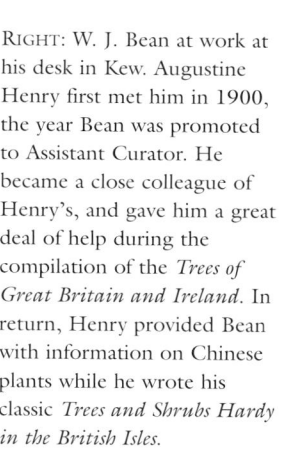

RIGHT: W. J. Bean at work at his desk in Kew. Augustine Henry first met him in 1900, the year Bean was promoted to Assistant Curator. He became a close colleague of Henry's, and gave him a great deal of help during the compilation of the *Trees of Great Britain and Ireland*. In return, Henry provided Bean with information on Chinese plants while he wrote his classic *Trees and Shrubs Hardy in the British Isles*.

variety of routes up thousands of steps. Monks lived in a monastery midway up the mountain, and they guarded a shrine that sheltered the famous footstep on the summit. Henry reached the top of the mountain after hiking 34 km (21 miles), and returned the same distance the next day. It was a spectacular spot; the mountain rose high above the surrounding jungle-covered plains and low-lying hills. Rhododendrons formed forests at this point, and, when in bloom, it seemed as though the peak was strewn with vermilion.

From Sri Lanka, Henry travelled on to the Nilgiri Hills in southern India, where Stewart and Mary Crum had a coffee plantation. His stay there was brief, however, as Henry was keen to get back to Europe, and first made his way to England. In London, he based himself near Kew, where he spent the following year working on his Chinese collections. There, he befriended the new Assistant Curator, William Jackson Bean, a great authority on hardy trees and shrubs. Bean's most notable publication, *Trees and Shrubs Hardy in the British Isles*, was first published in 1914. It is still available today, and, for many, it is the 'bible' of woody plants cultivated in British and Irish gardens. Both Bean and Henry learned much from each other during that year at Kew, and, in later years, Henry gave him much help when he was writing up his notes on new trees and shrubs from China.

The year at Kew also allowed Henry to plan ahead for the future. He had returned from China a little at odds about what best to do with the rest of his life. One thing was certain: whatever path he might follow, it would be for the benefit of Ireland. It gradually occurred to him that forestry might be an option. He had an interest in the subject, and in Britain and Ireland, unlike continental Europe, it was practically an unknown science.

In 1900, Ireland was the least forested country in Europe. Remnant pockets of ancient woodland survived here and there, and many of the great estates had been densely planted by enthusiastic landlords during the 18th and 19th centuries. Despite this planting, just 1.5 per cent of Ireland remained wooded. Thus, forestry became a new interest and Henry determined that, if he was going to be of use to Ireland, then it would be through forestry and the establishment of great forest reserves. Throughout his travels in China, he had often despaired to see how rapidly areas were becoming deforested. It saddened him to see ancient forests felled, and, in a letter to Evelyn Gleeson, he had the following to say:

The calm way in which man expirates animals and ruins forests annoys me. Man is an uncanny beast, he wants the earth. The necessity that will always exist for timber will however necessitate in the future great forest reservations in countries where forests can thrive. So there is hope. A forest is the finest thing in the world, it is the expression of nature in its highest form, it is so full of beauty and variety.[1]

Forestry was only beginning to make headway as a science in Britain and Ireland, and most of the books published on the subject were based on continental experience, which was far from applicable to the very different conditions of climate, soil, labour and market that existed on the two neighbouring islands.

Arthur K. Bulley with his wife Harriet. As a result of Henry's visit to Ness, Bulley employed George Forrest and Frank Kingdon Ward to collect for him in China.

Bulley and the great plant hunters

It was in the autumn of 1901, while returning to London from Ireland, that Augustine Henry paid a visit to Arthur K. Bulley. Bulley had just built a new house at Ness, on the western side of the Wirral Peninsula in rural Cheshire, England. Henry liked Bulley and his wife, Harriet. The couple planned to open a commercial nursery and seed shop (Bees Ltd) in the near future, and Henry provided Bulley with scores of ideas.

The most appealing of these was his suggestion to hire a man to collect plants in China. Henry was quick to remind the Liverpool businessman of how well Wilson's work was progressing in central China, and the benefits that the Veitch firm would reap. North-west Yunnan Province, Henry prompted, was virtually untouched and a great number of hardy and very beautiful plants remained to be introduced. 'Send a man to Tengchong' was his advice. Henry had once hoped to be based there himself, in the newly opened Customs House, but those plans never

materialised. Nevertheless, he assured Bulley it would be a perfect base for plant hunting and the district was easy to access from British-controlled Burma.

The result of Henry's visit to Ness was that Bulley was later to employ George Forrest (1873–1932), a young herbarium assistant at the Royal Botanic Garden, Edinburgh, to collect plants for him in China. One of the most dedicated and successful plant hunters of all time, Forrest mounted seven expeditions, mainly in Yunnan, between 1904 and 1932 and introduced a rich harvest of new, ornamental plants, especially *Rhododendron* and *Primula*. Just as Wilson was to introduce Henry's finest discoveries from Hubei and Sichuan provinces, Forrest sent seeds of many of Delavay's plants, but also discovered many himself.

Forrest was not Bulley's only man in the field. In 1911,

Bulley's first recruit, the great Scottish plant hunter, George Forrest. He is pictured here in a moon gate at his base in Dali in north-west Yunnan Province.

he sponsored Captain Frank Kingdon Ward (1885–1958) to collect for him, too, in Yunnan Province, thus kick-starting another brilliant career, and, from 1913 to 1916, Roland Edgar Cooper (1890–1962) explored parts of Bhutan and Sikkim sending back large consignments for Bees Ltd. Cooper, though less well known than Forrest and Kingdon Ward, discovered many new garden plants, including the wonderfully red-striped *Rhododendron rhabdotum* from Bhutan.

Henry followed the pursuits of all these men with great interest and was permanently on hand to provide help. Always a great letter writer, he wrote to George Forrest on at least one occasion during his first expedition to China to offer help and support.[2] Forrest worried that his was not exactly a virgin field, and that earlier collectors would be remembered as the real pioneers. In November 1913, he confided to his new sponsor, J. C. Williams:

I have always the intense longing to get into an entirely new area; a sort of new world where everything was new [...] to have such an opportunity as had Delavay or Henry.[3]

Forrest need not have worried. His name ranks alongside those of Delavay, Henry and Wilson as one of the greatest plant hunters of all time.

Augustine Henry continued to press the case for the exploration of China. In March 1902, he was guest of honour at a dinner of the Horticultural Club in London. Sir William Thiselton-Dyer proposed Henry's health in 'a capital speech', and, according to the *Gardeners' Chronicle*, Henry's speech, too, was outstanding. Once again, he pointed out that vast areas of China remained to be explored, stating that he had been the wrong person to take on the task and that his education had not prepared him for botanical work, 'an extensive knowledge of ancient Greece [...] being of no aid whatever'. He hoped that the Royal Horticultural Society would finance such an expedition, asserting that there still were many hardy plants that would excel anything yet introduced. Wilson returned to England in April 1902 with an enormous collection of seeds and bulbs. Harry Veitch was so pleased with the results that he sent him on a second, two-year expedition from 1903 to 1905.

In October 1902, Augustine Henry moved to Nancy, France, where he enrolled in the national school of forestry (École nationale forestière de Nancy). The subject had been grossly neglected in Britain and Ireland for centuries, but France and Germany were world leaders, and the course at Nancy was considered to be the best in Europe. Lessons

were in French, and Henry was keen to see how their forests were managed under the French Forest Service. Forests, he claimed, were not the affair of one generation, and forestry should be managed through state care. About this time, the British Government was buying back land from Anglo-Irish landlords, and many of the great Irish estates were soon to be broken up. Henry hoped that much of the mountainous uplands and bogs from this sale would be retained in state ownership for forestry purposes, rather than handing it back to small farmers who could do little or nothing with it. In France, all the very poor land was in state ownership, and the forests that had been planted over these regions were a commercial success. Ireland could do the same.

Captain Frank Kingdon Ward, the longest-serving professional plant hunter in the field. He began his career with Bulley in 1911, and is particularly famous for his explorations in south-east Tibet.

Augustine Henry with his co-author Henry J. Elwes. Over the course of ten years, they produced the seven-volumed *Trees of Great Britain and Ireland*. It remains, to this day, a classic; an accurate and authoritative work and a beautiful guide to trees.

The Trees of Great Britain and Ireland

In April 1903, Henry had a visit from the renowned English author and dendrologist, Henry John Elwes (1846–1922), a wealthy landowner from Colesbourne Park in Gloucestershire. Henry first met him in July 1901 at the Horticultural Society's Lily Show, where he was chairman during Henry's lecture on Chinese lilies. A passionate naturalist and a tireless traveller, Elwes visited the Middle East, Russia, the Himalaya, Tibet, China, Taiwan, Japan, North America, Mexico and Chile over the course of his 76 years. In those distant regions, he collected insects, birds and plants, and went big game hunting. Many of the trophies from these hunts adorned the walls of his house on the immense Colesbourne Estate.

Elwes was born with abundant energy and his lifetime of expeditions greatly increased the present-day knowledge within various branches of ornithology, entomology and botany, and his contribution to horticulture and forestry cannot be underestimated. In 1870, having read *Himalayan Journals*, he travelled to India to follow in the footsteps of Sir Joseph Dalton Hooker's famous 1849 expedition through Sikkim, and even made the same daring – and unauthorised – incursion into Tibet that Hooker had carried out more than two decades previously.

Two birds were named from his Sikkim adventure. In the lower valleys, he discovered Elwes' crake, *Amaurornis bicolor*, while, close to the Kongra Lama Pass, he found the high-altitude *Otocoris elwesii*, better known as Elwes' horned lark.[4] He made frequent return visits to the

ABOVE: In the winter of 1901–2, Elwes travelled through the temperate rainforests of southern Chile. There, he studied native trees, such as the Chile pine or the monkey-puzzle *Araucaria araucana*, pictured here at Conguillío in the Chilean Lake District. From the Andes of Chile, he introduced many new plants, including the deciduous southern beech *Nothofagus obliqua*.

Himalaya, all for the purpose of scientific exploration. No fewer than 15 species of butterfly commemorate his name, and his plant collections from around the world yielded a number of new plants, most notably the lovely *Galanthus elwesii* from Asia Minor. As Augustine Henry was to point out, many years later, almost every country Elwes visited yielded a new plant. For example, in 1874, he found six new species of *Crocus* in Asia Minor, and, while exploring Taiwan, he discovered *Tricyrtis formosana* var. *stolonifera*.

On inheriting the Colesbourne Estate in 1891, Elwes began to create a garden of great renown. As a gardener, his generosity was said to be overwhelming. Despite its trying soils and climate, Colesbourne became noted for its collection of bulbs (at one time, the largest in the world) and succulents, and the grounds were planted with many rare trees, shrubs and perennials gathered on his numerous expeditions. Although a keen horticulturist, Elwes never acquired a technical knowledge of botany. One of his greatest works, the *Monograph of the Genus Lilium*, appeared in 1880, but the scientific descriptions were the work of the Kew botanist, John Gilbert Baker (1834–1920).

311

ABOVE: The title page of *The Trees of Great Britain and Ireland*.

ABOVE RIGHT: A 2,000-year-old tree of *Ginkgo biloba* by a temple near Chongqing in central China. The photograph was taken by Henry's friend Mrs Archibald Little, and featured in *The Trees of Great Britain and Ireland*.

BELOW RIGHT: The Rocky Mountain fir, *Abies lasiocarpa*, in its native Montana. Elwes and Henry spared no effort in obtaining the very best images of trees, both in cultivation and in their native habitats.

BELOW: The seven-volumed *Trees of Great Britain and Ireland*. These copies, now at Glasnevin, once belonged to Lord Barrymore, a friend of Elwes and Henry. Barrymore created one of the finest arboretums in Europe at Fota in County Cork.

Elwes' love of trees developed late in life; it was not until 1888, while travelling through Mexico and California, that his interest began. A turning point occurred in 1900, when he visited the Drina Valley in Bosnia to see *Picea omorika*, and, in the winter of 1901–2, he visited southern Chile, where he travelled through great forests of *Araucaria araucana* and collected seeds of many of the southern beeches, including *Nothofagus obliqua*, which he introduced to cultivation. Fine trees of the latter, raised from Elwes' seeds, still grow at Kew and Glasnevin.

The reason Elwes had travelled to France was to discuss a project with Augustine Henry. He proposed publishing an authoritative work on trees that grew, or would grow, in the gardens and arboreta of Britain and Ireland, with reference to their native countries and their forestry value. The work was to be illustrated with good-quality photographs and would necessitate visits to the trees in their native habitats. Elwes was not prepared to take on such work on his own, and Henry, with his expert knowledge of trees and botany, would act as a perfect co-author.

Henry needed little time to think the matter over. He had gathered enough theoretical knowledge on forestry by then, and needed to supplement this with practical experience, which he could only get through visiting different places where forestry was being carried out. Henry Elwes was prepared to finance the entire project, and so research began for their classic work, *The Trees of Great Britain and Ireland*.

The seven volumes appeared, one by one, between 1906 and 1913, and remain, to this day, as the most remarkable books on trees that have ever been published. The purely botanical parts were entirely the work of Augustine Henry, but the pages dealing with distribution, history and cultivation were divided in varying proportions between the two authors, the share of each being shown by his initials.

Printed on 2,022 pages of heavy, creamy paper, the volumes were illustrated with 414 superb black-and-white photographs of trees either in cultivation or in their native habitats. The completion of the work required more than ten years of strenuous labour from the two authors, and, during its compilation, Elwes and Henry visited every notable arboretum in Britain and Ireland. Elwes maintained that they wore out two cars driving the length and breadth of both islands.

Based on their travels through every country in Europe, through nearly all the states of North America, Canada, Japan, China, India, western Siberia, Mexico and Chile, Elwes and Henry could assert that Britain and Ireland contained a greater number of fine trees from the temperate regions of the world than any other country. While many of the historic trees of England and Scotland had previously been scattered in various publications, those from Ireland had been almost

Augustine Henry photographed, in the summer of 1904, beneath a common alder, *Alnus glutinosa*, in the 18th-century Deer Park at Kilmacurragh in County Wicklow. Henry and Elwes worked frantically during this time to visit every major tree collection in Great Britain and Ireland. Many of the trees they recorded at Kilmacurragh still exist.

totally neglected. Augustine Henry therefore paid special attention to the trees of his homeland, and Elwes too was well acquainted with Ireland and was a close personal friend of Sir Frederick Moore, Director of Glasnevin Botanic Gardens. Irish estates were full of fine trees, particularly places like Castlewellan, Fota, Glasnevin, Kilmacurragh, Mount Usher and Powerscourt. The tree measurements were carried out by the authors themselves, and, since many of these trees still exist today, their records are all the more interesting.

The end result was widely acclaimed by dendrologists and horticulturists. Ellen Willmott was so impressed that she purchased three sets of volumes. Most subscribers were universities, botanic gardens, aristocratic landowners and wealthy gardeners. Henry's friend Lord Kesteven, whom he had first met in Yichang, also purchased a copy, as did his friend in Paris, Maurice de Vilmorin. *The Trees*, as it became known, was the first completely accurate account of trees that could be grown in Britain and Ireland. The volumes contained a wealth of knowledge on many of the new introductions from around the world, and Henry was well placed to describe in detail the many new Chinese trees entering the trade from Veitch's Coombe Wood nursery, where E. H. Wilson's collections from Hubei and Sichuan provinces were being raised and distributed.

The last major publication on trees was John Claudius Loudon's *Arboretum et Fruticetum Britannicum* (1838), a catalogue of woody plants that had been cultivated in Britain. *The Trees* attempted much more, and was based on first-hand practical knowledge. It makes, even today, a fascinating read and is every bit as useful as when it first appeared a century ago. Only 300 copies of the *Trees of Great Britain and Ireland* were ever printed and sets fetch huge sums at auction today. Augustine Henry's personal copy, full of annotations and news cuttings about trees, is housed in the rare book room at the National Botanic Gardens, Glasnevin.

Sir Frederick and Phylis, Lady Moore. Sir Frederick brought Glasnevin to the pinnacle of its fame, and he and Lady Moore were close friends of Augustine Henry.

Following his meeting with Augustine Henry in August 1903, David Fairchild decided to send collectors to China. The first he was to employ was Frank Nicholas Meyer.

David Fairchild and the American plant hunters

In August 1903, when Henry had returned from France and based himself in the Cambridge Cottage at Kew to begin work on *The Trees of Great Britain and Ireland*, he met with the American plant collector, David Fairchild. In 1900, while on a visit to China, Fairchild had got in touch with Henry to enquire about economic plants in China. As head of the plant introduction department of the United States Department of Agriculture (USDA), Fairchild was responsible for introducing new cereals, vegetables and fruits into the USA and he was keen to get Henry's advice on potential new crop plants that might be transplanted to North America. Henry replied, sending him a copy of his *Notes on Economic Botany of China*.

In his letter, Fairchild asked Henry how the USDA could procure seeds and plants from the interior of China. Henry's advice was simple: 'Don't waste money on postage – send a man'. Those words of wisdom made a deep impression on the American plant collector, and had a great influence on his policy when he returned to the USA. Largely on this advice, Fairchild inaugurated an exploration of China.[5]

Augustine Henry's role in having plant hunters sent to China cannot be underestimated, and it was fortunate that

he was based in London while Fairchild was visiting England. Fairchild had the following to say of their meeting:

Doctor Augustine Henry, the great authority on Chinese plants, had returned to England and was living near Kew Gardens. He was a fascinating person, rather small in stature, with the nervous manner which I have often noticed in scientific explorers who are more accustomed to plants than people. He received me most cordially and helped me to fill one of my notebooks with information, even writing in it many Chinese characters and notes of his own […] My main object in calling on Doctor Henry had been to discuss exploration in China. I asked him whether he would consider a proposition to return there. He replied that Professor Sargent had already offered him a thousand pounds a year and his expenses if he would go back and collect for the Arnold Arboretum, but that he had written saying that he was tired of China and did not want to return. He was, however, most enthusiastic about the possibilities of the western provinces, particularly Yunnan and Szechwan. He declared that these provinces 'are immense plains irrigated by many rivers; seven crops a year are raised'. Doctor Henry also told me of wild pear and peach varieties, hardy bamboos, 80 species of the genus rubus to which the blackberry and raspberry belong, and a persimmon in Peking, which the dealers ripen by puncturing the skin with a small stick to let in the air [...]

The industry of this unusual man was evident by a manuscript of his which he showed me – a dictionary containing 20,000 Chinese names of plants, including references from the principal Chinese botanical books. Moreover, he told me he was working on a dictionary of the Lolo language, the Lolos being a simple, independent people living in the interior of China, about whom little was known.

That afternoon spent with Doctor Henry had far-reaching results. The information which he gave me made a great impression on me, and subsequently, when I was directing the plans and policy of the Office, it determined me to send explorers into China.[6]

The man chosen by Fairchild was the Dutch-born Frank N. Meyer (1875–1918). It was David Fairchild who first saw the potential in Meyer as a plant collector, and asked him to travel to East Asia in search of crop plants. Over the course of four expeditions, between 1905 and 1918, he send back to the USA about 2,500 plant introductions, including notable crops such as soybean, many types of cereal, fruits, vegetables, fodder crops, wind-break trees, bamboo shoots, bean sprouts and water chestnuts. On reaching Yichang in 1917, during his final expedition to China, Meyer remarked to Fairchild, 'I am now on *Terra Sancta*. Mr Wilson and Dr Henry had Ichang as headquarters for many years. I feel like a Christian in Palestine or a Mohammedan in Mecca'.

Meyer proved himself to be a hardworking plant hunter of simple means. His very last letter, written to Fairchild, was from Yichang. In June 1918, Meyer drowned in the Yangtze while travelling on a steamer plying its route from the Hankow district of Wuhan to Shanghai. His body was found in the river a few days later, a sad and pathetic end for such a passionate collector of plants. No evidence of foul play was ever found and the events of his death and drowning remain a mystery to this day. He lies buried in Shanghai.

Meyer was not Fairchild's only collector in China. In 1922, he sent Joseph Rock (1884–1962) to Yunnan Province, and, for the next 27 years, Rock continued to explore vast areas of western China before he was finally forced to leave by the communist army.

In England, Henry became a regular garden visitor. He was a great friend of Ellen Willmott, who gardened at Warley Place in Essex, and of his fellow countryman William

Kilmacurragh House in County Wicklow. The handsome Queen Anne house was designed by the famous Irish architect Sir William Robinson in 1697, and was surrounded by extensive gardens and parkland.

Robinson, who had created another famous garden at Gravetye Manor in West Sussex. Then there was the buzz and excitement of the Chelsea Flower Show, and he also became a familiar face at Veitch's Coombe Wood nursery. Henry's first visit to the nursery was in the summer of 1903, when he travelled to see how seedlings from E. H. Wilson's first expedition to China were faring. He was also keen to keep in contact with other explorers, and, in October 1904, was visited by Antwerp Pratt. The last time both men had seen one another was in mountains around Changyang in south-west Hubei Province 16 years previously.

In the spring of 1905, Henry travelled back to Ireland to deliver a series of lectures, and stayed in Dublin with Sir Frederick and Lady Moore at the National Botanic Gardens, Glasnevin. Then a sister garden of both Kew and Edinburgh, Glasnevin was ranked with these institutions as one of the three great botanic gardens in the world. A share of seeds from Wilson's first expedition for Veitch had been sent to Sir Frederick Moore by Harry Veitch, and some of the perennials were already flowering at Glasnevin. Over the following years, Glasnevin would raise thousands of seedlings from Wilson's successive expeditions and from those of other plant hunters in China. Henry must have been delighted to see so many of his discoveries from central China growing with such vigour in his native Ireland.

From Glasnevin, he travelled south to the famous Kilmacurragh Estate in County Wicklow, where Thomas Acton (1826–1908), under the guidance of Sir Frederick Moore and his father Dr David Moore, had created the largest private collection of trees and shrubs in Ireland. Kilmacurragh was a lovely old place, full of rare and choice trees raised from seeds collected by plant hunters all over the world. Near Kilmacurragh, Henry also visited Powerscourt, the last great formal garden to be laid out in Europe. Professor Sargent came to Ireland that same spring, and Henry took him, Henry Elwes and Sir Frederick Moore on a visit to five of Ireland's incomparable gardens:

Castlewellan, Mount Usher, Fota, Derreen and Glasnevin.

A few months later, Augustine Henry was presented with the Royal Horticultural Society's ultimate accolade: the Victoria Medal of Honour (VMH). Generally seen as the most prestigious horticultural award in the world, the medal can be held by only 63 people at any one time. Other recipients included the directors of Glasnevin, Kew and Edinburgh Botanic Gardens, and various individuals such as Henry Elwes, E. H. Wilson and George Forrest were also later awarded the medal (in 1988, Roy Lancaster OBE, and author of this book's foreword, was too). Henry did not let it go to his head.

Exploring the great forests of North America

Henry's study of trees took him across North America in 1906; he travelled extensively along the Pacific coast from California, into Oregon, Idaho, Montana and Washington, before crossing into Canada to visit forests near Vancouver in British Columbia and near Winnipeg in Manitoba. He camped out most of the time, and trekking proved to be tough as there were no trails and horses were useless in mountain ascents. Unlike the trips he carried out in China, he had no 'coolies' to carry equipment, so, in his backpack he carried a blanket and provisions such as bacon and coffee, and flour to make pancakes. Early on the trip, one of the party killed a white mountain goat and a black bear, and this, no doubt, was added to their rations.

He received a lot of help from the United States Forest Service. However, in a letter to Sir David Prain (1857–1944), the new Director at Kew, he complained bitterly about the Great Northern Railway, with its interminable delays, due to accidents. In less than a year, 45 men had been killed along the mountainous section of the railway, including someone Henry knew from Ireland. He actually dreaded travelling along the line, since many of the wrecks still lay scattered along the way.

BELOW: Augustine Henry was greatly impressed by the forests of North America. Though lacking the variety of their Chinese counterparts, trees from western North American forests reached enormous dimensions and great age. These included the Sierra redwood, *Sequoiadendron giganteum*, seen here in the Mariposa Grove in Yosemite National Park, California.

Henry was particularly interested in collecting seeds of the west American larch, *Larix occidentalis*, to establish forestry plots in Britain and Ireland, and it was abundant on the northern Rocky Mountains. Around Flat Head Lake in northern Montana, it reached 76 m (250 ft) high and produced fine-quality timber. In the same area, *Larix lyallii* grew at high elevations on north-facing slopes. Henry stayed for a week in a biological station on the shores of Flat Head Lake, and on his return to Europe he hoped to propose a similar institution for the west of Ireland.

He thoroughly enjoyed the USA and its people. He got on very well with the forest rangers and trappers, though the New World forests differed in many respects from their Chinese counterparts. In north-west America, the forest growth was luxuriant, but the number of tree species was few, and these, for the most part, were practically all conifers. In many cases, these conifers were giants compared to their Asian cousins. Around Flat Head Lake, he was left in awe of gargantuan specimens of the Douglas fir, *Pseudotsuga menziesii*, more than 91 m (300 ft) tall. Henry also encountered the grand fir, *Abies grandis*, in Montana. In its native haunts, this tree grows with amazing speed and soon projects its crown 61 m (200 ft) into the forest canopy.

The Western red cedar, *Thuja plicata*, reached similar dimensions. Henry collected specimens near Lake MacDonald, and the tree had long been popular as a timber source with Native Americans. Western red cedar's great bulk, and its resistance to rot, led to its use for crafting canoes and giant totem poles. Entire villages built from huge logs of this tree lined the Pacific north-west coast when Captain Cook sailed that stretch of coast in 1778. Lodgepole pine, *Pinus contorta* ssp. *latifolia*, also interested Henry. Native Americans used it for the central pole of their huts, and it grew well on poor, badly drained soils. In the same forest, he made collections of the Western hemlock, *Tsuga heterophylla*. Again, it formed enormous specimens that compared in height to the Western red cedar, and, in undisturbed forests, trees as old as half a millennium could be found.

From Montana, Henry travelled westwards to Seattle in Washington and visited Mount Rainier to study the Nootka cypress, *Xanthocyparis nootkatensis*. From there, his journey took him south to Oregon, where he stayed with a gold miner. There, he had the opportunity to see Brewer's weeping spruce, *Picea breweriana*, in its native habitat. Henry regarded it as the most beautiful of all the spruces, and those who are familiar with this fine tree would no doubt agree. It is also America's rarest spruce and grows at high altitudes in northern California and southern Oregon, where trees can live for at least 900 years and reach heights of up to 52 m (170 ft). The beautifully weeping habit of this tree is an

Near Crescent City, Oregon, Henry visited forests of the coast redwood, *Sequoia sempervirens*. The trees featured here form the Cathedral Grove in Muir Woods, near San Francisco, and are the tallest trees in the world.

adaptation to shed snow loads in the depths of winter.

Even more impressive were the forests of *Chamaecyparis lawsoniana*, the Lawson cypress or Port Orford cedar. The timber of this tree was extremely valuable and was much esteemed by American foresters. Like the Douglas fir, the Lawson cypress is one of the giants of the Oregon forests and can live for up to 600 years, reaching heights of up to 61 m (200 ft). Of broadleaved evergreens, Henry reckoned that the most remarkable tree he saw was the 'headache tree' or Californian laurel, *Umbellularia californica*. In the damp forests of Oregon, it towered to 30 m (100 ft) overhead and could reach 1.5 m (5 ft) in diameter. The timber harvested from this tree was used in making furniture. In European gardens, it rarely makes more than a medium-sized tree and is a great favourite with Head Gardeners, who often indulge in extravagant stories of horrendous headaches brought on by the aromatic leaves.

While based in Oregon, Henry travelled to the coast to Crescent City, near which grew the most northerly population of the famous coast redwood, *Sequoia sempervirens*. One of the vegetable wonders of the world, Henry cannot but have been left in awe of the giants he saw. In Oregon and California, trees more than 2,200 years old have been recorded, and it is a humbling experience to stand beneath a grove that soars anything from 91 to 110 m (300 to 360 ft) overhead. Of all the world's forest trees, the coast redwood produces timber at a phenomenal rate, far more than any tropical rainforest tree. It had long been the mainstay of the west coast forestry industry, and grew alongside other great timber trees such as Sitka spruce, Douglas fir, Western red cedar, grand fir and Western hemlock.

The Sitka spruce, *Picea sitchensis*, fascinated Augustine Henry. The largest of all the spruces, it clung to a 2,900-km (1,800-mile) stretch of coast, from its namesake, Sitka, in Alaska to a narrow, fog-bound belt in California. Few other trees so tolerated wet feet. Two-thirds of the tree's year was likely to be cloudy, and precipitation in many of its habitats approached 2,540 mm (100 in.) – conditions very similar to parts of the west of Ireland and Scotland. In British Columbia, trees of more than 97 m (320 ft) could still be found. Henry immediately recognised its potential as a timber tree worthy of trial on the blanket bogs of Ireland and the Scottish highlands, and he very accurately predicted that clones from the coastal regions of Oregon would suit the Irish climate best.

From Oregon, he made a brief trip to Mount Shasta in California to see the Western yellow pine, *Pinus ponderosa*. A widespread and variable species across several states in western USA, it grew with greatest vigour on the western side of the Sierra Nevada, and the finest trees within that region were found on the slopes of Mount Shasta. There, it formed enormous trees of striking appearance with reddish-brown bark with a broad, round-headed crown.

Of all the regions he visited in North America, it was the forest trees of coastal Oregon that interested Henry most. The maritime climate of the region roughly equated to that of Ireland, and Henry was convinced that if a successful forestry industry was to be established in Ireland, then it should be based on trees from this region and not species from continental Europe, which did not show the same vigour in cultivation.

He learned a great deal from his trip to the USA and Canada. In 20 years, he reckoned, there would not be left in North America a single uncut forest, and the timber question would become acute and lumber prices would rise enormously. He was determined to see that Ireland would be replanted with suitable fast-growing trees.

Henry returned to Europe by the Canadian Pacific, branching off at Winnipeg to Cass Lake in Minnesota, where he stopped briefly to study *Larix laricina* and the Jack pine, *Pinus banksiana*, the most northerly distributed American pine. From there, he travelled on to Boston and Washington, DC. In Boston, he stayed with Professor Sargent on his Holm Lea Estate and visited the last fragment of primeval forest left in New England.

From the USA, Henry travelled home via Gibraltar. His studies were not yet quite done; he planned to collect specimens of the Spanish fir *Abies pinsapo* in its native habitat. It was once a widespread tree, but by the time of Henry's visit, in December 1906, it clung to inaccessible spots on only three mountaintops, where it grew with *Pinus halipensis* and *Pinus pinaster*.

From Gibraltar, he set sail across the Mediterranean to Naples, and, from there, visited Rome and Florence. In Florence, he found much of interest in the city herbarium, including Père Giuseppe Giraldi's collections from Shaanxi Province in central China. His next destination was Corsica, where he spent almost two weeks in mountains visiting forests

Sir Harry James Veitch, the foremost nurseryman of his day. Veitch employed E. H. Wilson to travel on two expeditions to China, and raised his collections in the family's Coombe Wood nursery. Henry visited the nursery on several occasions.

RIGHT: Avondale House, the ancestral home of Charles Stewart Parnell – and birthplace of forestry in Ireland.

by then liberally sprinkled with early falls of snow. He spent the New Year of 1907 on Corsica before heading off once again, this time to study the Algerian fir *Abies numidica*, which occupied a small mountainous area in the east of Algeria. Such was Henry's energy and enthusiasm that, after spending months trekking through the forests of North America, the Mediterranean and North Africa, all he had to say was 'the work is rough on boots, but my health is splendid'.[7]

Back in England, in May 1907, Henry and Elwes visited Veitch's Coombe Wood nursery, where Wilson's collections from Hubei and Sichuan provinces were flourishing. It must have given Henry great pleasure to see so many of his discoveries firmly established in cultivation.

In August of that year, he was appointed Reader (later, Professor) of Forestry in the newly established School of Forestry at Cambridge. His second career was on a sure footing, and he had established an international reputation in a new field. Elwes endowed the new school with a generous fund and E. H. Wilson sent timber specimens of various trees from China, including logs of *Keteleeria davidiana*. Henry used his global network of contacts for the benefit of the new forestry school. Cambridge could soon claim to have the largest collection of wood specimens for use in forest botany in the world, and a rapidly expanding forestry herbarium. The timber specimens were unrivalled for their variety and they illustrated problems encountered in silviculture. Research in timber began along scientific lines.

A degree of M.A. *honoris causa* was conferred on Augustine Henry by the University of Cambridge in 1908. The same year, he travelled to Denmark, Norway and Sweden to visit the great Scandinavian forests and botanic gardens. During that trip, he visited Uppsala University's botanical gardens and saw the original *Populus nigra* planted by the famous Swedish botanist, Carl Linnaeus.

The founding father of Irish forestry

Meanwhile, in Ireland, slow advances in forestry were being made. In 1904, the state purchased Avondale, a wooded estate of 223 ha (551 acres) near Rathdrum in County Wicklow. Avondale was the 18th-century home of Samuel Hayes (1743–95), an enthusiastic tree planter and author of the first book on trees in Ireland. It was also the birthplace of his descendant, Charles Stewart Parnell (1846–91), one of Ireland's great patriots and political leaders.

By the first decade of the 20th century, it was estimated that 1.5 per cent of Ireland was covered with woodland – and even that figure was steadily shrinking. The comparison with Europe was striking. Finland still had 73 per cent forest cover, Austria had 32 per cent, while, in France and Belgium, the figure was 17 per cent. Denmark, an agricultural country and just half the size of Ireland, had double the acreage of wooded land. Iceland was the only European country whose proportion of woodlands fell below that of Ireland.

Even then, that figure was steadily shrinking. The 'Land War' organised by Charles Stewart Parnell had resulted in the second of the Land Acts, passed in 1881, and these rocked the confidence of landlords who saw in them a forewarning of a transfer of ownership of Irish land over the following decades. The breaking up of large Irish estates lessened the interest of many of these landlords in maintaining forested areas, and the same Acts made little provision for the protection and preservation of estate woodlands being sold to tenants. These stately woods soon fell under the axe and saw, and a great number of 'travelling mills' came over from England and Scotland to begin the wholesale destruction of demesne timber. Desperate to balance their losses, Anglo-Irish landlords welcomed the income from the sale of these once-preserved woodlands.

In 1906, A. C. Forbes was appointed Forestry Expert at

Avondale, and was instrumental in creating a new forest experimental station on the lines of a continental forest garden for demonstration and experimental purposes, that could be used for education and training and as a resource for Irish arboriculturists. Forbes laid out 104 plots, each of about an acre, planting both natives and exotic trees to test their suitability for commercial planting and economic value. An arboretum was laid out near the old house and a tree nursery was established. A century later, visitors can wander through mature forests of oak, beech, ash, giant and coastal redwoods, Douglas fir, Western red cedar and towering eucalyptus laid out along a grand south-east axis called the Great Ride, the focus of which is an Irish cairn. Avondale's was a landscape laid out on an ambitious scale. From the cairn, the axis shifted southwards to reveal a sweeping vista of the lovely Avonmore River.

In November 1907, not long after the very first group of forestry students graduated from Avondale, a committee on afforestation met to devise a national forestry policy, and the report they published the following year established the future of forestry in Ireland.[8] Finally, the question of reforestation was being taken seriously – and not before time. Evidence was heard from 48 people, most of whom were connected with the timber industry or forestry. It was the far-seeing recommendations given to the committee by Augustine Henry that established forestry as a successful and viable industry in Ireland. Henry's view was that no forestry should be attempted unless it paid. Planting slow-growing trees, such as oak, elm and ash, would not bring a return of any kind until the distant future. Certainly, it was a safe investment, but not really remunerative. The quicker the return, the better. People would see there was something in it, thus also encouraging the private sector. As to the choice of trees, most experts giving evidence to the committee favoured Scots pine, European larch, Norway spruce and hardwoods, all because European forestry methods during that period favoured European conifers. Exotics had been used in the past, though with little success because virtually no thought had been put into their selection, choice of site, shelter, maintenance and aftercare. Many foresters felt a prejudice against these exotics, due to the indiscriminate way in which they had then been praised in the past.

Given correct conditions, exotic trees grow remarkably well in Ireland. In his evidence, Henry referred to Irish gardens and arboreta such as Castlewellan in County Down, Mount Usher and Kilmacurragh in County Wicklow, Derreen in County Kerry and Fota in County Cork. These historic demesnes, he pointed out, were world famous for the sheer variety of luxuriantly growing trees and shrubs, many of which were rarely found in England and not at all in the colder climates of Germany and Austria. In County Kerry, one could find lichens growing in the wild

that were not met with again until Madeira. The question of suitable forest trees needed to be settled by experience in Ireland, he said. German books on forestry were absolutely useless for application in Ireland.

Henry's recommendations included the planting of unproductive bogs and marginal uplands. Under the operation of the Land Purchase Acts, large tracts of mountain land and peat bogs were passing into the hands of peasants without the capital or knowledge to carry out improvements. In Henry's opinion, ownership of these uneconomic holdings would only bring misery, and an amendment to the Acts was required so that all such waste land sold by landlords should be used for forestry purposes, as this would give employment to local labourers in rural districts. He advised the committee to plant large blocks of not less than 1,000 acres (405 ha), to provide adequate fencing against game and cattle, to establish shelter belts before the main planting was carried out and to use the correct choice of fast-growing conifers. It was this latter recommendation that proved to be Henry's most important contribution. In his opinion, if forestry was to be a success in Ireland, then foresters needed to forget continental experience and look to the Pacific north-west coast of the USA and Canada as a source of timber trees. He pointed out the similarities of climate and rainfall to prove his theory:

Prejudice should not exclude foreign trees. The question is whether they will grow, and whether if treated as forest trees they will do well. After I had gathered my facts as to exotic trees in Ireland I formed my theory, and my theory is this; that, owing to the insular position, extreme mildness and rainy nature of the winter, the Gulf Stream and the excessive rainfall, the climate of Ireland differs in every respect from the climate of Continental Europe […] Where we do have an analogous climate, the same species of trees do very well. In British Columbia, Washington and Oregon, there is a Gulf Stream, a rainy winter and a rainfall nearly parallel to that of the west half of the west of Ireland. If you look at the rainfall maps, you will see that the west half of Ireland is very rainy, and most of the waste land is in this rainy belt. In British Columbia, Washington, Oregon and California, the forests are the greatest forests in the world in many respects, and certainly they are the greatest in the North Temperate Zone, and all the trees without exception that grow on the Pacific Coast have done extremely well in Ireland and Wales and the west of Scotland and the south-west of England. The non-trial of fast-growing trees on a large scale is simply due to the innate conservatism of these islands, backed up by the imperfect knowledge of the remarkable and peculiar features of the climate of Ireland.[9]

The results of my observations show that we may accept as a general law that all trees native to the Pacific slope of North America from Alaska to Oregon are suitable for planting in Ireland, where they thrive amazingly [...] They find in Ireland a climate exactly like that in which they occur at home. They produce timber twice as fast as the native species. For the afforestation of waste lands conifers practically should be exclusively employed [...] For example, the Sitka spruce produces twice the volume of timber per acre than the common spruce [It] does well in wet soil and in the wet climate of Ireland, and should be exclusively employed in such situations.[10]

Henry's choice of conifers included Corsican pine (*Pinus nigra,* ssp. *laricio*), Douglas fir, Western red cedar, coastal redwood, giant redwood and, perhaps most importantly, Sitka spruce. The latter he suggested for planting in peat bogs in upland regions, having seen it thrive in similar conditions in North America.

He was also the first forester to highlight the importance of seed provenance of trees for Irish forestry. Choice of species alone was not enough to guarantee success. Many North American conifers, particularly Douglas fir and Sitka spruce, have an enormous range of distribution and therefore subpopulations required further study. In the case of the Douglas fir, he stated that trees of coastal origin were superior in vigour to those found in the mountains far inland. He also pointed out that trees from the most northerly range of distribution were not so vigorous as those from its southerly stations.[11]

Henry's advice was accepted and it was his proposals that led to the lucrative forestry industry that Ireland enjoys today. His list of suitable trees proved ideal. Sitka spruce has stood the test of time is now the most widely planted forest tree in Ireland. It grows on Irish boglands as happily as it does in North America, even colonising ground where native trees cannot survive. Pacific Coast species dominate the forests of Ireland, and will continue to be important trees in future forest planting. Conifers in Ireland grow six times faster than in the timber-producing countries of Scandinavia.

Because of his great contribution to the industry, Augustine Henry is remembered by foresters in his homeland as 'the founding father of Irish forestry'. In 1951, the Society of Irish Foresters and the state-run Forestry Division dedicated a grove of trees and shrubs at Avondale to Henry's memory, and erected a memorial stone in his honour. It was fitting that Avondale, the birthplace of Irish forestry, was where foresters chose to remember Augustine Henry.

BELOW: Sitka spruce thriving on blanket bog near Wicklow Gap, high in the Wicklow Mountains. An area of unproductive moorland where native trees cannot flourish, Augustine Henry rightly predicted that North American conifers could make regions like this productive and profitable in a relatively short time. His advice set the basis for a successful forestry industry in Ireland.

Henry the tree breeder

In 1907, E. H. Wilson was once again en route for China, this time under the auspices of the Arnold Arboretum. Henry took a keen interest in the activities of other plant hunters, none more so than Wilson. He was in the USA when he learned that Sargent had finally persuaded Wilson to collect for the Arnold. It seems Henry had been searching for a suitable post for Wilson at the time and had found a position in Canada. In November 1906, Henry wrote to Wilson from Washington:

> I have just come here from Boston […] I shall miss you: am sorry. I agree with Sargent that this expedition is to be a great one. Success to you![12]

In Shanghai, Wilson met up with Frank Meyer, and, from there, sailed up the Yangtze to Yichang, which was to be his base for the next two years. Henry was still keen to trial exotics for forestry purposes, and wrote to Sargent enquiring about how Wilson was getting on and requesting small quantities of any conifer seeds he collected.

Two years later, Veitch's nursery teamed up with the Arnold Arboretum and sent the English plant hunter William Purdom (1880–1921) to collect plants in north-west China. The number of ornamental plants introduced by Purdom are few, in comparison with his contemporaries, and some of his most notable finds were from his second expedition, which he carried out with Reginald Farrer. Purdom's best-known gift to gardeners has to be the wonderfully fragrant, winter-flowered *Viburnum farreri* from Gansu Province, which he introduced through Messrs Veitch.

E. H. Wilson (second row, first seated figure) on his houseboat *The Harvard* at Yichang during his first expedition for the Arnold Arboretum (1906–8). Henry wrote to Wilson, wishing him well.

In his letter to Professor Sargent, Henry went on to discuss European elms (*Ulmus* spp.) and their many hybrids. During the preparation of the section on elms in *The Trees of Great Britain and Ireland*, Henry was puzzled about how best to classify the many varieties of the species.

At Cambridge, he investigated the ancestry of many of these. In 1909, he sowed 90 different seed batches collected from trees in the south of England. Henry concluded that

On his second expedition to China, William Purdom travelled through Gansu Province with Reginald Farrer introducing *Viburnum farreri* to cultivation. One of Purdom's seedlings (pictured above) still grows at Glasnevin.

there were few pure species of elm in England, and based his theory on observations of the growth habits of seedlings. True species, such as *Ulmus glabra* (the wych elm), produced seedlings that were uniform in size and all other characteristics. In the majority of cases, so-called 'varieties' produced seedlings that were different in size and the arrangement of leaves. When he and his students sowed seeds of the Huntingdon elm at Cambridge, the progeny segregated out in the Mendelian ratio of 3:1 based on leaf examination: 732 seedlings bore opposite leaves and 239 had alternate leaves. Henry concluded that many of these 'varieties' were often simple Mendelian combinations of two existing species, and many of the elms studied were not varieties but hybrids.

It was during his work with elms that Henry realised the potential of artificially breeding hybrid trees for forestry purposes, and so began his pioneering work on genetics and hybridisation. His studies showed that vigorous hybrid trees, such as the Huntingdon elm, the Lucombe oak, the London plane and the common lime, were of accidental origin, the result of seeds produced by fertilisation of the flowers of one species by pollen of another wafted on the wind or carried by insects. The Huntingdon elm, *Ulmus* 'Vegeta', exhibited all the traits of hybrid vigour. It was one of the largest of all the elms and produced timber faster than any of the species. Impressed by these facts, he began experiments in the production of new trees by hybridisation in the hope of obtaining fast-growing kinds that would produce timber rapidly.

In 1912, Henry began a series of hybridisation trials using ash, alder, elm, larch and poplar. Poplars proved to be good trees to work with, as seedlings could be raised in the same year as the cross was carried out. In March of that year, he crossed *Populus deltoides* 'Cordata' with the pollen of the *Populus trichocarpa* (the black cottonwood), the fastest- and tallest-growing of the balsam poplars from western North America. By June, a few seeds had ripened, and these germinated the following October at Cambridge. In the spring of 1913, Henry had the seedlings (then 5 cm tall) sent to the National Botanic Gardens, Glasnevin, where they were planted in the walled fruit garden, and there they grew with astounding vigour. By the end of the season, the tallest of Henry's poplar seedlings was more than a metre (3.3 ft) tall, and, by September 1914, it was more than 3 m (10 ft) tall. This hybrid, later named *Populus* x *generosa*, was the very first deliberate cross between a black and balsam poplar, and, during the 1920s, it was cultivated for its timber in the south of France and in northern Italy. Though remarkably rapid in growth, it never became a success because of its susceptibility to bacterial canker.

Populus x *vernirubens* was another of Henry's trees, though, unlike *Populus* x *generosa*, it was not a deliberate hybrid but a chance hybrid raised, in 1914, from seeds

Augustine Henry's seedling of *Populus* x *generosa* in the walled garden at Glasnevin in 1914. The seedling, photographed with gardener Peter Daly, was then only two and a half years old.

gathered from an open-pollinated tree of the Carolina poplar, *Populus deltoides* 'Carolin', in the Kew collection. It is a far more handsome tree than *Populus* x *generosa*, and is a beautiful sight in April when the buds begin to open and its coppery-red foliage emerges. The specific epithet '*vernirubens*' was coined by Henry and means 'spring-red'. A magnificent tree still grows in the front garden of Henry's former residence at Ranelagh in Dublin, and is often admired by visitors to Helen Dillon's well-known garden next door. Another poplar associated with Henry is *Populus* x *canadensis* 'Henryana', a large, wide-spreading tree of unknown origin. It was named in recognition of Henry's work in bringing the group out of obscurity and for clarifying so many nomenclatural errors.

Henry's foresight and great knowledge of tree breeding has long since been widely recognised, and his work on the subject brought him worldwide fame. The American geneticist Dr Ernest Schreiner, who later carried on Henry's breeding work, had the following to say:

Augustine Henry was the first forester to realise the possibilities of creating better forest trees by scientific breeding and he was the first forester to do something about it.[13]

ABOVE: *Platanus* 'Augustine Henry'. The original tree grows near the Azalea Garden at Kew. It is probably the most ornamental of the planes, but is unavailable commercially.

RIGHT: Following his fourth expedition to China, E. H. Wilson settled at the Arnold Arboretum, where he became Keeper, following Professor Sargent's death in 1927.

Another fine tree that carries Henry's name is *Platanus* 'Augustine Henry', a striking plane received at Kew in 1878 from the Belgian nurseryman Van Houtte under the name '*Platanus californica*'. Augustine Henry first described this tree, calling its merits to attention and highlighting its confused identity. The original tree still grows near the azalea garden at Kew, and is one of the most beautiful trees in that part of the arboretum. Henry's plane can be distinguished from the London plane by its laxer lower branches, the smoother, more freely flaking bark, its better-developed central stem and the more elegantly toothed, large, sea-green leaves. *Platanus* 'Augustine Henry' is very rare in gardens, and, at present, is unavailable commercially, which is a pity since it is a remarkably beautiful tree in every respect.

Life could not have been better for Henry during his years in Cambridge. His work was pioneering and challenging, and, for a second time, he fell in love: Alice (Elsie) Brunton (1882–1956) was the daughter of a leading London physician. The couple married on Saint Patrick's Day, 17 March 1908, and Henry's friend Evelyn Gleeson sent him a sprig of shamrock from Ireland to wear on the day. The marriage, by all accounts, was a very happy one. Elsie became a great plantswoman under her husband's influence and regularly travelled with him to mainland Europe to study forest trees and gardens.

Botanic gardens in Great Britain and Ireland benefited enormously from Henry's global contacts in botany and forestry. He continually received seeds of trees from all over the world, and, in April 1909, for example, sent seeds of *Podocarpus totora* and *Agathis australis*, two of New Zealand's most noble trees, to Glasnevin and Kew asking that any duplicate seeds be sent on to Edinburgh. In 1909, the public-spirited Veitch nursery very generously distributed 15,000 of E. H. Wilson's herbarium collections from central China to Kew, Edinburgh, Dublin, New York, Paris, Hamburg, St Petersburg, the Smithsonian Institute, the Arnold Arboretum and a set was also sent to Augustine Henry.

In 1911, E. H. Wilson returned with his wife and daughter to England. Shortly before this, he had travelled from China to the USA following his fourth and final plant-hunting expedition. Wilson was recuperating from a near-fatal accident that had broken his leg in Sichuan Province. Before setting sail to Europe, he had begun work with Alfred Rehder on *Plantae Wilsonianae*, a catalogue of his Chinese collections, which totalled an amazing 65,000 herbarium specimens, 1,593 seed lots and 168 consignments of cuttings and scions.[14] Augustine Henry met Ernest Wilson in September of that year, and no doubt the former listened in awe to the tales from the latter's very last adventure in China.

In 1913, the final volume of *The Trees of Great Britain and Ireland* appeared. A set of seven volumes was gifted to Professor Sargent of the Arnold Arboretum by a group of Great Britain and Ireland's most distinguished horticulturists, including Professor Isaac Bayley Balfour (of Edinburgh), Sir Frederick Moore (Glasnevin), Sir David Prain and W. J. Bean (Kew), Edward A. Bowles, Lord Kesteven, Sir Edmund Giles Loder, Sir Harry Veitch, J. C. Williams and William Robinson. Each volume was bound by different native woods, including 14th-century beech removed from the foundations of Winchester Cathedral.

The end of exile – Henry returns to Ireland

In April 1913, Augustine Henry finally returned to his native Ireland, following 32 years of self-imposed exile. The Royal College of Science (now University College, Dublin) had established a Chair of Forestry. Henry was elated; at last, he was home, with good prospects and in a position to guide the still-embryonic forestry industry along its correct pathway. He bought a fine old townhouse in Ranelagh, one of the most desirable addresses in the south-side suburbs of Dublin, and, over the years, it became a gathering point for some of Ireland's best-known and most brilliant literary and political figures.

The house was surrounded by a decent-sized garden, and the Henrys immediately set to work on planning a new design. They had a few good trees to begin with – a fine yew, a walnut and some apple trees – and a long stretch of lawn. The latter was stripped and replaced with a series of box-edged borders, and these were filled with all sorts of rarities, including many of the hardy Chinese plants that had been named after Henry. These came as gifts from Glasnevin, Kew and from Sir Harry Veitch.

The garden became well known during the 1920s, and, within the confines of box-edged beds, visitors met fine plants, many of which carried Henry's name, including *Acer henryi*,

ABOVE: Alice and Augustine Henry in their garden at Ranelagh, Dublin, during the 1920s. The garden grew many of the plants that Henry had discovered in China, and, in the glasshouse, he grew *Corydalis saxicola*, which he had discovered on ledges on the cliffs of the Xiling Gorge above Yichang.

Cotoneaster henryanus, *Lilium henryi*, *Ligustrum henryi*, the ghostly white-stemmed *Rubus lasiostylus*, *Spiraea henryi*, *Viburnum henryi*, *Viburnum rhytidophyllum*, *Rhododendron augustinii*, *Hypericum beanii*, *Corydalis cheilanthifolia*, *Hamamelis mollis*, *Ribes henryi*, *Lysimachia henryi*, *Itea ilicifolia*, *Lonicera pileata*, *Androsace henryi*, *Deinanthe caerulea*, *Dipteronia sinensis* and *Sinowilsonia henryi*. Along the back walls of the house grew bushy vines of *Lonicera henryi*, *Parthenocissus henryana*, *Actinidia chinensis*, *Schisandra henryi* and, in the shelter of a small glasshouse, *Corydalis saxicola*, the *ai-huang-lien* that he had discovered in the gorges above Yichang in 1885, bore crowded racemes of yellow blossoms during the winter months. By the front gate of his house, he planted his hybrid cottonwood, *Populus* x *vernirubens*.

In Dublin, he continued his work breeding of hybrid timber trees, and, from time to time, used the facilities and

325

Lilium henryi in Augustine Henry's Ranelagh garden during the 1930s. The photograph was taken by J. W. Besant, Director of the National Botanic Gardens, Glasnevin.

Glasnevin in 1910. Augustine Henry was a regular visitor to Sir Frederick and Lady Moore, who lived in the Director's Residence, a fine, early Georgian house near the garden entrance.

Augustine Henry's house at Sandford Road, Ranelagh, in Dublin; a comfortable townhouse dating from the 1830s.

collections at Kew and Glasnevin for these purposes. He regularly brought his students to great Irish gardens, such as Powerscourt and Kilmacurragh, to study exotic trees, and one of his forestry students, H. M. Fitzpatrick, left the following impression of Henry towards the end of his life:

I first met professor Henry when I was a forestry student in 1926. I remember vividly his ebullient personality; he always arrived in college like a whirlwind, cheeks pink and blue eyes dancing with life behind a pair of old-fashioned steel-rimmed glasses. He was invariably clutching a bundle of letters [...] and wearing a pork-pie hat, a red tie, a faded green camel-hair overcoat, a pair of heavy boots and carrying a large walking stick. Although always in a hurry he seemed to have time to stop and talk. He was quite unpretentious, absolutely without a trace of snobbishness, and courteous to all.

It is his amazing physical energy and mental vigour which remains most clearly in my mind. His immediate interest filled his entire mind, nothing else mattered and conventions were forgotten. One day, wishing to have a word with a colleague driving into the college quadrangle, Henry gave several massive thumps with his stick on the side of the car.

I think it was the brilliant circle which surrounded him which appealed to his cultural taste and his delight in good conversation. His friends included Jack B. Yeats, the artist, A. E. or George Russell, the poet and economist, Richard Best, the Irish scholar, Henry Nixon [...] all remarkable men whose equals he would not have found in any other community. They were all great talkers, but Henry could hold his own and in the receptions in his house he would go from group to group taking part in the lively arguments. The Henrys were Co. Derry farmers and Augustine was the intellectual of the family.[15]

Sir Frederick Moore, one of Glasnevin's greatest directors, was also one of Henry's closest friends in Ireland,

A contemporary portrait of Augustine Henry commissioned by the National Botanic Gardens, Glasnevin, in recent years. The portrait is based on a photograph of Henry that appeared in the *Gardeners' Chronicle* in 1913, announcing his return to Dublin as Professor of Forestry. Henry was then aged 56.

It was on 29 September 1951, at Avondale in County Wicklow, that Irish foresters chose to commemorate Augustine Henry. Pictured at the unveiling of the monument and memorial grove is his widow Alice (far right), while Dr Thomas Walsh, Director of the National Botanic Gardens, Glasnevin, stands behind the memorial.

and he left the following impression:

> He was a great talker, and would sit for hours by the fire in my study during the long winter evenings telling of his many and varied experiences; he talked simply and without a trace of boastfulness. He was very patient in listening to others. He was very determined in carrying out work he undertook and very thorough and painstaking in his methods. I never saw him angry or perturbed, but he could be very firm. He had acquired an almost oriental calm of manner, especially when others became excited.[16]

Augustine Henry retired from University College, Dublin, in 1926. He was awarded many honours over his lifetime, though the tribute that gave him most pleasure was published in 1929 in the second volume of *Icones Plantarum Sinicarum*, a beautifully illustrated work on Chinese plants. Each volume was dedicated to an outstanding botanist, and the second was worded as follows:

> To Augustine Henry, through whose assiduous botanical exploration of central and south-western China, the knowledge of our flora has been greatly extended.

In a personal letter, Professor H. H. Hu of the Fan Memorial Institute of Biology in Beijing paid Henry the ultimate compliment:

> As a pioneer and veteran botanist of western China you have not only added to the world much scientific knowledge of the Chinese flora but you have set up a great example for Chinese botanical students. This dedication is our humble appreciation of what you have so humbly achieved.[17]

Towards the end of his life, Henry's memory began to fail, and so he decided to put his memory to the test and walked one day to Glasnevin. He returned, chuckling to himself, following the experiment. 'I went up to the Botanic Gardens,' he said, 'and could not remember the name of a single tree'.[18] It was a sad fate for a man long regarded as the world's greatest authority on trees of the north temperate regions.

Augustine Henry died in his house at Ranelagh, following a short illness, on 23 March 1930. He lies buried in Deansgrange cemetery in the south Dublin suburbs. Just seven months later, E. H. Wilson was killed in a car accident in Massachusetts, and, two years later, George Forrest died in the field in north-west Yunnan Province. A golden era in Chinese plant hunting had finally come to an end, and Forrest, Henry and Wilson – three of the greatest names in the exploration of the Chinese flora – passed into legend.

In his native Ireland, Augustine Henry remains the most famous plant hunter to have ever departed her shores. He is commemorated in several gardens in Ireland, and, at the National Botanic Gardens, Glasnevin, a tree of *Acer henryi* was planted by the herbarium building in 2000 to mark the centennial of his return from China.

ABOVE: Henry's passion for trees never diminished. He is pictured here at Kilmacurragh in 1929 with *Podocarpus hallii*.

RIGHT: Augustine and Alice Henry's tombstone at Deansgrange in Dublin. Photographed in July 2007 for the 150th anniversary of Henry's birth, it is draped with a bough of *Lithocarpus henryi*.

BELOW: Hubei's forestry headquarters at Yichang. Henry would have been pleased to know that central China's forests are now being managed in a more sustainable way.

Epilogue

In August 2003, staff from Wuhan Botanical Garden spent a month in Dublin as guests of the National Botanic Gardens, Glasnevin. Pictured here are Donal Synnott (then Glasnevin's Director), Miss Wang Qing, Mr Deng Wenqiang and Professor Ding Zhaohua.

By the summer of 2009, the Three Gorges reservoir will have reached its maximum level and the flooding of the main gorges and their many side glens and tributaries will be completed. The Three Gorges themselves will not be submerged, but they will lose part of their dramatic aura, as the muddy waters of the Yangtze climb their cold, grey cliff faces. The gorges' mysterious atmosphere will no doubt remain, but the region will have changed forever.

One of my most abiding memories of the Three Gorges region is from September 2002, when we sailed through the Qutang Gorge to the Shang Dynasty (*c*.1600–1027 BC) town of Wushan. It was an exciting entry for our group into 'Henry country', since it was just south of this town that Augustine Henry discovered the glabrous-leaved handkerchief tree, *Davidia involucrata* var. *vilmoriniana*. Wushan was an unpretentious market town and lay on a low-lying flood plain on the north bank of the Yangtze. We sailed into it as dawn broke over the town and the nearby Yangtze River. It was a spectacular, and somewhat emotional, sight as the coffee-coloured waters of the Yangtze reflected the early morning sunlight on the skeletal-like remains of the town. Wushan was, by then, almost completely demolished, and most of this work had been carried out by hand. We walked through its desolate streets as men and women hammered and chiselled buildings to the ground and carried salvaged bricks in wicker baskets on their backs, to be used in the construction of a new town on the mountain slopes above. We met many more towns and cities like this as we sailed through the gorges to Yichang.

It was remarkable to see the movement of people on such a massive scale, and to have visited the dam site in its latter phase of construction. Yet, it was sad to witness the flooding of such an historic and beautiful landscape. We revisited the region two years later, when the extent of flooding was very

Seedlings of *Lilium henryi*, from our 2004 expedition, germinating in the nursery at Glasnevin in the spring of 2005. The gardens at Kilmacurragh have been the greatest beneficiary of our Chinese travels.

A Hani couple strolling through a street in Yuanyang in southern Yunnan Province's Ailao Shan mountain range.

obvious, and most of the tributaries and side gorges had been partly submerged. Many of these have now completely disappeared beneath the new reservoir. In retrospect, I think those of us who sailed through the gorges in September 2002 feel a certain sense of achievement. Flooding began just a few weeks later, and we knew as we sailed towards Yichang that we would be the very last botanical expedition to travel down the Yangtze before the final section of the dam was put in place. Thus, we saw the region much as Henry and Wilson knew it. It was strange, yet exhilarating, to finally reach Yichang – and absolutely bizarre to arrive there the night before the very last building was demolished in the Foreign Compound where Augustine Henry and Ernest Wilson were once based.

We did not expect to stumble upon so many extant buildings mentioned by Henry in his letters. The old missionary church at Bankinsing in Taiwan was a wonderful find – though I was relieved that the locals had given up their headhunting ways! In Shanghai, a Customs House still dominates the Bund, and, in the Customs House at Mengzi, a wall plaque bears Augustine Henry's name. The people we met were every bit as wonderful as the places. Henry would be pleased to know that the ethnic minority groups of southern Yunnan Province still hold a strong cultural identity. Colourfully dressed Hani women continue to visit that marketplace at Mengzi, and one of the greatest highlights of all three expeditions was our unplanned visit to the little Yi school on Great Black Mountain.

Through these expeditions, we formed a network of friends and colleagues in various botanic gardens across China and Taiwan – and these relationships are reciprocal. In August 2003, a number of staff members from Wuhan Botanical Garden stayed in Dublin for a month as guests of the National Botanic Gardens, Glasnevin. During this period, they studied European botanic garden techniques and also visited some of Ireland's most notable gardens, such as Altamont, Kilmacurragh, Powerscourt and Mount Stewart, as well as national parks, including the Burren in County Clare. Another great

highlight was their visit to Helen Dillon's garden at Ranelagh. The Dillon Garden is regarded as the finest townhouse garden in the world, and Helen had travelled as a member of the 2002 team to Sichuan and Hubei provinces. A wonderful reception was hosted in the garden for the Chinese team, nearing the end of their stay in Ireland, and they were thrilled to be next door to the house in which Augustine Henry once lived.

Several thousand seedlings were raised from our Chinese collections, and these have found their way into various state-owned gardens around Ireland. One of the greatest benefactors has been the Kilmacurragh Botanic Gardens, Glasnevin's country estate in County Wicklow. Until the Great War, Kilmacurragh had the largest private plant collection on the island of Ireland, and acted as an unofficial annexe to Glasnevin. It contained the collections of Sir Joseph Hooker, William Lobb, Ernest Wilson, George Forrest, Frank Kingdon Ward and even grew a number of plants raised from seeds collected on the Cangshan range in Yunnan Province by Père Jean Marie Delavay during the 1880s. During the Great War, however, two successive owners (brothers) were killed, placing enormous financial pressure on the estate, and, sadly, the gardens slipped into decades of decline. Purchased by Glasnevin in 1996, it is now seeing better times.

At present, Kilmacurragh is being replanted using wild-origin material, including a good representation of our central China collections. It will take many of these 100 years or so to mature, but still, as I stroll past young trees of *Cunninghamia lanceolata*, *Emmenopterys henryi*, *Ginkgo biloba*, *Ilex forrestii*, *Magnolia sprengeri*, *Paulownia fargesii* and *Sorbus wilsoniana*, for example, I am temporarily transported back to that wonderful region. In the National Herbarium at Glasnevin, our dried specimens are now housed alongside those of Henry's and Wilson's. Plant exploration is an enjoyable prerequisite of working for the National Botanic Gardens, Glasnevin, and though my new focus is to be the flora of temperate South America, I look back on our many expeditions to China with great satisfaction and with many happy memories.

Augustine Henry's plants

Between 1885 and 1900, Augustine Henry collected more than 158,000 herbarium specimens from various locations throughout China and Taiwan. His very first collection was *Clematis henryi* from Yichang; his last was *Neolitsea sericea* from an island in the Shanghai delta. Henry's collections comprise more than 6,000 distinct species – almost 20 per cent of the entire Chinese flora, and the largest single collection ever made by a plant hunter in China.

Many plants have been named for Augustine Henry, under the guise of *austinii, augustinei, augustinii, augustiniana, henryi, henriana, henryana, henryanum* and *henryanus*, for example. In a few instances, '*henryi*' may commemorate other collectors, as is the case with *Rhododendron henryi*, which was named for its discoverer, the Rev. B. C. Henry, an American missionary based in south-east China during the late 19th century. In another case, *Chamaecyparis thyoides* var. *henryae* was named for that indomitable American plantswoman Mary Henry, founder of the Henry Botanic Gardens at Gladwyne, near Philadelphia, in the USA.

In recent years, I have been able to compile an almost-complete list of Augustine Henry's collections in China, including his many discoveries. To date, I have traced 1,338 new species, 30 new subspecies, 338 new varieties and 20 new forms – giving a grand total of 1,726 new plant discoveries in China. These are summarised below.

New families
Bretschneideraceae
Eucommiaceae
Sargentodoxaceae
Tetracentraceae
Trapellaceae

New genera
Ancylostemon
Archangiopteris
Burretiodendron
Chamydoboea

Craspedolobium
Cyphotheca
Dipteronia
Eleutharrhena
Emmenopterys
Hancockia
Hemiboea
Hemsleya
Huodendron
Itoa
Leptocanna
Loxocalyx

Neocheiropteris
Neomartinella
Notoperygium
Paralamium
Petrocosmea
Petrodoxa
Pittosporopsis
Plagiopetalum
Poliothyrsis
Psilopeganum
Saruma
Sichuania

Sindechites
Sinofranchetia
Sinojackia
Sinowilsonia
Styrophyton
Tapiscia
Trapella
Trirostellum
Tupistra

Plants named for Augustine Henry that are accepted in current botanical nomenclature

Acer henryi
Aconitum henryi
Actinidia callosa var. *henryi*
Actinidia henryi
Actinodaphne henryi
Aegopodium henryi
Allium henryi
Alnus henryi

Alstonia henryi
Amorphophallus henryi
Androsace henryi
Angelica henryi
Antrophyum henryi
Arachniodes henryi
Aralia henryi
Archangiopteris henryi

Argyreia henryi
Arisaema sikokianum var.
  henryanum
Asplenium henryi
Aster henryi
Astragalus henryi
Atalantia racemosa var.
  henryi

Balanophora henryi
Begonia augustinei
Begonia henryi
Belvisia henryi
Berberis henryana
Biondia henryi
Blumea henryi
Brachycorythis henryi

Buckleya henryi
Buxus henryi
Calamagrostis henryi
Calamus henryanus
Calanthe henryi
Camellia henryana
Campylotropis henryi
Canthium henryi
Capparis micrantha var.
　henryi
Carex henryi
Carlemannia henryi
Carpinus henryana
Caryodaphnopsis henryi
Castanea henryi
Chionanthus henryanus
Chloranthus henryi
Chrysosplenium henryi
Cirsium henryi
Clematis henryi
Clerodendrum
　colebrookianum var.
　henryanum
Clerodendrum henryi
Cochleria henryi
Codonopsis henryi
Coluria henryi
Colysis henryi
Connarus henryi
Corylopsis henryi
Cotoneaster henryanus
Craibiodendron henryi
Cyclobalanopsis augustinii
Cypripedium henryi
Dalbergia henryana
Davallia henryana
Delphinium henryi
Dendrobium henryi
Digitaria henryi
Elaeagnus henryi
Eleutherococcus henryi
Embelia henryi
Emmenopterys henryi
Eriobotrya henryi

Eriocaulon henryanum
Erycibe henryi
Euphorbia henryi
Eurya henryi
Ficus henryi
Ficus sarmentosa var.
　henryi
Fimbristylis henryi
Gentianella henryi
Geranium henryi
Gerbera delavayi var.
　henryi
Goodyera henryi
Grewia henryi
Guldenstaedtia henryi
Gutzlaffia henryi
Heliciopsis henryi
Hemiboea henryi
Hemipilia henryi
Hepatica henryi
Heracleum henryi
Huperzia henryi
Hymenophyllum henryi
Hypericum augustinii
Hypericum henryi
Hypolepis punctata var.
　henryi
Illicium henryi
Illigera henryi
Impatiens augustinii
Impatiens fissicornis var.
　henryi
Impatiens henryi
Indigofera henryi
Iris henryi
Isodon henryi
Ixora henryi
Lactuca henryi
Lasianthus henryi
Ligustrum henryi
Lilium henryi
Liparis henryi
Lithocarpus henryi
Lonicera henryi

Lysimachia henryi
Macaranga henryi
Magnolia henryi
Mazus henryi
Meliosma henryi
Microsorium henryi
Microtropis henryi
Monachosorum henryi
Munronia henryi
Mussaenda henryi
Neocheiropteris henryi
Notoseris henryi
Oreocharis henryana
Ormosia henryi
Ornithoboea henryi
Oryzopsis henryi
Osmanthus henryi
Parthenocissus henryana
Passiflora henryi
Pecteilis henryi
Pedicularis henryi
Pentapanax henryi
Peucedanum henryi
Philadelphus henryi
Phyllostachys henryi
Pimpinella henryi
Pinus tabulaeformis var.
　henryi
Pittosporum henryi
Platanus 'Augustine
　Henry'
Populus x canadensis
　'Henryana'
Premna henryana
Prenanthes henryi
Primula carolinehenryi
Prunus henryi
Psychotria henryi
Pteris henryi
Puccinia henryana
Pygeum henryi
Randia henryi
Rehmannia henryi
Rhamnus henryi

Rhododendron augustinii
Rhodoleia henryi
Ribes henryi
Rosa henryi
Rubus henryi
Sageretia henryi
Sambucus henriana
Saprosma henryi
Saruma henryi
Saussurea henryi
Saxifraga mengtziana
Schisandra henryi
Scrophularia henryi
Sindechites henryi
Sinojackia henryi
Sinowilsonia henryi
Smilacina henryi
Sorbus henryi
Spiraea henryi
Stellaria henryi
Sterculia henryi
Sticta henryana
Strobilanthes austini
Syzygium augustinii
Tetrastigma henryi
Thladiantha henryi
Tilia henryana
Toona ciliata var. henryi
Trisetum henryi
Tylophora augustiniana
Tylophora henryi
Uraria henryi
Urena lobata var. henryi
Urophysa henryi
Vaccinium henryi
Vernonia henryi
Veronica henryi
Viburnum henryi
Viola henryi
Vitex henryi
Wendlandia augustinii
Youngia henryi

Plant synonymy in relation to Augustine Henry's plants

Acanthopanax henryi = *Eleutherococcus henryi*
Alpinia henryi = *Alpinia hainanensis*
Alsophila henryi = *Alsophila gigantea* var. *polynervata*
Anemone henryi = *Hepatica henryi*
Antidesma henryi = *Antidesma montanum*
Aquilegia henryi = *Urophysa henryi*
Ardisia henryi = *Ardisia crispa*
Arisaema sazensoo var. *henryanum* = *Arisaema sikokianum* var. *henryanum*
Balania henryi = *Balanophora henryi*
Bauhinia henryi = *Bauhinia touranensis*
Bridelia henryana = *Bridelia affinis*
Buddleja henryi = *Buddleja forrestii*
Capparis henryi = *Capparis micrantha* var. *henryi*
Caprifolium henryi = *Lonicera henryi*
Carex longicruris var. *henryi* = *Carex henryi*
Carolinella henryi = *Primula carolinehenryi*
Carpinus tshonoskii var. *henryana* = *Carpinus henryana*
Castanopsis henryi = *Castanea henryi*
Catalpa henryi = *Catalpa ovata*
Catharinea henryi = *Atrichum crispulum*
Celastrus hindsii var. *henryi* = *Celastrus hindsii*
Cheiropteris henryi = *Neocheiropteris henryi*
Cirrhopetalum henryi = *Bulbophyllum andersonii*
Cleghornia henryi = *Sindechites henryi*
Cnicus henryi = *Cirsium henryi*
Coelogyne henryi = *Pleione bulbocodioides*
Cornus henryi = *Cornus walteri*
Cotoneaster rugosa var. *henryana* = *Cotoneaster henryanus*
Crataegus henryi = *Crataegus scabrifolia*
Crepis henryi = *Youngia henryi*
Cynanchum henryi = *Biondia henryi*
Desmodium henryi = *Podocarpium duclouxii*
Deutzia henryi = *Deutzia crassifolia*
Deyeuxia henryi = *Calamagrostis henryi*
Dichroa henryi = *Dichroa febrifuga*
Dioscorea henryi = *Dioscorea delavayi*
Dolichos henryi = *Dolichos junghuhnianus*
Epipactis henryi = *Goodyera henryi*
Eurya distichophylla var. *henryi* = *Eurya henryi*
Fedorovia henryi = *Ormosia henryi*
Ficus foveolata var. *henryi* = *Ficus sarmentosa* var. *henryi*
Fraxinus retusa var. *henryana* = *Fraxinus retusa*
Gentiana henryi = *Gentianella henryi*
Gerbera henryi = *Gerbera delavayi* var. *henryi*
Gymnogramme henryi = *Colysis henryi*
Habenaria henryi = *Platanthera minor*
Helicia henryi = *Heliciopsis henryi*

Hemsleya henryi = *Neoalsomitra integrifolia*
Henrya augustinianum = *Tylophora augustiniana*
Henryastrum augustiniana = *Tylophora augustiniana*
Henryettana mirabilis = *Antiotrema dunnianum*
Hiptage henryana = *Hiptage minor*
Hymenolepis henryi = *Belvisia henryi*
Hypericum patulum var. *henryi* = *Hypericum beanii*
Ilex henryi = *Ilex macrocarpa*
Ipomoea henryi = *Argyreia henryi*
Isopyrum henryi = *Urophysa henryi*
Jasminum urophyllum var. *henryi* = *Jasminum urophyllum* var. *wilsonii*
Koelreuteria henryi = *Koelreuteria elegans* subsp. *formosana*
Linociera henryi = *Chionanthus henryanus*
Lycopodium henryi = *Huperzia henryi*
Macaranga henricorum = *Macaranga denticulata*
Machilus henryi = *Phoebe tavoyana*
Maesa henryi = *Maesa montana*
Maianthemum henryi = *Smilacina henryi*
Mallotus henryi = *Macaranga henryi*
Nasturtium henryi = *Cochleria henryi*
Neohenrya augustiniana = *Tylophora augustiniana*
Oligobotrya henryi = *Smilacina henryi*
Paris henryi = *Paris delavayi*
Pasania henryi = *Lithocarpus henryi*
Pellaea henryi = *Pellaea nitidula*
Petrocosmea henryi = *Petrocosmea minor*
Phlegmariurus henryi = *Huperzia henryi*
Phoebe henryi = *Phoebe tavoyana*
Phylloboea henryi = *Paraboea rufescens*
Phyllomphax henryi = *Brachycorythis henryi*
Plagiogyria henryi = *Plagiogyria stenoptera*
Platanthera henryi = *Platanthera minor*
Plectranthus henryi = *Isodon henryi*
Pleione henryi = *Pleione bulbocodioides*
Polygonatum henryi = *Polygonatum cyrtonema*
Polypodium henryi = *Colysis henryi*
Prenanthes henryi = *Notoseris henryi*
Primula henryi = *Primula carolinehenryi*
Prismatomeris henryi = *Canthium henryi*
Prunus yunnanensis var. *henryi* = *Prunus henryi*
Pterostyrax henryi = *Sinojackia henryi*
Quercus augustinii = *Cyclobalanopsis augustinii*
Quercus henryi = *Lithocarpus henryi*
Rhodiola henryi = *Rhodiola yunnanensis*
Rhus henryi = *Rhus potaninii*
Rhynchosia henryi = *Dumasia villosa*
Salix henryi = *Salix heterochoma*

Sanicula henryi = *Sanicula orthacantha*
Sarcanthus henryi = *Robiquetia succisa*
Saxifraga henryi = *Saxifraga mengtziana*
Scolopia henryi = *Scolopia saeva*
Sedum henryi = *Rhodiola yunnanensis*
Selaginella henryi = *Selaginella repanda*
Selliguea henryi = *Colysis henryi*
Semiaquilegia henryi = *Urophysa henryi*
Senecio henryi = *Sinacalia tangutica*
Sinacalia henryi = *Sinacalia tangutica*
Sonerila henryi = *Plagiopetalum esquirolii*
Sorbus henryi = *Sorbus hemsleyi*
Speranskia henryi = *Speranskia cantonensis*
Steudnera henryana = *Steudnera colocasiifolia*

Stipa henryi = *Oryzopsis henryi*
Stranvaesia henryi = *Stranvaesia davidiana*
Strobilanthes henryi = *Gutzlaffia henryi*
Strychnos henryi = *Strychnos cathayensis*
Styrax henryi = *Styrax formosana*
Symplocos henryi = *Symplocos lucida*
Thea henryana = *Camellia henryana*
Tinus henryi = *Ardisia crispa*
Uraria henryi = *Desmodium hispidum*
Vanda henryi = *Vanda brunnea*
Vitis henryana = *Parthenocissus henryana*
Wendlandia henryi = *Wendlandia longidens*
Yinshania henryi = *Cochleria henryi*

Plants named for Augustine Henry's bases in China

Yichang
Campylotropis ichangensis
Citrus ichangensis
Elatostema ichangense
Indigofera ichangensis
Persea ichangensis
Polystichum ichangense
Rubus ichangensis
Thalictrum ichangense
Viburnum ichangense

Mengzi
Didymocarpus mengtze
Euonymus mengtseanus
Hoya mengtzeensis
Impatiens mengtszeana
Rhododendron mengtszense
Saxifraga mengtziana
Veratrum mengtzeanum

Great Black Mountain
Aster nigromontana

Yuanjiang
Clematis yuanjiangensis

Manmei
Ilex marneiensis
Polypodium manmeiense

Simao
Litsea pierrei var. *szemaois*
Premna szemaoensis
Syzygium szemaoense
Thalictrum simaoense

Wushan
Astragalus wushanicus
Stellaria wushanensis

Henry plants named for friends and colleagues

Caroline Henry
Quercus carolinae (now *Lithocarpus carolinae*)
Carolinella henryi (now *Primula carolinehenryi*)

Evelyn Gleeson (Dublin)
Keteleeria evelyniana

Ho (native plant collector)
Heptapleurum hoi (now *Schefflera hoi*)

Sir Robert Hart
Hartia sinensis (synonym of *Stewartia pteropetiolata*)

Emil Bretschneider
Bretschneidera sinensis

Charles Sprague Sargent (Boston)
Sargentodoxa cuneata

Sir William Thiselton Dyer (RBG, Kew)
Dipteronia dyeriana

Sir Arthur Hill (RBG, Kew)
Pilea hilliana

Sir Isaac Bayley Balfour (RBG, Edinburgh)
Diospyros balfouriana

William Botting Hemsley (RBG, Kew)
Aconitum hemsleyanum
Begonia hemsleyana
Biondia hemsleyana
Corydalis hemsleyana
Dioscorea hemsleyi
Euonymus hemsleyana
Hemsleya chinensis
Heracleum hemsleyanum
Lindera hemsleyana
Lysimachia hemsleyana
Machilus hemsleyi
Metaplexis hemsleyana
Paliurus hemsleyanus
Sloanea hemsleyana
Sorbus hemsleyi
Styrax hemsleyanus
Tetrastigma hemsleyanum

Professor Daniel Oliver (RBG, Kew)
Acer oliverianum
Meconopsis oliveriana
Thladiantha oliveri
Tilia oliveri

Appendix 2

Chinese place names

Throughout this book, I have opted to use the current Pinyin romanisation system for Chinese place names, giving the older romanisations – Wade–Giles or, rarely, Post Office – as applicable. Thus, 'Yichang' appears, on first mention, as 'Yichang (Ichang)' and 'Kaohsiung' is given as 'Kaohsiung (Takow)'.

For additional reference, the lists below feature present-day place names that may be easily found on modern maps presented alongside older or local names with which Augustine Henry and his contemporaries will have been familiar.

Provinces, autonomous regions, islands

Anhui (Anhwei) Province
Fujian (Fukien) Province
Gansu (Kansu) Province
Guangdong (Kwangtung) Province
Guangxi (Kwangsi) Zhuang Autonomous Region
Guizhou (Kweichow) Province
Hainan Dao (Hainan Island), Hainan Province
Hebei (Hopei) Province
Hubei (Hupeh) Province
Jiangsu (Kiangsu) Province
Jiangxi (Kiangsi) Province
Lamay Island (Xiao Liuqiu, Hsiao Liuchiu, Golden Lion Island), Taiwan
Lanyu (Botel Tobago, Orchid Island), Taiwan
Shaanxi (Shensi) Province
Shanxi (Shansi) Province
Sichuan (Szechuan, Szechwan) Province
Taiwan (Formosa) Island
Zhejiang (Chechiang, Chekiang) Province

Municipalities, prefectures, counties, cities, districts, towns, villages

Badong (Patung) County, Hubei Province
Bankinsing (Bankinsing, Wanchin, Wanjin), Taiwan
Baokang (Paokang) County, Hubei Province
Baoxing (Mupin) County, Sichuan Province
Beijing (Peking) Municipality
Changleping (Changlo), Hubei Province
Changyang Tujia Autonomous County (Changyang), Hubei Province
Chengde (Jehol), Hebei Province
Chengdu (Chengtu), Sichuan Province
Chongqing (Chungking, Chung-ching) Municipality; formerly part of Sichuan Province
Dachang (Taning Hsien) Town, Wushan County
Dachang Hui Autonomous County, Hebei Province
Dali (Tali) City, Yunnan Province
Dali Bai Autonomous Prefecture, Yunnan Province
Danzhou (Nodoa) City, Hainan Island
Dazhuang (Tachuang), Yunnan Province
Emei County (Omei Hsien), Sichuan Province
Fang County (Fang Hsien, Fang Xian), Hubei Province
Fengchunling (Feng Chenlin),
Yunnan Province
Garzê Tibetan Autonomous Prefecture, Sichuan Province
Guangzhou (Canton) City, Guangdong Province
Haikou (Hoihow) City, Hainan Province
Hankou (Hankow) District, Wuhan City
Honghe Hani and Yi Autonomous Prefecture (Honghe Hanizu Yizu Zizhizhou), Yunnan Province
Hsinchu County (Xinzhu Xian), Taiwan
Huangpu (Whampoa) District, Guangdong Province
Jianshi (Chienshih) County, Hubei Province
Kangding (Dartsedo) City, Garzê Tibetan Autonomous Prefecture
Kangding (Tachienlu, Dardo) County, Garzê Tibetan Autonomous Prefecture
Kaohsiung (Gaoxiong; Takow, Tako) City Municipality, Taiwan
Kaohsiung County, Taiwan
Kunming (Yunnan Fu) City, Yunnan Province
Lanyu Township, Taitung County
Lao Cai (Laokay) City, Lao Cai Province, Vietnam
Leshan (Kia ting Fu) City, Sichuan Province

Lichuan County (Lichuan Xian), Jiangxi Province

Liantuo (Nanto) Village, Hubei Province

Lijiang (Likiang) Town, Yunnan Province

Liouciou Township (Liuqiu Xiang), Pingtung County

Luding (Lu-ting-chiao) County, Garzê Tibetan Autonomous Prefecture

Mahuanggou (Mahuangpo) City, Sichuan Province

Maoba (Modaoqi) Town, Hubei Province

Maoping Town, Zigui County

Mengzi (Mengtze) County, Yunnan Province

Nanjing (Nanking) City, Jiangsu Province

Ningbo (Ningpo, Mingzhou) City, Zhejiang Province

Oluanpi (South Cape, Cape Eluanbi), Taiwan

Pingshanba (Pin-shan-pa) Village, Hubei Province

Pingtung City (Pingdong Shi, Pingtung Shih), Taiwan

Pingtung County, Taiwan

Pu'er (Puerh, Pu'er Shi) City, Yunnan Province

Qiongshan (Chiungshan, Kiungshan) District (Qiongshan Zu), Haikou City

Qiongzhou (Kiungchow); now Qiongshan

Sandouping (Santoup'ing) Town, Hubei Province

Shanghai Municipality

Shennongjia (Shengnengchia) Forestry District (Shennongjia Linqu), Hubei Province

Shiping (Shih Ping) County, Yunnan Province

Simao (Szemao) City, Yunnan Province

Simao (Simao Qu, Cuiyun) District, Yunnan Province

Taipei (Taibei) County (North County), Taiwan

Taitung (Taidong, Hou Shan) County, Taiwan

Tamsui (Tamsui) Township, Taiwan

Tengchong County (Tengchong Xian), Yunnan Province

Tengyue Town (Momein), Tengchong County

Three Gorges Reservoir Region (Sanxia), Chongqing Municipality/Hubei Province

Tongguan (Talang), Yunnan Province

Wuhan (Hankou, Hanyang, Wuchang) City, Hubei Province

Wushan County (Wushan Xian), Chongqing Municipality

Xingshan (Hsingshan) County, Hubei Province

Xishuangbanna (Sipsongpanna) Dai Autonomous Prefecture, Yunnan Province

Ya-an City (Ya-chou Fu), Sichuan Province

Yichang (Ichang) City, Hubei Province

Yiling District (Yiling Qu), Yichang City

Yuanjiang Hani, Yi and Dai Autonomous County (Yuanjiang, Yuan Chiang), Yunnan Province

Yuanyang County (Yuanyang Xian), Yunnan Province

Zigui (Kuei) County, Hubei Province

Rivers

Babian Jiang (Black or Papien River), Yunnan Province

Chang Jiang (Yangtze River, lower), eastern China

Dadu He (Tung River), Sichuan Province

Daning River (Taning River), Sichuan Province

Han Jiang (Han River), Hubei Province

Jinsha Jiang, (Yangtze River, upper), central and western China

Lancang Jiang (Mekong River), Yunnan Province

Min Jiang (Min River), Sichuan Province

Nu Jiang (Salween River), Yunnan Province

Qing Jiang (Tsing Kiang), Hubei Province

Yuan Jiang (Red River), Yunnan Province

Mountains and hills

Daba Shan (Tapa Shan) range, central China

Dahei Shan (Great Black Mountain), Yunnan Province

Emei Shan (Mount Omei), Sichuan Province

Gongga Shan (Minya Konka), Sichuan Province

Moji Shan (The Dome), Hubei Province

Wanshoushan (Ape's Hill, Shoushan), Taiwan

Yushan (Mount Morrison, Mount Yu, Jade Mountain), Taiwan

Appendix 3

Augustine Henry (1857–1930) – a chronology

1857 2nd July: born in Dundee, Scotland. In August, the Henry family return to Ireland.

1871 Augustine Henry's mother dies.

1877 Graduates from Queen's College, Galway (now the National University of Ireland, Galway).

1878 Obtains a Master of Arts degree from Queen's College, Belfast. Moves to London for a year.

1880 Qualifies as a doctor through the University of Edinburgh.

1881 Joins the Chinese Imperial Maritime Customs Service. Moves to Shanghai.

1882 Transfers to Yichang in Hubei Province. Hunts for fossils in the surrounding hills and glens.

1884 Begins to botanise around Yichang.

1885 Makes contact with Sir Joseph Dalton Hooker at Kew. Hires his first native plant collector and gathers specimens from Badong and Yichang.

1886 Sends his first consignment of more than 1,000 specimens to Kew. Introduces *Rhododendron mariesii* to cultivation.

1887 Dr Ernst Faber visits Henry at Yichang and travels on to explore Emei Shan in Sichuan Province. Later that year, Antwerp Edgar Pratt reaches Yichang with his family. Henry discovers *Lilium henryi*.

1888 Henry's grandmother dies. He embarks on a six-month long expedition to explore the mountains north and south of the Yangtze River. Discovers *Davidia involucrata* var. *vilmoriniana* in south Wushan County, Sichuan Province. Henry's 'Chinese names of plants' is

published in the *Journal of the China Branch of the Royal Asiatic Society*.

1889 Transfers to Hainan. Departs Yichang having discovered more than 500 new species and 25 new genera. Introduces *Lilium henryi* to cultivation via Kew. Begins collecting in Hainan; contracts malaria and returns to Ireland. Corresponds with Père Jean Marie Delavay. Visits Kew and is surprised to be received there as a celebrity. Bases himself at Kew Gardens.

1891 Augustine Henry's father dies. Marries Caroline Orridge, returns to China. Caroline contracts tuberculosis.

1892 Caroline Henry temporarily moves to Japan to recuperate, and collects plants there for Kew. Henry meets the English plant collectors and explorers Captain H. Bower and Dr W. G. Thorold, who have returned from Tibet. He also meets the American explorer W. Woodville Rockhill, who is shortly to return to Tibet. Writes *Notes on Economic Botany of China*, which was later republished in America by David Fairchild. Meets the Irish plant hunter William Hancock. Transfers to Taiwan.

1894 Caroline Henry moves to Colorado; dies that autumn. Augustine Henry leaves Taiwan and travels to the USA, where he meets Professor Sargent at the Arnold Arboretum in Boston, Massachusetts.

1895 Henry returns to China, and is based for a third time in Shanghai.

1896 Receives a new post at Mengzi in Yunnan Province. Collects on the Daweishan mountain range. Begins to study ethnic groups. Collects for the Arnold Arboretum. Hires 'Old Ho', a native plant collector. Discovers wild tea. Receives a letter from Arthur Kilpin Bulley.

1897 Sends his native plant collector to the Daweishan range and explores the Ailaoshan range.

1898 Transfers to Simao. Urges Kew and the Arnold Arboretum to send a professional collector to China. Is shocked at the rate of deforestation in the Mekong valley.

1899 Henry's native plant collector 'Old Ho' dies of malaria. Ernest Henry Wilson arrives in Simao to meet Henry.

1900 Henry departs China on 31 December, having discovered 1,726 new plants and collected 158,050 herbarium specimens.

1901 Visits Sri Lanka and climbs Adam's Peak. Travels to India to meet his sister, Mary. Meets A. K. Bulley in England; persuades him to send collectors to China.

1902 Caroline Henry commemorated in *Carolinella henryi* (now *Primula carolinehenryi)*. Moves to France to study forestry. Joseph Hooker dedicates a volume of *Curtis's Botanical Magazine* to Augustine Henry.

1903 Henry is visited by Henry Elwes in France. Bases himself at Kew to begin work on *The Trees of Great Britain and Ireland*. Visited at Kew by David Fairchild; as a result, Fairchild later sends Frank Meyer and Joseph Rock to China. Henry's native plant collector, 'Old Ho', is commemorated in *Heptapleurum hoi* (now *Schefflera hoi*). *Quercus carolinae* (now *Lithocarpus henryi*) is named for Caroline Henry and *Keteleeria evelyniana* is named in honour of Henry's friend in Ireland, Evelyn Gleeson.

1904 Writes letters of advice to George Forrest.

1905 Presented with the Victoria Medal of Honour (VMH), the most prestigious award in the fields of botany and horticulture.

1906 Explores the forests of North America. First volume of *The Trees of Great Britain and Ireland* is published.

1907 Appointed Reader (and, later, Professor) of Forestry at Cambridge. Advises a National Committee on suitable species for commercial forestry purposes; his advice is far reaching and establishes a lucrative forestry industry in Ireland.

1908 Marries Alice (Elsie) Brunton on Saint Patrick's Day.

1911 Meets Ernest Henry Wilson following his final expedition to China.

1912 Begins to breed hybrid trees.

1913 Final, seventh volume of *The Trees of Great Britain and Ireland* published. Returns to Ireland to take the post of Professor of Forestry at University College, Dublin.

1926 Retires from University College, Dublin.

1929 A wing of the Fan Memorial Institute of Botany in Beijing is dedicated to Henry. Also, the second volume of *Icones Plantarum Sinicarum* is dedicated to him.

1930 Augustine Henry dies, following a short illness, at his home in Ranelagh, Dublin.

Appendix 4

Select glossary

acuminate leaves gradually tapering to a point at the tip

albumen the storage tissue for oily or starchy nutritive material; a food supply for the embryo

anther the pollen-bearing part of the stamen

apomict a plant that reproduces asexually (by seed), thus reproducing clonally by seed; seedlings are identical to the parent plant and belong to the same clone

aroid group of plants belonging to the family Araceae with flowers carried in a spadix

axil the angle formed by a leaf or lateral branch with a stem, or a vein with a midrib

axillary produced in the axil

bipinnate leaves twice pinnate

bract a modified leaf at the base of a flower stalk or flower cluster

bulbil a small bulb or bulb-like growth

calyx a collective term for sepals that form the outer whorl of the floral envelope

capsule a dry, several-celled seed vessel

compound composed of two or more similar parts

cordate shaped like a heart, e.g. the base of a leaf

corymb a flat-topped flowerhead with the outer blossoms opening first; *see also* cyme

culm the stems of grasses and bamboos

cyme a flat topped flowerhead with the inner blossoms opening first; *see also* corymb

dichotomous branching regularly by forking repeatedly in two

dioecious male and female flowers carried on separate plants

endosperm the albumen, when it is stored inside the embryo sac

epilithic growing on rocks

epiphyte growing on plants without being parasitic

ethnobotany the study of the use of plants by indigenous peoples and societies

fenestrate irregularly perforated by numerous openings or translucent zones

fluviatile growing in or by a river or stream

genus the principal rank in the taxonomic
(pl. **genera**) hierarchy between family and species

herbarium a systematic collection of dried plants used for scientific study

homonym a scientific name given to two or more plants in a similar genus but belonging to quite different species; the names are identical, but not the species

indumentum a dense, hairy covering

labellum the lip or enlarged third petal of an orchid

lanceolate lance-shaped, widening above the base and long tapering towards the apex

liana a woody, climbing vine

lignotuber the swollen, woody base of a number of trees and shrubs adapted to withstand fire

lithophyte a plant that grows on rocks or stony soil, deriving its nourishment from the atmosphere rather than from the soil

lobe any protruding part of an organ, e.g. corolla, calyx, leaf

materia the science of substances, including plants
medica and animals, used in medicine

midrib the central vein or rib of a leaf

monogeneric of a family containing a single genus

monotypic a genus or family containing a single species

neotropical belonging to the tropics of the New World; *see also* paleotropical

ovate	broadest below the middle (like a hen's egg)
paleotropical	belonging to the tropics of the Old World; *see also* neotropical
panicle	a branching raceme
pantropical	belonging to tropical regions of the Old and New Worlds
pedicel	the stalk of an individual flower in an inflorescence
peltate	a leaf that is more or less circular and flat with the stalk inserted in the middle
petal	one of the separate segments of a corolla
petiole	the leaf stalk
pinnate	with leaflets arranged either side of a central stalk
pistil	the female organ of a flower comprising the ovary, style and stigma
pseudobulb	a water-storing, thickened, bulb-like stem found on many orchids
raceme	a simple, elongated inflorescence with stalked flowers
rhizome	a specialised, swollen, underground stem lying close to the soil surface that produces roots and aerial parts, such as the leaves, stem and inflorescence
scales	a minute leaf or bract; or, a flat, gland-like appendage on the surface of a leaf, flower or shoot
sepal	one of the segments of the calyx
sessile	not stalked, as in leaves and flowers
spadix	the fleshy axis of a spike, often subtended by a spathe
spathe	a large bract subtending and often ensheathing an inflorescence; applied only in monocotyledons
species	the category of taxa found beneath genus level and usually containing closely related,

	morphologically similar individuals often found within a distinct geographical range; the basic unit of naming, it is often further divided into subspecies (subsp. or ssp.), variety (var.) and forma (f.); the species itself is given a specific epithet or trivial name
spike	a simple, elongated inflorescence with sessile flowers
stamen	the male organ of a flower containing the filament and anther
stigma	the summit of the pistil, which receives the pollen
stolon	a trailing stem that produces new plants at its tip
style	the elongated central part of the pistil between the ovary and stigma
tendril	a slender, modified branch, leaf or axis attaching itself by twining or adhesion; a means of support used by many climbing plants
thyrse	a compact, narrow panicle
tomentum	a dense covering of matted hairs
trifoliate	three-leaved
tuber	a swollen underground stem or root used for storage
umbel	a flat-topped inflorescence in which the pedicels all arise from a common point
umbellate	flowers in umbels
unisexual	with flowers of one sex only
variety (var.)	the category of taxa intermediate between subspecies (subsp., ssp.) and forma (f.)
whorl	three or more flowers arranged in a ring
xerophytic	adapted to withstand drought

Notes

The endnote numbering below refers to corresponding citations in the main text; *see also* Appendix 6, Select bibliography.

Chapter 1
1. Nelson, 1995: 1
2. Moore, 1942: 10–15
3. Nelson & Walsh, 1984: 87
4. Lancaster, 1993
5. Bishop, 1996: 179
6. Bretschneider, 1898, vol. 2: 874

Chapter 2
1. Pratt, 1892: 17
2. Pratt, 1892: 20
3. Wilson, 1913: 12
4. Morley, 1979: 34
5. Wilson, 1913: 12
6. Bonavia *et al.*, 2004
7. Henry, 1894a: personal communication
8. Wilson, 1913: 12
9. Morley, 1979: 38
10. Wilson, 1913: 29
11. Pratt, 1892: 12
12. Morley, 1979: 40
13. Bretschneider, 1898, vol. 2: 638.
14. Werner, 1928: 555
15. Nelson & Walsh, 1984: 71
16. Veitch (J. H.), 1906: 84
17. Wilson, 1913: 12
18. Desmond, 1999: 107
19. Henry, 1885: personal communication
20. Thiselton-Dyer, 1905: viii
21. Henry, 1890: 93–94
22. Heude, 1894: 244
23. Henry, 1902: 3
24. Bean, 1989, vol. 1: 456
25. Sargent, 1916: 382
26. Henry, 1893a: 20
27. Henry, 1893a: 64

Chapter 3
1. Pratt, 1892: 12
2. Wilson, 1913: 29.

3. Henry, 1903a: 217
4. Veitch (J. H.), 1906: 422
5. Hooker, 1891: t. 7191
6. Howard, 1980: 113
7. Oliver, 1888: 75 (fig. 1.) and Oliver, 1889: 134
8. Sargent, 1913: 414
9. Bretschneider, 1898, vol. 1: 954
10. Pratt, 1892: 7
11. Pratt, 1892: 9
12. Morley, 1979: 55
13. Morley, 1979: 56
14. Wilson, 1925: 78
15. Hsu, 2006: 30–35
16. Hinkley, 1999: 209
17. Henry, 1893a: 49
18. Morley, 1979: 58

Chapter 4
1. Sargent, 1913: 346
2. Pratt, 1892: 49
3. Pratt, 1892: 49
4. Henry, 1893a: 44
5. Sargent, 1916: 395
6. Henry, 1893a: 25
7. Shaw, 2002 (in Stearn, 2002): 280
8. Henry, 1893a: 44
9. Hemsley, 1912: t. 8432. *See also* Dode, 1908: 406
10. Wilson, 1916 (in Sargent, 1916): 257
11. Bean, 1989, vol. 4: 85
12. Bean, 1989, vol. 4: 701
13. Kingdon-Ward, 1954: 77
14. Henry, 1888a: personal communication
15. Wilson, 1913: 34
16. Wilson, 1913: 32
17. Wilson, 1913: 46
18. Henry, 1888b: personal communication
19. Wilson, 1913: 51
20. Henry, 1902: 4
21. Skvortsov, 1998: 109
22. Hinkley, 1999: 286

23. Bretschneider, 1898, vol. 2: 790
24. Igarashi & Fukuda, 1997
25. Farrer, 1922
26. Pim, 1984: 37

Chapter 5
1. Zheng, 1983: 177–187
2. Xu *et al.*, 2000: table
3. Donohue, 2002: 14
4. Zich, 1997: 20
5. Henry, 1893a: 46
6. Valder, 1999
7. Hsu, 2006: 31
8. McAllister, 2005: 94
9. Oldfield, 2007
10. Cicuzza *et al.*, 2007
11. Bartholomew *et al.*, 1983: 2
12. Ge *et al.*, 1997: 342

Chapter 6
1. Bishop, 1996
2. Hemsley, 1892: 298–301
3. Pratt, 1892: 49
4. Lancaster, 1993: 86
5. Pratt, 1892: 110
6. Wilson, 1913: 250
7. McAllister, 2005: 84
8. Sargent, 1913: 528
9. Wilson, 1913: 251
10. Henry, 1889d: personal communication
11. Pratt, 1892: 126.
12. Wilson, 1913: 209
13. Cribb, 1997: 274–83
14. Le Lievre, 1994: 238–47
15. Wilson, 1913: 220
16. Pratt, 1892: 224
17. Hemsley, 1892: 299

Chapter 7
1. Buckley & Samagalski, 1994
2. Davidian, 1992: 313
3. Barwick, 2004: 220
4. Henry, 1889a: personal communication

5. Henry, 1889c: personal communication
6. Henry, 1889b: personal communication
7. Morley, 1979: 71
8. Shephard, 2003: 224
9. Pim, 1984: 41
10. Henry, 1891b: personal communication
11. Henry, 1891a: personal communication
12. Bretschneider, 1898, vol. 2: 806
13. Bretschneider, 1898, vol. 2: 808
14. Henry, 1892a: personal communication
15. Nelson, 1986 (in Henry, 1893a): xiii
16. Henry, 1892a: personal communication
17. Bretschneider, 1898, vol. 2: 770
18. Soó, 1927: 143
19. Henry, 1892b: personal communication

Chapter 8
1. Henry, 1896a: 2
2. Henry, 1893b: personal communication
3. Desmond, 1995: 210
4. Bretschneider, 1898, vol. 2: 709
5. Bretschneider, 1898, vol. 2: 739
6. Henry, 1896a: 3
7. Henry, 1896a: 38
8. Barwick, 2004: 236
9. Henry, 1902: 6
10. Morley, 1979: 24
11. Anon, 1867: 599–601
12. Henry, 1902: 3
13. Keng, 1996: 412
14. Schneider, 1916 (in Sargent, 1916): 495
15. Henry, 1894b: personal communication
16. Henry, 1894d: personal communication
17. Jackson, 1901: 31
18. Henry, 1894c: personal communication

Chapter 9
1. For the correct nomenclature of this tree, *see* Whitehouse, 2007: 112
2. Storey, 2001: 18

3. Li *et al.*, 1975: 1–13
4. Henry, 1896a: 1–118
5. Hsieh & Shen, 1994: 7–16
6. Anon, 2002

Chapter 10
1. Henry, 1895: personal communication
2. Henry, 1896b: personal communication
3. Henry, 1896c: personal communication
4. D'Orléans, 1898: 18
5. Henry, 1896d: personal communication
6. Henry, 1896e: personal communication
7. Nelson, 1982–83): 29
8. Handel-Mazzetti, 2001 (1927): 54
9. Henry, 1896f: personal communication
10. Henry, 1903b: 98
11. Henry, 1903b: 98
12. Mayhew *et al.*, 2002
13. Henry, 1903b: 97
14. Lancaster, 1993: 209
15. Henry, 1903c: 100
16. Henry, 1896g: personal communication
17. McLean, 1997: xi
18. McLean, 1997: 22
19. Henry, 1897a: personal communication
20. Henry, 1897b: personal communication
21. Henry, 1903c: 408
22. Henry, 1897c: personal communication
23. Henry, 1897d: personal communication
24. Henry, 1897–8: 411

Chapter 11
1. Henry, 1898a: personal communication
2. Henry, 1899a: personal communication
3. Henry, 1897e: personal communication
4. Henry, 1897f: personal communication
5. Henry, 1898b: personal communication
6. Henry, 1899b: personal communication
7. Henry, 1899c: personal communication

8. Briggs, 1993: 12
9. Wilson, 1926: 275
10. Henry, 1899d: personal communication
11. Wilson, 1901: 127
12. Veitch (J. H.), 1906: 93
13. Henry, 1899f: personal communication
14. Wilson, 1913: viii
15. Nelson, 1982–83: 21
16. Veitch (J. H.), 1905: personal communication
17. Veitch (J. H.), 1900a: personal communication
18. Veitch (J. H.), 1900b: personal communication
19. Shephard, 2003: 258
20. Veitch (H.), 1899: personal communication

Chapter 12
1. Kaiyun & Zhekun, 1998: 3
2. Feng *et al.*, 1998: 9
3. Goodman, 2000: 4
4. Wu, 1999: 11
5. Shui & Chen, 2002: 205–312
6. Yunnan Society of Ecological Economics *et al.*, 1992
7. Shultes & von Reis, 1995: 145

Chapter 13
1. Henry, 1899e: personal communication
2. McLean, 2004: 58
3. Forrest, 1913: personal communication
4. Henry, 1923: ii
5. Fairchild, 1941 (1938): 157
6. Fairchild, 1941 (1938): 284
7. Henry, 1907: personal communication
8. Anon, 1908: 1–169
9. Anon, 1908: 165
10. Anon, 1908: 32
11. O'Driscoll, 1981: 21
12. Nelson, 1982–83: 36
13. Mooney, 1970: 82
14. Briggs, 1993: 77
15. Morley, 1979: 23
16. Moore, 1942: 12
17. Moore, 1942: 15
18. Morley, 1979: 24

Select bibliography

Anon (1867) Cormorant on the coast of Formosa. *Illustrated London News*, 15 June 1867.

Anon (1908) Report of the Departmental Committee on Irish Forestry. Dublin, Ireland: Alexander Thom & Co. (Department of Agriculture and Technical Instruction, Dublin).

Anon (2001) Monkey business at Takao Hill. *Taipei Times*, 29 January 2001.

Bartholomew, B., Boufford, D. E., Chang, A. L., Cheng, Z., Dudley, T. R., He, S. A., *et al.* (1983) The 1980 Sino-American botanical expedition to western Hubei Province, People's Republic of China. *Journal of the Arnold Arboretum*, **64**(1): 1–103.

Barwick, M. (2004) *Tropical and Subtropical Trees*. London, UK: Thames & Hudson.

Bean, W. J. (1989) *Trees and Shrubs Hardy in the British Isles*, vols 1–4. London, UK: John Murray.

Bishop, G. (1996) *Travels in Imperial China – The Intrepid Explorations and Discoveries of Père Armand David*. London, UK: Cassell.

Bonavia, J., Hayman, R., Bishop, K., Booz, P. & Holdsworth, M. (2004) *The Yangzi River and the Three Gorges*, 7th edit. (illustrated). Hong Kong: Odyssey Publications, Airphoto International.

Bretschneider, E. (1898) *History of European Botanical Discoveries in China*, vols 1–2. London, UK: Sampson Low, Marston & Co.

Briggs, R. W. (1993) *Chinese Wilson: A Life of Ernest H Wilson, 1876–1930*, London, UK: The Stationery Office (Royal Botanic Gardens, Kew; Royal Botanic Garden Edinburgh).

Buckley, M. & Samagalski, A. (1994) *China (Lonely Planet Travel Survival Kit)*, 4th rev. edit. London, UK: Lonely Planet Publications.

Cicuzza, D., Newton, A. & Oldfield, S. (2007) *The Red List of Magnoliaceae*. Cambridge, UK: Fauna and Flora International.

Cribb, P. (1997) *The Genus Cypripedium*. Portland, OR, USA: Timber Press (in association with the Royal Botanic Gardens, Kew).

Davidian, H. H. (1992) *The Rhododendron Species*, vol. 3: Elepidotes (series *neriiflorum* to *thomsonii*). Portland, Oregon, USA: Timber Press.

Desmond, R. (1995) *Kew: the History of the Royal Botanic Gardens*. London, UK: Harvill Press & Royal Botanic Gardens, Kew.

Desmond, R. (1999) *Sir Joseph Dalton Hooker – Traveller and Plant Collector*. Woodbridge, Suffolk, UK: Antique Collectors' Club (with Royal Botanic Gardens, Kew).

Dode, L.-A. (1908) *Davidia vilmoriniana. Revue Horticole*, **80**: 406.

Donohue, M. (2002) Villages of the dammed. *Irish Times* magazine, **3**(19).

Fairchild, D. (1938) *The World Was My Garden: Travels of a Plant Explorer*. (First published, 1938.) New York, NY, USA: Charles Scribner's Sons.

Farrer, R. (1922) *The Rainbow Bridge*. London, UK: Arnold.

Feng, Z. Z., Yang, S. Z. & Wang, D. M. (1998) *Rare Trees in Yunnan Province*. Beijing, People's Republic of China: Esperanto Press.

Forrest, G. (1913) Personal communication to John Charles (J. C.) Williams, 29 November 1913. Archives of the Royal Botanic Gardens Edinburgh.

Ge, J.-W., Wu, J.-Q., Zhu, Z.-Q. & Zhao, B.-Y. (1997) Studies on plant diversity and present situation of conservation in Shennongjia Biosphere Reserve, Hubei, China. *Journal of Wuhan Botanical Research*, **15**(4): 341–352 (in Chinese).

Goodman, J. (2000) *The Exploration of Yunnan*. Kunming, Yunnan, China: Yunnan People's Publishing House.

Handel-Mazzetti, H. (2001) *A Botanical Pioneer in South West China: Experiences and Impressions of an Austrian Botanist during the First World War*. D. Winstanley (trans). First published as *Naturbilder aus Südwest China* (1927); Vienna: Österreichischer Bundesverlag.

Hemsley, W. B. (1892) A botanical collection made in western China. *Journal of the Linnean Society of London (Botany)*, **29**: 298–301.

Hemsley, W. B. (1902) *Carolinella henryi*. In: Thiselton-Dyer, W. T. (ed.) *Hooker's Icones Plantarum*, ser. 4, **8**(2), plate 2726.

Hemsley, W. B. (1912) *Davidia involucrata* var. *vilmoriniana* Hemsl. *Curtis's Botanical Magazine*, **CXXXVIII (138)**: t. 8432.

Henry, A. (1885) Personal communication to Joseph Dalton Hooker, 7 September 1885. London, UK: Archives of the Royal Botanic Gardens, Kew.

Henry, Anderson (1881) *Primula* x. *henryi*. *Gardeners' Chronicle*, n. ser. 15: 404. London, UK.

Henry, A. (1888a) Personal communication to William Thiselton-Dyer, 29 June 1888. London, UK: Archives of the Royal Botanic Gardens, Kew.

Henry, A. (1888b) Personal communication to William Thiselton-Dyer, 9 October 1888. London, UK: Archives of the Royal Botanic Gardens, Kew.

Henry, A. (1889a) Personal communication to William Thiselton-Dyer, 17 May 1889. London, UK: Archives of the Royal Botanic Gardens, Kew.

Henry, A. (1889b) Personal communication to William Thiselton-Dyer, 9 August 1889. London, UK: Archives of the Royal Botanic Gardens, Kew.

Henry, A. (1889c) Personal communication to William Thiselton-Dyer, 14 August 1889. London, UK: Archives of the Royal Botanic Gardens, Kew.

Henry, A. (1889d) Personal communication to William Thiselton-Dyer, 19 November 1889. London, UK: Archives of the Royal Botanic Gardens, Kew.

Henry, A. (1890) Notes on two mountain antelopes of central China. *Proceedings of the Zoological Society of London*, **8**: 93–94.

Henry, A. (1891a) Personal communication to William Thiselton-Dyer, 20 May 1891. London, UK: Archives of the Royal Botanic Gardens, Kew.

Henry, A. (1891b) Personal communication to William Thiselton-Dyer, 24 October 1891. London, UK: Archives of the Royal Botanic Gardens, Kew.

Henry, A. (1892a) Personal communication to William Thiselton-Dyer, 15 January 1892. London, UK: Archives of the Royal Botanic Gardens, Kew.

Henry, A. (1892b) Personal communication to William Thiselton-Dyer, 15 October 1892. London, UK: Archives of the Royal Botanic Gardens, Kew.

Henry, A. (1893a) *Notes on Economic Botany of China*. Shanghai, China: The Presbyterian Mission Press.

Henry, A. (1893b) Personal communication to William Thiselton-Dyer, 3 March 1893. London, UK: Archives of the Royal Botanic Gardens, Kew.

Henry, A. (1894a) Personal communication to William Thiselton-Dyer, 18 March 1894. London, UK: Archives of the Royal Botanic Gardens, Kew.

Henry, A. (1894b) Personal communication to Sargent, 31 May 1894. Archives of the Arnold Arboretum Horticultural Library, Harvard University, Boston, MA, USA.

Henry, A. (1894c) Personal communication to Sargent, 30 October 1894. Archives of the Arnold Arboretum Horticultural Library, Harvard University, Boston, MA, USA.

Henry, A. (1894d) Personal communication to William Thiselton-Dyer, 31 October 1894. London, UK: Archives of the Royal Botanic Gardens, Kew.

Henry, A. (1895) Personal communication to Evelyn Gleeson, 11 January 1895. Archives of the National Botanic Gardens, Glasnevin, Dublin.

Henry, A. (1896a) A list of plants from Formosa, with some preliminary remarks on the geography, nature of the flora and economic botany of the island. *Transactions of the Asiatic Society of Japan*, **24** (December 1896 supplement): 1–118.

Henry, A. (1896b) Personal communication to Evelyn Gleeson, 5 March 1896. Archives of the National Botanic Gardens, Glasnevin, Dublin.

Henry, A. (1896c) Personal communication to Evelyn Gleeson, 11 May 1896. Archives of the National Botanic Gardens, Glasnevin, Dublin.

Henry, A. (1896d) Personal communication to William Thiselton-Dyer, 28 May 1896. Archives of the Royal Botanic Gardens, Kew, London.

Henry, A. (1896e) Personal communication to William Thiselton-Dyer, 14 July 1896. Archives of the Royal Botanic Gardens, Kew, London.

Henry, A. (1896f) Personal communication to Evelyn Gleeson, 29 August 1896. Archives of the National Botanic Gardens, Glasnevin, Dublin.

Henry, A. (1896g) Personal communication to Evelyn Gleeson, 14 November 1896. Archives of the National Botanic Gardens, Glasnevin, Dublin.

Henry, A. (1897a) Personal communication to Sargent, 13 January 1897. Archives of the Arnold Arboretum Horticultural Library, Harvard University, Boston, MA, USA.

Henry, A. (1897b) Personal communication to William Thiselton-Dyer, 29 January 1897. Archives of the Royal Botanic Gardens, Kew, London.

Henry, A. (1897c) Personal communication to Evelyn Gleeson, 20 February 1897. Archives of the National Botanic Gardens, Glasnevin, Dublin.

Henry, A. (1897d) Personal communication to Evelyn Gleeson, 25 May 1897. Archives of the National Botanic Gardens, Glasnevin, Dublin.

Henry, A. (1897e) Personal communication to William Thiselton-Dyer, 3 June 1897. Archives of the Royal Botanic Gardens, Kew, London.

Henry, A. (1897f) Personal communication to William Thiselton-Dyer, 19 July 19 1897. Archives of the Royal Botanic Gardens, Kew, London.

Henry, A. (1897–8) A budget from Yunnan. *Bulletin of Miscellaneous Information*. London, UK: Royal Botanic Gardens, Kew.

Henry, A. (1898a) Personal communication to William Thiselton-Dyer, 8 June 1898. Archives of the Royal Botanic Gardens, Kew, London.

Henry, A. (1898b) Personal communication to William Thiselton-Dyer, 29 November 1898. Archives of the Royal Botanic Gardens, Kew, London.

Henry, A. (1899a) Personal communication to William Thiselton-Dyer, 30 March 1899. Archives of the Royal Botanic Gardens, Kew, London.

Henry, A. (1899b) Personal communication to Sargent, 1 April 1899. Archives of the Arnold Arboretum Horticultural Library, Harvard University, Boston, MA, USA.

Henry, A. (1899c) Personal communication to Evelyn Gleeson, 1 May 1899. Archives of the National Botanic Gardens, Glasnevin, Dublin.

Henry, A. (1899d) Personal communication to Sargent, 21 July 1899. Archives of the Arnold Arboretum Horticultural Library, Harvard University, Boston, MA, USA.

Henry, A. (1899e) Personal communication to Evelyn Gleeson, 31 July 1899. Archives of the National Botanic Gardens, Glasnevin, Dublin.

Henry, A. (1899f) Personal communication to Sargent, 14 November 1899. Archives of the Arnold Arboretum Horticultural Library, Harvard University, Boston, MA, USA.

Henry, A. (1902) Midst Chinese forests. *Garden*, **61**: 3–6.

Henry, A. (1903a) Some new trees and shrubs of western China. *Flora and Sylva*, **1**.

Henry, A. (1903b) The Lolos and other tribes of western China. *Journal of the Anthropological Institute of Great Britain and Ireland*, **33**.

Henry, A. (1903c) Botanical exploration in Yunnan. *Bulletin of Miscellaneous Information*. London, UK: Royal Botanic Gardens, Kew.

Henry, A. (1907) Personal communication to David Prain, 3 January 1907. Archives of the Royal Botanic Gardens, Kew, London.

Henry, A. (1923) Obituary notice of Henry John Elwes. *Proceedings of the Royal Society, London*.

Heude, P. (1894) *Kemas henryanus*. In: *Mémoires concernant l'Histoire Naturelle de l'Empire Chinois*, vol. 2.

Hinkley, D. J. (1999) *The Explorer's Garden*. Portland, Oregon, USA: Timber Press.

Hooker, J. (1891) *Rehmannia rupestris. Curtis's Botanical Magazine*, **CXVII** (**117**): t. 7191.

Howard, R. (1980) E. H. Wilson as a botanist. Part 1. *Arnoldia*, **40**(3): 102–138.

Hsieh, C. & Shen, C. (1994) Introduction to the Flora of Taiwan. Geography, geology, climate and soils. *Flora of Taiwan* 1: 7–16. National Science Council of Taiwan.

Hsu, E. (2006) Elusive *Emmenopterys henryi. The Plantsman*, **5**(1): 30–35.

Igarashi, S. & Fukuda, H. (1997) *The Life Histories of Asian Butterflies*, vol. 1. Tokyo, Japan: Tokai University Press.

Jackson, B. D. (1901) A list of the collectors whose plants are in the Herbarium of the Royal Botanic Gardens, Kew, to 31 December, 1899. *Bulletin of Miscellaneous Information*: 1–80. London, UK: Royal Botanic Gardens, Kew.

Kaiyun, G. & Zhekun, Z. (eds) (1998) *Highland Flowers of Yunnan*. Kunming, Yunnan, People's Republic of China: Kunming Institute of Botany, Chinese Academy of Sciences (Science Press).

Keng, H. (1996) *Flora of Taiwan*, vol. 2, 2nd edit. Taipei, Taiwan: Editorial Committee of the Flora of Taiwan, Department of Botany, National Taiwan University.

Kingdon-Ward, F. (1954) *Berried Treasure: Shrubs for Autumn and Winter Colour in Your Garden*. London: Ward Locke & Co.

Lancaster, R. (1993) *Plantsman's Paradise: Travels in China*. Reprint (with addendum). Woodbridge, Suffolk, UK: Antique Collectors' Club.

Le Lièvre, A. (1994) Prince Henri of Orléans: explorer and plant-hunter. *The New Plantsman*, **1**(4): 238–247.

Li, H.-L. *et al.* (1975) *Flora of Taiwan*, vol. 1, 1st edit. Taipei, Taiwan: Epoch Publishing Co.

Mayhew, B., Huhti, T. & Miller, K. (2002) *South-West China*, 2nd rev. edit. London, UK: Lonely Planet Publications.

McAllister, H. (2005) *The Genus Sorbus – Mountain Ash and other Rowans*. London, UK: Royal Botanic Gardens, Kew (Kew Publishing).

McLean, B. (1997) *A Pioneering Plantsman – A. K. Bulley and the Great Plant Hunters*. London, UK: Royal Botanic Gardens, Kew; Royal Botanic Gardens Edinburgh.

McLean, B. (2004) *George Forrest – Plant Hunter*. Woodbridge, Suffolk, UK: Antique Collector's Club (in association with the Royal Botanic Gardens Edinburgh).

Mooney, O. V. (1970) The Augustine Henry Memorial Grove – a record. *Irish Forestry*, **27**(2).

Moore, F. (1942) Augustine Henry, 1857–1930. *Journal of the Royal Horticultural Society*, **67**(1).

Morley, B. D. (1979) Augustine Henry: his botanical activities in China, 1882–1890. *Glasra*, **3**.

Nelson, E. C. & Walsh, W. F. (1984) *An Irish Flower Garden Replanted: the Histories of Some of Our Garden Plants*. Kilkenny, Ireland: Boethius Press.

Nelson, E. C. (1982–3) Augustine Henry and the exploration of the Chinese flora. *Arnoldia*, **43**(1). Boston, MA, USA: Arnold Arboretum of Harvard University.

Nelson, E. C. (1986) Introduction. In: Henry, A. *Notes on Economic Botany of China*, 1893. Kilkenny, Ireland: Boethius Press.

Nelson, E. C. (1995) *The Cause of the Calamity: Potato Blight in Ireland, 1845–1847, and the role of the National Botanic Gardens, Glasnevin*. Dublin, Ireland: The Stationery Office.

O'Driscoll, J. (1981) Henry – the tree breeder. *Irish Forestry*, **38**(1).

Oldfield, S. (2007) *Great Botanic Gardens of the World*. London, UK: New Holland Publishers.

Oliver, F. W. (1888) On the structure, development, and affinities of *Trapella, Oliv.*, a new genus of pedalineae. *Annals of Botany*, **2**(1).

Oliver, F. W. (1889) On a new form of *Trapella sinensis*. *Annals of Botany*, **3**(1).

d'Orléans, Prince H. (1898) *From Tonkin to India by the sources of the Irawadi: January '95–'96*. H. Bent (trans). London, UK: Methuen & Co.

Pax, F. A. (1905) *Primula henryi*. In: Engler, A. *Das Pflanzenreich*, IV, **237**(22): 47.

Pim, S. (1984) *The Wood and the Trees: a biography of Augustine Henry*, 2nd edit. Kilkenny, Ireland: Boethius Press.

Pratt, A. E. (1892) *To the Snows of Tibet through China*. London, UK: Longmans, Green & Co.

Sargent, C. S. (ed.) (1913) *Plantae Wilsonianae: An Enumeration of the Woody Plants Collected in Western China for the Arnold Arboretum of Harvard University During the Years 1907, 1908, and 1910 by E. H. Wilson*, vol 1. Publications of the Arnold Arboretum, No. 4. Cambridge, UK: Cambridge University Press.

Sargent, C. S. (ed.) (1916) *Plantae Wilsonianae: An Enumeration of the Woody Plants Collected in Western China for the Arnold Arboretum of Harvard University During the Years 1907, 1908, and 1910 by E. H. Wilson*, vol. 2. Publications of the Arnold Arboretum, No. 4. Cambridge, UK: Cambridge University Press.

Sargent, C. S. (ed.) (1917) *Plantae Wilsonianae: An Enumeration of the Woody Plants Collected in Western China for the Arnold Arboretum of Harvard University During the Years 1907, 1908, and 1910 by E. H. Wilson*, vol. 2. Publications of the Arnold Arboretum, No. 4. Cambridge, UK: Cambridge University Press.

Schneider, C. K. Alnus Henryi. In: Sargent, C. S. (1916) *Plantae Wilsonianae*, vol. 2. Cambridge, UK: Cambridge University Press.

Shaw, J. In: Stearn, W. T. (2002) *The Genus Epimedium and other Herbaceous Berberidaceae*. London, UK: Royal Botanic Gardens, Kew.

Shephard, S. (2003) *Seeds of Fortune – A Gardening Dynasty*. London, UK: Bloomsbury Publishing.

Shui, Y.-M. & Chen, W.-H. (2002) *Microtropis* (Celastraceae) from the Daweishan Range, S.E. Yunnan, China. *Botanical Bulletin of Academia Sinica*, **43**.

Shultes, R. E. & von Reis, S. (1995) *Ethnobotany – Evolution of a Discipline*. Portland, OR, USA: Dioscorides Press.

Skvortsov, A. K. (1998) Taxonomic notes on *Betula* – II. Two Chinese birches described by A. Franchet in 1899 and misunderstood by subsequent authors. *Harvard Papers in Botany*, **3**(1): 109–112.

Soó, R. (1927) The *Melampyrum* species of East Asia. *Journal of Botany*, **65**: 138–145.

Storey, R. (2001) *Taiwan*. London, UK: Lonely Planet Publications.

Thiselton-Dyer, W. (1905) Historical note to 'Index Florae Sinensis – an enumeration of all the plants known from China Proper, Formosa, Hainan, Corea, the Luchu Archipelago, and the Island of Hongkong'. 3 vols (1886–1906). F. B. Forbes & W. H. Hemsley, *Journal of the Linnean Society of London* (*Botany*), **xxxvi:** vii.

Valder, P. (1999) *The Garden Plants of China*. London, UK: Weidenfeld & Nicholson.

Veitch, H. (1899) Personal communication to William Thiselton-Dyer, 19 December 1899. Archives of the Royal Botanic Gardens, Kew, London.

Veitch, J. H. (1900a) Personal communication to E. H. Wilson, 8 January 1900. Archives of the Arnold Arboretum Horticultural Library, Harvard University, Boston, MA, USA.

Veitch, J. H. (1900b) Personal communication to E. H. Wilson, 16 February 1900. Archives of the Arnold Arboretum Horticultural Library, Harvard University, Boston, MA, USA.

Veitch, J. H. (1905) Personal communication to E. H. Wilson, 6 February 1905. Archives of the Arnold Arboretum Horticultural Library, Harvard University, Boston, MA, USA.

Veitch, J. H. (1906) *Hortus Veitchii*. London, UK: James Veitch & Sons.

Werner, E. (1928) *Autumn Leaves*. Shanghai, China: Kelly & Walsh.

Whitehouse, C. (2007) A *Bauhinia* renamed. *The New Plantsman*, 6(2): 112.

Wilson, E. H. (1901) *Gardeners' Chronicle*, ser. 3. London, UK.

Wilson, E. H. (1913) *A Naturalist in Western China*, vol. 1. London, UK: Methuen & Co.

Wilson, E. H. (1916) *Davidia involucrate* var. *vilmoriniana*. In: Sargent, C. (ed.) (1913) *Plantae Wilsonianae*, vol. 1. Cambridge: Cambridge University Press.

Wilson, E. H. (1925) *The Lilies of Eastern Asia*. London, UK: Dulau & Co.

Wilson, E. H. (1926) *Aristocrats of the Garden*. Boston, MA, USA: The Stratford Company

Wu, Q. (1999) *Wild Flowers of Yunnan in China*. Beijing, China: China Forestry Publishing House.

Xu, T.-Q., Wu, J.-Q., Ye, Q.-G., Wang, C.-H. & Huang, R. (Wuhan Institute of Botany, The Chinese Academy of Sciences) (2000) A study on the endemic vascular plant species of the Three Gorges Reservoir Area of the Changjiang River. *Journal of Wuhan Botanical Research*, 18(3).

Yunnan Society of Ecological Economics, Xishuangbanna Nature Reserve Administration & Yunnan Forestry Investigation and Plan Institute (eds) (1992) *Xishuangbanna – A Nature Reserve of China*. Beijing, China: China Forestry Publishing House.

Zheng, Z. (1983) The characteristics of the flora and an outline of the distribution of plants in Hubei Province, People's Republic of China. *Journal of Wuhan Botanical Research*, 1(2): 165–75.

Zich, A. (1997) China's Three Gorges: before the flood. *National Geographic*, 192(3): 2–33.

Index of plants

Additional plants associated with Augustine Henry are listed in Appendix 1.

Index of places and people

For additional reference, Appendix 2 lists contemporary Chinese place names used in this book alongside the older or local names with which Augustine Henry and his collectors will have been familiar.